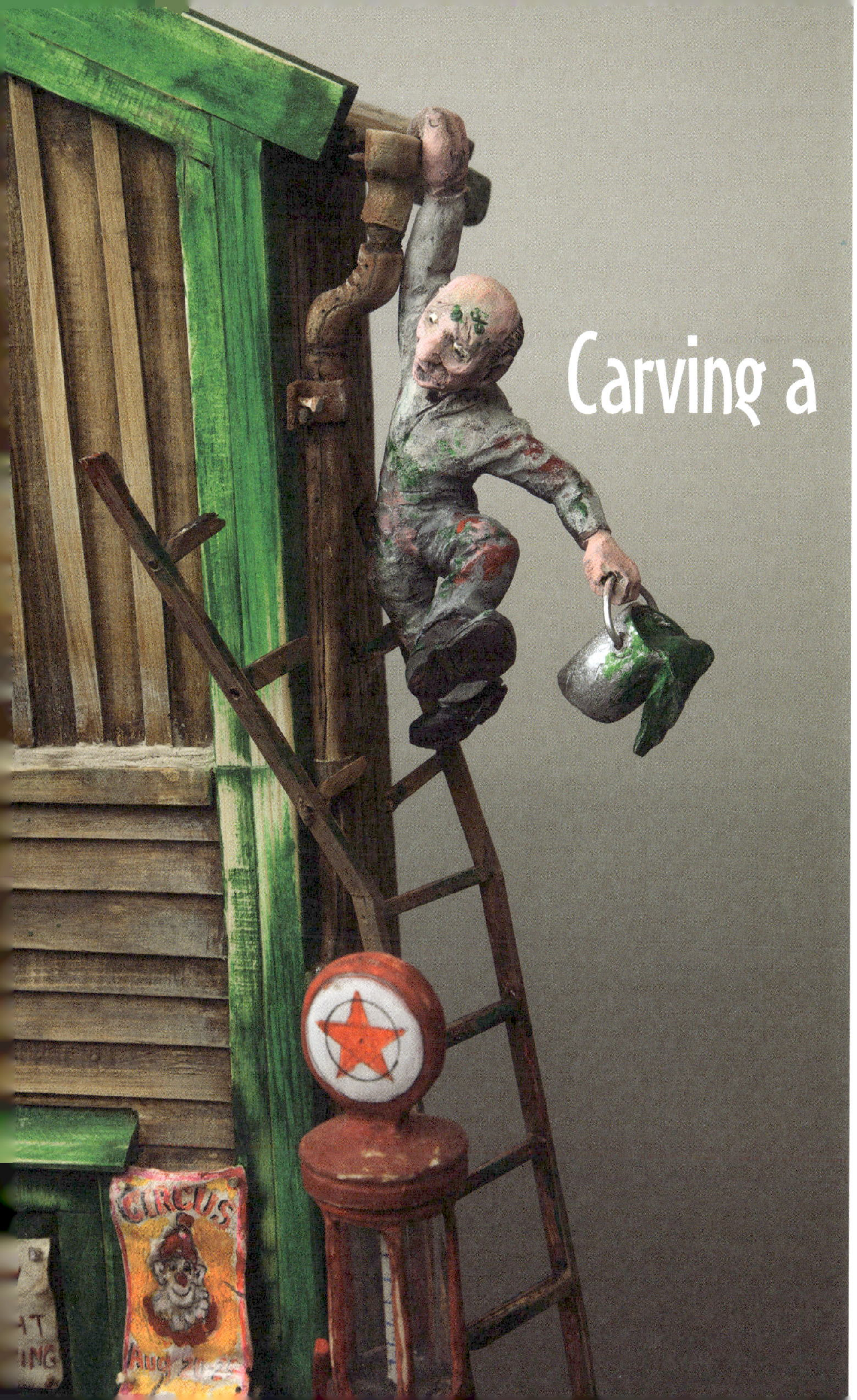

Carving a 1930s Street Scene

Caricature Carvers of America

Schiffer Publishing Ltd
4880 Lower Valley Road • Atglen, PA 19310

Library of Congress Control Number:

Designed by RoS
Type set in MisterEarl/Zurich BT

ISBN: 978-0-7643-4601-9
Printed in The United States of America

CCA Book Committee: Bob Travis, Editor; Randy Landen, Associate Editor; Sandy Smith, Associate Editor; Jack A. Williams, Associate Editor.

Cover and studio photographs: Jack A. and Carole Williams; Step-by-step photographs by Douglas Congdon-Martin.

Acknowledgment: We wish to express our sincere gratitude to Debra Northrup of Hawthorn Suites by Wyndham, Sacramento, CA, for her gracious hospitality and assistance in our marathon photography session for this book.

Published by Schiffer Publishing, Ltd.
4880 Lower Valley Road
Atglen, PA 19310
Phone: (610) 593-1777; Fax: (610) 593-2002
E-mail: Info@schifferbooks.com

For our complete selection of fine books on this and related subjects, please visit our website at **www.schifferbooks.com**. You may also write for a free catalog.

This book may be purchased from the publisher. Please try your bookstore first.

We are always looking for people to write books on new and related subjects. If you have an idea for a book, please contact us at proposals@schifferbooks.com.

Schiffer Publishing's titles are available at special discounts for bulk purchases for sales promotions or premiums. Special editions, including personalized covers, corporate imprints, and excerpts can be created in large quantities for special needs. For more information, contact the publisher.

This book is dedicated to the memory of six CCA members who contributed greatly to promoting the art of caricature carving: Claude Bolton, Tom Brown, Dave Dunham, Tex Haase, Will Hayden, Dave Rasmussen, and Joe Wannamaker.

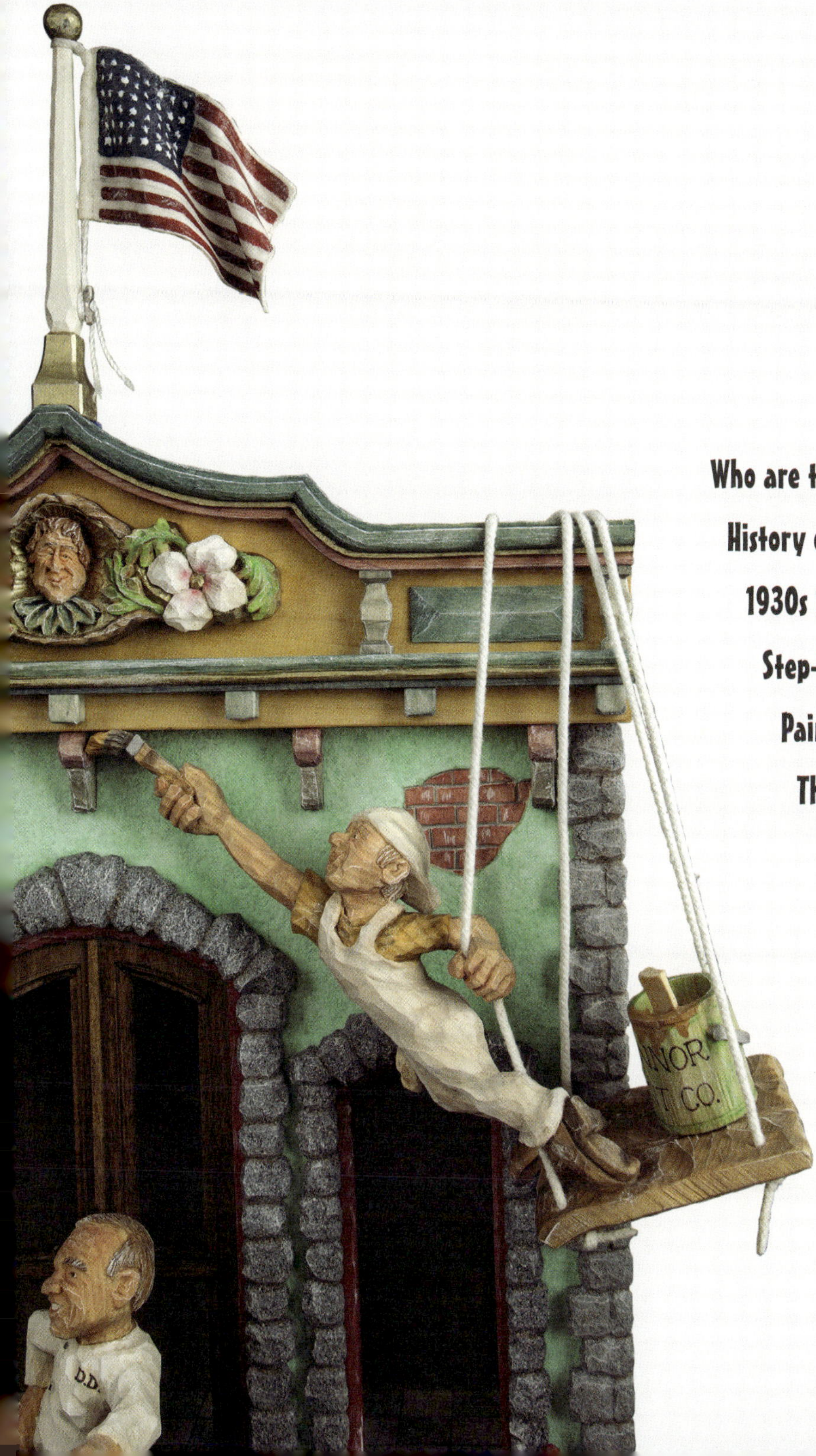

CONTENTS

Who are the Caricature Carvers of America?

Active Members 2013

Vicki Bishop
Phil Bishop
David Boone
Mitch Cartledge
PJ Driscoll
Gary Falin
Gene Fuller
Chris Hammack
Bruce Henn
Eldon Humphreys
Randy Landen
Pete LeClair
Don Mertz
Keith Morrill
Ryan Olsen
Steve Prescott
Floyd Rhadigan
Joe Schumacher
Sandy Smith
Dave Stetson
Dennis Thornton
Bob Travis
Jack A. Williams
Tom Wolfe
Joe You

Emeritus Members

Gary Batte
Harold Enlow
Desiree Hajny
Marv Kaisersatt
Peter Ortel
Vic Otto
Jack Price
Doug Raine
Harley Refsal
David Sabol
Harley Schmitgen
Gerald Sears
Cleve Taylor
Rich Wetherbee

Deceased Members

Claude Bolton
Tom Brown
Dave Dunham
Tex Haase
Will Hayden
Dave Rasmussen
Joe Wannamaker

History of the Caricature Carvers of America

This book, *Carving a 1930s Street Scene*, marks our 6th book publication since the Caricature Carvers of America (CCA) was established in 1990. The CCA is a non-profit educational organization whose mission is to promote the art of caricature woodcarving through seminars, competitions, exhibits, and publications.

To that end, the CCA has worked diligently over the past twenty-two years to expose people to the art of caricature carving, using a variety of media. For over ten years, CCA carvings were on display at the National Carving Museum in Custer, South Dakota. Our "Full Moon Saloon" has toured the country through its owner, Woodcraft Supply Corporation, which displays the saloon at its stores throughout the country. "The Circus" is on permanent display in Harmony, Minnesota. The "CCA Signature Collection," completed in conjunction with our 10th Anniversary in 2000, is currently on display at one of the country's largest woodcarving galleries, Peter Engler Designs, located in Branson, Missouri. In 2010, the "CCA Train" and "Full Moon Saloon" were featured exhibits at Silver Dollar City's 50th Anniversary Celebration, where they were seen by many of the quarter of a million visitors to the event. Currently, the 1880s "Train" is on loan to the California Railroad Museum, where it will be on display through the end of 2013. It is anticipated that over 300,000 visitors to the museum will see the 100+ caricature carvings and train that make up the project.

For the past ten years, the CCA has sponsored the National Caricature Carving Competition. The competition encourages caricature carvers, new and experienced, to exhibit their work on a national platform. The CCA also hosts its annual three-day carving workshop during the competition, offering a variety of caricature classes taught by members of the CCA. Individually, CCA instructors offer an assortment of caricature carving classes around the country throughout the year.

Finally, the CCA has, with the printing of *Carving a 1930s Street Scene*, published six books which promote the art of caricature carving. *Carving the Full Moon Saloon* (1995), *Carving the CCA Circus* (1997), *Caricature Carvers Showcase* (2007), *Carving an 1880's Western Train* (2009), and *Caricatures in Motion* (2011) are unique books that carefully outline the process of the various projects from inception to completion, through photos, drawings, patterns, and text.

The CCA is proud to be a part of the carving community. Any contributions we've made, however small, are simply intended to encourage carvers and to promote the art of caricature carving. As we move forward from here, down whatever road carving takes us, we remain committed to our original goals. For additional information on CCA projects, members, the competition, or upcoming seminars and exhibits, please visit our website at www.cca-carvers.org.

1930s Street Scene: The Project

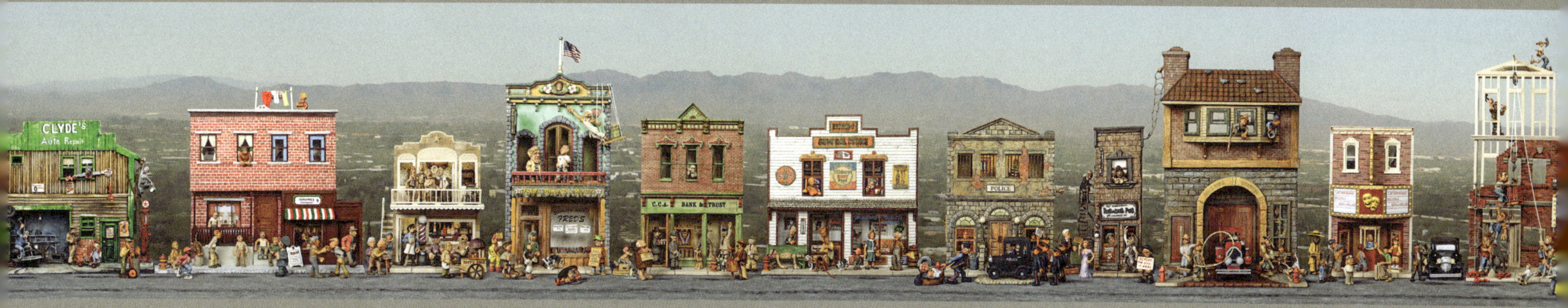

The idea for a 1930s street scene as the next CCA book project was discussed as early as 2010. In late 2011, at the annual meeting in Boise, Idaho, we decided to go ahead with the venture. At an impromptu meeting and group discussion on a street scene, it became apparent there was strong interest in the idea. Within a few minutes people were volunteering to create a variety of specific buildings. Our secretary began a list, and in a short time eleven buildings were claimed by members. Some buildings were constructed by one member, others by groups of two or more. Those not working on buildings carved figures and ancillary pieces to fill out the specific scenes.

We're frequently asked, "How do you coordinate a project of this magnitude?" The simple answer is, "We don't." Most of us are separated by great distances and don't have an opportunity to work together during the year. We agree on a theme, set the scale, return home, and work individually on the project until the next annual meeting. In this case, those not working on specific buildings had the advantage of knowing what structures would be included in the project, and could carve figures and accessories specifically designed for the building or scene. Finally, we scheduled a work day in conjunction with our annual meeting to set up the project. Jack Williams arrived two days early to paint the street canvas so that it would be ready for our work day. Members brought their contributions and we spent the day finalizing the placement of the figures and buildings. After several hours of arranging, rearranging, and then rearranging again, the project was finished. We took reference photos, made some notes, and called it a day.

Step-by-Step Instructions for Carving a Caricature Figure

With PJ Driscoll

The variety of carving styles represented by our membership make the Caricature Carvers of America a unique organization. From the thought process and design, to carving and finishing a piece, the diversity among members is striking. This will become evident as the reader peruses the following chapters. Since there is limited space in this book we cannot provide detailed instructions for every carving. In lieu of that, we offer detailed step-by-step instructions for one representative carving.

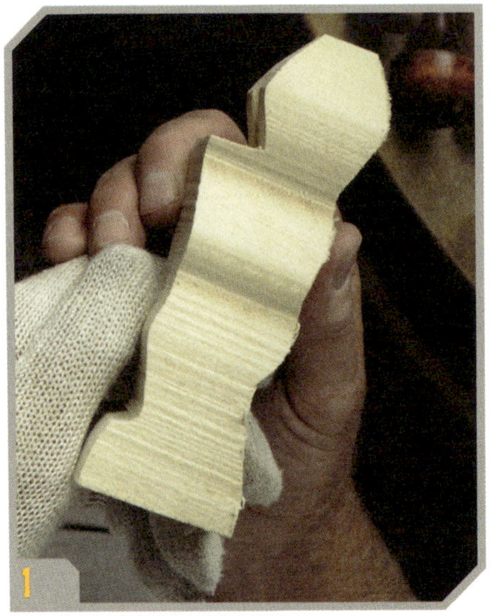

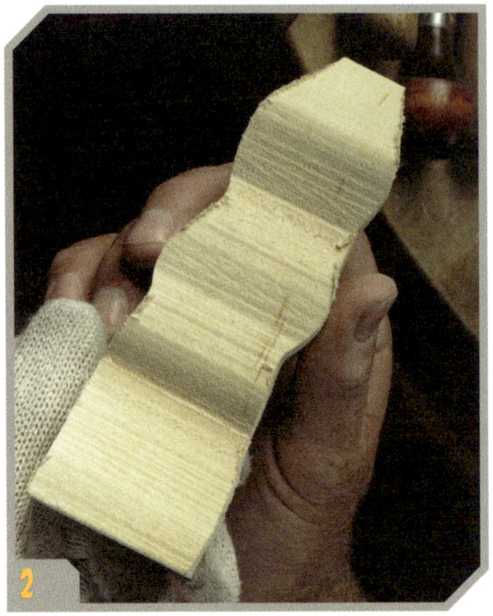

1-3) Cut the blank using the pattern on page 167

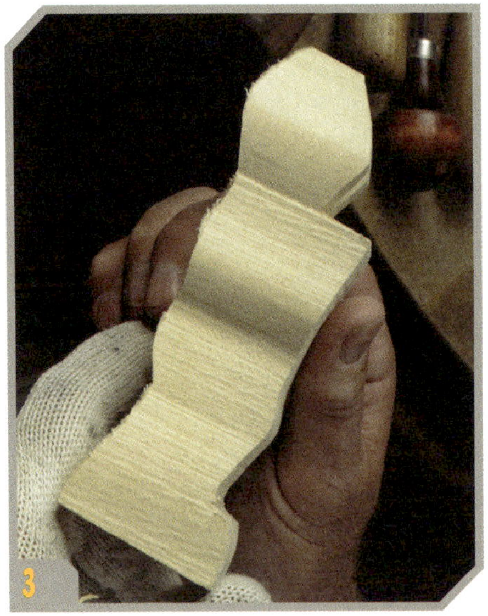

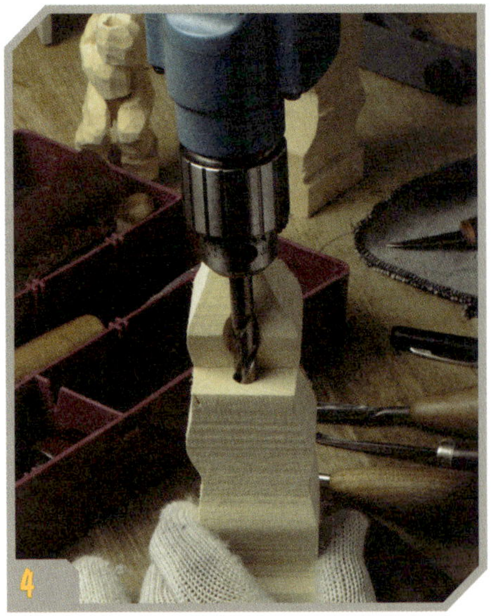

After cutting the blank on a band saw, drill a hole for the pole. I use a 3/8″ bit.

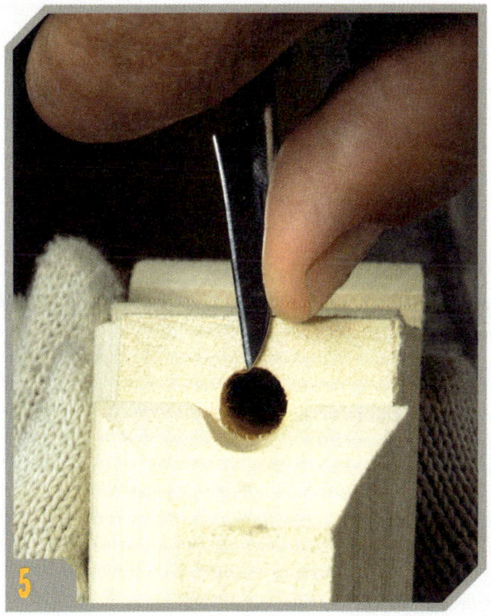

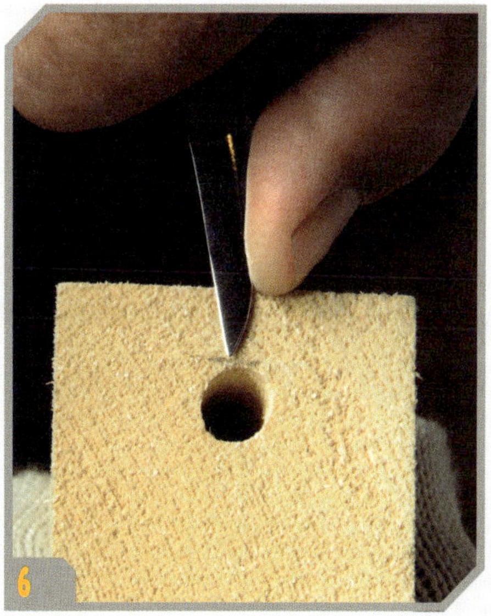

5-6) Be sure the holes are centered and the same distance from the front edge of the blank at the top and the bottom.

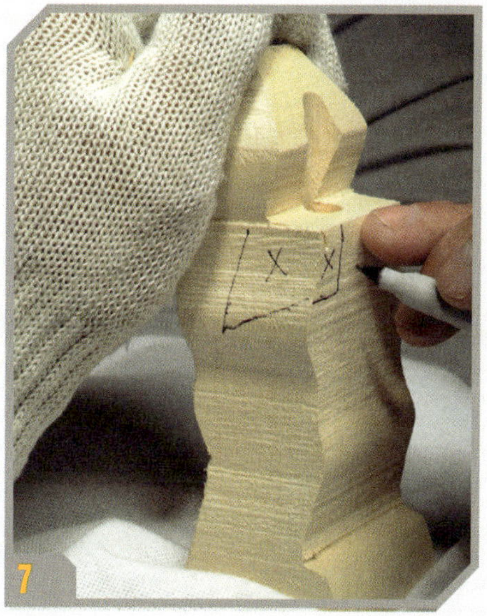

Mark the front right…

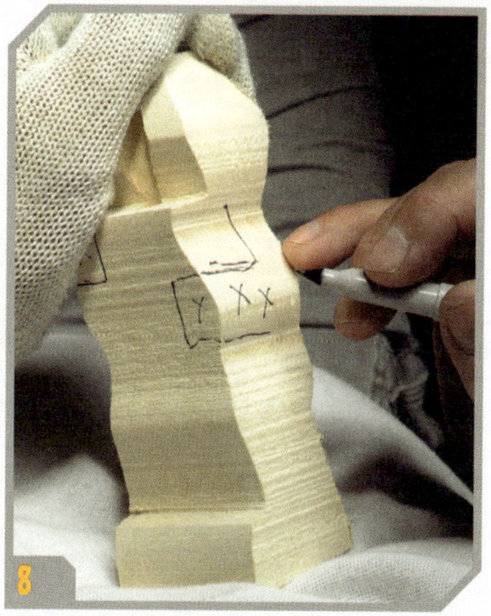

and front left for removal.

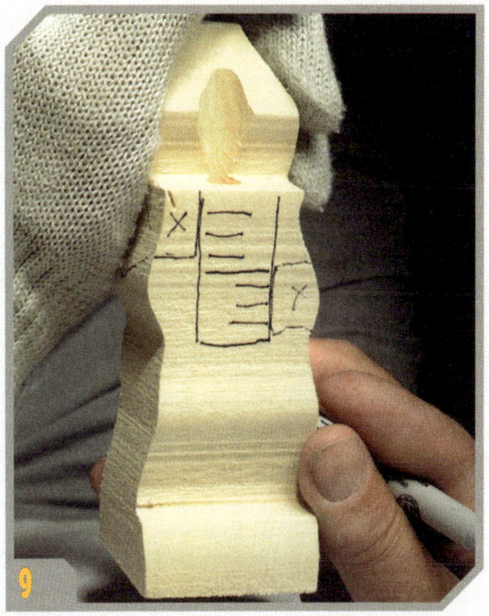

The area between will be the hands, which are marked next.

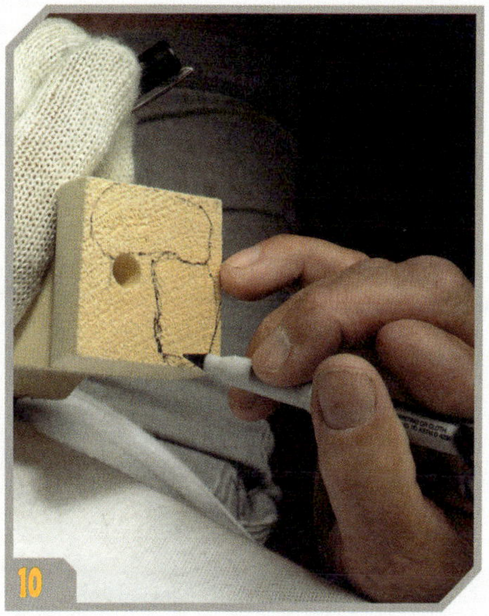

Mark the soles of the feet.

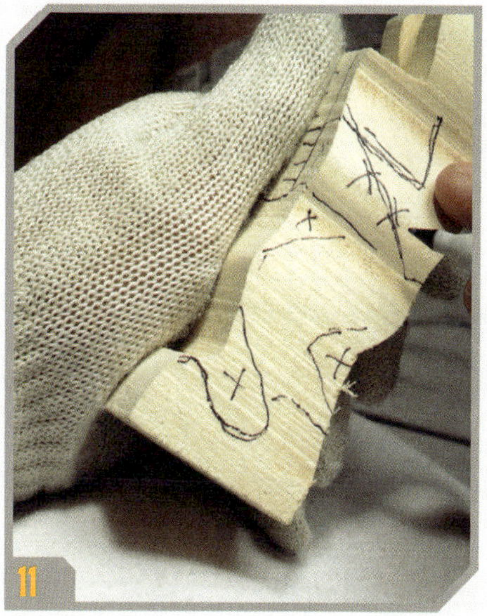

Mark areas to be removed on the left leg…

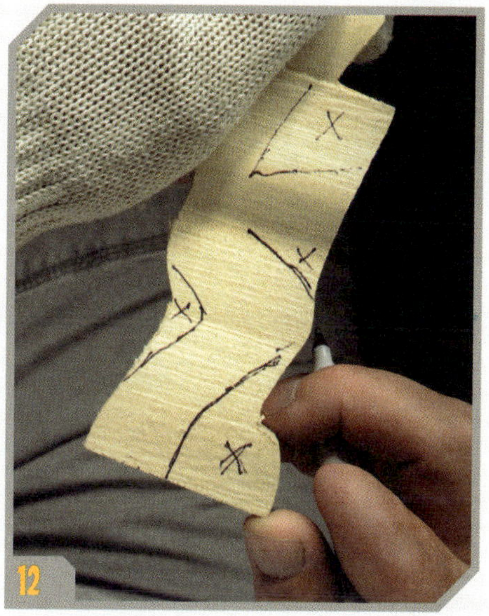

and the right leg.

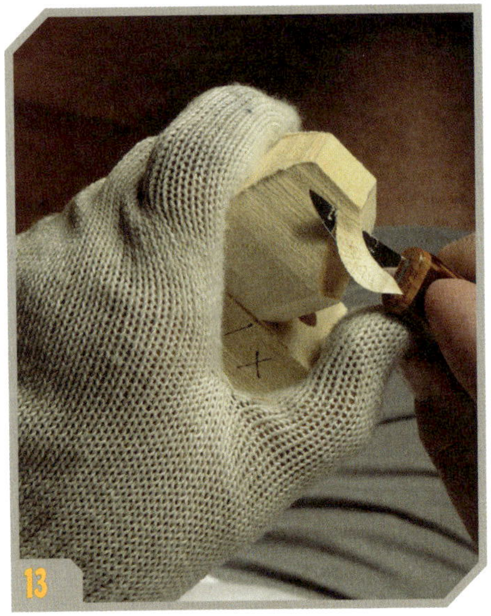

Trim away the square corners around the whole carving, beginning on the head...

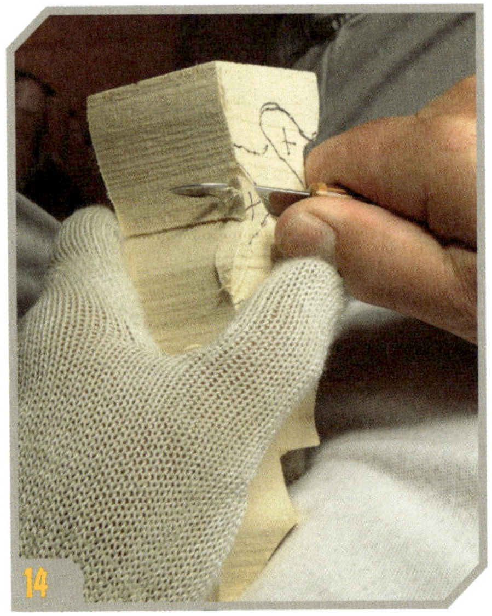

and continuing with the body.

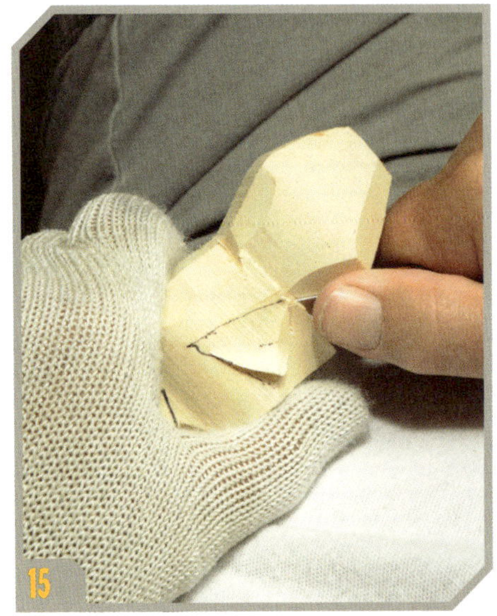

On areas that are to be removed, you can go deeper.

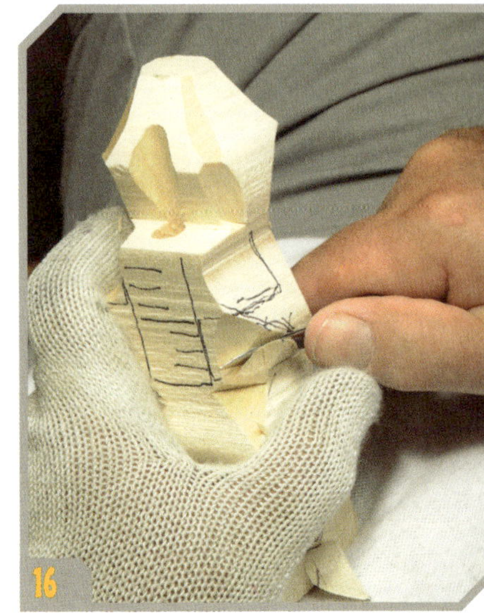

Block in the arms.

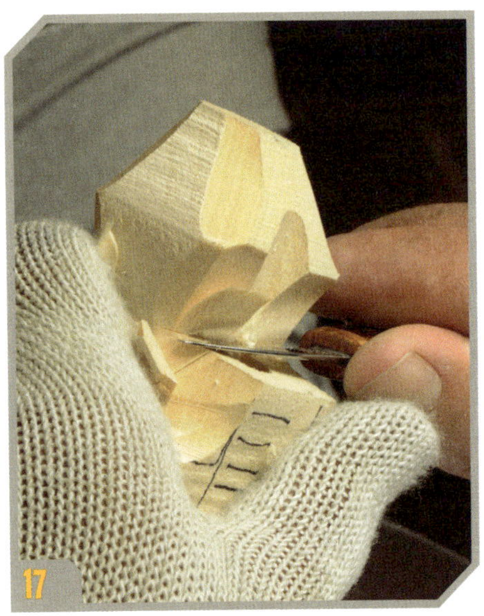

Next, remove some of the head to bring the arms out.

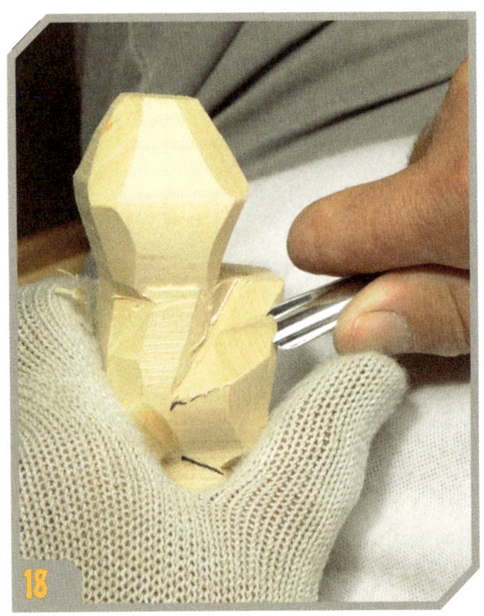

Use a gouge to bring out the top of the hands.

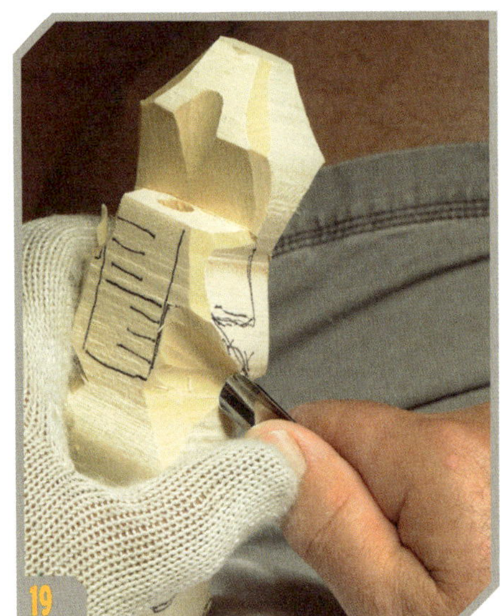

Repeat on the other side.

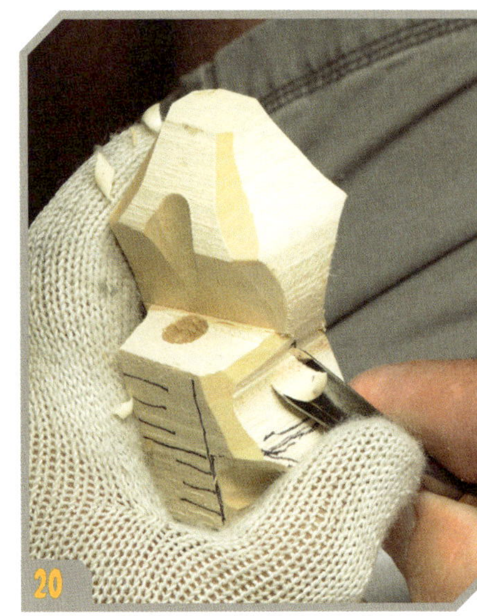

Continue to bring out the shoulder with the gouge.

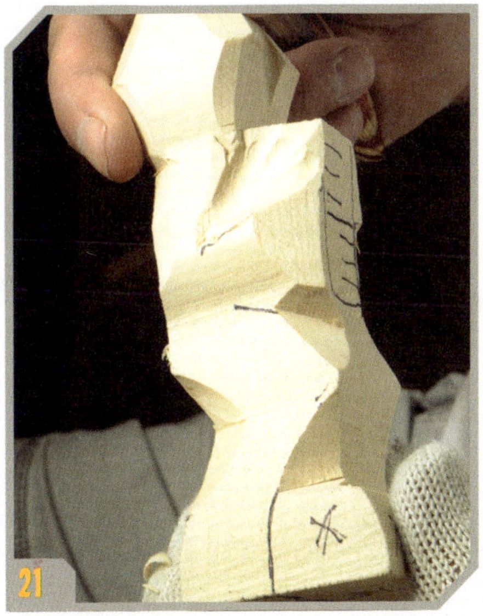

21

Progress.

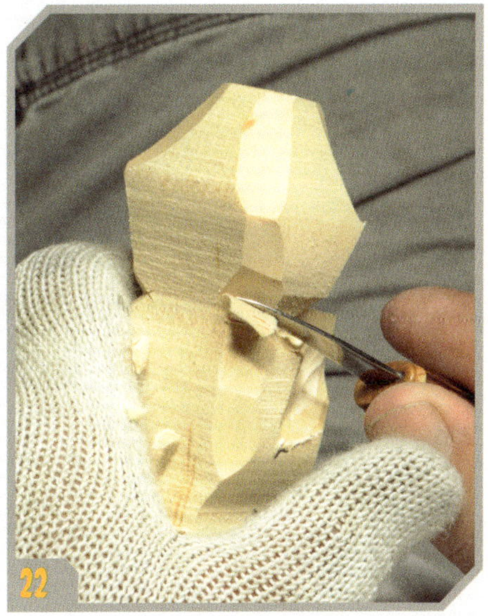

22

Use the knife to define the shoulder at the neck.

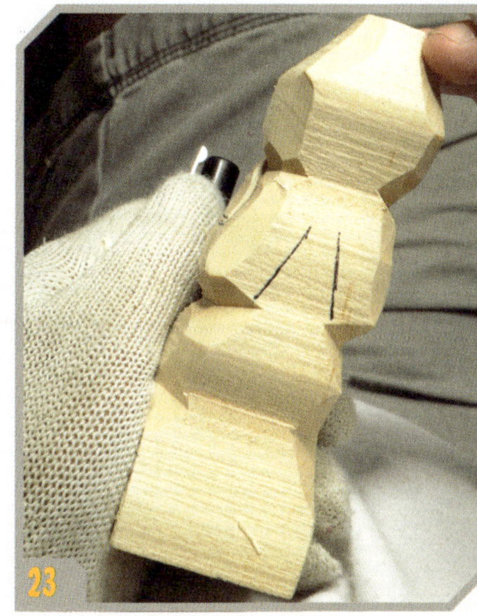

23

On the back, make the upper arms equal length, then mark the back of the arms.

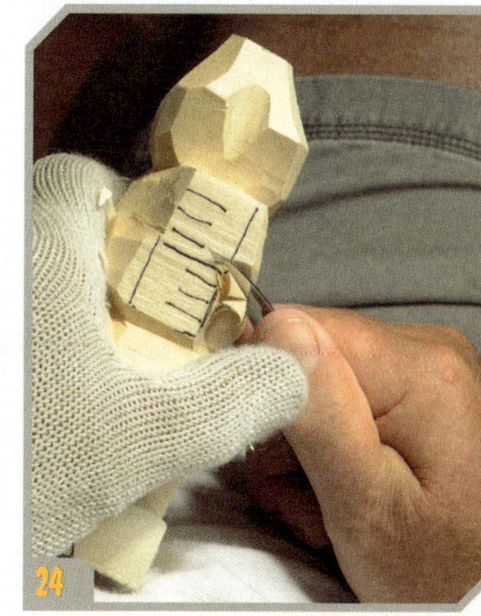

24

Continue to block in the hands.

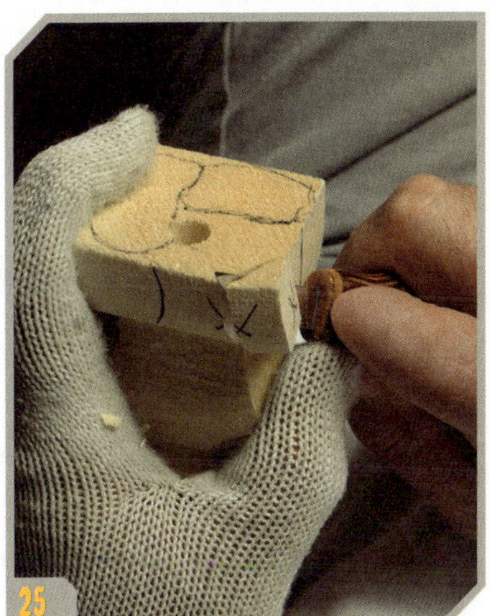

25

Remove the wood between the feet.

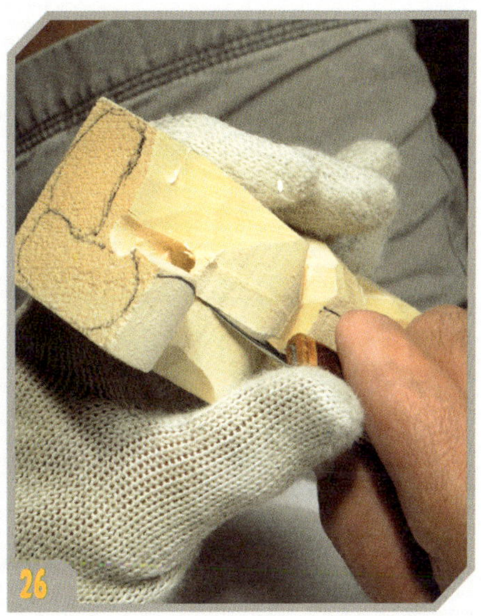

26

Separate the legs, making two stop cuts...

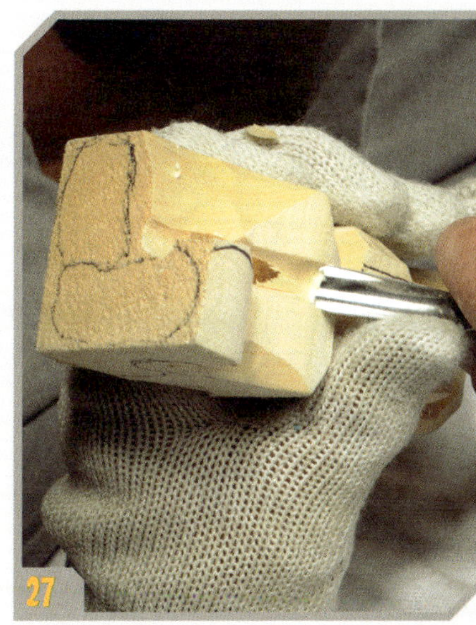

27

and cleaning it out with a gouge.

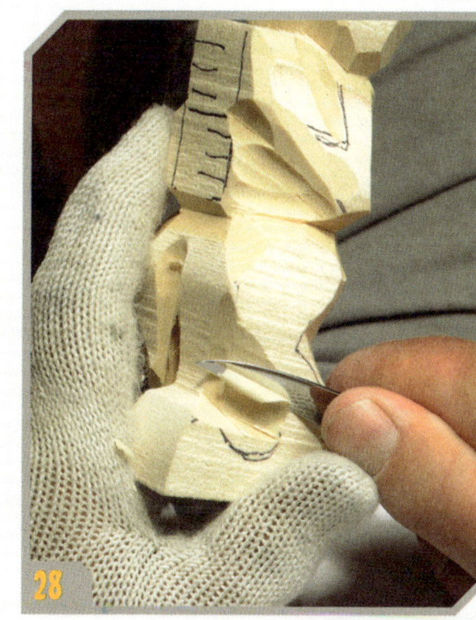

28

Shape the side of the left leg from the knee to the ankle. This is the harder foot because it is behind the pole—the "brake" foot.

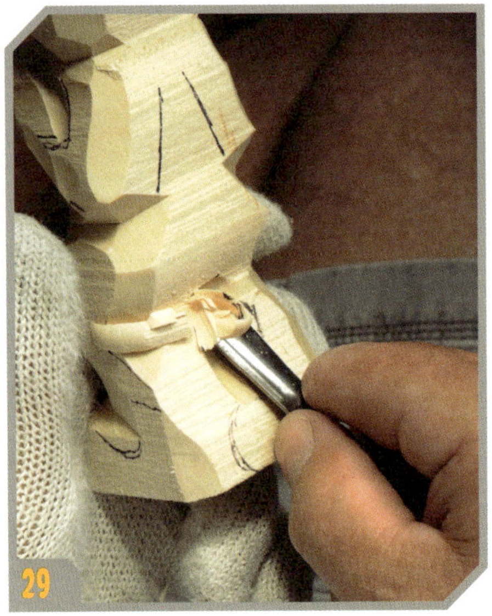

Continue to bring out the brake foot on the back using a gouge.

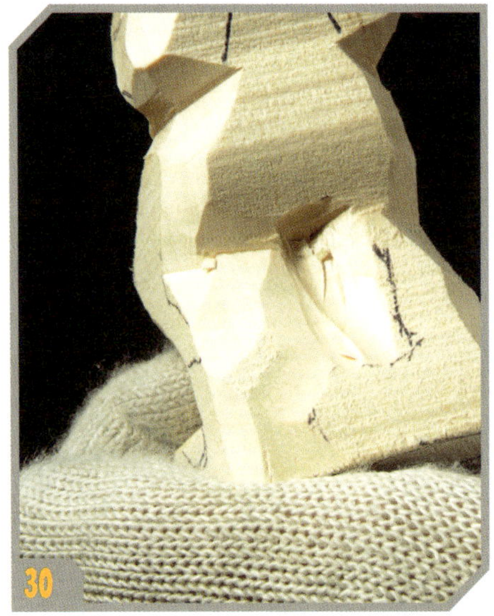

Progress on the back…

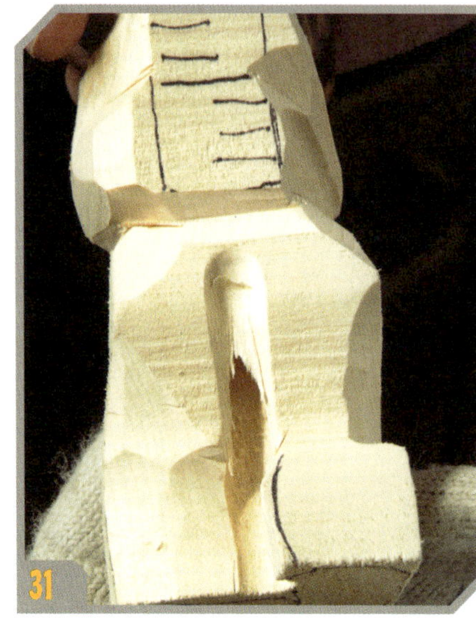

and the front.

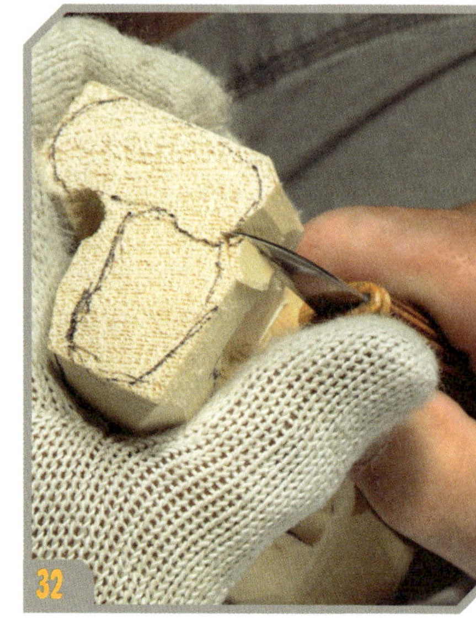

Continue to separate the legs and shape the foot. Gradually, I work my way all the way through.

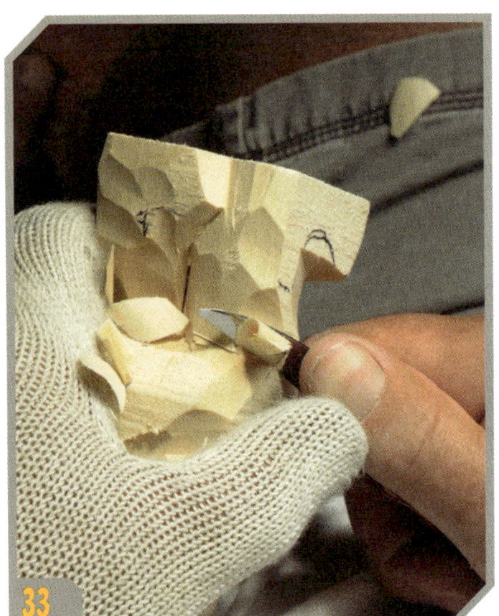

Shape the lower legs.

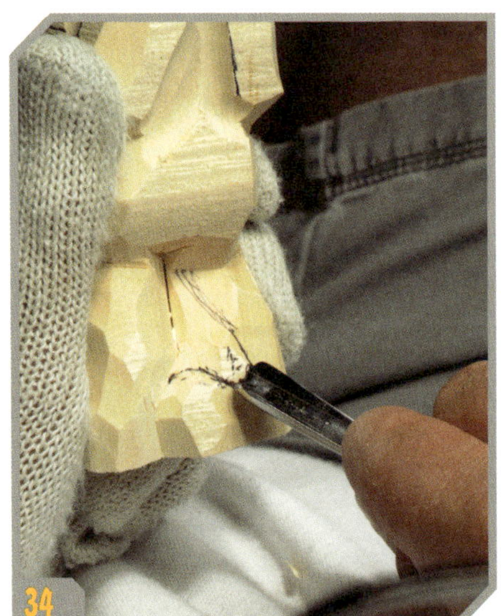

Redraw the brake foot outline and shape it with the gouge.

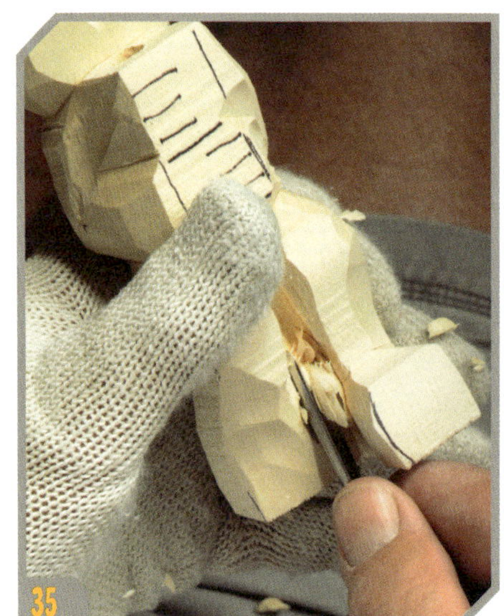

Break through the legs, working from the back…

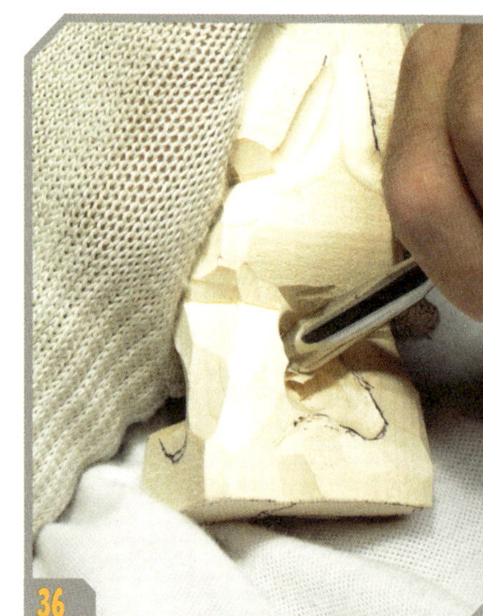

and the front.

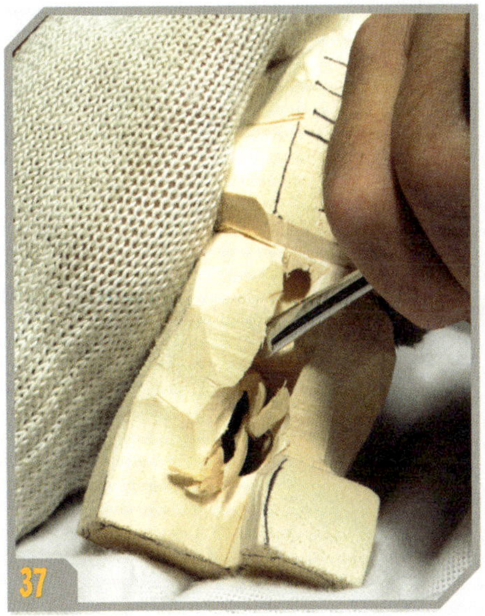

After breaking through, enlarge the opening from the front and the back.

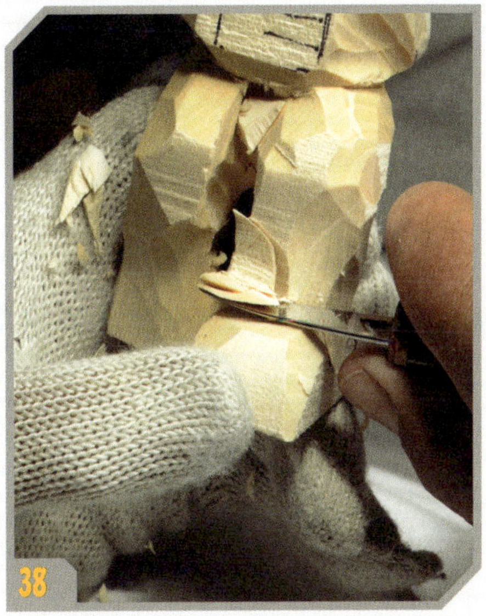

Shape up the foot and carve the space above the foot to bring out the shoe.

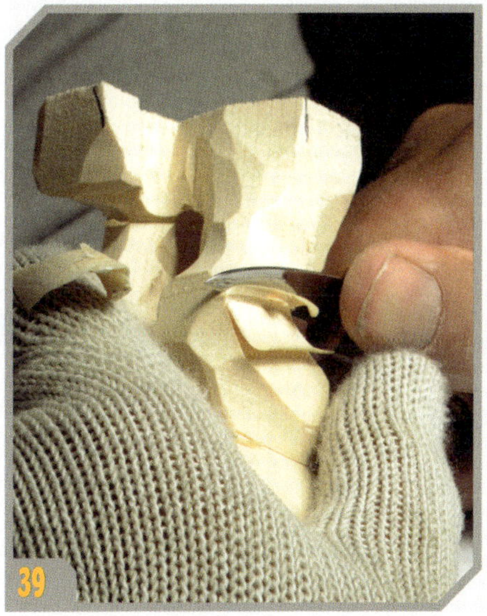

Continue to shape, removing saw marks as you go.

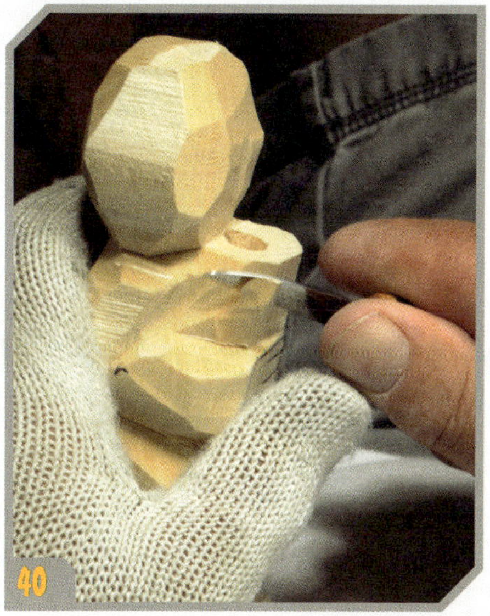

Set the four planes of the fingers.

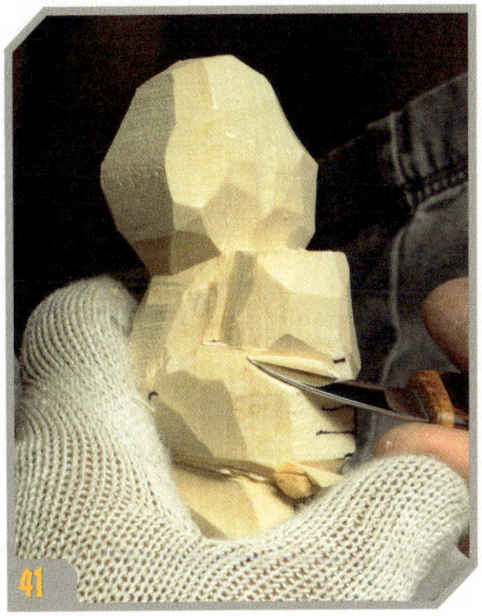

Create the separation between the top and bottom hand.

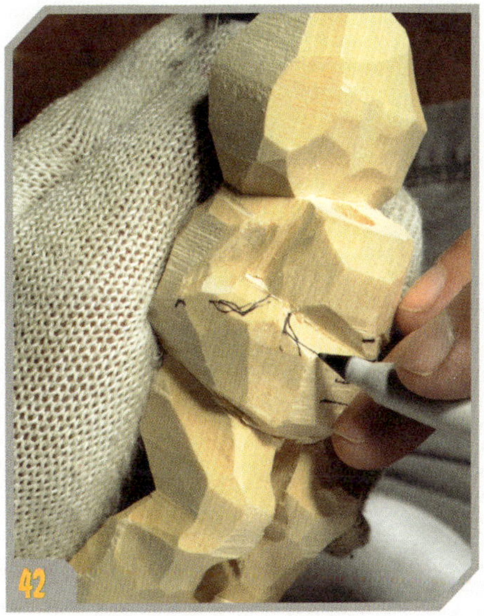

Mark the thumbs as they go around the pole, top...

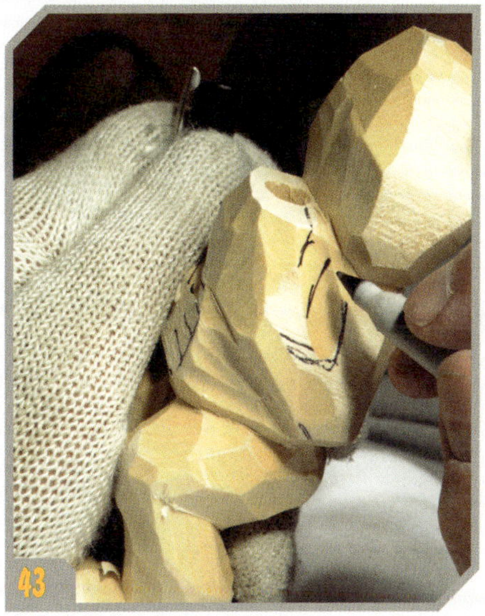

and bottom.

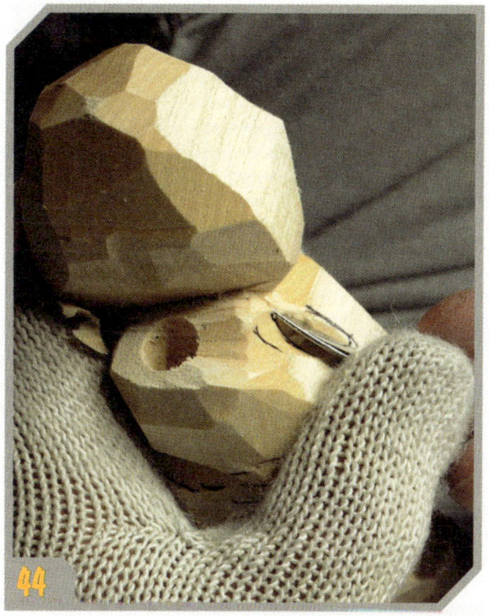

Shape the upper hand to bring out the thumb.

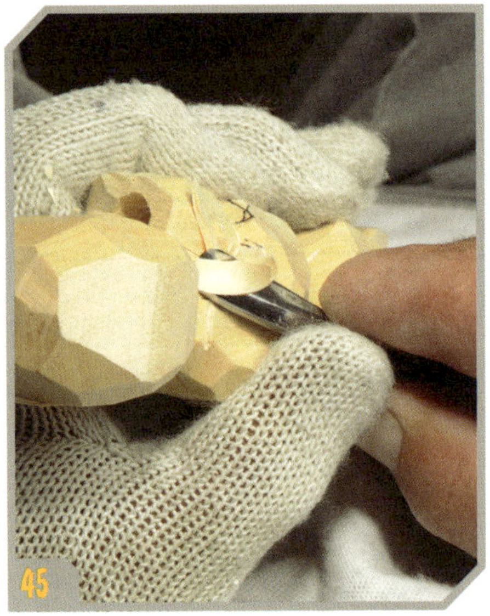

Shape the arm from the hand.

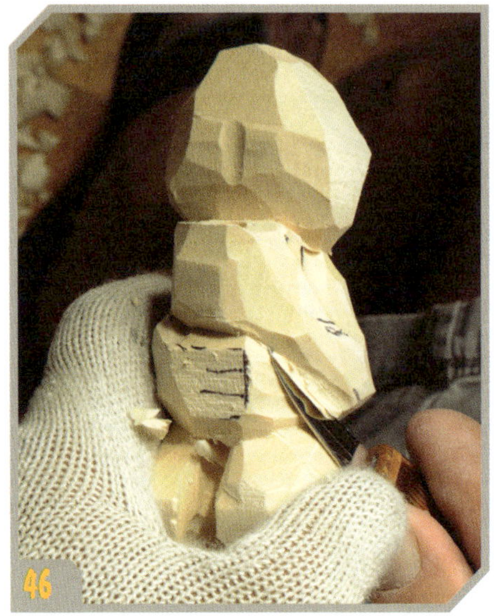

Continue to separate the upper and lower hands and arms.

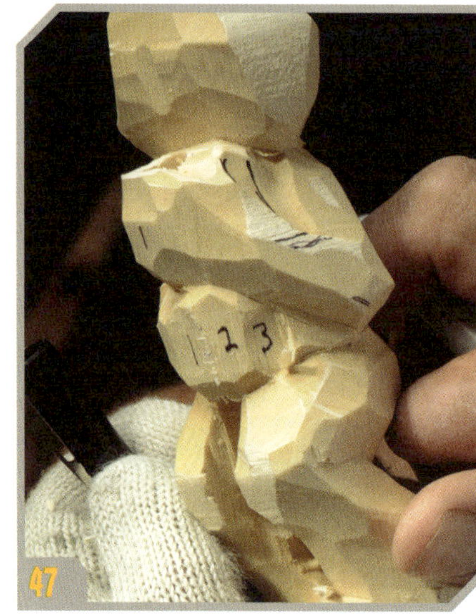

The three planes of the hands established.

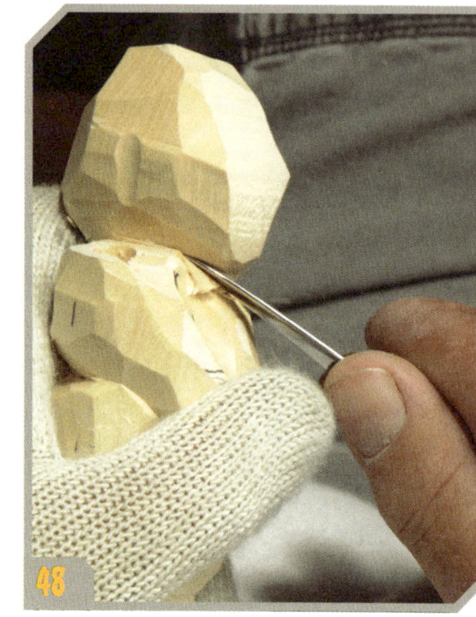

Deepen the line between the head and the hands.

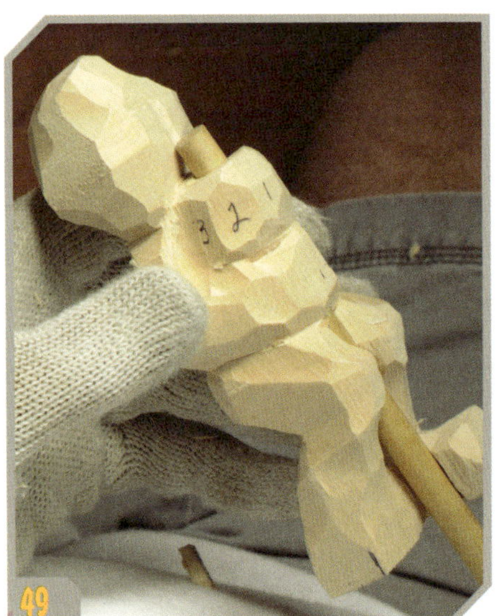

Check with the pole regularly to make sure the hands look natural.

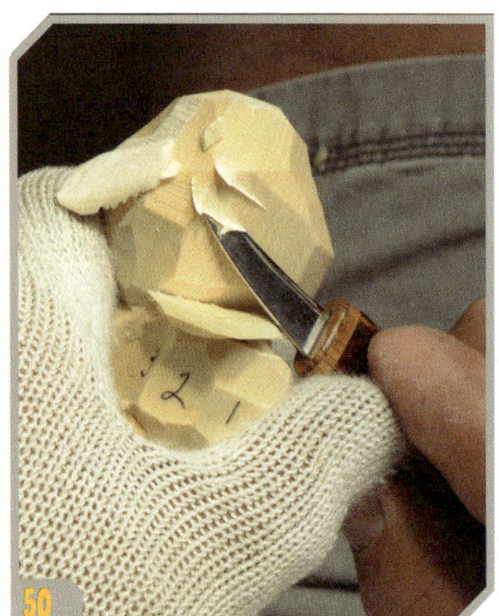

The pole was hitting the side of the head, so it needs a little trimming.

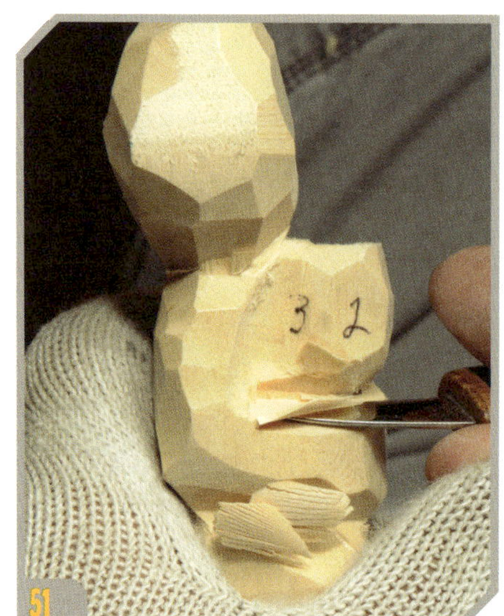

Deepen the line between the two arms.

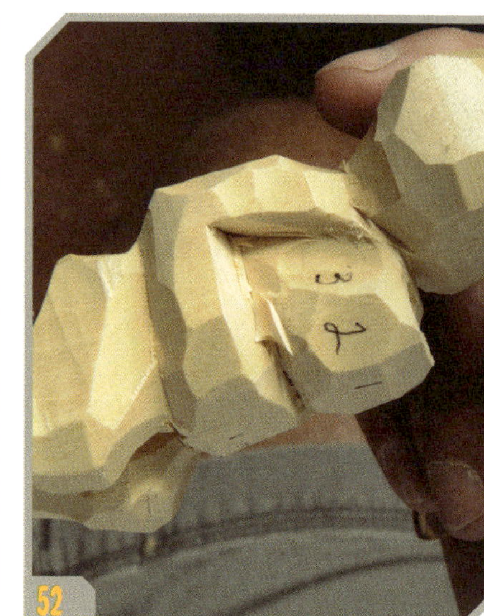

Progress.

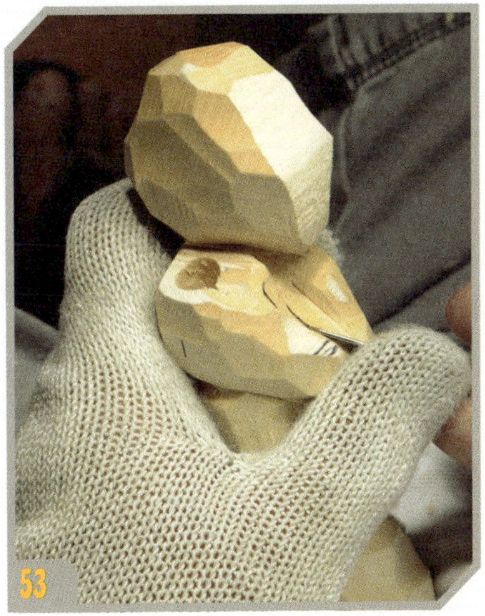

Trim the arms so they have the same basic shape.

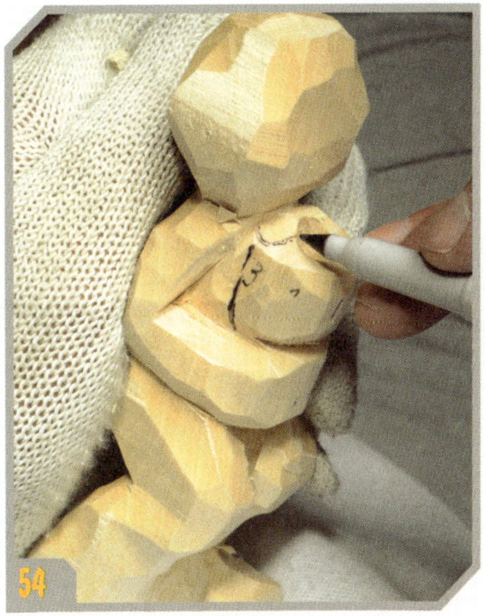

Redraw the thumb and hand. The thumb goes behind the pole and is a little higher than the fingers.

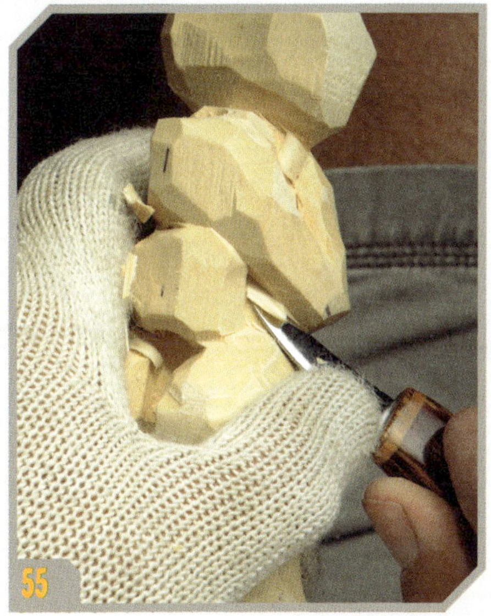

Continue to deepen the edges of the hand, bringing them out from the body.

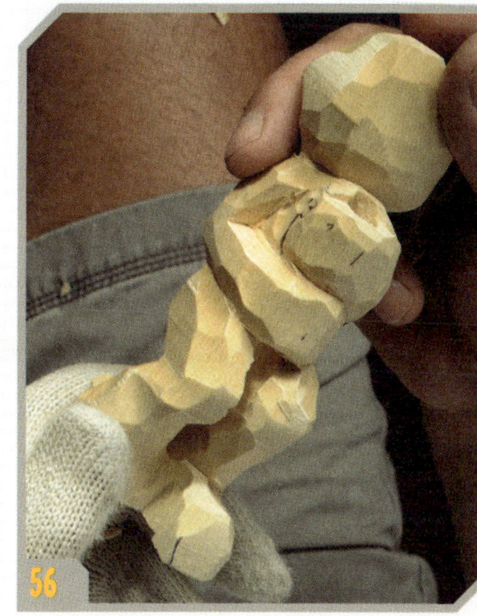

Progress. I keep turning the carving to look for places that need more work.

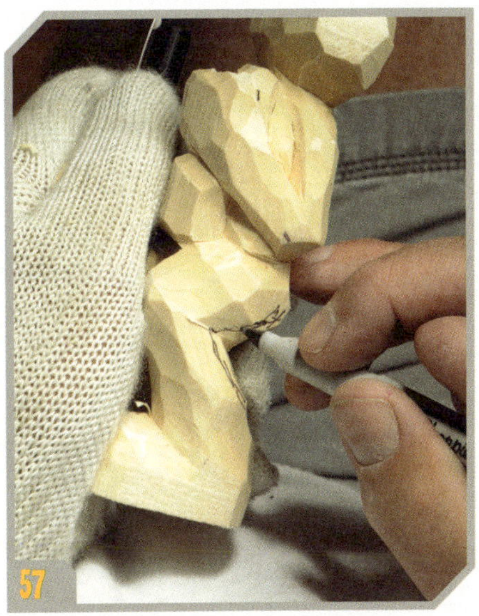

The hip and the back of the leg need to be brought in and up.

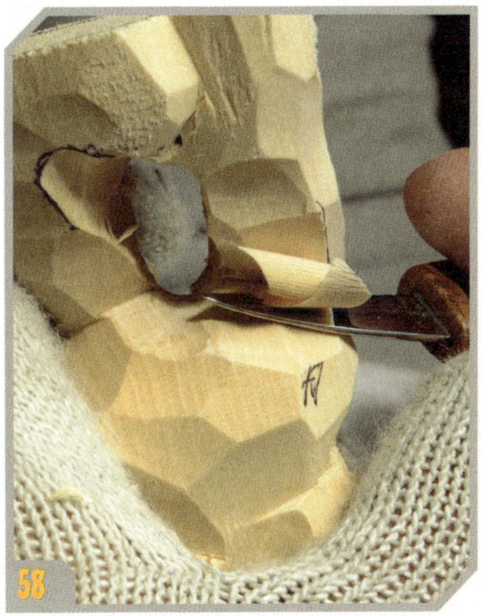

Trim the back of the both legs.

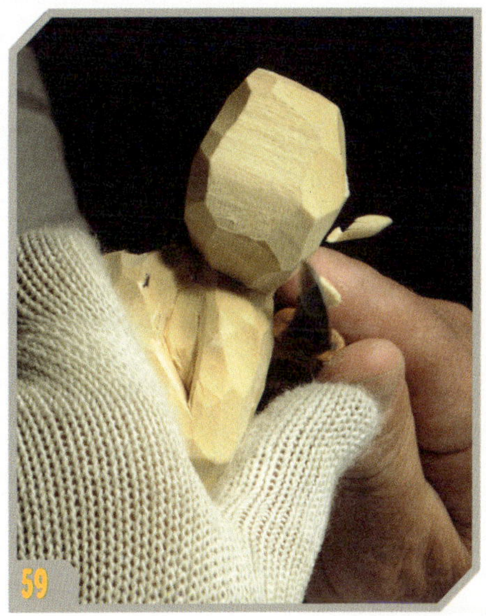

With the basic shape established, I go over the piece and thin it down. I use short, roll cuts for this to get the effect I am after.

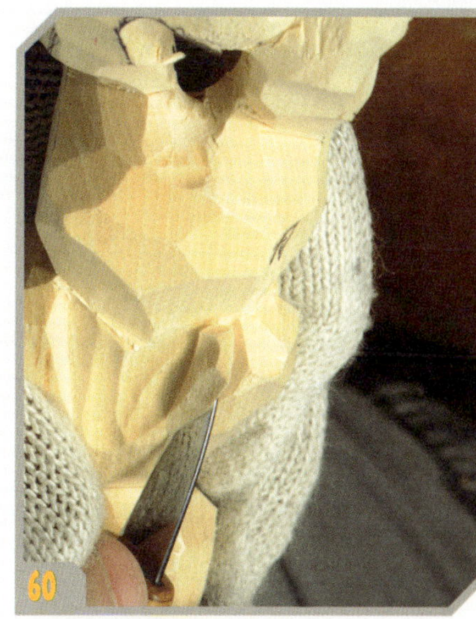

I want to deepen the space between the arm and the body to create shadow and dimensionality. Sometimes I go all the way through, but this is not always necessary.

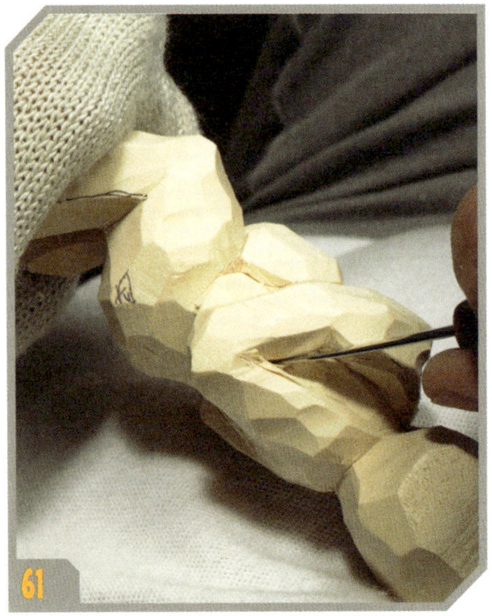

61 I use what I call a triangle cut to deepen the elbow. The three cuts are: one down the lower arm into the elbow…

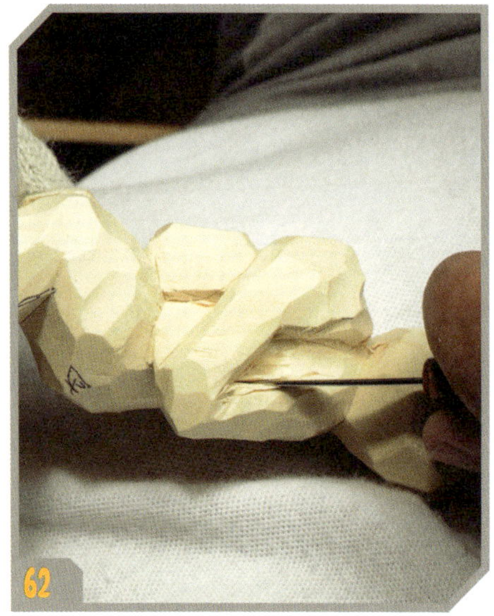

62 another along the upper arm…

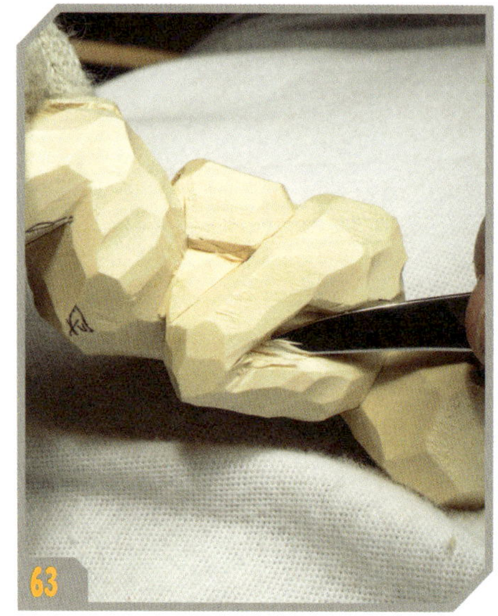

63 then a fairly deep slice along the surface of the body. I repeat this several times until, eventually...

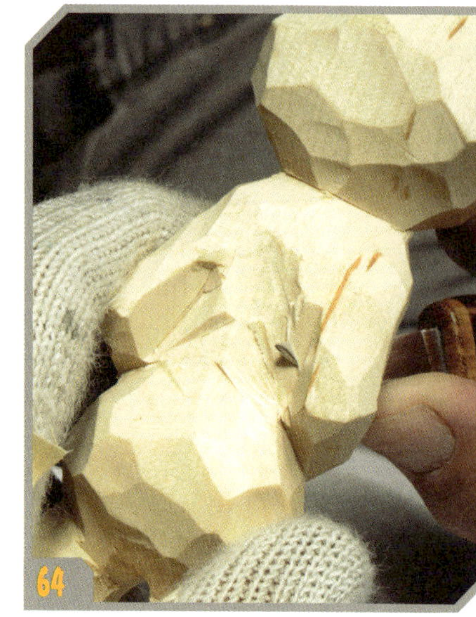

64 I come through.

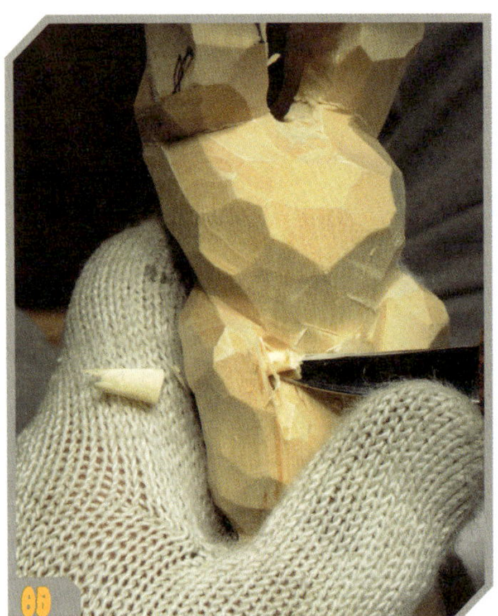

65 Clean up the back side of the elbow with a triangle cut the other way. Repeat on the other arm.

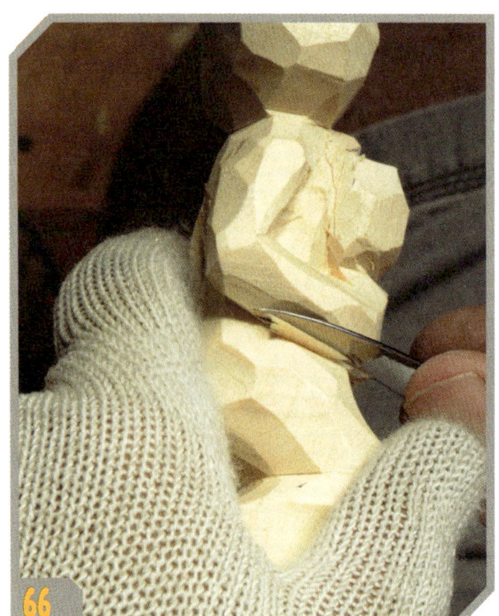

66 Mark spots that need opening up and trim them.

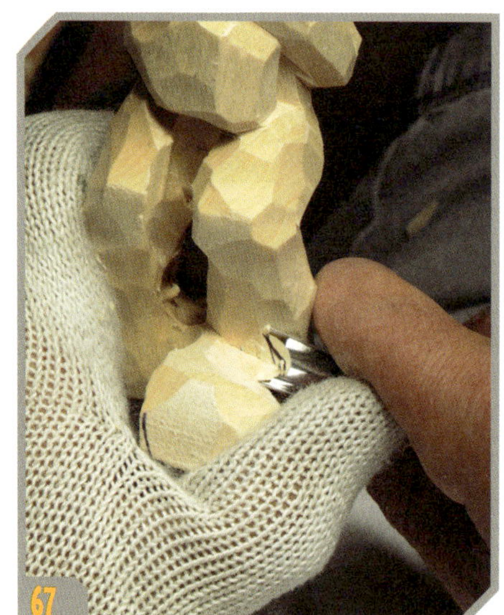

67 Where the foot meets the leg, I open it up with a gouge.

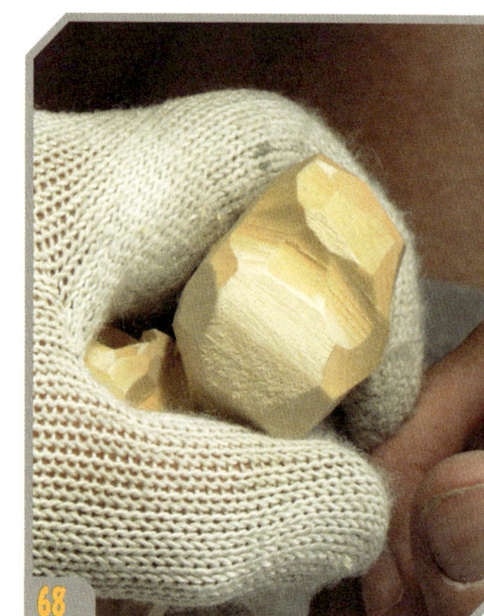

68 Moving to the head and face, about a third of the way down, gouge the eye sockets.

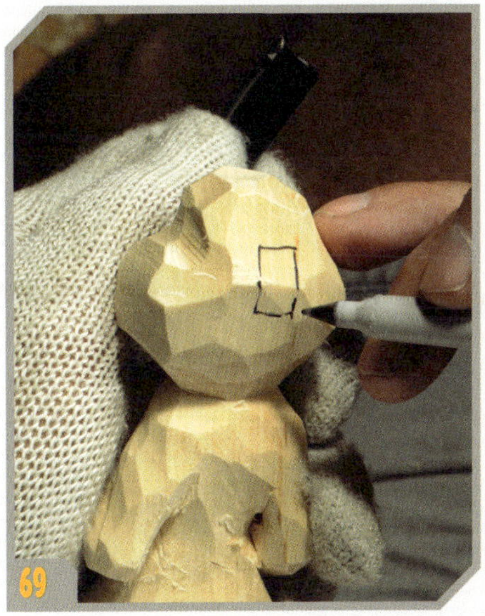

Mark the ear at the center of the head, with the top of the ear even with the eyes.

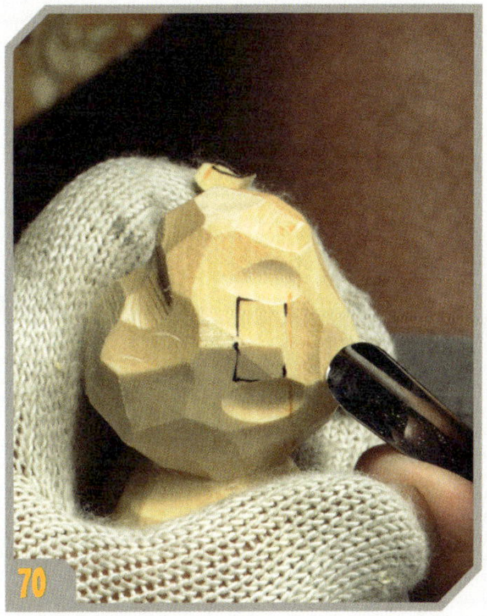

Gouge around the top, back and bottom of the ear.

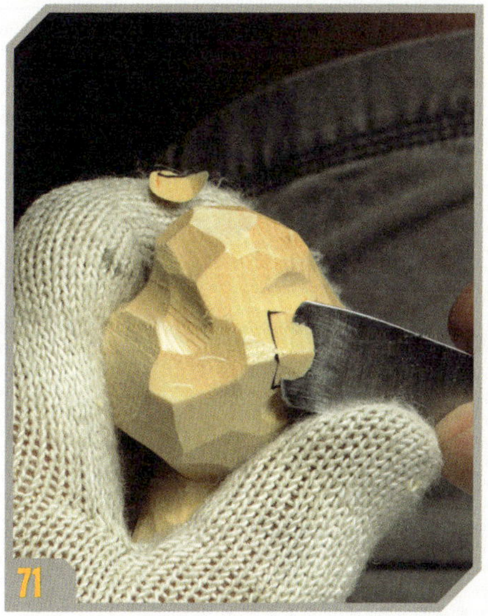

With a flatter gouge, cut the surface of the ear toward the front.

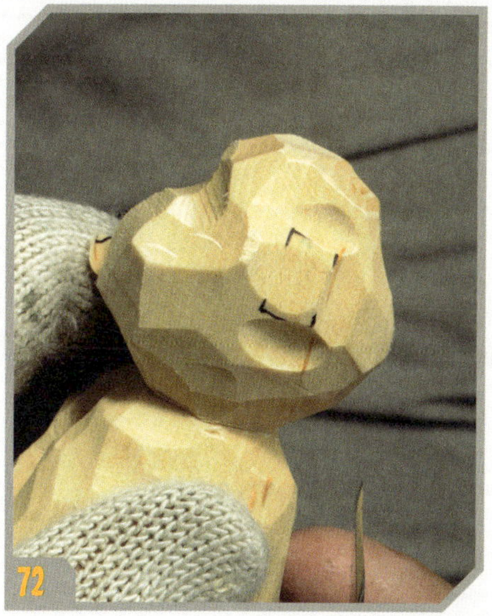

Progress.

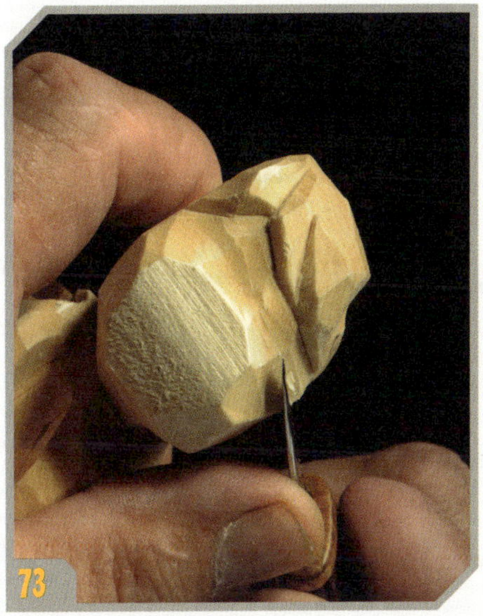

Block in the hairline and establish the part in the hair.

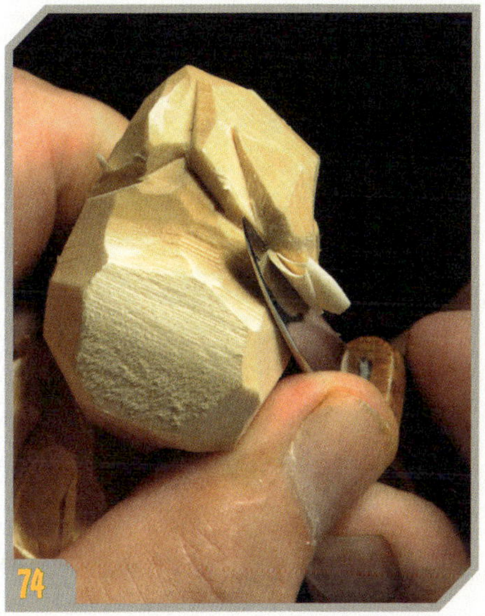

Shape the face back to the hairline.

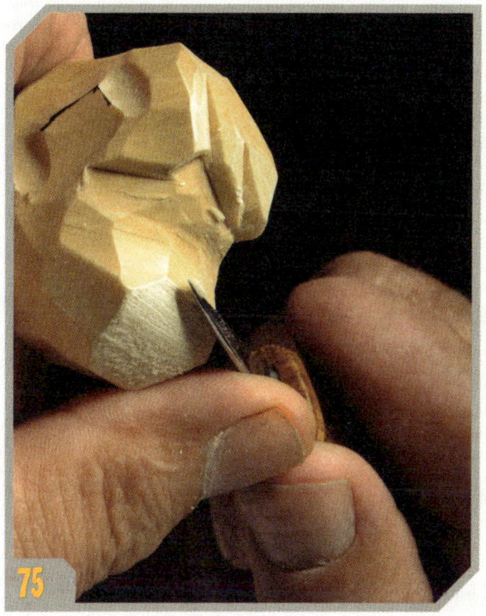

Lower the nose a little bit.

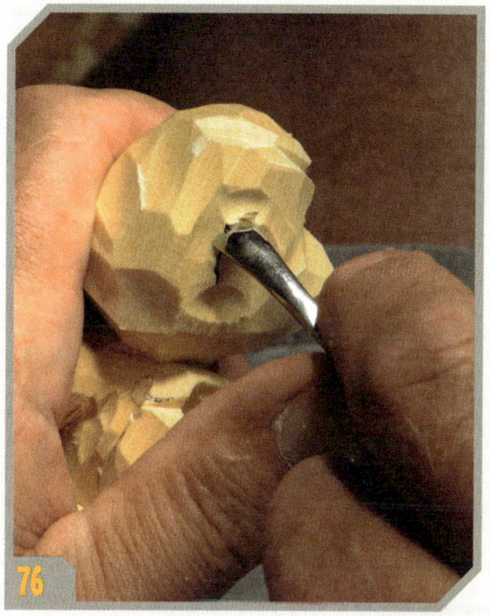

Use a gouge to define the ear with three stop cuts. Press the gouge in at the top of the ear with the cup toward the ear.

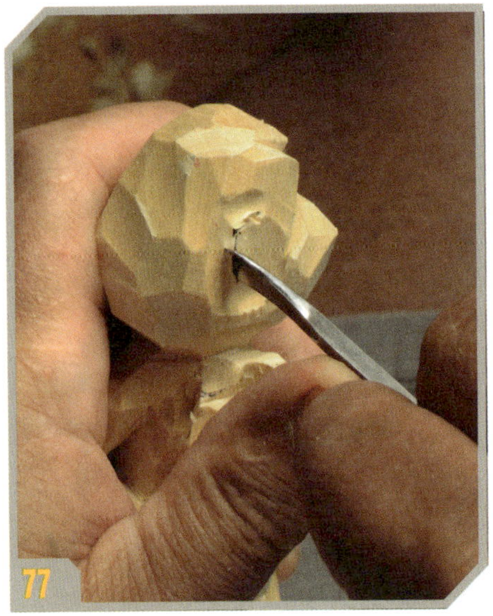
77

Then cut in at the bottom back of the ear with the cup out.

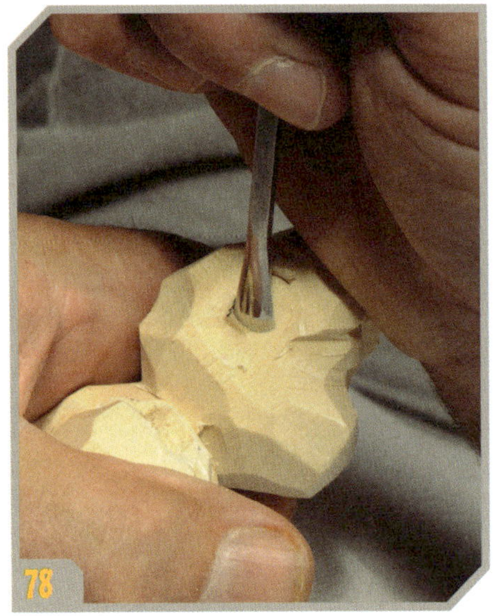
78

Finally, cut the lower lobe with the cup in.

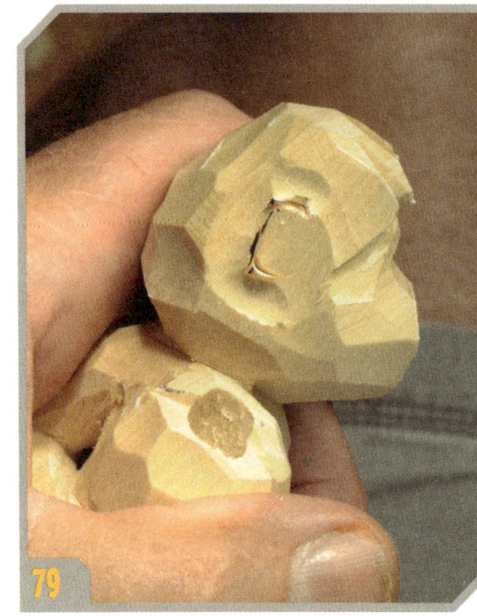
79

The result.

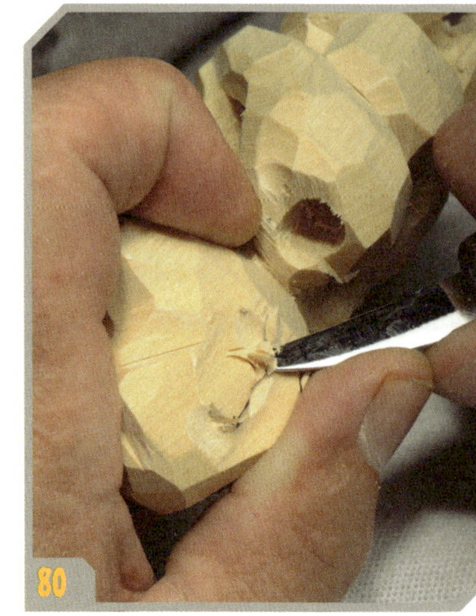
80

Relieve around the ear with a knife. Repeat on the other ear.

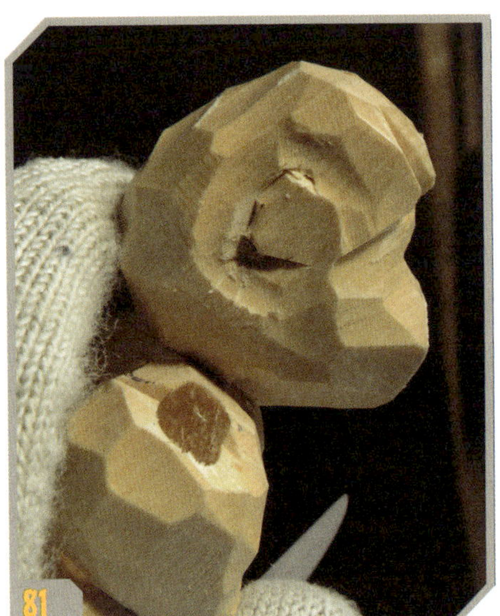
81

Progress on the ear.

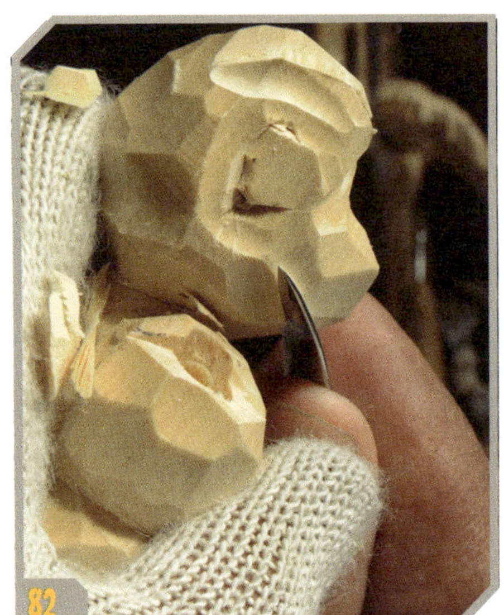
82

Cup out the jaw line.

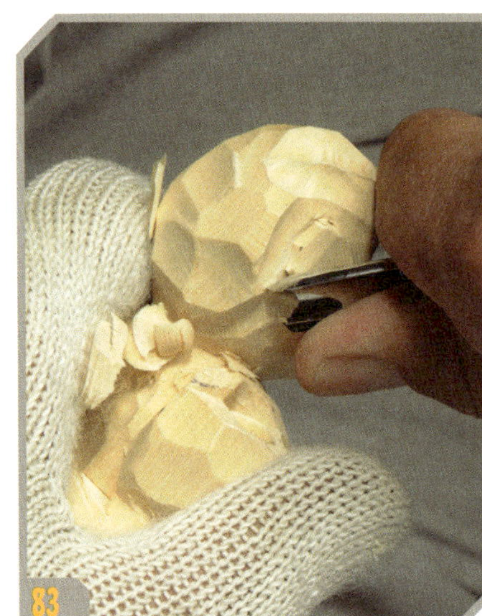
83

With a gouge behind the ear, form the hairline at the neck.

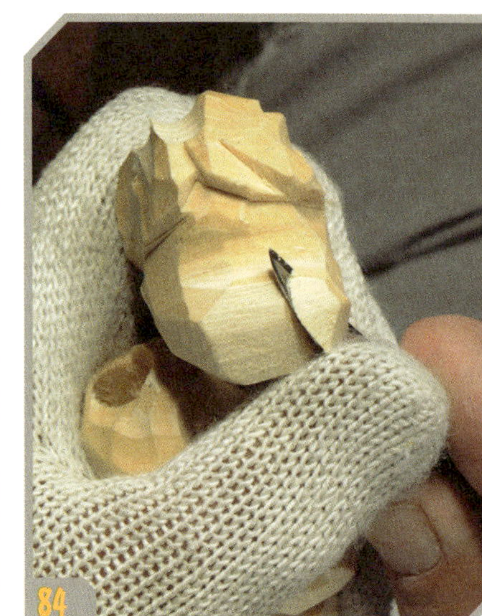
84

84-85) Shape the front of the face, knocking off the corner on one side...

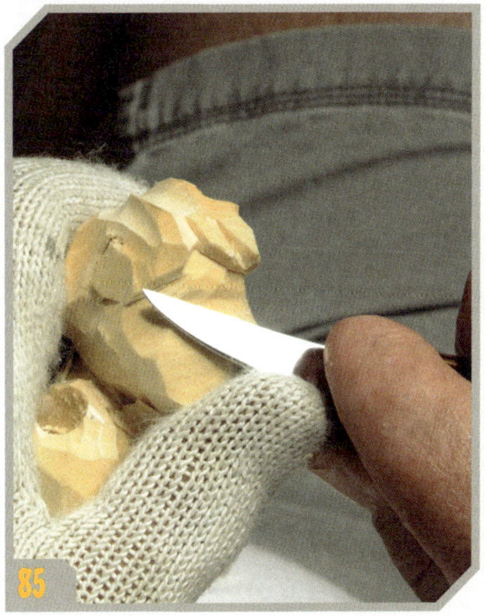

and the other...

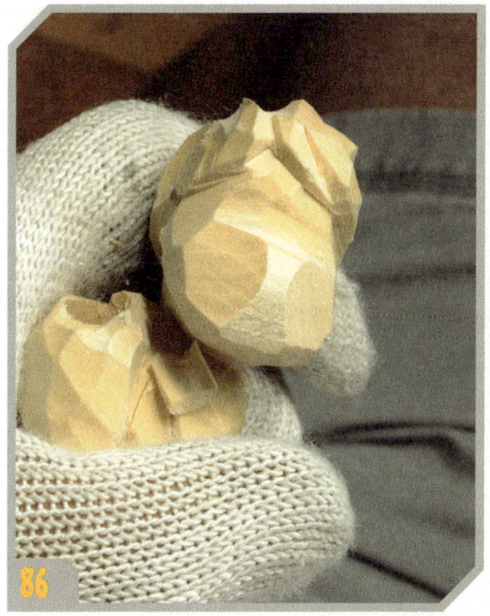

for this result.

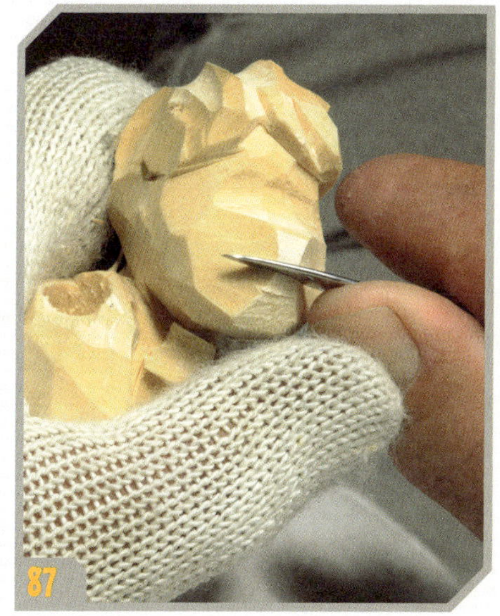

Make a stop at the bottom of the nose.

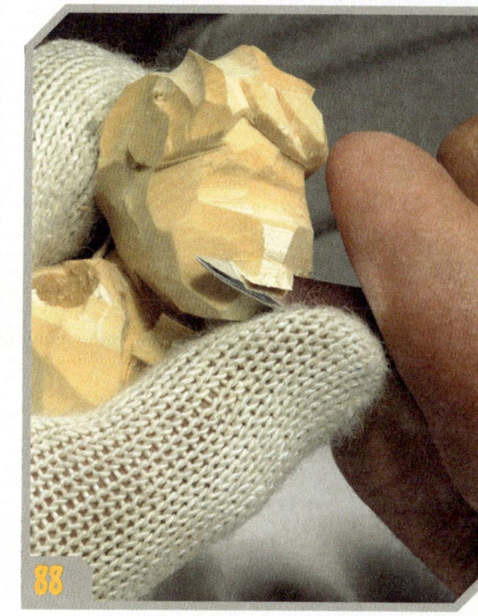

Cut back to it from the lip.

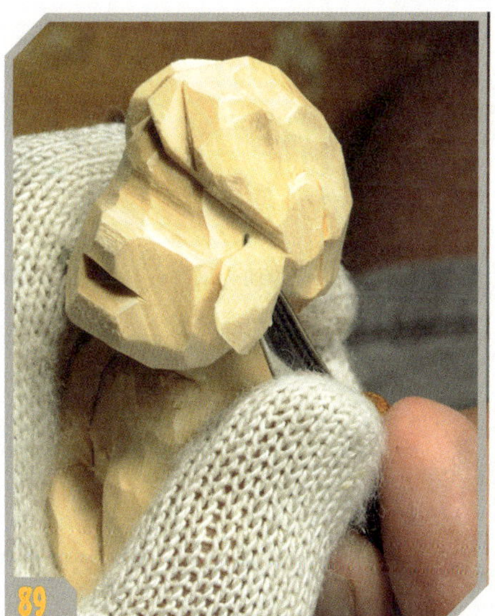

Shape the cheek back to the hairline on both sides.

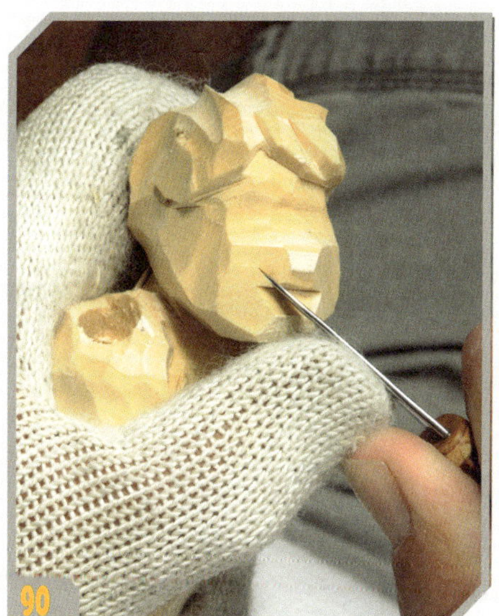

On each side, cut the bottom of the nostrils at 45 degrees.

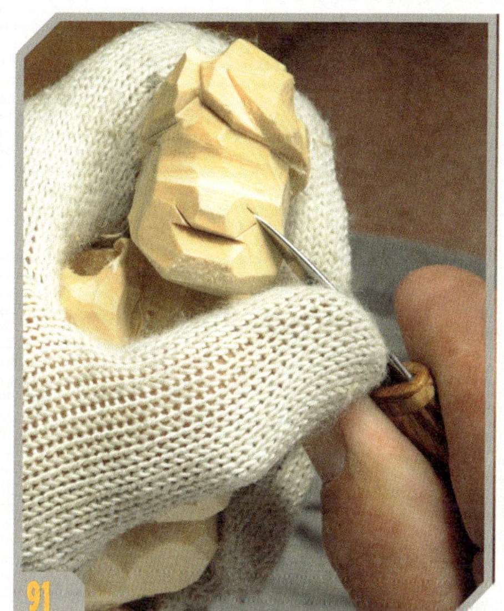

Make a stop cut along the cheek line.

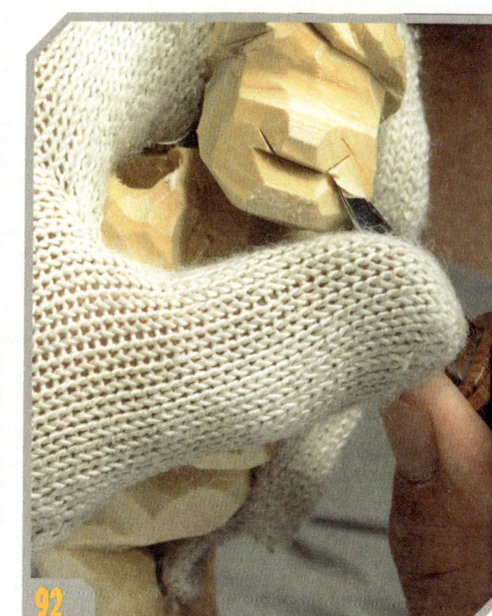

Carve along the lip back to the cheek line...

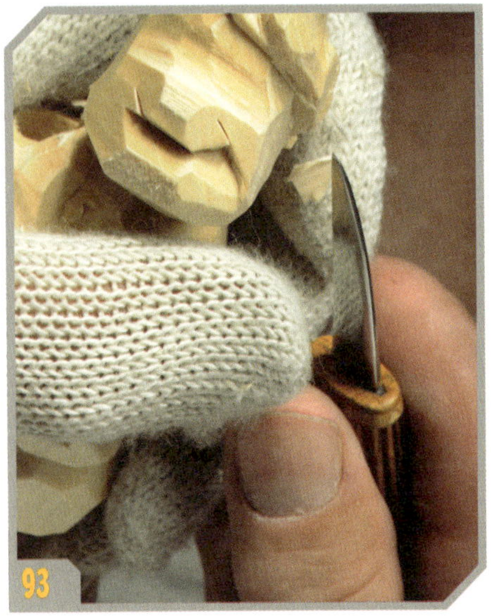

for this result. Repeat on the other side.

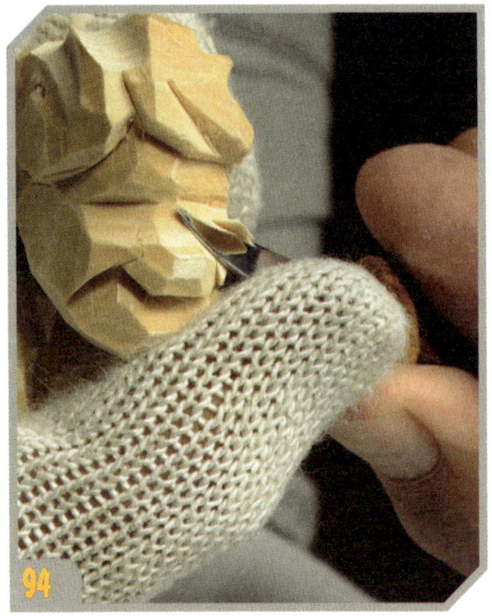

Use a roll cut along the nose to define the plane of the cheek.

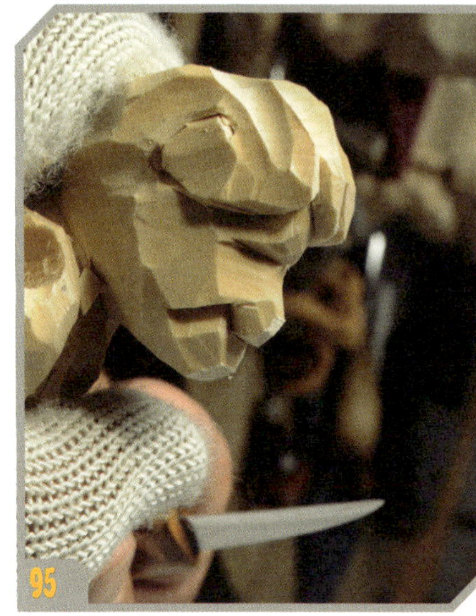

Progress.

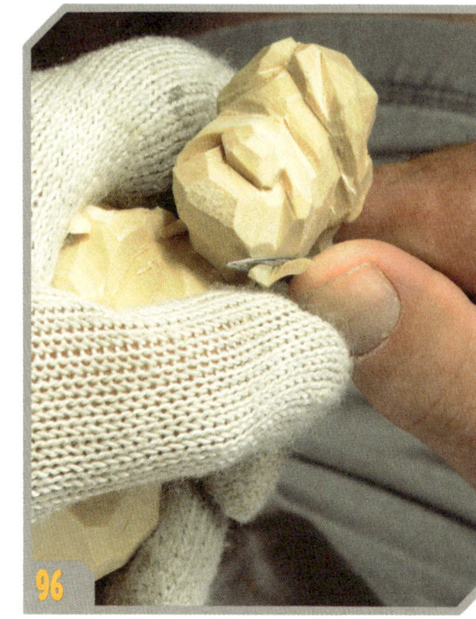

Shape the mustache area...

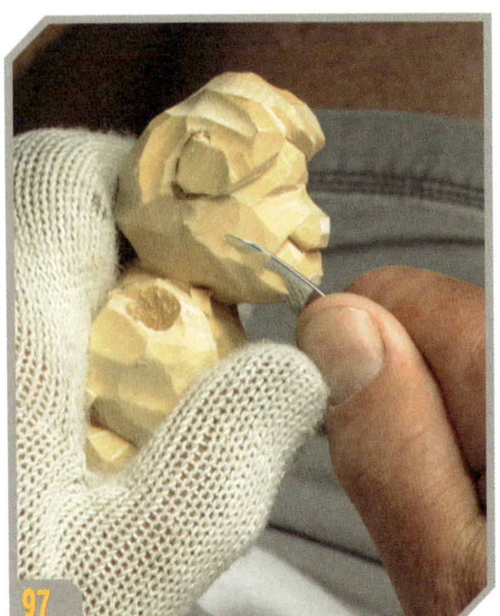

and the lower cheek.

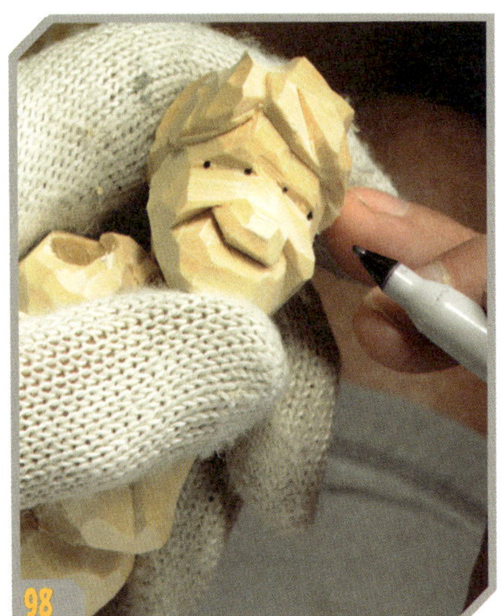

I like to put a dot at the inner and outer corners of the eyes to help me visualize where I am going.

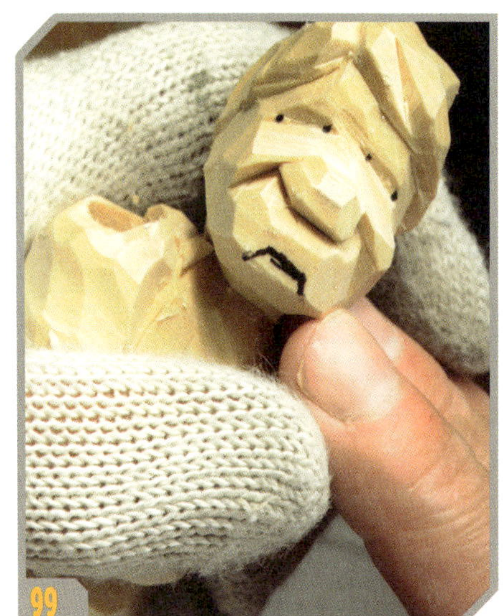

Also make a guideline for the mouth.

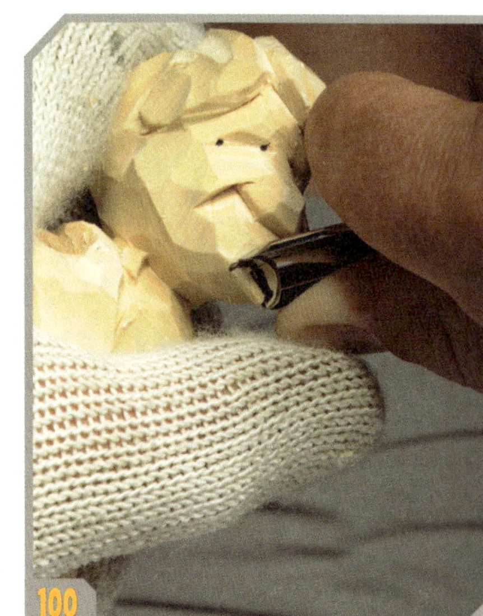

Use a gouge to clean out the mouth area.

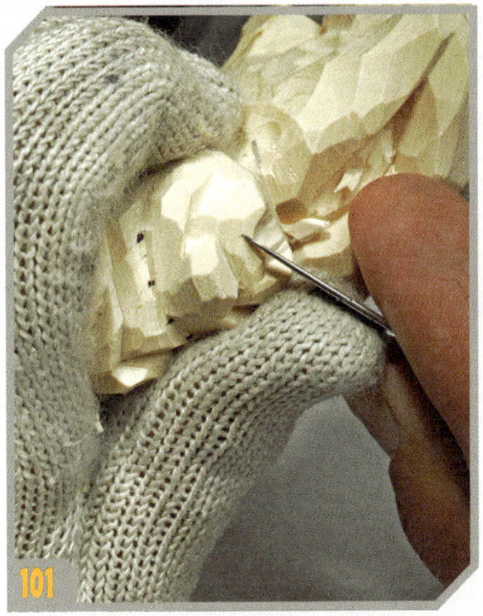

At the corners of the mouth define the mustache with three cuts. One along the side of the moustache…

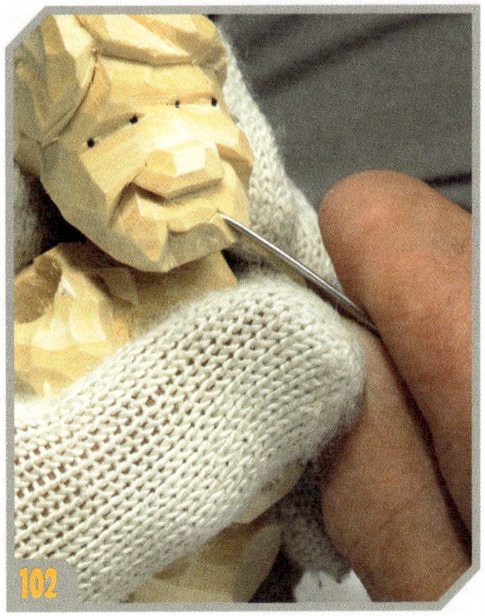

one along the bottom edge…

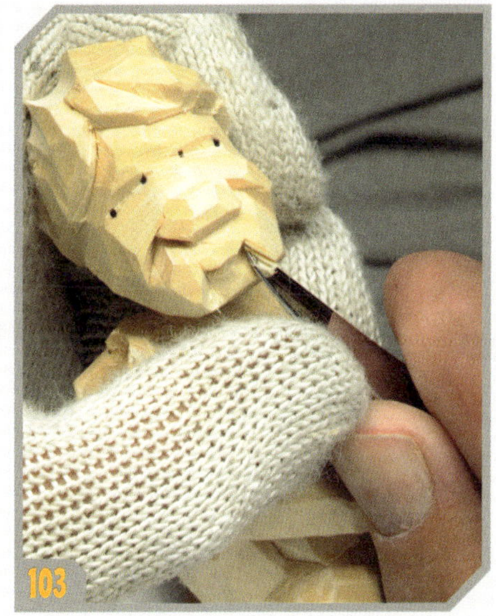

and then one cutting back along the surface of the lip to free the chip.

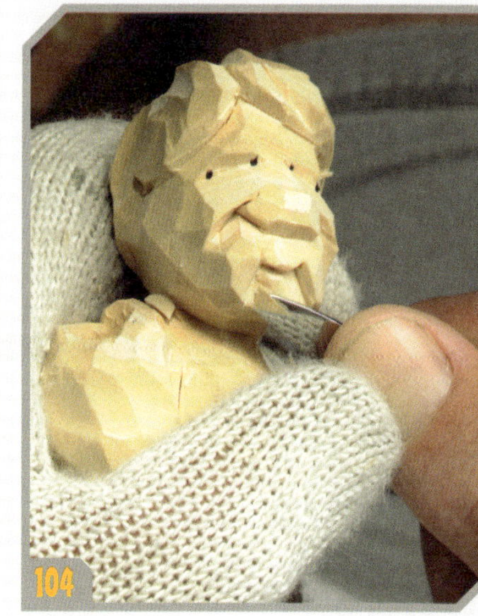

Make a scooping cut under the lip on both sides…

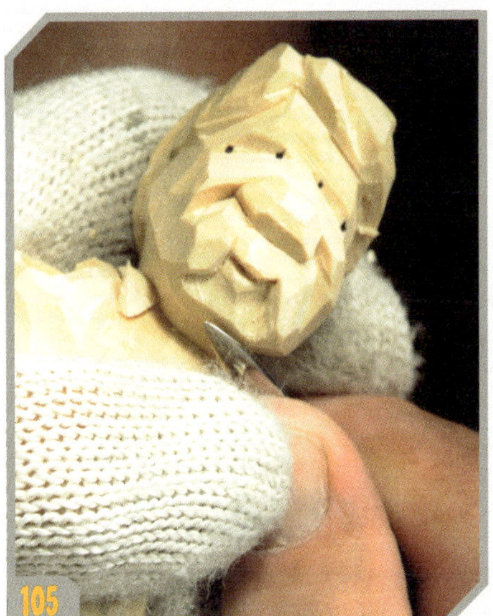

for this result.

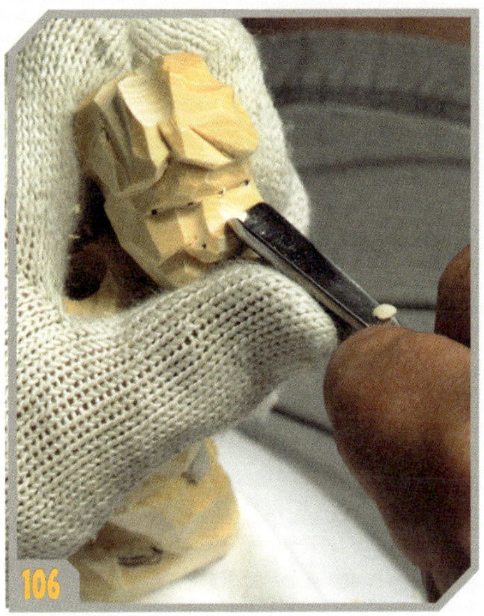

Use a gouge to cut along the side of the nose up to the eye socket on both sides.

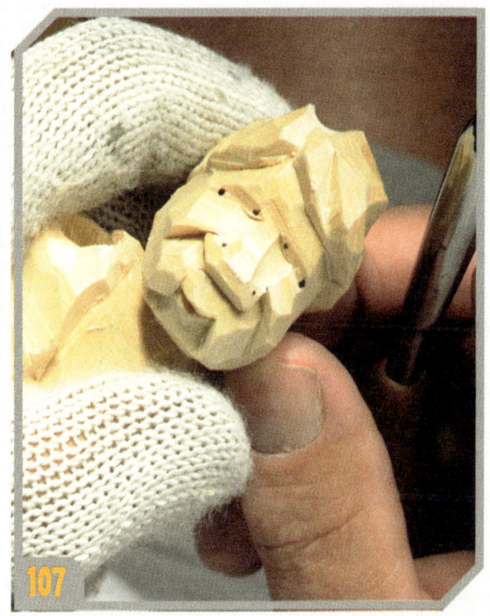

The result.

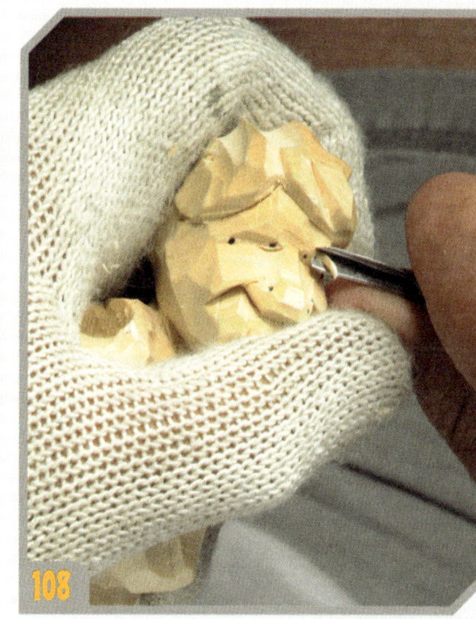

With a small v-tool, start at the outer edge of the eye and cut toward the center, going up toward the middle...

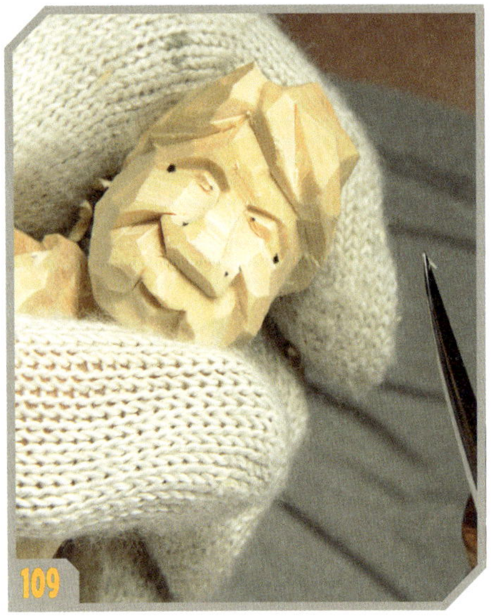

and down to the inside corner for this result.

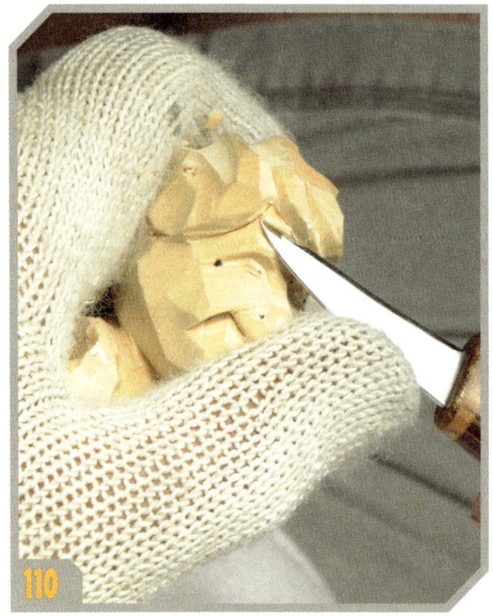

From the top of the eyebrow, make a roll cut toward the hairline to bring out the eyebrow.

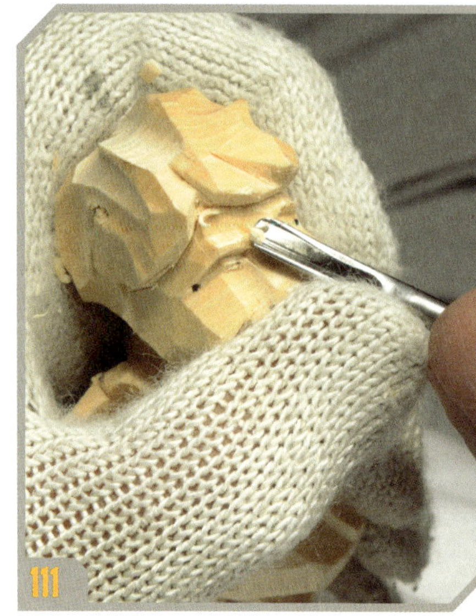

Separate the eyebrows using the same gouge.

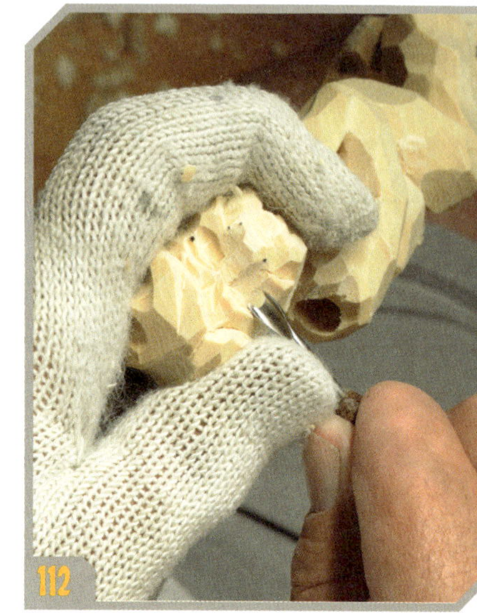

With a small u-gouge, scoop under the eye, moving from the outside. Repeat on the other side.

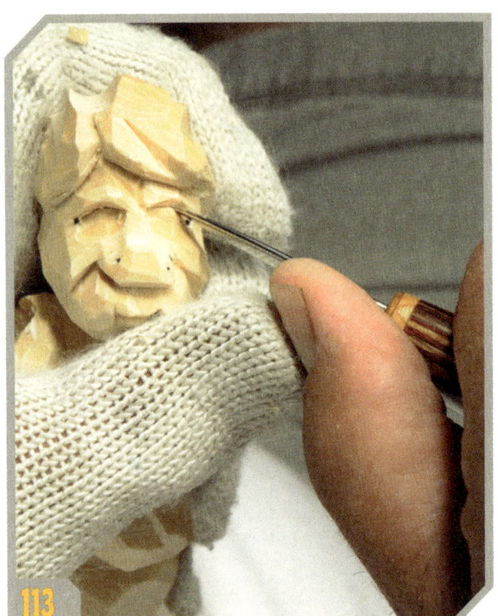

Make a stop cut with a knife under the upper lid.

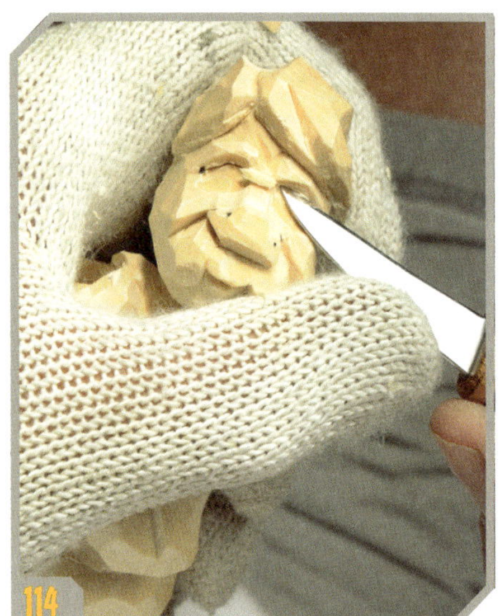

Relieve the cut from the eyeball.

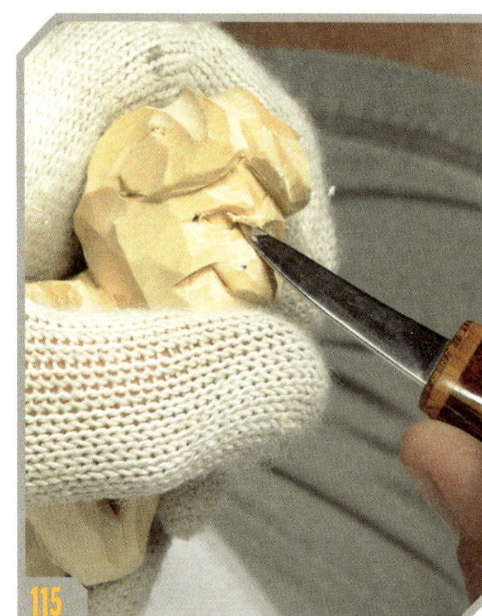

Decide how wide the eyeball should be and make stop cuts in the corner.

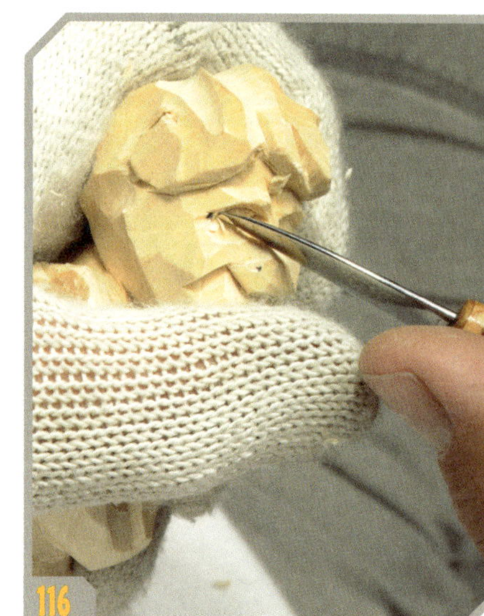

Relieve it from the eyeball. Repeat on the other side.

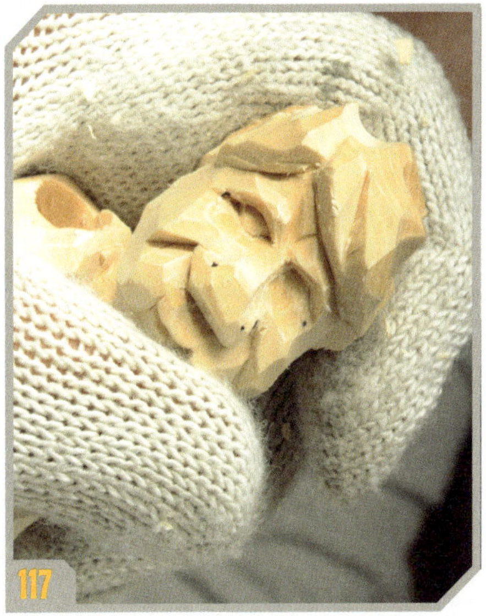

117

The result.

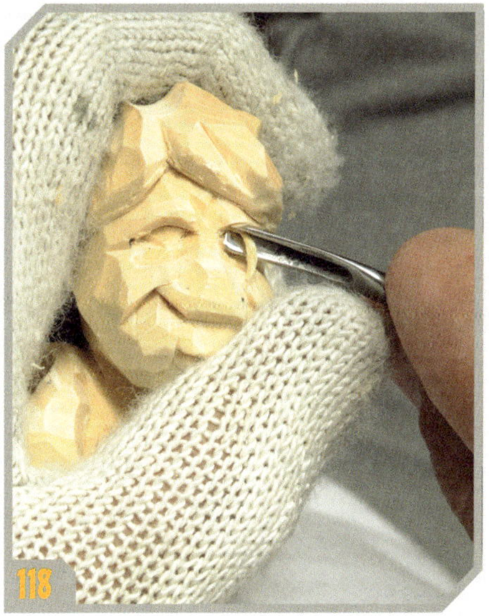

118

Use a v-tool to shape the upper lid...

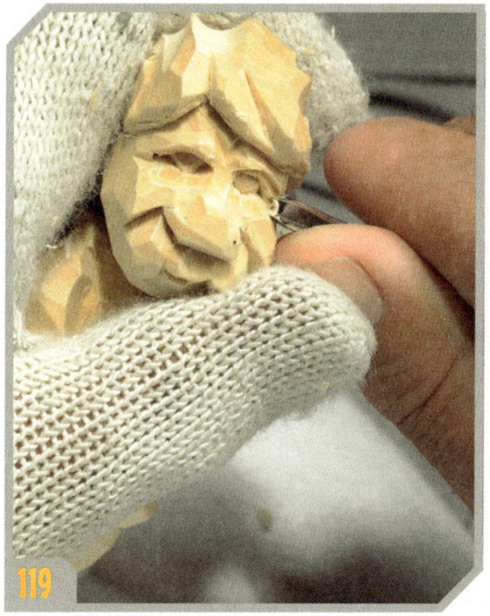

119

and cut the crow's foot at the corner.

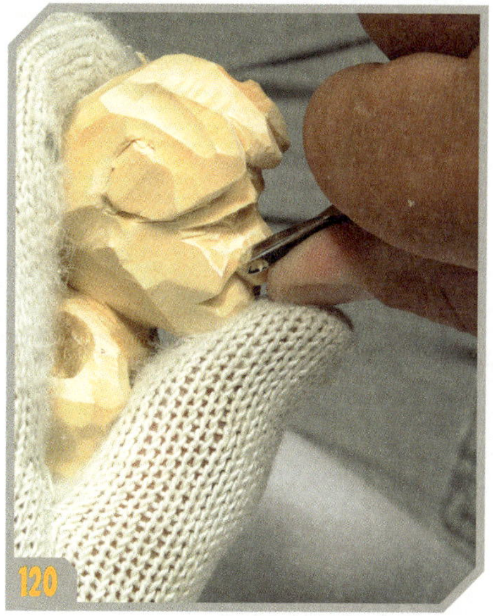

120

Shape the upper edge of the nostril with the same v-tool.

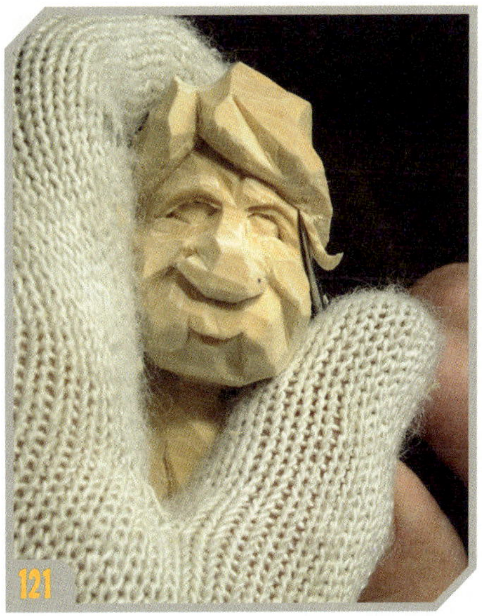

121

Trim the temple area.

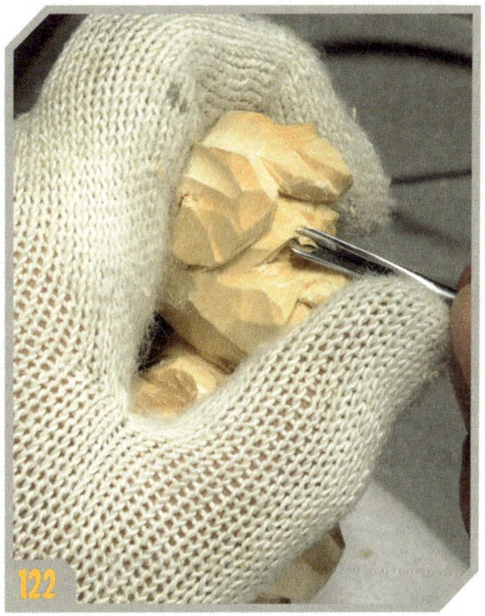

122

Use the v-tool to make the hairlines in the eyebrows.

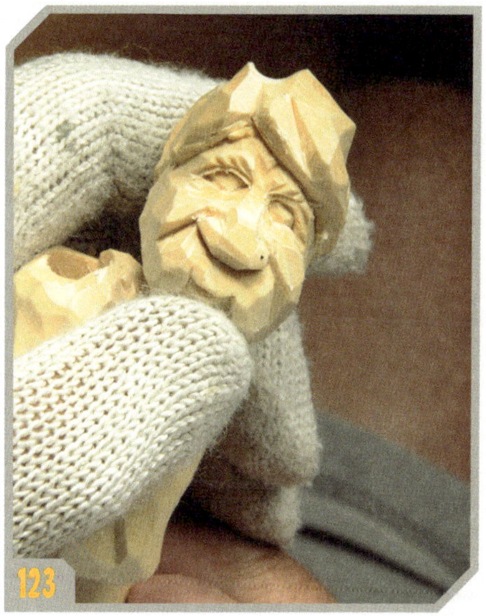

123

The result.

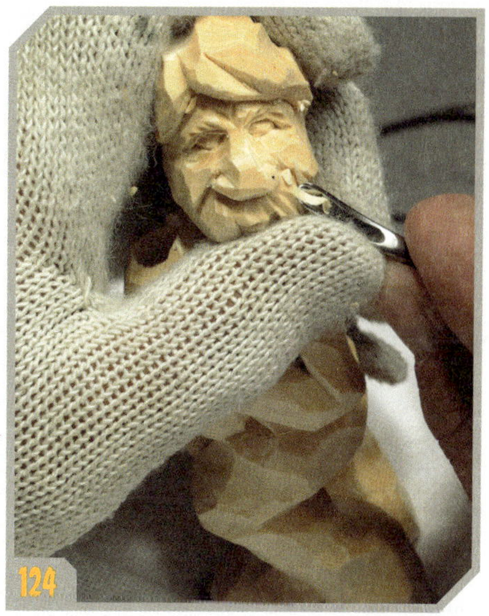

124

Use the same method to make hairlines on the mustache.

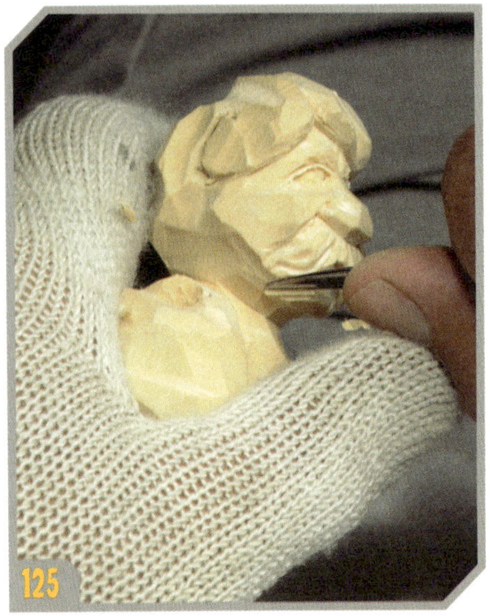

Define the chin where it meets the mustache.

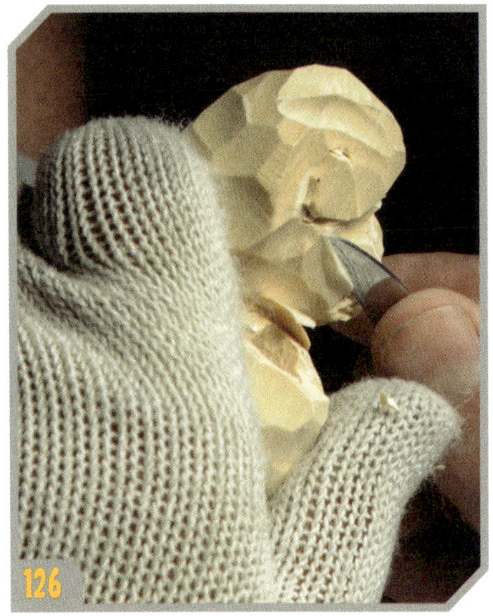

Shape the lower cheek and jaw.

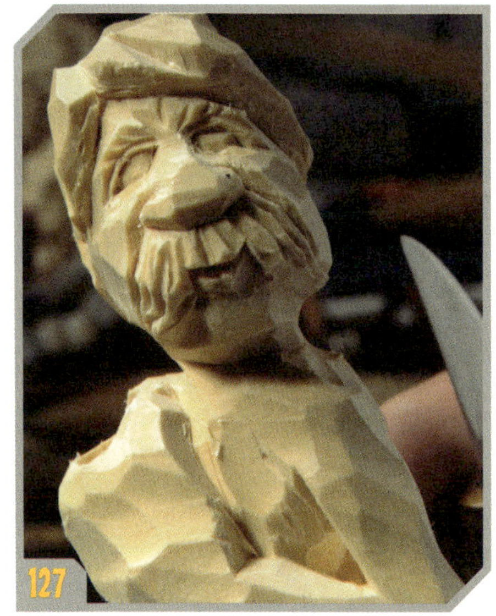

Progress on the face..

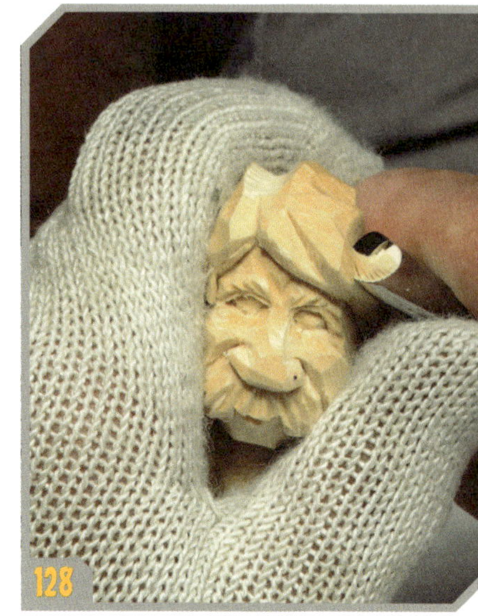

I use a series of three or four gouges to detail the hair, starting with a bigger one to form the general contour. Avoid straight lines.

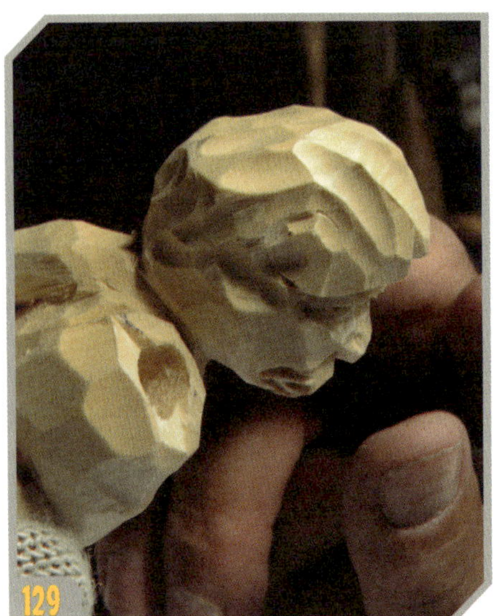

The result.

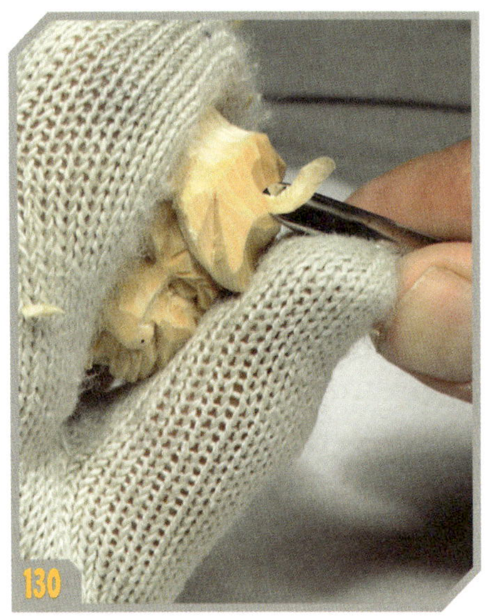

Add details with a smaller gouge. It is easy to get too busy in the hair, so be careful.

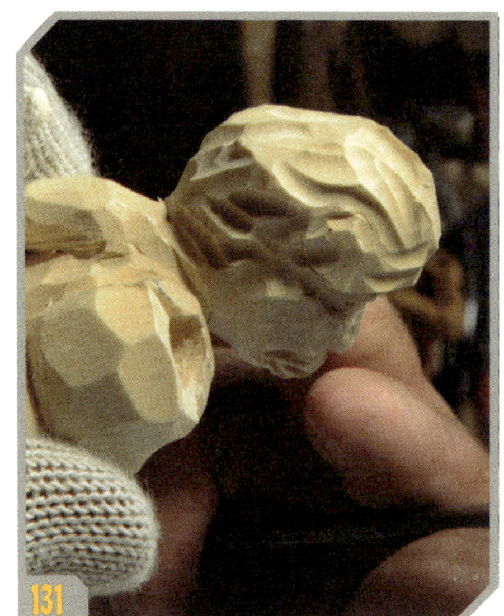

Progress.

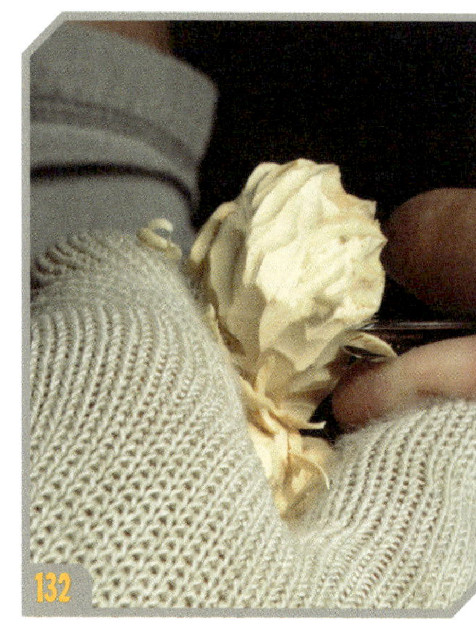

The final gouge adds a nice touch.

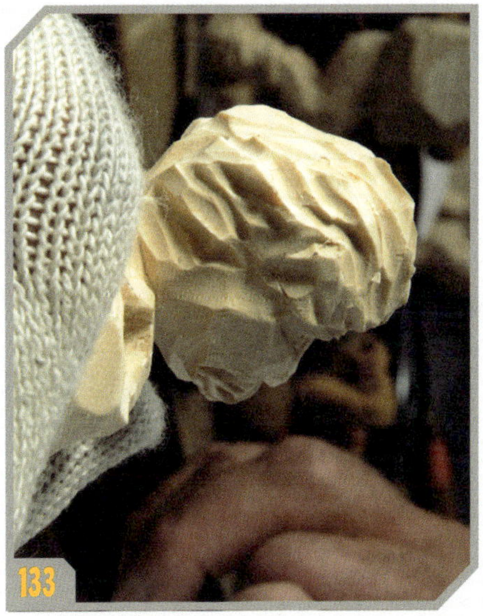

133 The result.

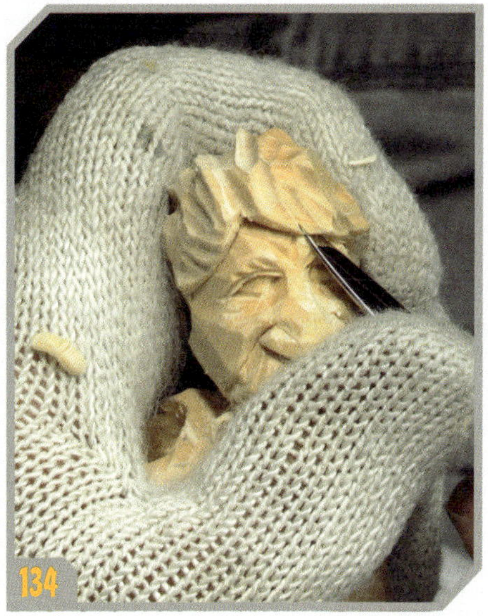

134 With a knife, go back and add some notches to break up the hairline and give it detail.

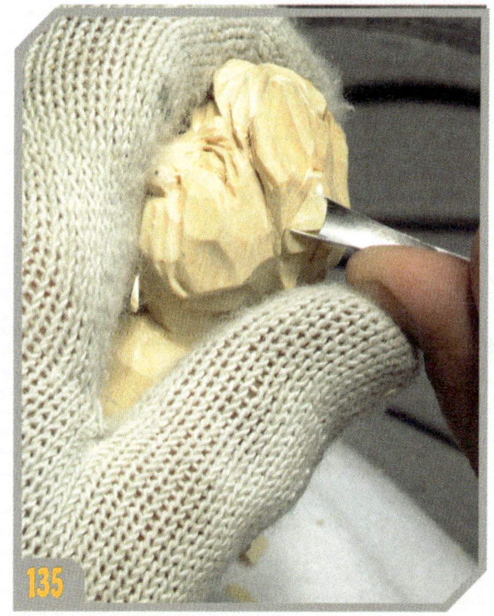

135 Cup the surface of the ear with a gouge.

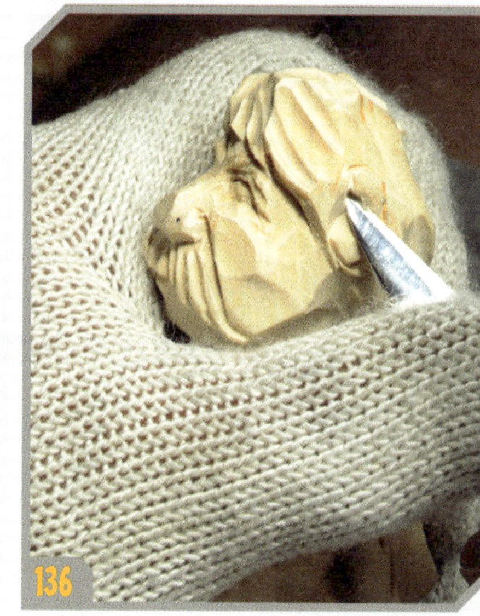

136 Make a triangle cut at the top corner…

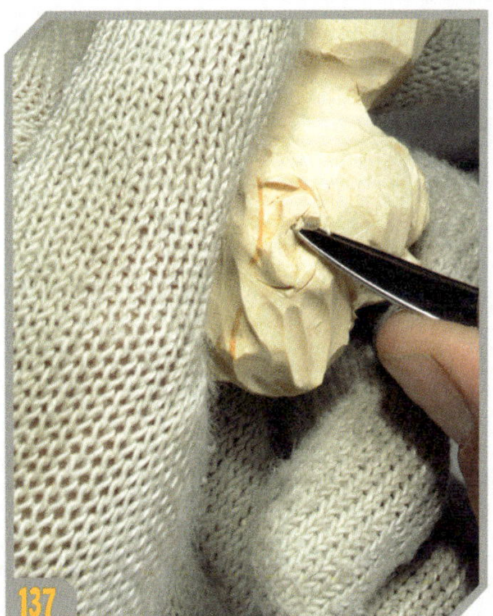

137 and the bottom to create shadow.

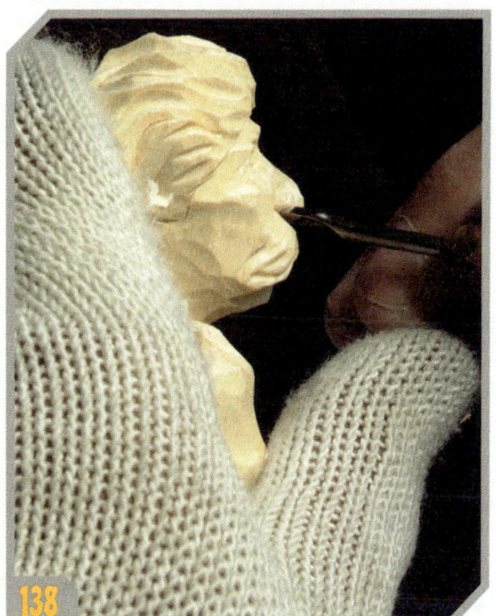

138 Gouge out the nostrils.

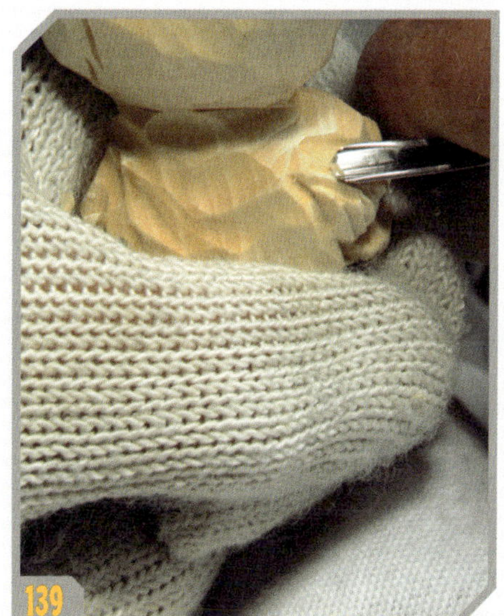

139 Clean up the head. I usually like to use a gouge to undercut the hairline and the moustache, giving the piece better shadows.

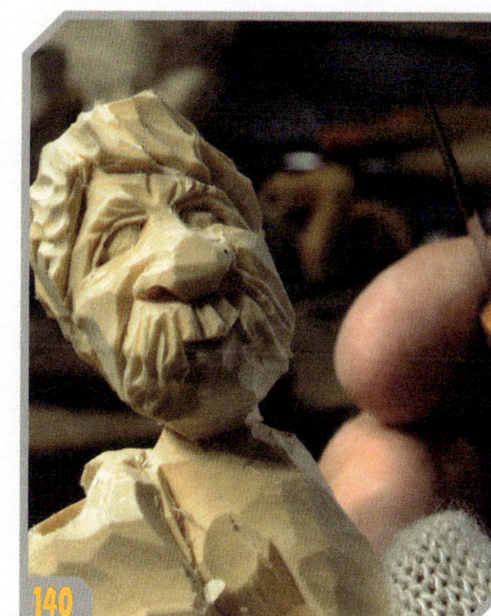

140 The result from the front...

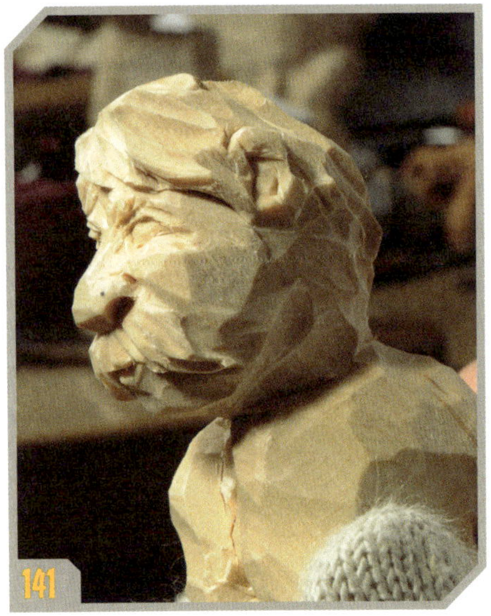

and the side.

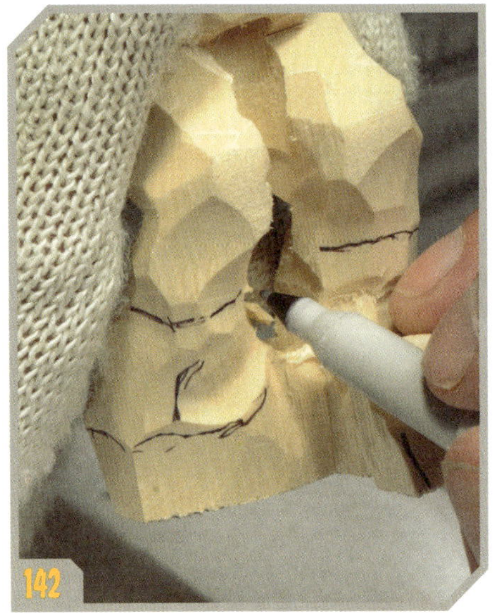

Clean up the surface of the body, then draw in the top of the boot…

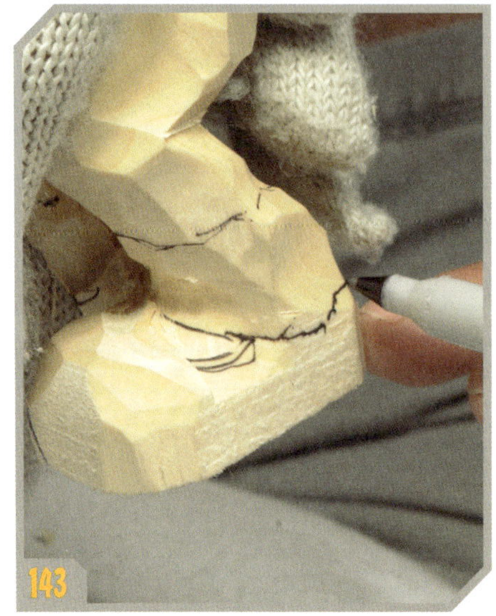

and bottom of the cuff, where it is folded down.

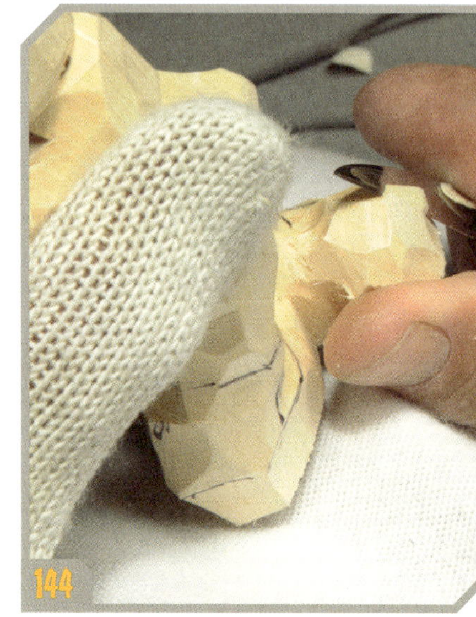

Shape foot of the boot. Remember the outside of the shoe is always the low side and the inside is the high side.

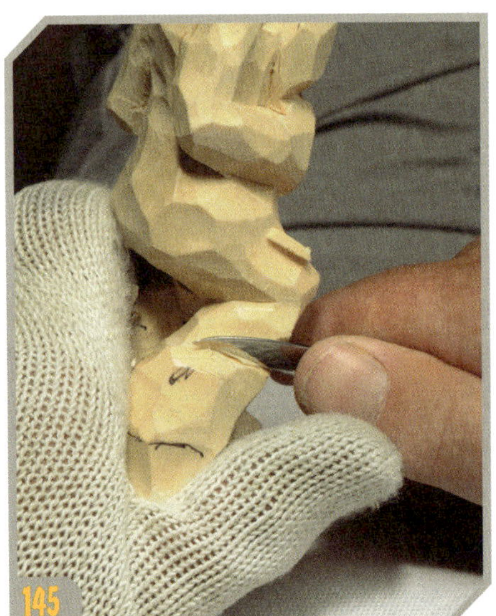

The pants are tucked into the boot, so make a stop cut around the top of the boot and trim the pants back to it.

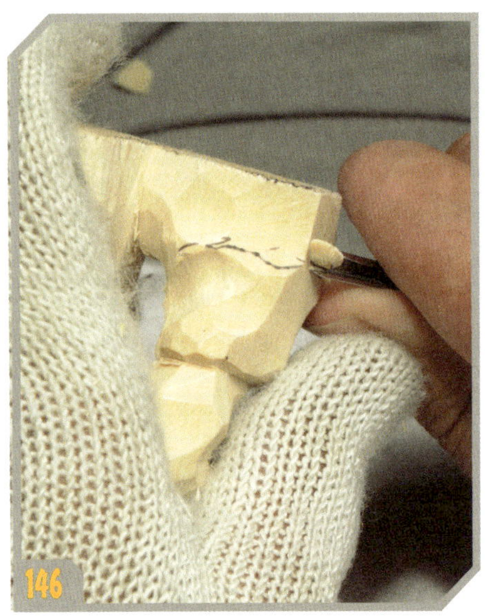

Run a v-tool around the fold-down and the top of the boot.

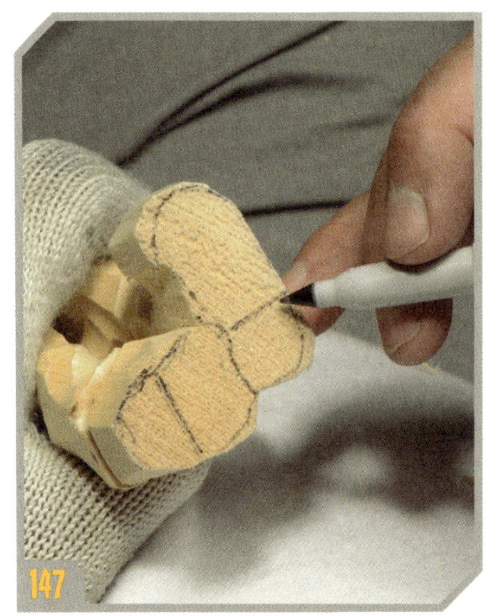

Mark the heel of the boot…

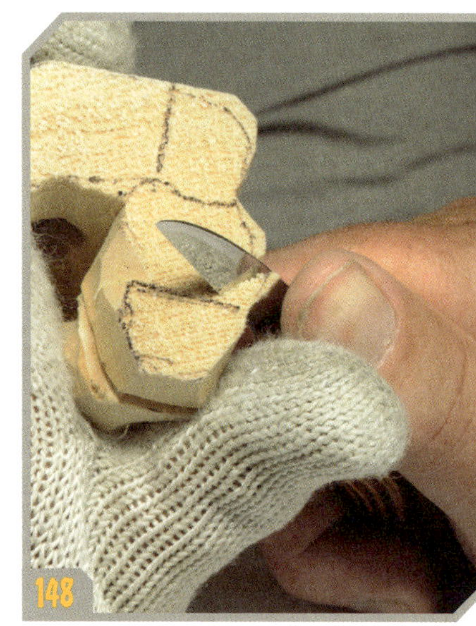

and take a notch out on the inside and outside.

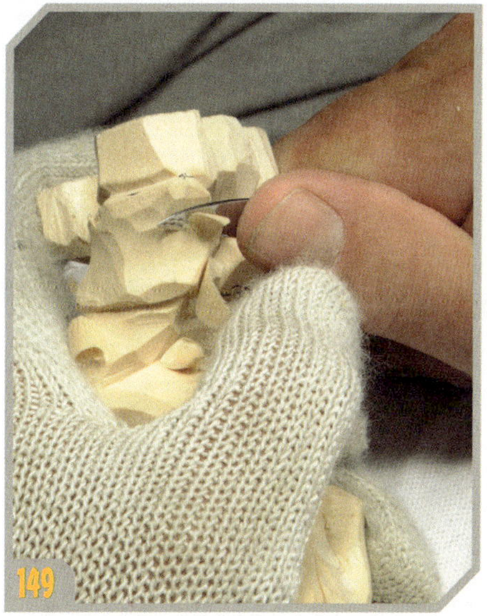

149 Roll-cut the surface of the cuff to cup it.

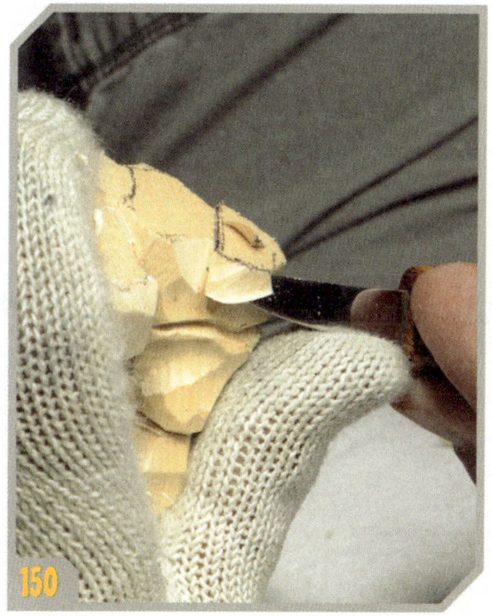

150 Thin the heels and cut the sole back to the heel.

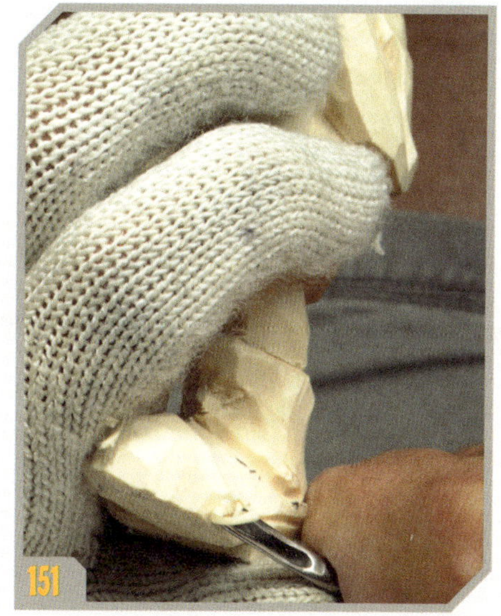

151 Use a v-tool to define the top edge of the sole.

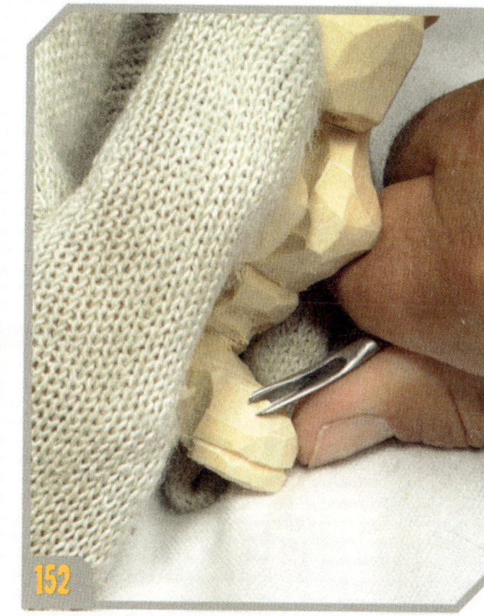

152 With the same tool, mark the steel toe cap of the boot.

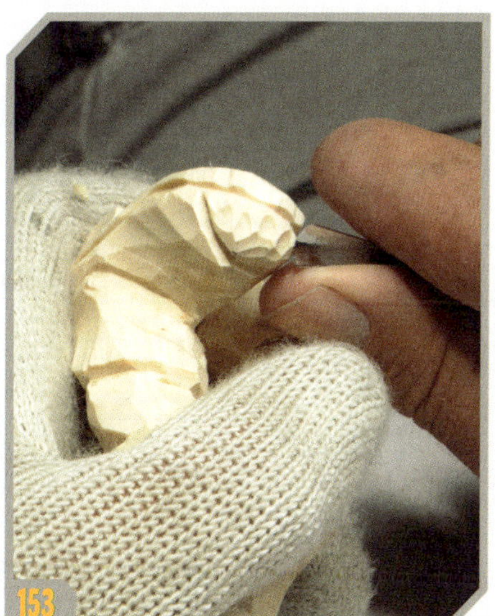

153 Use the v-tool to make some folds in the rubber.

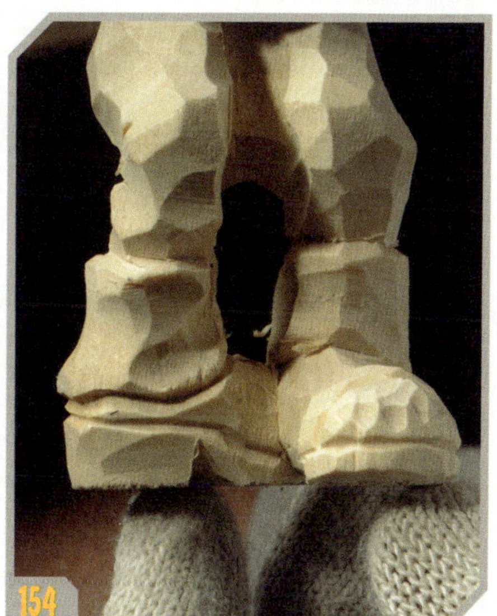

154 The feet finished.

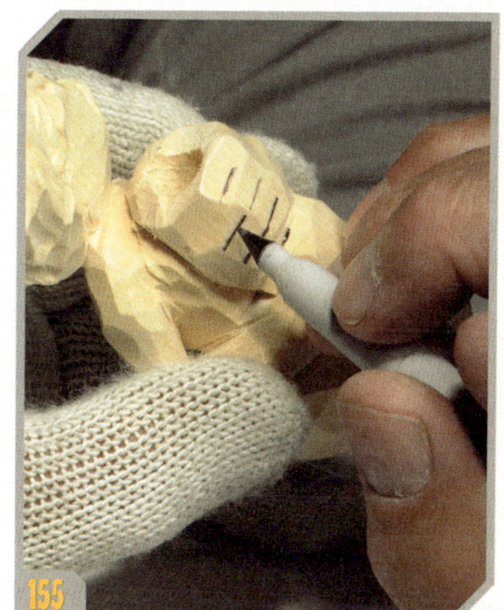

155 The fingers are marked, beginning with the center line and adding one to each side.

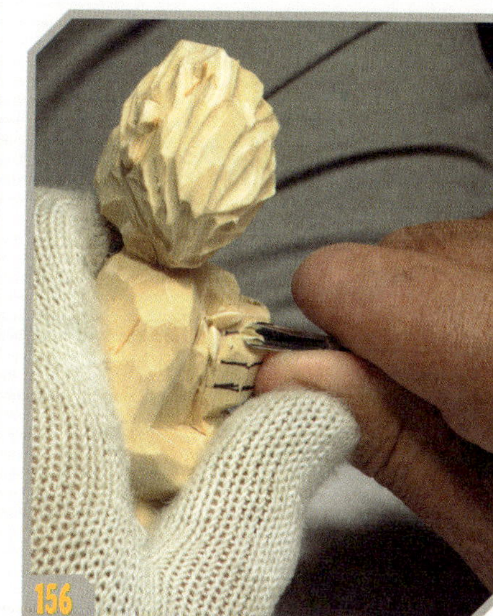

156 Each line is followed with a v-tool making a scoop cut for each segment of the fingers.

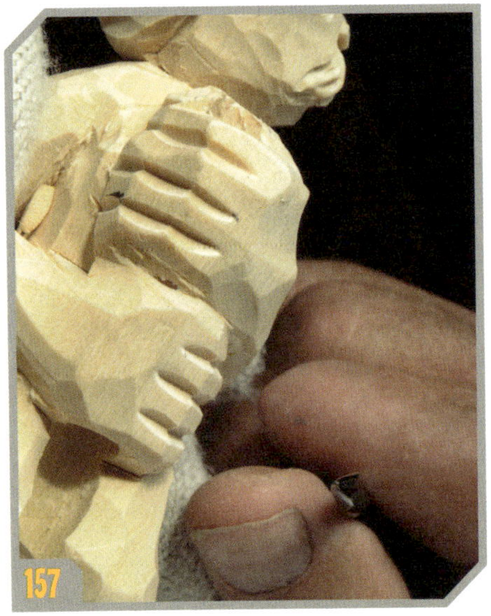

157

The result.

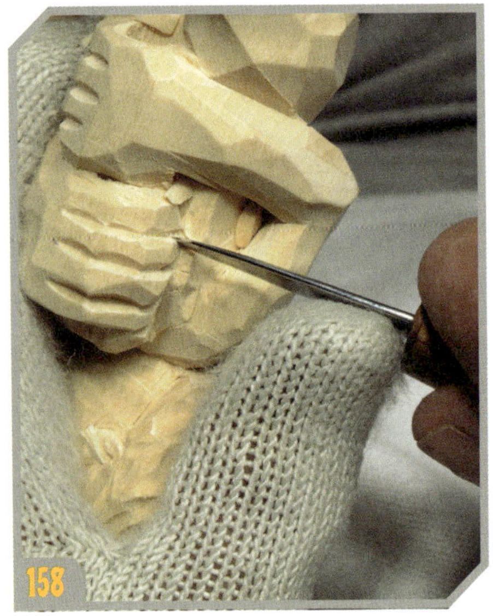

158

Make a notch between the fingers at the end to separate them.

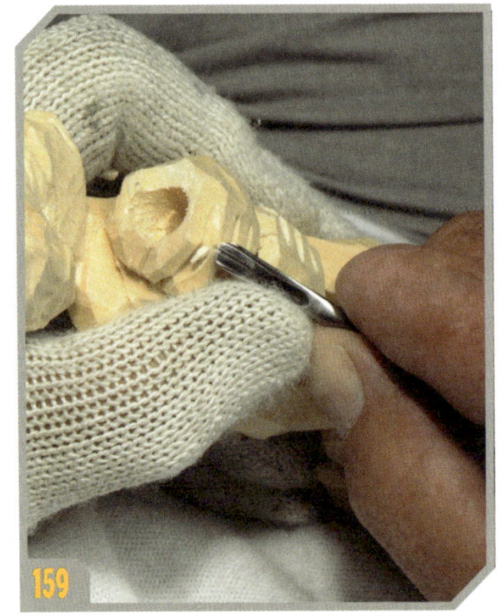

159

Detail the joints with a gouge, make a straight cut across the middle and a curved cut above and below that.

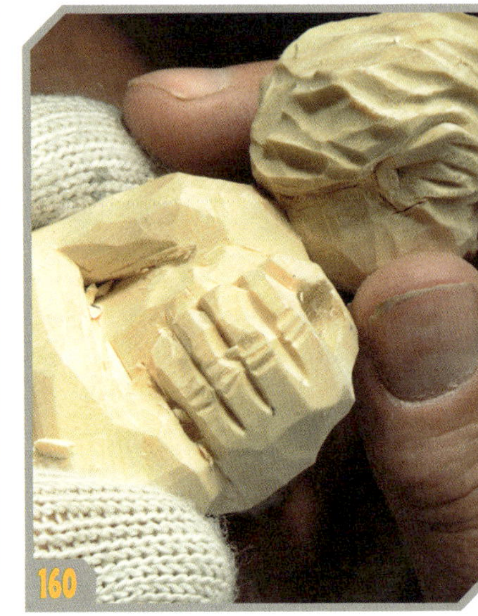

160

The result.

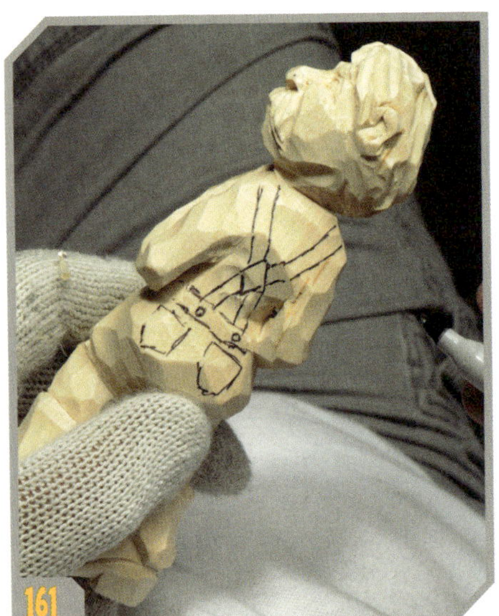

161

Draw in the details of the pants and suspenders. Back...

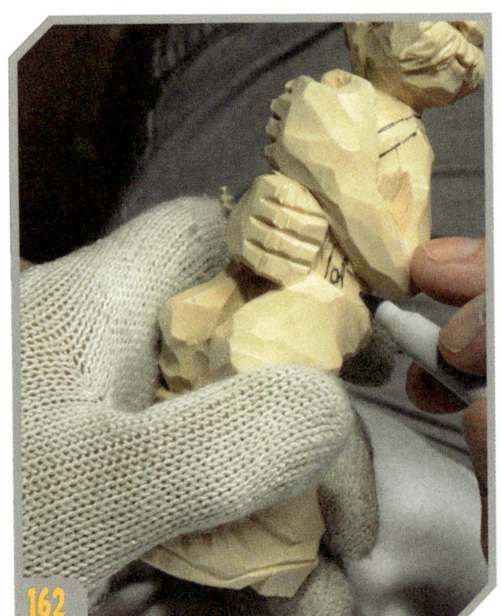

162

and front. If you've left room continue the suspenders to the waist in front.

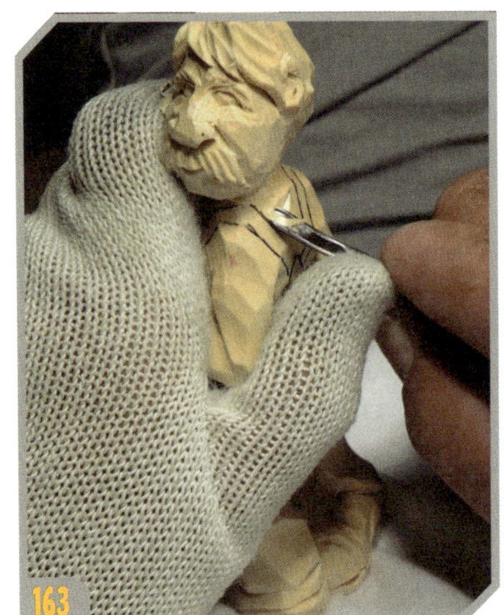

163

Follow the lines with a v-tool.

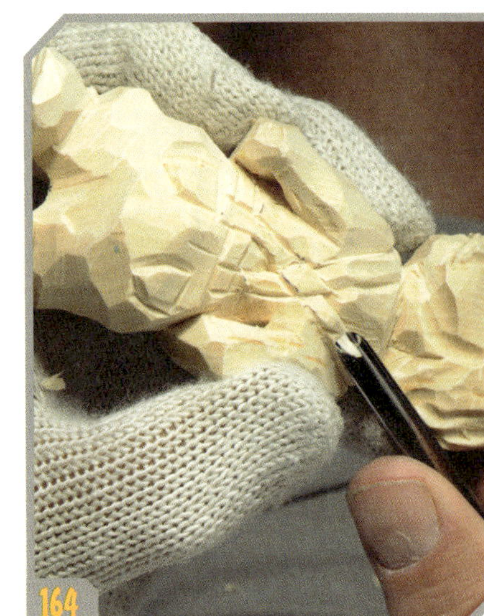

164

Use the gouge to add some shape to the suspenders.

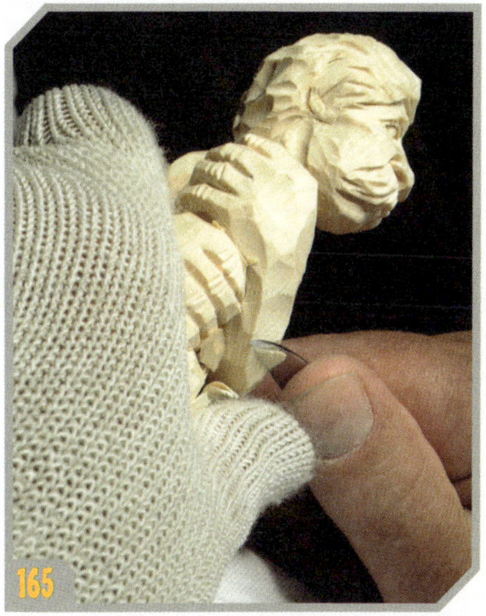

165

Go back and refine your carving.

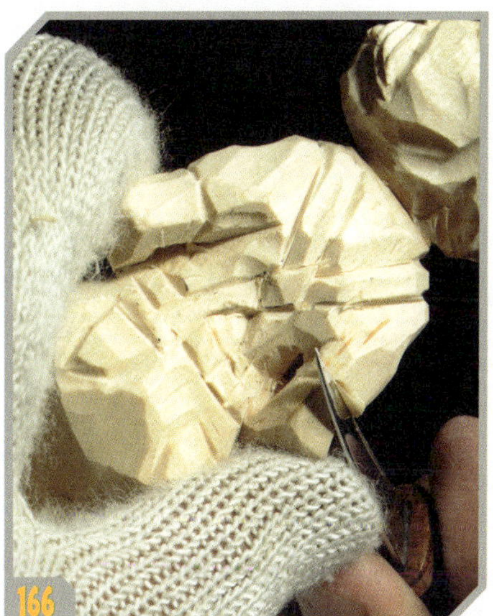

166

Cut the line of the short sleeve shirt and trim the arm back to it.

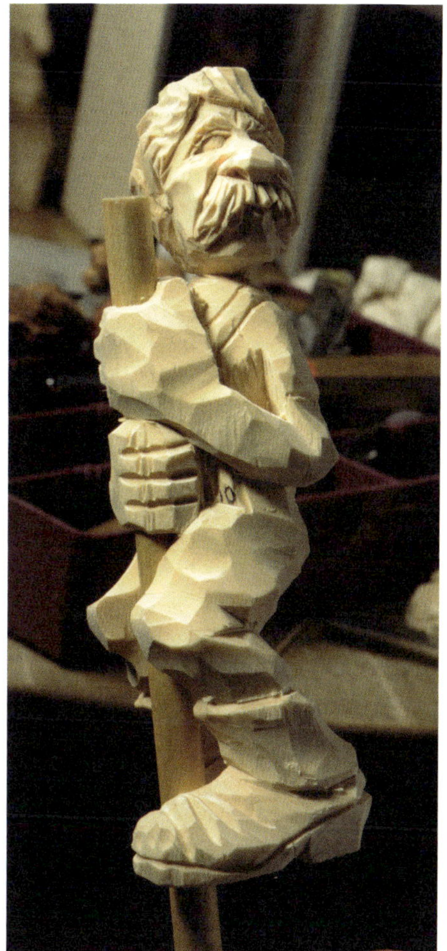

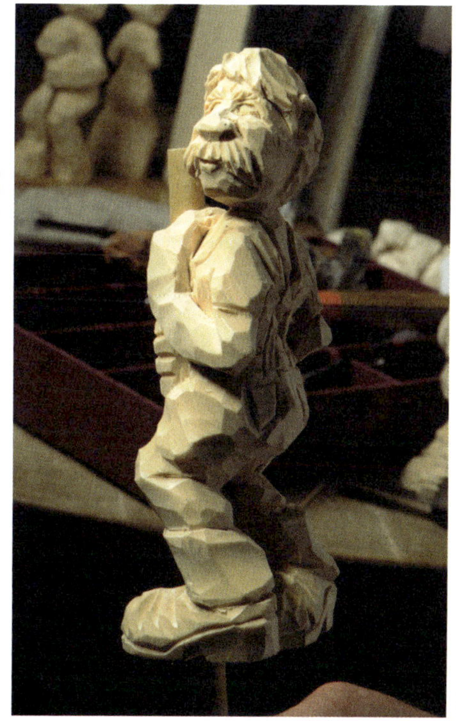

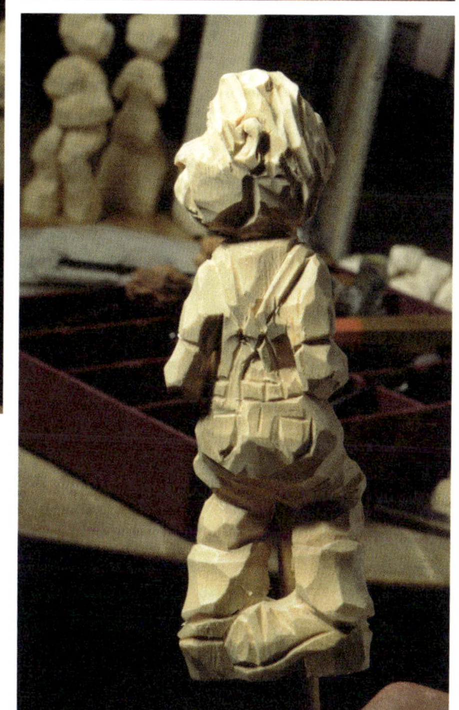

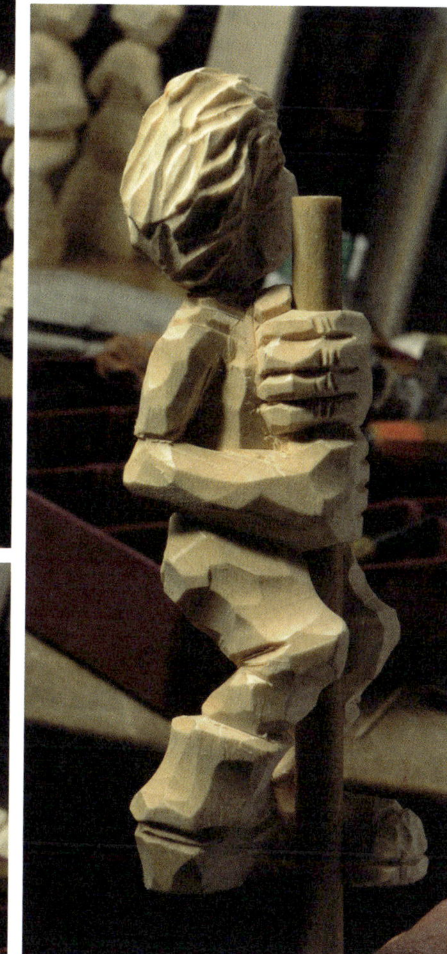

The finished carving.

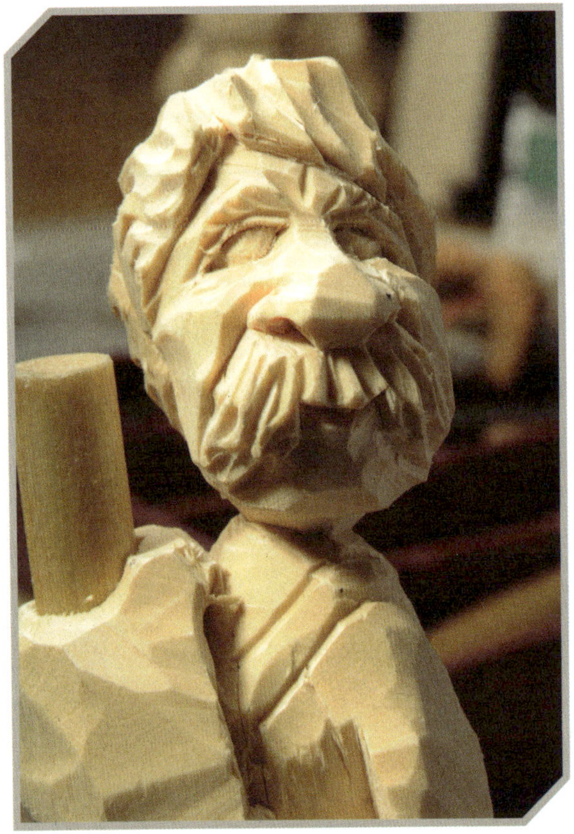

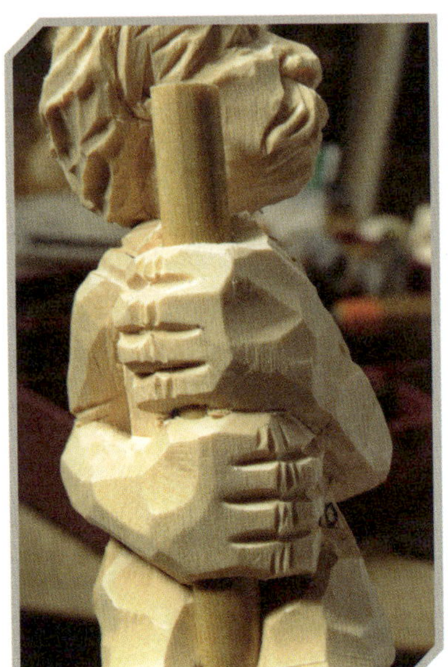

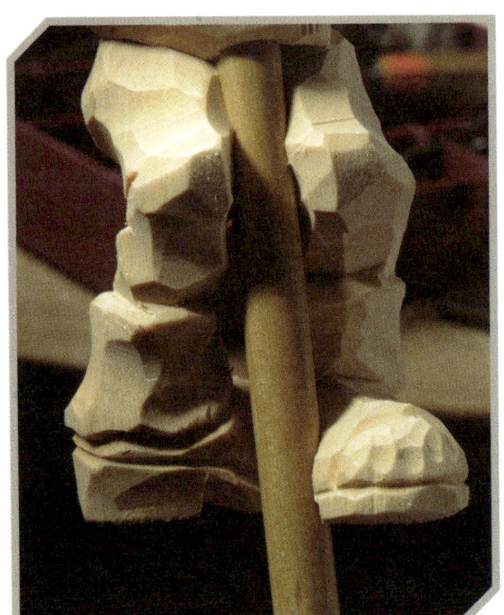

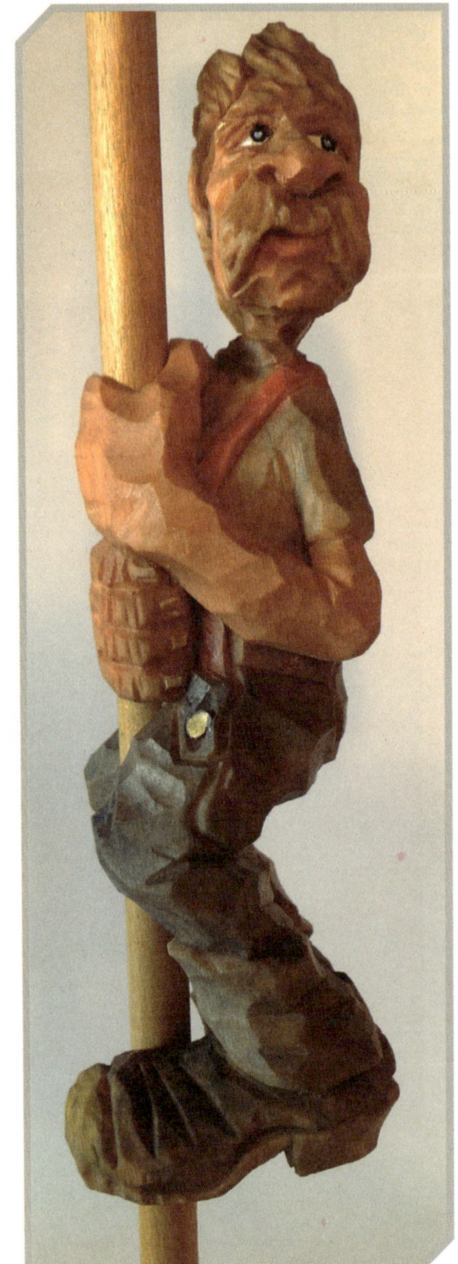

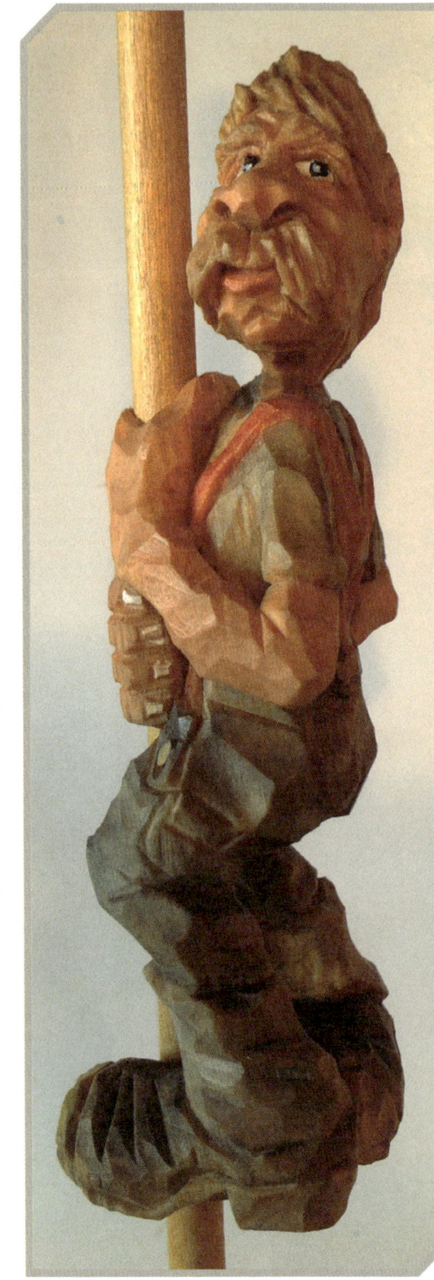

The painted fireman.

Painting and Finishing Caricature Carvings

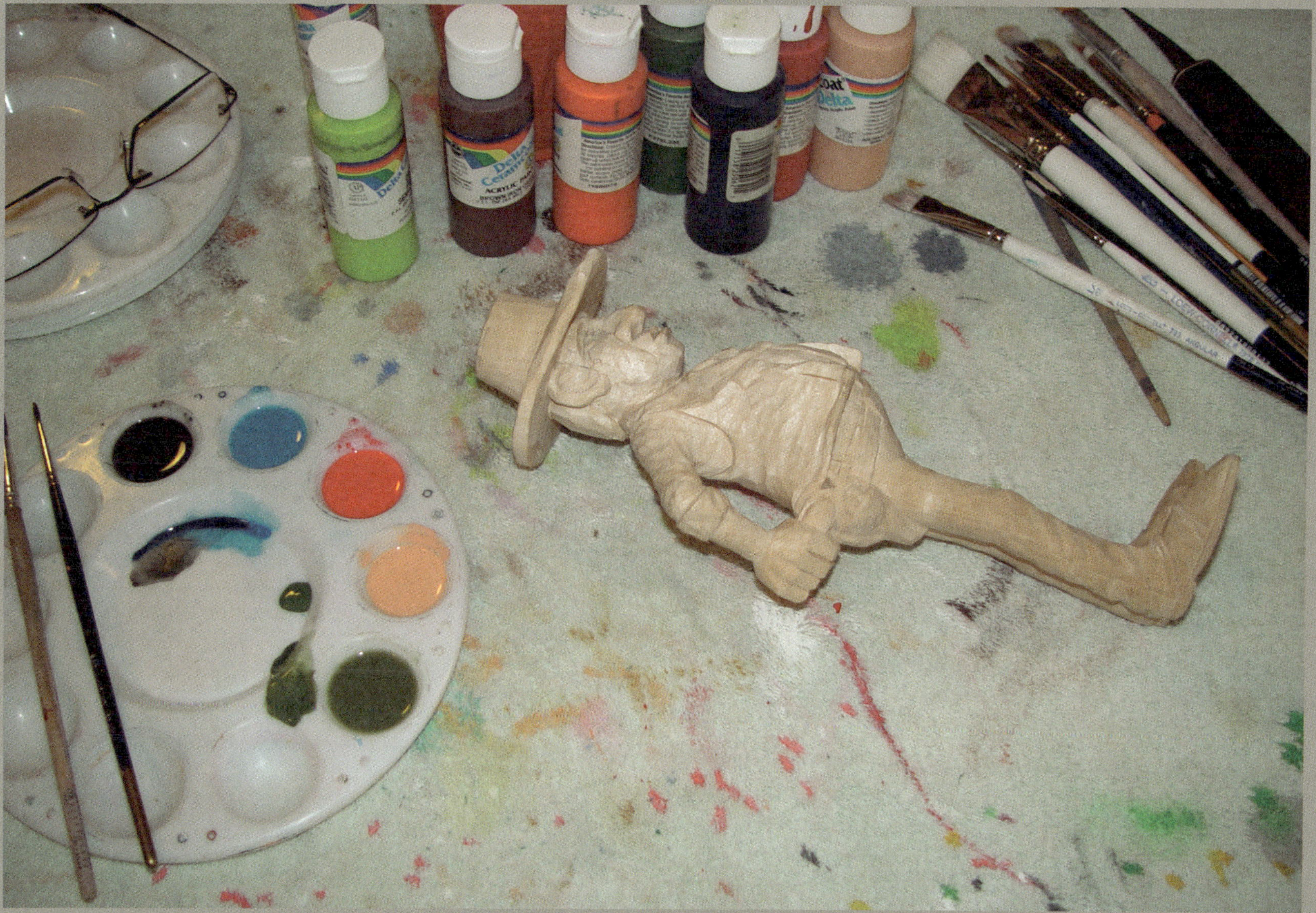

Listening to a discussion on painting techniques among caricature carvers will quickly suggest that there is no best way to paint a carving. It becomes apparent that each carver believes their method is best. Judge for yourself as you read what the carvers featured in this book have to say about painting.

Phil Bishop

I use Delta Ceramcoat acrylic paint thinned with water to a light wash. After painting, I rub the high points of the faceted cuts with a small piece of t-shirt cloth to lighten the color. To create light, medium, and dark values on my carvings, I use a darker shade of the same color to bleed into the wrinkles of the clothing, and dry brush the worn areas of clothing with white. To finish the carving, I use a mixture of one quart boiled linseed oil and ¼-inch burnt sienna artists' oil paint. I add the oil paint to the mixing vessel and blend with a brush into an ounce or two of the oil. After the paint is dissolved, I add the rest of the linseed oil.

Vicki Bishop

Wash the carving with Simple Green and water using a denture brush to scrub off any dirty spots. Paint the carving while it is still wet. Do not let it dry as this will raise the grain. The paint serves as a sealer and will prevent the grain from raising. Use watered-down acrylic paints to paint the piece, and then rub it down with a wet piece of T-shirt. Then darken the color and shade the wrinkles to give you three tonal values: light, medium, and dark. After the paint is dry, dip the piece in boiled linseed oil with a small amount of burnt sienna oil paint dissolved in the linseed oil.

Mitch Cartledge

Before painting, I inspect the piece to make sure that the areas to receive different colors of paint are separated by deep knife cuts. This helps prevent paint bleeding and also provides crevices for the antiquing mixture to accumulate. I prefer very light washes of color. I pretreat the carving with a mixture of ¼ boiled linseed oil, ¼ mineral spirits, and ½ Minwax natural (#209). I encourage experimenting to see what works for your taste. Before the treatment fully dries, I paint with an acrylic wash heavily thinned with water. Note that color does "brighten" as it dries. I will sometimes apply additional coats of paint to get more color if necessary. The carving is then sealed with satin polyurethane and allowed to dry for a couple of days. My last step is to brush on Briwax "golden oak" wax with a toothbrush as my antique. I wipe off the excess with paper towels and pick out any heavy clumps that may have collected in crevices.

PJ Driscoll

I really don't think there is a right or wrong way to paint. There are some ways that appeal to the eye more than others. I have tried oils and acrylics. I enjoy the painting process as much as the carving process. Patience is the key. Use the method and type of paint with which you feel most comfortable.

Before applying any paint to my carving, I always test the colors on the same type of wood from which the carving was made. Sometimes it takes several attempts before the right color is achieved. Paint lightly in order to allow the wood grain to show. My preference is soft colors and earth tones.

Following are the steps I use: 1. Wash the carving with a toothbrush, using warm water and Dawn liquid soap detergent. Let dry at least 24 hours. 2. I paint the whites of the eyes first with undiluted acrylic paint, then paint the rest. 3. Next, I coat the entire carving with a mixture of boiled linseed oil and a small amount of raw sienna artists' oil paint. When I say "small," I can't emphasize it enough. 4. I allow the carving to dry at least six hours. If I am rushed, I will dry it with paper towels. The drying period allows the wood to take the paint evenly.

Painting can be a very creative process. Many light washes may suit the carving better than one heavy one. After the painting process is finished, I let the carving set for a few days before checking again for areas that may need touching up. When I am satisfied that the painting is complete, I spray the carving very, very lightly with Deft semi-gloss spray lacquer. This finish helps protect the carving from getting soiled. The semi-gloss dries to a flat finish if it is sprayed on very lightly.

Harold Enlow

This project was painted with acrylics thinned with water and allowed to dry. It was antiqued with a mixture of boiled linseed oil and raw umber artists' oil paint. Wipe the mixture off immediately after applying, leaving some in the deep cuts to create an antique appearance. Allow the antiquing to dry thoroughly. Because linseed oil is highly susceptible to spontaneous combustion, always be sure to immediately submerge rags or paper towels used for antiquing in water, then spread and allow to dry before discarding. The finished project may be sprayed lightly with a clear satin spray lacquer, if desired.

Gene Fuller

I use acrylic paints that are diluted with water to a milky consistency in a painter's palette. The carving is washed under the tap and scrubbed using a denture brush and a mild detergent. It is painted while still wet and is kept wet during most of the painting process. Eyes and teeth are painted dry, with undiluted paints. Flesh tones are derived by mixing about three drops of medium flesh with one drop of shading flesh and perhaps ten drops of water. A highly diluted tomato spice is used to further define shaded areas around the mouth, eyes, and neck. Parts of the carving may be dry brushed. A small amount of white paint is picked up on a brush, lightly passed over a paper towel to remove most of the paint and then passed lightly over the carving to define carving facets on pants, shirt, etc. The dry carving is coated with an equal mixture of paint thinner and boiled linseed oil, allowed to dry overnight, then given a coat of Watco natural wax. If desired, a mixture of equal parts dark and natural Watco wax may be applied as an antiquing solution. Be sure to let each coat dry between applications.

Bruce Henn

I prefer to use watered down acrylic paint. After the paint is dry, I coat the carving with a mixture of boiled linseed oil and a small amount of burnt umber oil paint. Think "light washes" so your carving does not look like it is ceramic.

Eldon Humphreys

I use acrylic paints, usually watered down to a wash. I first coat the carving with a mixture of boiled linseed oil and raw sienna oil paint. (Mix 1 inch of paint squeezed from the tube to ½-pint of boiled linseed oil.) I then apply the acrylic wash over the initial coating. Upon completion, I leave the completely painted carving to dry for about seven days before waxing with a paste finishing wax. I brush and buff the piece to a shiny finish.

Randy Landen

Before painting, clean up any "fuzzies" and erase or shave off any pencil marks. To ensure the paint absorbs evenly into the wood, wash the carving with dish soap and warm water. I do not use any sealer before painting. I paint with acrylic paints (Ceramcoat), watered down to a wash, with some exceptions, like the eyes and teeth. I begin with the lightest colors and progress to the darker colors, blending colors to accent variations in depth or texture. Blending colors is easiest while the paint is still damp or wet. Also while the paint is still damp, I use a wet rag to rub some of the paint away on the clothing, boots, hat, belt, etc. This technique highlights the tops of wrinkles, and gives clothing and leather a worn look. I let the piece dry completely and dry brush the appropriate areas and then antique the carving using boiled linseed oil and a mixture of burnt sienna and burnt umber artists' oil paints.

Pete LeClair

I use a combination of acrylic paints and Minwax #209 containing a small amount of raw sienna artists' oil paint. I have a three-part video on YouTube on painting a bottlestopper head. Go to YouTube and type in peteleclair.

Keith Morrill

My painting techniques, like my carvings, have changed over time as a result of observing what other carvers are doing and trial and error experimenting. Currently I use acrylic paints that have been watered down considerably. I personally prefer it to be obvious that the figure is wood when painted. I don't wash or seal the wood before painting, other than dipping the carving in water before beginning. I find the paint penetrates the wood more evenly and is easier to work on moist wood. I stopped using linseed oil long ago; preferring to antique simply by applying watered down, brown paint. This can be done right after painting. Next I apply water-based polyurethane without waiting for the antiquing to dry. By not using linseed oil I avoid the odor, long periods of waiting for drying, and the danger involved in disposing of oily rags.

Ryan Olsen

I scrub the carving and then let it dry. After the grain has been raised a bit, I smooth the carving by rubbing it with a wad of blank printer paper, and then dip it in boiled linseed oil. I prefer to use a light colored wood as it makes it easier to get a good skin tone. After the oil has dried for a day or so, I begin painting using very thin washes. I build the colors slowly and shade the edges with darker colors to give the carving depth. I consider contrast and overall color composition. Not every color looks good on wood. Experiment to learn which colors you prefer. I avoid stark black or white and try to stay with earth tones, unless I am trying to highlight something. Midnight blue makes a great shadow color for the male face. It can be used to suggest five o'clock shadow. When painting clothing, I use reference photos as a guide. Instead of making broad generalizations of color and texture, find specific, authentic colors and designs and make your carving unique. It is very easy when you are "in the moment" to overdo it on the blush or shading or dry brushing. Step back, take your time, and develop a technique that you trust.

Peter Ortel

With other CCA projects such as the Full Moon Saloon and The CCA Circus, I used dilute washes of acrylic paints, which leave the carvings with a flat color surface. But for this project, I wasn't comfortable with that method of painting. The variety of final finishes that carvers use, such as sealing, antiquing, or waxing, didn't feel quite right for the fire truck project.

Over the years, having heard comments from kids about the big shiny red fire trucks, I wanted to keep that look. So, I painted my fire truck a bright shiny red. It was modeled in the style of a pre-1930s American LaFrance. I finished it off with multiple coats of acrylic high gloss, similar to the finishes of that era.

Steve Prescott

I first clean the finished carving to remove any hand oils, dirt, and pencil marks. I use a dishwashing liquid that cuts grease. Do not waterlog the carving. Pat it dry. Sometimes, painting on damp wood works better. I paint directly on the raw, clean, unsealed wood. I use thin washes of acrylic paint (Ceramcoat by Delta) to paint major surfaces. I use full-strength paint on white (eyes) and metallic (buckle) surfaces. Shading is accomplished by adding midnight blue or burnt umber to the diluted base color. I also use an antiquing solution of boiled linseed oil and oil-based burnt umber to finish the carving and seal the wood. If the finished carving is be handled a lot, you may want to use a sealer or wax. Just be sure it's a matte finish. People are not supposed to be shiny!

Joe Schumacher

After the carving phase is complete I clean the carving with mild soap and water to remove any dirt and oil left on the wood. I use watered down acrylics and finish with a dry brush of a light color to enhance the facets of the carvings. Dry brushing can give the appearance of age, so I did not dry brush the faces of the boy or girl shown in this book—I wanted to keep their youthful look. After dry brushing, I spray my carvings with light coats of matte sealer. Have fun, make somebody smile or laugh, and keep carving.

Sandy Smith

To finish a carving, I use acrylic paints thinned with Minwax's water-based wood stain clear tint base. The "magic water" turns the acrylic paint into an acrylic stain and stays wet a bit longer than water; this allows colors to blend better. The eyes are painted with undiluted paint. Because most of the caricatures have pieces that could be easily broken off if the carving was waxed then buffed, Deft satin finish spray lacquer or Delta Ceramcoat's satin water-based varnish were used as a final protective sealer.

Dennis Thornton

I use acrylic paints and seal with a spray matte finish. It is important to allow your carvings a day or two to dry before applying the matte finish. I have seen freshly painted carvings develop a gray or cloudy shade when sprayed wet. If this happens, your only choice would be to start the painting process all over again.

Bob Travis

I prefer dilute washes of acrylic paints. Artists' acrylic colors that come in tubes work well, as do most of the bottled acrylic paints that can be purchased in craft stores. Remember, a small amount of paint goes a long way. Test your washes first on a piece of the same wood that you used for your carving. You should be able to see the grain of the wood through the paint. A good rule of thumb is that when you think your paint is sufficiently diluted, add a little more water. If you get it too diluted, you can always apply additional washes. If you get the paint on too thick, your only recourse is to carve it off. I paint directly on the dry wood surface. I use an antiquing mix of boiled linseed oil containing a small amount (¾-inch of paint per quart of linseed oil) of artists' oil paint to finish the carving. I prefer burnt umber paint in my antiquing mix; however, other earth tones such as burnt sienna, raw sienna, and raw umber will work. The only difference in the end result is that the toning on your carving will vary with the color that you add to your antiquing mix. Experiment on the block of wood that you used to test your paints before antiquing your carving. A light spray coat of Workable Fixatif, 1306 by Krylon will seal in much of the linseed oil odor.

THE STREET SCENE

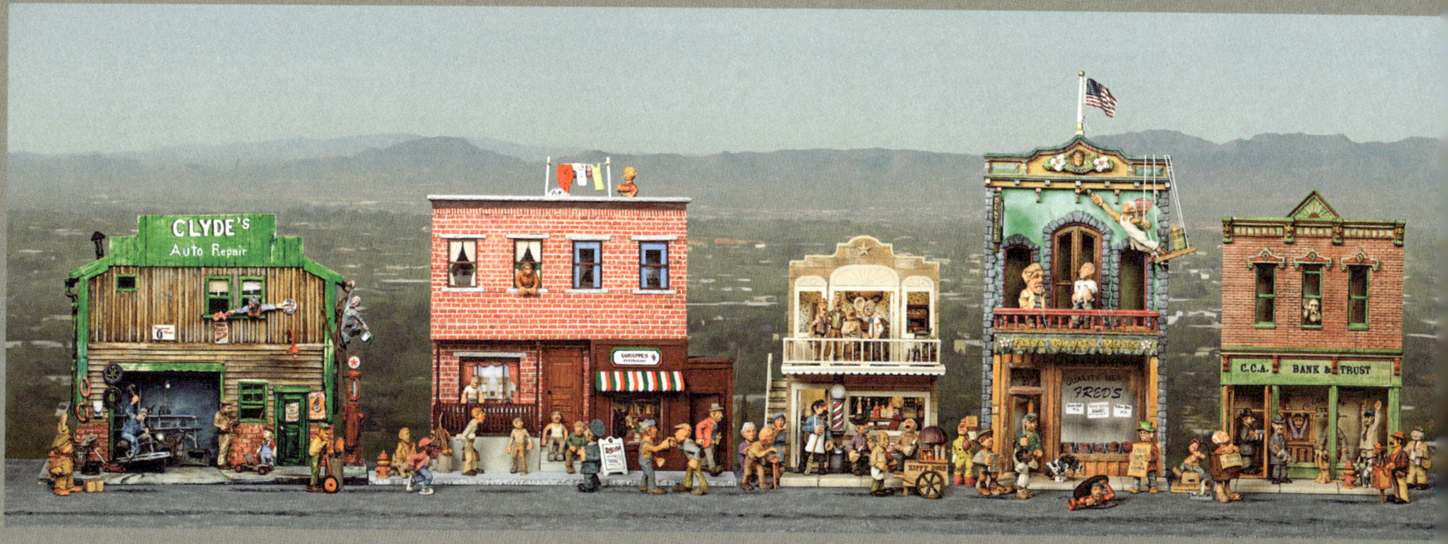

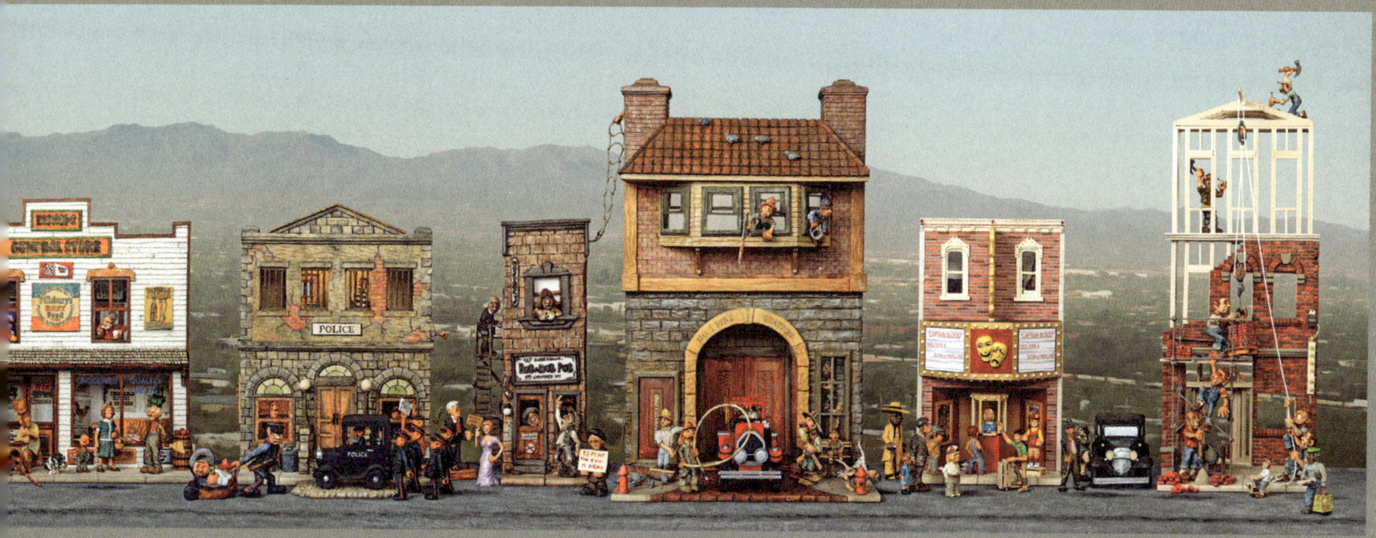

CLYDE'S AUTO REPAIR

David Boone

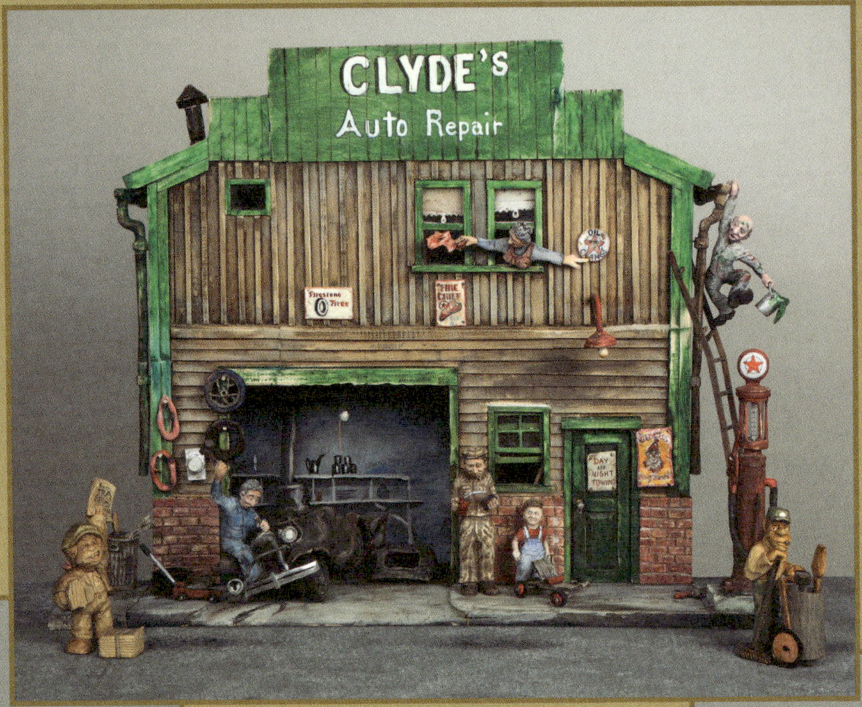

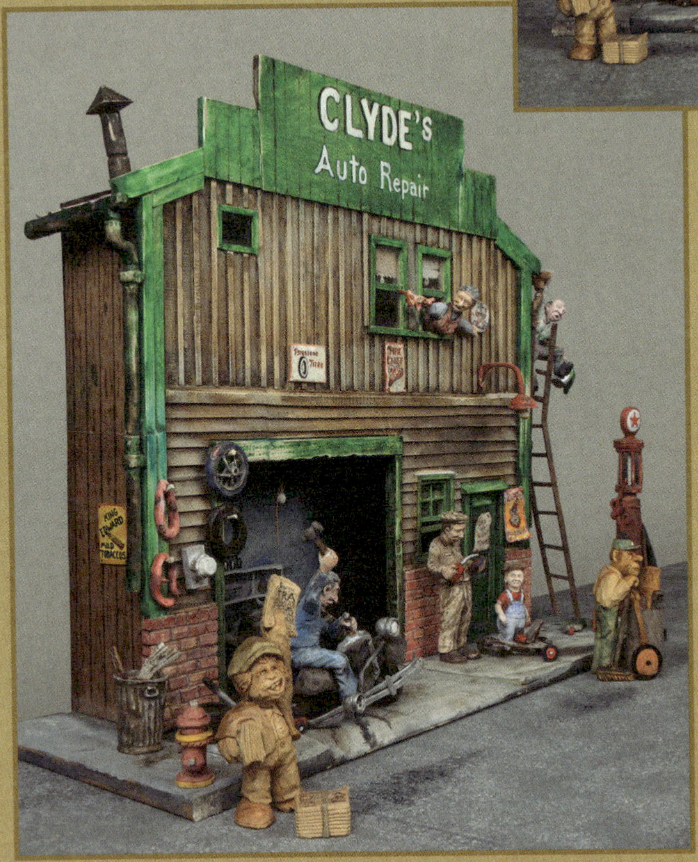

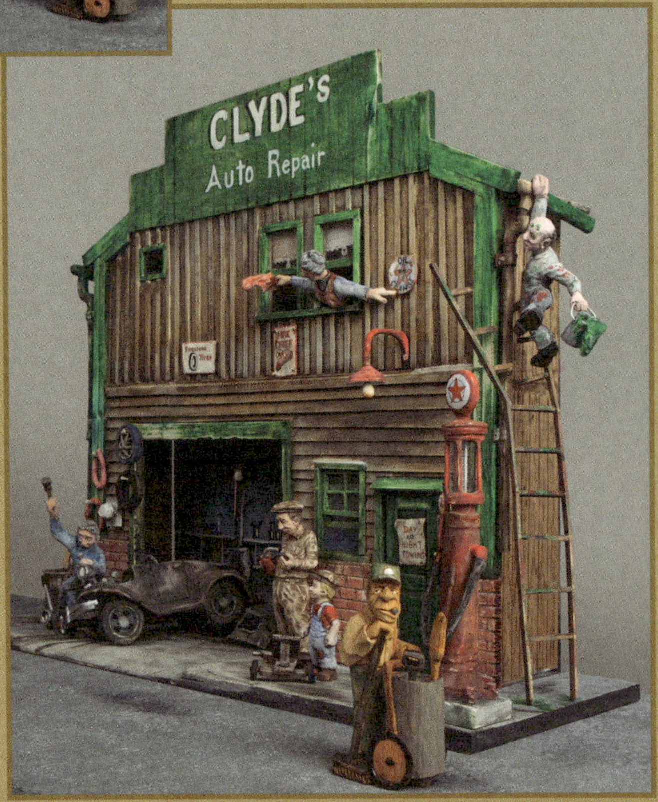

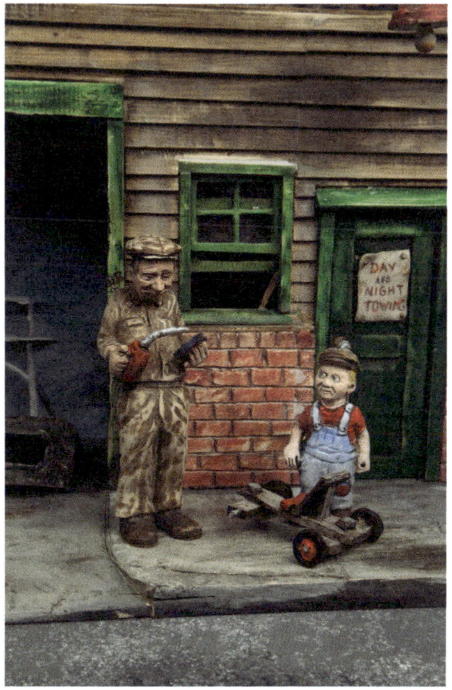

Man and boy with go-cart

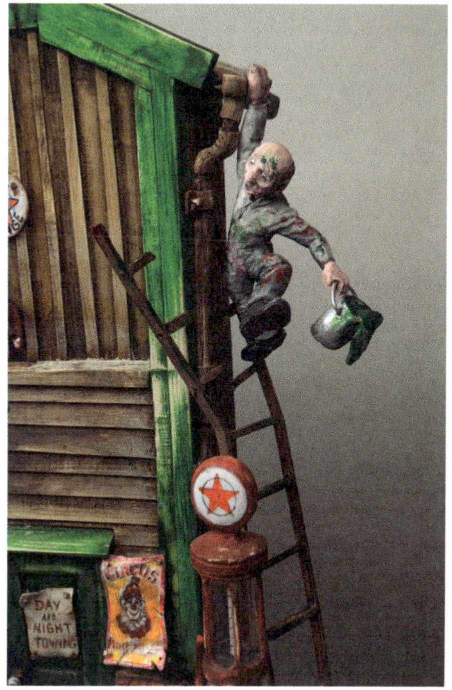

OOPS!

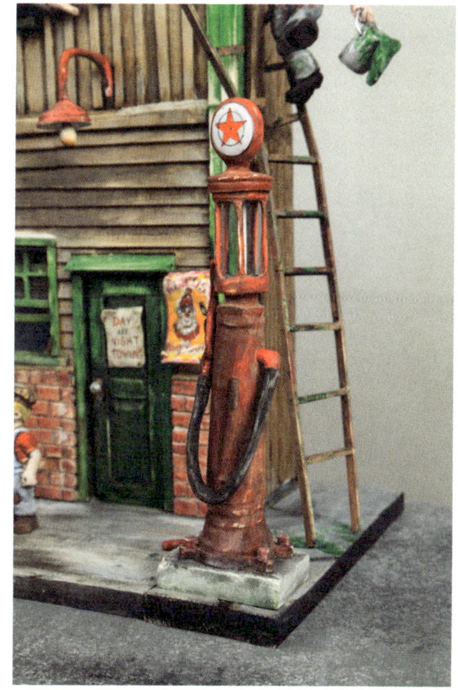

Gas pump

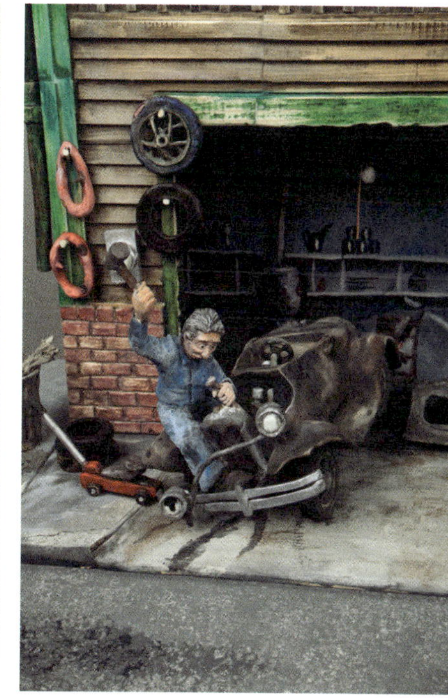

Shade tree mechanic

Woman at window

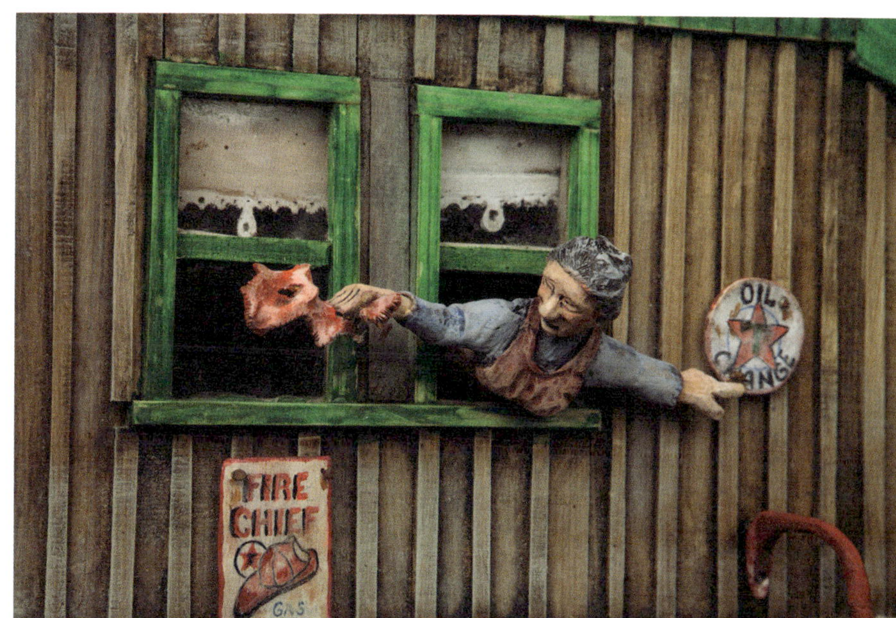

Last year David was asked by the Burnsville Little Theater to play the part of "Clyde," a garage worker in the play "Dearly Departed." He was very excited to be an actor. The play was hilarious and the community responded with a full house every night for two weeks. When the "30s Street Scene" was chosen by the CCA, David loved the idea. He decided to do a garage that would be called "Clyde's Auto Repair." He studied scenes on the internet and cars driven in those days. He went to a local gas station that had an old gas pump and took photos. David then began to draw his scene and patterns for his characters. He carved "Clyde" working on an old car, with a jack to lift the car, and an old man with an oil can repairing a small boy's wagon wheel. He carved a lady in the window waving to alert the man on the ladder that he was falling. Many details on the building such as the signs, light fixtures, and the plumbing were done the way they looked in the 30s. David had a great time doing this piece.

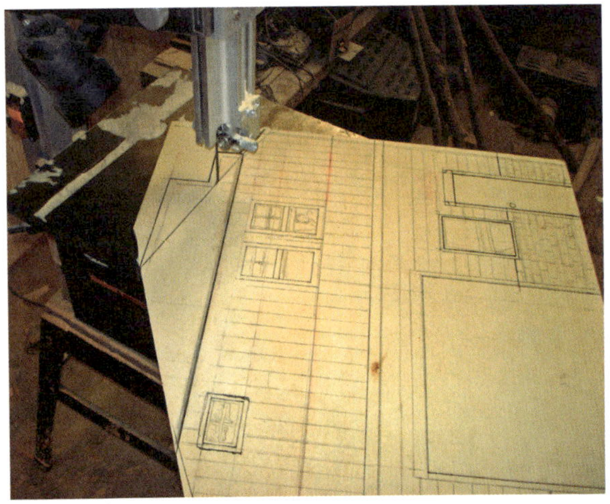

Cutting out the front

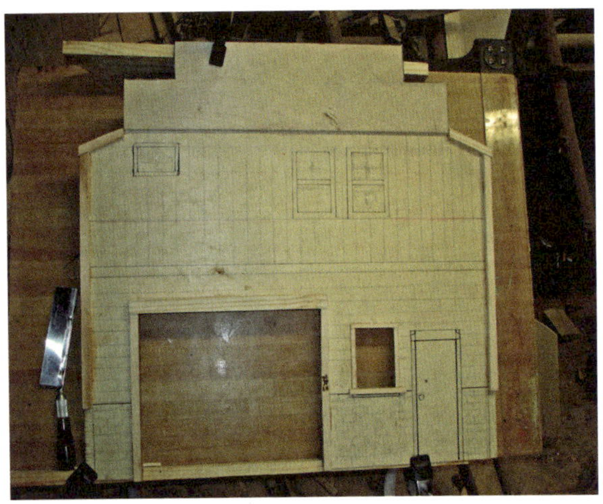

Front cut out

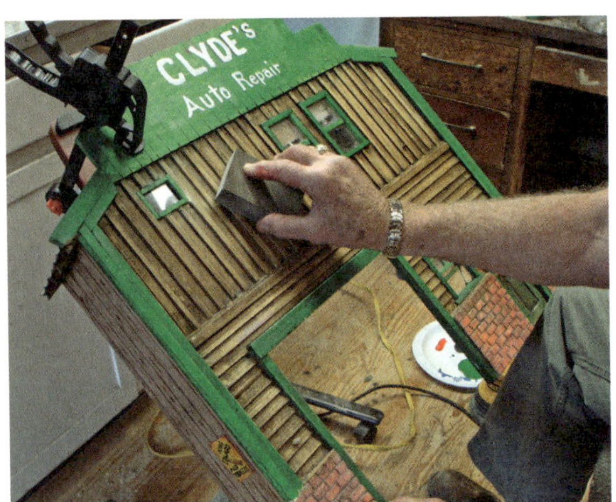

Aging the front

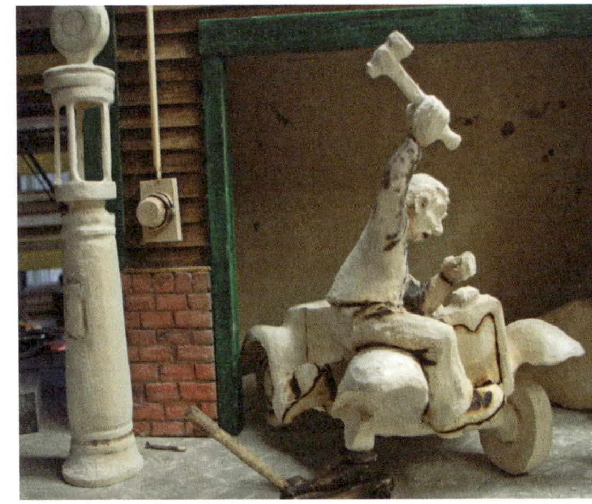

Wood burning car and mechanic

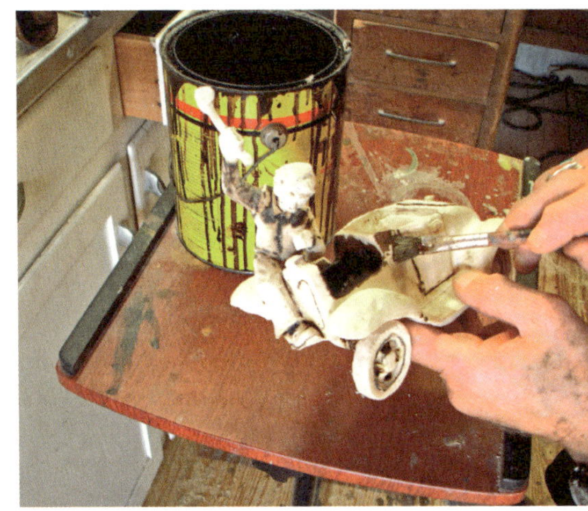

Beginning staining car and mechanic

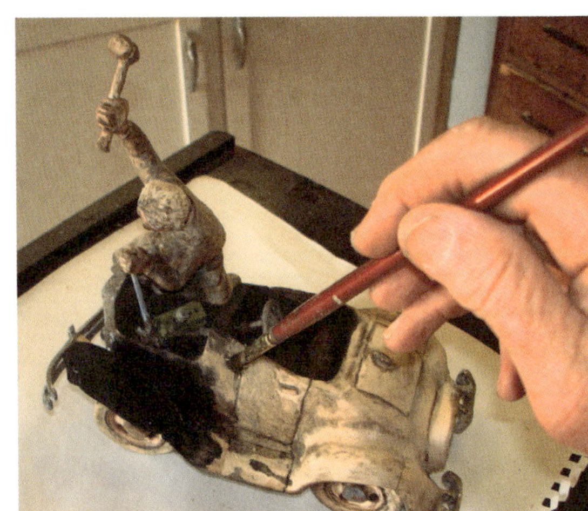

Finish staining car and mechanic

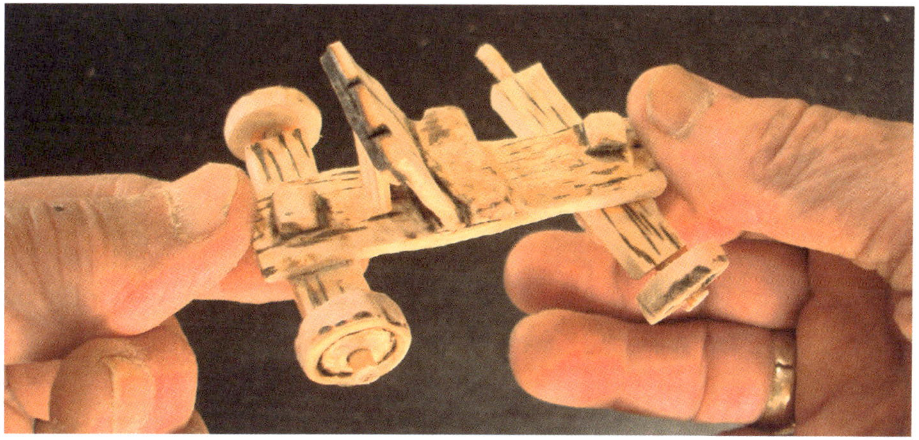

Go-cart frame

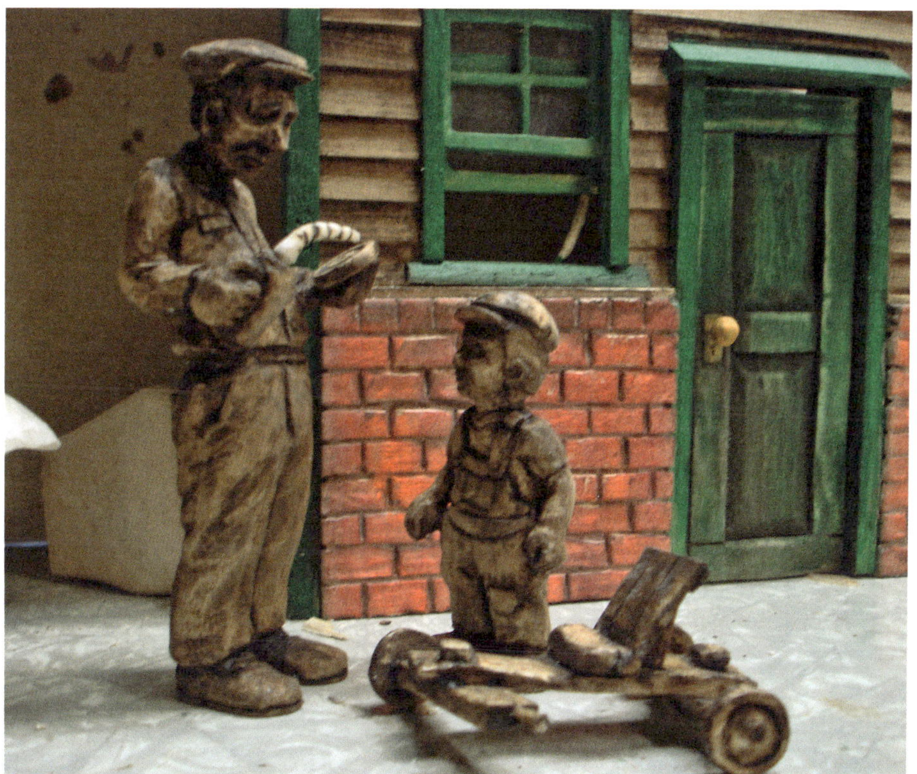

Go-cart ready to paint

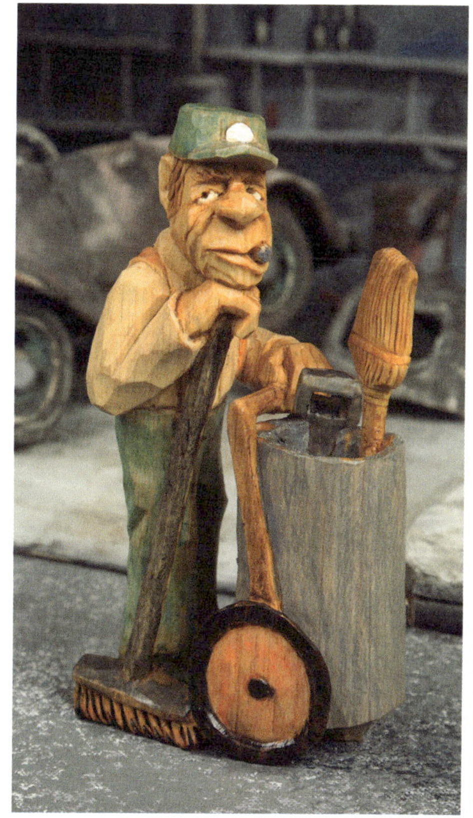

Street sweeper by Don Mertz

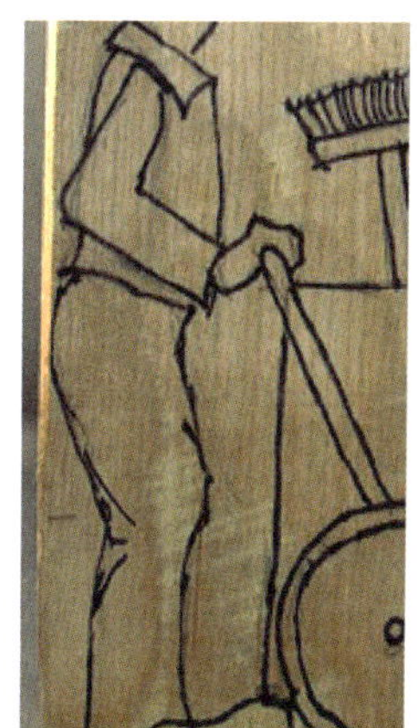

Pattern on wood, left side

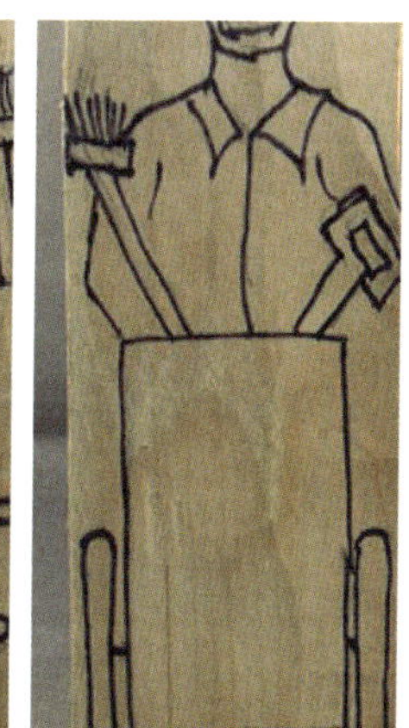

Pattern on wood, front

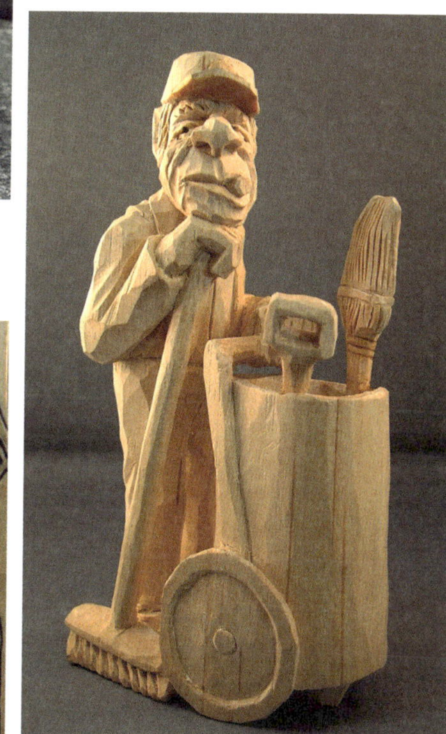

Ready to paint

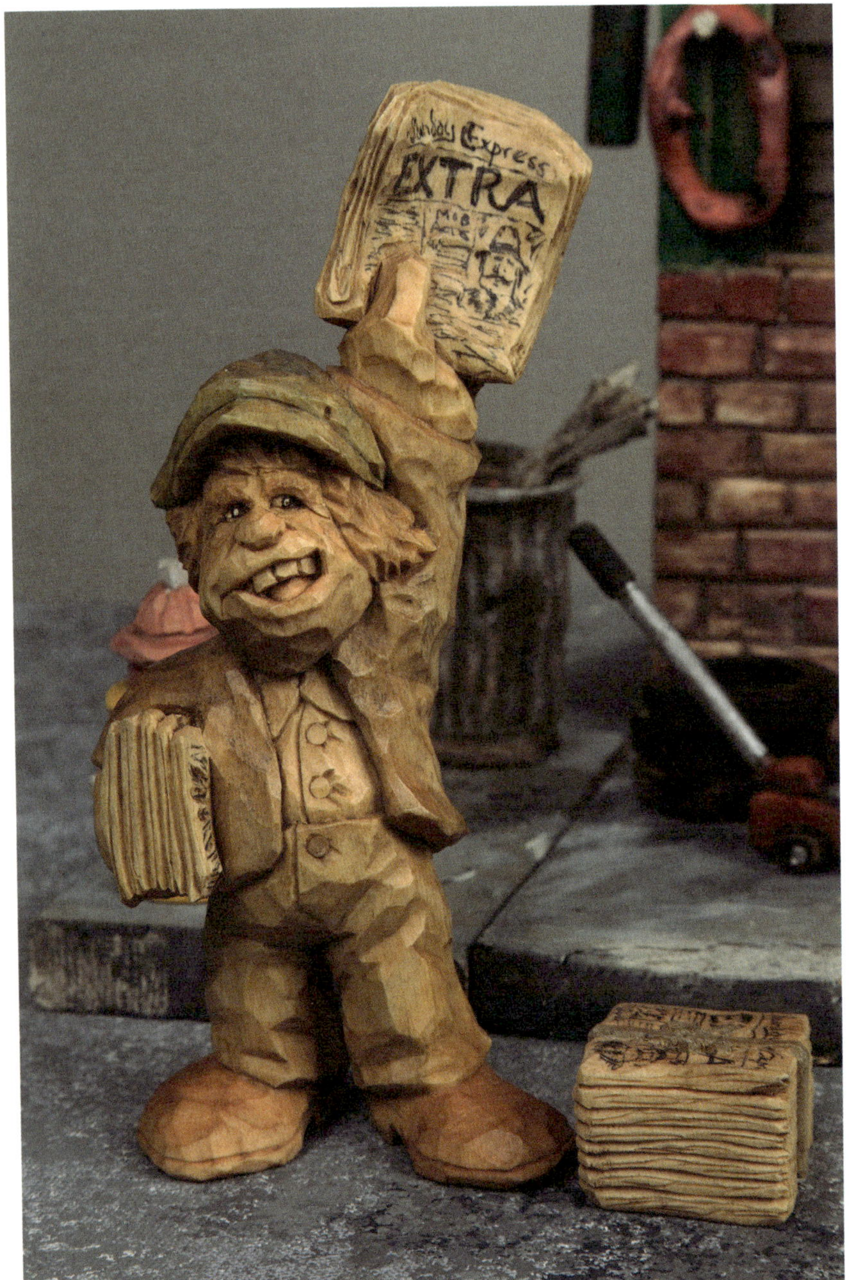

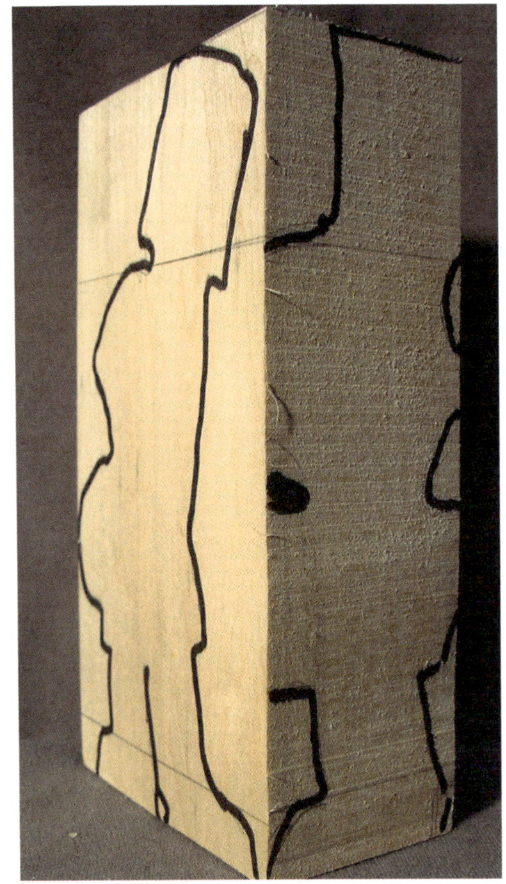

Pattern drawn on block

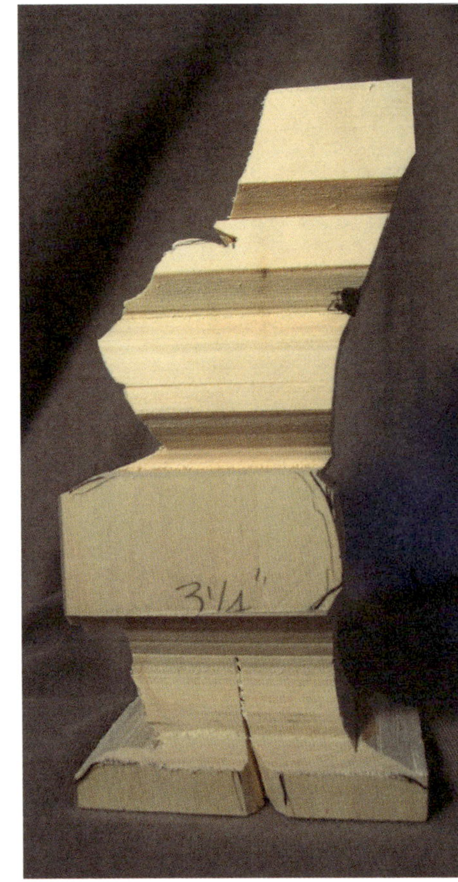

Band sawed blank, front

Newspaper boy by Mitch Cartledge

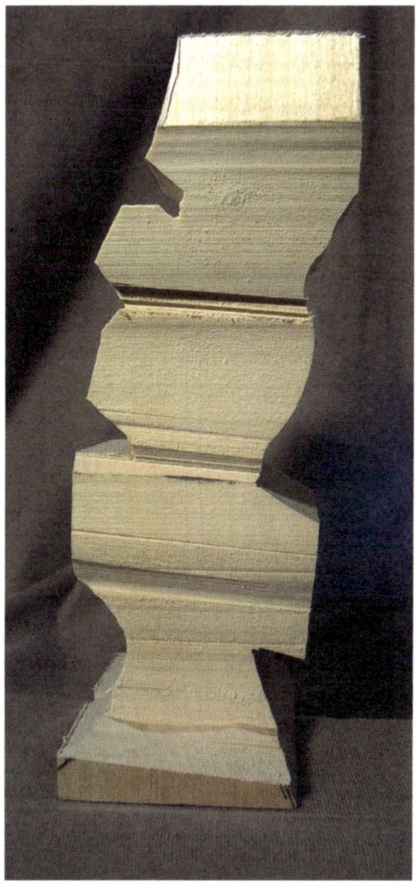

Band sawed blank, side

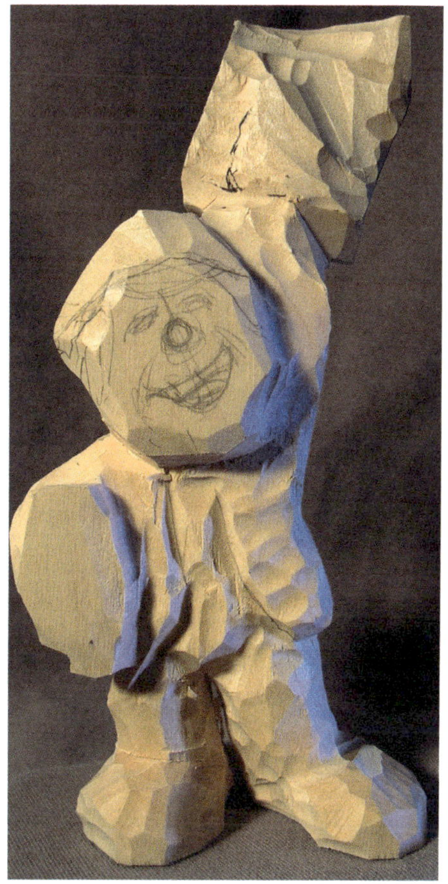

Partially roughed out

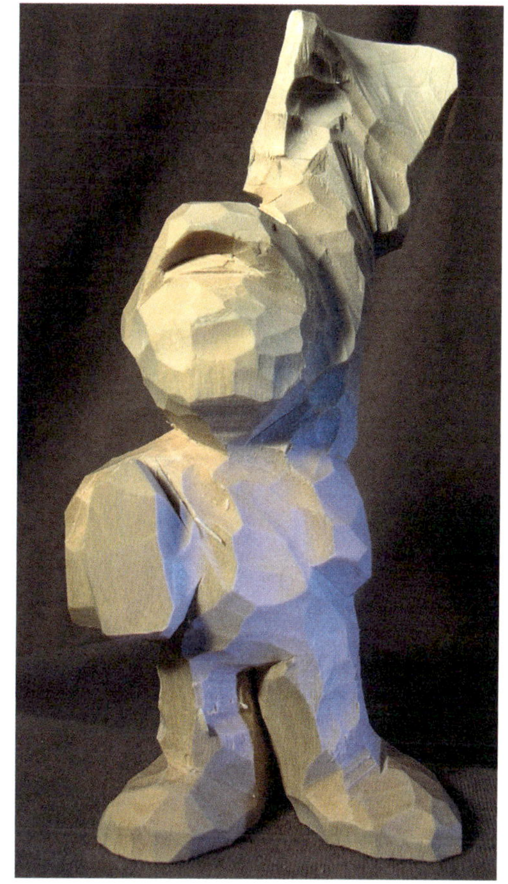

Roughed out, front

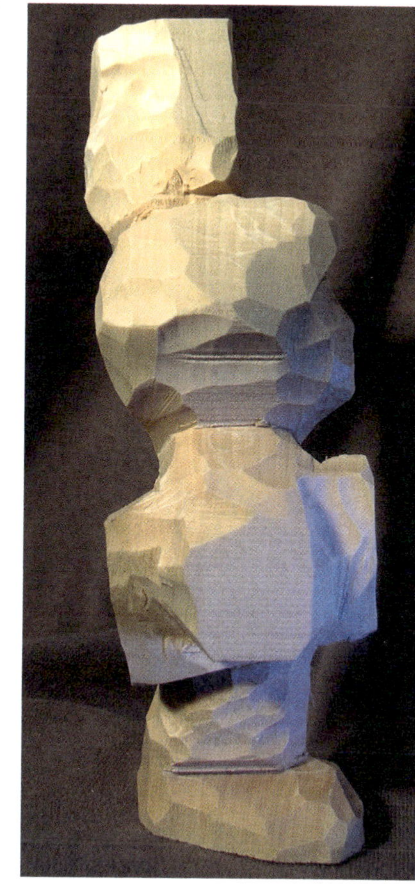

Roughed out, right side

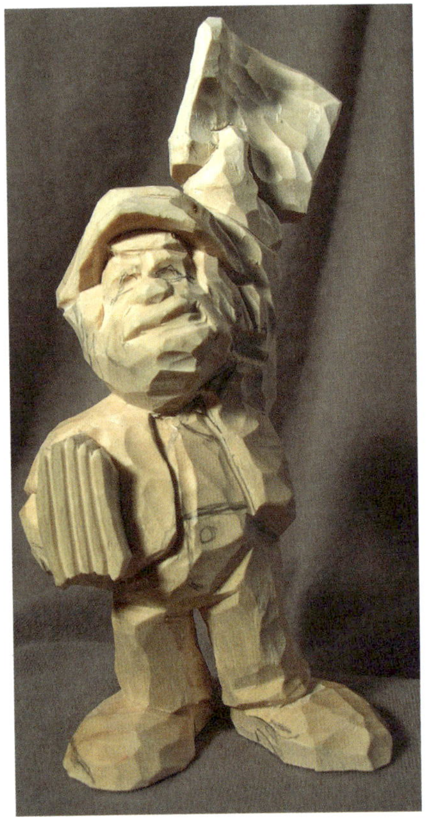

Beginning detail, front

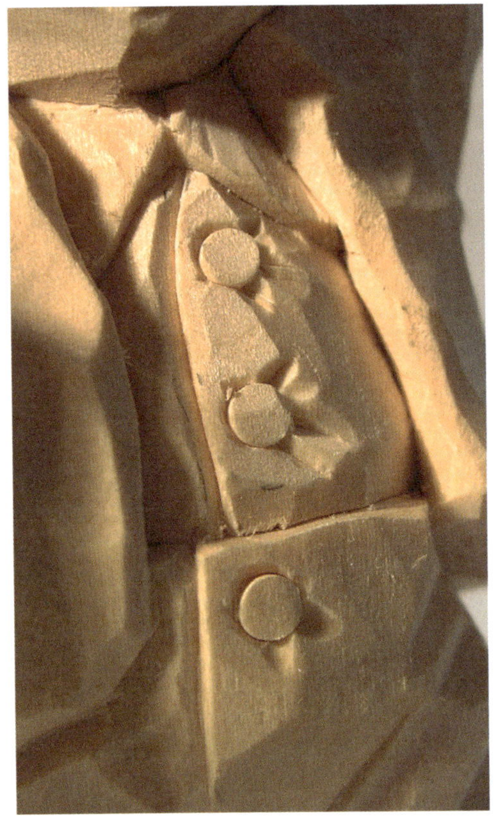

Shirt and waist detail

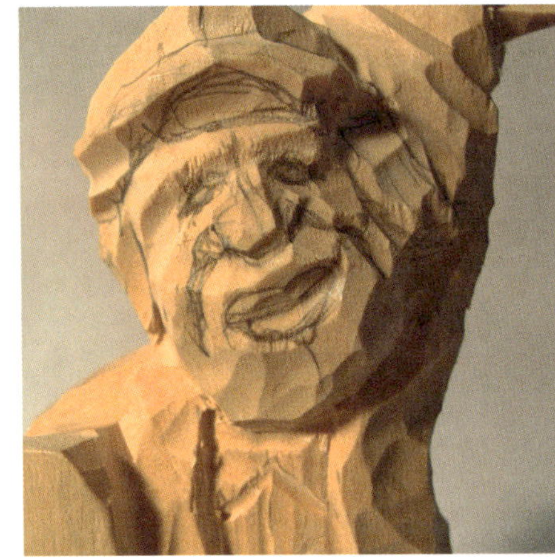

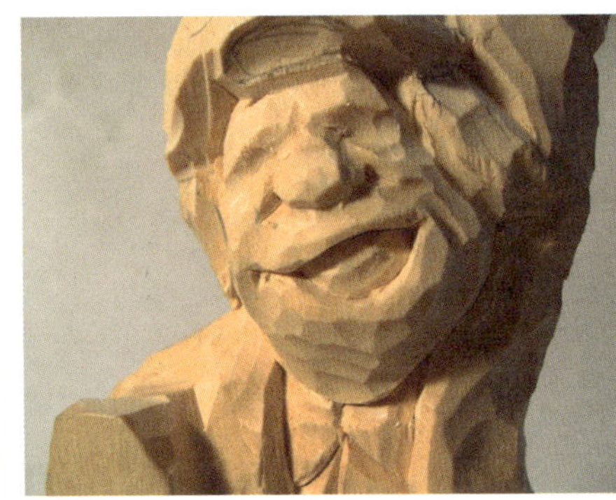

Facial details

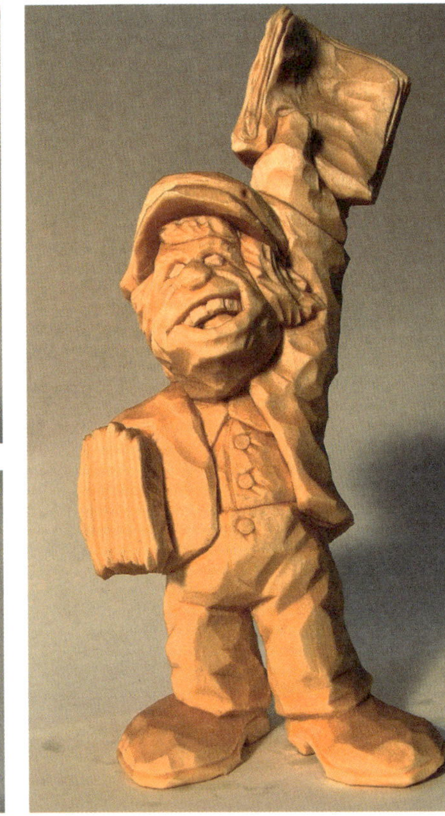

Ready to paint

Tip from Mitch Cartledge

- Don't be afraid to try new things and make mistakes. Expect to throw some things away. It was not until I learned this that I really evolved as a carver.

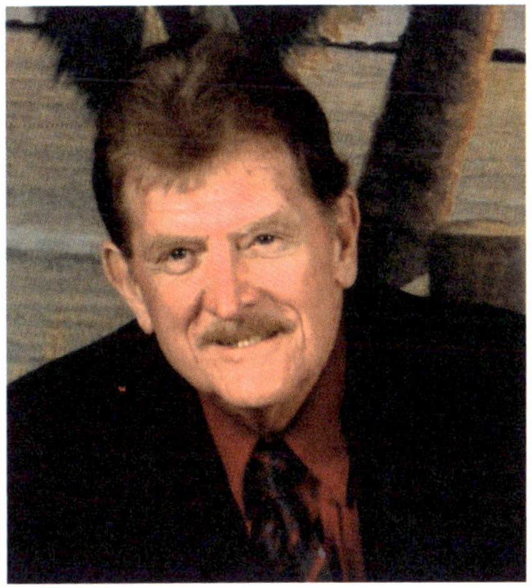

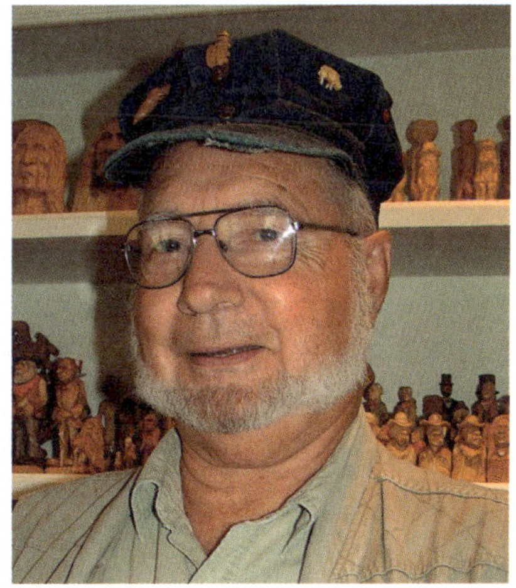

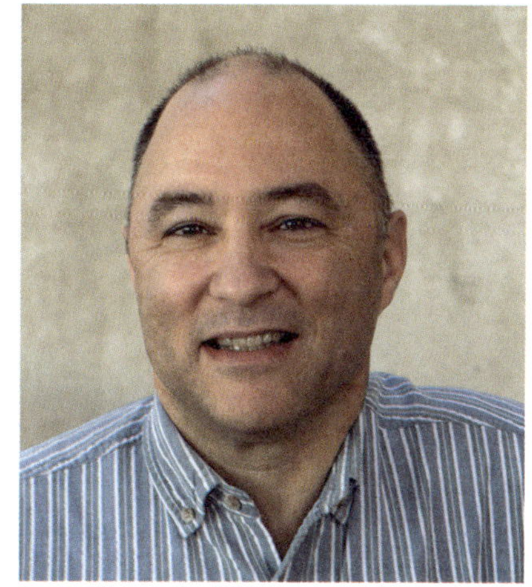

David Boone

David was born with the gift of artistic ability. His third grade teacher recently presented David with a framed drawing that he drew in her class.

David first tried woodcarving about 25 years ago. Experiencing life in the mountains of North Carolina has provided the inspiration for many of his carvings. He likes to produce a carving that tells a story. He loves humor and would walk a mile to play a joke on his friends. When he worked at Glen Raven Mills in Burnsville, he would draw cartoons of co-workers who experienced hilarious situations, and then display them on the bulletin board. When he left, the office gave him a photo album of those cartoons.

David has no formal training in carving. He loves to do caricatures because he can get expressions of people in unusual and funny circumstances.

Don Mertz

Donald K. Mertz, the Wood Bee Carver, has been carving seriously since 1975 when he joined the National Wood Carvers Association. Carving primarily with a knife, Don has developed a carving style he calls "Whittle-Carving." He has written instructional articles for *Chip Chats, Wood Carving Illustrated,* and *Carving Magazine* and publishes a woodcarving blog at www.woodbeecarver.com, a journal-diary of his carving activities through photographic and instructional postings.

Don was elected to CCA in 2009 and currently serves as Secretary.

Don's motto as the Wood Bee Carver is: "Would be carvers would be carvers if they would carve wood," which means that carving is a "learn by doing activity" and "the more one carves the better one carves."

Mitch Cartledge

Mitchell began drawing cartoons as a teenager to keep busy. In the early 1980s, carving became a way to produce gifts. Time constraints limited his carving early on, but the interest was always there. In the mid-1990s, after meeting Tom Wolfe and joining a local carving club, he was able to combine the early drawing and carving interests into caricature carving.

The camaraderie from the club energized him, but it has been within the last 10 years, after a move to his current home in Morganton, North Carolina, that Mitchell really started to devote consistent attention to carving.

Carving is still a hobby for Mitchell. He works full-time as the Director of Quality for Green Textile in Spartanburg, South Carolina. He teaches carving classes on a limited schedule.

A & K BOARDING HOUSE and GUISEPPE'S RESTAURANT

Pete LeClair and Keith Morrill

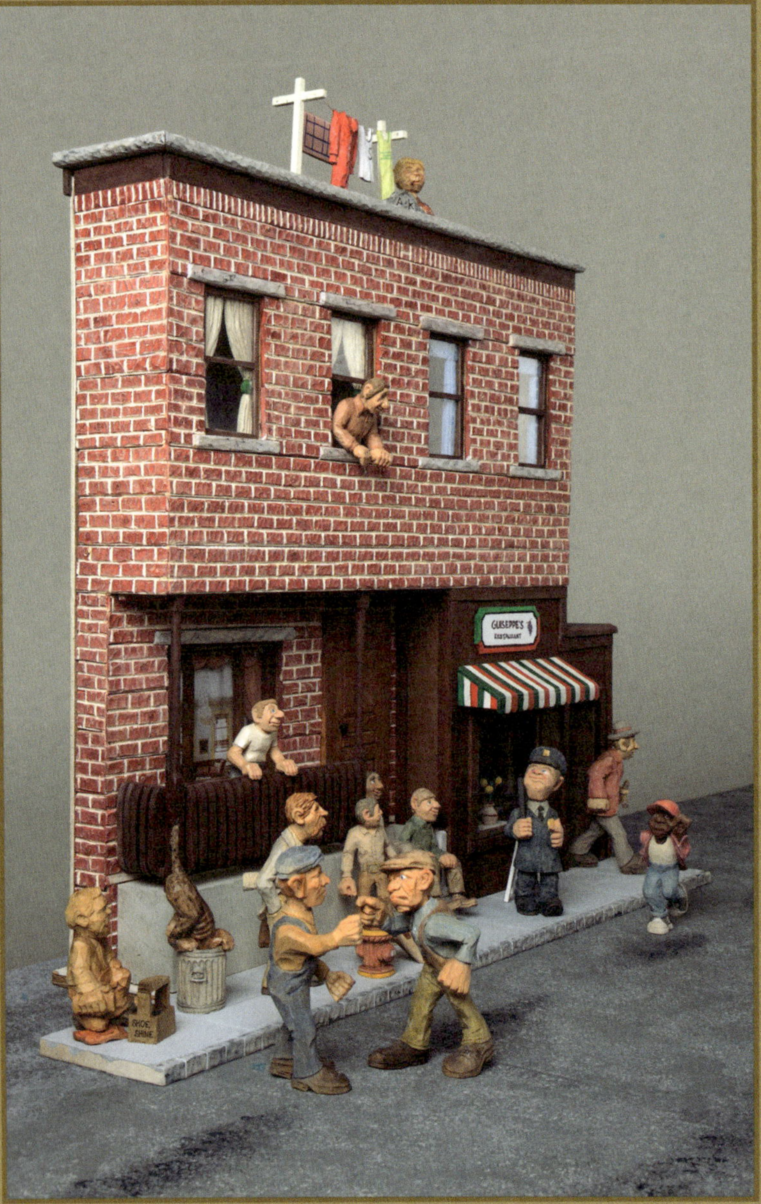

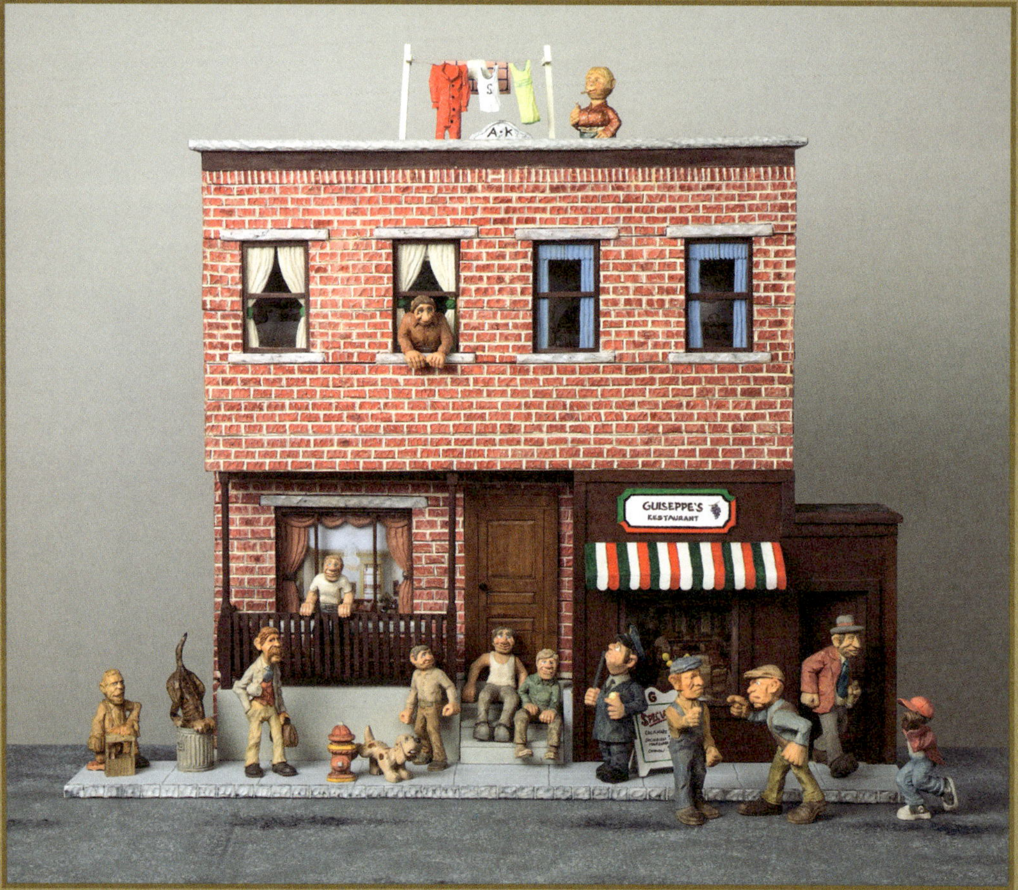

The project idea was based on an A&K building consisting of four apartments and a restaurant owned and operated by Giuseppe and Janna Brasili. I chose the A&K building because I have so many wonderful memories of the 1950s. In those days you knew everyone in your neighborhood. Every school day my friends Len Hill, Edsel Johnson, Angelo Brasili, Jack Clifford, and I would meet in front of Giuseppe's and walk to school. In 1960, after being discharged from the Navy, I rented the top left apartment for two years before buying a home.

—Pete LeClair

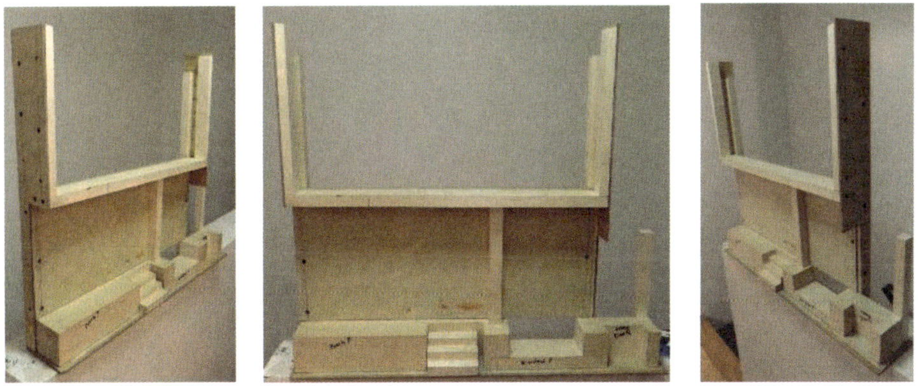

The beginning

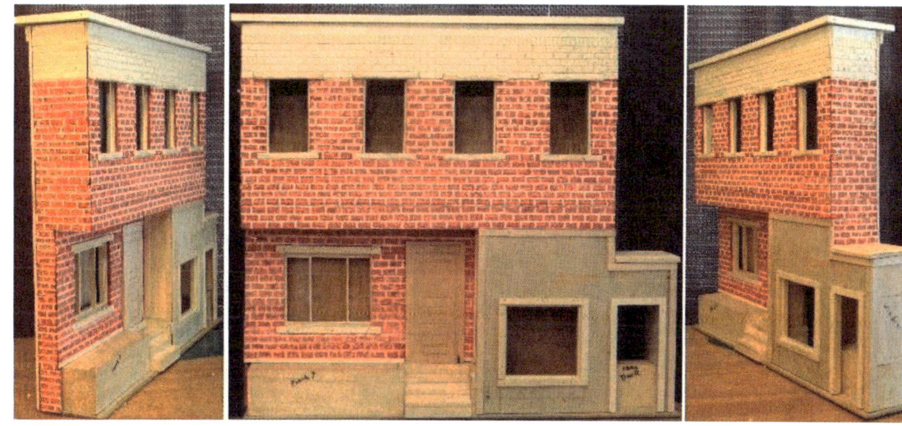

Nearly finished

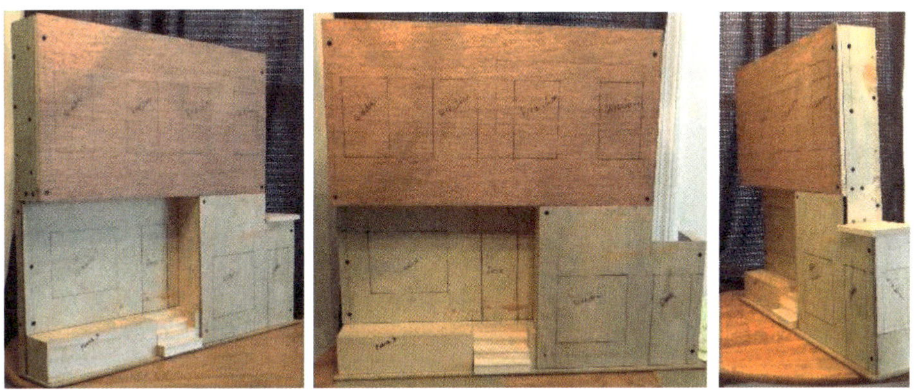

Roughed out

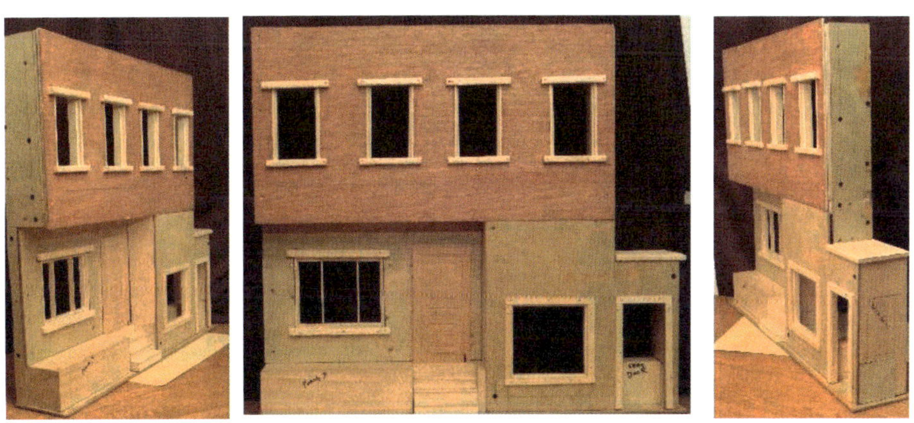

On schedule

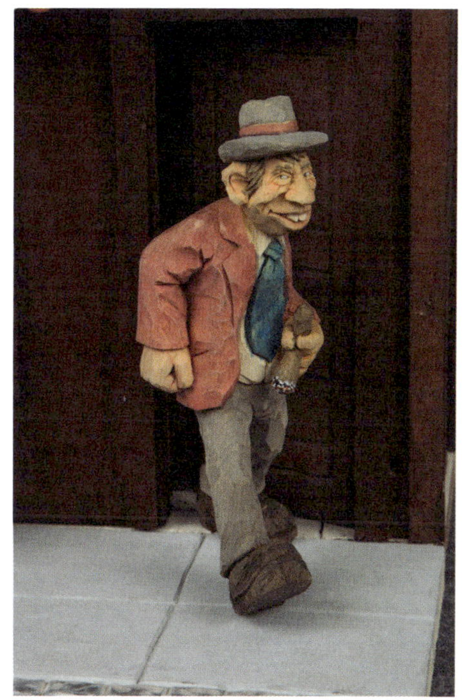

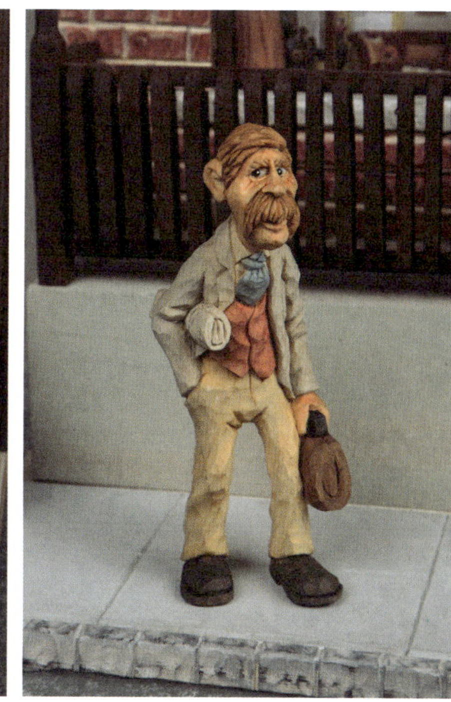

After searching the internet for ideas for 1930s clothing, hairstyles, etc., I chose to carve two figures. I also discovered that there were a lot of buildings with rooftop clotheslines in those days.

—Pete LeClair

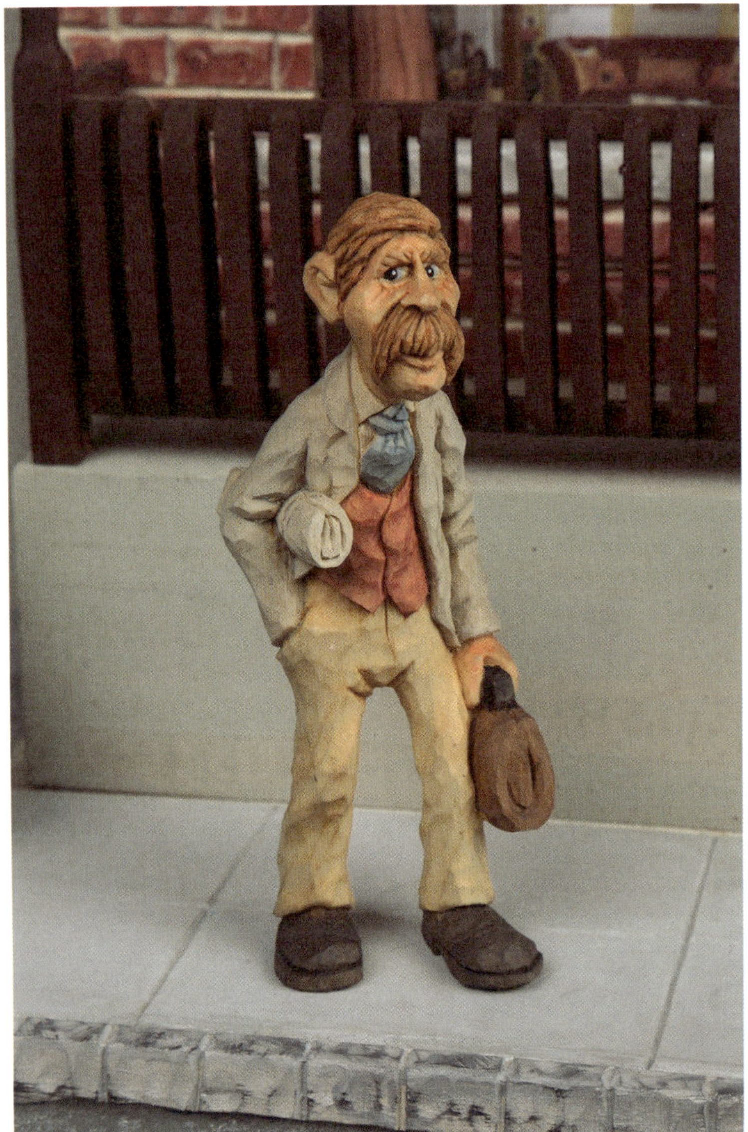

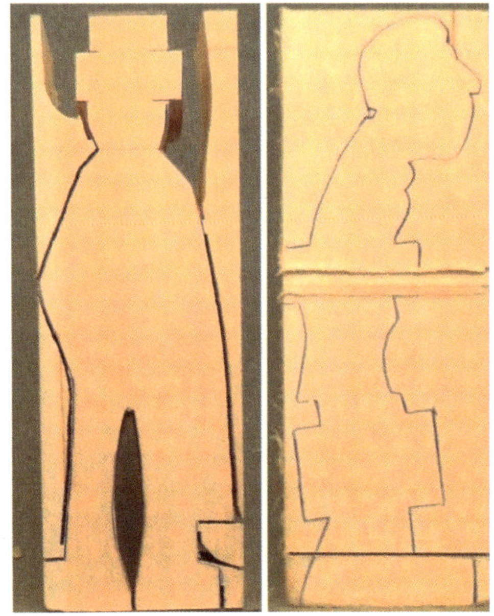

Pattern on wood

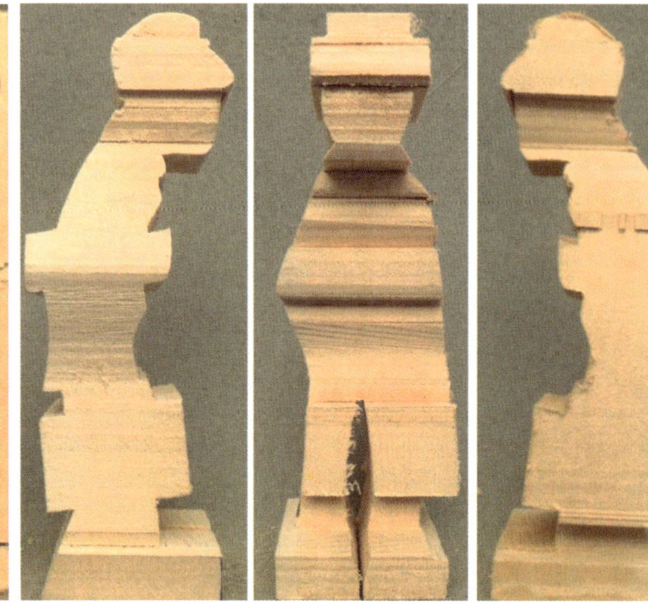

Cut out

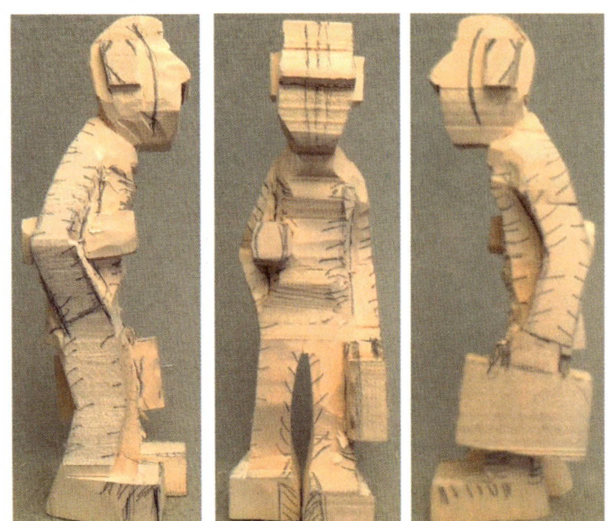

Blocked out

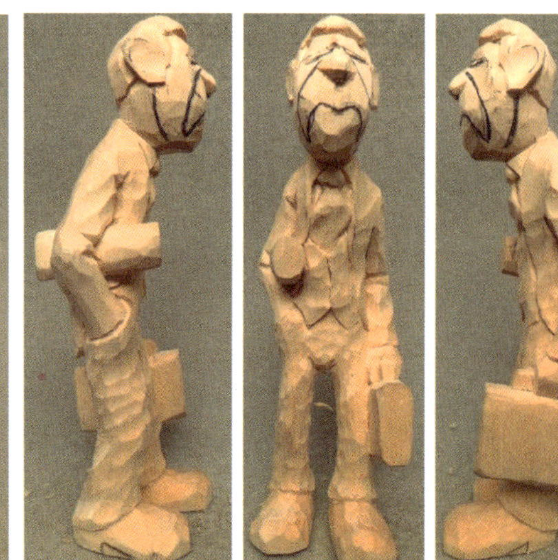

Begin detail

Try carving this guy. Use your imagination as you carve. Be creative, change his clothes and give him a different expression. He doesn't have to look just like the carving in the picture.

—Pete LeClair

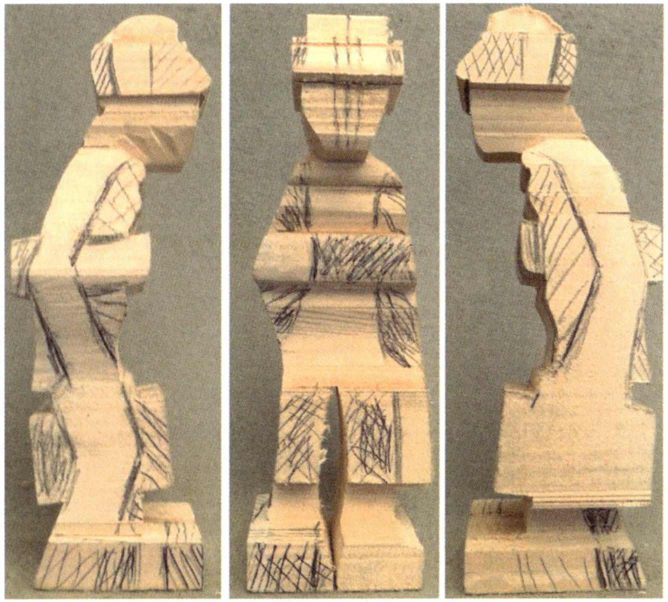

Areas marked for blocking

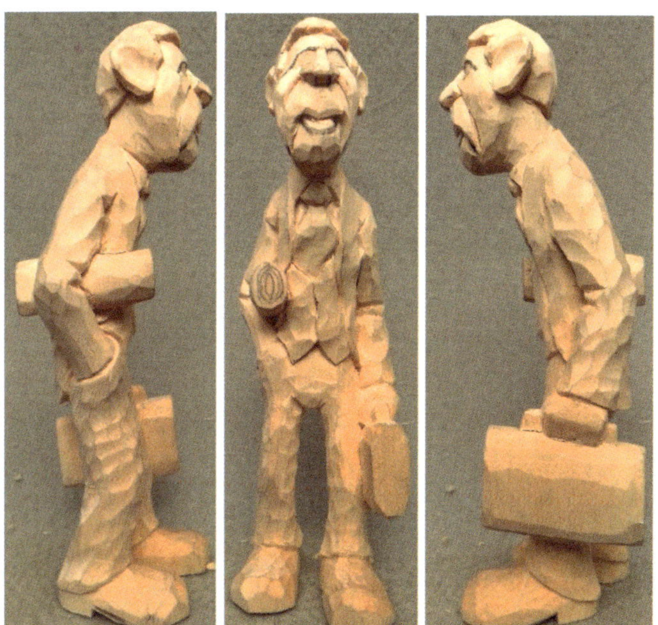

Ready to paint

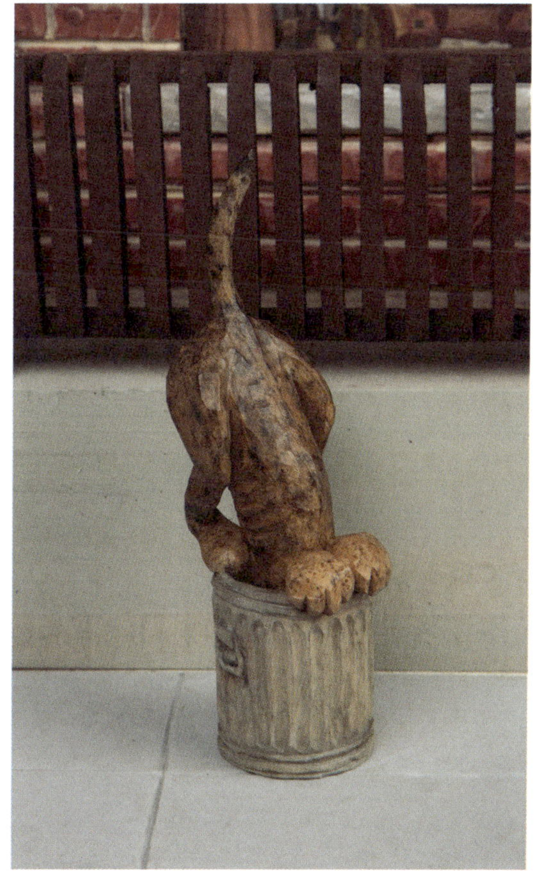

Dog in trash can by Sandy Smith

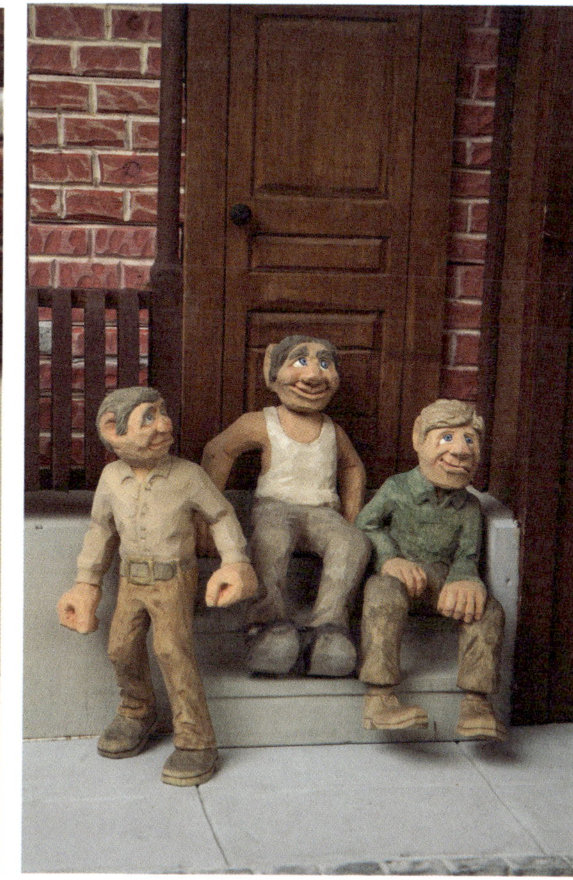

Men sitting on steps by Keith Morrill

Tips from Pete LeClair

- I find that many carvers use dull tools and poor quality wood. Learn how to sharpen your tools and use them safely, and purchase good basswood.
- When using your knife, have your thumb on the wood, not on the knife. This provides better control and is safer.

If you look through carving magazines and "how to" books available today, it is apparent that a majority of carvers, myself included, often carve figures that are standing upright, arms at sides, with their heads pointing straight ahead. The obvious reason is that carving with the grain is easier and presents fewer problems than when body parts and clothing are sticking out. Carving across the grain, where things have a tendency to break off, is more difficult and requires planning and patience.

—Keith Morrill

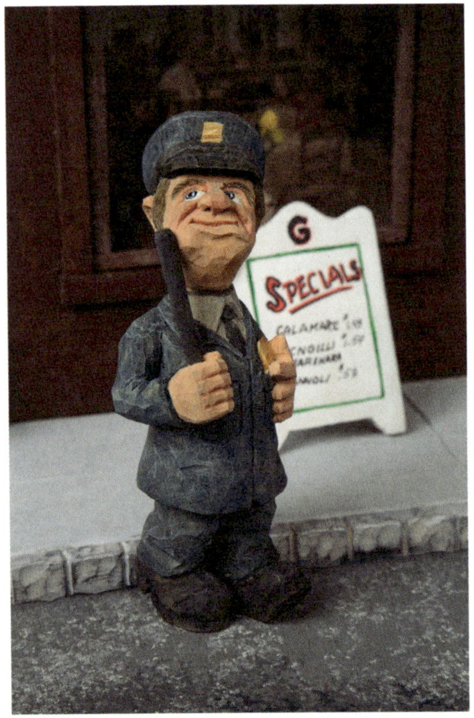

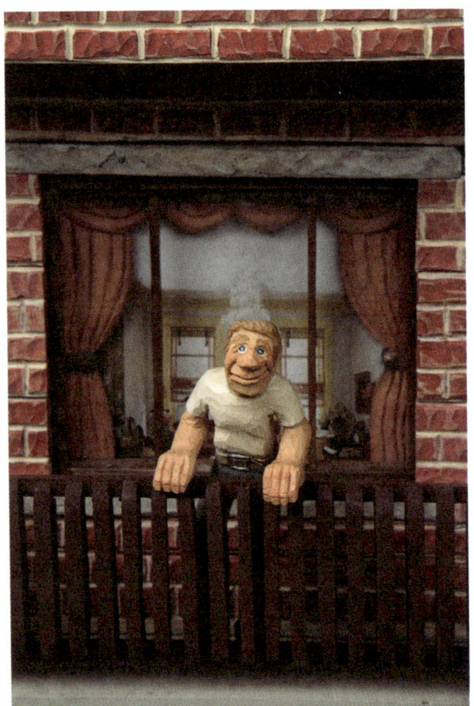

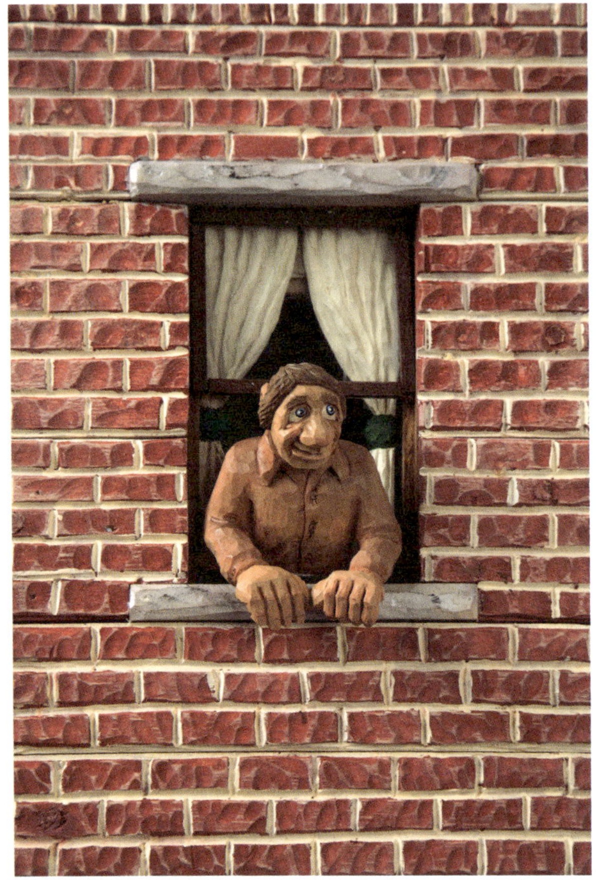

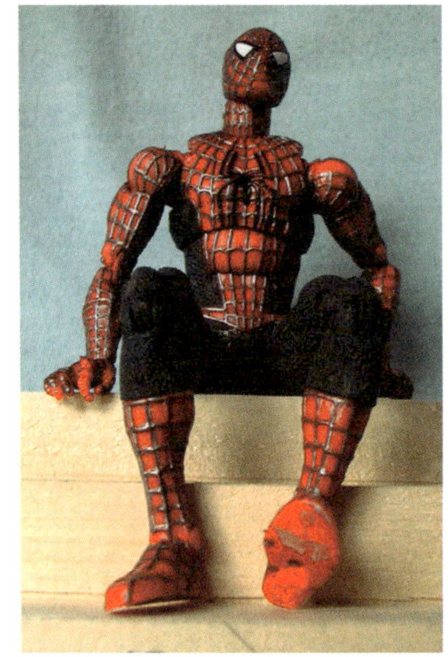

Spiderman

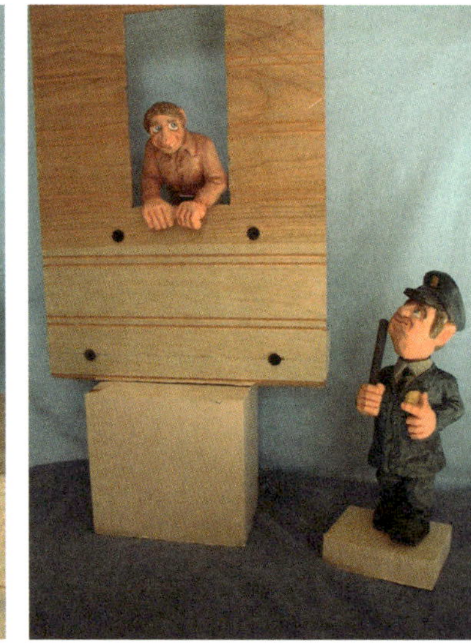

Setting the scene

As you carve and gain confidence in your ability, you will begin to try other challenging projects that require additional planning and precise carving techniques. It helps if you can "see" what's in the wood and are able to start cutting away what doesn't belong.

—Keith Morrill

Over the years, I've used a variety of techniques to assist me in making a rough pattern: clay, mannequins made of cardboard, wire, pipe cleaners, and wood. More recently, I've taken advantage of the many action figures on the market for kids. My favorite is Spiderman because the figure usually has the most articulations, or movable joints, compared to other action figures. Spiderman can easily be manipulated to achieve almost any pose. This enables you to see where grain direction problems can best be avoided before the actual carving begins. The action figure is also a big help to me in sketching my pattern.

—Keith Morrill

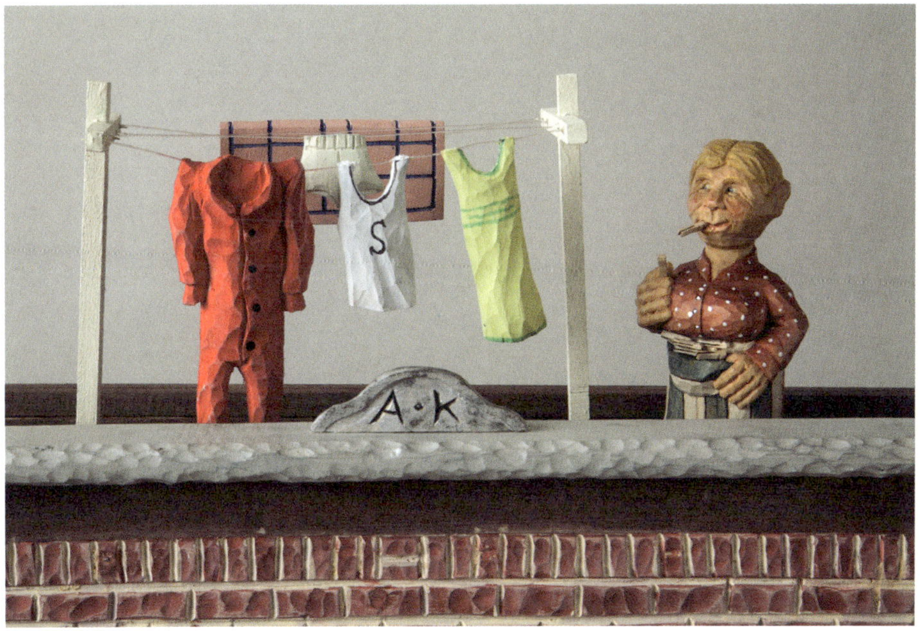

The clothes dryer hadn't been invented by the 1930s, so hanging the clothes out to dry was a common sight. This matronly lady seems to be enjoying her work.

—Gary Falin

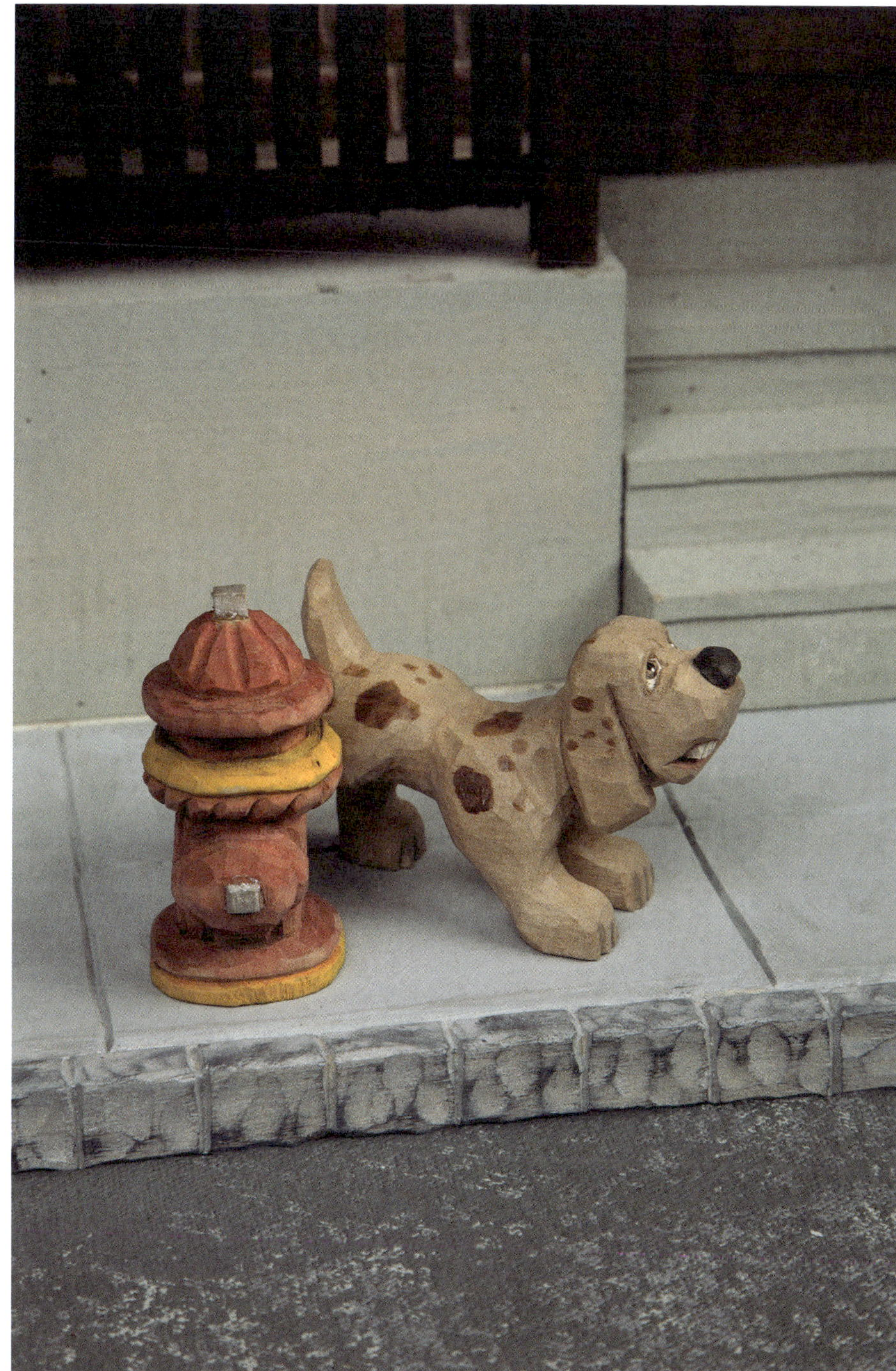

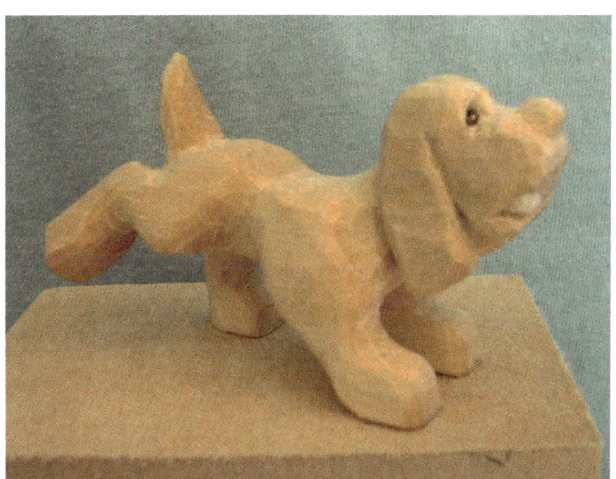

Marking his territory by Keith Morrill

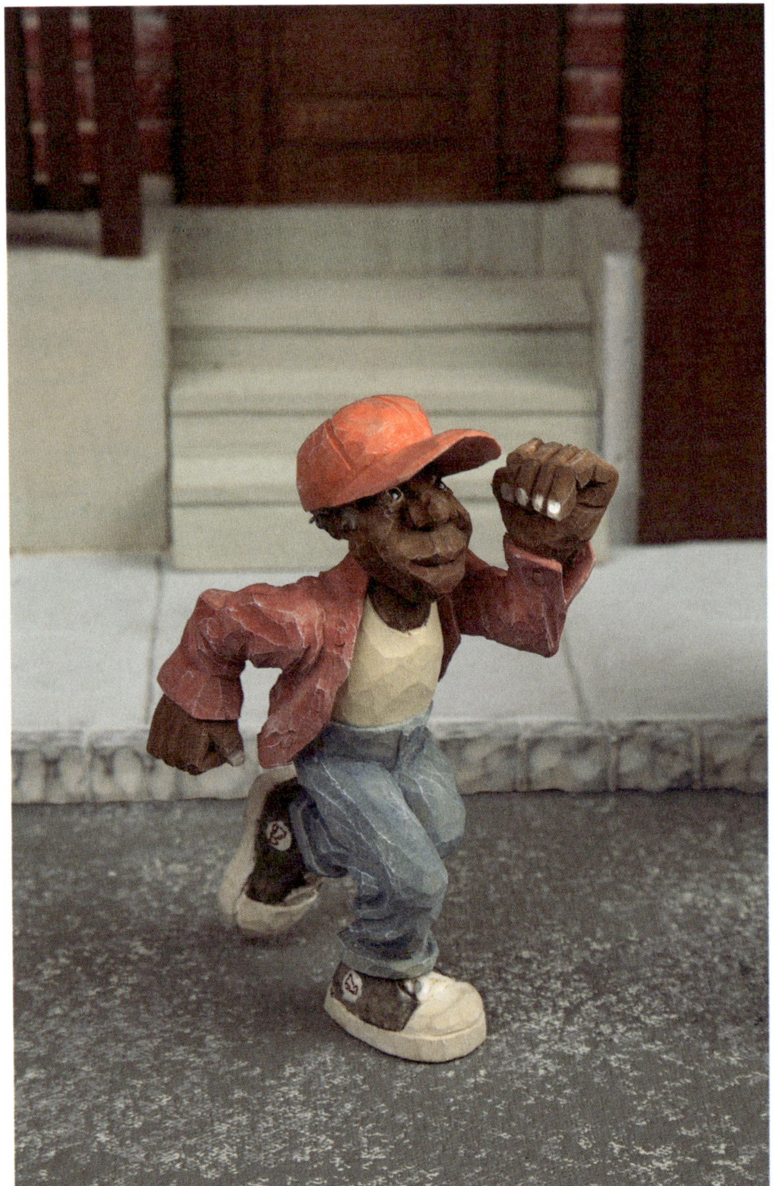

Something that all small towns in the USA have in common is kids playing and dreaming. That's how the idea of the boy running came about. All of my figures start as a rough sketch and evolve to a refined drawing.

—Joe Schumacher

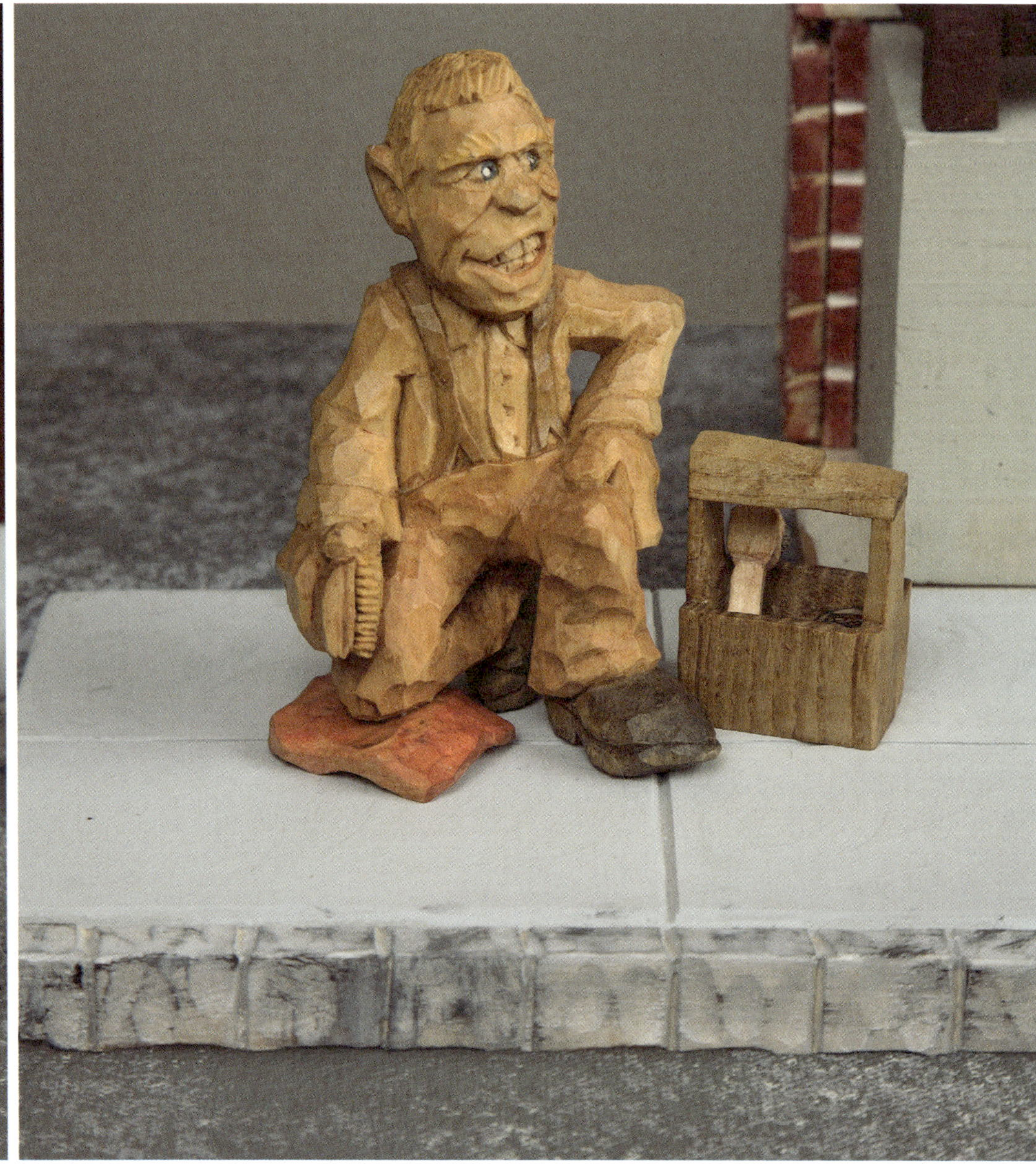

The shoeshine boy was a common street corner vendor during, and after, the "Great Depression."

—Mitch Cartledge

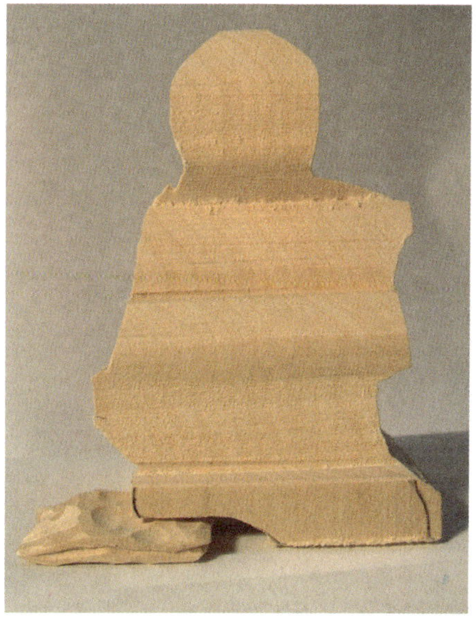

Blank, front view

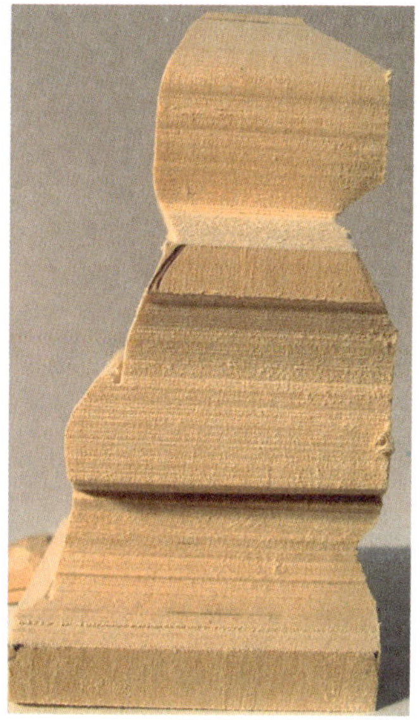

Blank, side view

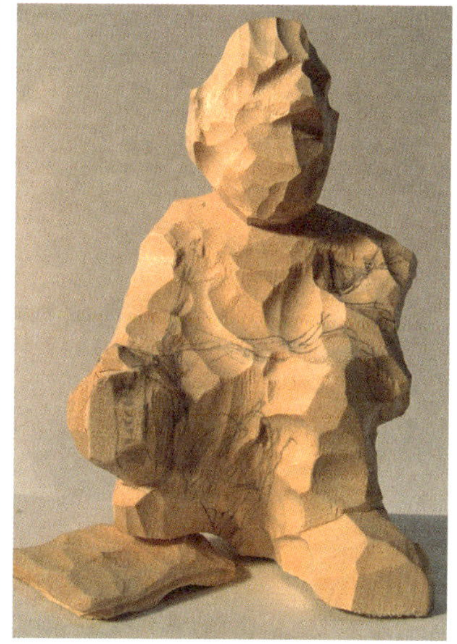

Roughing out, front view

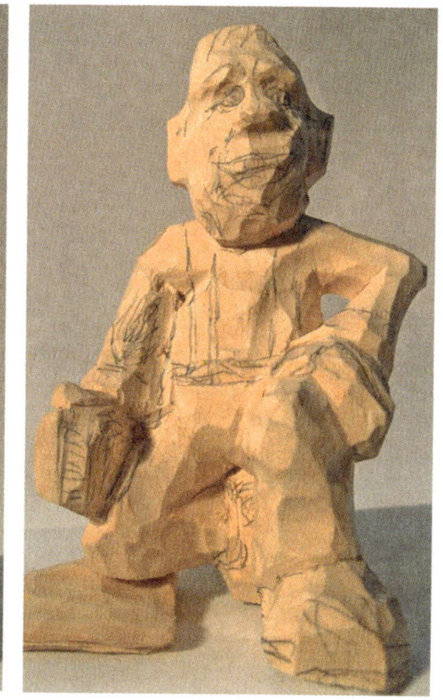

Ready to block, front view

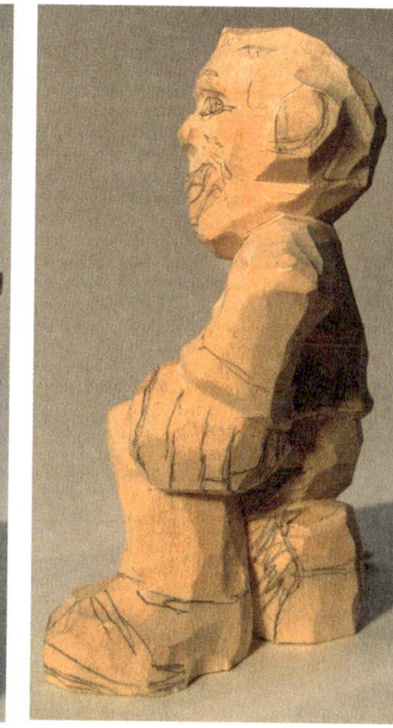

Ready to block, left side

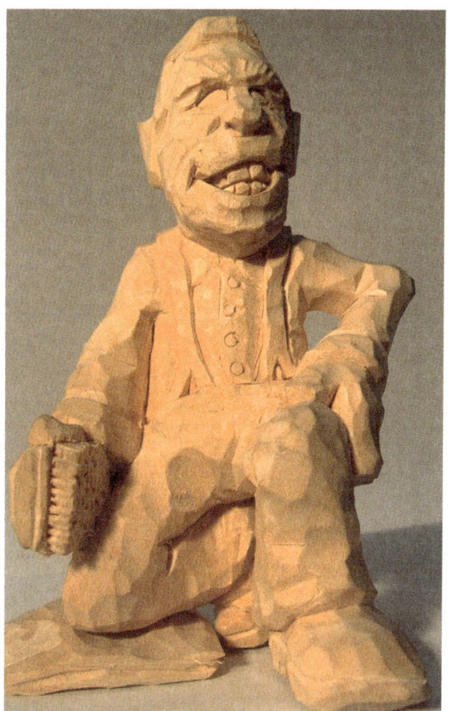

Detail being added

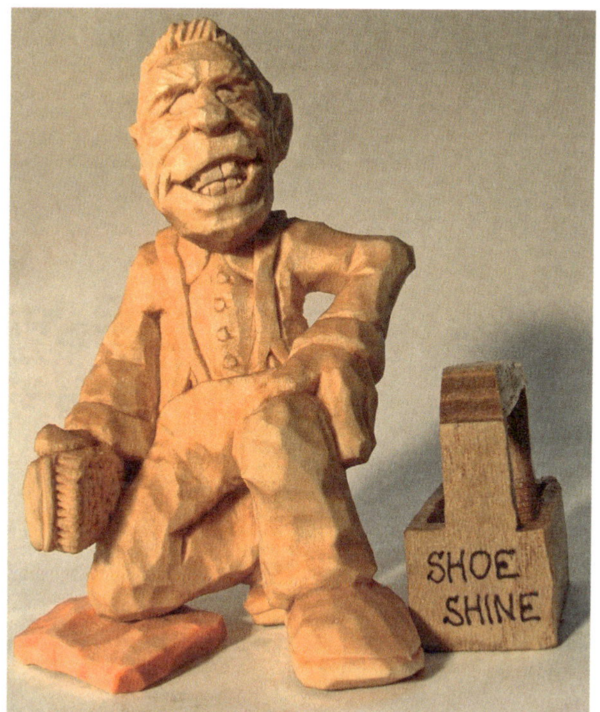

Ready to paint

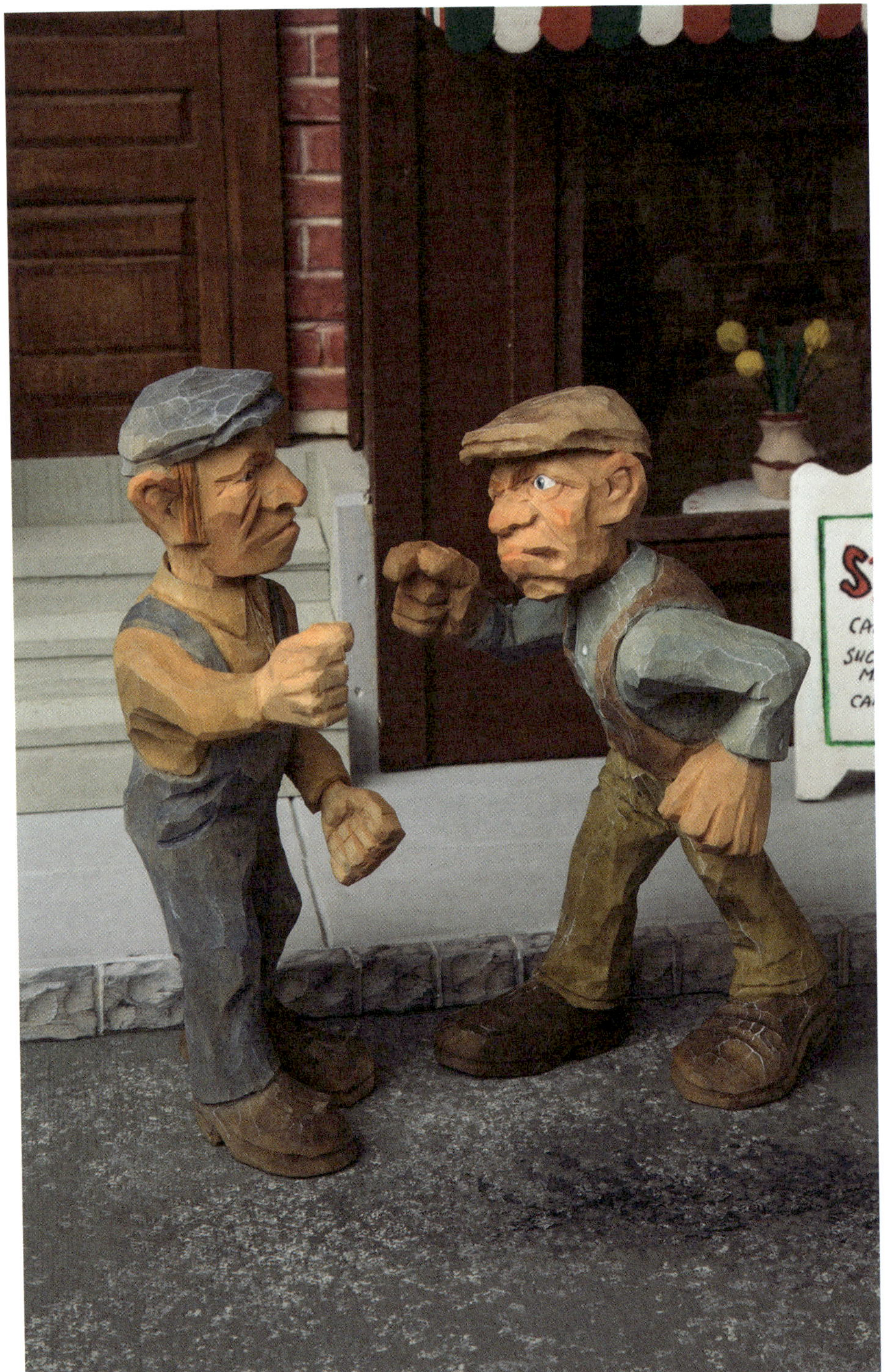

The 1930s was a period of great despair, seasoned with faith and hope for a better future. My carvings reflect the human response to the realities of an economic future impacted by the Great Depression, but encouraged by the leadership of a powerful new president. Examples of my carvings depicting the reality of the times can be found throughout this book. Here two men feud over political matters. So while our 1930s scenes are done in caricature, there remains the stark reality of the time period, its uncertainties and difficulties.

The two feuding men are carved in an aggressive posture with tight fists, one with a jabbing finger, and both with angry expressions. Each is carved from just two pieces of wood, making up the head and body. They are to be arranged toe to toe, as if ready to exchange blows. Seems to be in keeping with the current political discourse, does it not?

—Gene Fuller

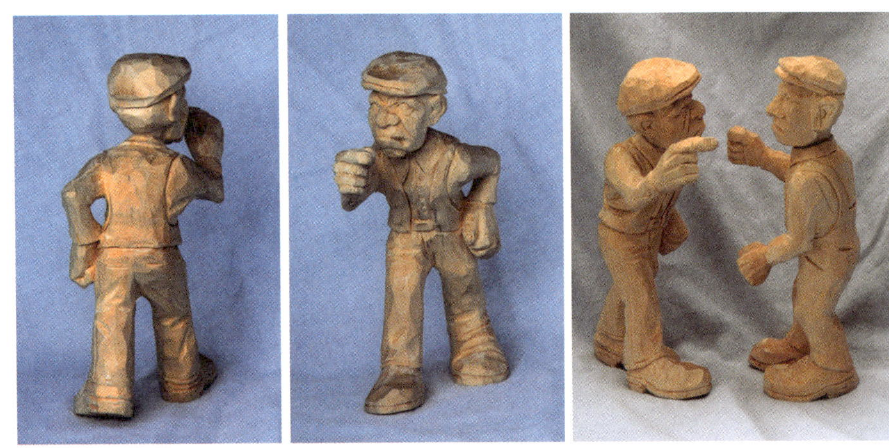

Ready to paint

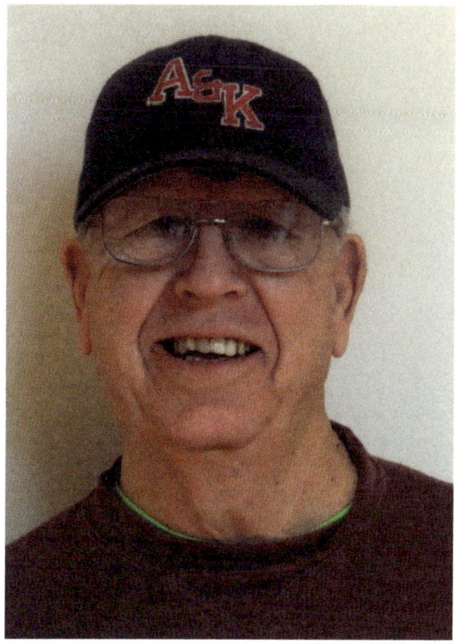

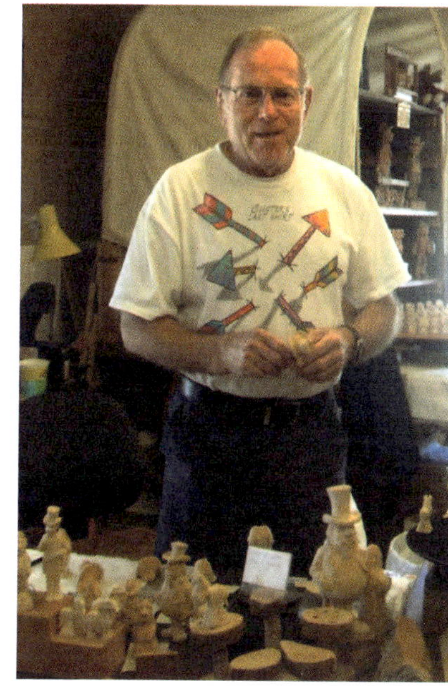

Pete LeClair

I started carving in the early 1970s. After seeing a picture of an Andy Anderson carving, I thought I would like to try woodcarving. Without carving clubs in my area, I had to learn on my own. It was slow going but I enjoyed it.

I participated in my first carving show in 1990. At that show I was asked if I would teach a two-day seminar in upstate New York. Working full-time, I could only do a few seminars a year, but, in 1998, I retired and started teaching more seminars.

I have taught seminars throughout the United States, Canada, Australia and England.

Keith Morrill

Keith is a South Dakota native. He spent his vocational life as a biology teacher, first at the high school level and then, for the majority of his teaching career, at South Dakota State University. Upon retiring, he moved to the Black Hills, and currently resides in Custer, South Dakota.

As a kid, Keith developed an interest in wood, spending time building model airplanes when they were wood rather than the plastics of today. His interest in wood eventfully led him to the Doane College Experience woodcarving classes in Crete, Nebraska. From that point forward, carving has been a serious hobby for Keith. Over the years, he has attended and taught many workshops throughout the country.

Keith has been a member of the CCA for over 20 years and the Carver in Residence at the National Museum of Woodcarving in Custer for over 25 years.

LONE STAR BARBER SHOP

Steve Prescott and Ryan Olsen

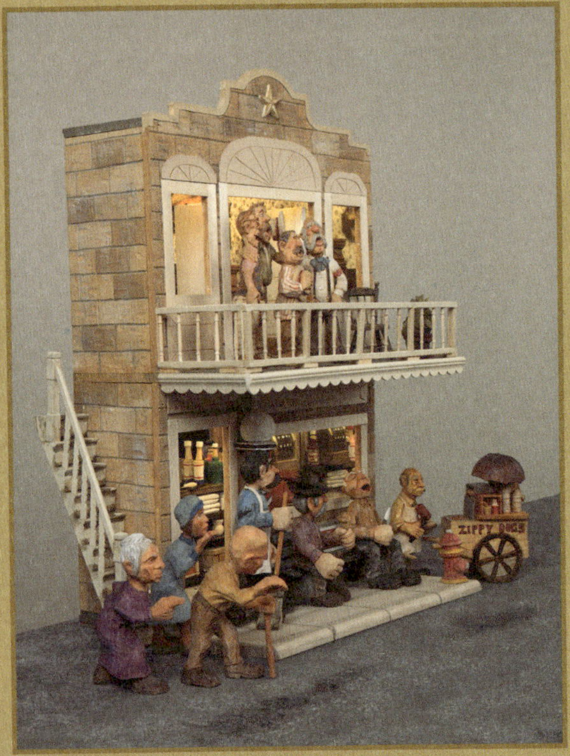

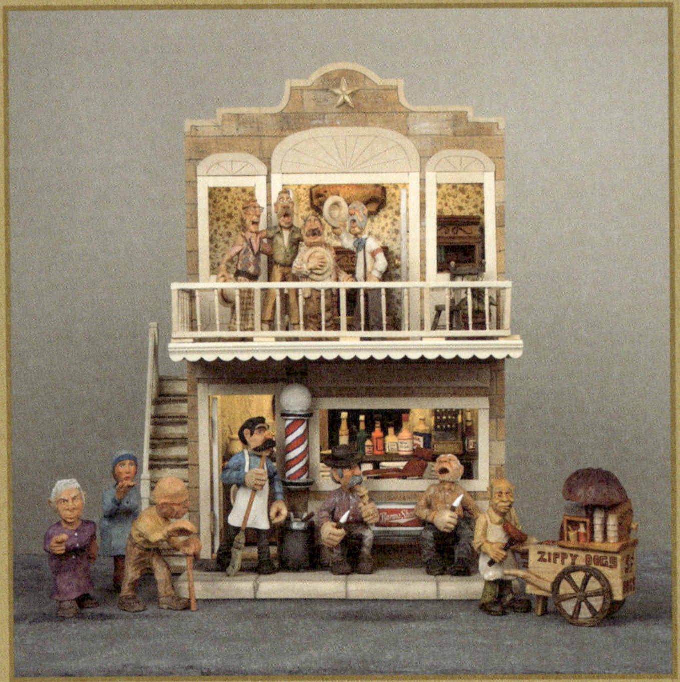

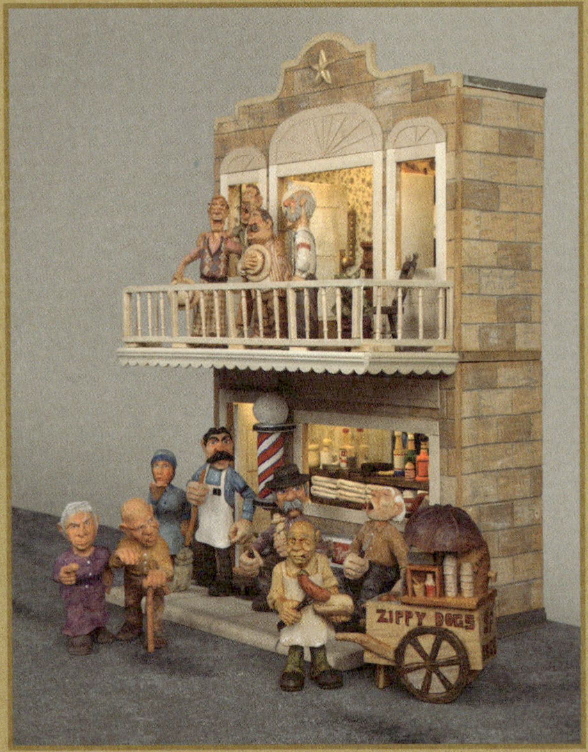

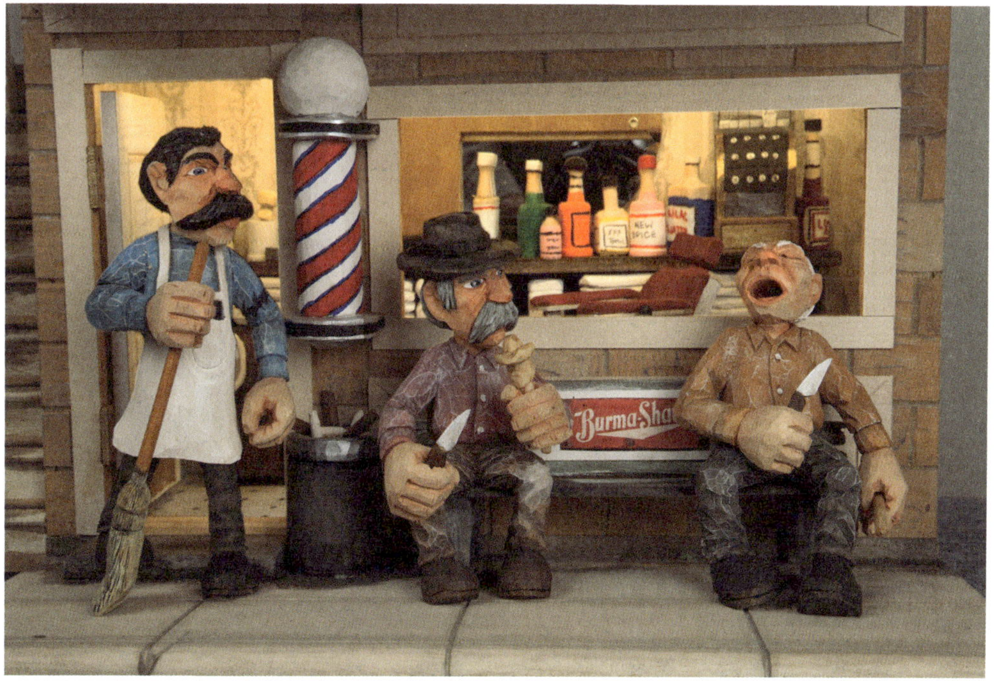

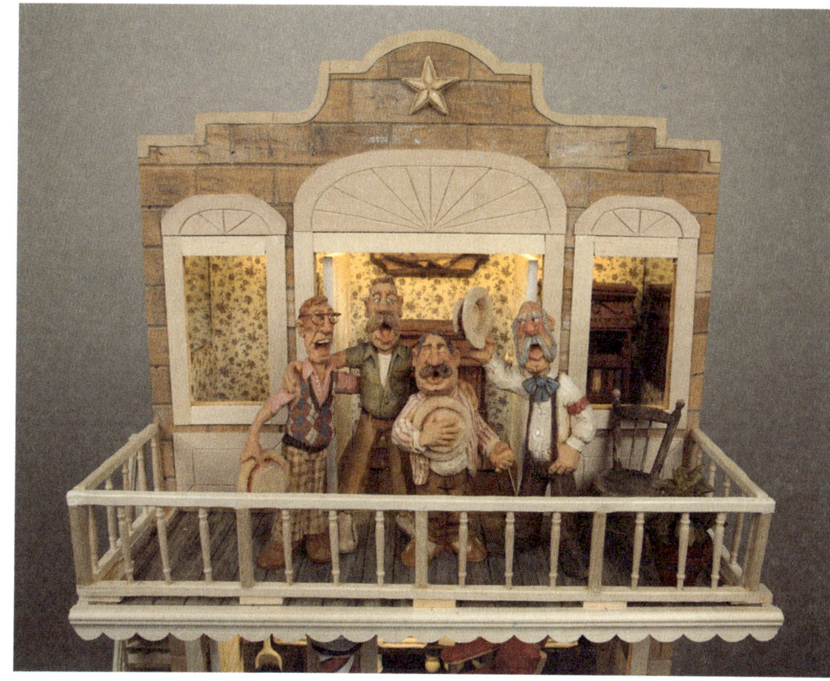

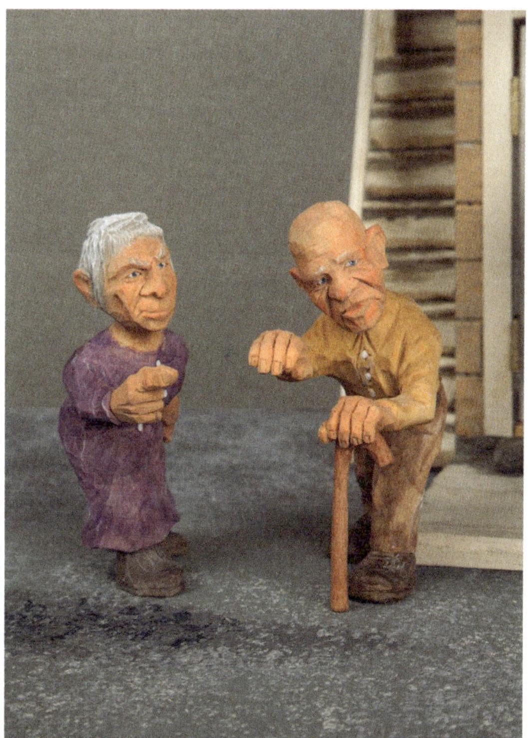

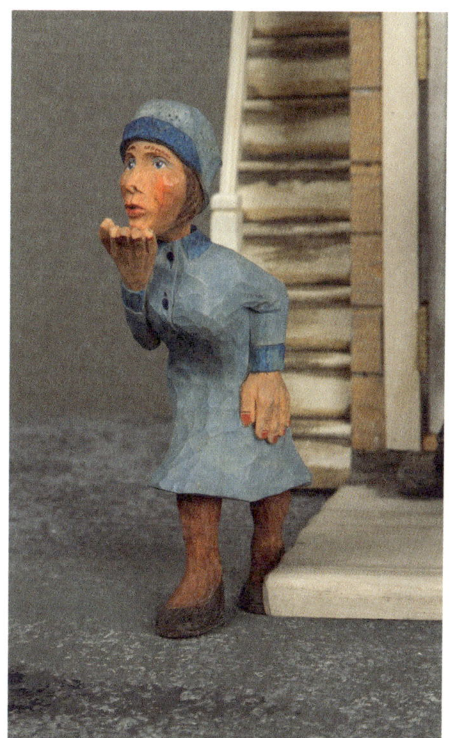

Barber and whittlers by Steve Prescott
Elderly couple and woman blowing kiss by Gene Fuller
Barbershop quartet by Ryan Olsen

When the CCA proposed doing a 1930s Street Scene, I immediately volunteered to do a barber shop. I recently inherited my grandfather's barber equipment. I have displayed his handmade razor strop, straight razor, sharpening stone, scissors, shaving mug and brush, duster brush, and hand clippers in a shadow box. It was a natural fit for me.

I built the barber shop structure with help from a carving friend who has better carpentry skills than I. The style is called Mission Revival and it is still popular here in Texas, because it resembles the Alamo. I teamed up with one of the CCA's newest members, Ryan Olsen from Idaho, making a blend of the CCA's oldest and newest members.

—Steve Prescott

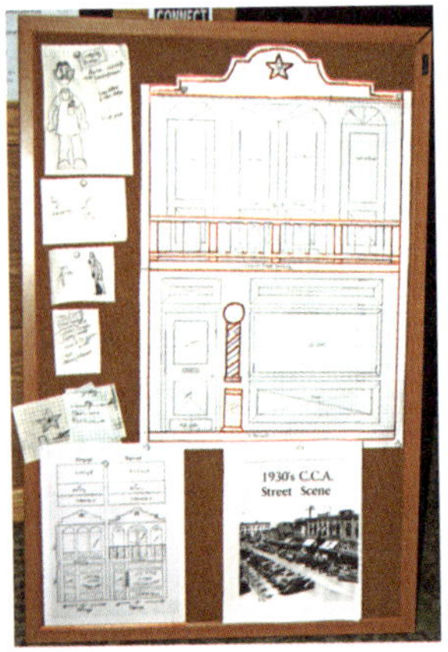

Plans

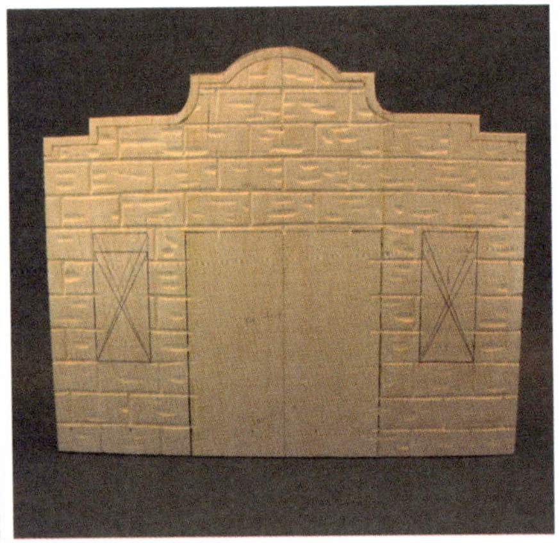

Front board

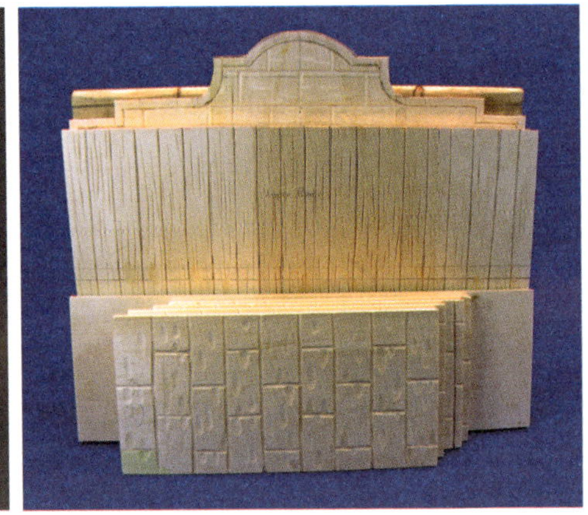

Ready to assemble

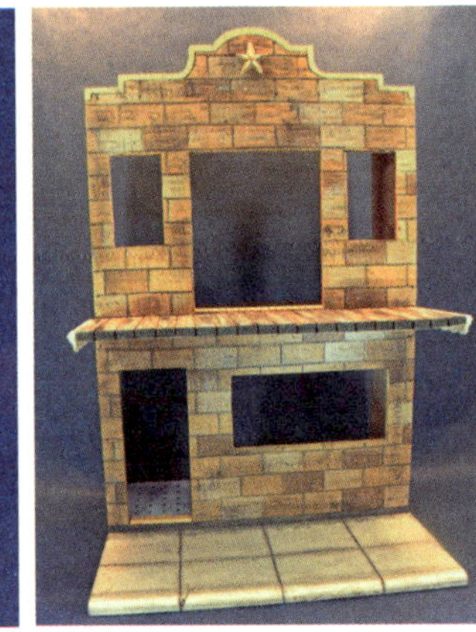

Assembled, front

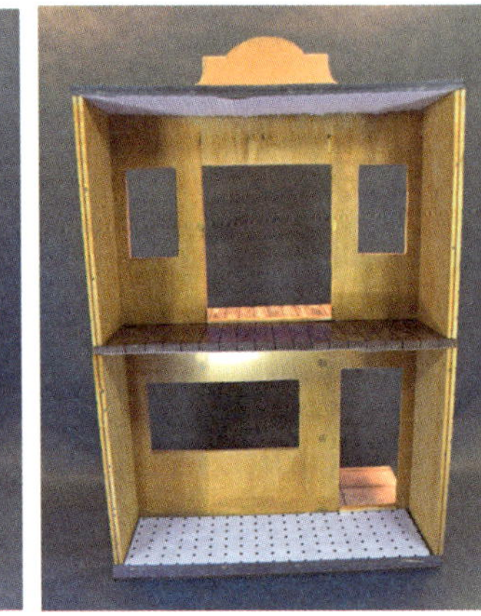

Assembled, back

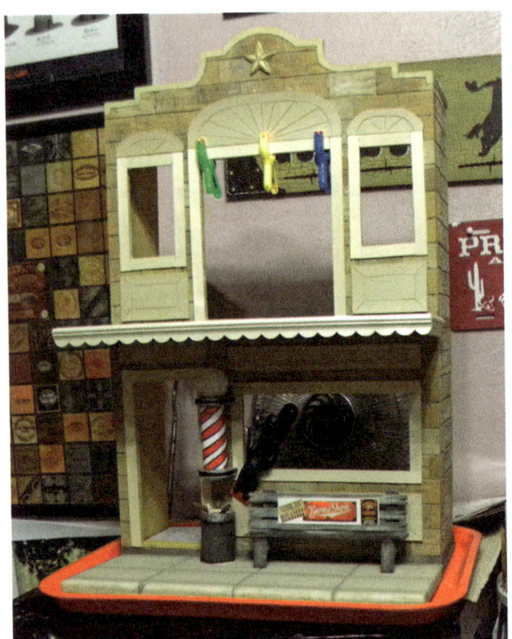

Adding trim

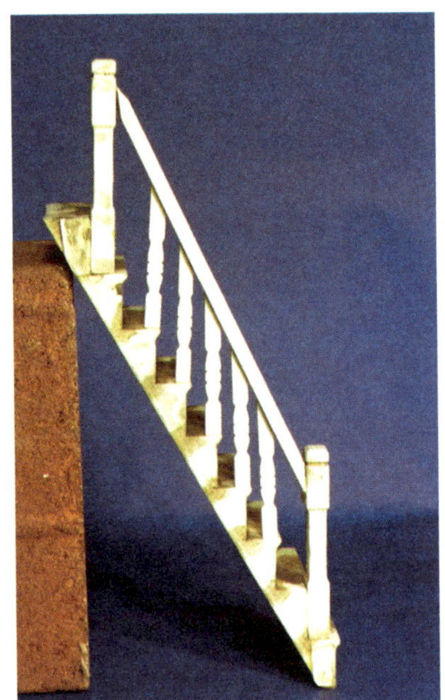

Stairs

Tips from Steve Prescott.

• Take a chip carving class. It is great training in learning to make good, clean, precise cuts. Having said that—I hate to chip carve!

• Take a tole painting class to learn to shade properly. Tole painting is done on a variety of flat objects and even though it is a heavier style of painting than caricature woodcarving, it is great for learning shading techniques. Shading your three dimensional carving will really make the cuts and colors pop.

• Always carry a small sketch book to record ideas. If I don't write it down, I'll forget it and it is gone forever. (This trait is getting worse as I age, too.)

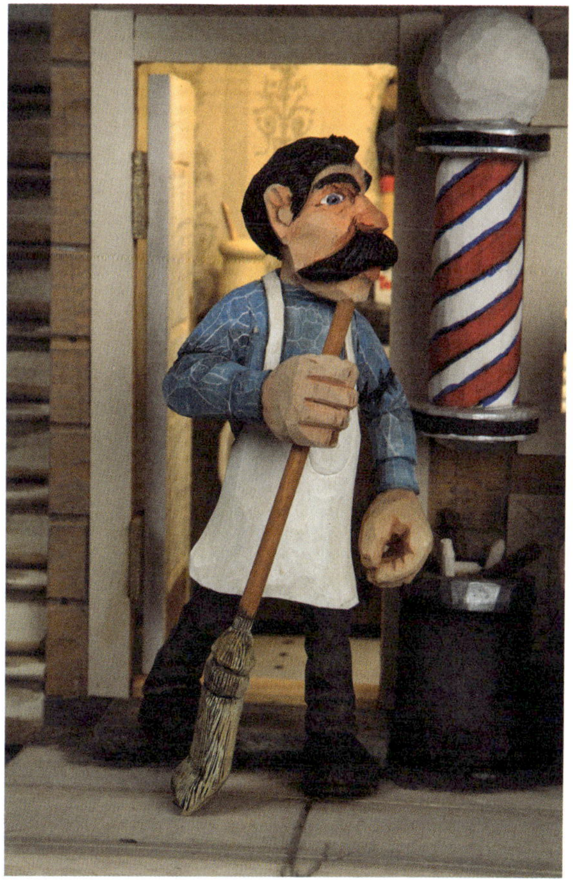

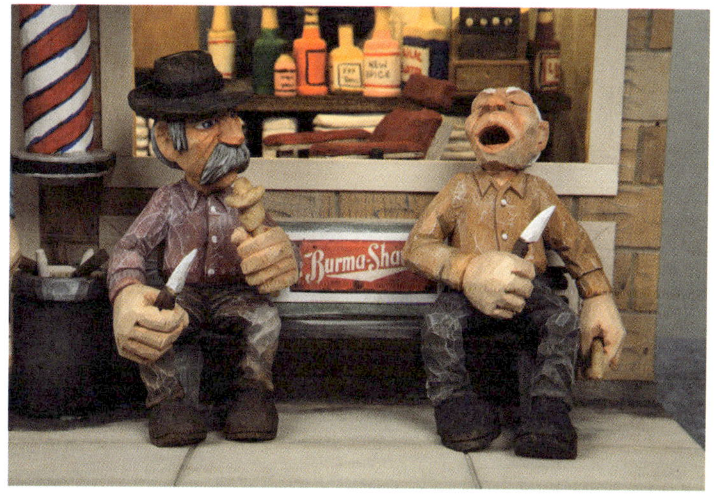

The perturbed barber is storming out to sweep up the mess created by the two whittlers seated on the bench out front. One whittler is looking astonished at his buddy, who has fallen asleep during mid-stroke. This seems to occur more often to me as I age. The focus of this caricature scene is on the sleeping woodcarver.

—Steve Prescott

The barber adds some action to the scene. He is caught in mid-stride as he steps off the front step. His posture and expression shows his disapproval and frustration at having to re-sweep his sidewalk. Notice that the hair is shiny from his hair tonic. His waxed handlebar mustache is required for this era. The broom is added as were the arms and head.

—Steve Prescott

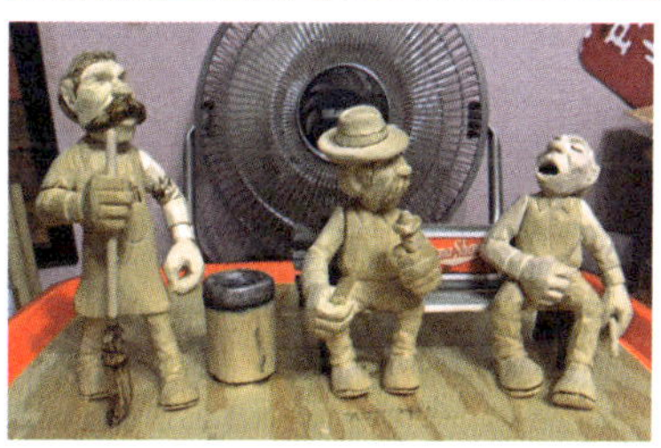

Barber and whittlers

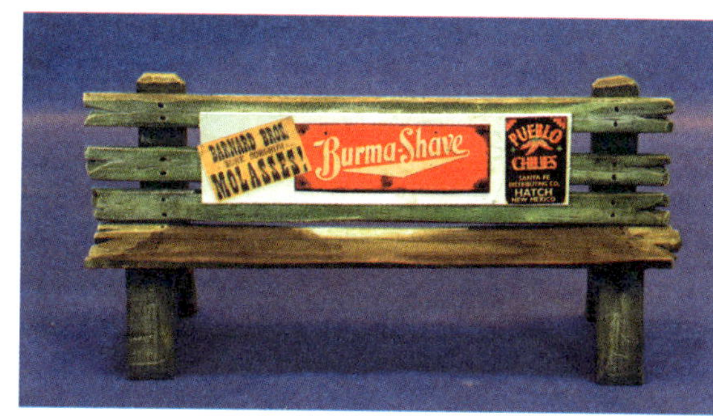

Sidewalk bench

The counter, cluttered with all those multicolored and multi-shaped bottles, brings back memories of the smells of all those hair tonics and colognes, as well as cigars and cigarettes. The barber chair was modeled after my own carving shop barber chair, with maroon leather and chrome. I also added a couple wall mirrors to reflect lights on the dark interior. These objects left little room for figures inside the barber shop.

—Steve Prescott

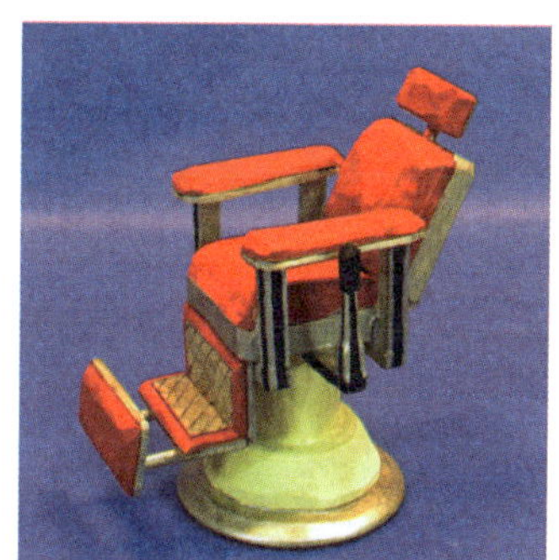

Barber chair

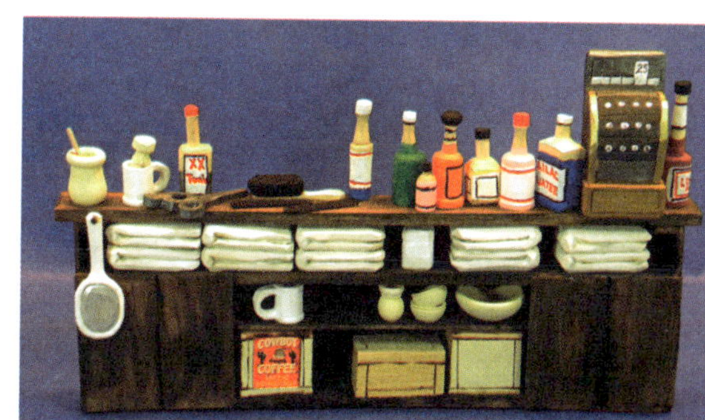

Counter with supplies

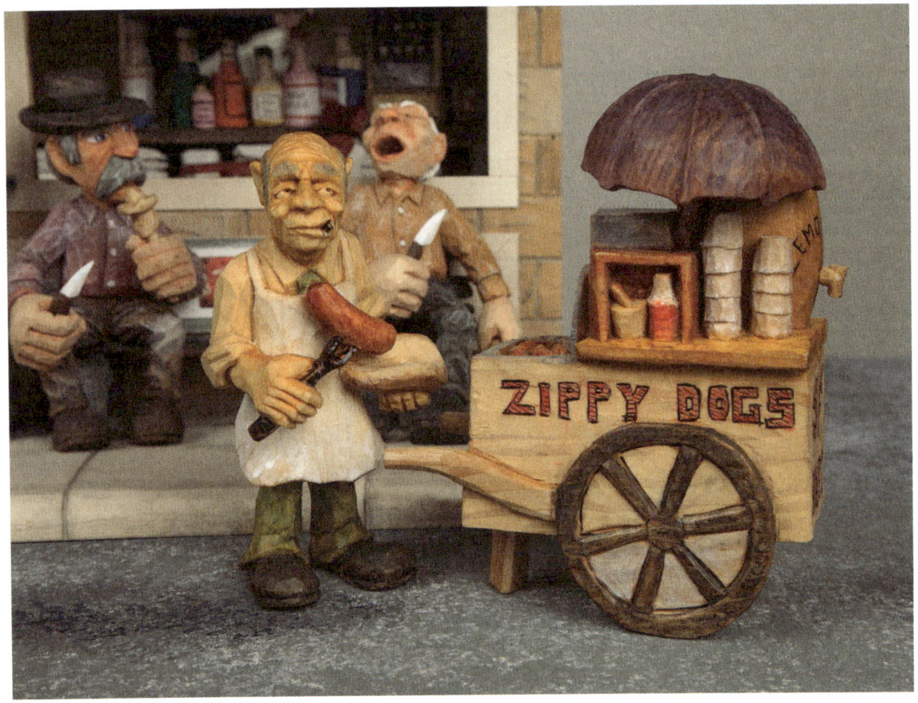

The hot dog vendor was carved separately from the hot dog cart, but it is evident that he belongs with the cart. The cart and its equipment were representative of what would be on a vendor's cart without being too explicit in presenting all necessary equipment. In other words, artistic license, exaggeration, and imagination played an important part in the mental image that goes into each carving.

—Don Mertz

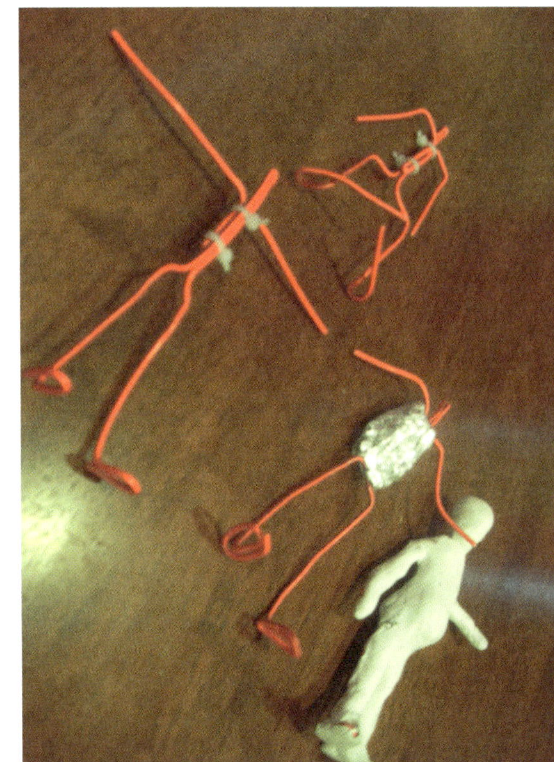

Wire Armatures

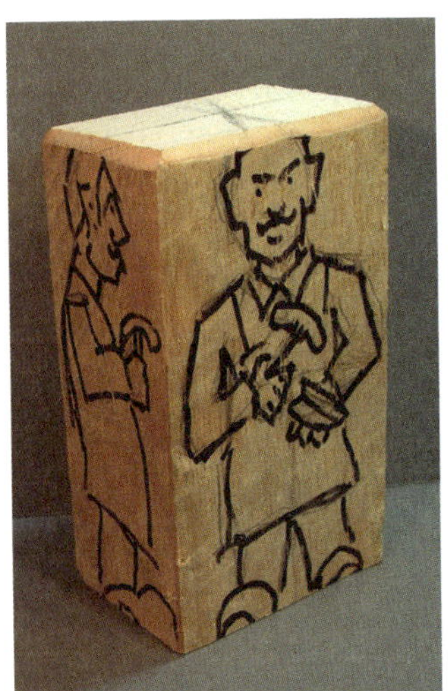

Pattern on wood

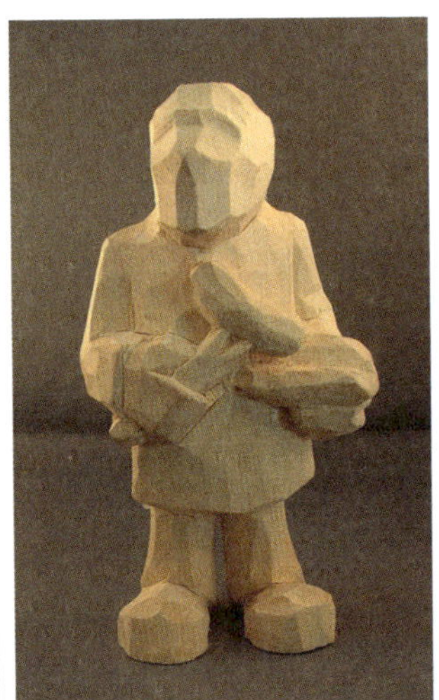

Roughed out, front

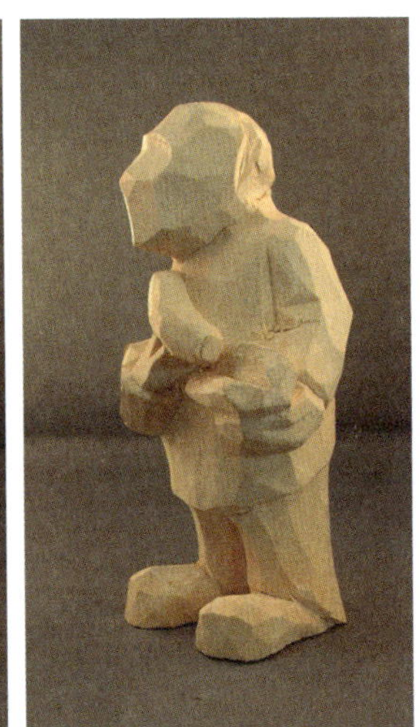

Roughed out, side

In my opinion, it is virtually impossible to carve an effective multi-figure piece without some real planning. I like to mold a sketch in clay before I begin to carve, to help plan the movement proportions. Last year, Joe You showed me a great way to make an armature out of wire. After creating the armatures, I filled the figures out with aluminum foil and Sculpey brand clay. I baked the figures to keep them from moving as I worked with them.

—Ryan Olsen

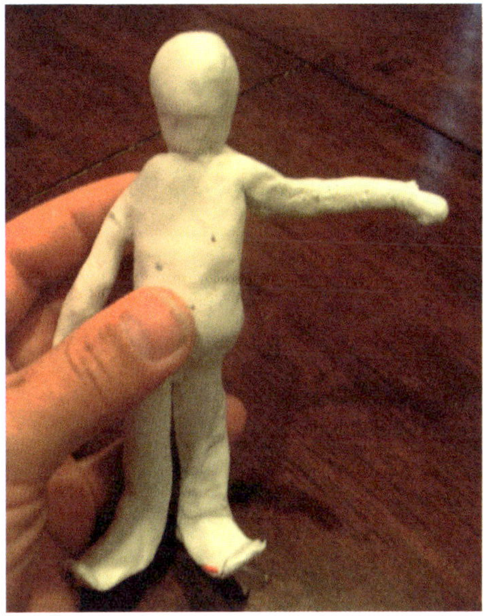

Clay model. First singer on left

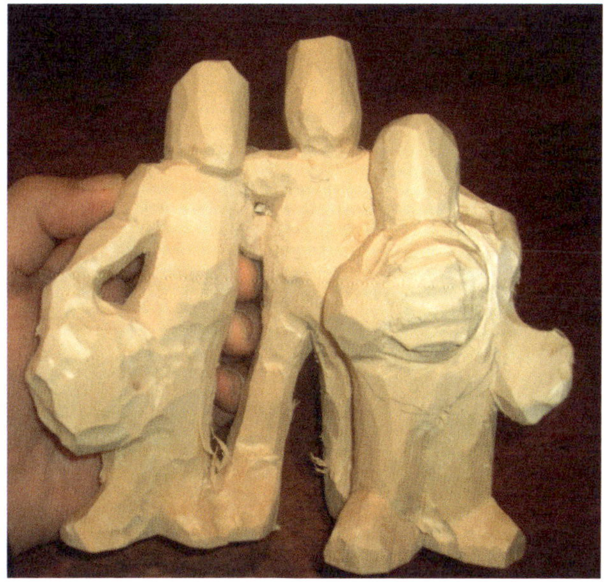

Trio roughed out in wood

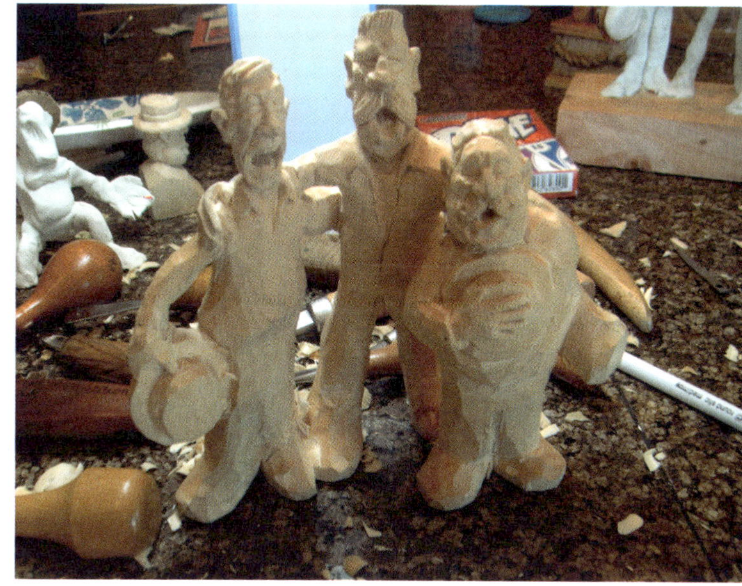

Trio partially carved

I decided to do the barbershop quartet from one piece of wood, in order to create interaction. The difficulty increased significantly, but the end product was worth it. I wanted the quartet to look as though they were singing and moving as one unit. Unfortunately, I miscounted the figures and only ended up with a trio, and so I had to add one more figure to make a quartet.

—Ryan Olsen

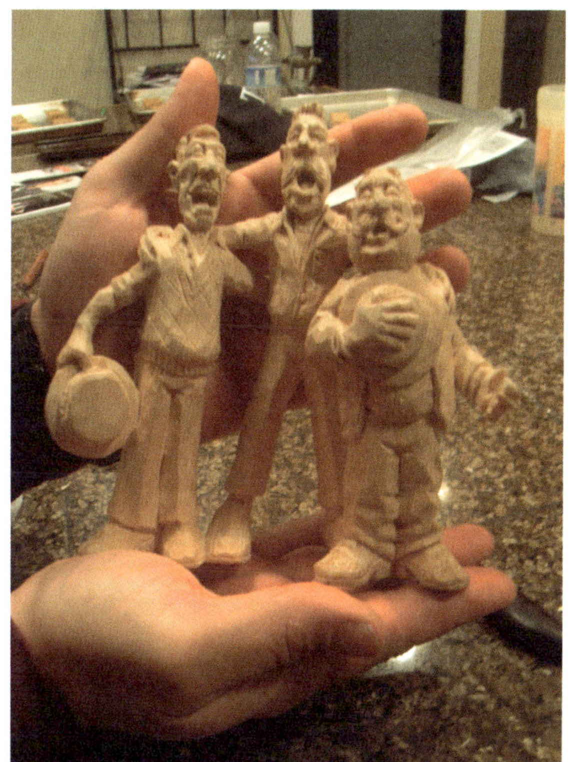

The silhouette was drawn on two sides of a block of wood and the excess wood was removed with a band saw and a drill gun. I slowly removed wood, using the sculpture as a guide and taking great care to leave plenty of wood for the details. I worked all of the figures together, first, with large shapes and movement in mind, and then slowly worked in more and more details. Carving a multi-figure work like this is a real challenge, because there are more eyes, ears, and noses that have to be right. It requires a lot of breaks, problem solving, and a slow, methodical approach.

—Ryan Olsen

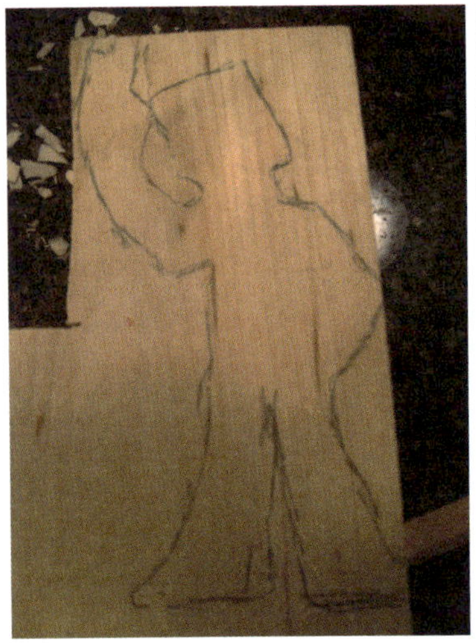

Fourth singer, pattern on wood

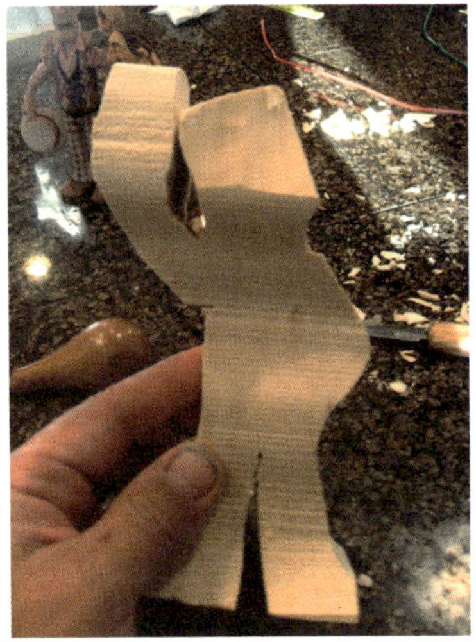

Cut out

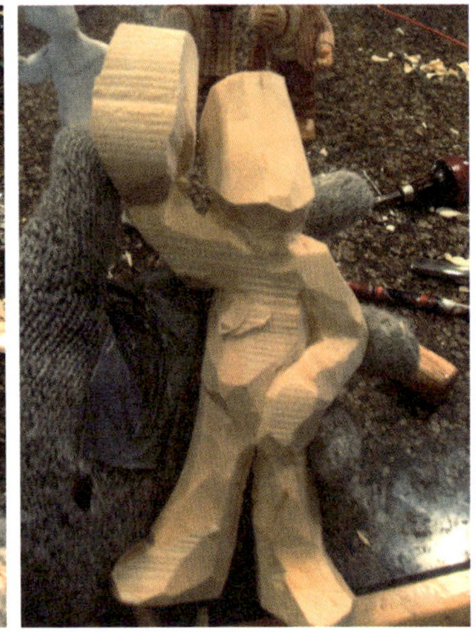

Partially roughed out

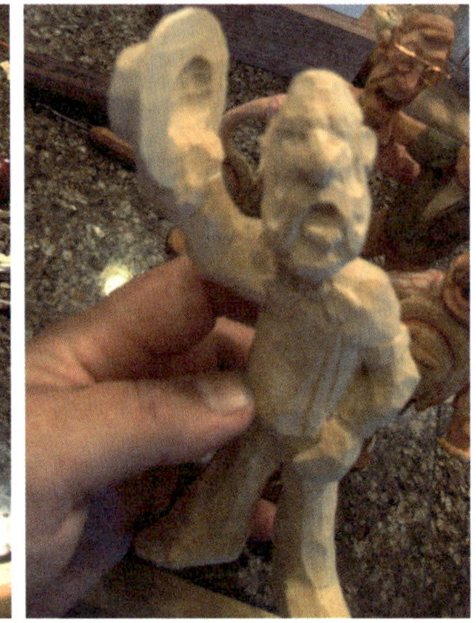

Closing in on it!

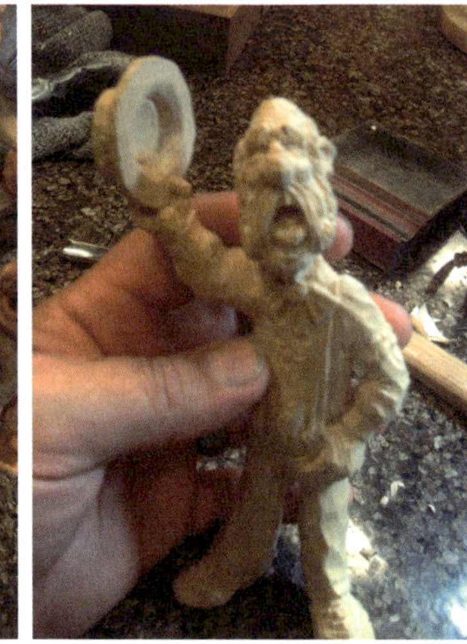

Ready to paint

For me, a good light source is critical. I like to carve directly under a full-spectrum lamp. I never rough out and carve detail in the same sitting. Taking a break lets my brain rest. The break usually involves catching up on the chores that I put off while carving.

—Ryan Olsen

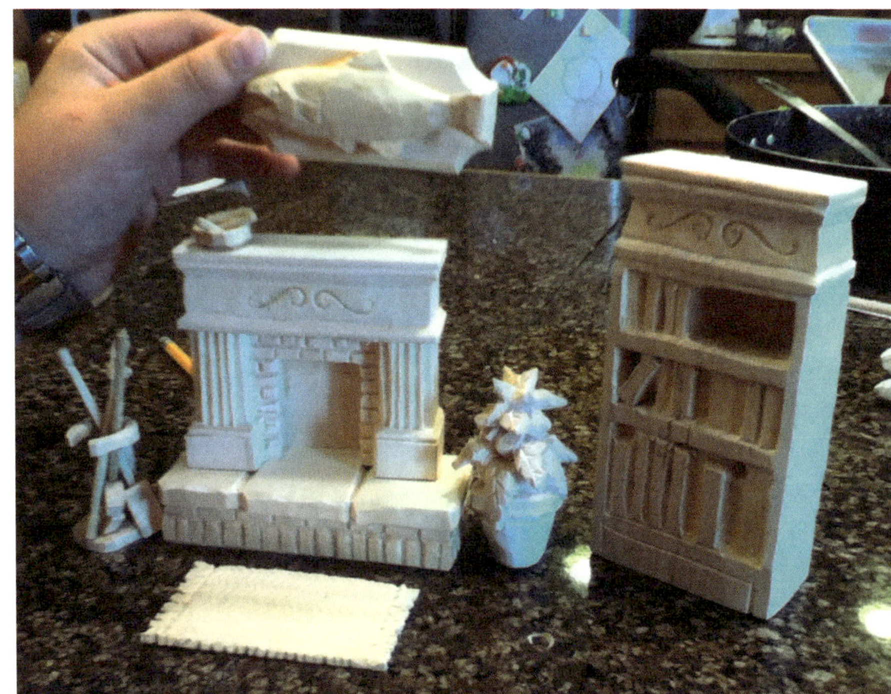

Furniture ready to paint

Steve and I decided to do some furniture inside of the barbershop and upstairs gentlemen's club to make it more authentic. Steve has always said that it is the little details that make the scene and I completely agree. We had to be careful not to overpower the figures with the furniture and the details. After all, it's the figures and their interaction that make a scene really work.

—Ryan Olsen

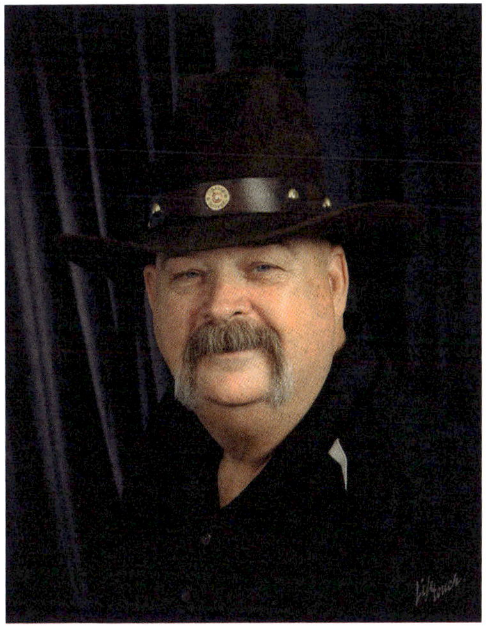

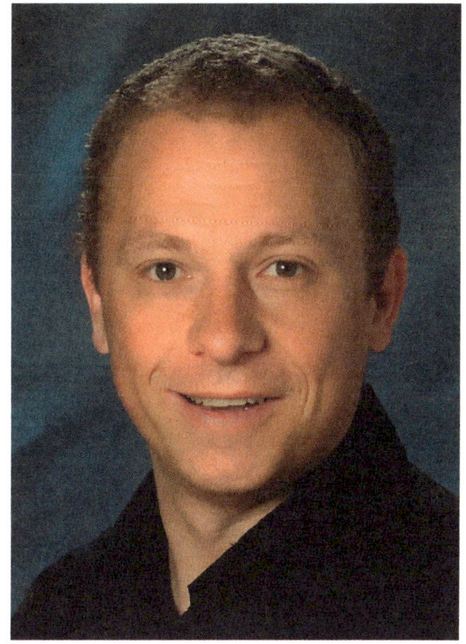

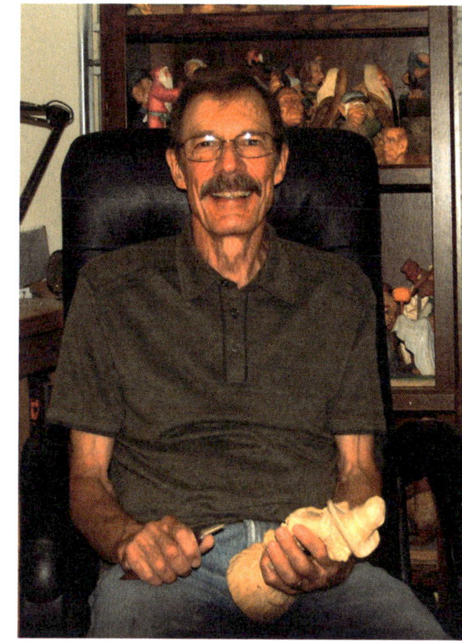

Steve Prescott

Steve Prescott is a founding member of the CCA. He is a retired teacher and coach, with over thirty years of experience. Steve has been carving since 1981. In addition to his CCA activities, he actively participates in other carving activities such as shows, competitions, teaching classes/seminars, writing woodcarving books/articles, and judging woodcarving shows.

Steve has been married to Pat for more than forty years. She shares an active role in Steve's woodcarving, as well as managing to spoil four beautiful grandchildren, whose outstanding intelligence and good looks are directly attributed to the prepotency of their grandsire.

Ryan Olsen

Ryan first became interested in carving when he was very young. When he was only seven, he found a pocket knife and kept it hidden from his parents. He began carving seriously while he was earning his master's degree in opera at the Cincinnati Conservatory of Music. His favorite tools were snap-off razor blades because "they always had a sharp point." After too many snap-off accidents, he upgraded to X-acto knives and sharpened steak knives.

Ryan stays busy performing opera and teaching middle school choir and orchestra. He has also been teaching opera at Boise State University for the last 10 years. Ryan, his wife, Amy, and their four children live in Melba, Idaho. His advice to caricature carvers is "Carve what you know and love!"

Gene Fuller

Gene Fuller was a professor of biology at Boise State University, where he retired in 2000 after 33 years of teaching. He was introduced to wood carving by Cleve Taylor and Vic Otto. Gene is active in the Idaho Woodcarvers Guild. He has chaired several local woodcarving shows, served as a judge, taught classes, and helped organize several carving jamborees. In 2005, he was elected to CCA and has served as the treasurer for four years. He was pleased to have the opportunity to host the 2010 annual CCA meeting in Boise.

Aside from carving, Gene enjoys the classes and book club activities at the Boise State Emeritus Guild, fly fishing, hiking, trips to McCall, Idaho, with Jackie, his wife of 45 years, and visiting his two sons in Portland, Oregon.

DUNHAM'S DENTISTRY & FRED'S MEAT MARKET

Bob Travis and Joe You

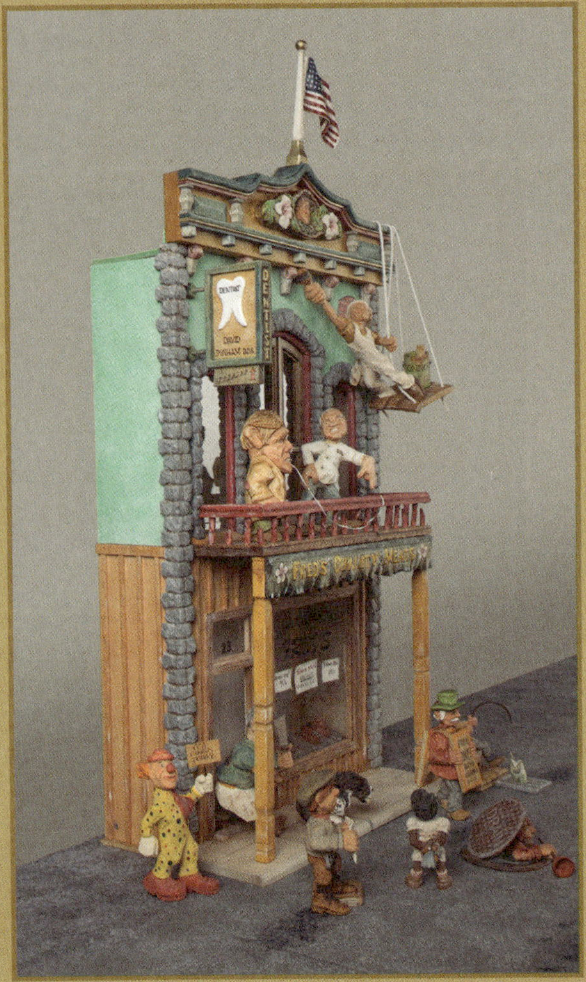

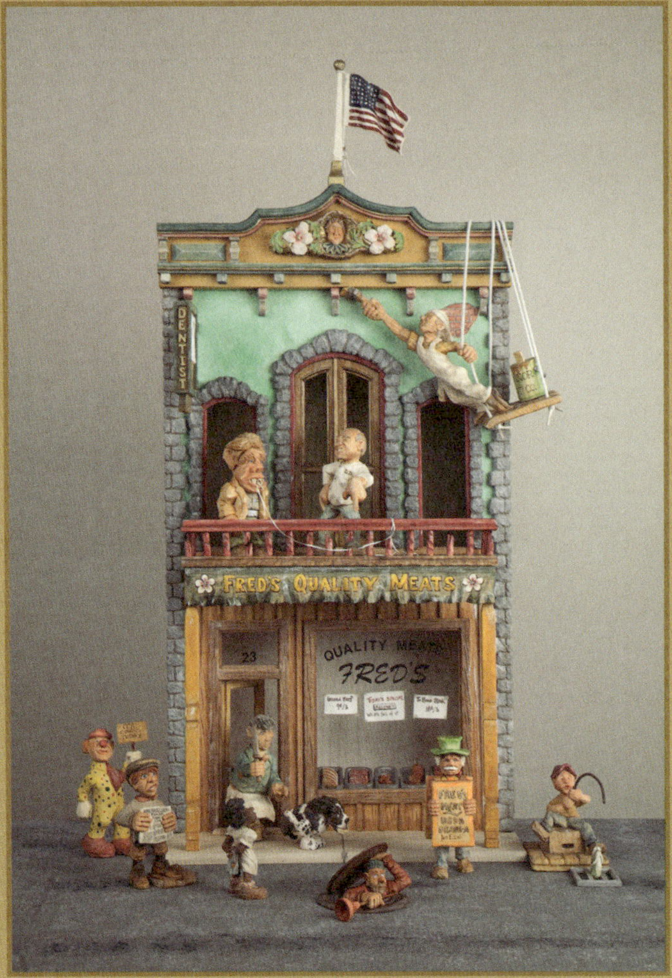

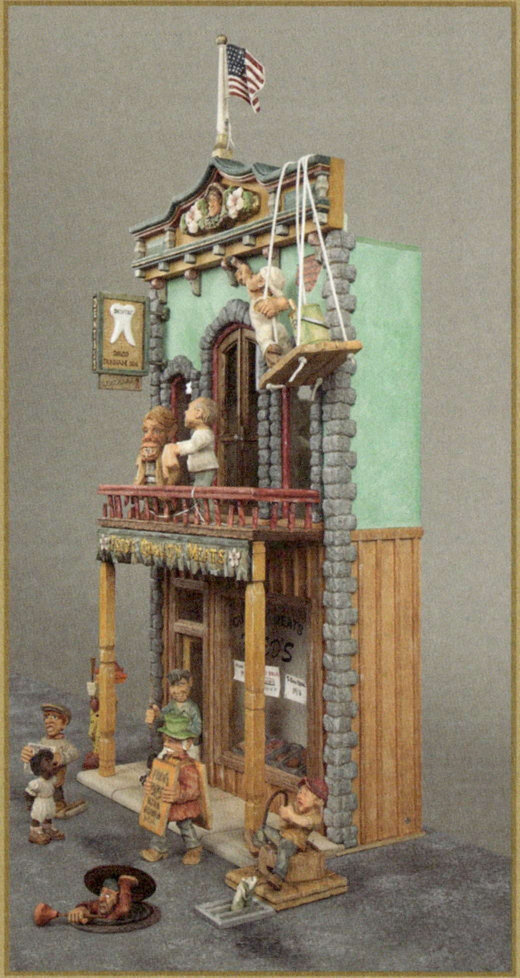

Bob Travis and Joe You were collaborators in constructing a two-story building to honor two people. The second-story honors a friend and one of the best caricature carvers ever, Dr. Dave Dunham from Cleburne, Texas. Dave happened to be an orthodontist, but his office on the second floor is that of a general dentist.

The ground floor honors Joe's father, Fred You, who owned a meat market in Sacramento, California. Throughout high school and his undergrad college days, Joe spent many a weekend working behind a meat counter and selling meat. Fred clearly does not appreciate the dog (carved by Sandy Smith) who just took off with one of his prized T-bone steaks. Who knows, if Joe's dad catches the dog, it may end up as tomorrow's special.

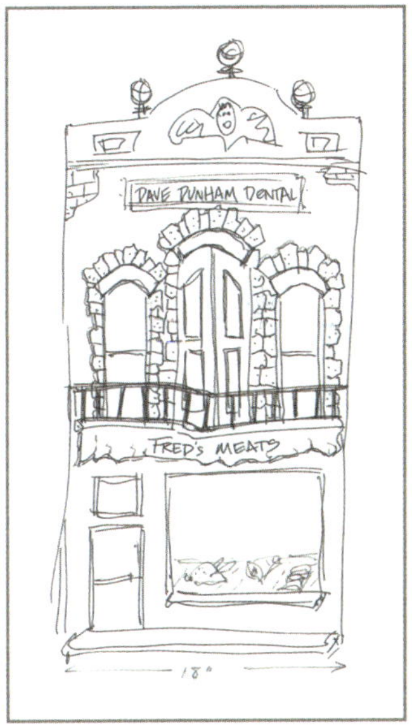

Original sketch by Joe You

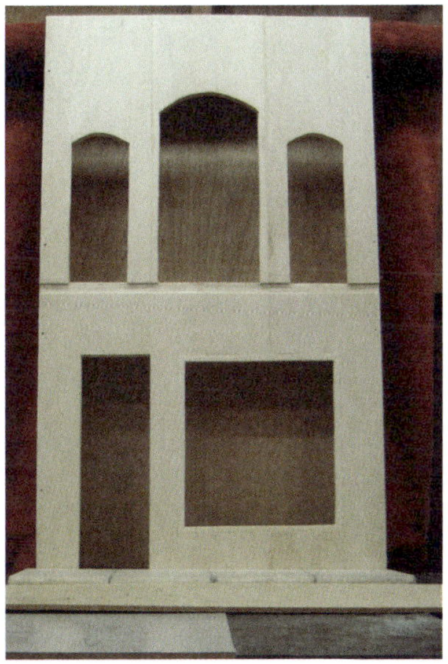

Building unpainted

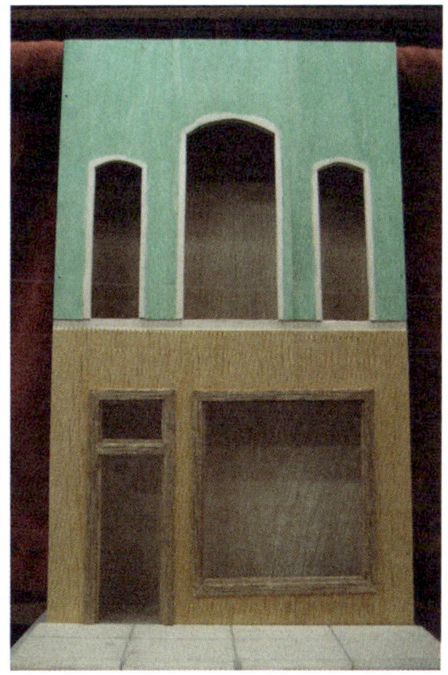

Base coat paint

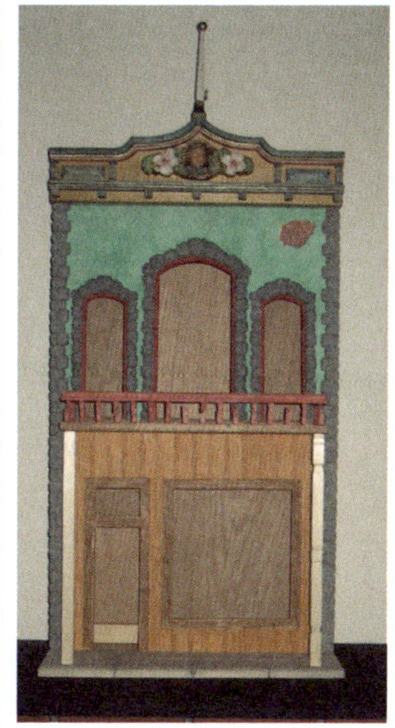

Porch added

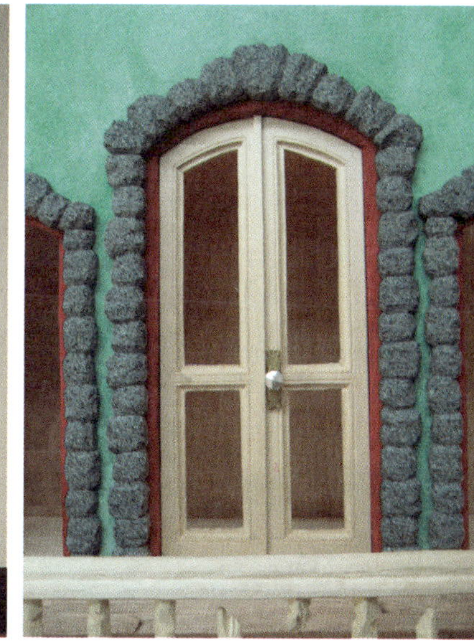

Dental office door

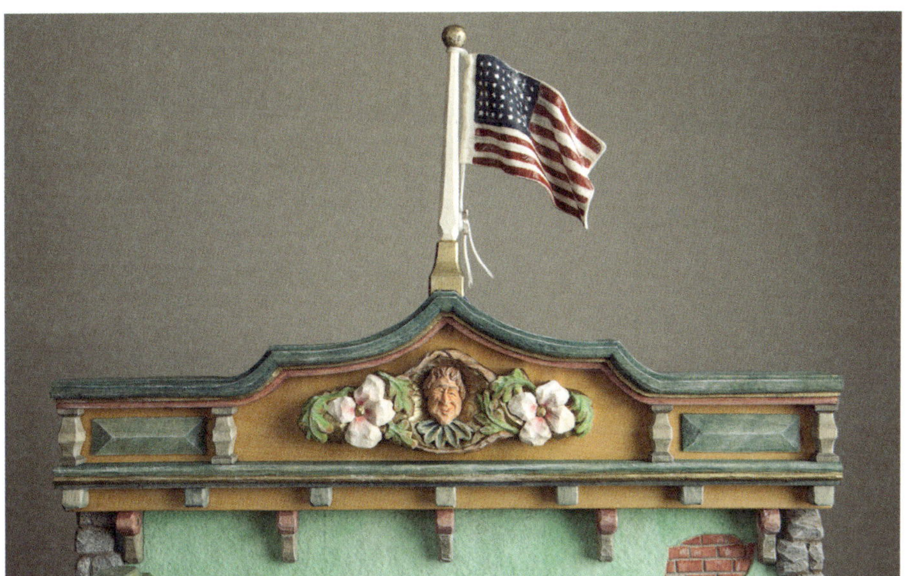

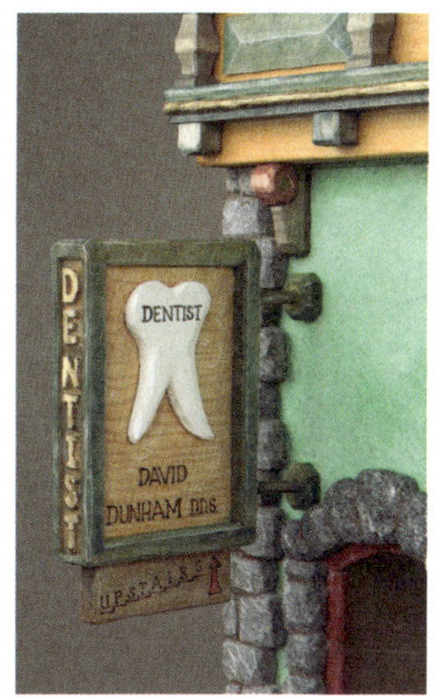

A word about the building. The cornice of the building was carved in separate pieces. The building is topped off with a flag made of cloth and painted with forty-eight stars. The flag's position was held by wrapping the cloth around dowels and applying several coats of clear urethane.

—Joe You

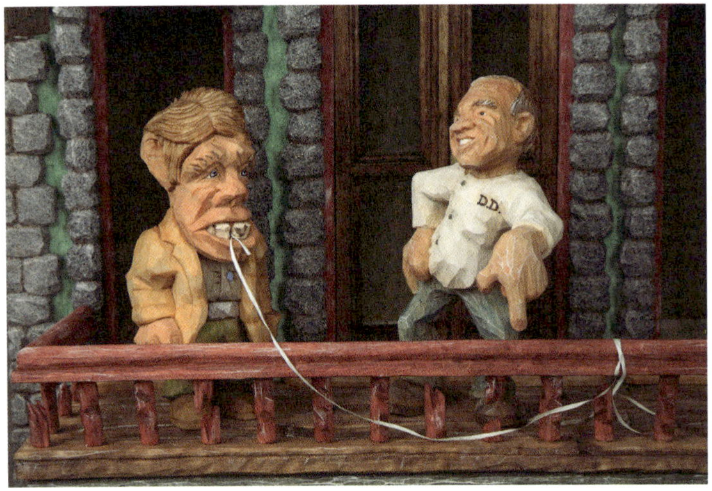

Patient by Bob Travis;
Dr. Dave, painter, and boy fishing by
Joe You

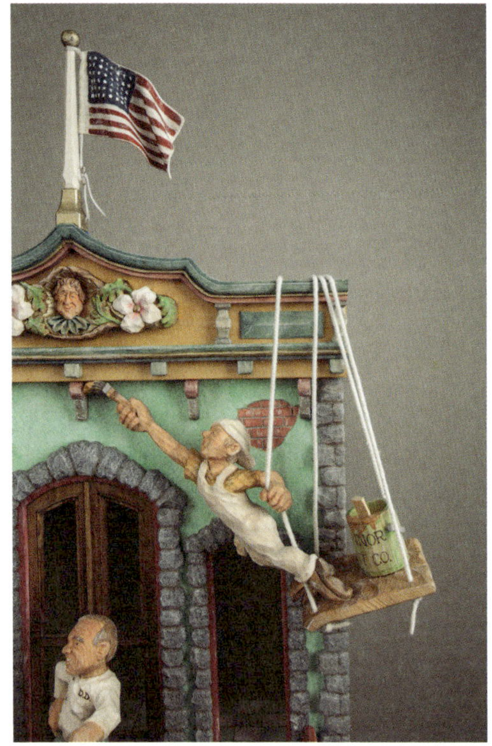

Since Dave probably had little experience extracting teeth as an orthodontist, his method of extraction was to tie a string around the tooth with the other end tied to a rail, and have his patient jump. That's what he is instructing his patient to do. We are not sure his patient is buying into that idea.

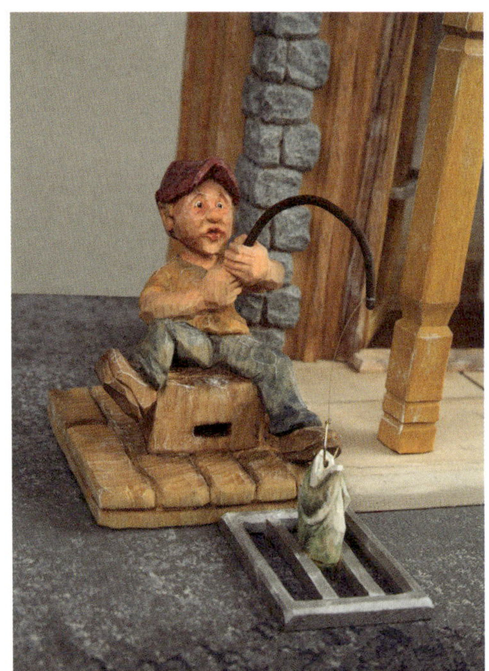

This boy is catching fish in a street drain. As a fisherman since he was young, Joe had many dreams of pulling fish out of improbable spots.

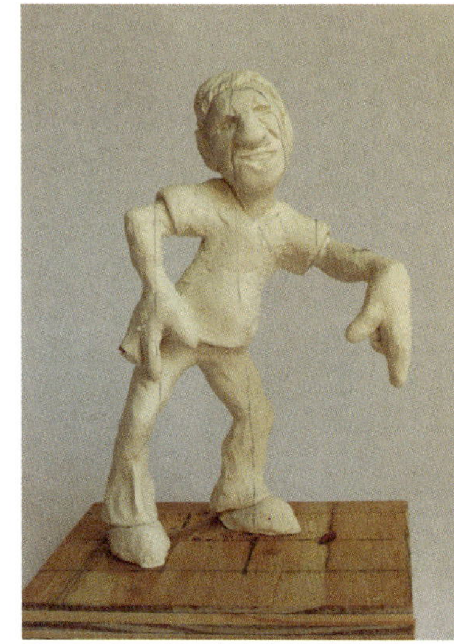

Dr. Dave
clay model

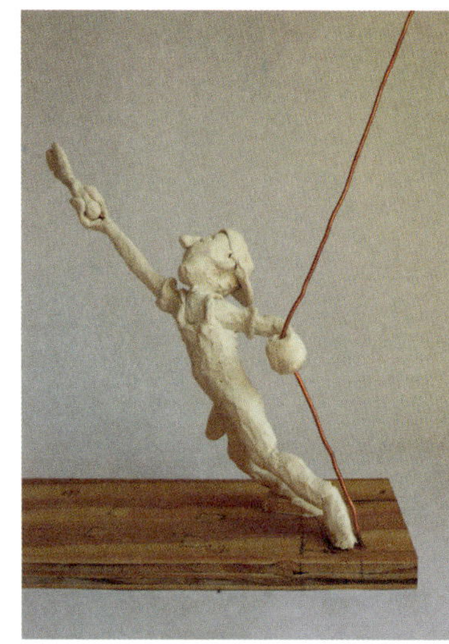

Painter
clay model

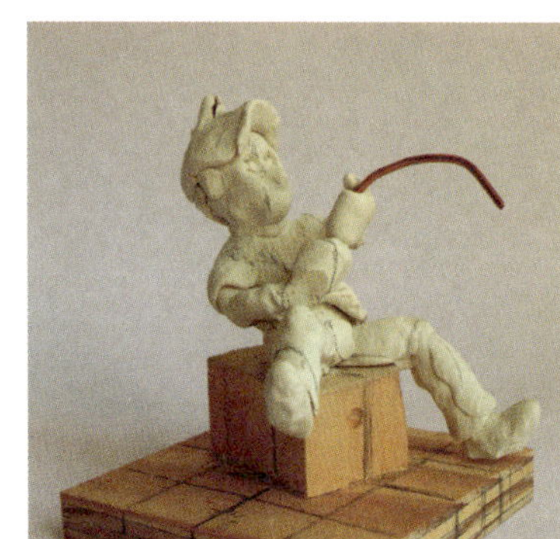

Fishing boy
clay model

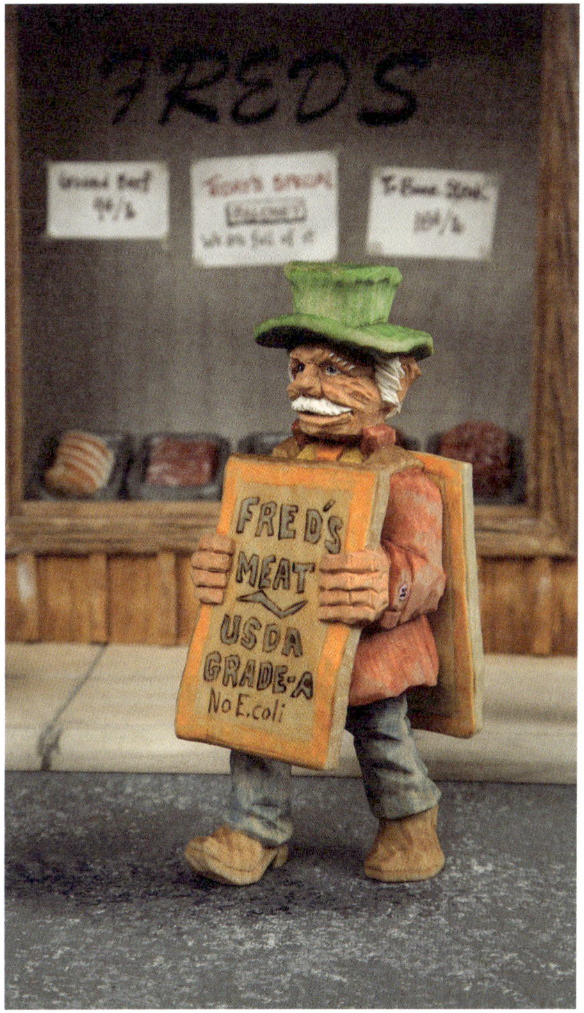

Signboard man by Bob Travis

Hired by Fred to advertise his top quality meat, this guy has little positive to say about Fred's competitor down the street.

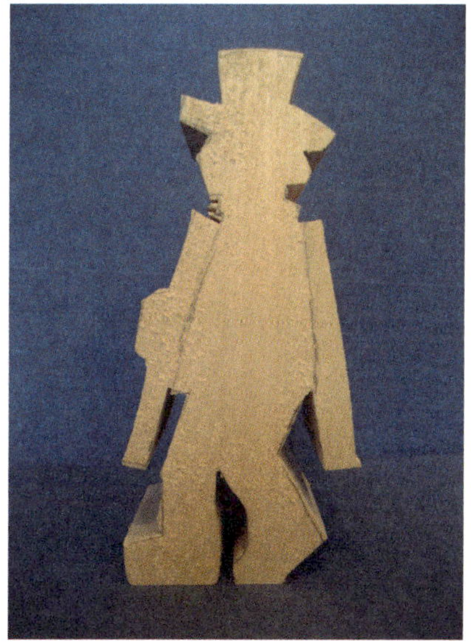

Cut-out, Side view

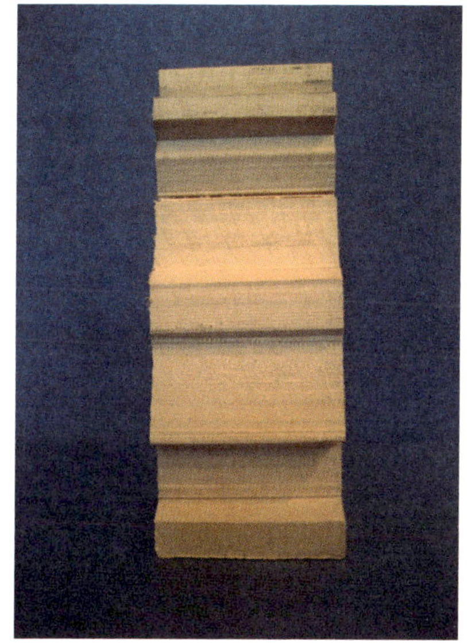

Cut-out, Front view

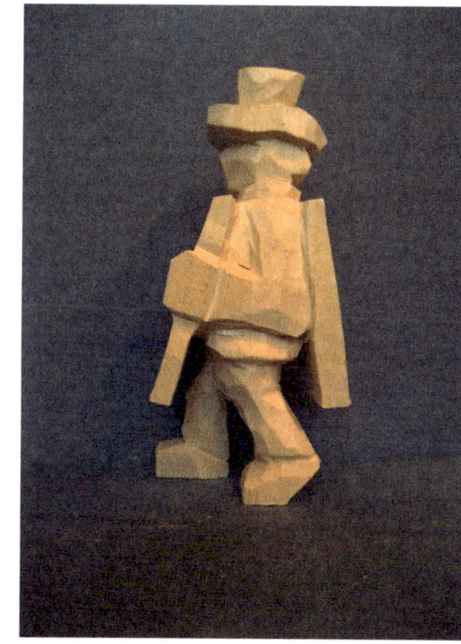

Roughed out

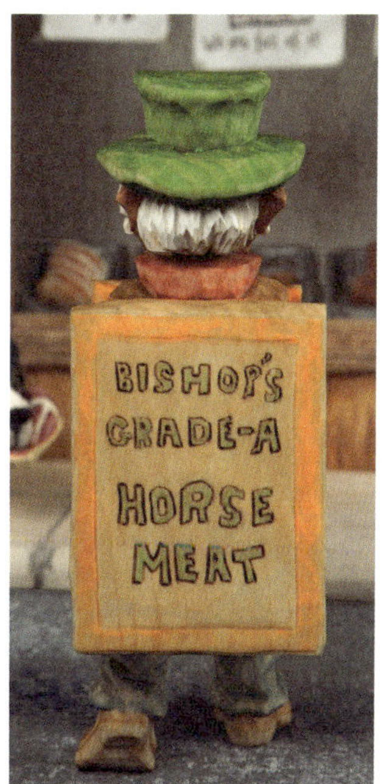

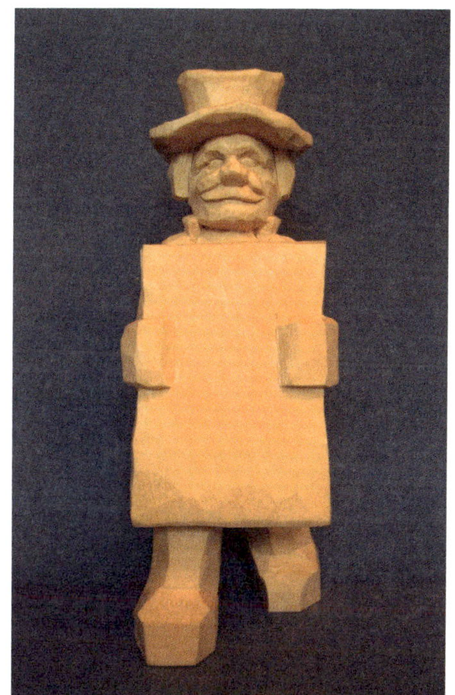

Facial detail

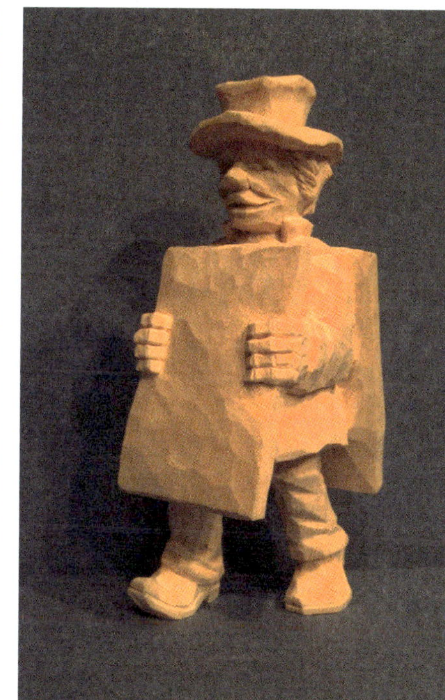

Ready to paint

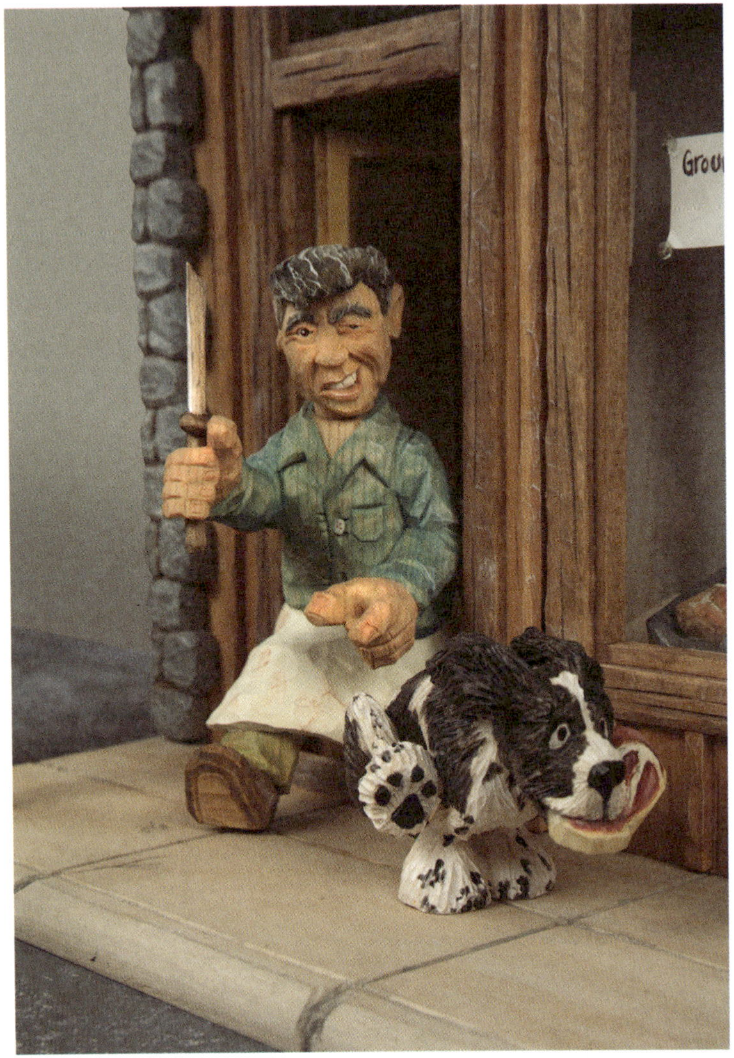

Butcher by Joe You; dog by Sandy Smith

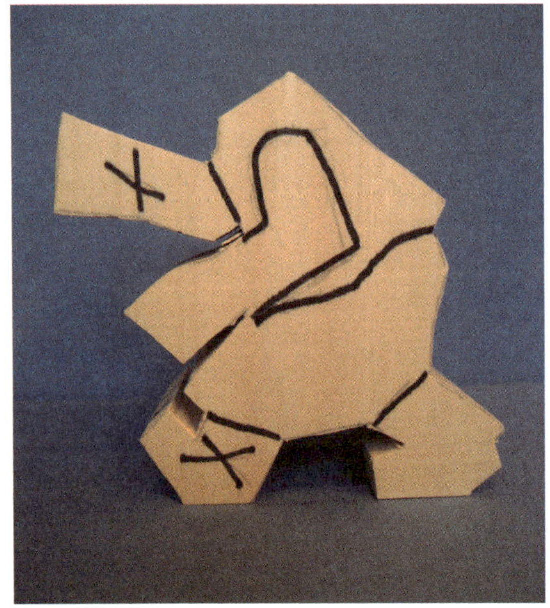

Butcher cut-out with guidelines

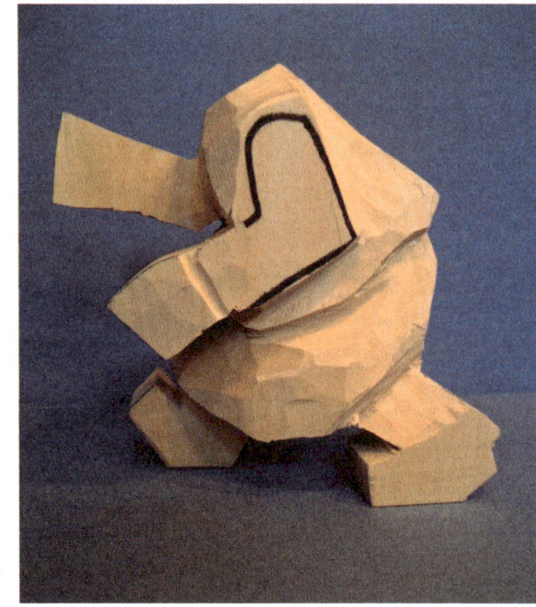

Blocked out

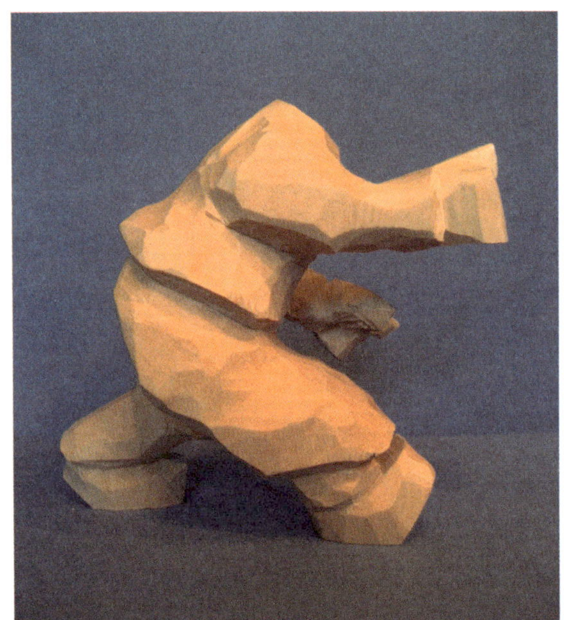

Roughed out

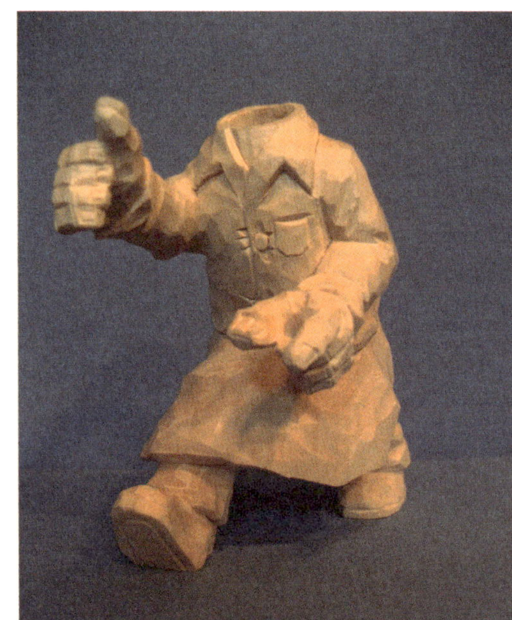

Ready to paint

Do you suppose Fred will catch the thief?

Fred was carved with a separate head. I volunteered to carve the butcher, but Joe wanted a likeness of his father. So I carved the body and Joe carved the head. This can easily be made a one-piece carving, but because it was already a two-piece carving, the butcher knife was added later.

—Bob Travis

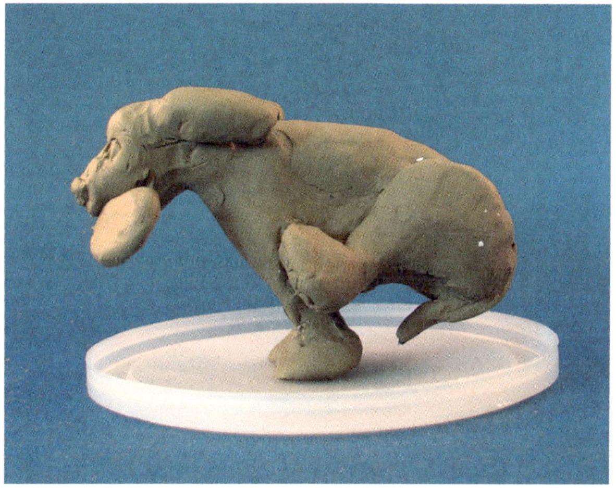

Sandy's clay model

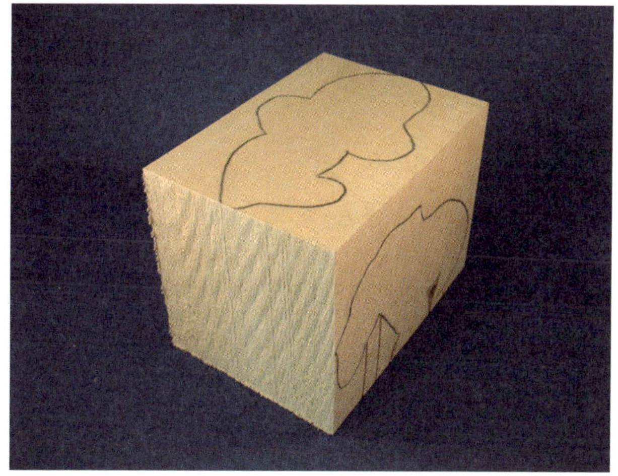

Pattern on wood

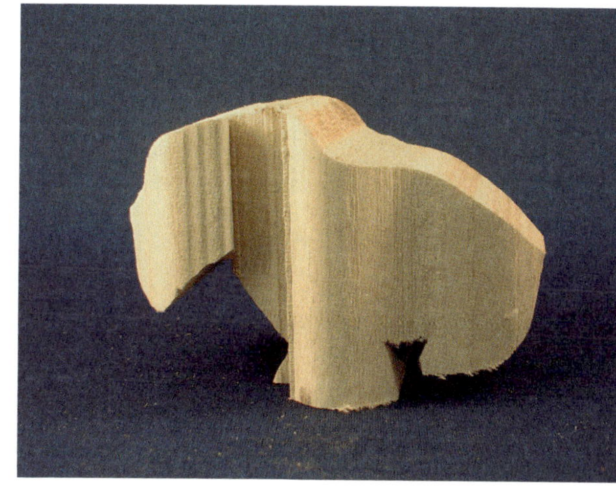

Cut-out

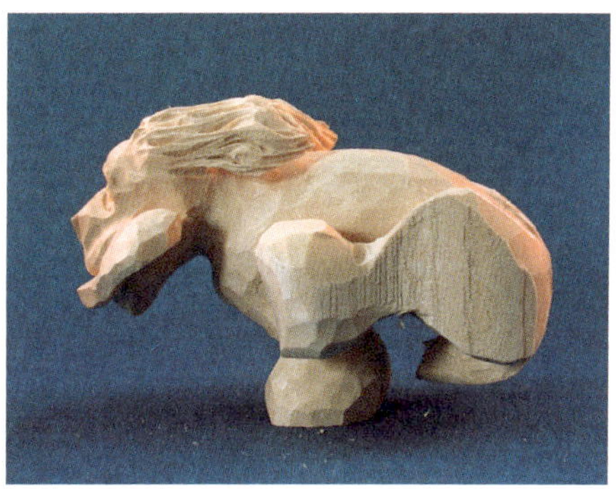

Roughed out

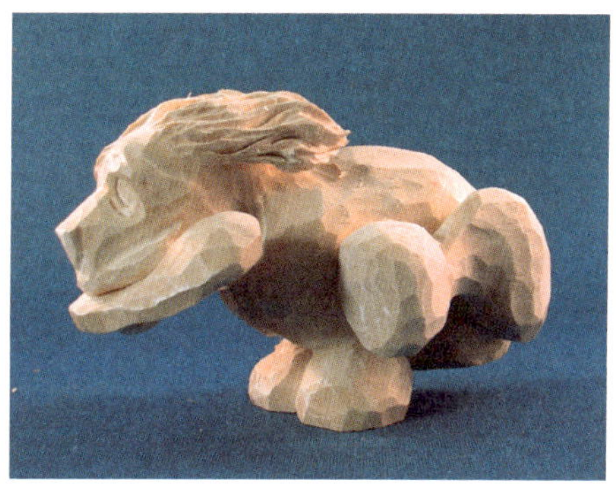

Nearing completion

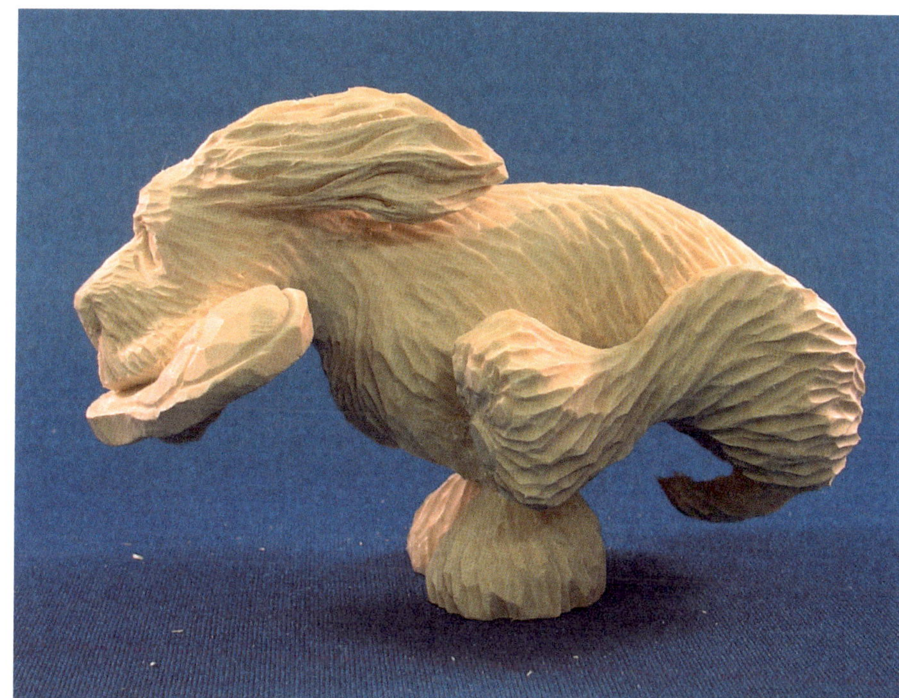

Detailed

Tip from Sandy Smith

• No matter how careful I am not to cut off parts of carvings that protrude (such as a dog tail), if the wood grain is running across thin areas, chances are these protrusions will break. To prevent this from happening, a piece of the "same" wood is glued to the main section prior to carving, making sure that the grain runs away from the main body. A little planning on how the direction of the grain runs will help prevent breakage while carving and then while dusting after the carving is complete.

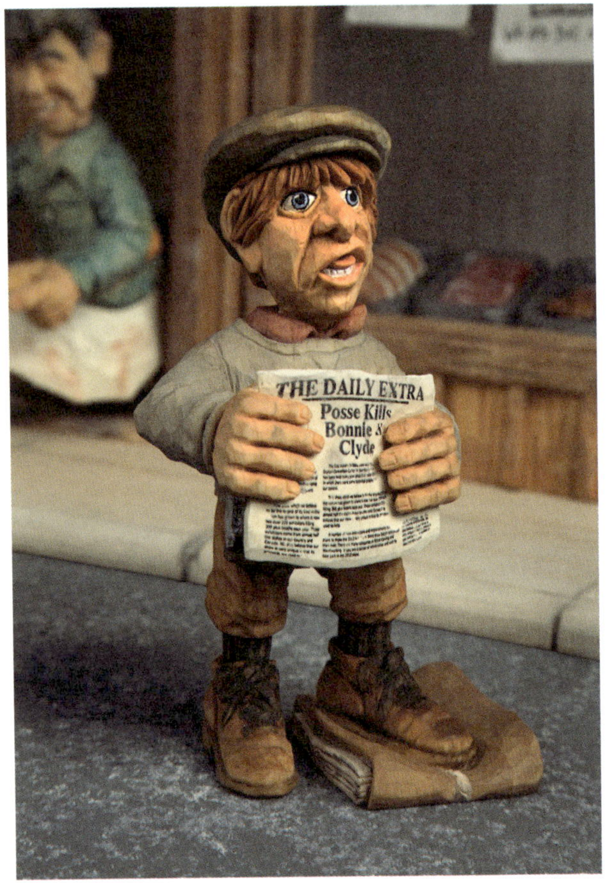

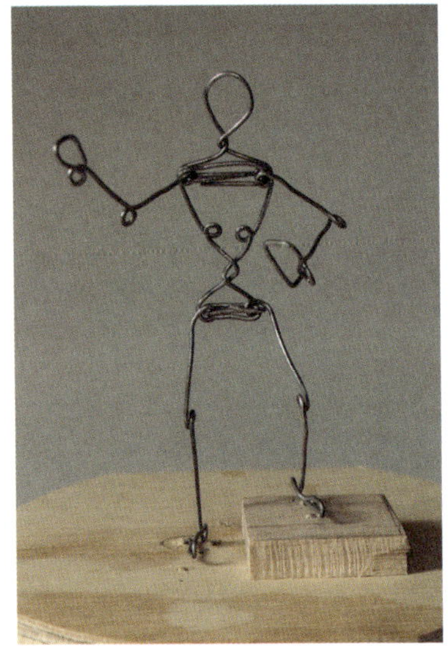

Jack's wire armature

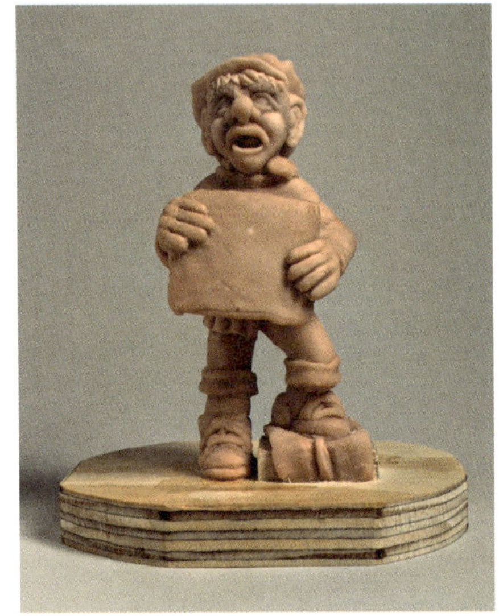

Clay model, front view

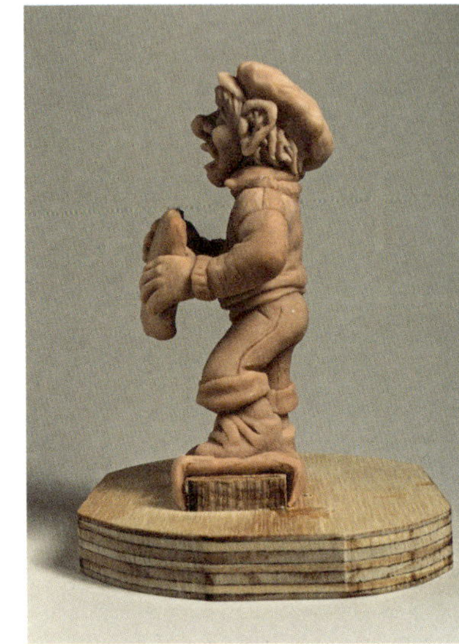

Clay model, side view

Revenues for newspapers swiftly declined after the stock market crash. Circulation managers responded with one of the few resources at their command—cheap juvenile labor. At the tender age of 8, I began carrying a newspaper route. The route opened the door to the working world. Earning spending money and setting aside a portion each week to a mandatory savings account taught discipline and management skills. More importantly, once or twice a year all the carriers were treated with visits to the newspaper office to see the operation of newspaper production.

—Jack Williams

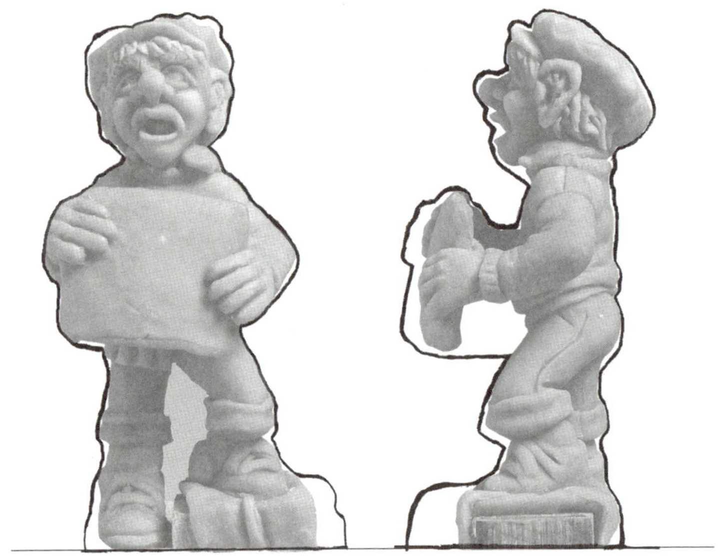

From clay to pattern

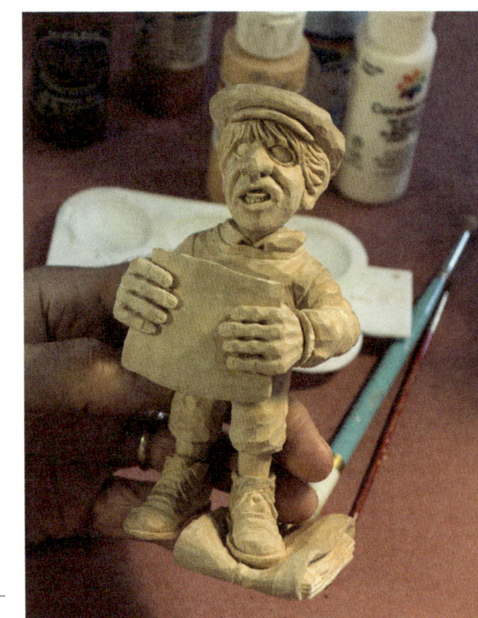

Ready to paint

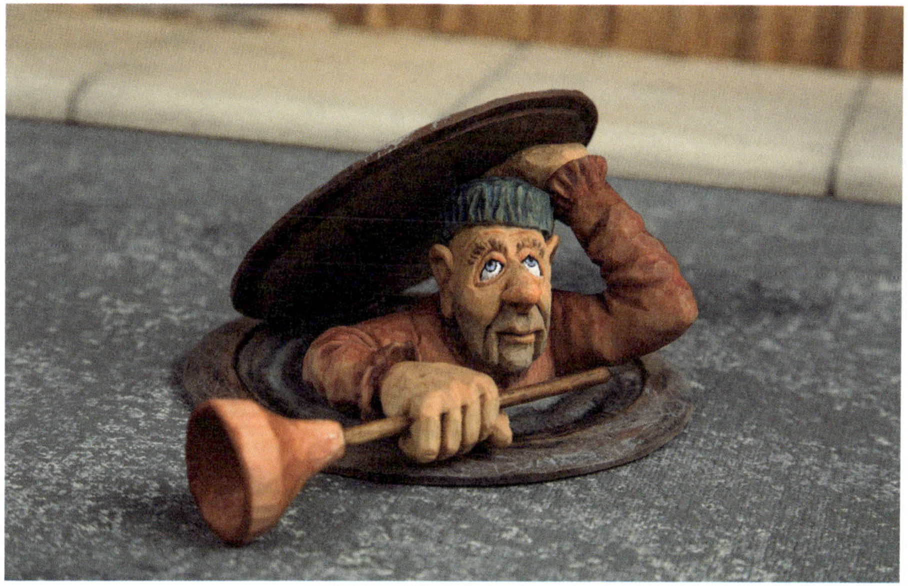

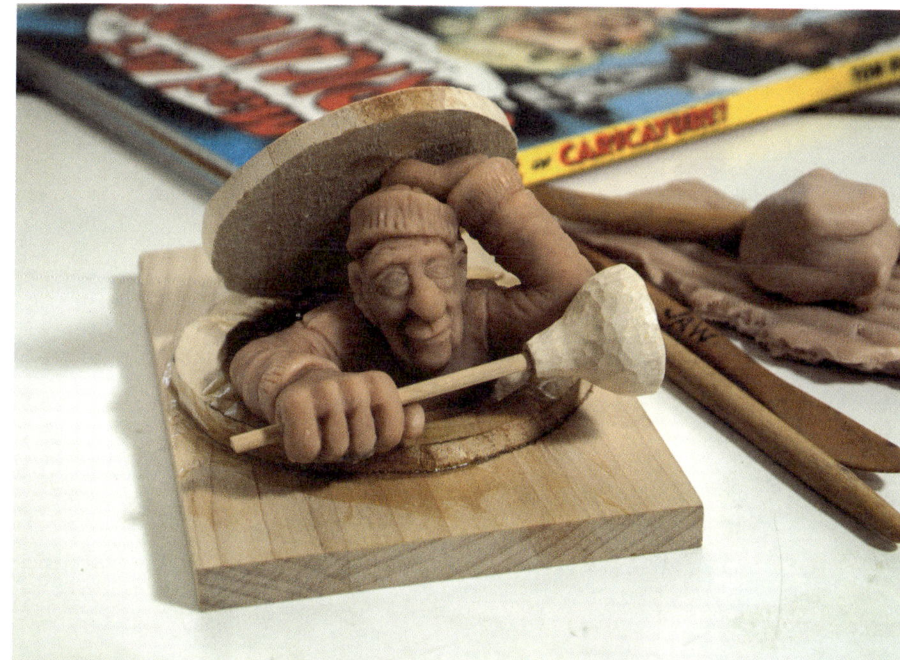

Jack's clay model

How many times have we set out to do a task with the wrong tool? Well this 1930s public servant seems to have done just that. Before he knew it he was in trouble up to his chest. Just like all of us when this happens, he didn't think about the depth of the problem.

—Jack Williams

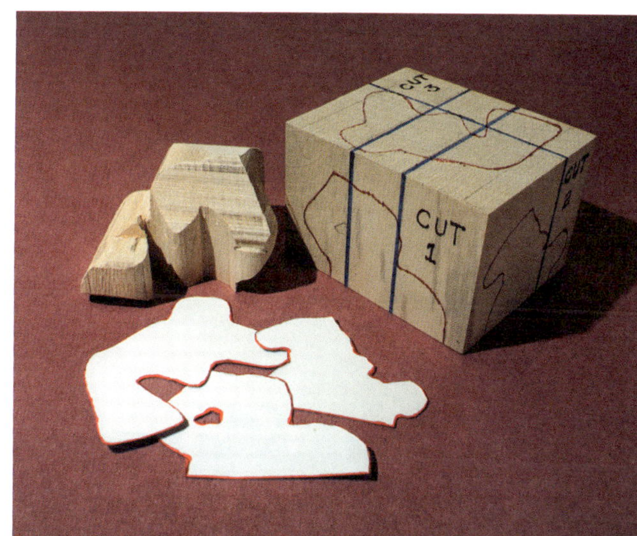

Ready to carve

Tip from Jack Williams

- Jack creates his own reference material by taking a photograph of someone in the same pose and clothing that he has in mind for a carving. He makes a wire armature the exact size of the carving. Using Super Sculpey, he works out the details and possible problems and then makes a pattern from the model, usually making the pattern larger for the hands, feet, or head. The larger pattern offers the option of giving it more of that caricature look when carving.

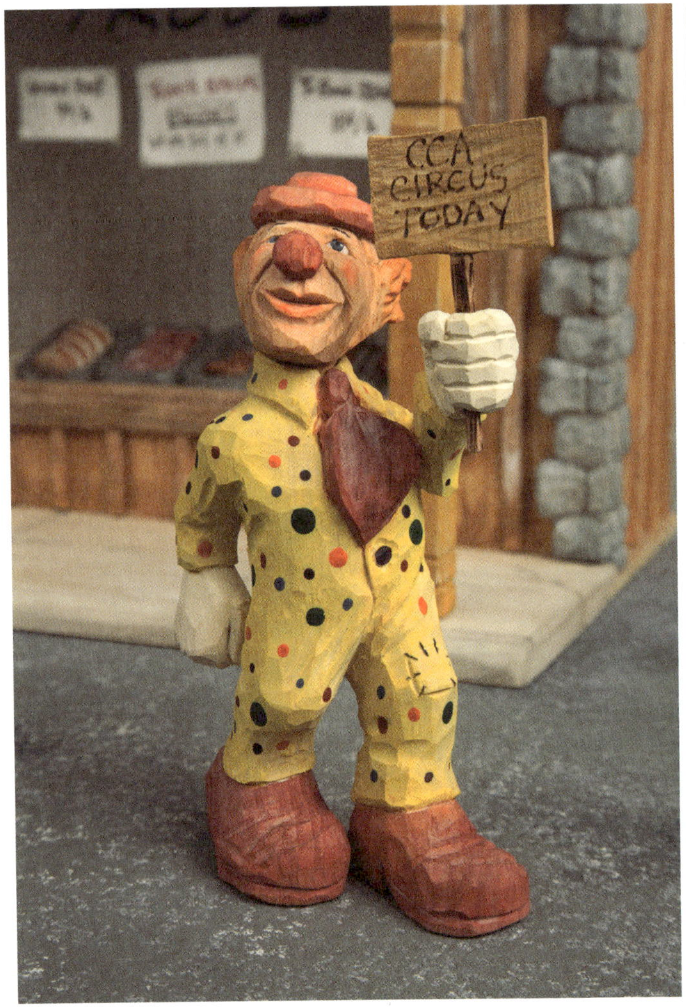

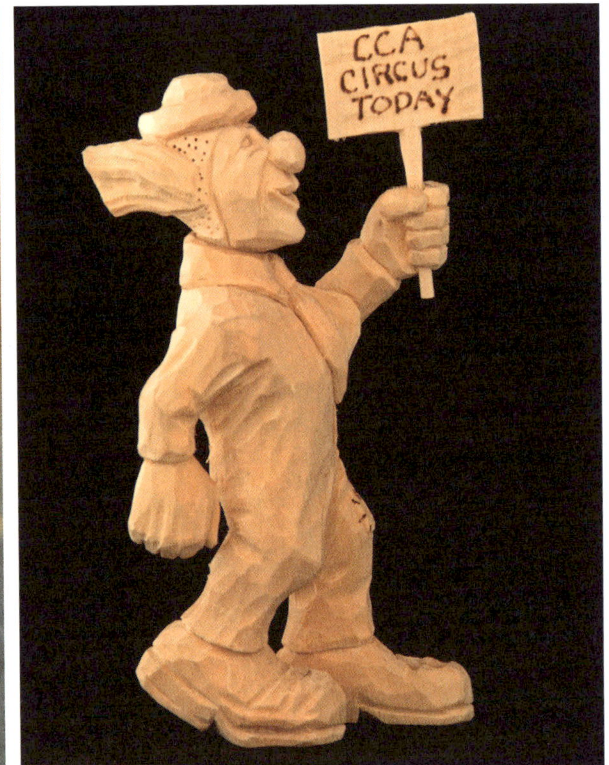

The CCA Circus is coming to town. The clown may be the most fun to carve and paint because one can take so much liberty in the choice of apparel and color schemes. Notice that he is pictured in a joyful full stride proudly displaying his sign inviting all to attend the CCA Circus. The choice of carving patches provides an opportunity to introduce yet another color pattern into an already busy carving.

—Gene Fuller

Tips from Gene Fuller

- Plan your carving and do the research necessary to understand your subject, but do not be afraid to alter your plan if the wood suggests a variation.
- Never underestimate the value of extremely sharp tools. Nothing will destroy a carving quicker than dull tools. Accordingly, always wear a safety glove.

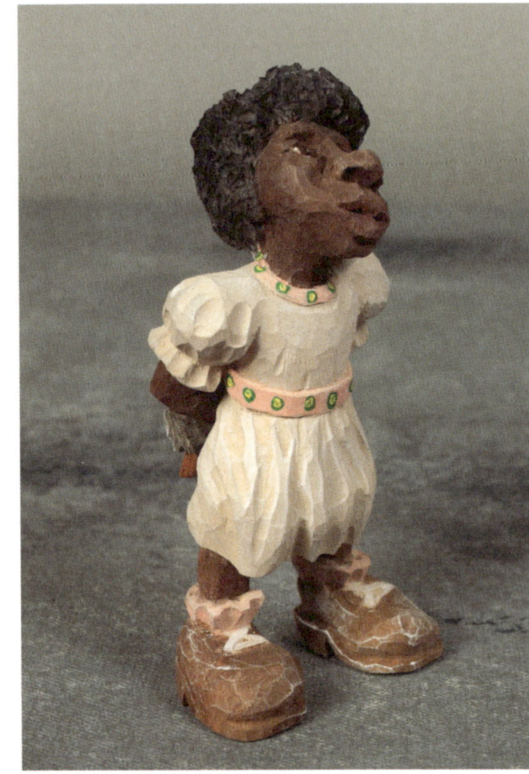

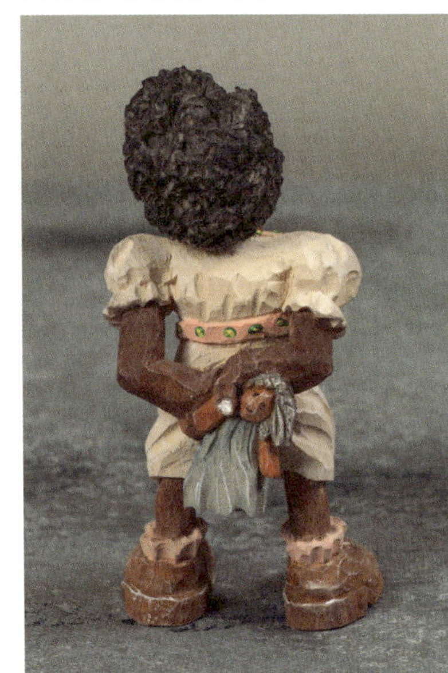

Little girl looking up, by Joe Schumacher

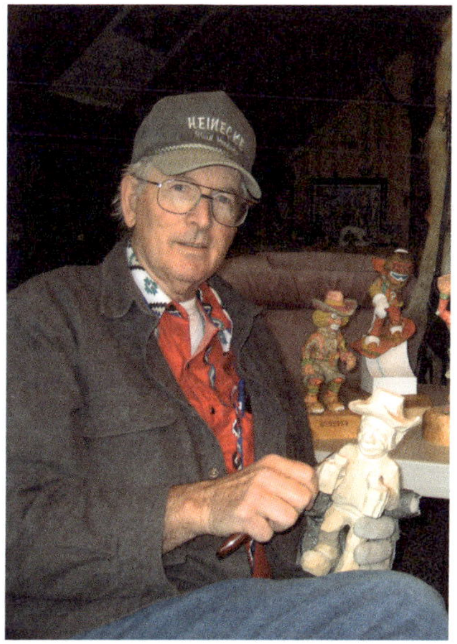

Bob Travis

Bob is a retired Professor of Plant Sciences at the University of California, Davis. He is a founding member of CCA and has served two terms as president. He has served as the project editor for all six CCA books.

Teaching caricature carving has been one of Bob's favorite activities. He has taught seminars from coast to coast (if you live and teach in California and do a couple of seminars in Connecticut and Massachusetts, that qualifies for the coast to coast claim) and has been on the Doane Experience teaching staff in Crete, Nebraska, since 1990. Bob has also served as a judge for numerous carving shows. Caricature carving has been a large part of his life since the late 1970s.

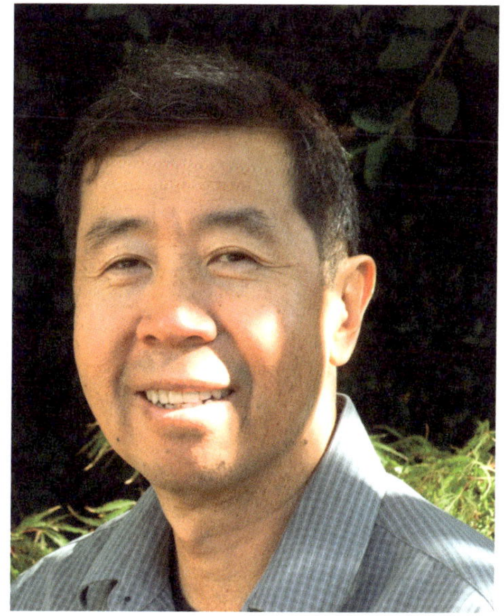

Joe You

Joe became hooked on caricature carving by being caught in a perfect storm. There were three elements to this perfect storm. First, in 1994, he viewed a collection of CCA carvings at Bob Travis' home. Second, he took a series of carving classes. Third, Joe's prior interest in art could now be coupled with his newfound interest in woodcarving.

Joe loves the endless forms and expressions in caricature carving. Working out positions and action is a welcome challenge. Recently, Joe has enjoyed the next level in challenges by carving a true caricature of actual people.

Joe and his wife, Chris, have three grown children, and have recently entered the grandparents' club. They live in Sacramento, California.

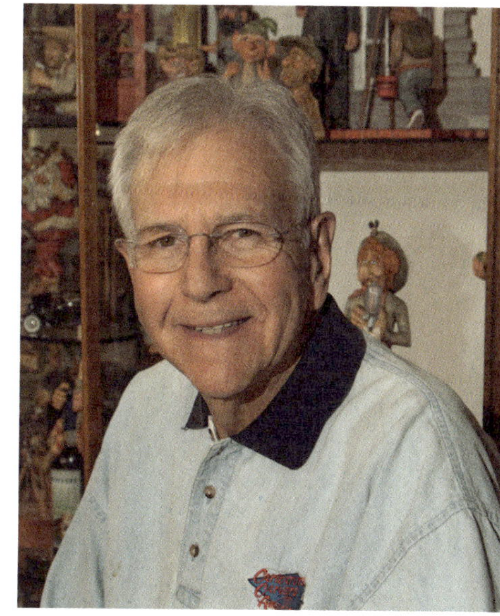

Jack A. Williams

In 1988, Jack attended a workshop with CCA member Harold Enlow, which piqued his interest in caricature carving. One of Jack's proudest moments was when he became a member of CCA in 2003. Others include the Independent Publisher Book Award he and Vic Hood received in 2003, and being awarded the Ron Ryan Award from the Artistry in Wood Show at Dayton, Ohio, in 2004.

Before retiring, Jack was a professional photographer, which accounts for his interest and involvement in photographing woodcarvings for books and carving publications. Now retired, Jack lives with his wife, Carole, in Arizona. Jack's carvings have all been claimed by his three children and seven grandchildren, which explains why Jack's carvings aren't for sale.

CCA BANK & TRUST

Floyd Rhadigan

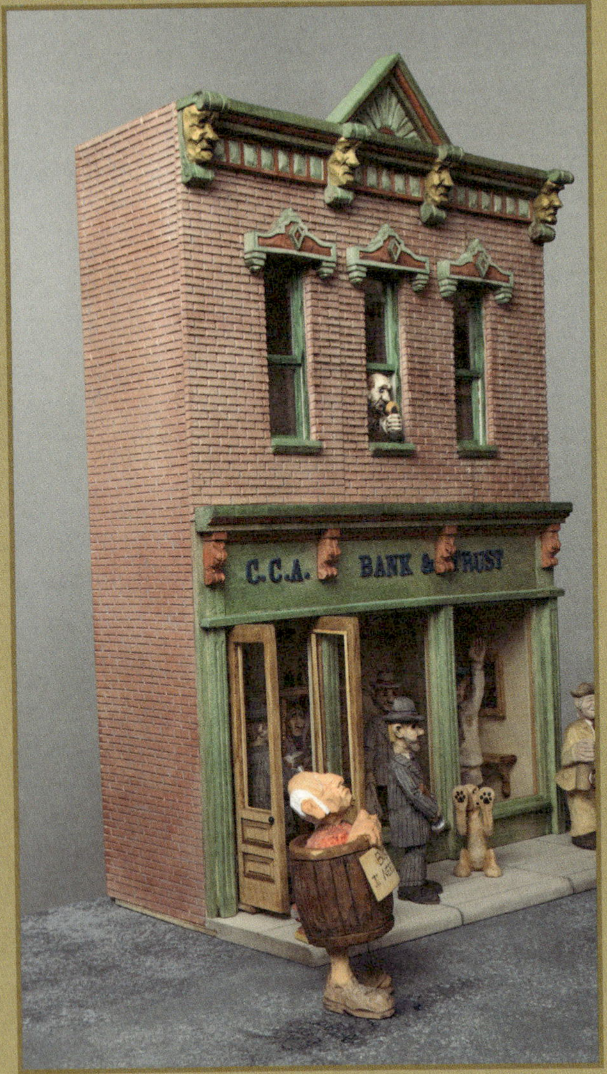

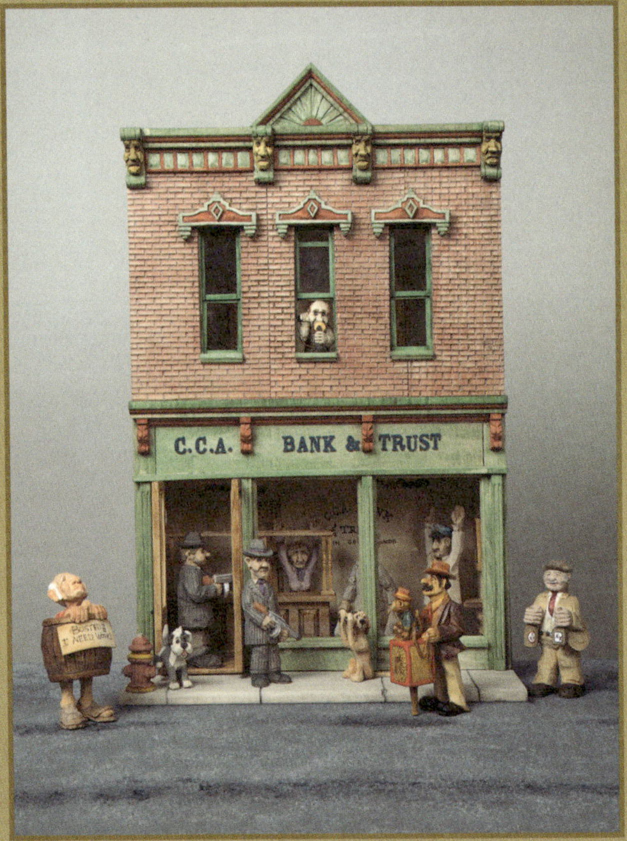

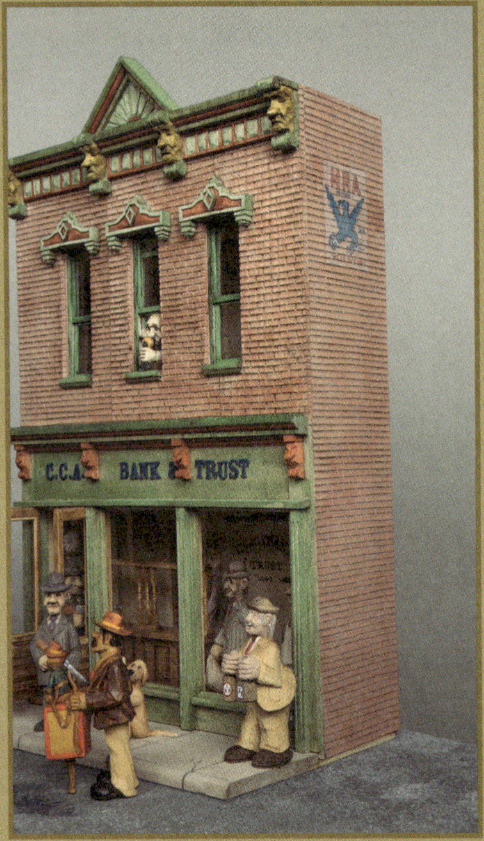

The choice for me was easy. I own a bank in Clinton, Michigan, that was built in 1873. It has seen many uses over the years, hardware store, antique shop, stained glass shop, and now it's a carving studio and store.

In 1909, most of downtown Clinton burned. The roof of the bank was destroyed by the fire, but the two-foot thick walls saved the building. I was told the bank was robbed in the 1930s. So my scene depicts how the robbery may have happened.

—Floyd Rhadigan

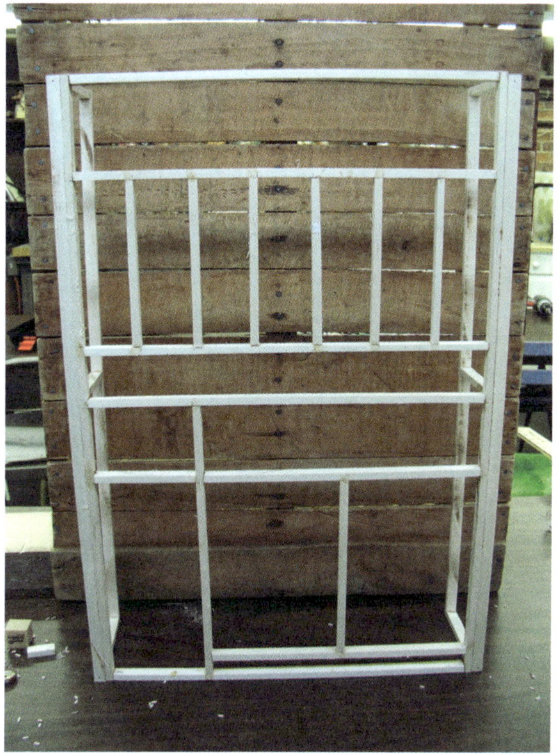

Bank framing

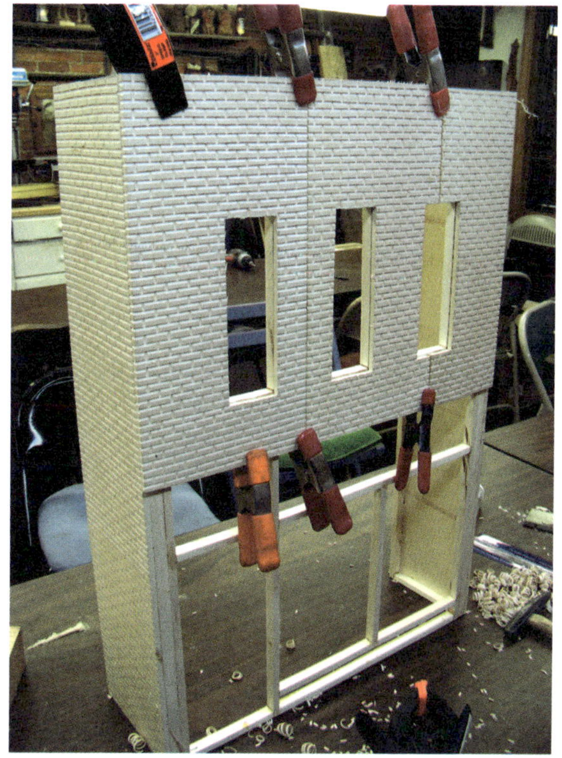

Under construction

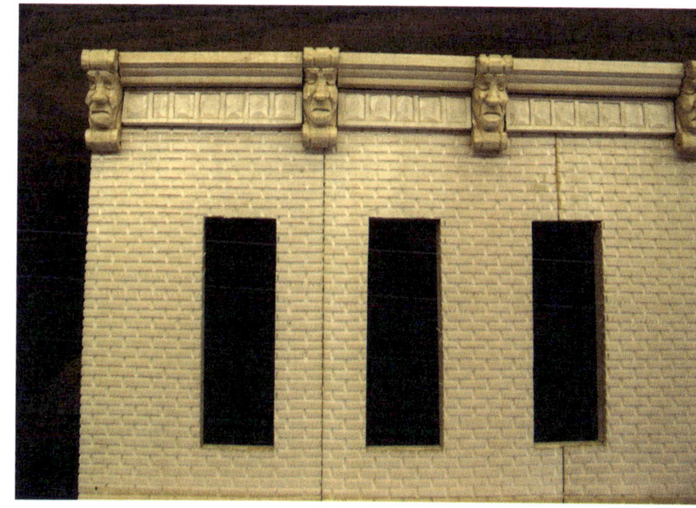

Cornice

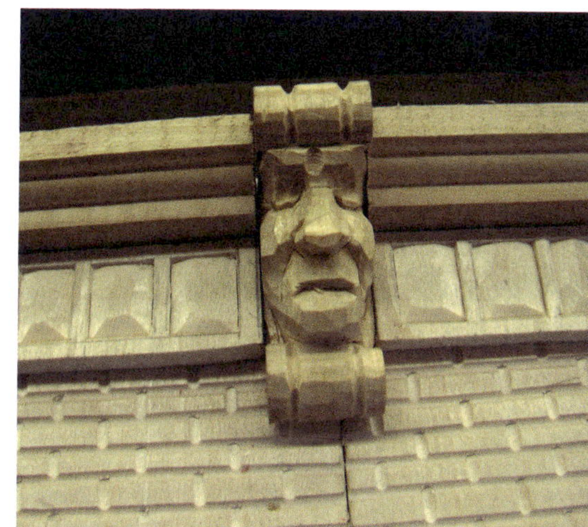

Corbel

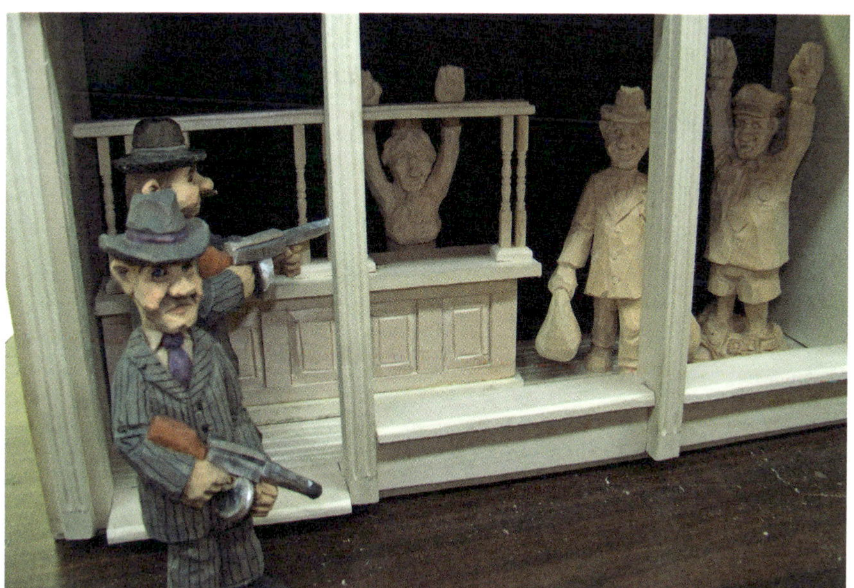

Painting in progress

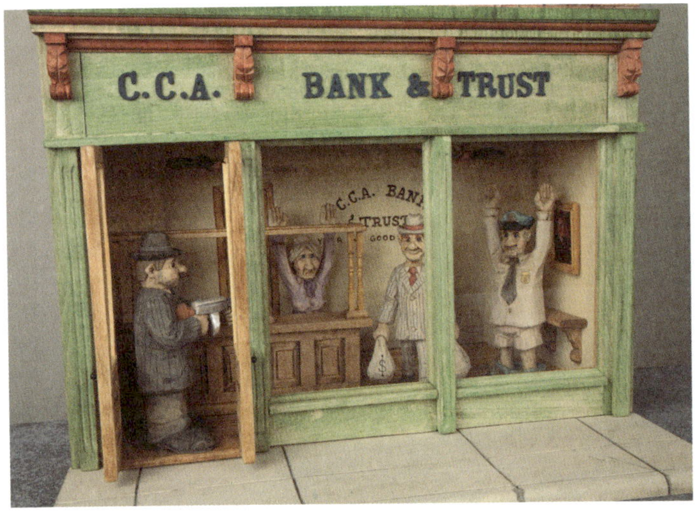

Hold-up scene

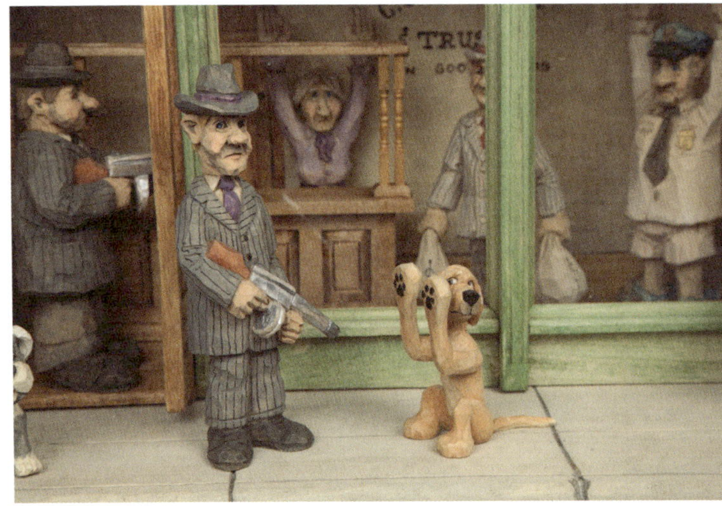

Man holding up dog. Man by Floyd Rhadigan; Dog by Sandy Smith

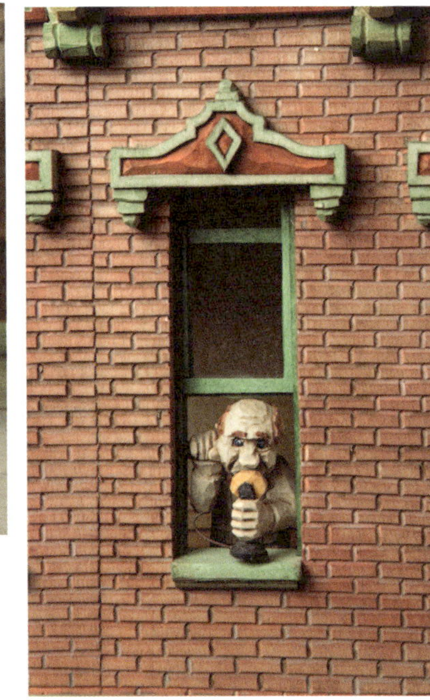

Callin' the cops by Floyd Rhadigan

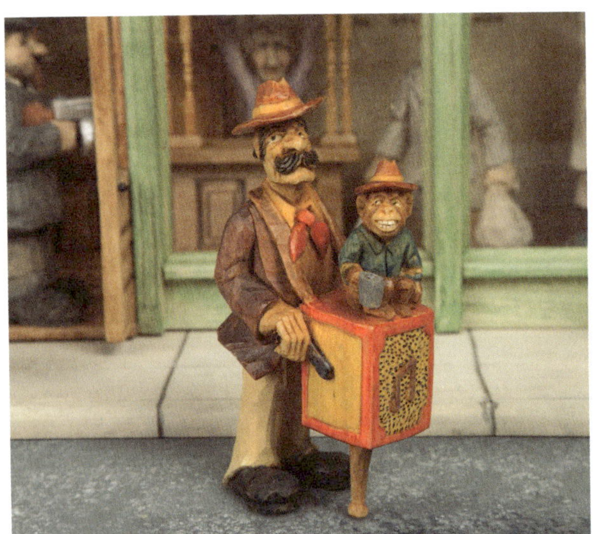

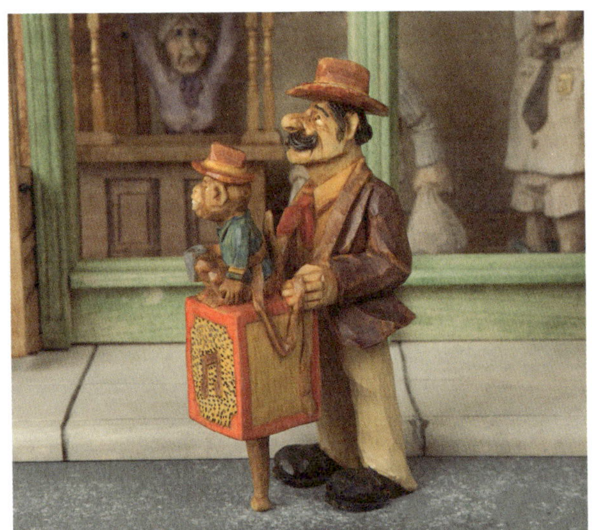

Organ grinder by Don Mertz

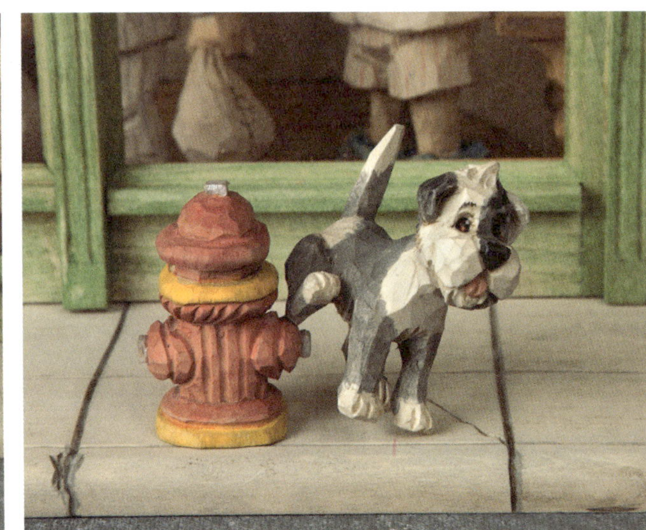

Dog and fire hydrant by Floyd Rhadigan

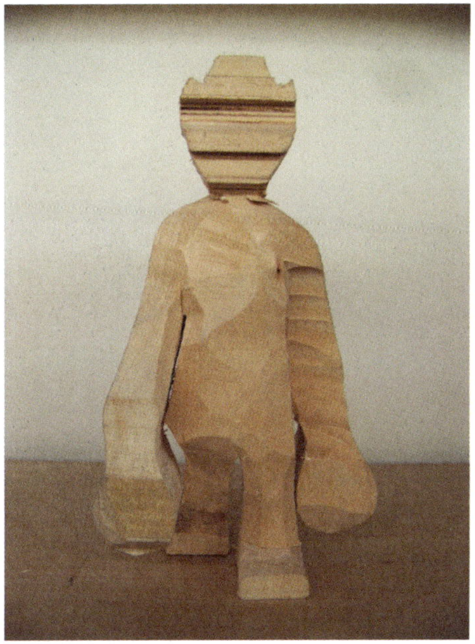

Robber. Roughed out

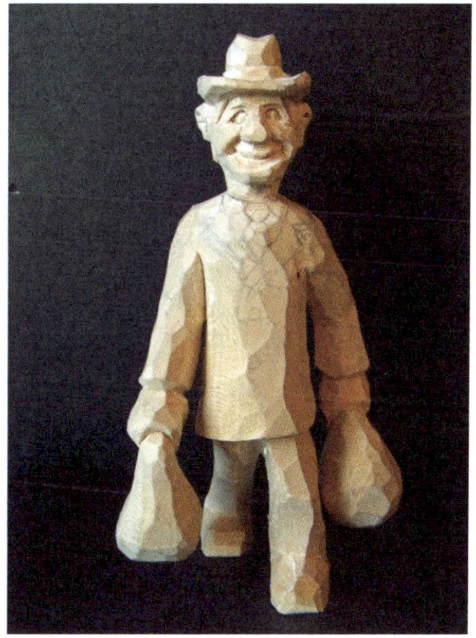

Partially carved

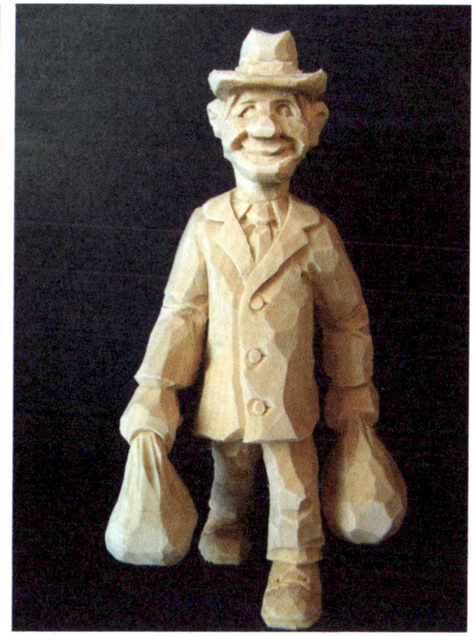

Ready to paint, front

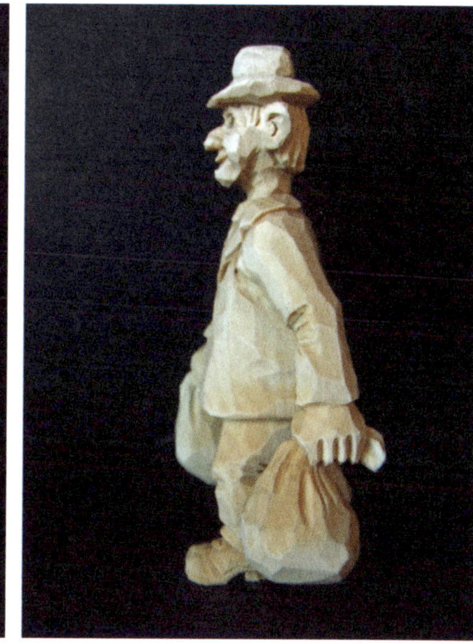

Ready to paint, left

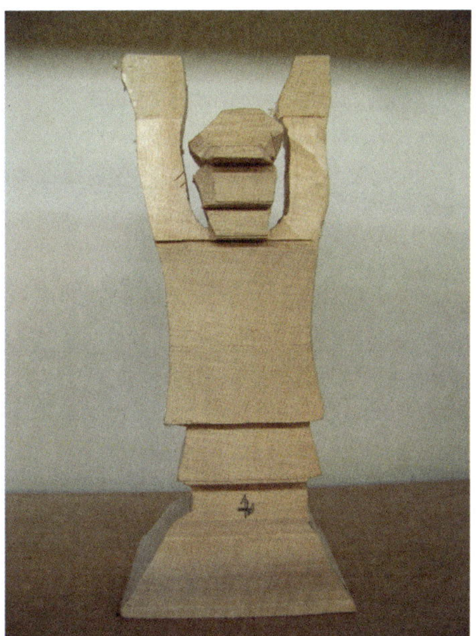

Security Guard, cut out

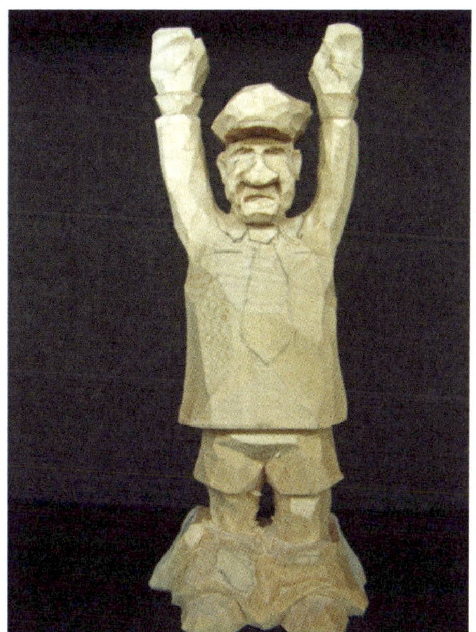

Roughed out, front

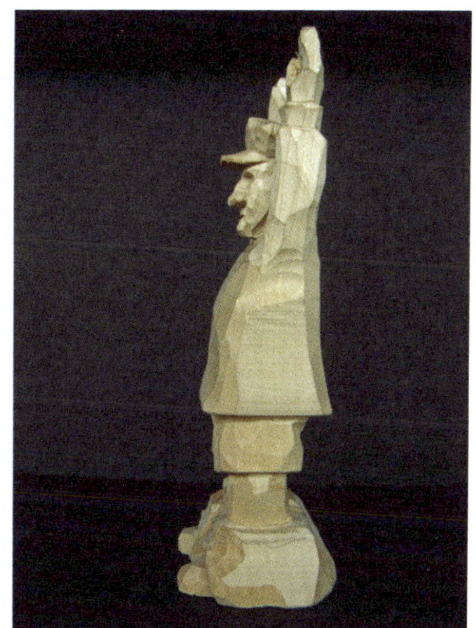

Roughed out, left

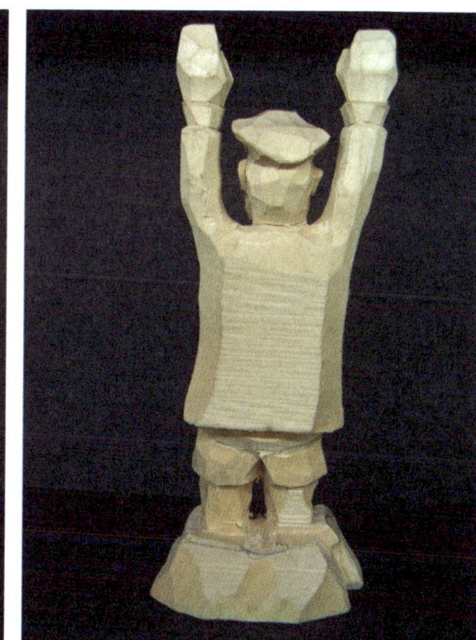

Roughed out, back

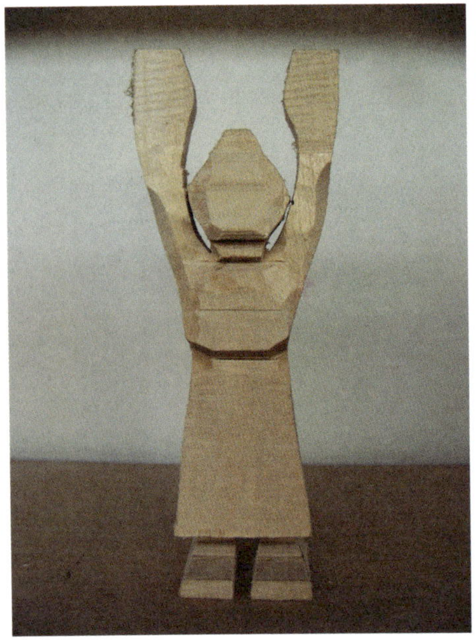

Teller, cut out

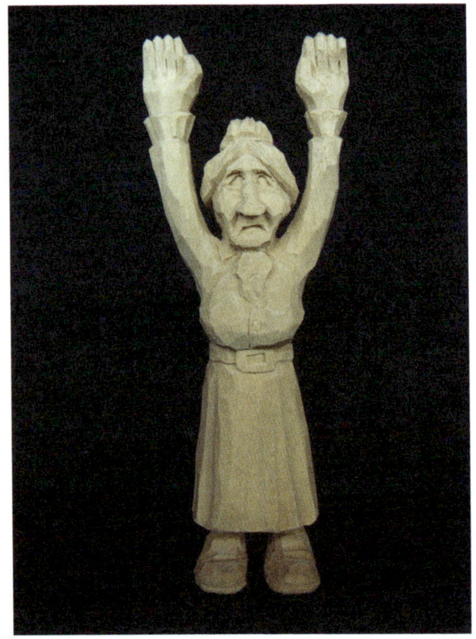

Ready to paint, front

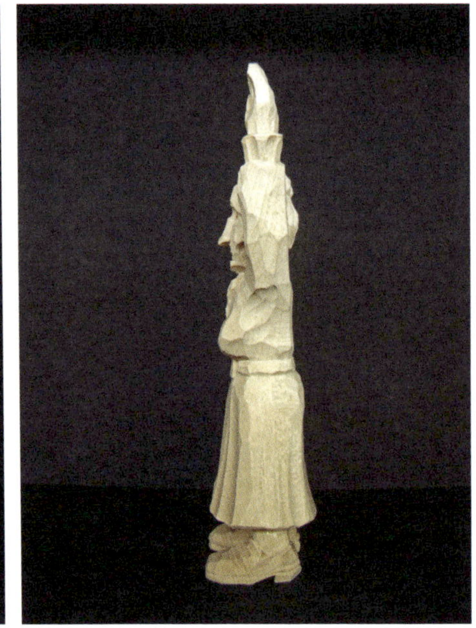

Ready to paint, left

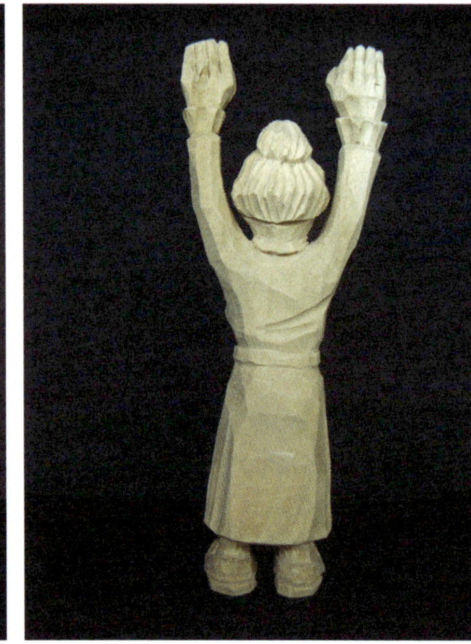

Ready to paint, back

Tips from Bruce Henn

• The grain of the carving runs vertically for strength. However, the extended arms are cross-grain, so care must be taken when carving them. A spot of super glue can add strength to the cross-grain.

• It's always a good idea to strop your knife and gouges before adding detail.

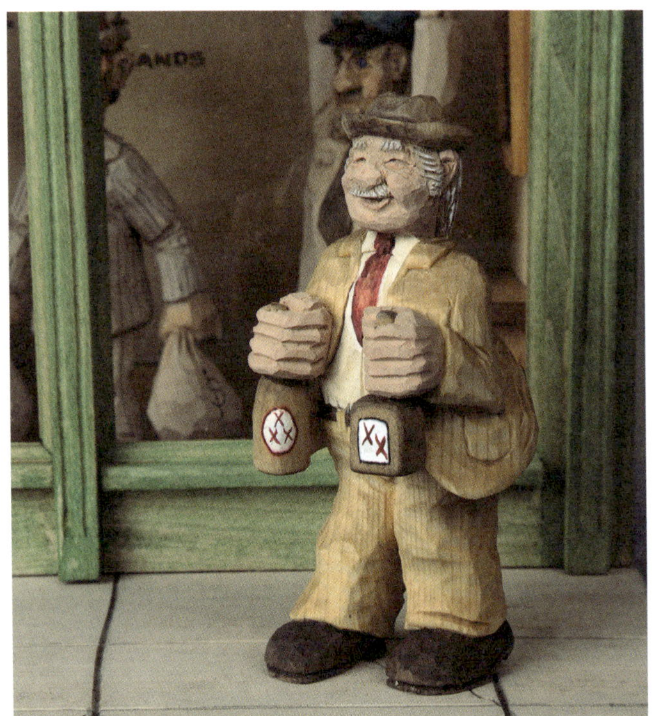

I wanted to do an intoxicated man walking on the sidewalk. I used a wooden mannequin to establish the pose for drawing the pattern, and then band sawed the blank. He has two bottles, one in each hand and a small flask in his hip pocket for a spare. He has a big smile on his face and, in his intoxicated condition, he's happy and without a care in the world. I rounded his body leaving his arms extended out, and then removed the wood between, above, and under his arms. I started on his hat brim and the top of his hat, and moved down to establish his coat line. His legs were carved next, removing wood in front of his left leg and in back of his right leg. I worked around the body and moved up to his head, establishing where the face, ears, and hair were located, and carved the final details. The bottles were carved separately and inserted.

—Bruce Henn

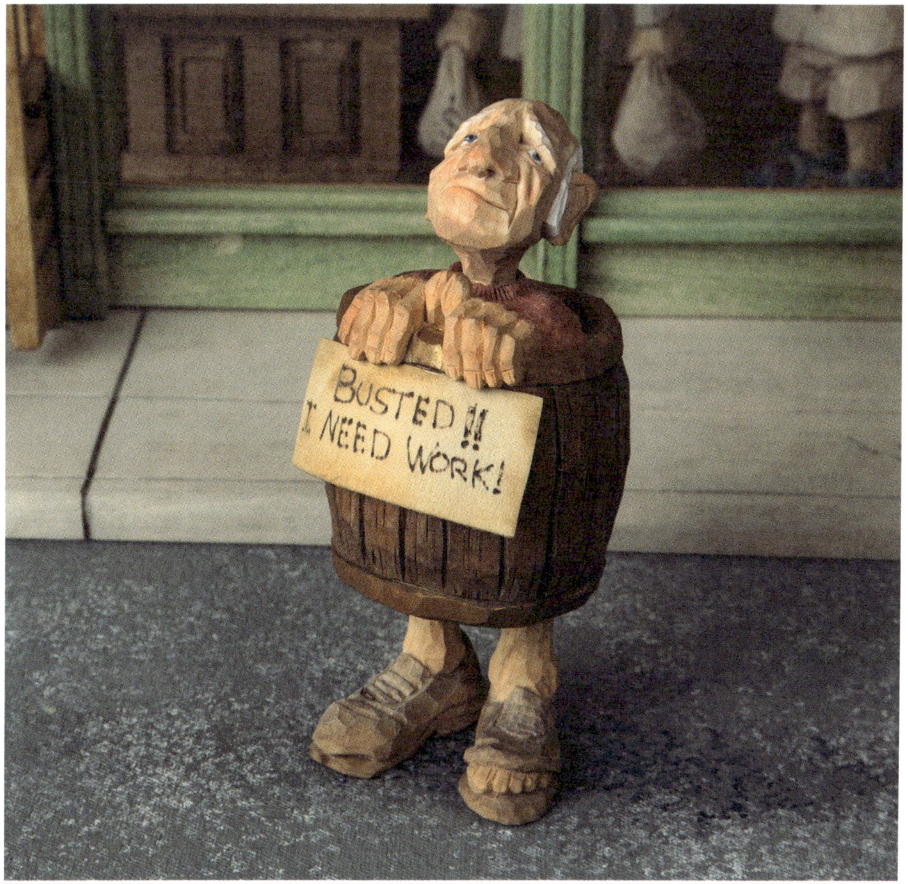

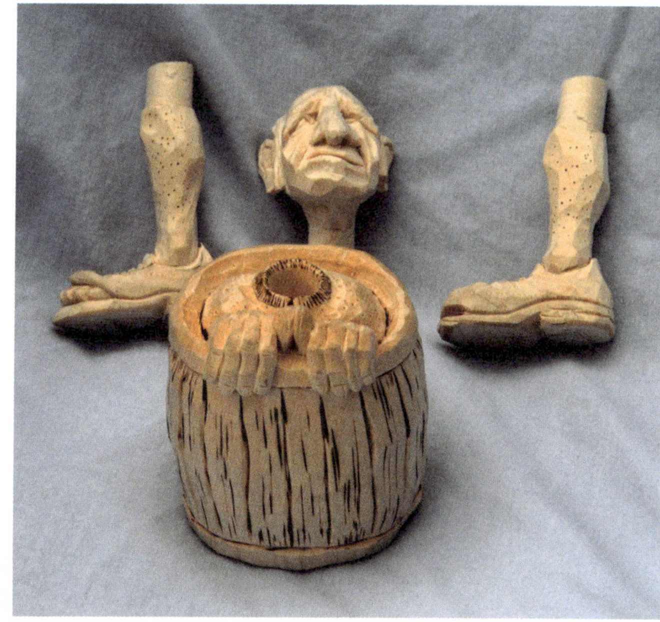

Four pieces

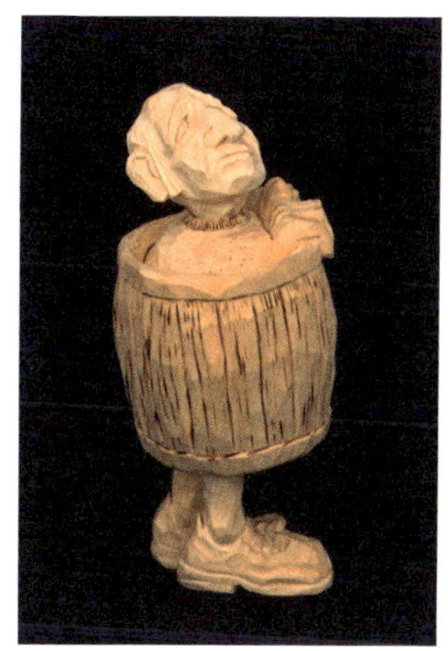

Right side view

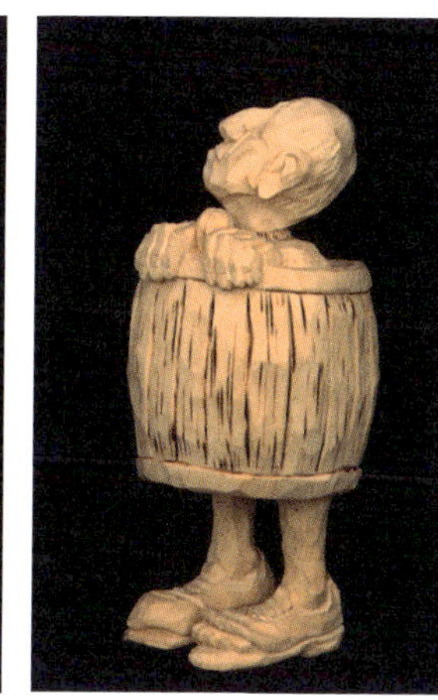

Left side view

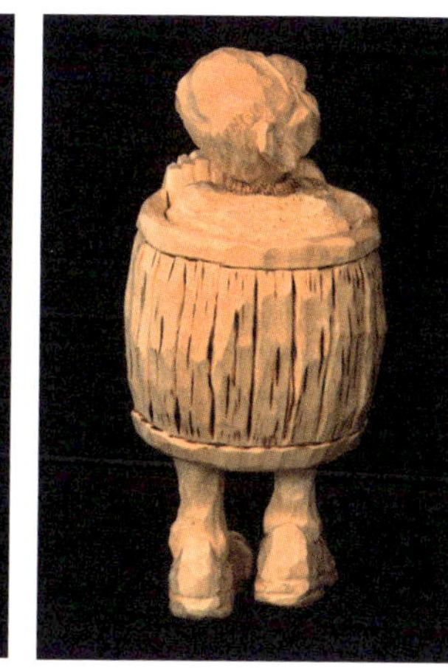

Back view

The man in a barrel was carved in four pieces. This requires that holes be drilled in the barrel as shown in the pattern to accommodate the head and two legs. The top of the barrel must be carved to define the shoulders, neck, hands, fingers, and knuckles. The bottom of the barrel was carved out to countersink the legs. Carving the shoes so that the toes protrude on only one side adds interest without overwhelming the carving. Be sure to define the ankle bones. After rounding the barrel, outline the rim and each of the slats with a v-tool and use a wood burner to define them. Create a slender space under the fingers in which to insert the sign, complete with a message asking for assistance. I chose to carve the head hatless, nearly bald, and with a face that has an expression of desperation. You may elect a different approach.

—Gene Fuller

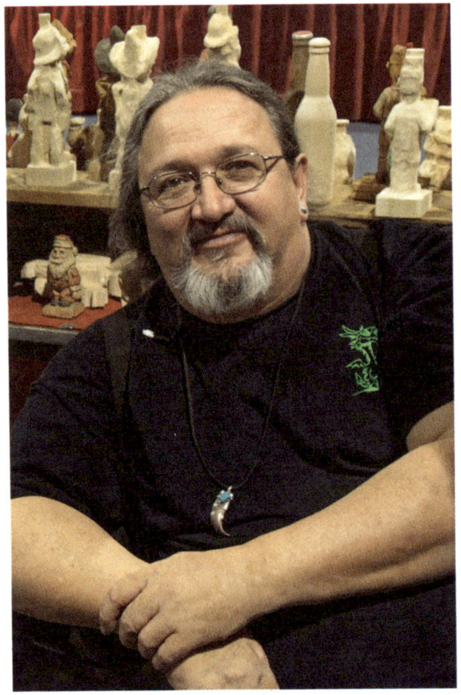

Floyd Rhadigan

I hail from the town of Clinton in southeastern Michigan. I have been carving for 40 years, and teaching for 35. Although I have carved in many styles, my first love has always been caricature.

With the help from books by Andy Anderson and Harold Enlow, I have come a long way.

The biggest event in my career was becoming a member of the CCA. It is like belonging to an association where all my heroes are members. It has been my privilege to be the President of the CCA for the last three years.

I have a woodcarving store and studio where I teach. I also have a great collection of carvings done by fellow members. Stop in and carve a while.

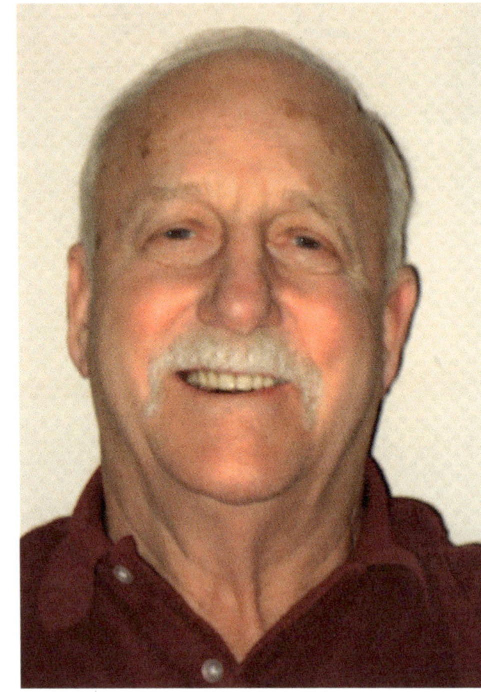

Bruce Henn

As a carver for 40-plus years, and having taught for more than 20 years, I still learn from every class I teach or take. In the summer of 1970, while on a camping vacation, I picked up a piece of firewood out of boredom, which happened to be redwood. At the time my pocket knife was not sharp enough to cut this grainy wood. I found a utility knife in my tool box, which was sharp enough to cut the wood and each of my fingers at least once. After an afternoon of carving, and numerous band-aids, a rabbit emerged. Not a great carving, but recognizable as an animal. I was hooked and started on my journey of woodcarving.

I am a member of the Dayton Woodcarvers Guild and the Brukner Nature Carvers of Troy, Ohio. I am also a member of the National Woodcarvers, E.W.C.C. of Converse, Indiana, and the Affiliated Woodcarvers, Ltd. I was inducted into the Caricature Carvers of America in 2006 and currently serve as President.

BISHOP'S GENERAL STORE

Phil and Vicki Bishop

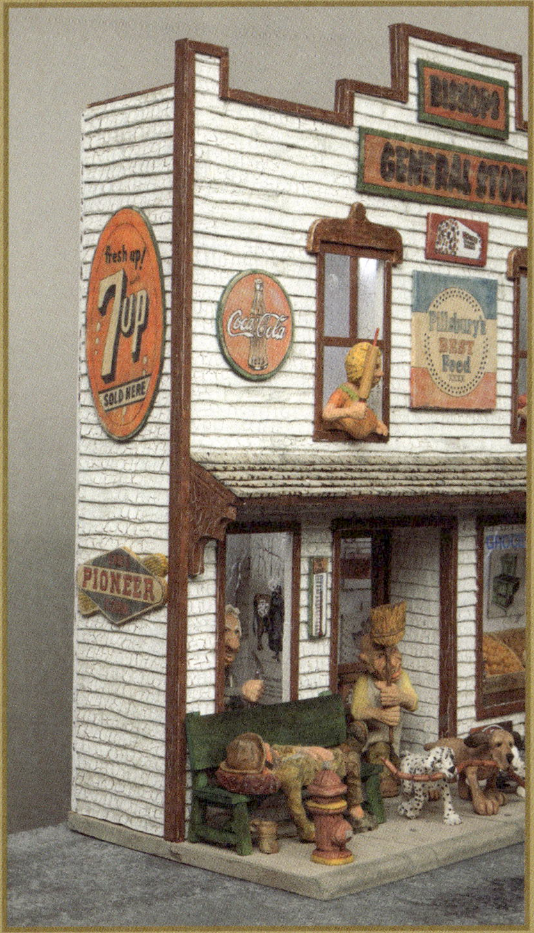

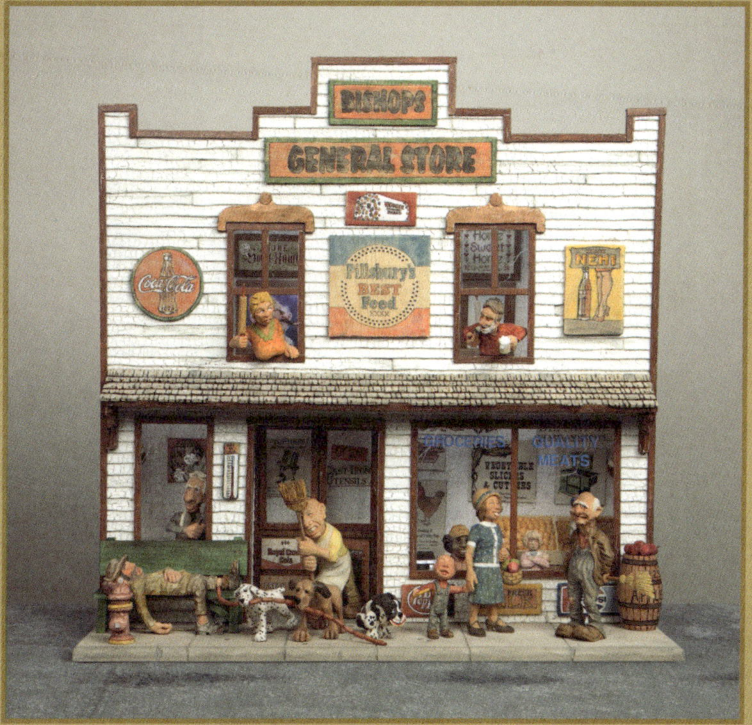

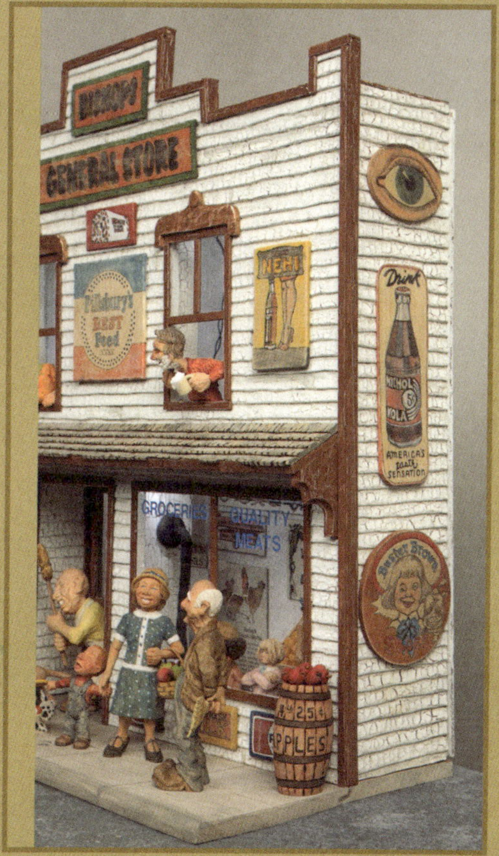

A general store is a collection of household items that your family needs. Selections were limited and prices were fixed. Credit was at the merchant's option. Goods were purchased by merchant, based on what they thought their customers might need. There were few luxuries, because people had little disposable income and merchants didn't want to invest in items that might not sell.

Many early merchants had to depend on their family to mind the store and participate in clerking, stocking, selling, and keeping the store clean. It was not uncommon to find a wife and her husband together inside the store.

—Phil and Vicki Bishop

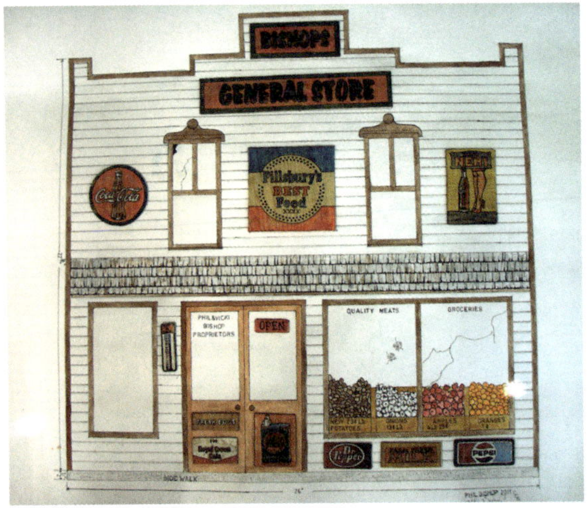

Store plans

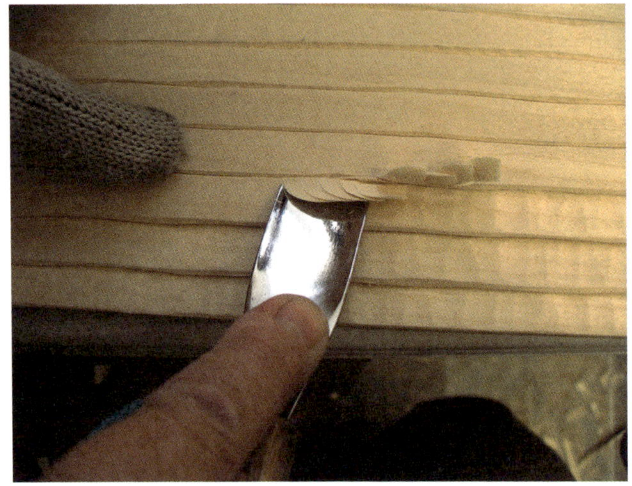

Carving the siding

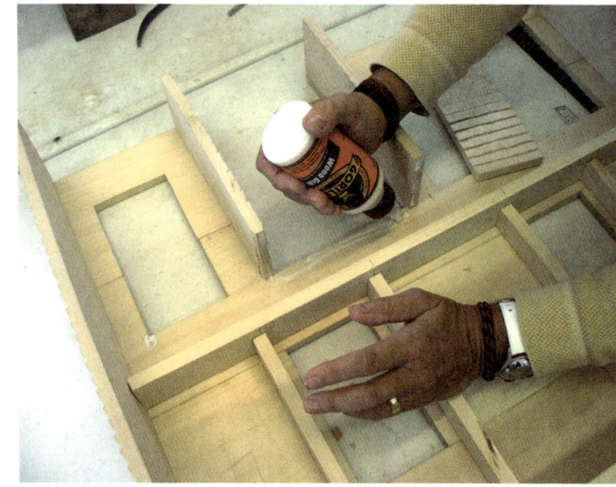

Construction

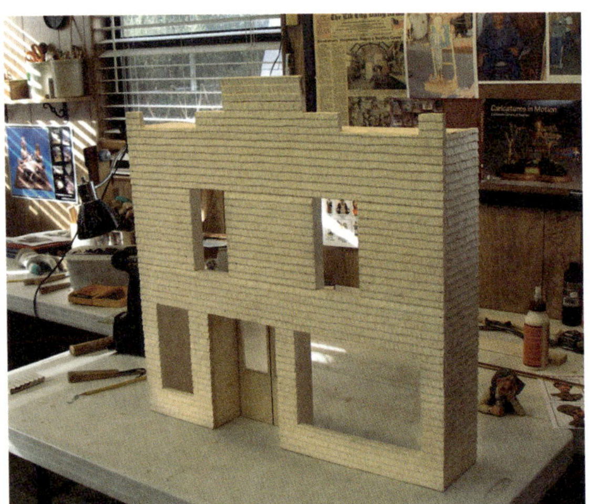

Store front

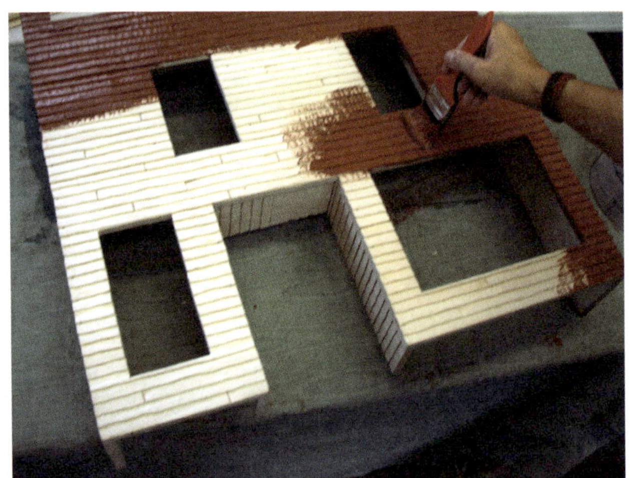

Painting the store

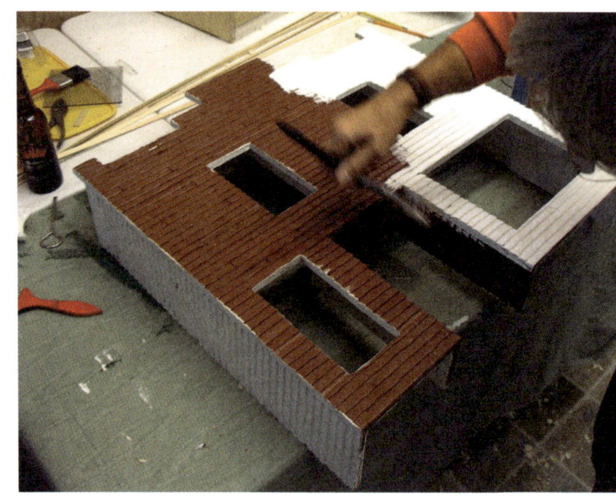

Applying the finish

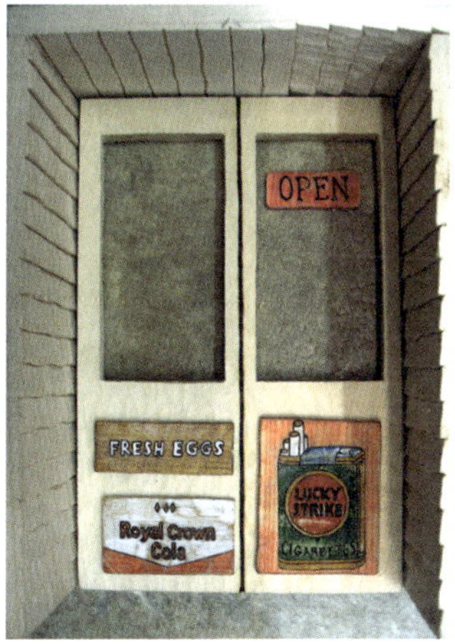

Doors

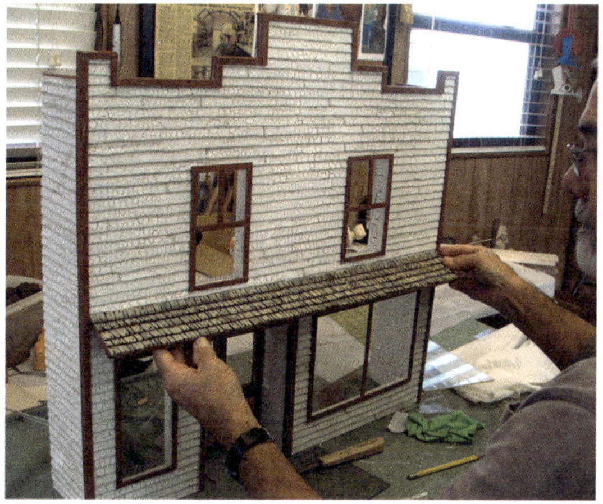

Adding trim

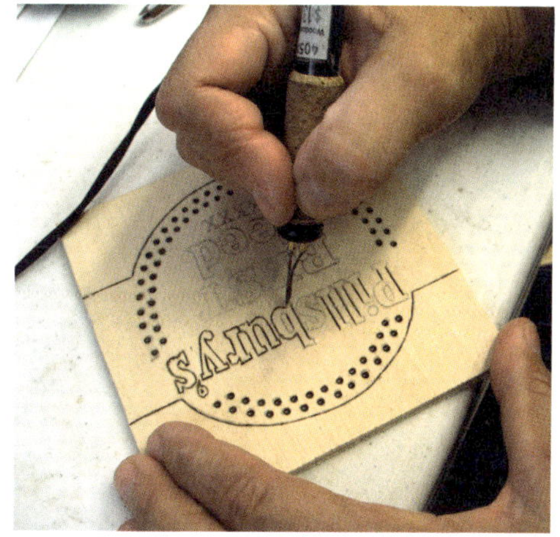

Wood burning a sign

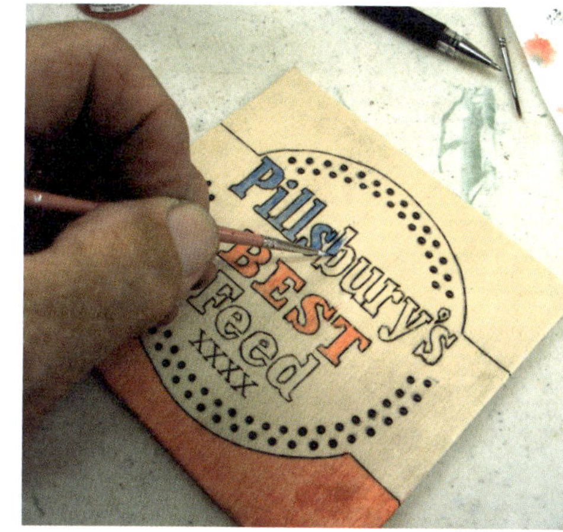

Painting a sign

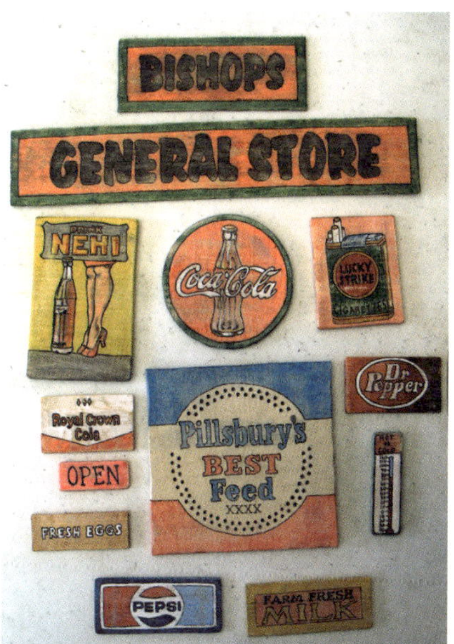

Advertising signs

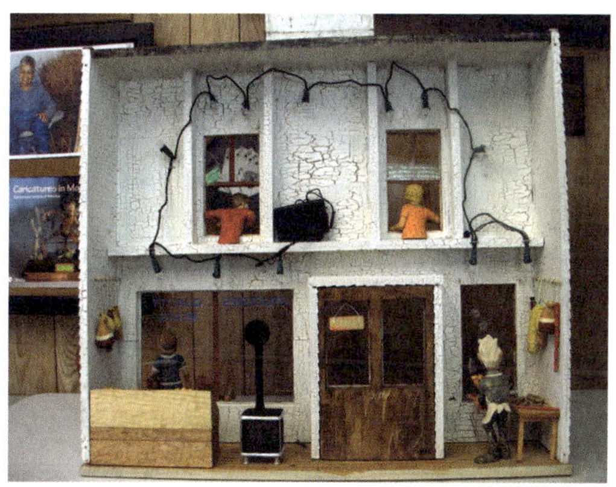

Back of store

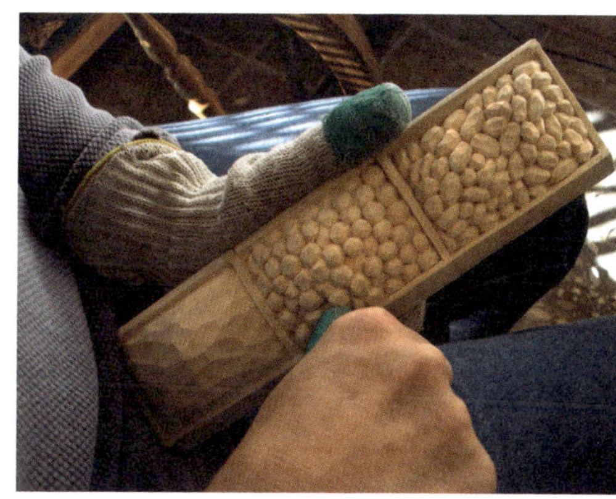

Tater bin

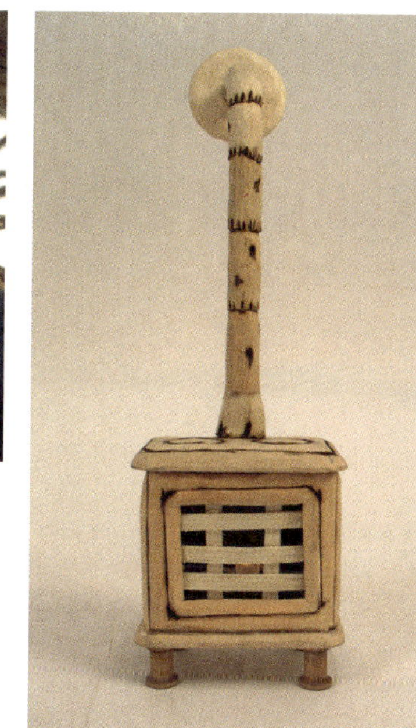

Winter warmth

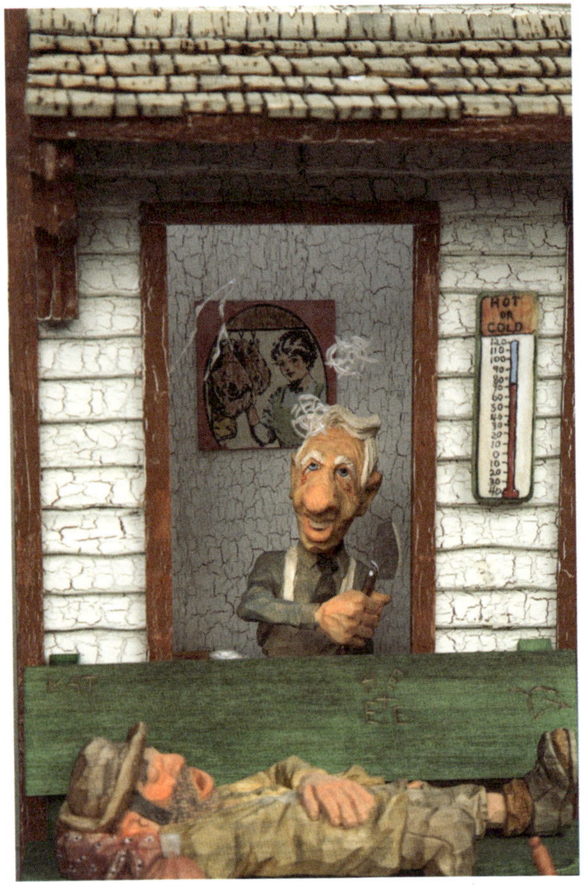

Bartoe

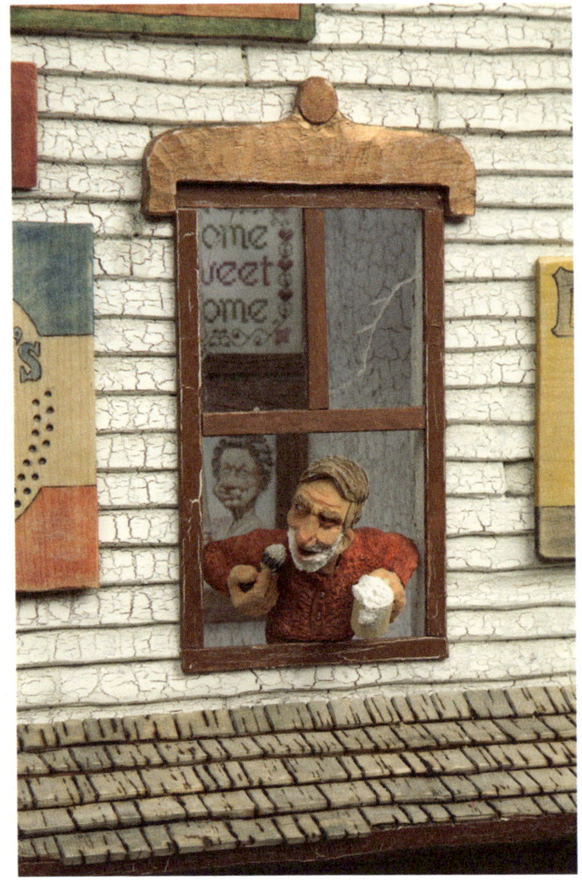

Claude

Tip from Phil Bishop

- Stretch your imagination to the limit and love what you do.

Claude is in the upper apartment window, busy shaving and trying to get ready, so he can please the love of his life, Ella Mae. He doesn't know what she's upset about, but he knows he needs to keep her happy.

The shaving cream on Claude's face, brush, and mug is Snowtex. Claude was carved from the waist up, because that's all you see of him.

—Phil Bishop

Bartoe, the butcher, baker, and sausage maker of the thirties, also existed in the general stores of the forties and fifties. My childhood memories of the good old days provided great inspiration for this project. I frequented this kind of store and these characters are etched in my memories

The cleaver and the chicken were carved separately and added later.

Everybody knows Alfred as the store's friendly jack-of-all-trades, willing to help stock the shelves, run the register, or sweep the floors. He was known to swat a dog or two with his broom for trying to get away with a few sausages.

The broom is carved and added later.

—Phil Bishop

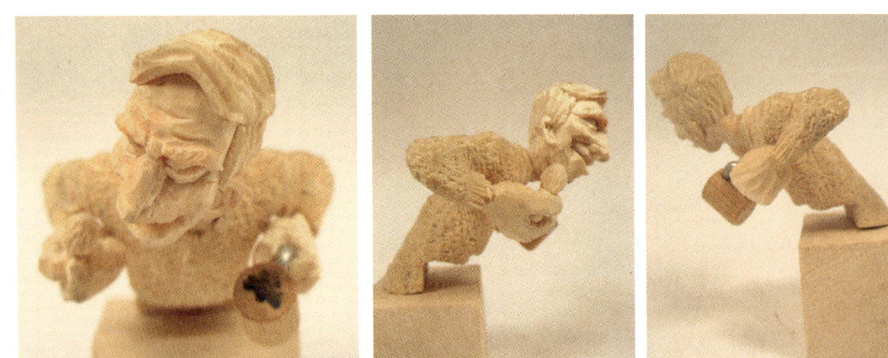

Claude ready to paint

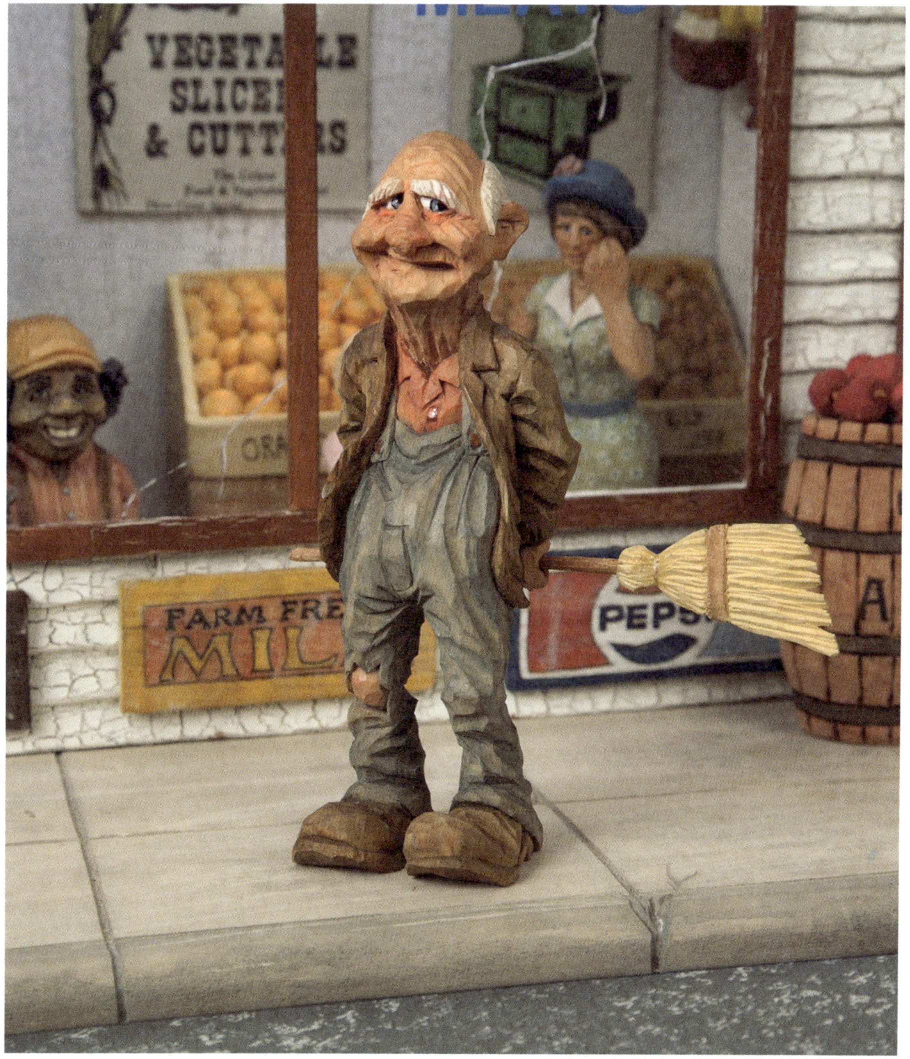

Alfred

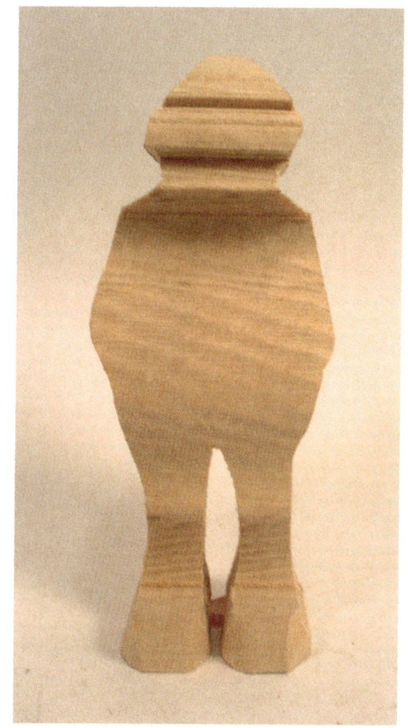

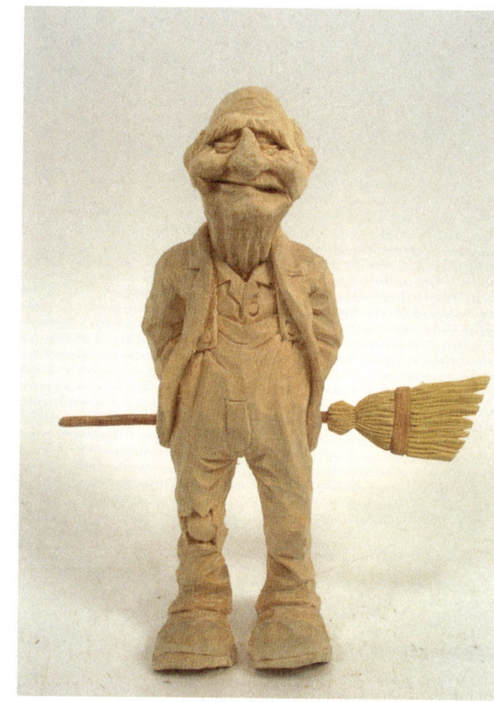

The designs for the patterns start with a front and side view drawing, which is traced on a block of wood and band sawed out.

Begin the process by roughing the basic overall form, and then draw the details on the roughed-out shape and carve them with knives, gouges and v-tools.

—Phil Bishop

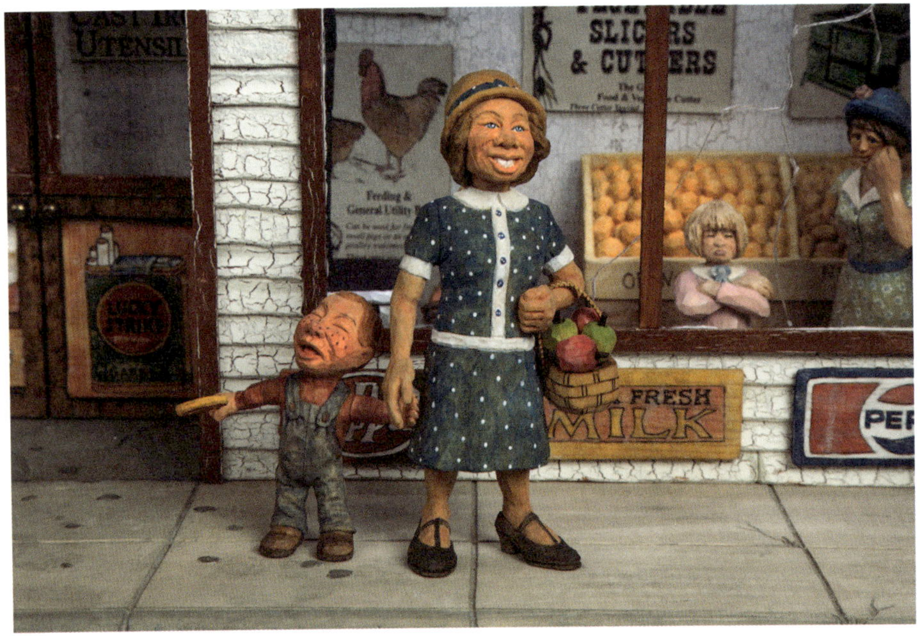

Bunny and Wheezer

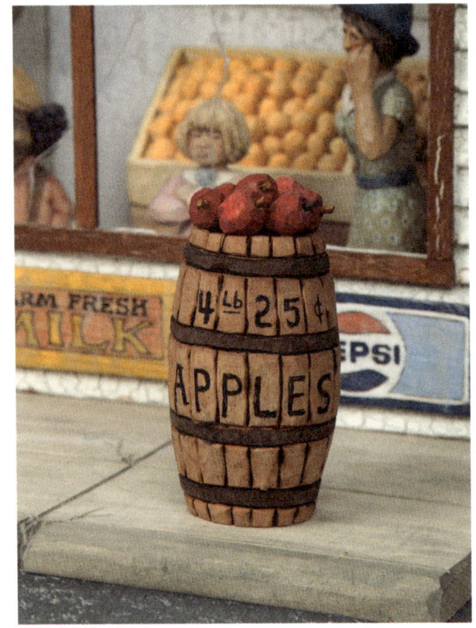

Apple barrel

Tip from Vicki Bishop

- Don't be afraid to step out of your comfort zone. Carve things that you normally wouldn't carve. This will help your carving and your creativity.

Bunny and Weezer came to be from watching the movie "Oh Brother, Where Art Thou" and some old "Little Rascals" movies. The design for the patterns start with a crude mock-up in clay and are then transferred to wood to be cut into a band sawn blank.

The general store needed a shopper and she needed to be dragging a snotty nosed little kid with her. The handle on her basket is made of flat basket reed and was added later. This material can be soaked and bent. The apples and the sucker were also carved and glued in later.

—Vicki Bishop

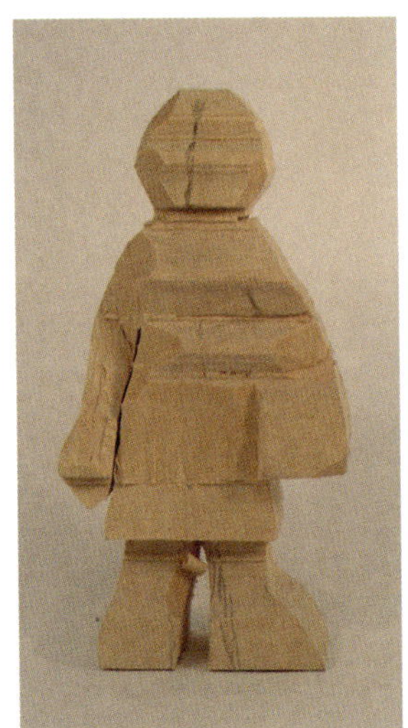

Bunny cut out, front

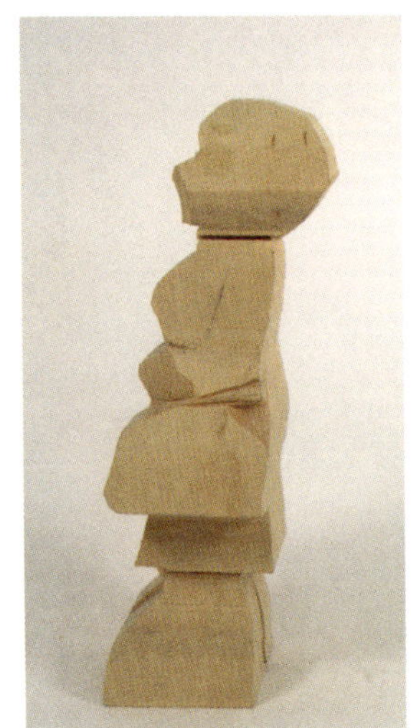

Bunny cut out, side

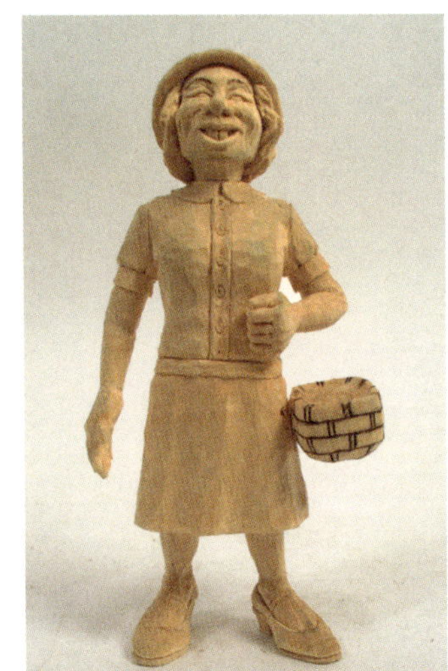

Ready to paint, front view

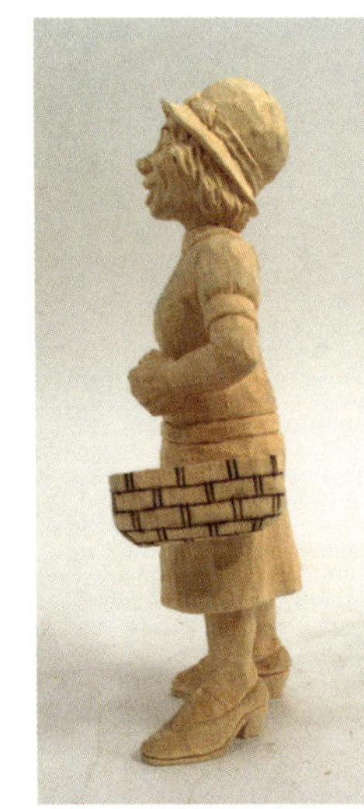

Ready to paint, side view

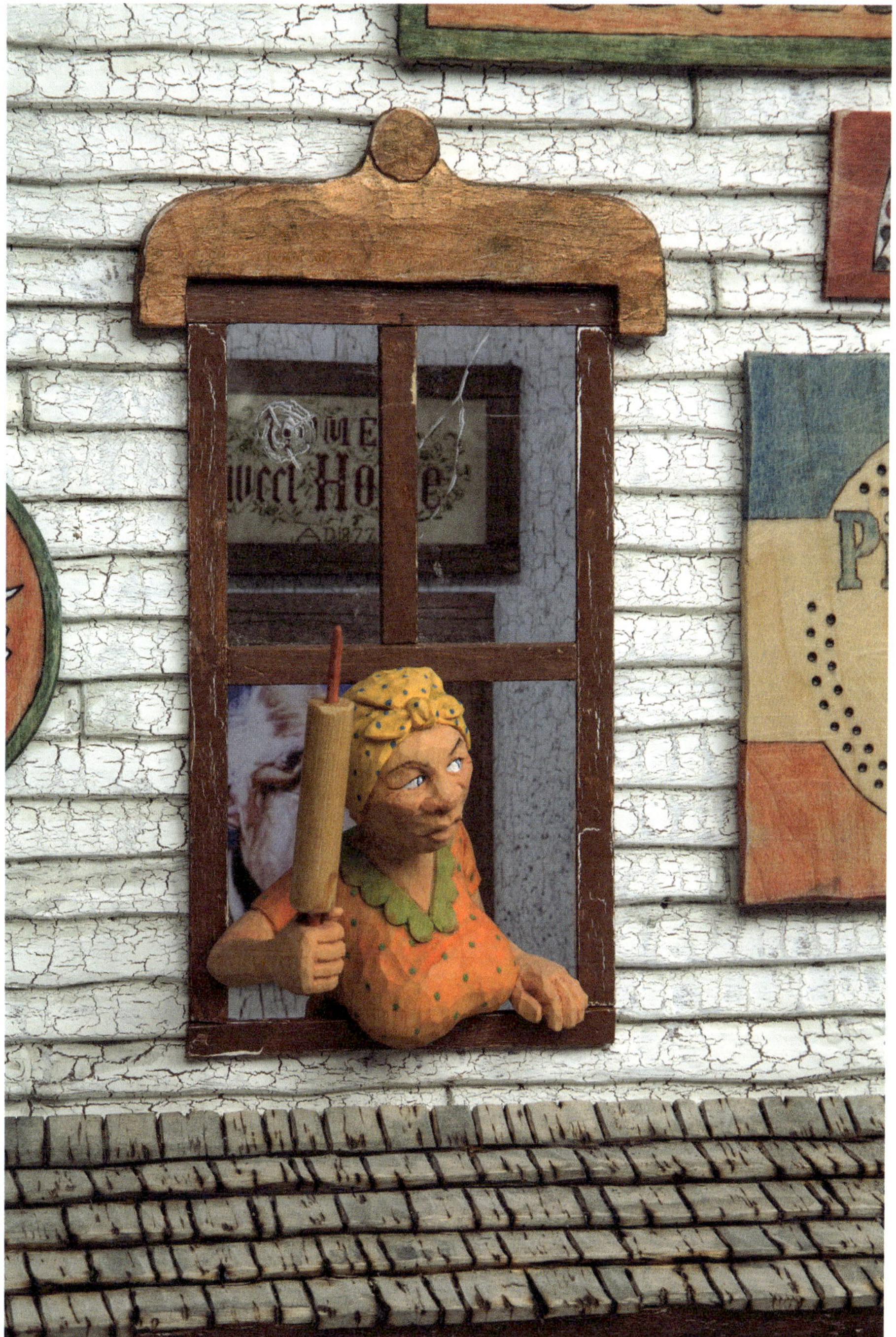

Ella Mae

The store is a two-story building, so the upper floor became an apartment. Ella Mae came into being as the disgruntled wife of Claude. She is upset with Claude about who knows what, and is threatening him with her trusty rolling pin. She had to fit over the window ledge, so clay came in handy for the design. She didn't need a lower body, because like Claude, all you can see is her torso. It took a couple of attempts at carving her to get her to fit over the window ledge.

—Vicki Bishop

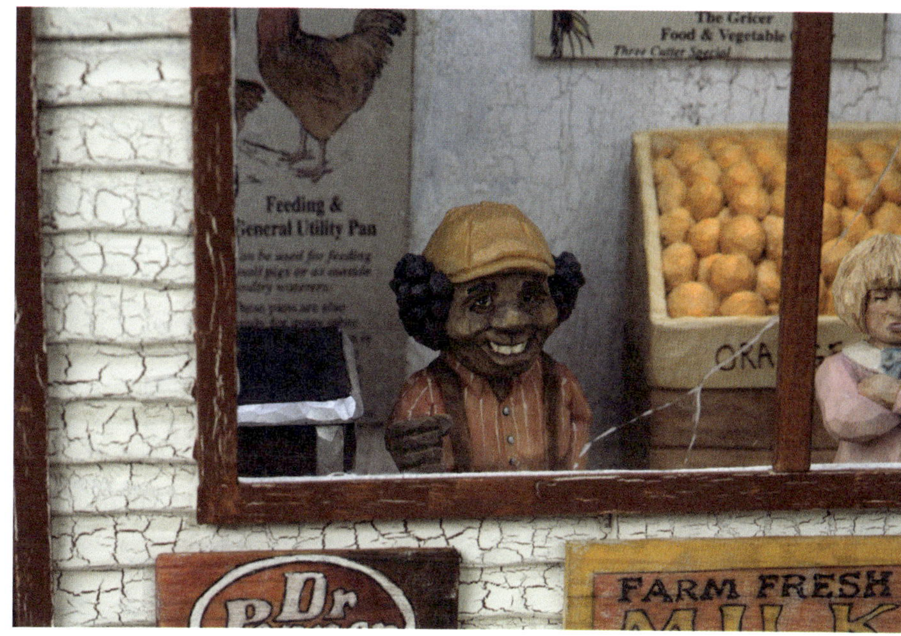

Little boy in store, Gary Falin

The idea for my carvings came from the "Little Rascals." Perhaps this little guy is deciding what kind of candy he will purchase with the lone penny in his pocket, or maybe, like most children during the Great Depression, he was just daydreaming of what it would be like to have enough money to buy candy.

—Gary Falin

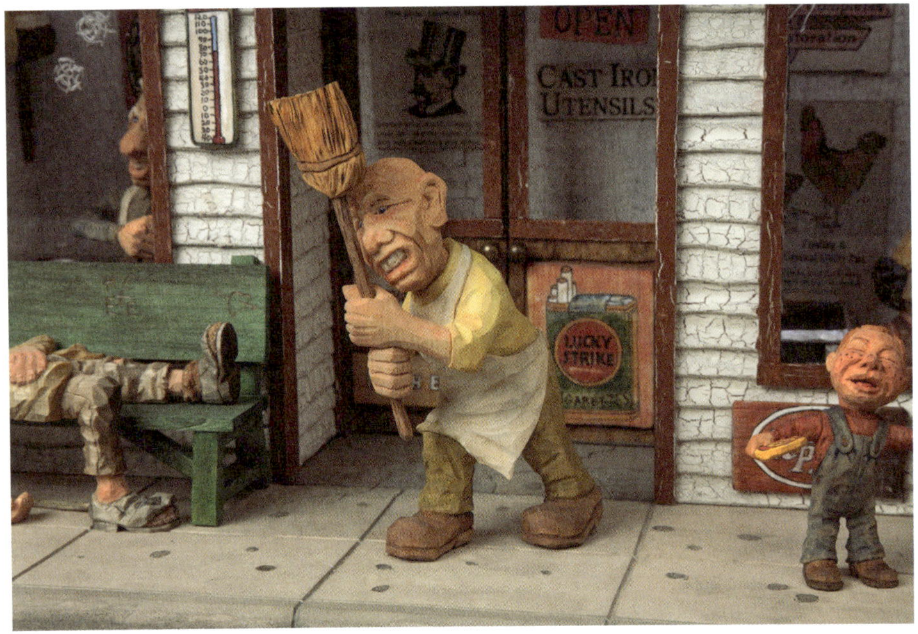

Sweeping up, Gene Fuller

Tips from Harold Enlow

- Follow your dreams! Enjoy life!
- Be happy! Make lots of friends!
- Always keep your carving tools sharp!

The1930s were a difficult time for many Americans. Not only were things tough for people, but meals were few and far between for dogs. Brooms came in handy for keeping the shop clean, as well as keeping the canines under control. I wonder how this man was employed before the depression?

—Gene Fuller.

Hobos, cowboys and hillbillies have always been my favorite caricatures to carve. Hiram is all stretched out on a bench after a long day on the road. He's using his pack, which holds his few possessions, for a pillow. His stick, which carries the pack and his rusty can from which he drinks, are under the bench.

—Harold Enlow

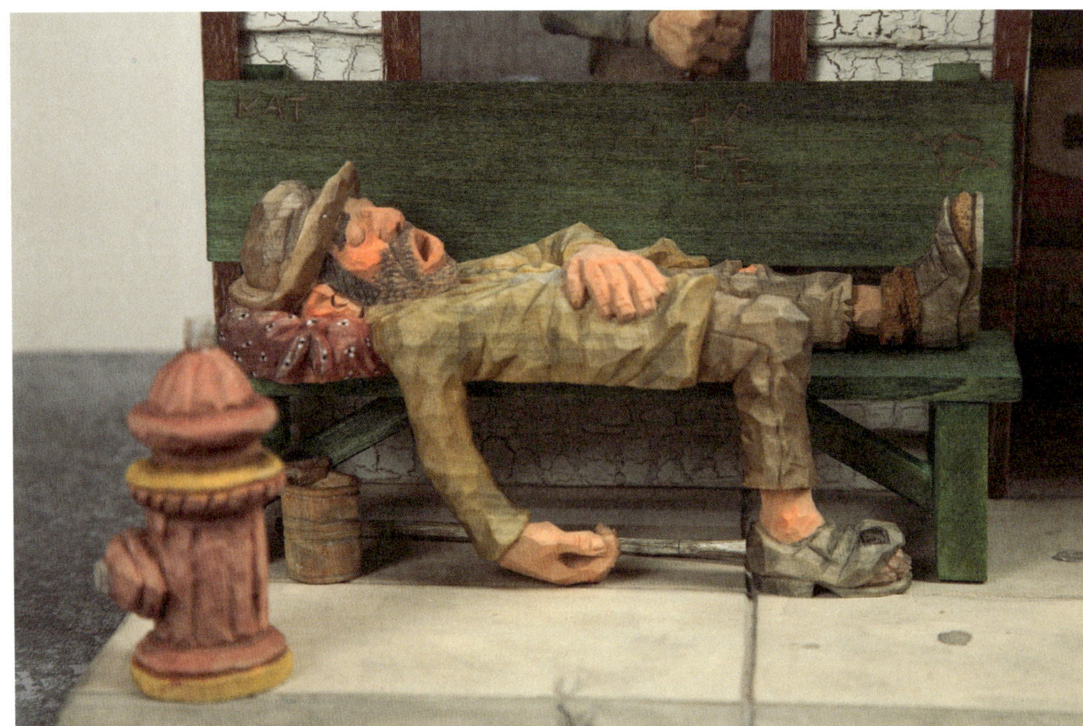

Hiram by Harold Enlow

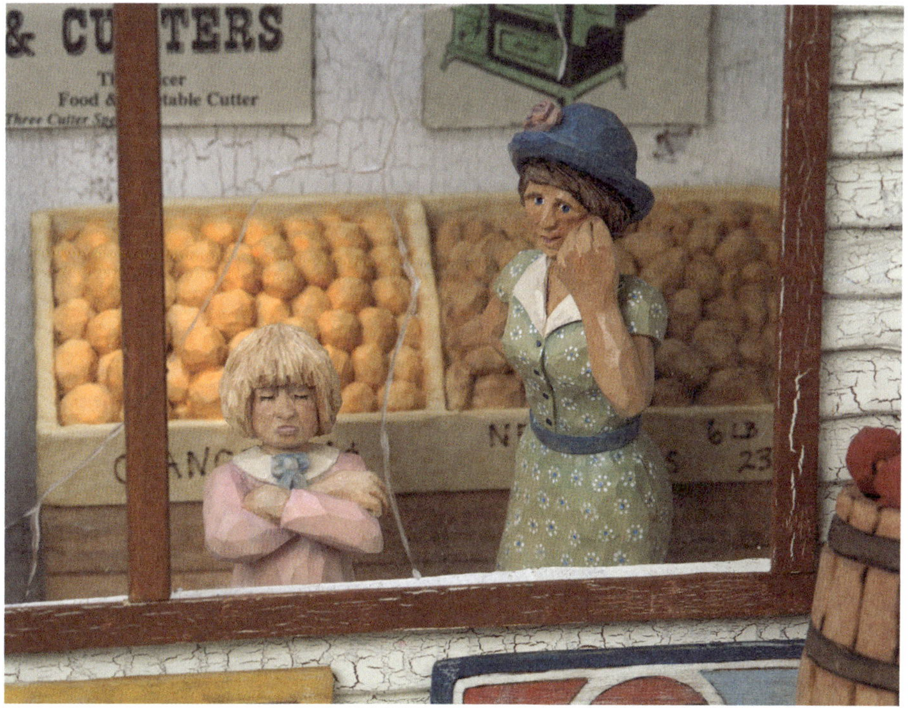

Shopper and pouting girl

Shopper from armature to pattern by Sandy Smith

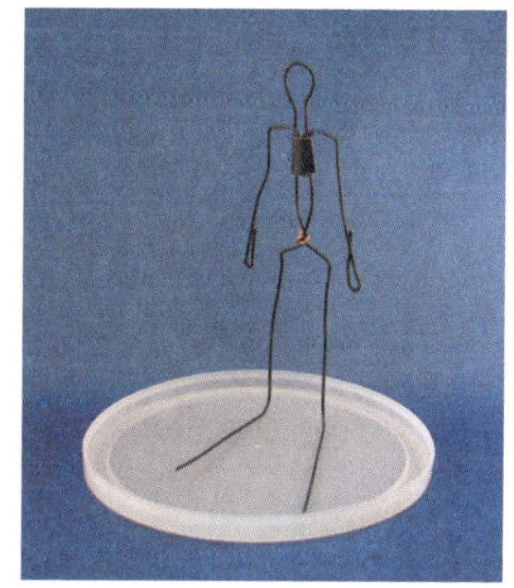

Shopper armature

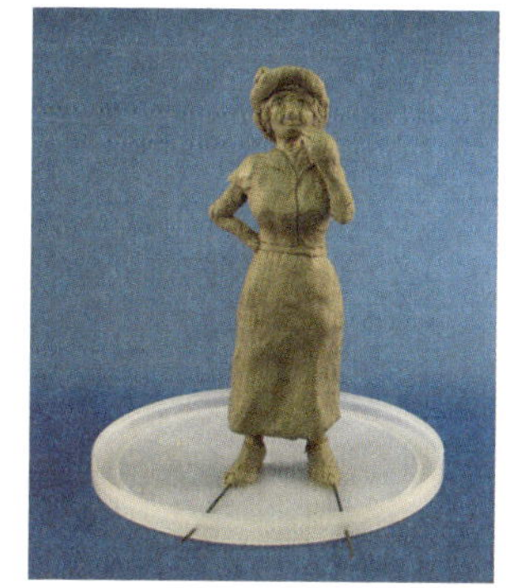

Clay, front

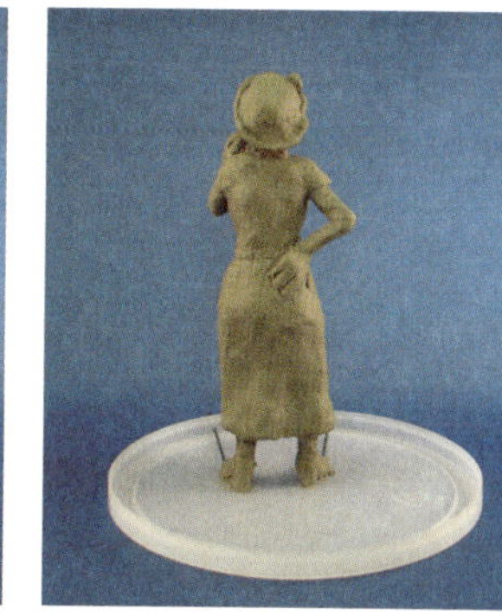

Clay, back

Bishop's General Store needed customers, so I carved an indecisive lady and a pouting little girl to help fulfill that requirement. Both caricature designs began with wire armatures and clay to use as go-bys. The mom is in serious thought about what she wants to purchase, while the sweet little tyke stands close by with her bottom lip pooched out, her chin tucked in, and arms crossed. My mom would never let me get by with that!

—Sandy Smith

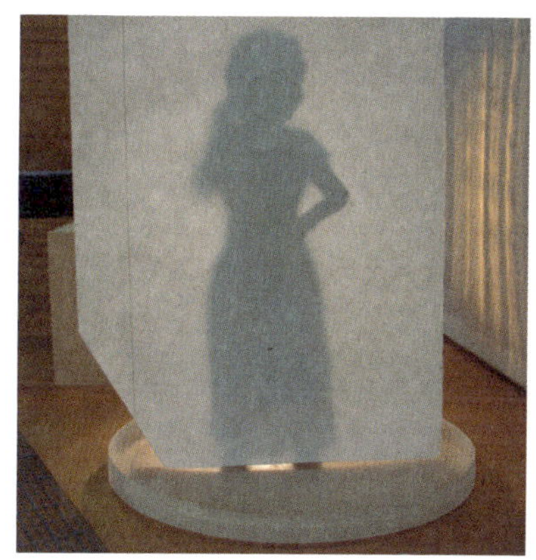

Pattern shadow

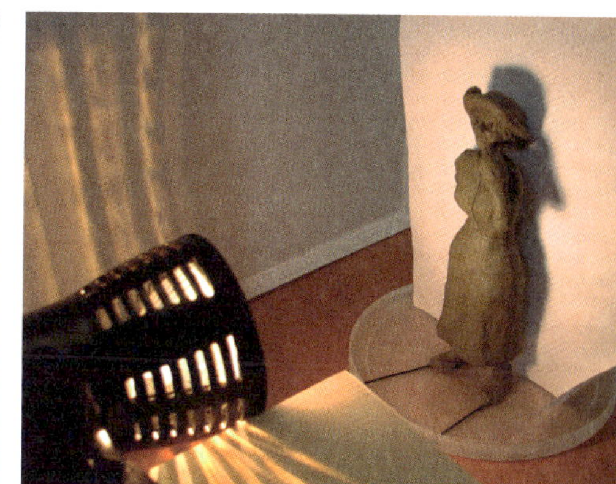

Pattern shadow

Pouty girl from clay to wood by Sandy Smith,

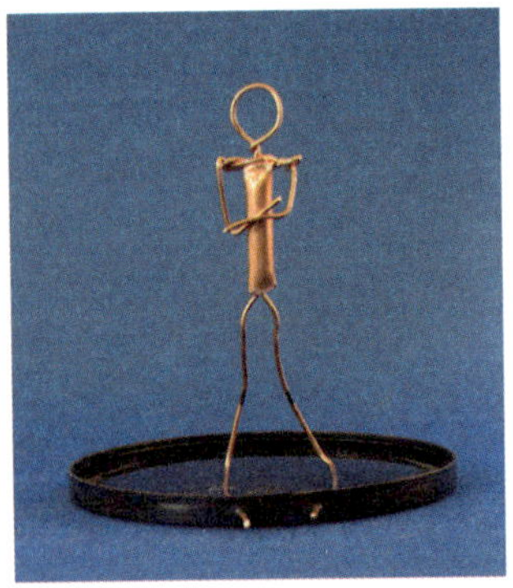

Pouty girl armature

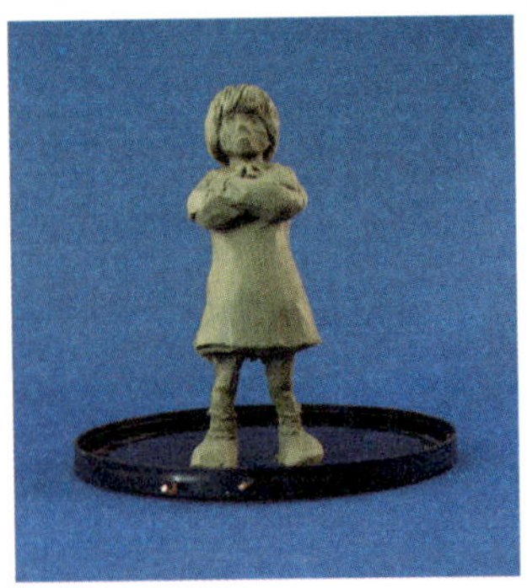

Clay, front

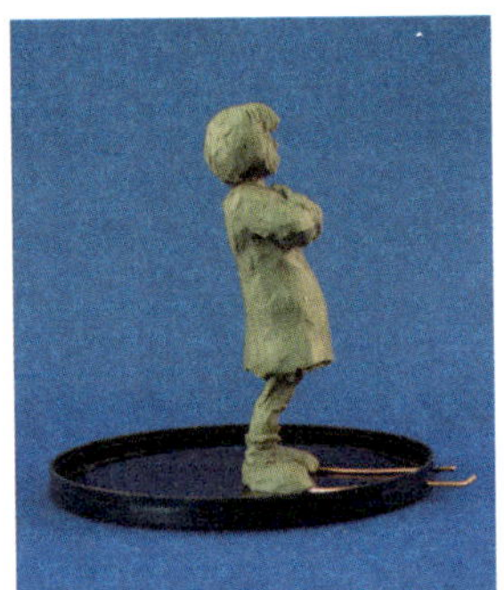

Clay, right side

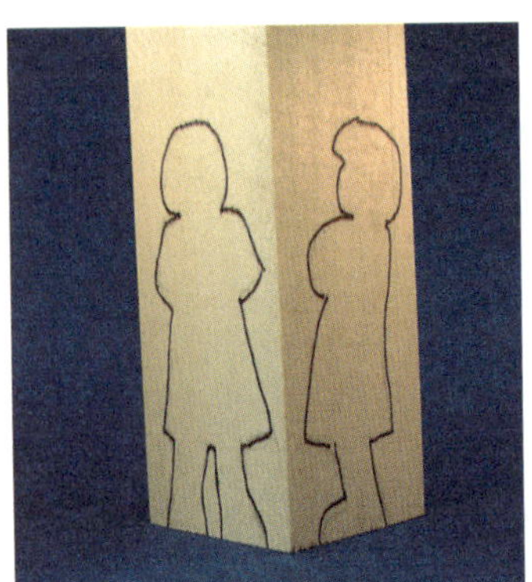

Pattern on wood

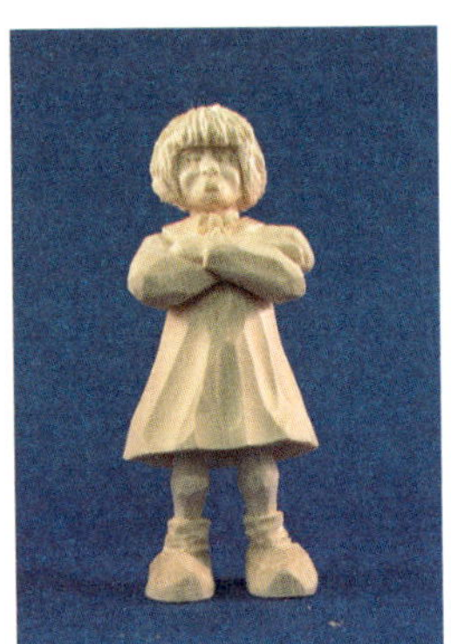

Ready to paint

Sandy's sausage thieves from armature to clay

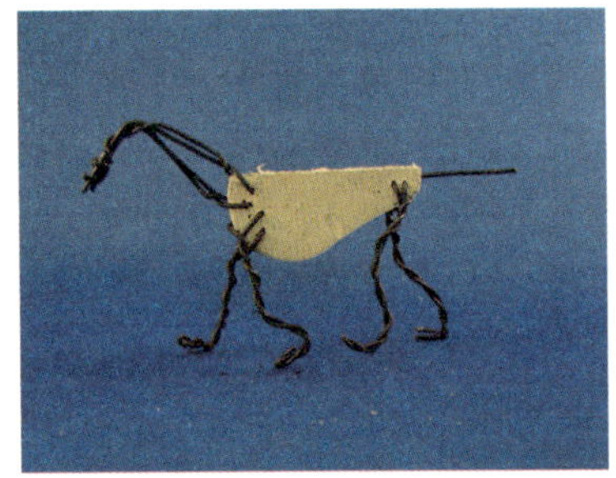

Armature

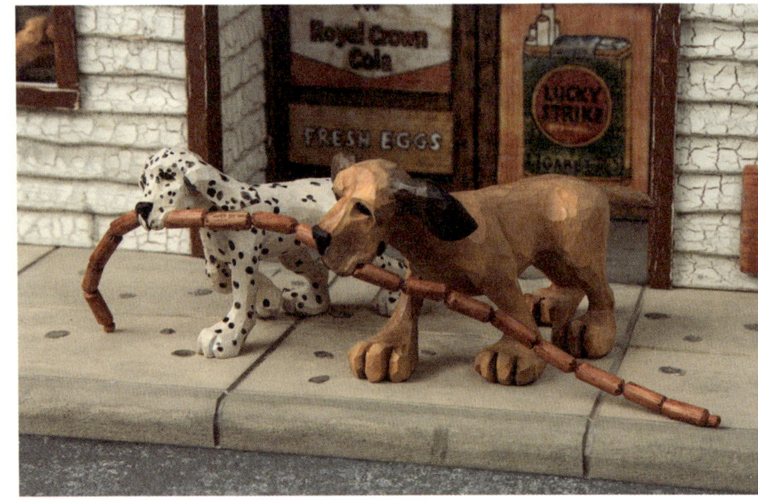

Sausage thieves

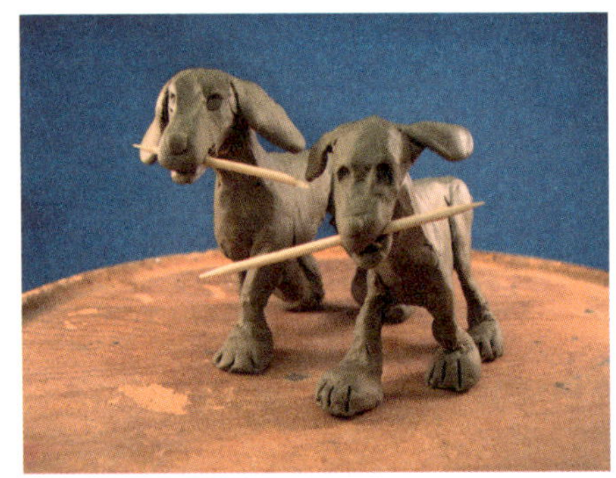

Clay, front view

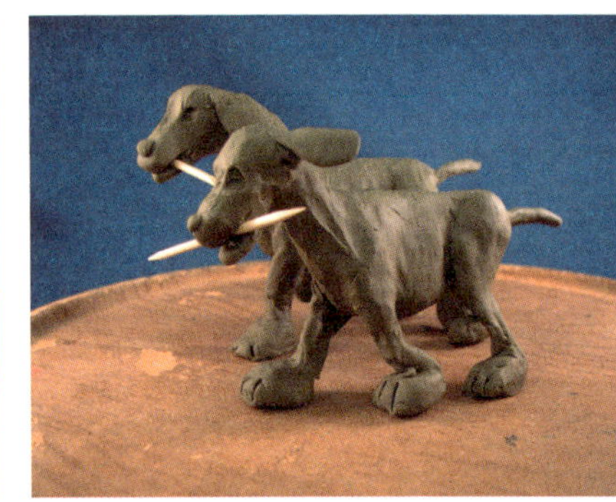

Clay, left side view

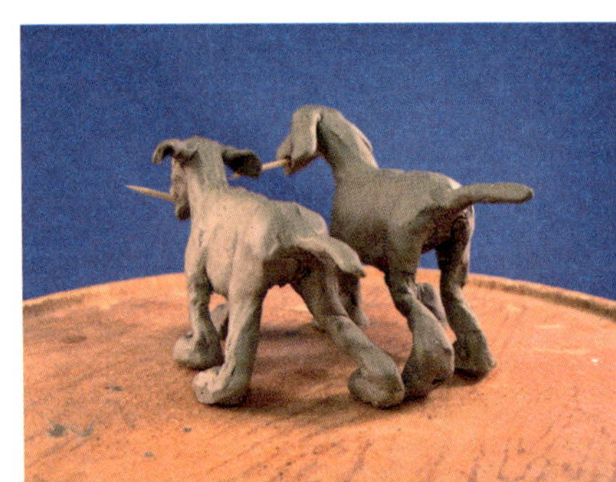

Clay, rear view

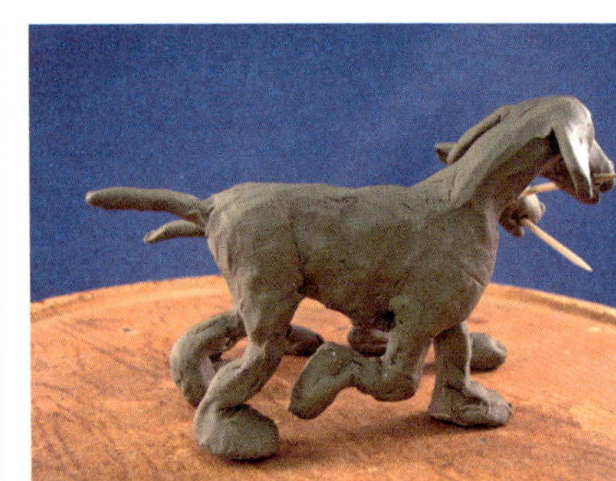

Clay, right side view

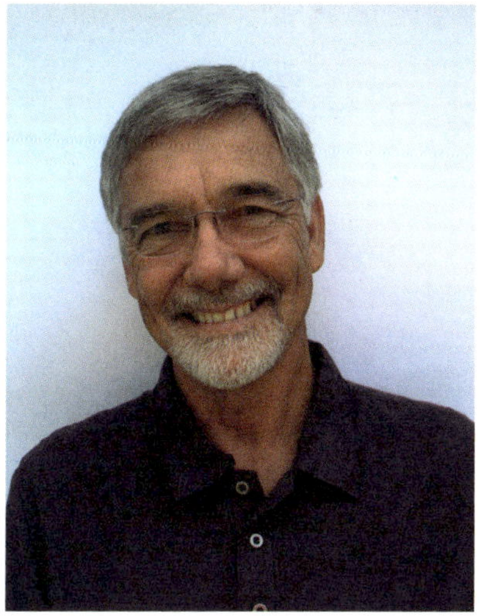

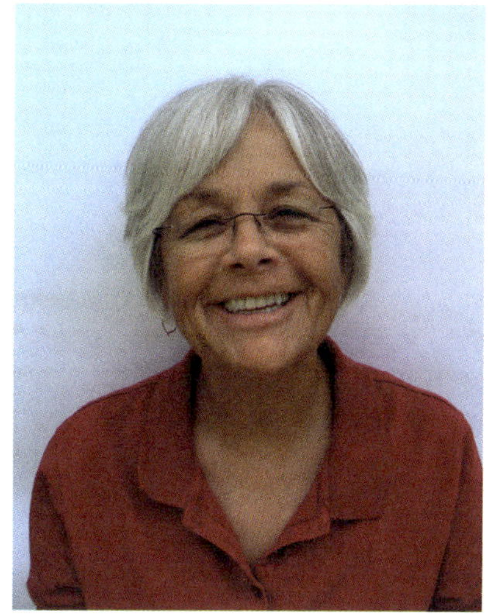

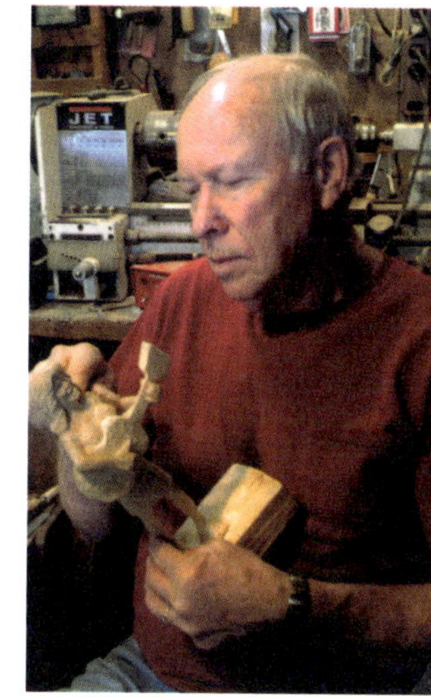

Phil Bishop

Phil Bishop, Elk City, Oklahoma, was a full-time woodcarving instructor along with his wife, Vicki. Phil credits Ed Zinger for giving him the opportunity to begin teaching at the Rendezvous in Branson.

Phil was inspired by the carving books of Steve Prescott, Cleve Taylor, Harold Enlow, Tom Wolfe, and also by the work of Randy Landen and Dave Dunham. He also admires the cartoons of Herb Mignery, and the work of Chris Hammack, Gene Zesch, and many other caricature artists.

The Bishops sold their roughout business in 2012 and retired from teaching. They continue to attend woodcarving shows and are having a great time with old friends. Phil continues to create new, one-of-a-kind pieces. Phil became a member of the Caricature Carvers of America in 1998, accepted Emeritus status in 2006, and returned to active membership in 2010.

Vicki Bishop

Vicki Bishop, Elk City, Oklahoma, was introduced to caricature carving through her husband, Phil. Phil had encouraged Vicki to carve for years, because he could see her natural talent. In 1999, while Phil was teaching in Michigan, Vicki took Dave Stetson's night class. Michele Stetson sat next to Vicki and helped her with her piece. Needless to say Vicki was hooked forever.

With Phil's encouragement, more experience, and confidence, she started to assist Phil at the seminars. Before long she was a full-time carving instructor. The carving duo was away from home 200 days a year, teaching approximately 25-30 seminars a year. They have since retired from the woodcarving circuit and are devoting their time to carving original pieces. Vicki became a member of the Caricature Carvers of America in 2008.

Harold Enlow

As a child, Harold liked to draw and make his toys out of wood or other things he could find. Harold joined the Army in 1957, and spent 18 months in Okinawa, Japan, where he became seriously interested in woodcarving.

He married Elaine in 1960. In the early 1960s he met Peter Engler, who was a great inspiration to Harold's woodcarving career.

Harold and Elaine opened a woodcarving shop at Dogpatch, U.S.A. in 1968, and spent several years carving Al Capp's Lil' Abner characters. After leaving Dogpatch in 1975, Harold began teaching carving classes. He taught thirty-five to forty classes each year, all over the United States and Canada, retiring in 2005.

A founding member of Caricature Carvers of America, Harold continues to carve and teach on a very limited basis while pursuing his new hobby of blacksmithing.

POLICE STATION and JAIL

Randy Landen, Dennis Thornton and Eldon Humphreys

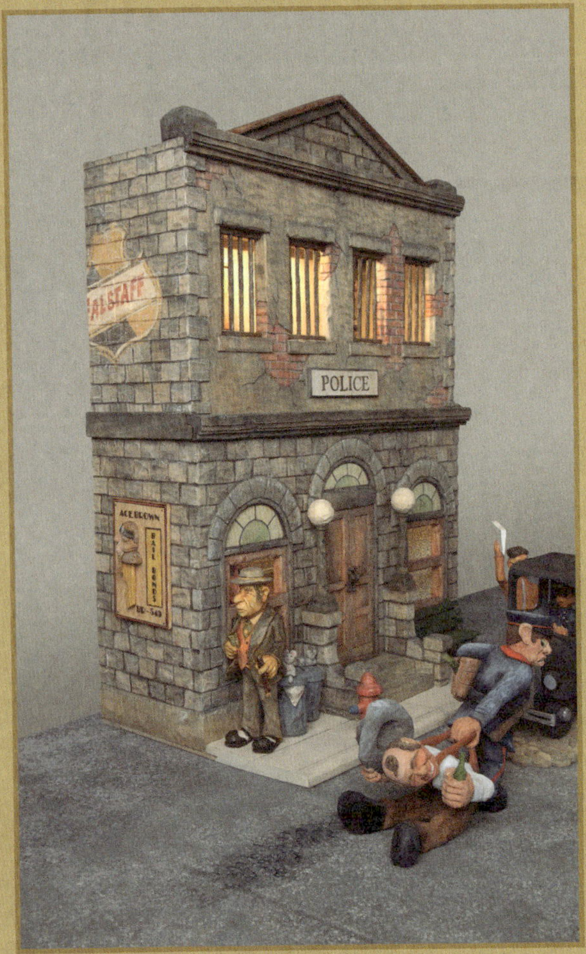

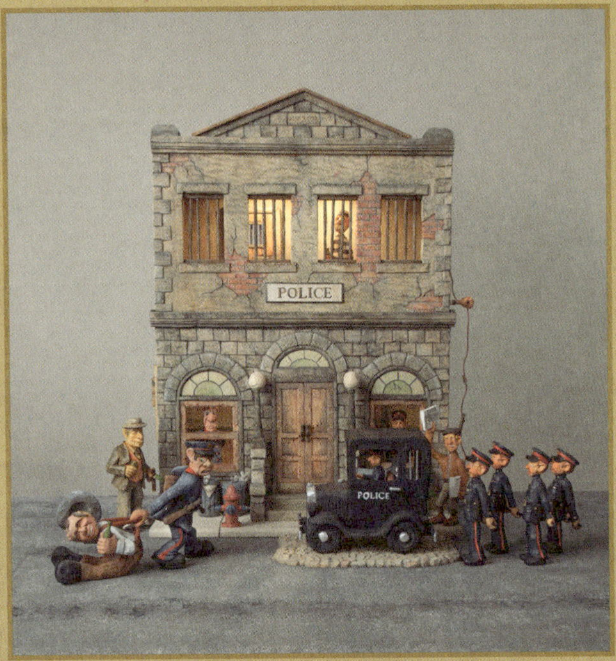

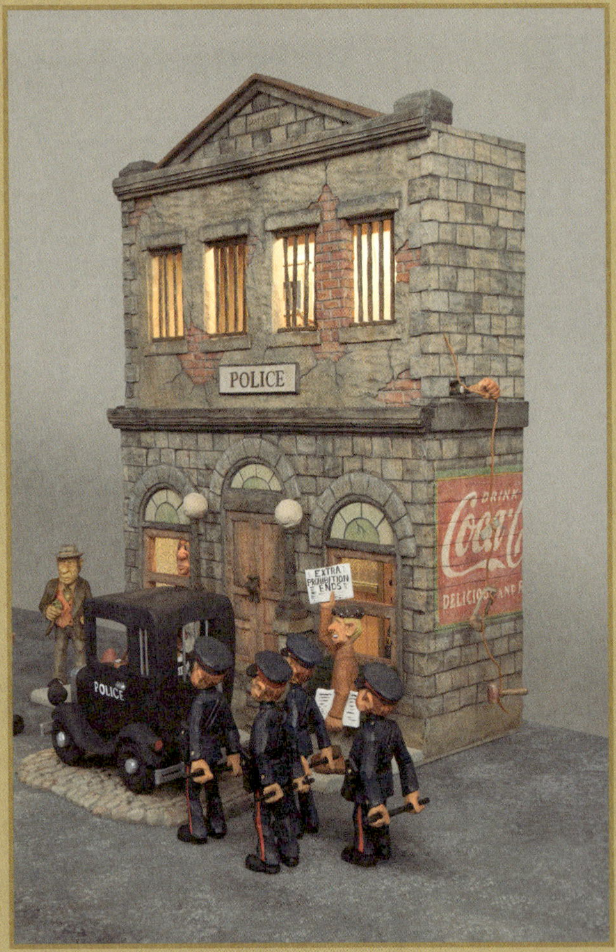

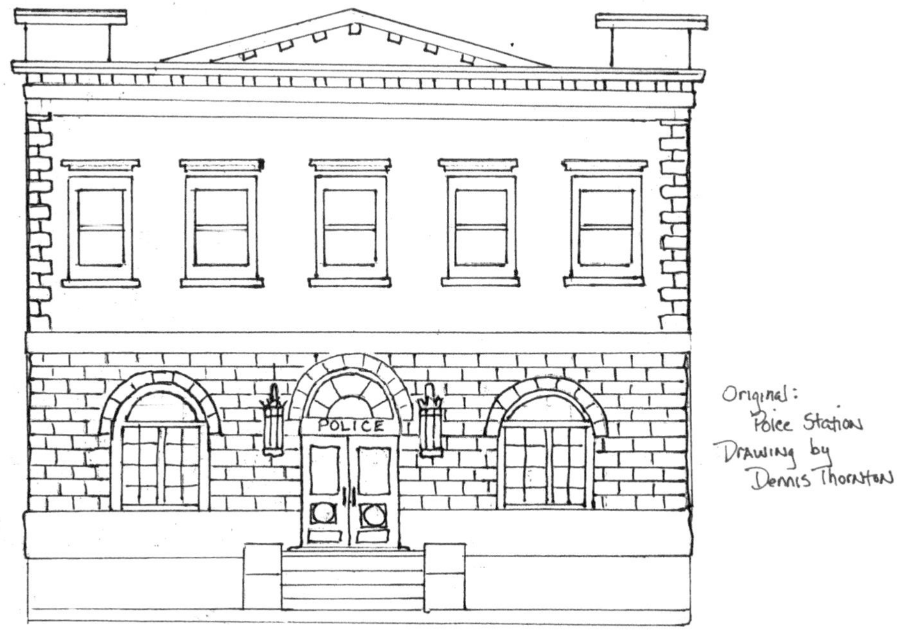

Original plans

When the CCA decided to carve a 1930s town there was never a question as to what Dennis, Eldon, and I wanted to do for our part of the project. All three of us are cops (Dennis and Eldon are retired), so the choice for us was easy.

The original plan for the police station was drawn by Dennis Thornton, based on research he'd done on period buildings. It was originally 24 inches tall and 24 inches wide. I liked the basic plan, but reduced the width by 6 inches, and put a jail on the second story, to give the building more of a caricature look. The completed building is 18 inches wide, 27 inches tall, and 6 inches deep, not counting the sidewalk.

Long before I started, overachievers Phil and Vicki Bishop had their grocery store, figures, and shipping box completely done. In talking with them I learned that they had problems with the thin wood warping during the painting process, so I opted to make my main building walls from $\frac{3}{4}$-inch basswood. I justified my decision by reasoning that an old police station and jail would have thick walls anyway.

All of the exterior surfaces are carved. The lower level is carved to resemble granite blocks, and the upper level a combination of granite, stucco, and exposed brick. To give the piece added interest, I painted partial logos for 1930s beer and pop on the sides of the buildings, using period pictures I found on the internet. I transferred them to the building using graphite paper, and painted them with water-based acrylic washes. The process is fairly simple, but takes quite a bit of time. A sign for the local bail bond company, carved by Tom Brown, is posted on the lower level.

I'd like to say I had a plan for the inside, but that wouldn't be true. I designed the inside as I went, based on what you could see from the exterior. The interior on both levels has doors, which were carved separately and glued to the back wall. The lower level has a chair rail, wainscoting, and wallpaper. The wallpaper is actually scrapbooking paper, cut into $2\frac{1}{2}$-inch strips, and mismatched at the seams. The floor is carved to look like oak plank flooring. I debated using plexiglass for the windows, but decided to leave them open to be consistent between the jail and the police station. Ultimately the interior was too dark, so I found a low voltage LED light that I mounted to the ceiling on the upper level.

As with my carving, the building is painted with water-based acrylic paint, dry brushed, and sealed with a linseed oil antiquing stain.

—Randy Landen

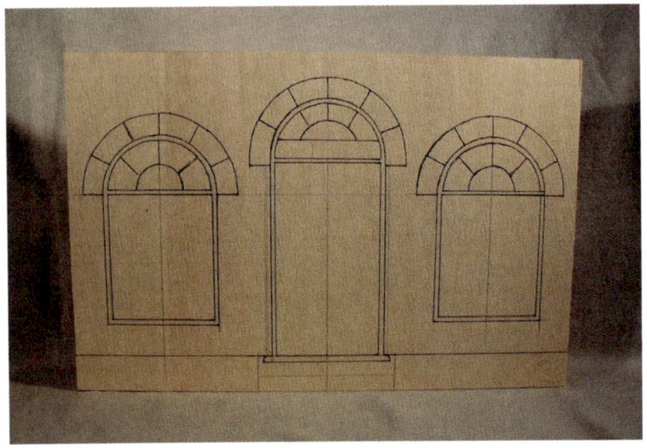

Ready to carve

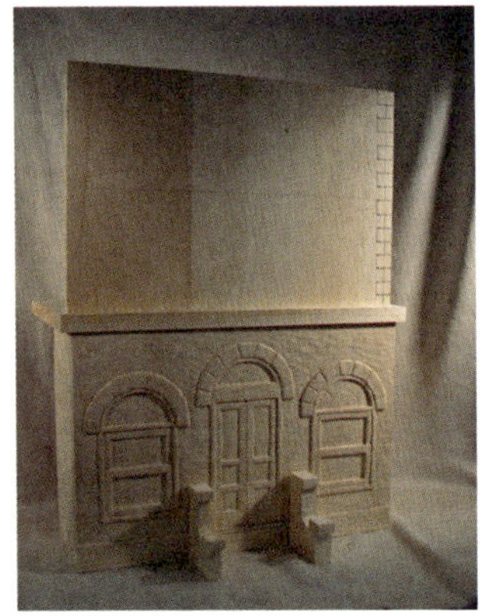

Downstairs carved

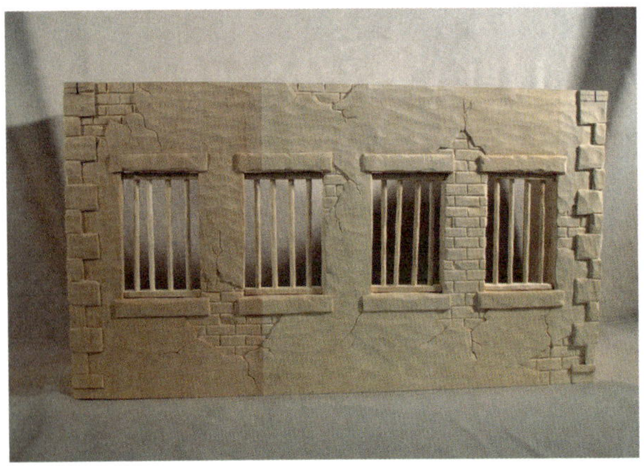

Upstairs carved

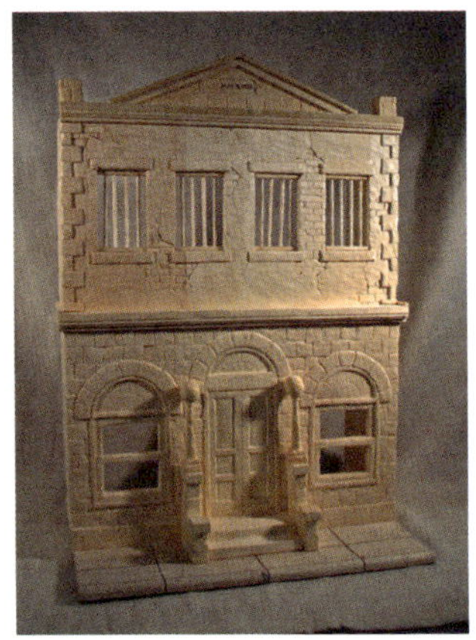

Ready to paint

Tip from Randy Landen

Painting signs and lettering:

• To create the titles or signs for my carvings, I use one of the varieties of fonts available in most computer word processing programs. The program helps with letter size, spacing, and centering. For specific brands or logos I use photocopies from old magazine ads, or search the internet (typically Google images) for pictures of a particular sign. For both lettering and logos, I trace them onto the wood using a wax-free transfer paper. The paper is available at most hobby shops or woodcarving supply stores. The outline provides a guide during painting, and can be erased with a soft gum eraser. To give the signs a weathered appearance, I rub them with a damp cloth and dry brush lightly over the top. Examples of two of these signs can be seen on either side of the 1930s Police Station and Jail.

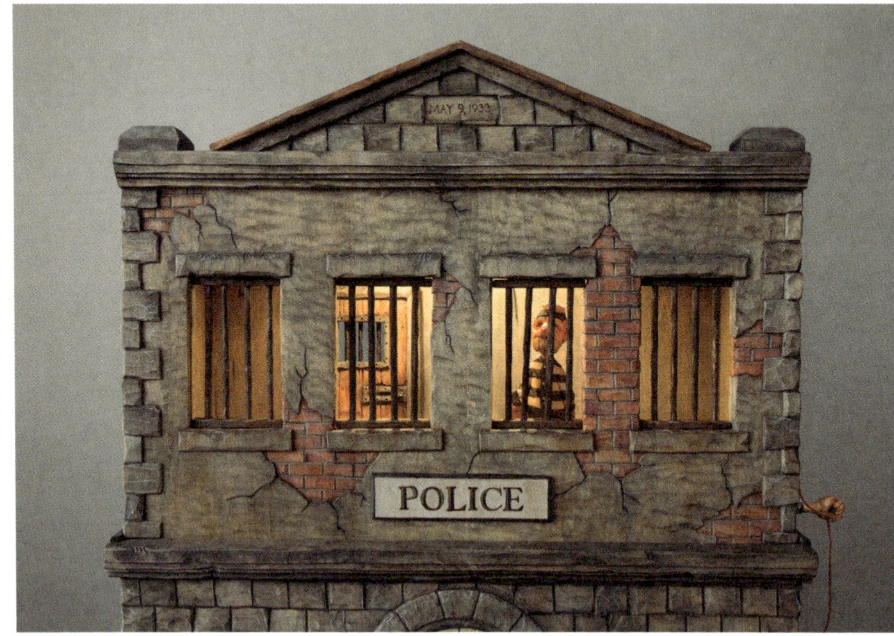

Prisoner

After deciding to add a jail as the second story of the police station, I wanted to have a prisoner looking out through the bars. Illuminating the lower level limited the construction of a floor in the jail, so I opted to mount the prisoner on a shelf, eliminating the need to carve a full figure. As a result, I carved about 75% of the prisoner. In retrospect, it would have been just as easy to do the whole carving, but it seemed like a good plan at the time.

I sketched a front view and side view of the prisoner on the basswood block, using horizontal lines to make sure the top of the head and chin lined up between the views. From there, I used a band saw to cut the front view first, leaving about 1 inch of the wood uncut at the bottom. That helps hold the wood together as you cut the side view. After the side view has been cut, I finish the front cut. The result is a band saw blank that eliminates a lot of the roughing-out time.

The prisoner and the file in his hand are carved from one piece, and finished with water-based acrylic washes. Because the black and white paints tend to bleed over to one another, I used a wood burner on a low heat to score the lines between the stripes on the shirt and pants. The line helps stop the paint from wicking into the next area. After the carving is painted and dry brushed, it was sealed with an antiquing stain made of boiled linseed oil tinted with burnt sienna and burnt umber oil paint.

—Randy Landen

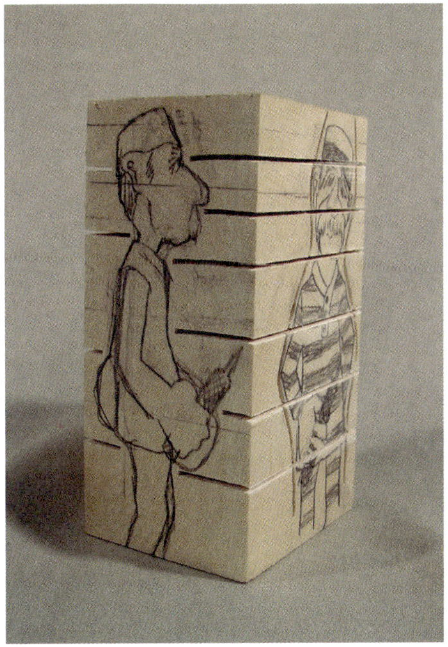

Pattern on wood

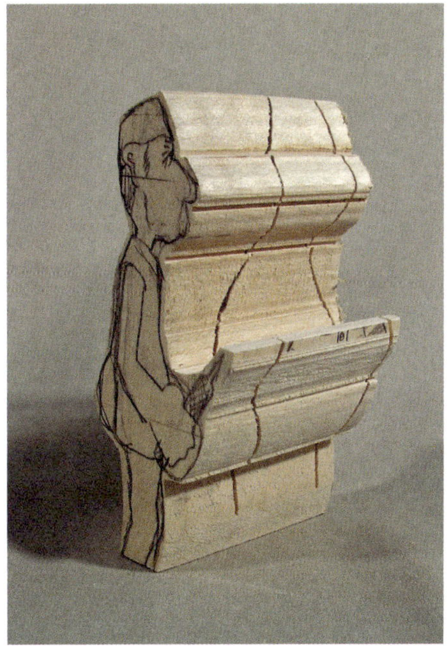

Cut out

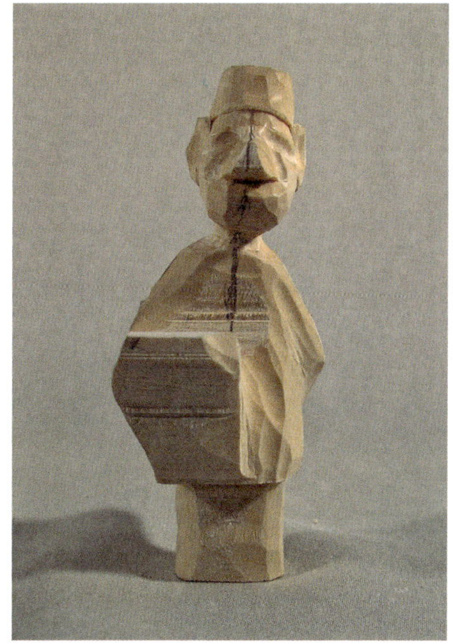

Roughing out, front

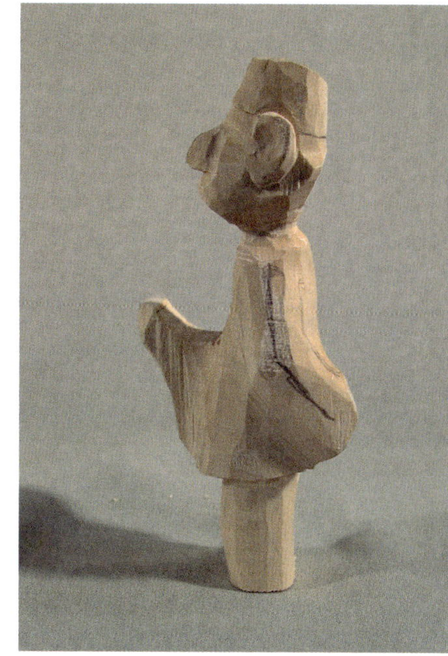

Roughing out, side

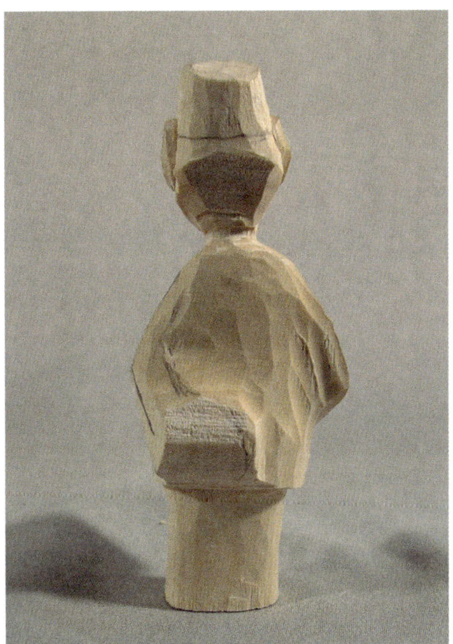

Roughing out, back

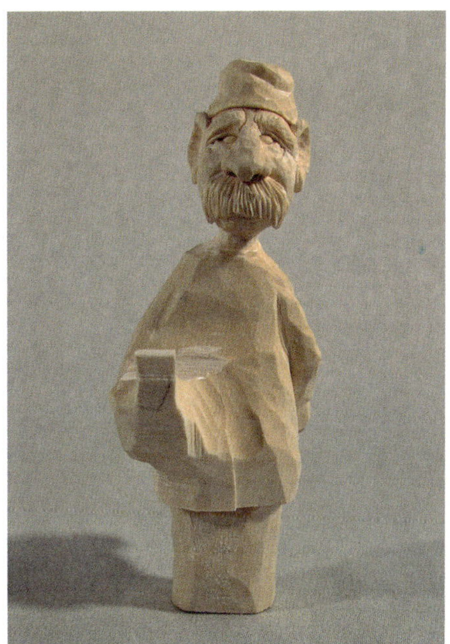

Nearly finished, front

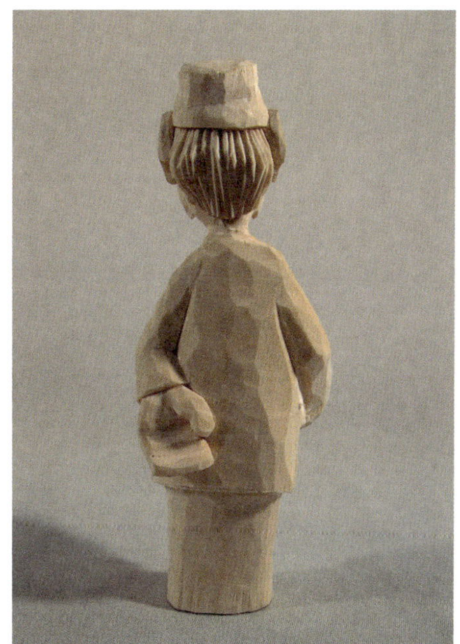

Nearly finished, back

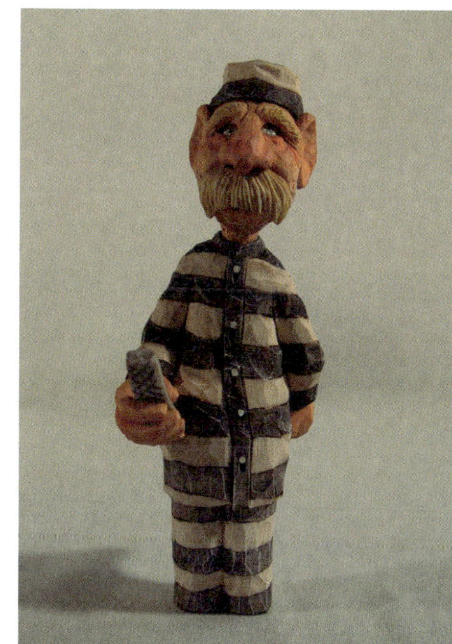

Finished prisoner by Randy Landen

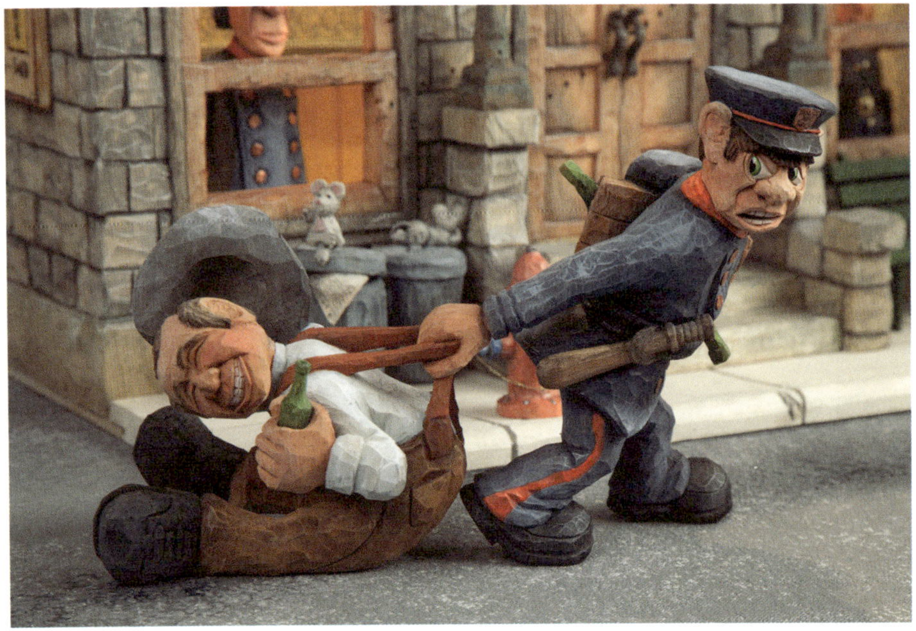

"Home, James"

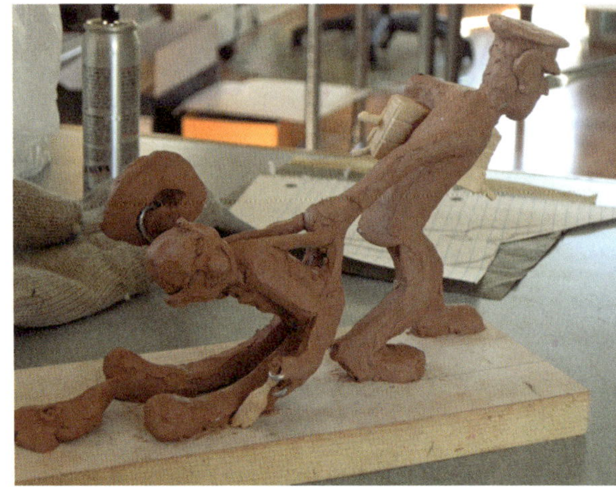

Clay model

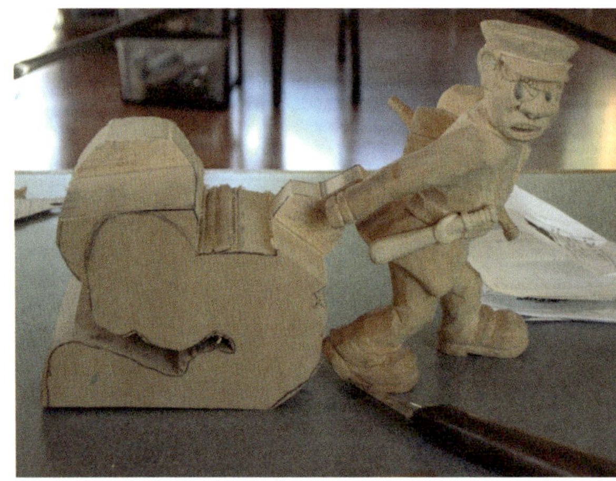

Pattern on wood. One figure carved

When this project was proposed and we heard a police station was in the works, Randy, Eldon, and I knew we had to work together. Being police officers with more than 100 years of police experience, the ideas just flooded in. My first carving, "Home James," is a diligent officer dragging a drunk to jail. The officer has confiscated the partier's case of wine. This carving offered me a chance to show significant action with subtle humor.

—Dennis Thornton

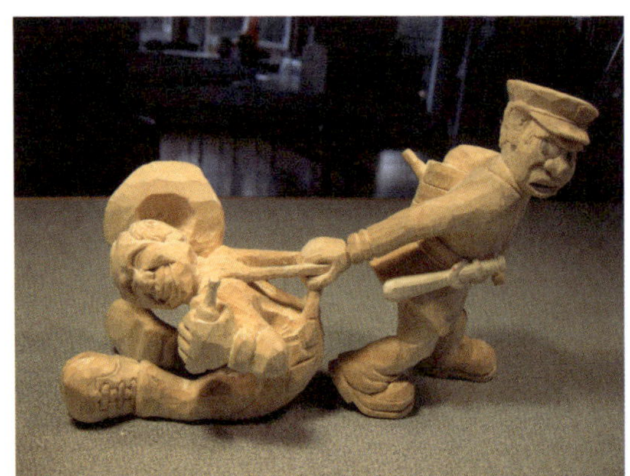

Ready to paint, front

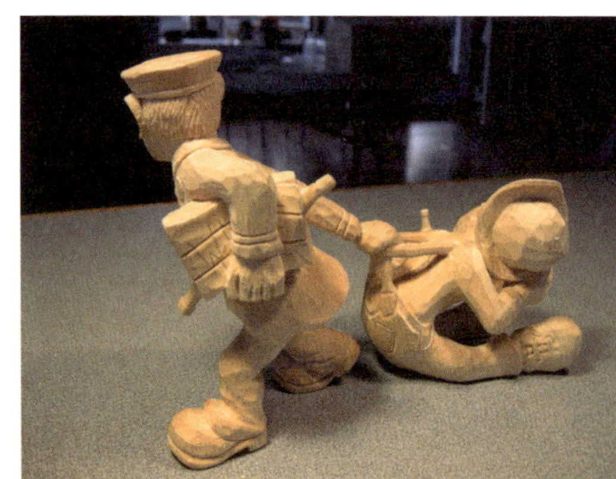

Ready to paint, back

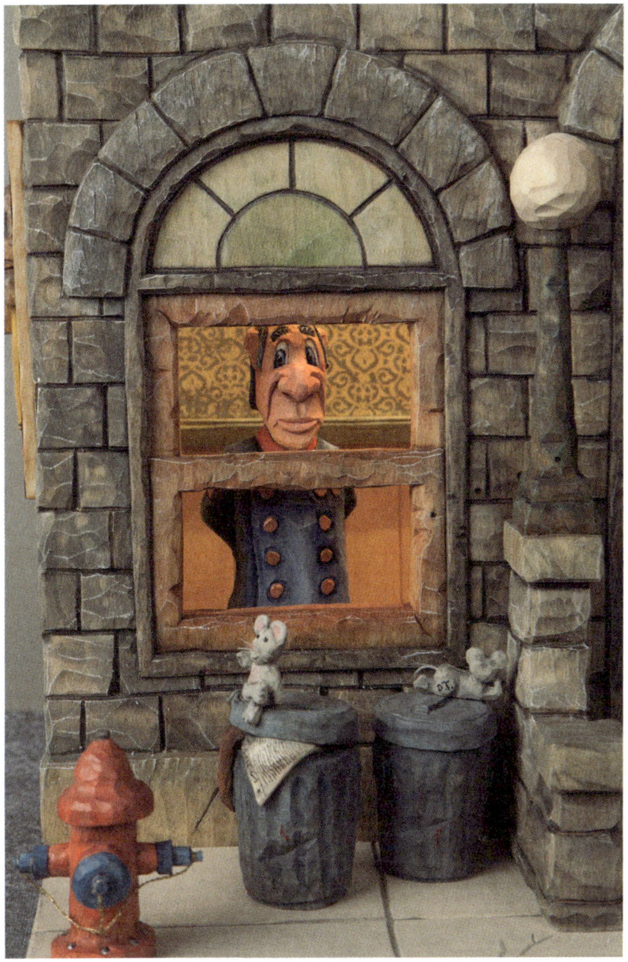

Tour Commander Jimmie O'Dea by Dennis Thornton

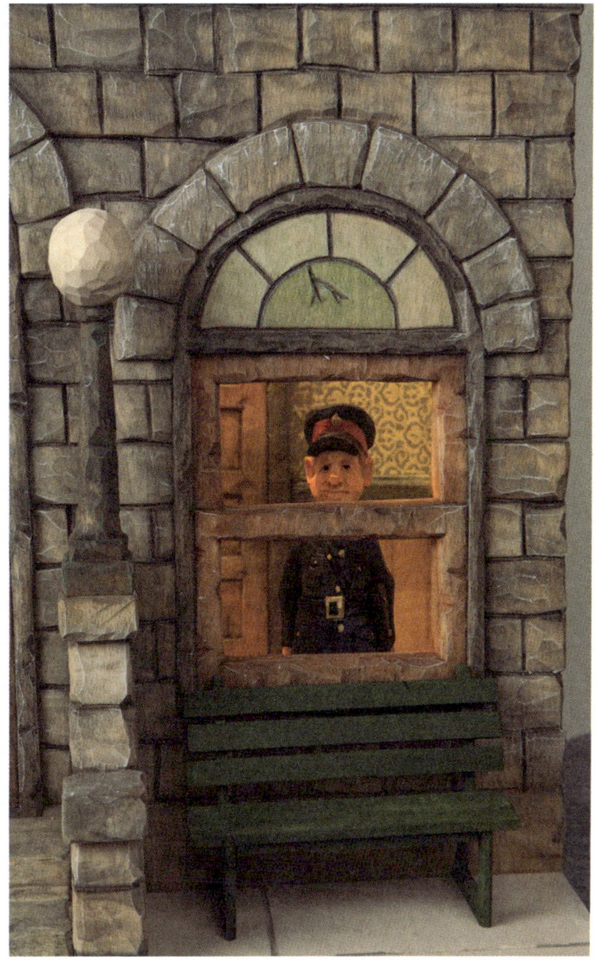

Police officer by Eldon Humphreys

Tips from Dennis Thornton

• I use a #2 lead pencil on my block of wood. It helps me see how much wood I want to remove, and it can help illustrate movement, positions of the body, and the center of the carving. It is easy to make a bad cut without a pencil line to show you the way.

• Removing dirt and pencil marks at the conclusion of carving is an important step that is often forgotten. I normally use a soft toothbrush, mild dish soap, and a little water to help wash away dirt. I dry the carving with a towel. Take care not to use too much water, as this can warp thin areas of wood.

• While carving caricatures, I like to keep the carving clean by removing fuzzies and other marks before moving on to a new area. Not only does this save time, but you'll see more clearly where you may need to make adjustments.

"Sgt. Jimmie O'Dea" is a Tour Commander inside the building. Like all of the carvings in this project, we worked with a scale that has to be spot-on when they are added to the buildings. This is a challenge, but easy enough to do if you keep the scale in mind. Additional carvings were added to the police station by CCA members Sandy Smith, Gene Fuller, and Don Mertz.

We decided to place trash cans in front of station, so I added two rats to the cans, watching the action on the street. These small details keep the project interesting.

—Dennis Thornton

The decision to divide the 30s Street Scene into separate building projects allows us display it as one large scene, or as individual building scenes. This allowed CCA members to specialize in carving pieces that they were more familiar with and interested in doing.

—Eldon Humphreys

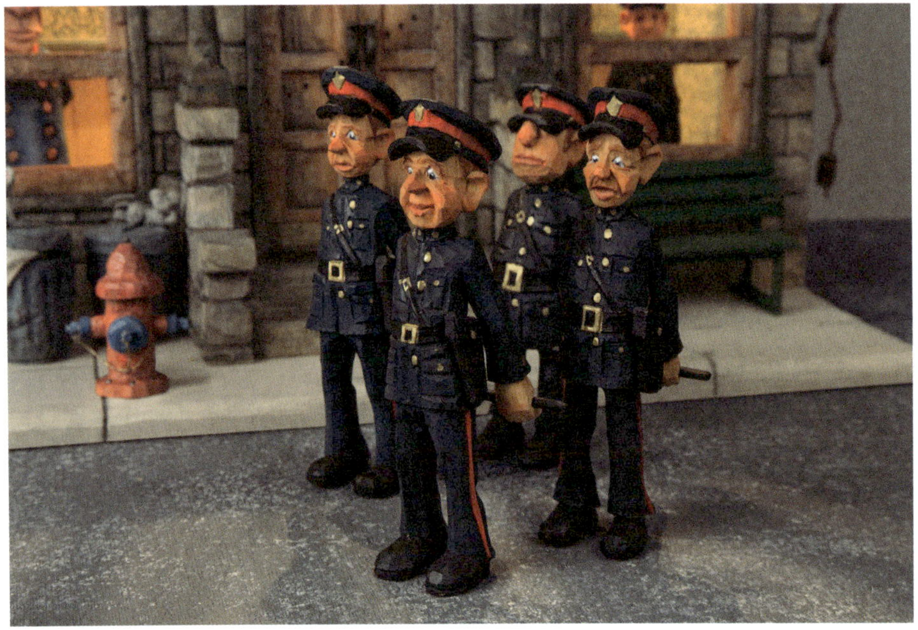

Cops

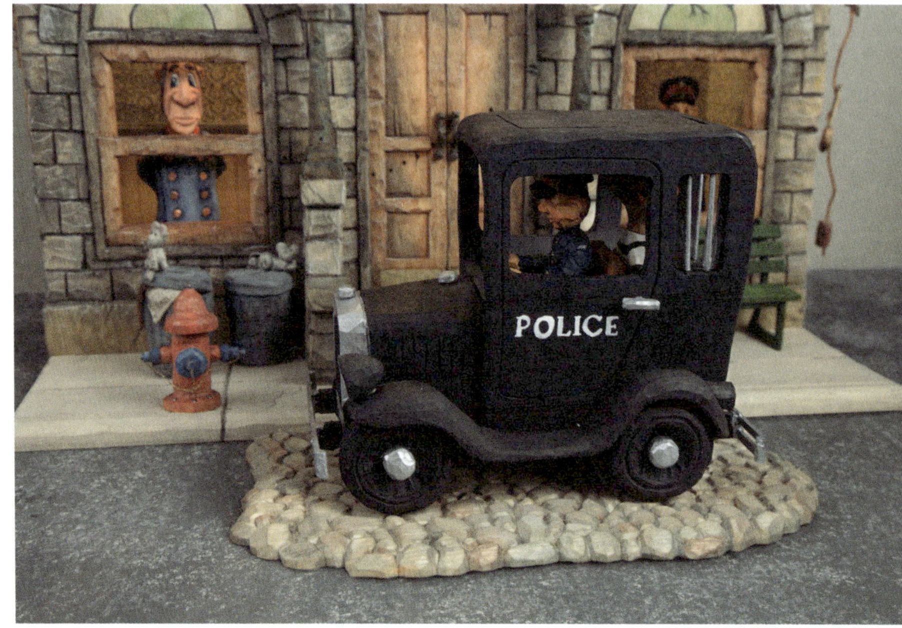

Paddy wagon

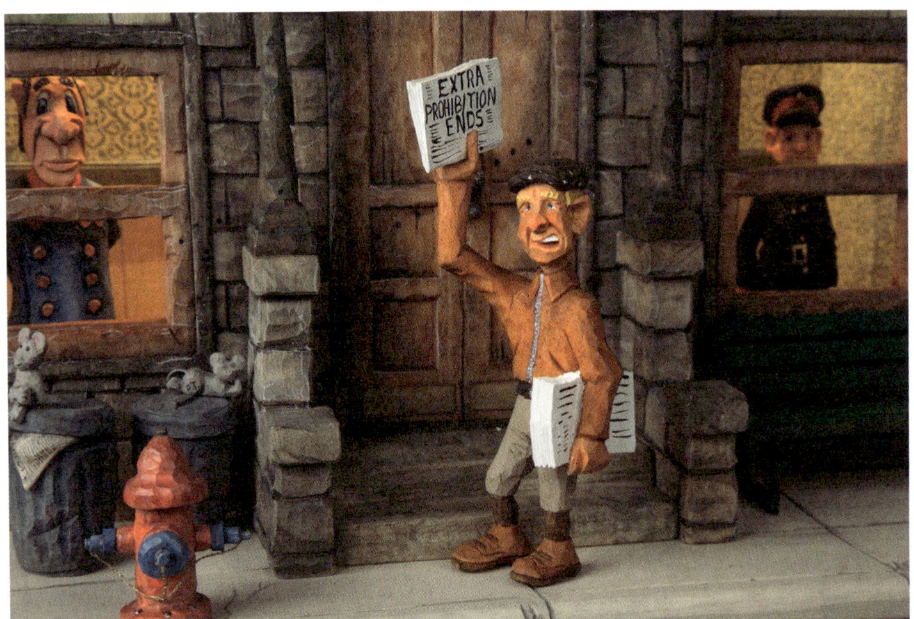

Newspaper boy

It did not take long after the decision was made to carve a street scene for members to begin joining together in various interest groups. Randy Landen, Dennis Thornton, and I, all being either current or retired police officers with more than 100 years of service between us, immediately selected the police station and its accompanying figures and accessories.

My prisoner van is a caricature of what I thought it would look like if Henry Ford had made one from a Model "A." I assembled and glued the van together from several pieces, rather than using one piece of wood. I did this to eliminate having to carve out the inside of the vehicle. I simply had to slim down the side pieces, making room for the driver and a prisoner.

—Eldon Humphreys

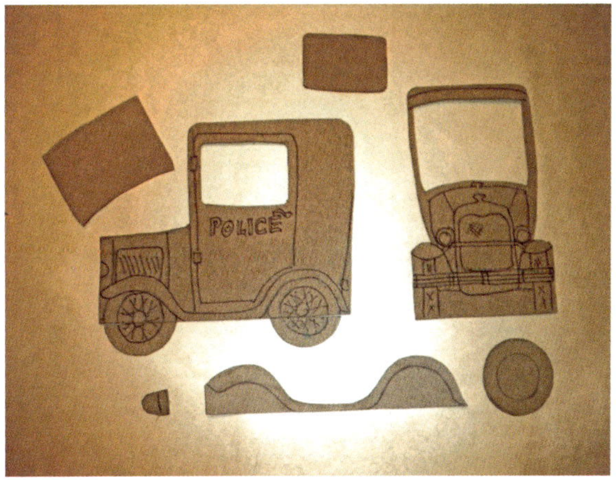

Paddy Wagon Plans

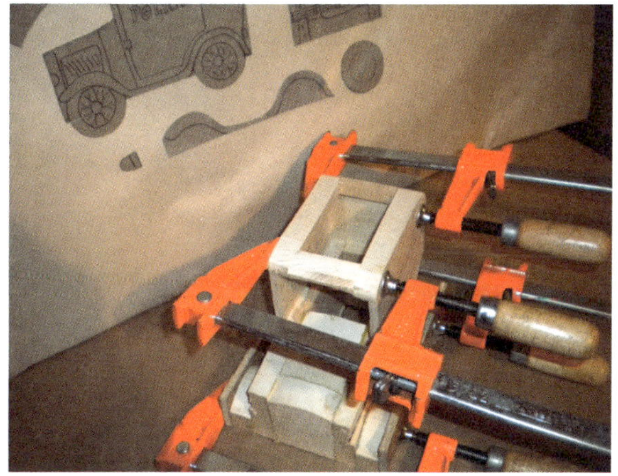

Gluing up

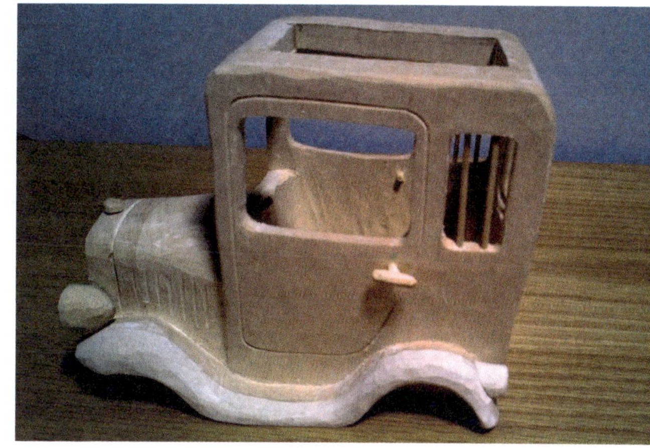

Body

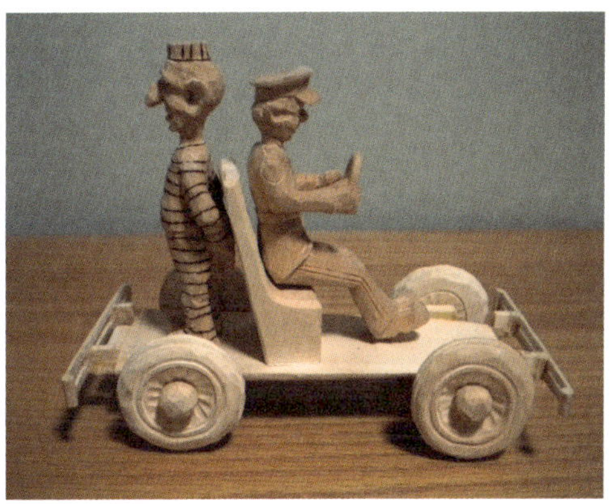

Frame, officer, and perp

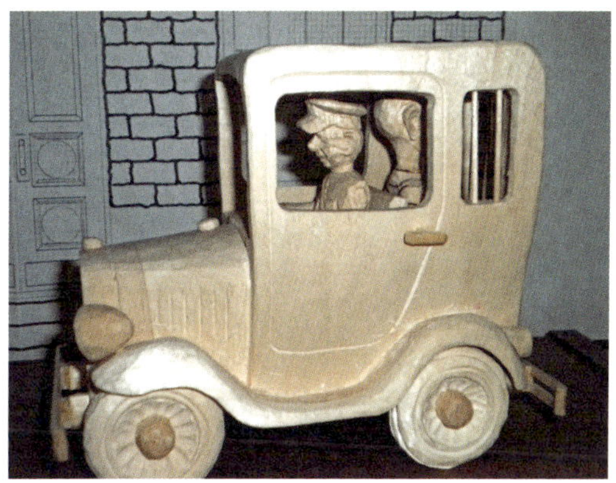

Officer and perp

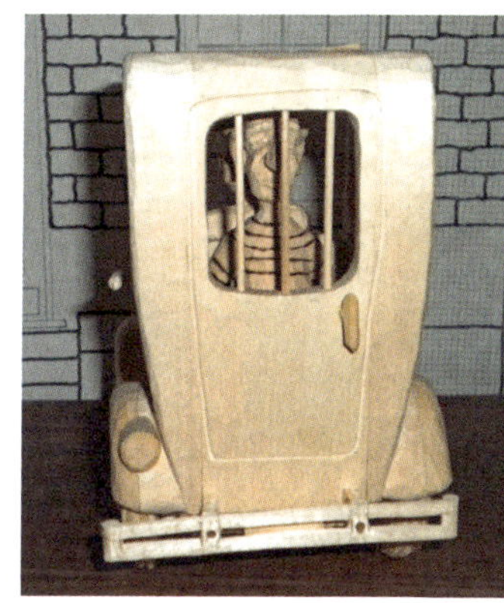

Perp goes for ride

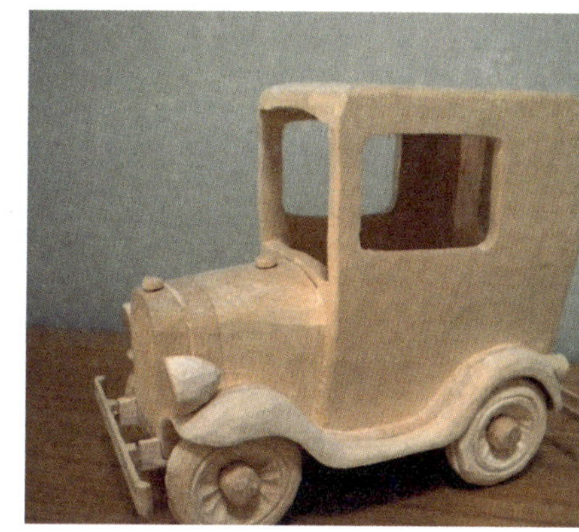

Ready to paint

Tip from Eldon Humphreys

• I rough draw the subject first, usually from a stick figure, and then flesh it out. I place the rough drawing on a light table, and using it as a guide, I draw the final detailed figure to be used as the pattern on a piece of cardboard.

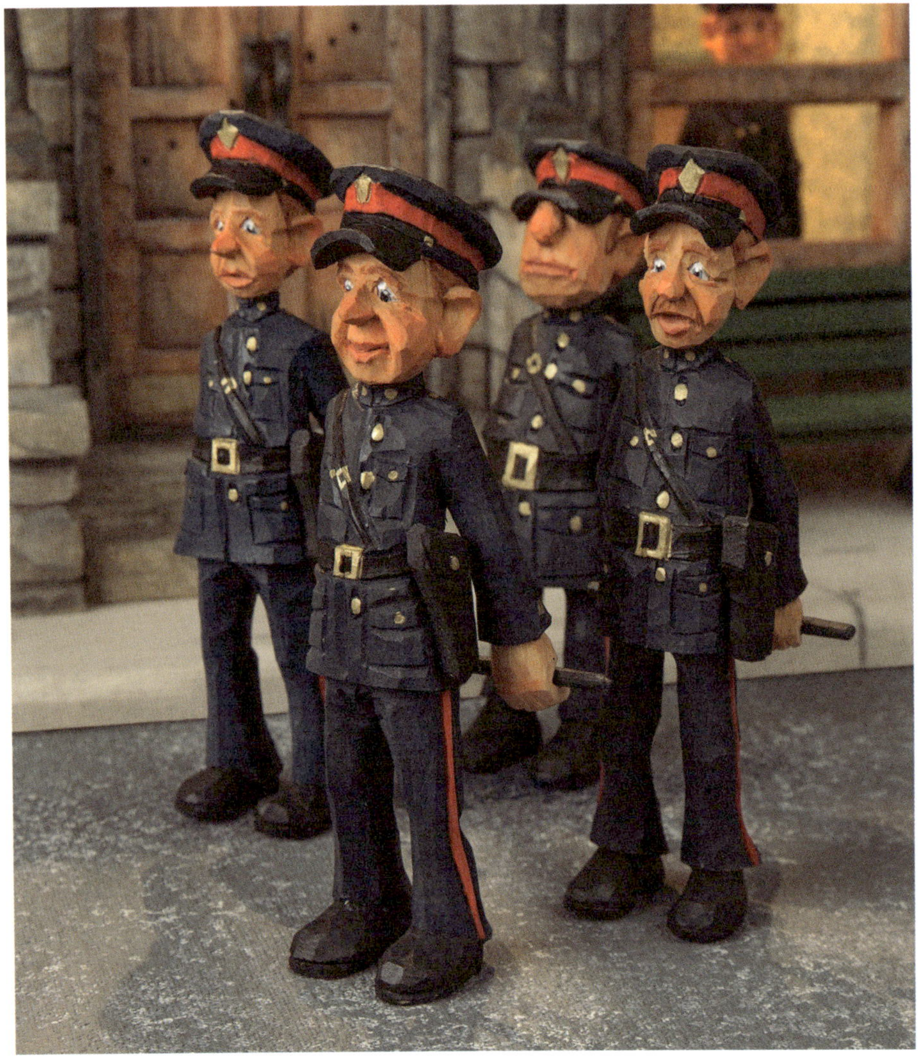

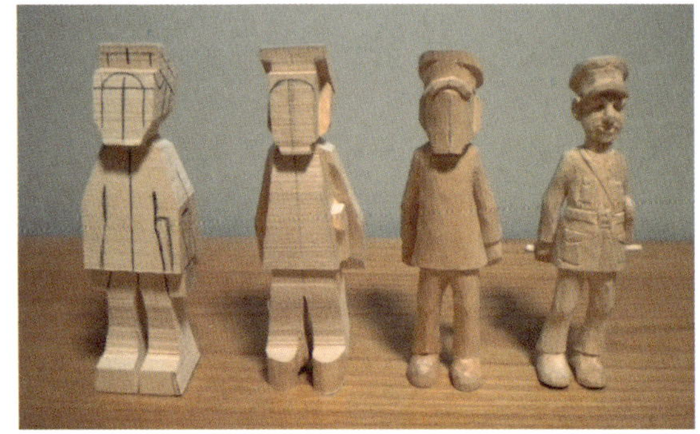

Cop with baton, front

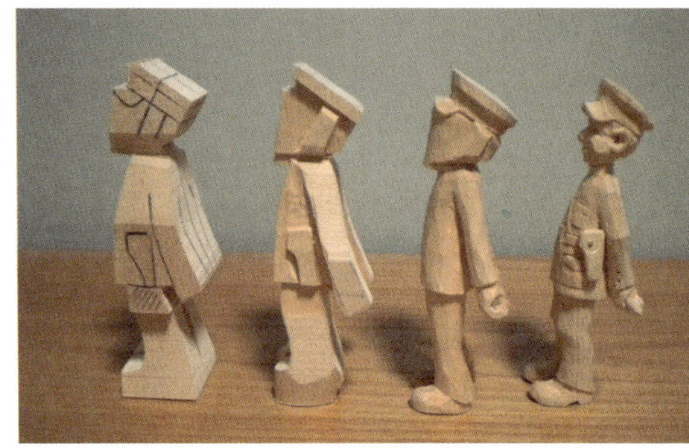

Cop with baton, left side

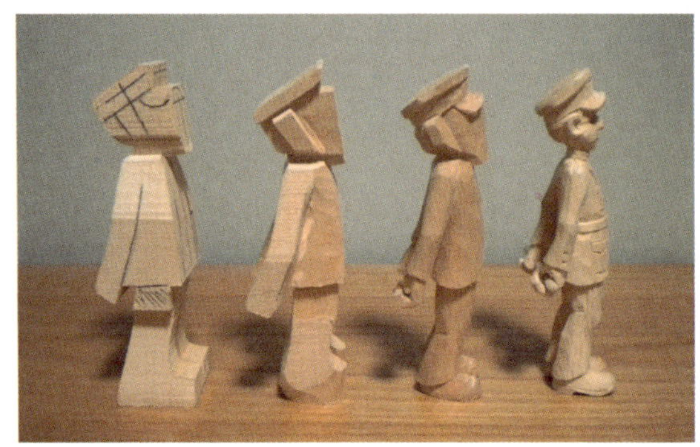

Cop with baton, right side

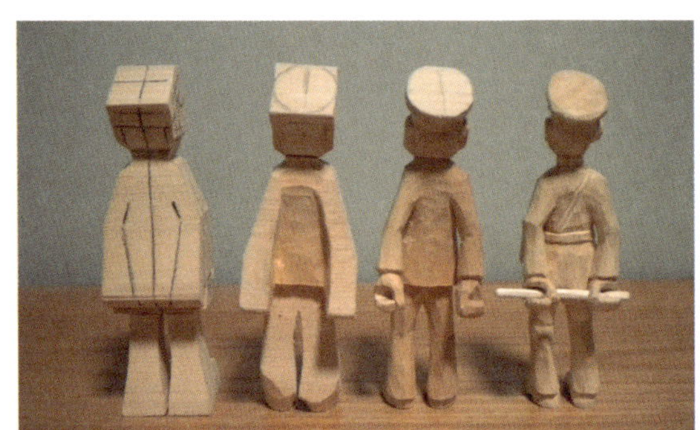

Cop with baton, back

The figures are carved mostly from one piece of wood, following the regular routine of blocking out, rounding, and detailing as demonstrated in the various pictures of the standing police officer.

—Eldon Humphreys

I love challenges ... and carving for the 1930's Street Scene certainly has been an enjoyable "double-dog dare." The possibilities were endless. My goal was to fill a need for caricatures to go along with the buildings that had been previously chosen. After settling on an idea, I visit the "images" section of the internet or use the library to research photos/illustrations. If I have a specific pose in mind for a human caricature, I persuade my husband to pose for me, or to take pictures of me in the desired posture. The next step is to construct an armature as a skeleton to support the weight of a clay model. I use illustrations of human or animal skeletons for the correct proportions. Utilizing a computer graphics program I can scale a drawing to the size required, print it and then transfer the measurements with calipers to the armature. I use a non-hardening clay (Plastalina) to create a "go-by." A tip that my mom taught me is to scratch a bar of soap (such as Ivory) to fill in under your nails before using the clay. It prevents the clay from accumulating under your nails and makes clean up quick. Creating a model in clay takes carvings to the next level. Any detail added to the clay will be a constant reminder of what not to carve away.

—Sandy Smith

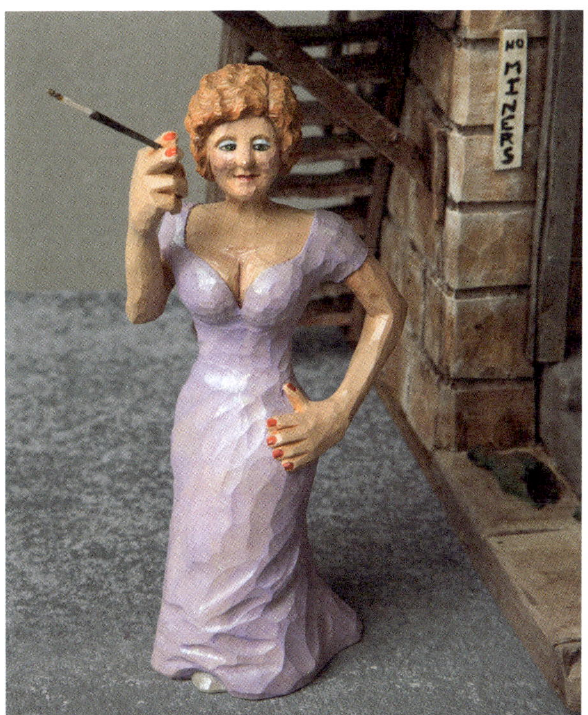

Lady of the evening

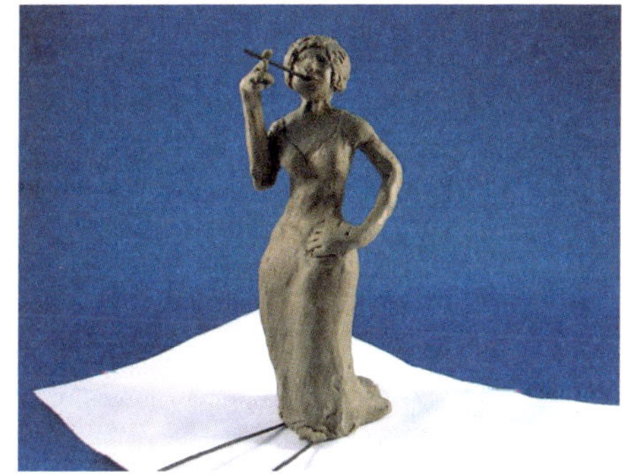

Clay, front

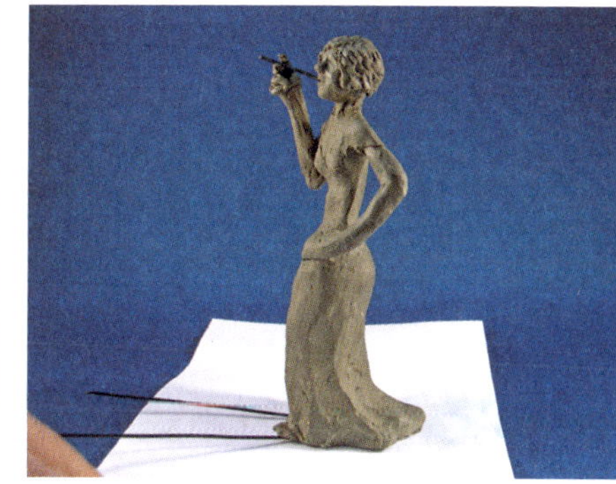

Clay, left side

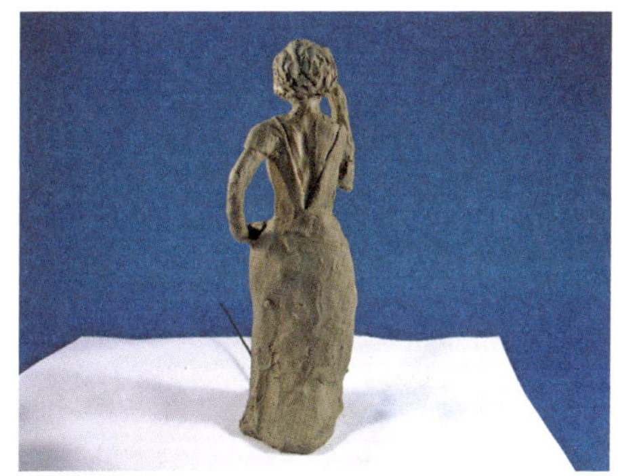

Clay, back

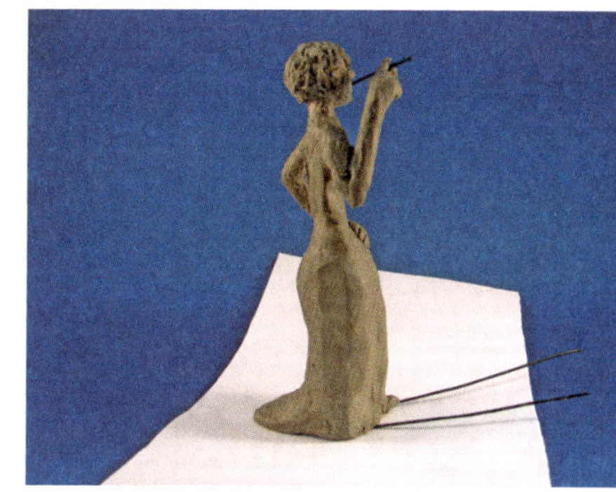

Clay, right side

Having a model to view from all angles (not just from sketches) is invaluable. When the clay "go-by" is to my liking, I will either photograph or trace around the model from two adjacent sides. If the figure is not too big, I will shine a bright light from behind the model so it casts a shadow on index paper. I draw around the shadow to create a pattern. The pattern can be transferred onto the basswood by using carbon paper or by cutting out the pattern and tracing around it. Make sure that the adjacent sides of your wood match up to the corresponding sides from which the patterns were drawn. If the carving is relatively small, I will use a scroll saw. Otherwise, a band saw is used to cut out the blank. I make certain that the centerlines are defined before I begin the carving.

—Sandy Smith

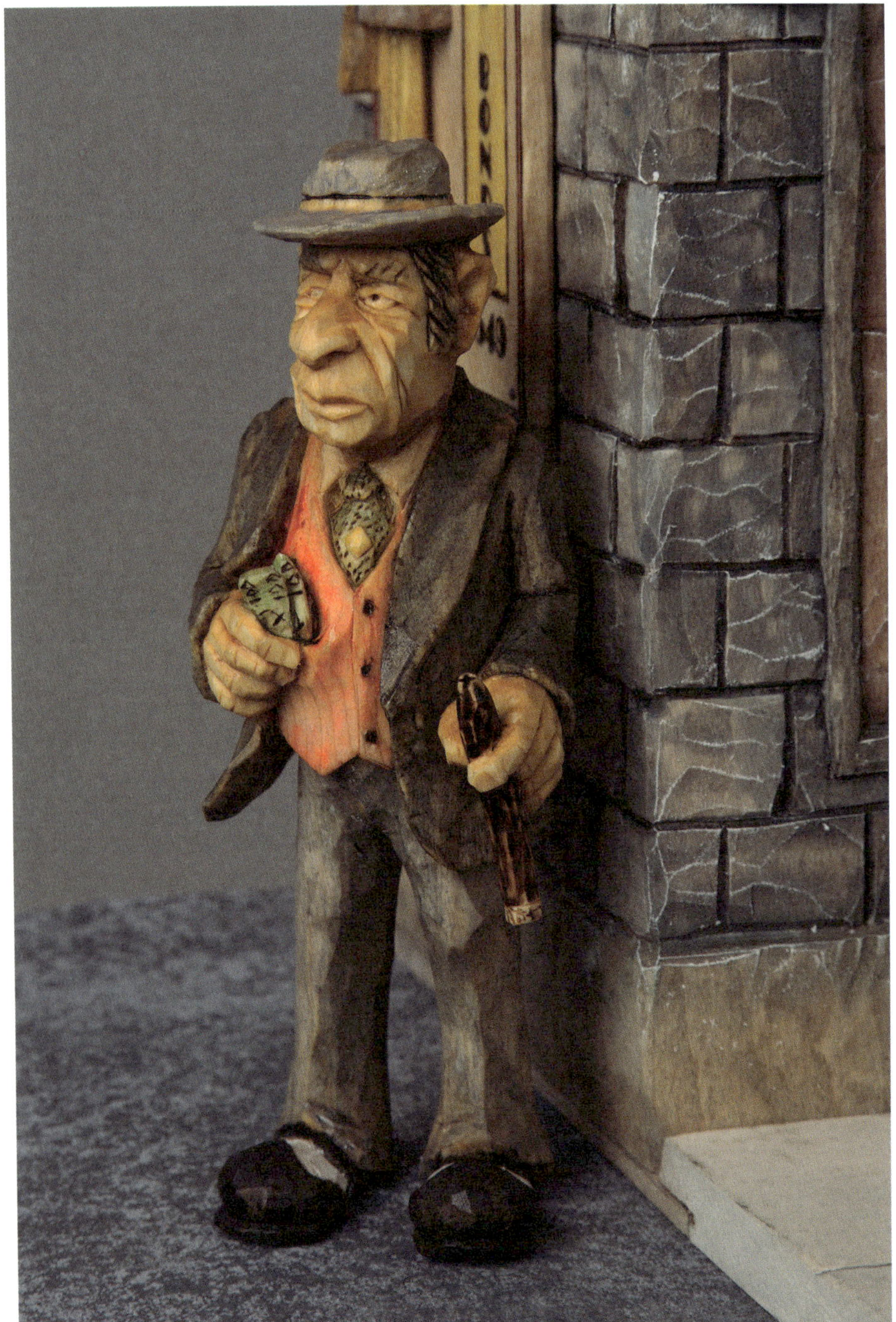

Politician

The ideas for individual figures for the 1930s Street Scene came by thinking about who would be on the sidewalks of a typical street in the 1930s. From a list of ideas, I chose four; an organ grinder with a monkey (CCA Bank), a street sweeper (Clyde's Auto Repair), a hot dog vendor (Lone Star Barber Shop), and a politician. In my initial research, I looked for period photographs of the subjects. These pictures, combined with my mental images, were melded together to form the genesis of the carving process. The period photographs gave clothing style as well as equipment identifiable with each figure. The politician has a wink in his eye and is busy poking money into a vest pocket, all while sporting a diamond stick pin in his tie, and smoking a long, expensive cigar.

—Don Mertz

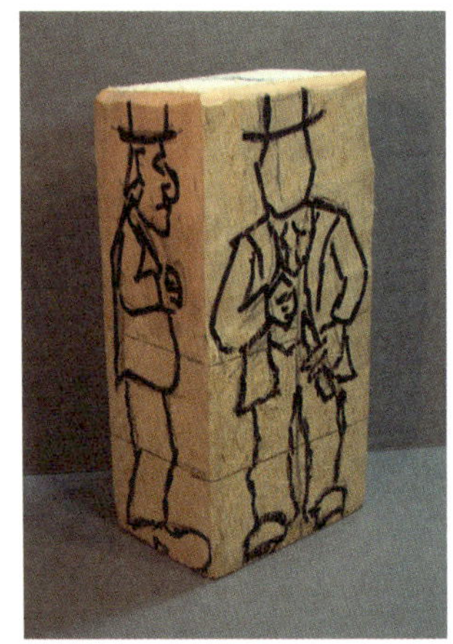

Pattern on wood

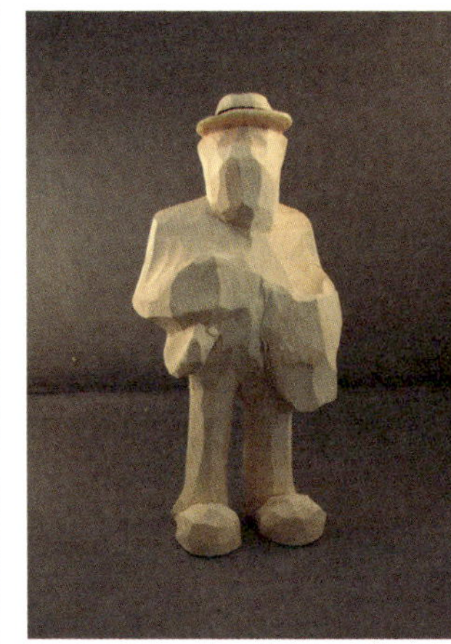

Roughed out, front

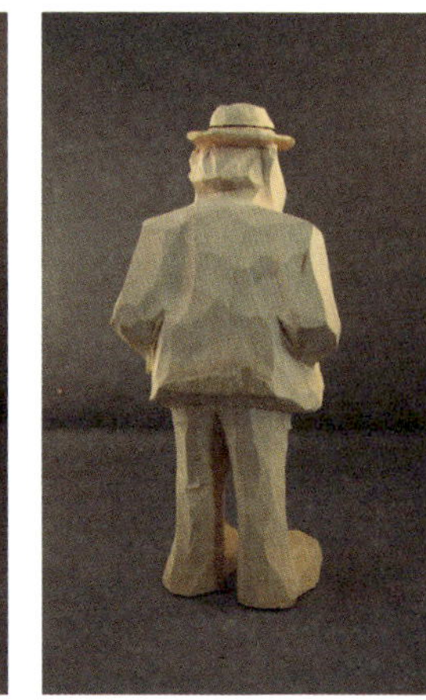

Roughed out, back

Tip from Don Mertz

• Ninety-five percent of a carving project is to carve basic form. Five percent is carving the details—the icing on the cake. To put icing on a half-baked cake would be the same as carving the details before there is a proper foundation to take the details.

Once the subject is carved to its basic silhouette image form, a good foundation exists to carve individual areas of the whole form in detail. Treat each area as a new and separate carving. For example, each shoe is a block form that is ready to receive the details that make it a shoe. Each hand is a form with angles and planes that can illustrate features of fingers, knuckles and wrinkles that make it a hand. Detail carving is the reward the carver gives himself for having a proper foundation upon which to add details.

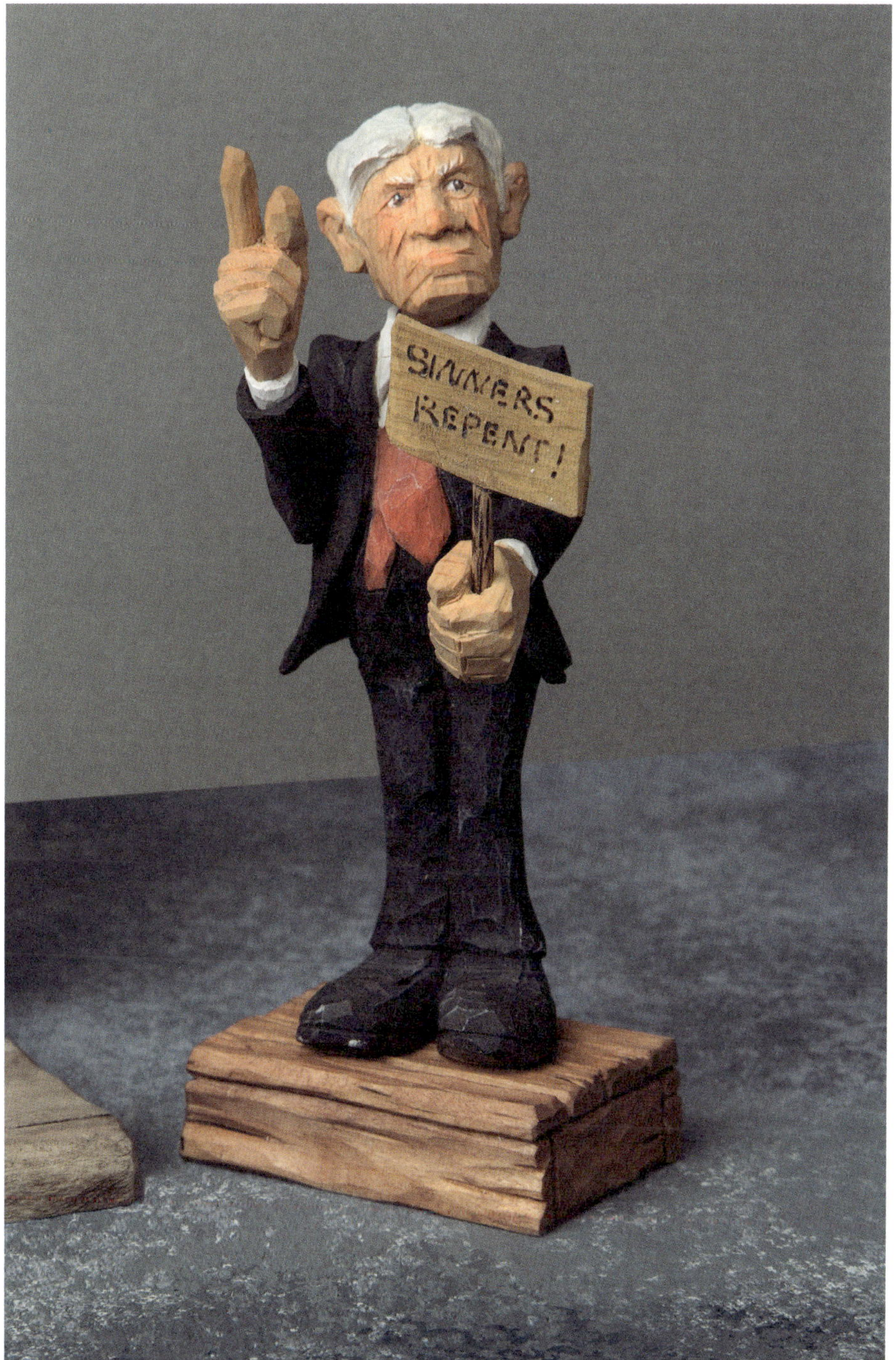

Protestor

The outraged protestor was carved with the extending finger larger than normal to emphasize his extreme displeasure with the activities in the massage parlor and its clientele. Although the hands and head were carved separately, all could be carved as one piece. The rigid stance was intentionally selected to suggest his state of mind. The "soap box" was carved to provide a platform for his discourse.

—Gene Fuller

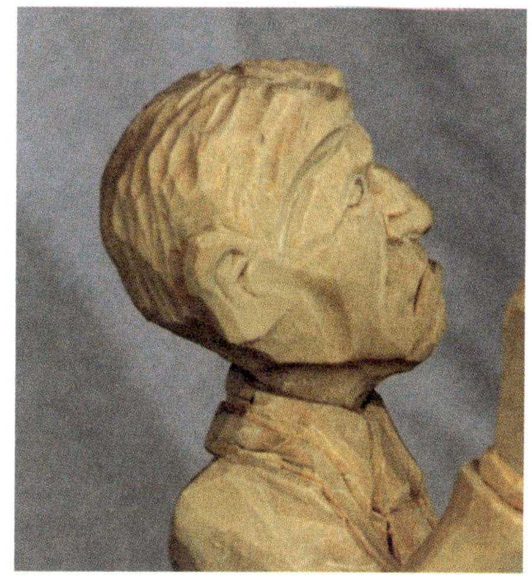

Head close-up

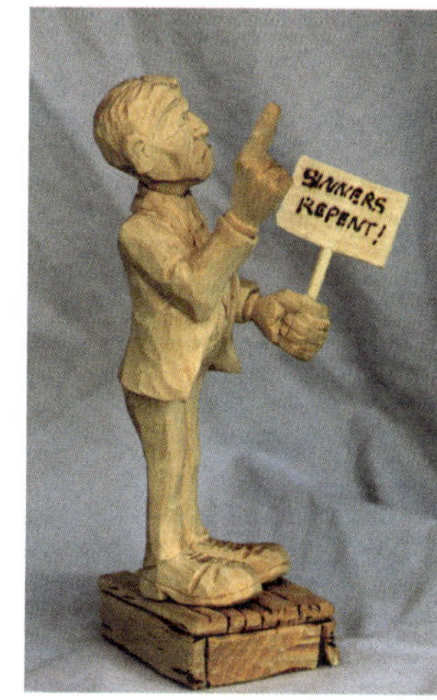

Ready to paint

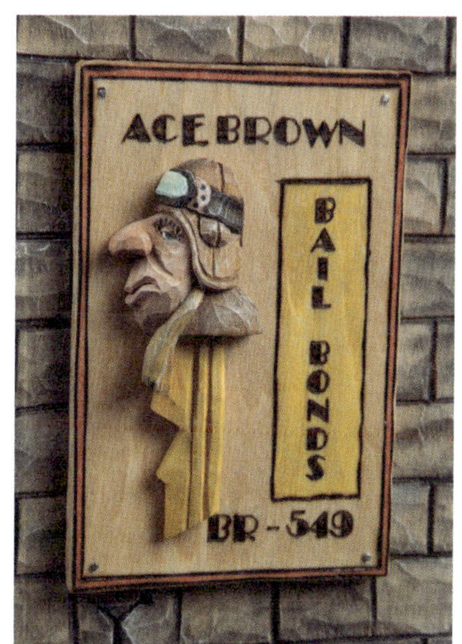

Tom Brown has always been fascinated by pilots. If you've seen Tom's work, you already know that. The sign, Ace Brown's Bail Bonds, incorporates Tom's distinctive carving style and his unique sense of humor. Plus the information is a necessity for those poor innocent souls spending time in the jail.

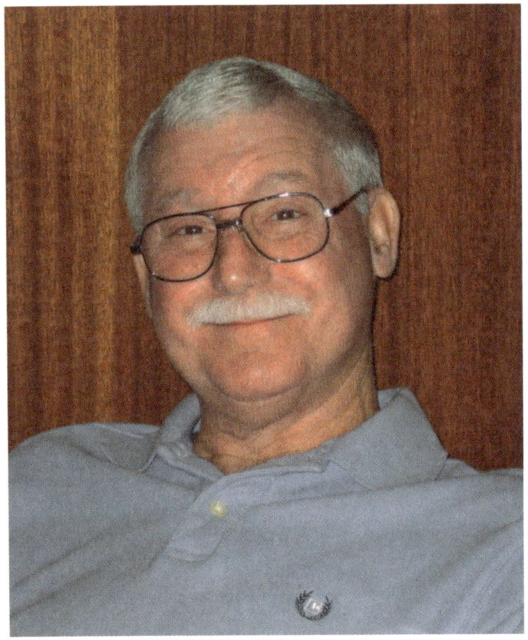

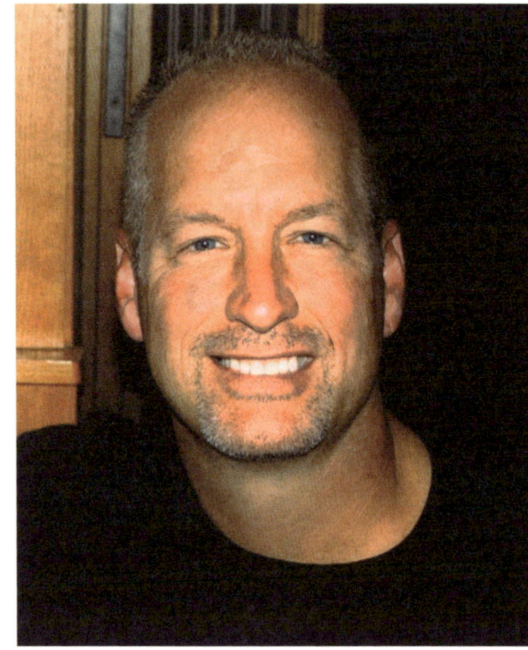

Tom Brown

Tom Brown lived in Converse, Indiana, with his wife, Suzi. As a young man, Tom joined the U.S. Navy, in 1963, and served aboard the aircraft carrier U.S.S. *Essex*. He later worked at and retired from the Chrysler Corporation in 1989. In addition, Tom was an Eagle Scout and Scoutmaster, where he first encountered woodcarving. Inspired by Harold Enlow, Dave Dunham, and other founding members of the CCA, Tom decided to carve caricatures. Tom founded the Eastern Woodland Carvers Club (EWCC) in 1988. The EWCC is host to the CCA's National Caricature Carving Competition. Tom is most proud of being elected to the CCA in 1995. He taught classes across the U.S., specializing in teaching beginning carvers how to sharpen and use their tools. Tom also served as a judge at shows throughout the country, including the International Woodcarvers Congress and the CCA's National Competition.

Randy Landen

Randy Landen lives in Derby, Kansas, just south of Wichita. He and his wife, Carol, collect wood carvings, and as you might suspect, caricatures dominate their collection.

Randy began carving in 1990. Many of the ideas for his carvings come from the situations he's seen in over 32 years as a police officer. Randy currently serves as a captain, in charge of the Wichita Police Department's Vice and Narcotics Unit.

Being a part of the CCA since 1994 has allowed him the opportunity to carve with many of the people who influenced and encouraged him as a new carver. Randy teaches carving and painting seminars on request. He enjoys repairing damaged and broken carvings, and buys and sells carvings on the secondary art market through his website at www.landenwoodcarving.com.

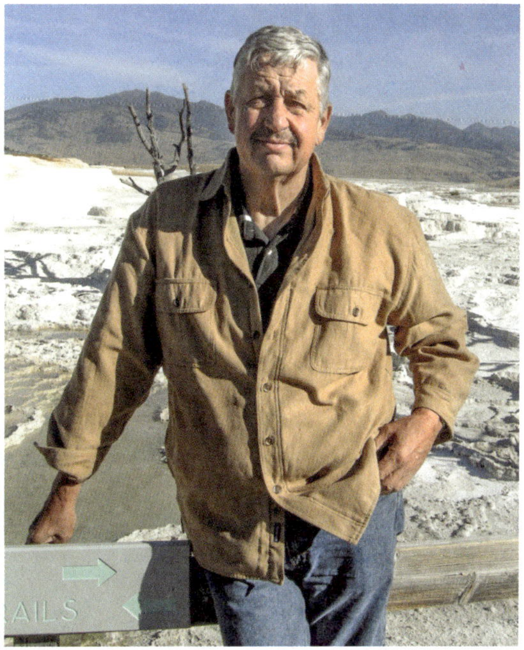

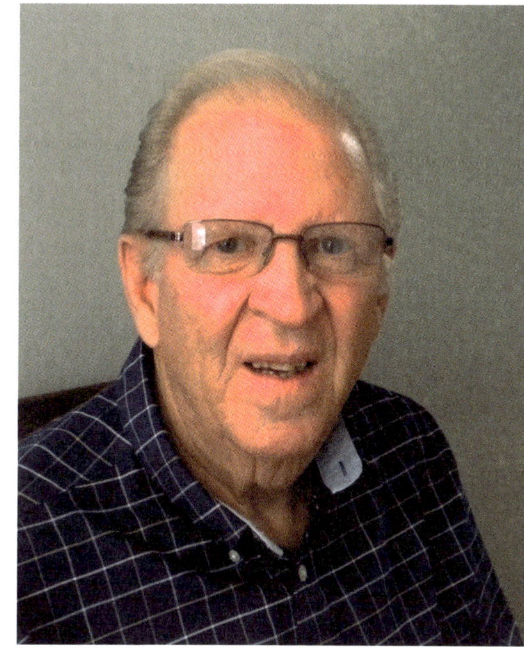

Dennis Thornton

For almost 20 years, Dennis has been enjoying caricature carving around the country, an art you could say he found by accident. Toward the end of a 30-plus year career as a police officer, he was involved in a head-on car crash while working. During his two-year recovery a friend pointed him to a woodcarving school. While learning how to carve he soon found caricatures and the laughs and humor they gave him and others.

Within two years he had begun competing in carving competitions and won his first of many Best of Show Awards. Dennis began traveling around the country with his wife, Susan, exhibiting his work and instructing at seminars.

In 2000 he was inducted into the Caricature Carvers of America, where he has served as the Treasurer, Vice President, President, and Past President.

Eldon Humphreys

Eldon has been carving for nearly 30 years. He became interested in woodcarving while searching for something to keep him busy once he retired, after serving thirty-five years on the Ontario Provincial Police Force.

He developed his skill by taking a series of classes over many years at the Woodcarving Rendezvous in Branson, Missouri; with Marv Kaisersatt in Minnesota; and also with other teachers who were expert in caricature carving. He was invited to become a member of the CCA in 1996.

Eldon lives with his wife, Carol, in Guelph, Ontario. He continues to share his enthusiasm for woodcarving by encouraging new carvers to experience the art of woodcarving in general and caricature in particular, by teaching throughout North America.

PUB and MASSAGE PARLOR

Chris Hammack

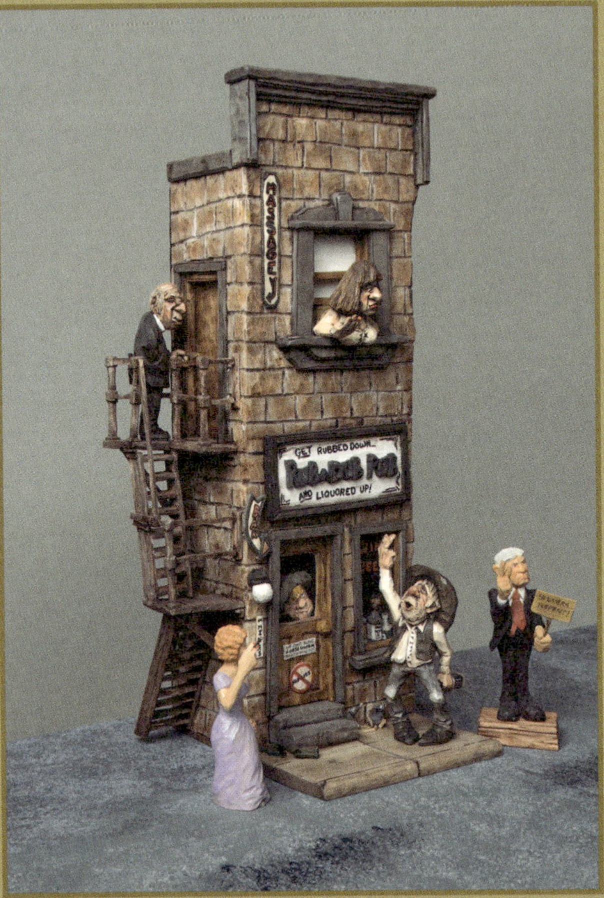

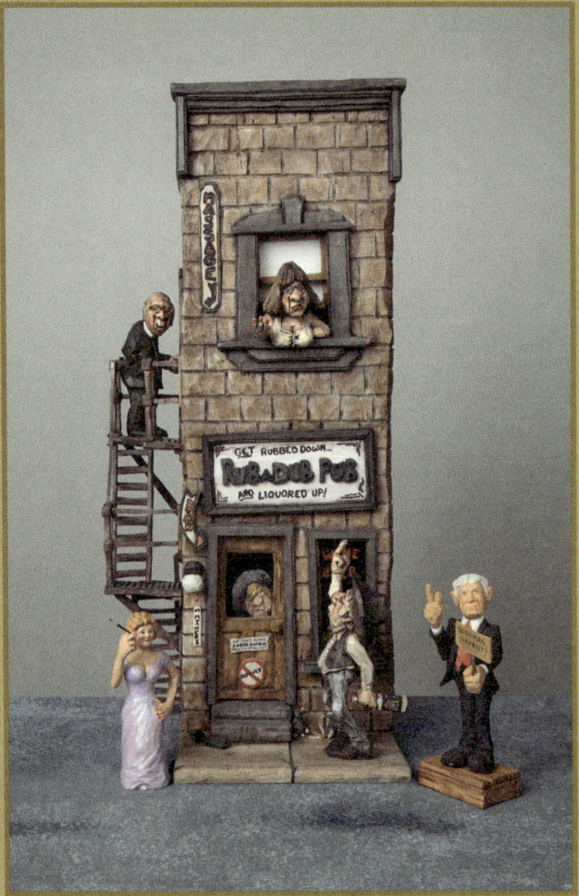

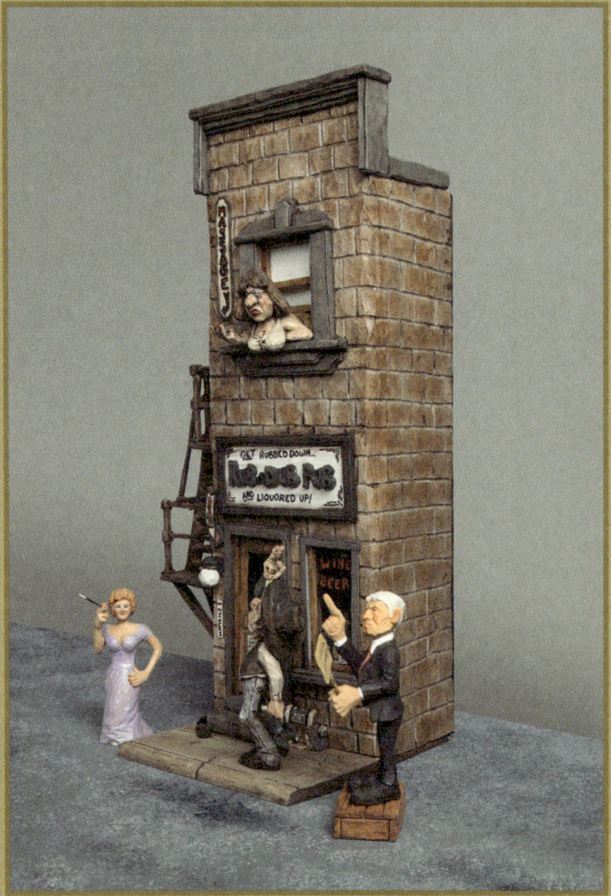

Being a western artist, when the CCA decided to do a thirties street scene, I immediately thought, "What would the cowboys I know and carve do, and where would they go if they found themselves in the big city in the 1930s?" Well, it didn't take me long to figure out the answer to this question. That became the initial inspiration for this carving of an old cowboy doing a little big city "negotiating." His buddy, obviously a bit over-served, is still inside the bar seemingly having a bit of trouble finding the door handle.

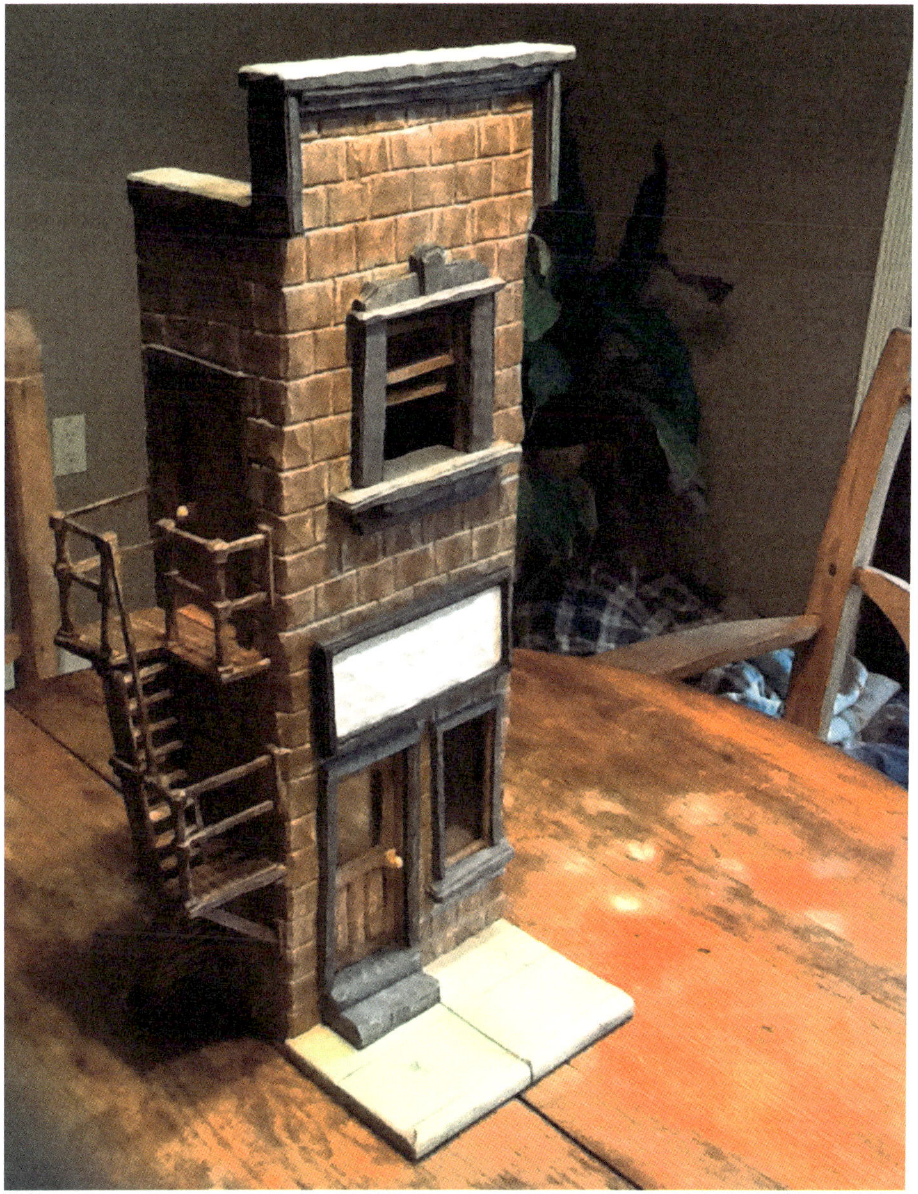

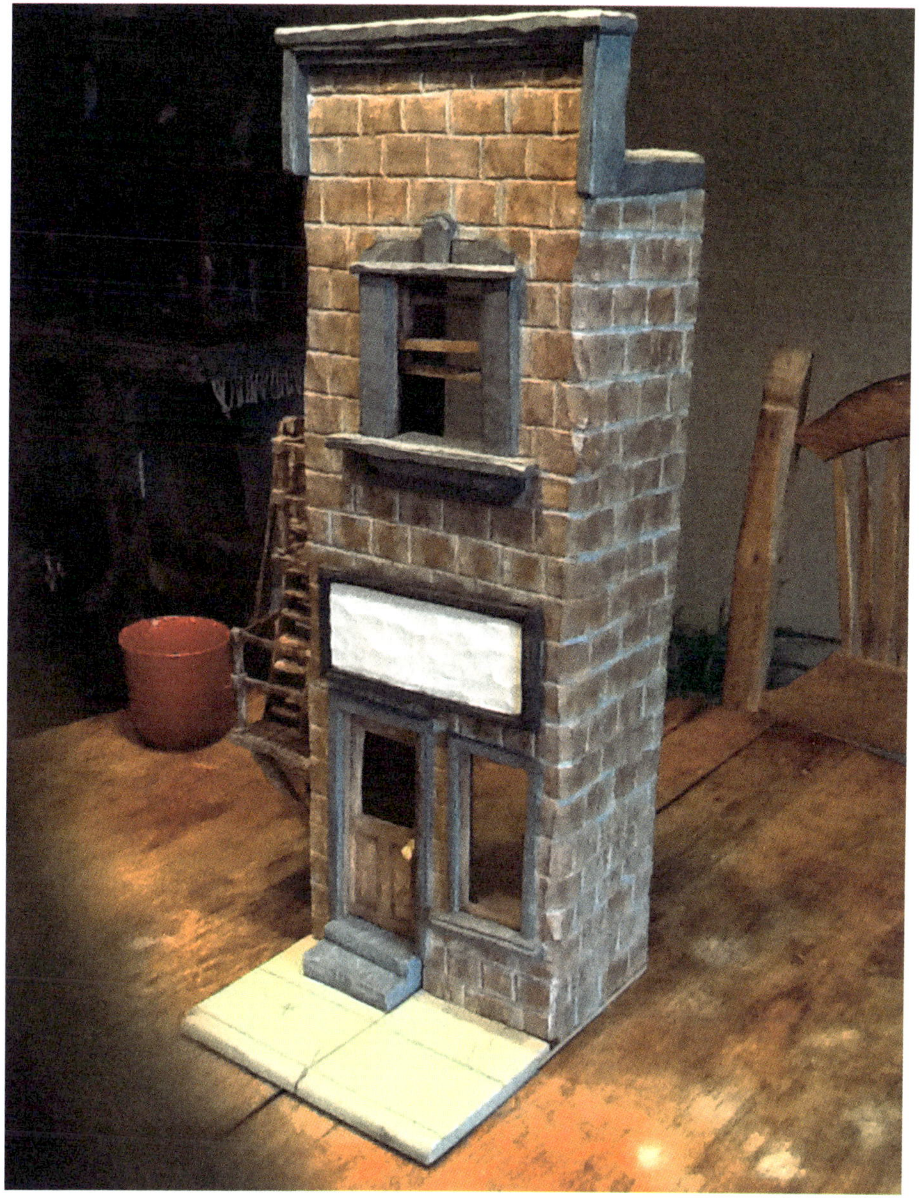

I roughed in the outside of the building using ½" plywood, and covered that with 3/8" basswood to carve in the bricks and other architectural elements. The building is roughly 8" wide, 24" tall, and 10" deep, including the 5" sidewalk. The stairway is just pieced together one stair step and one railing at a time. Super glue, some spray accelerator, and a mild sedative were of great help in constructing this part of the scene.

When deciding where this building should be placed, it seemed only logical it should be near the source of its main clientele. Naturally, that put it right between the police station and the firehouse.

I like the little details of a carving so I added a couple of drunken street rats to the scene and an apprehensive client on the alley stairway to give added interest.

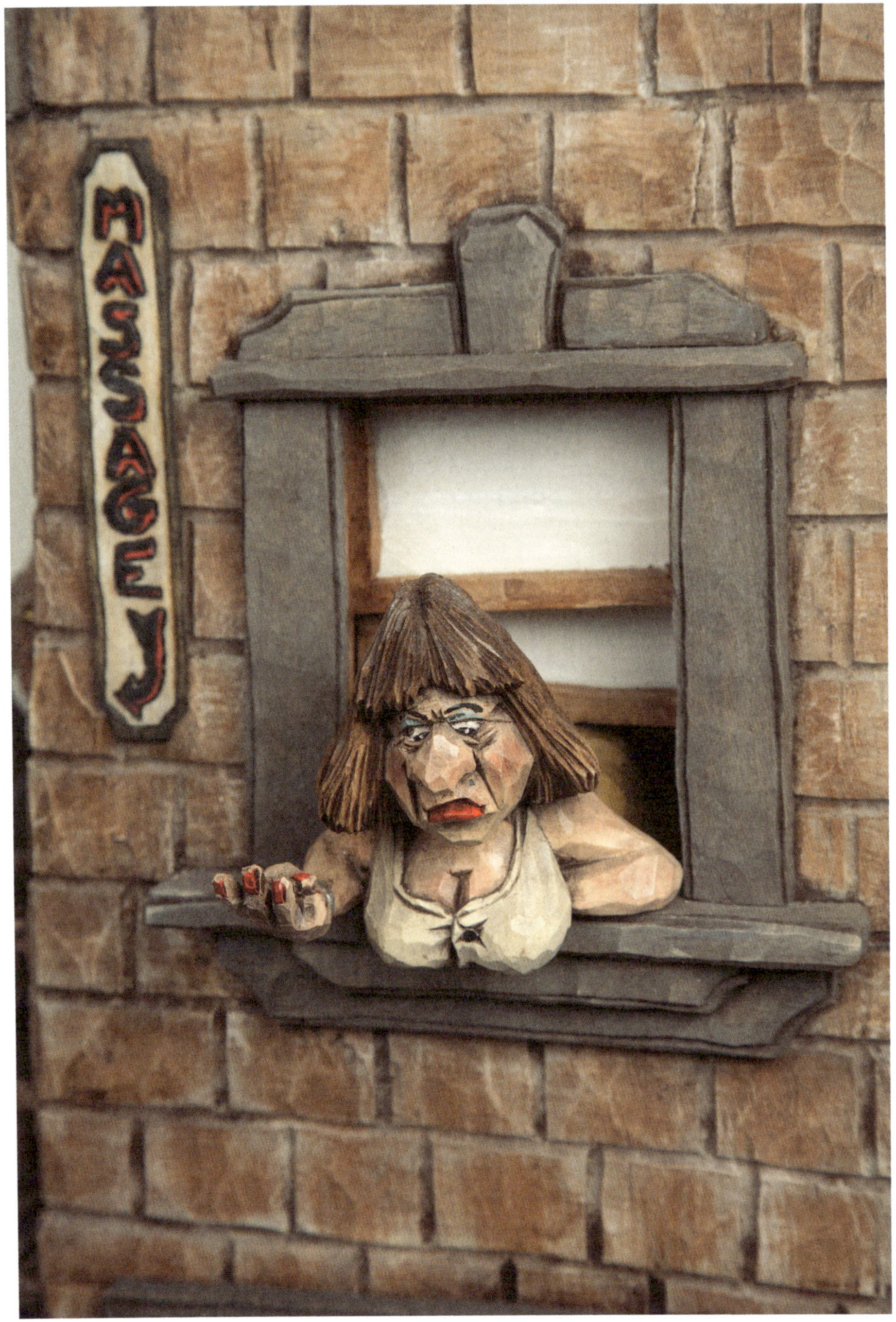

Masseuse

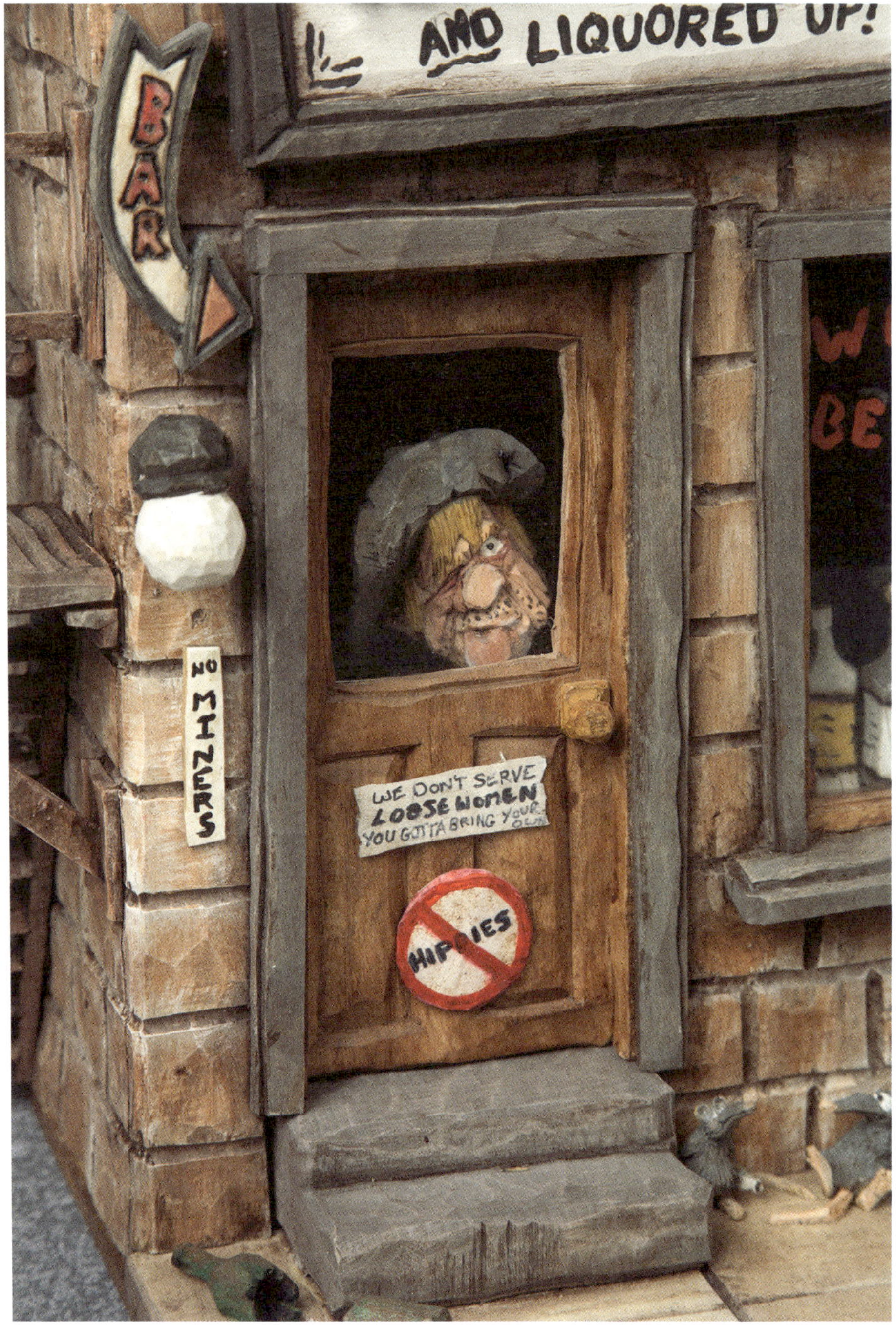

Face in door window

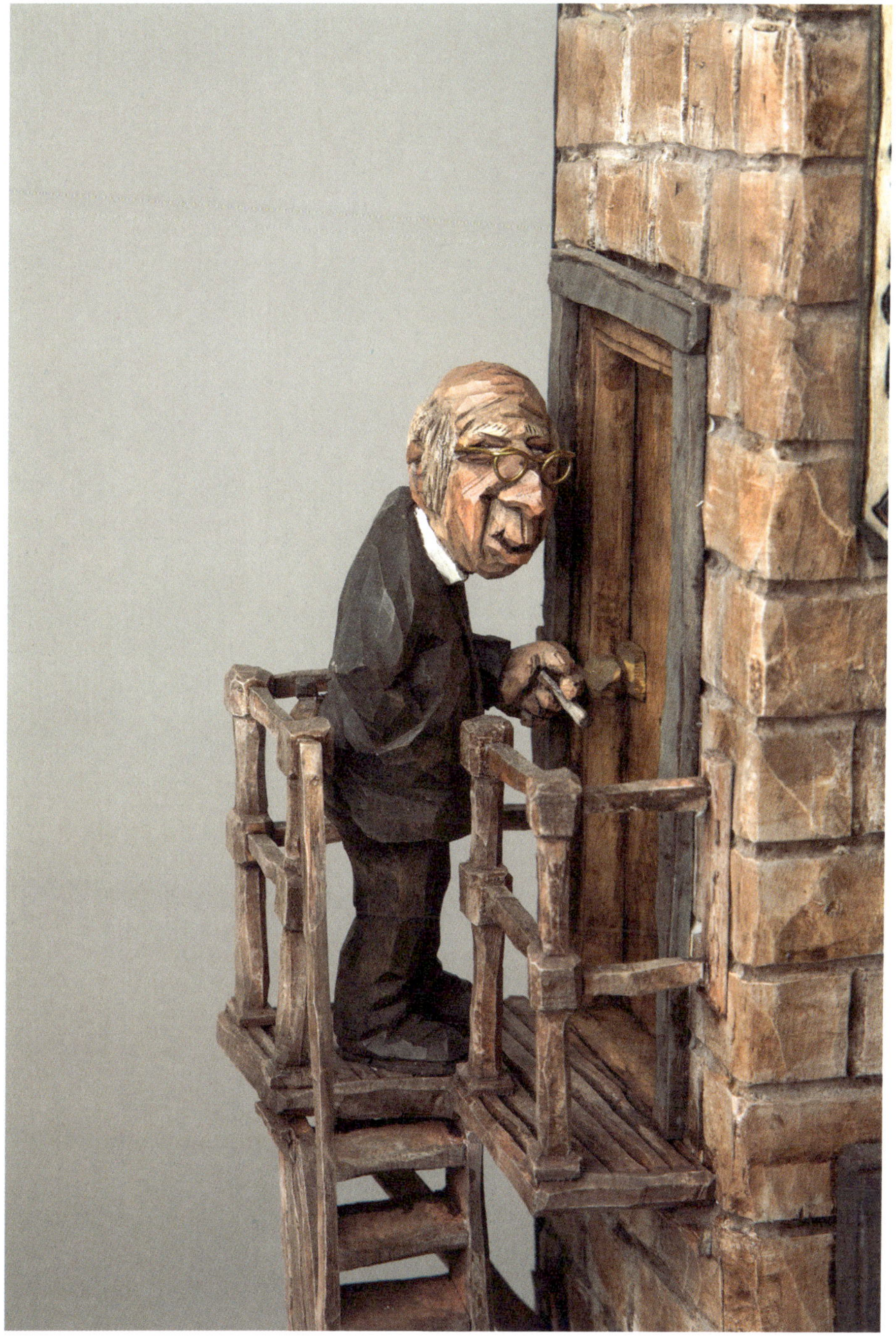

Preacher

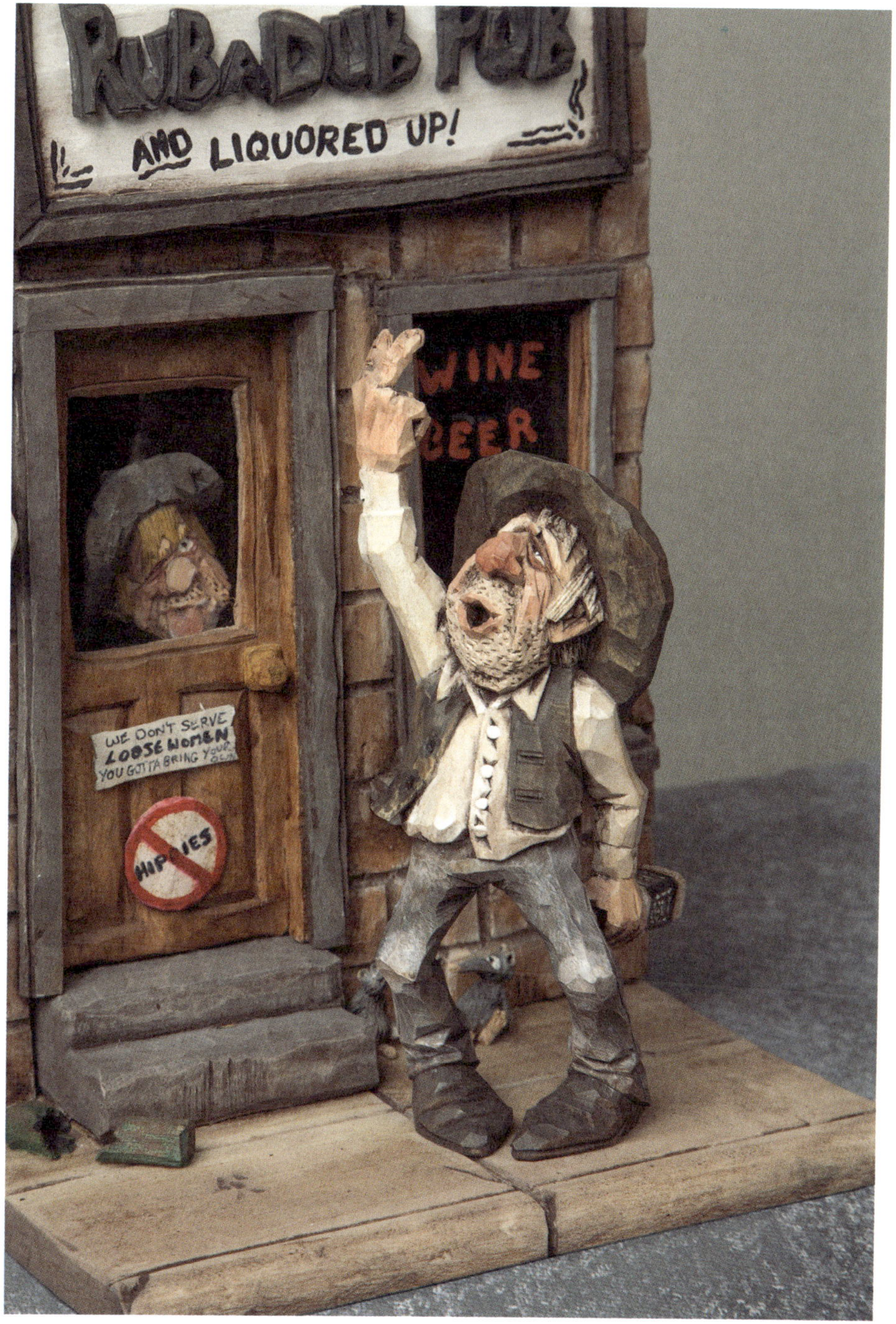

Negotiating cowboy

Good luck carving this snapshot of a big city "negotiation" cowboy style.

—Chris Hammack

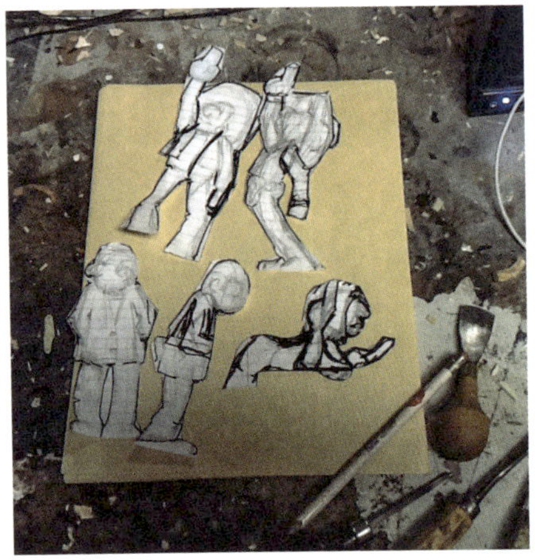

Start with sketches

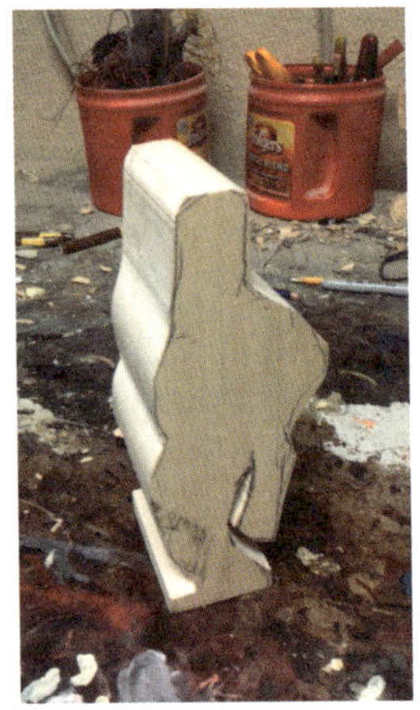

Band sawed blank

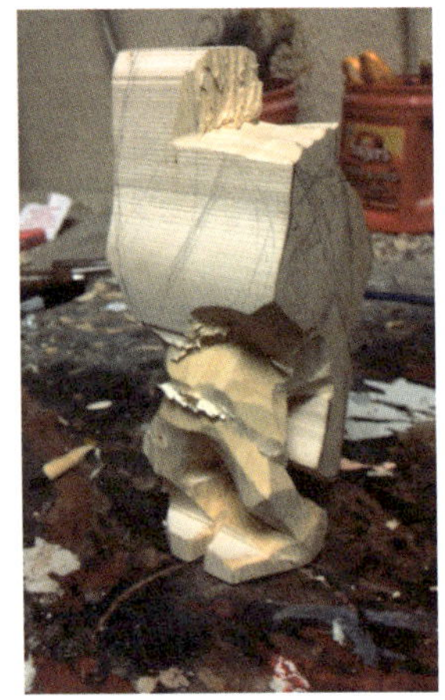

Legs roughed out

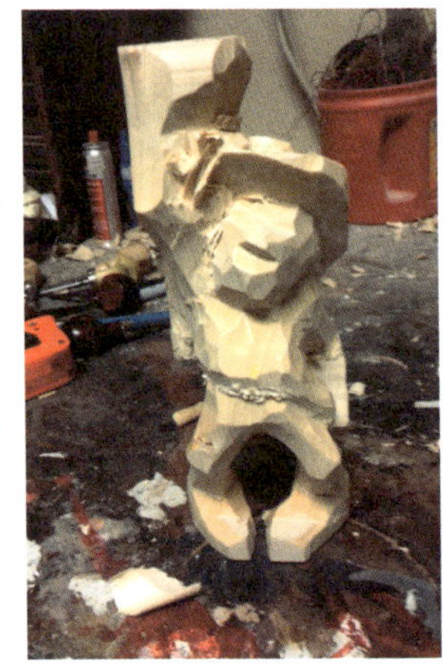

Legs, chest, head roughed out

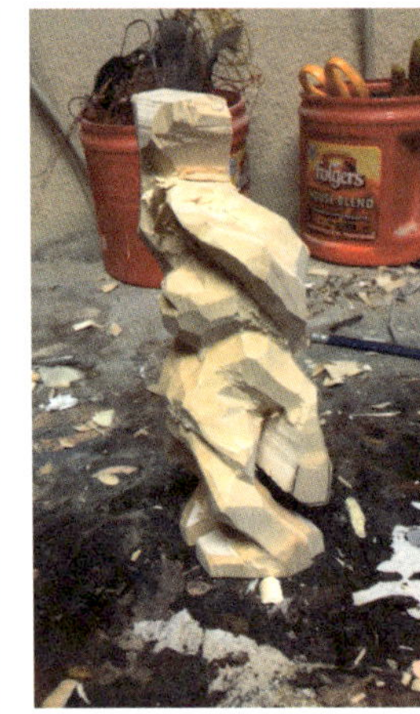

Side view

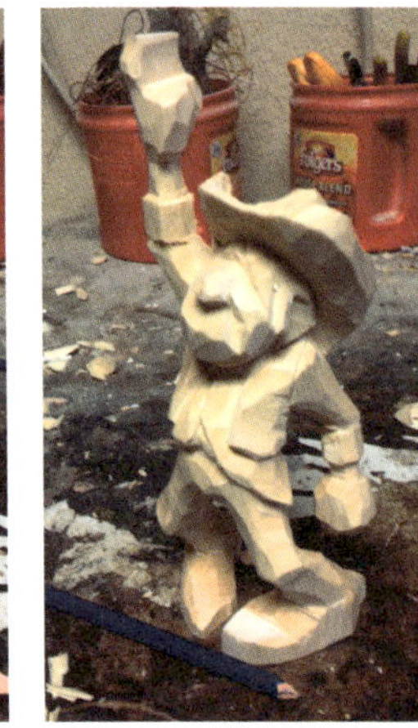

Mostly roughed out, showing hand

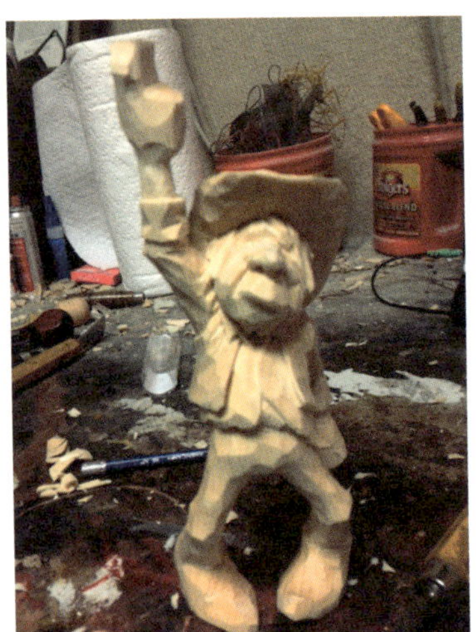

Face roughed out

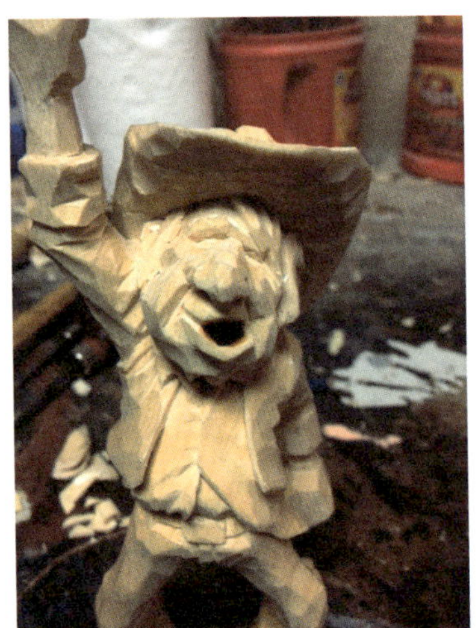

Facial detail

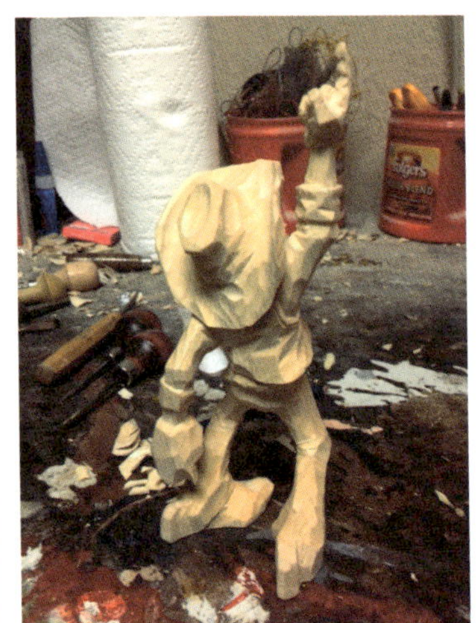

Mostly roughed out, back view

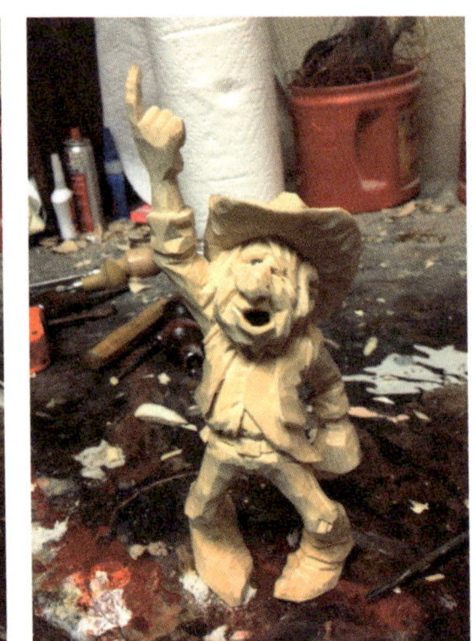

Almost ready to paint

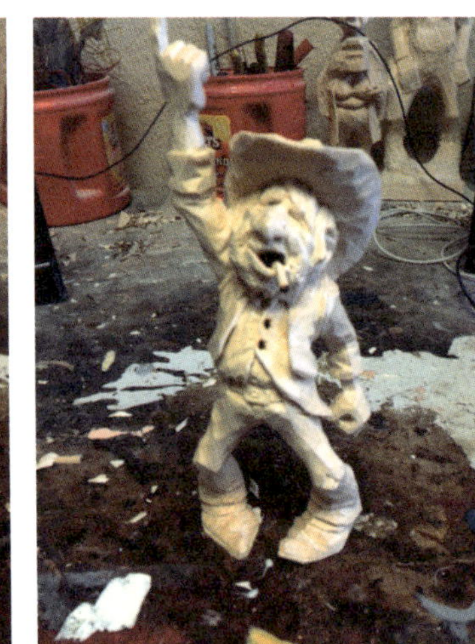

Ready to paint, cigarette added

First thoughts

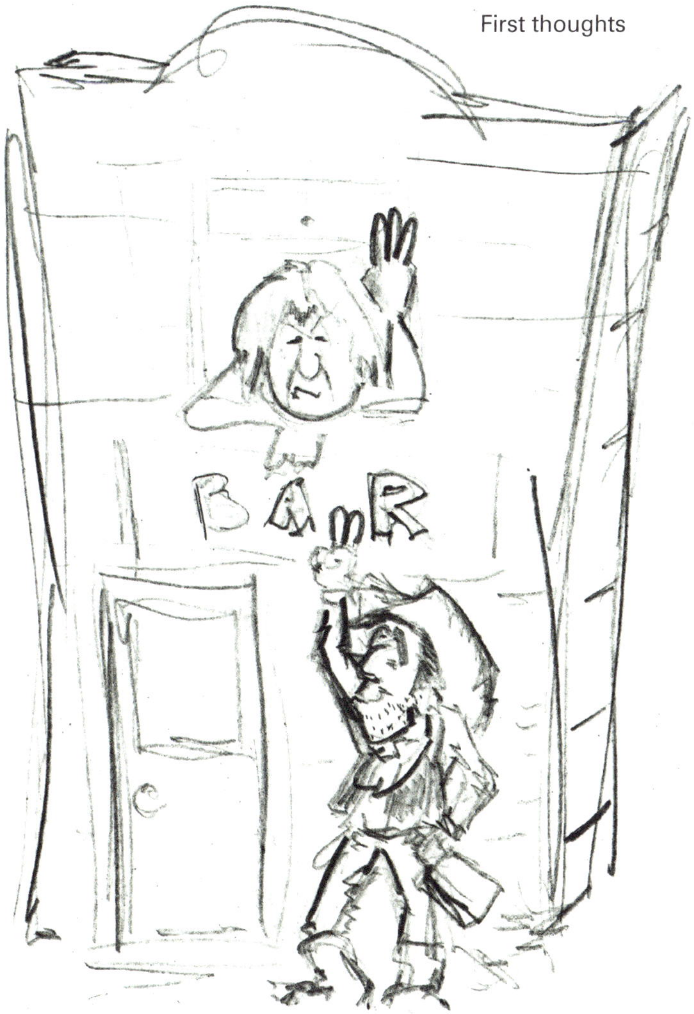

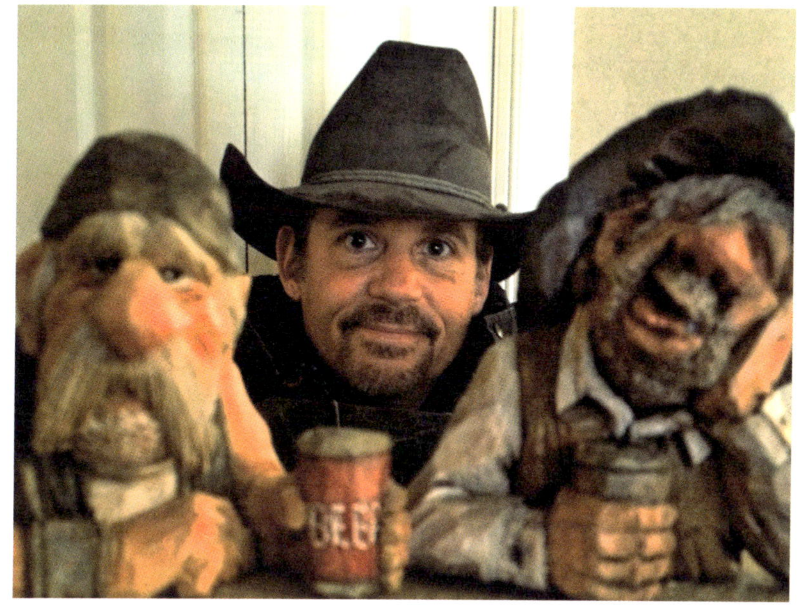

Tip from Chris Hammack

•Keep your knife sharp, wash your hands often so your carving won't be so dirty, and don't whittle naked.

Chris Hammack

Chris' carving career began 28 years ago, after a thirty-foot fall landed him in the hospital. During a five-month convalescence, he picked up a piece of firewood and a pocket knife and began carving caricatures, the same caricatures he sketched as a young boy growing up in Texas. Within two years, Chris began competing in carving competitions, winning numerous first place awards. The following years brought national seminars and carvings presented to U.S. Senators, mayors, and actors. Chris' artwork has been featured on Leanin' Tree cards for over twenty years. Chris operated a successful business in Colorado, distributing his artwork around the globe. Today, Chris is back to his roots in Texas (Cow Town, USA) continually creating exciting new characters and scenes from a fresh block of wood. Through his artwork, Chris shares his intuitive understanding of the cowboy lifestyle and sense of humor.

FIRE STATION

PJ Driscoll, Peter Ortel and Sandy Smith

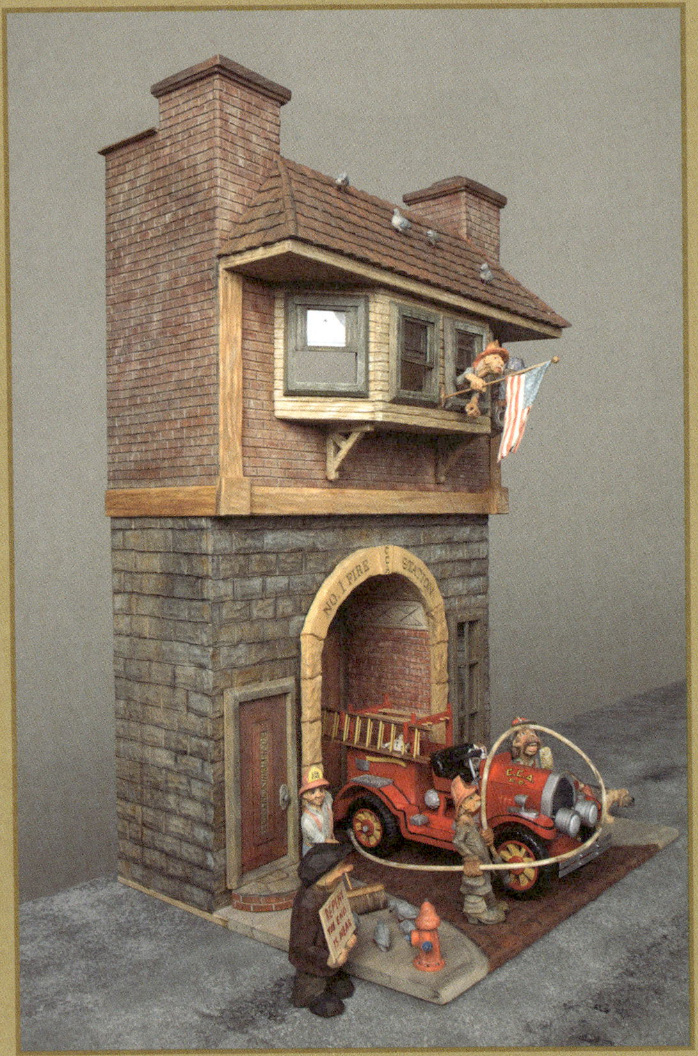

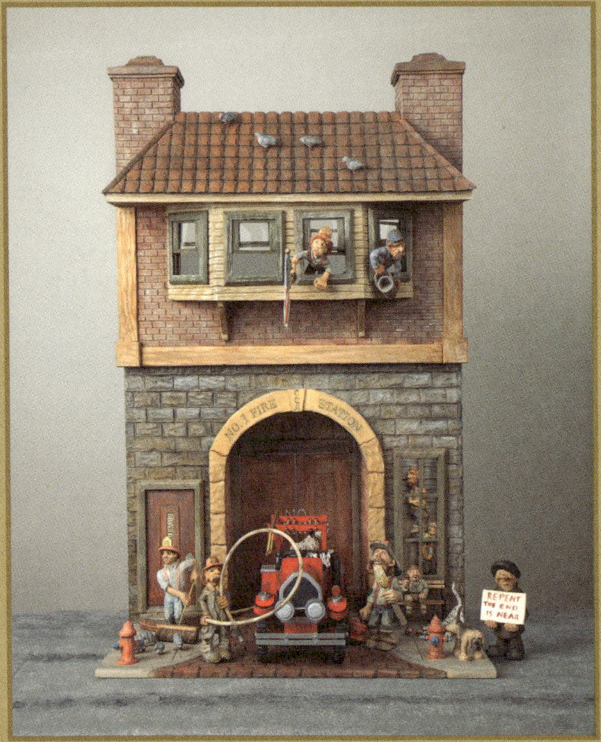

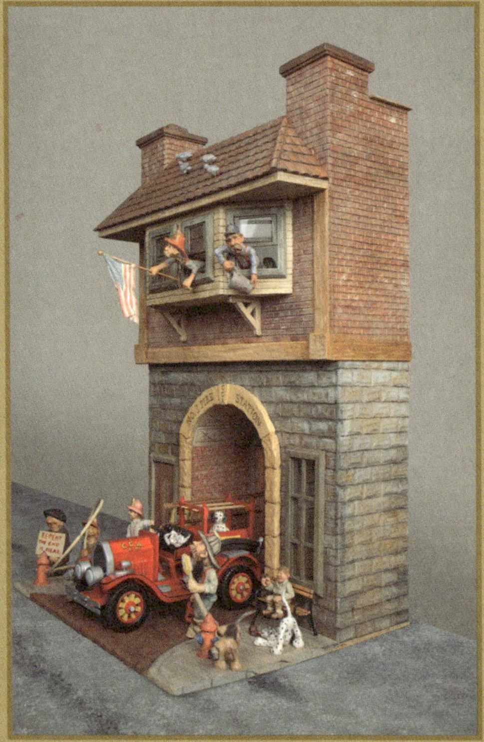

When the idea for this book popped up, the only thing that came to my mind was a 1930s fire station. What better people to have working with you on this scene than Peter Ortel, retired from the New York City Fire Department, and one of our newest members, Sandy Smith. These two great carvers made the project enjoyable.

After the meeting in September, 2011, we kicked the ideas around in our minds for a couple months, and then everything began to happen. After searching the web and e-mailing back and forth, Sandy sent the blueprint for the fire station. After a couple of adjustments by the three of us, I moved forward with the blueprint in my hand and the idea in my head. I had no idea how difficult this project would be, given the distance between us. Thank goodness we had e-mail and telephones. While building the fire station, Peter said, "What is a fire station without a fire truck?" So he started building the truck. In the meantime, Sandy continued to help by carving whatever firehouse caricature or accessory was needed.

—PJ Driscoll

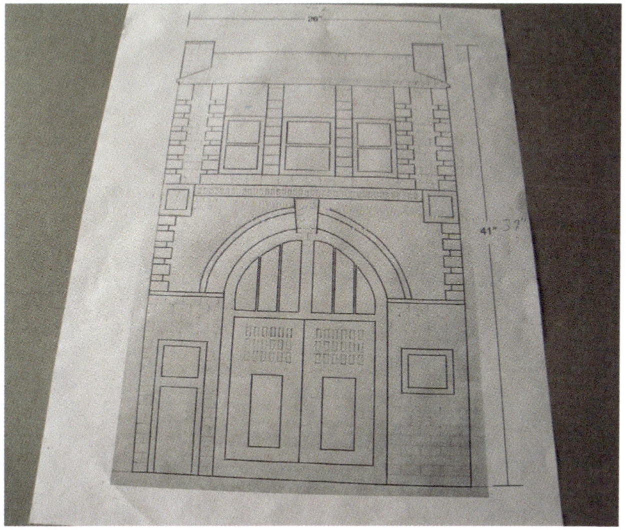

Plans

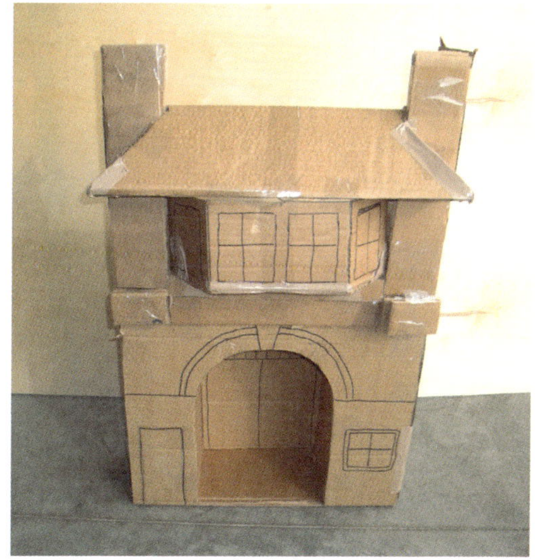

Cardboard model

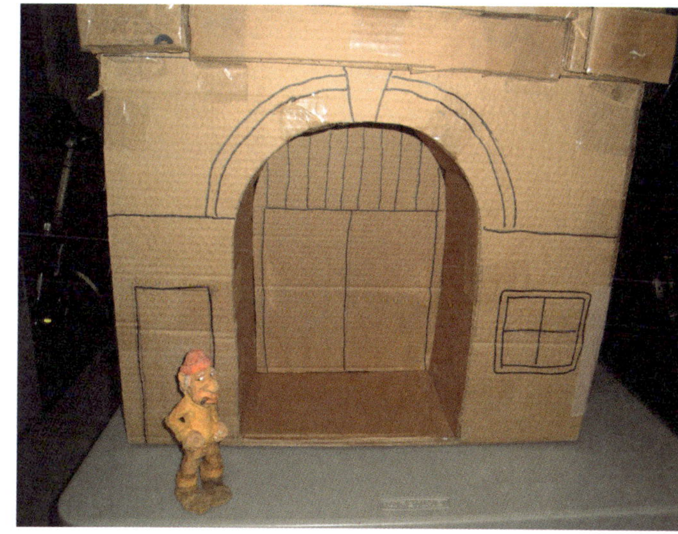

Model, ground floor

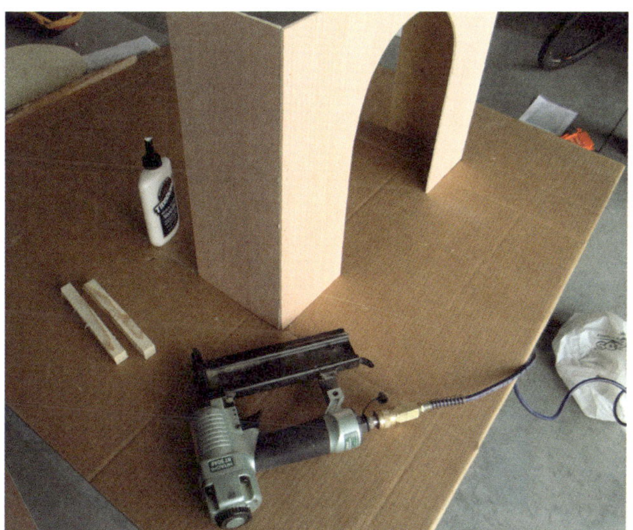

Construction underway

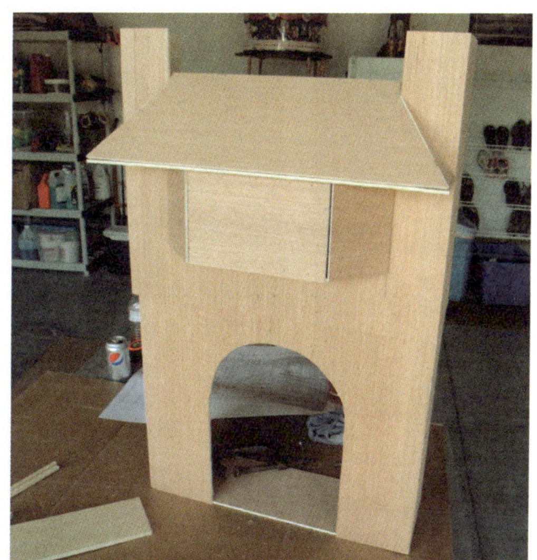

Making progress

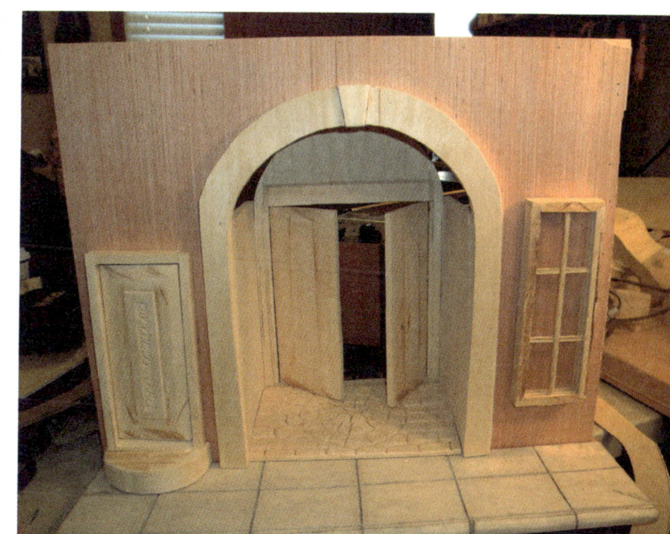

Doors and windows

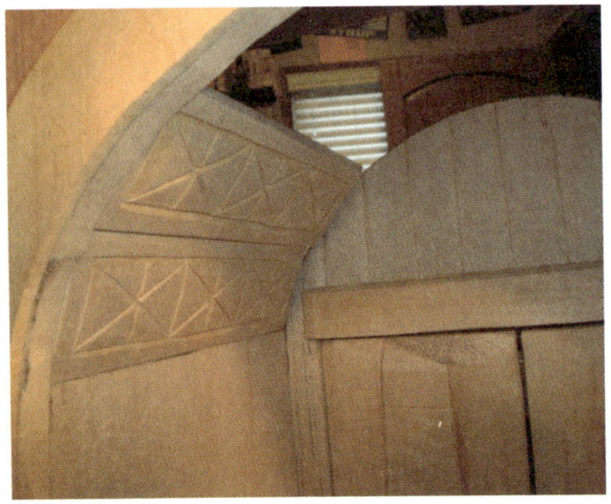

Entrance detail

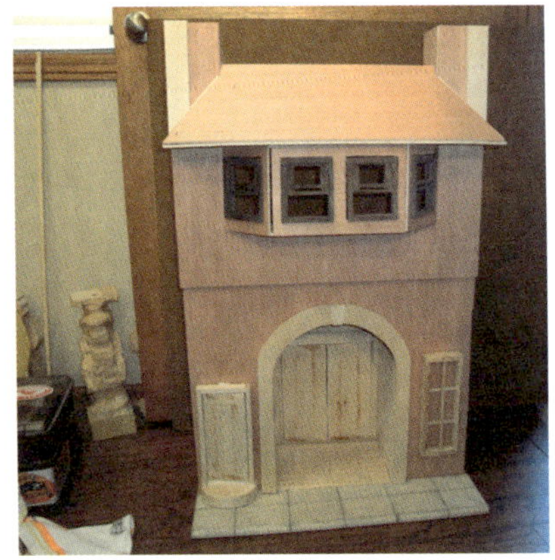

Taking shape

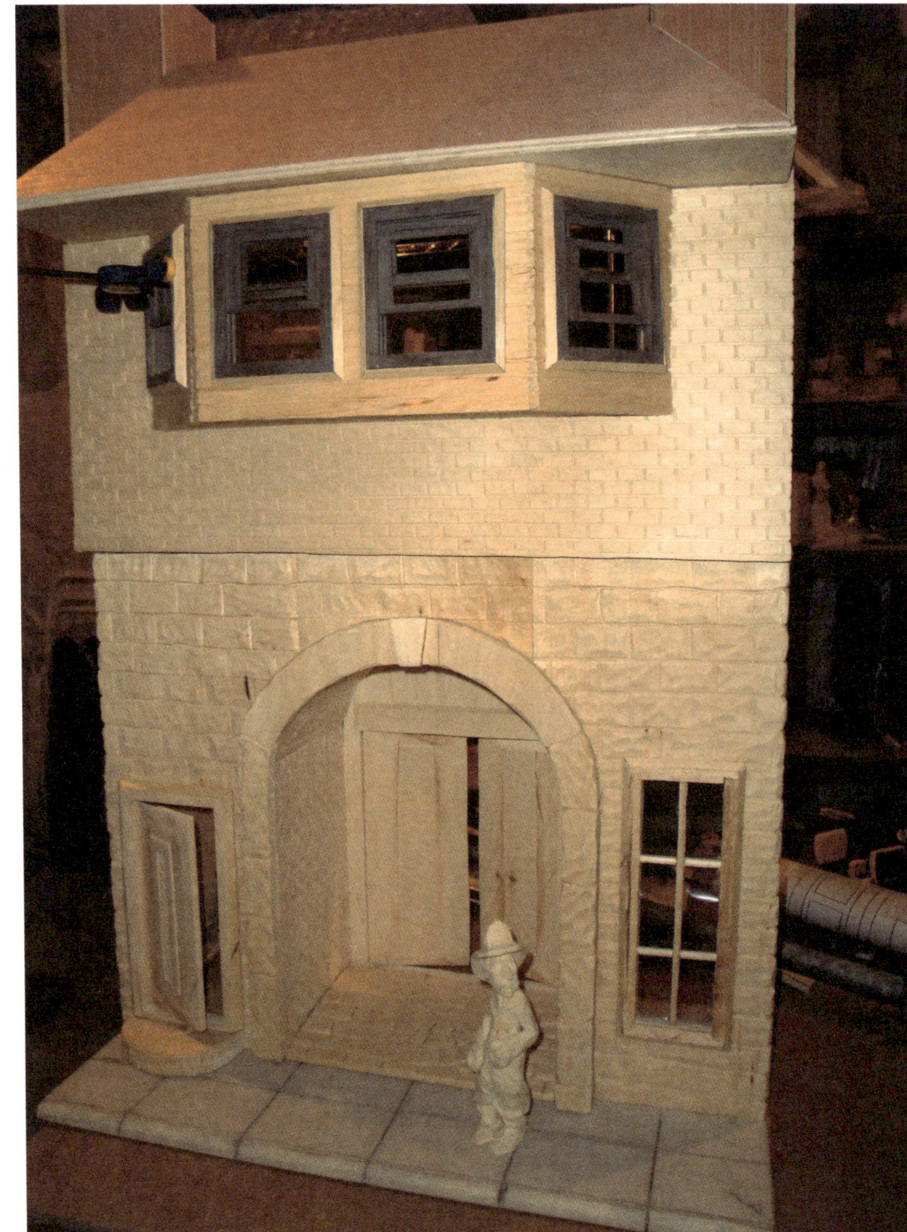

Window installation

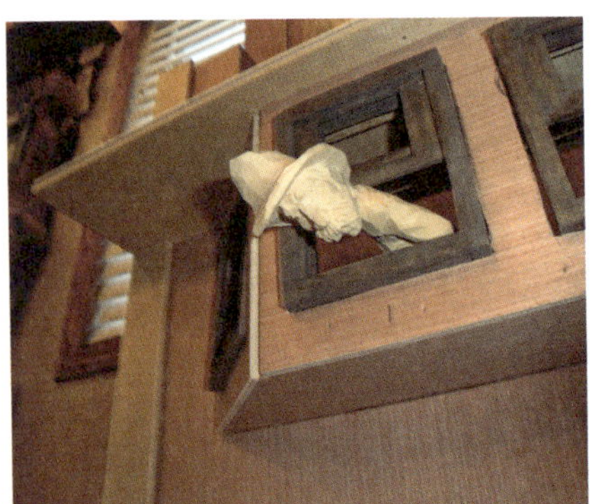

Fireman at window

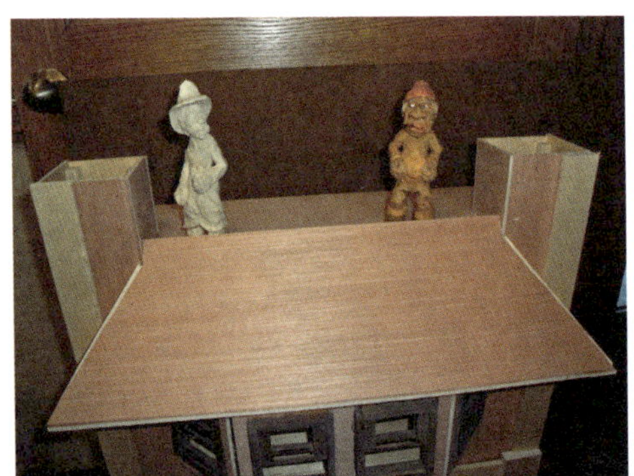

Roof under construction

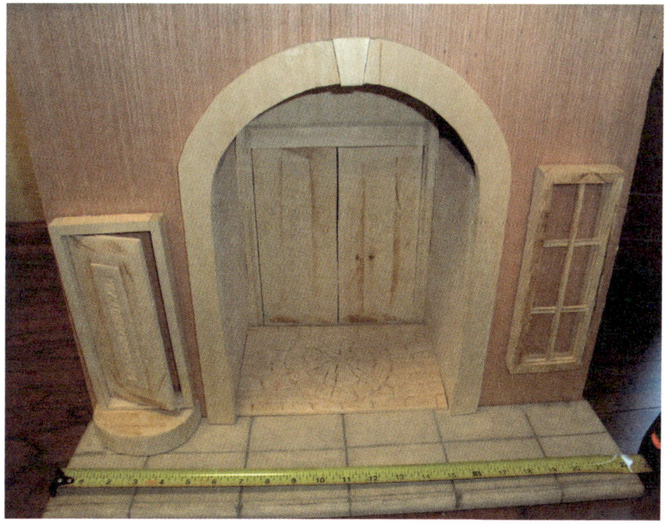

Front entry

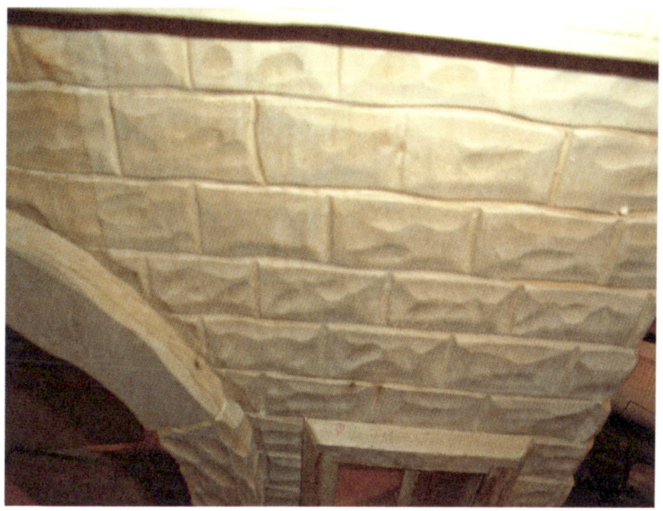

Building block detail

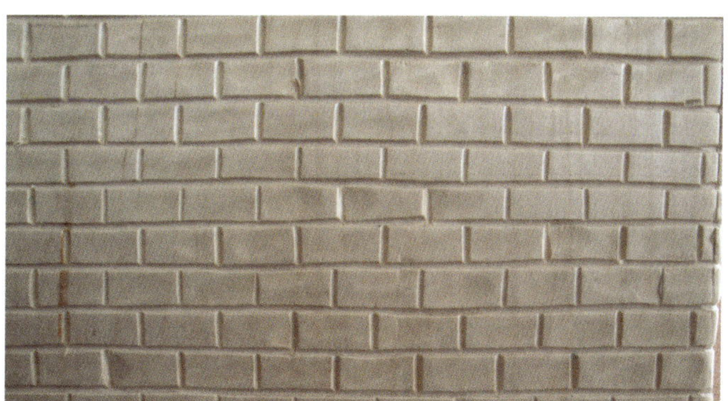

Brick detail

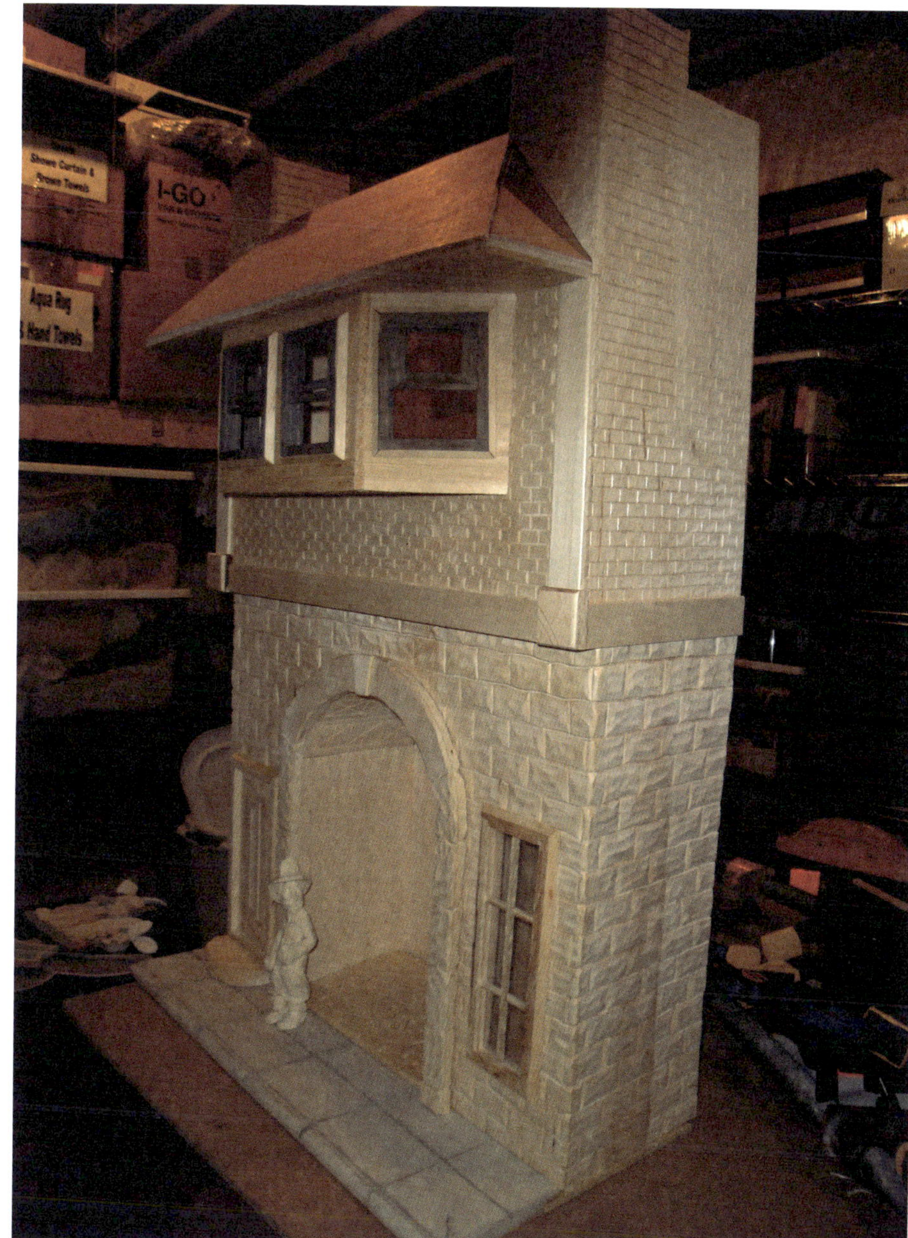

Ready to paint

The guidelines for the street scene limited us to a specific scale. While talking to Peter, we realized that all fire stations are essentially the same, no matter where they are in the country. Firefighters all like to play practical jokes when they're not responding to emergencies. Everyone lives as a family, so you have to try to get along. Once in a while a bucket of water is dumped on someone to cool them off. Not all fire stations have a fire pole, but I was determined to get one inside our firehouse. Sliding the pole was always a challenge. You have to develop your own style. I always had one foot behind the pole and the other in front. The back foot worked as my brake. Often you were half asleep, but if you were the first person on the pole, you knew there was someone sliding behind you and you had to get out of the way quickly. That's the short story behind our firehouse.

—PJ Driscoll

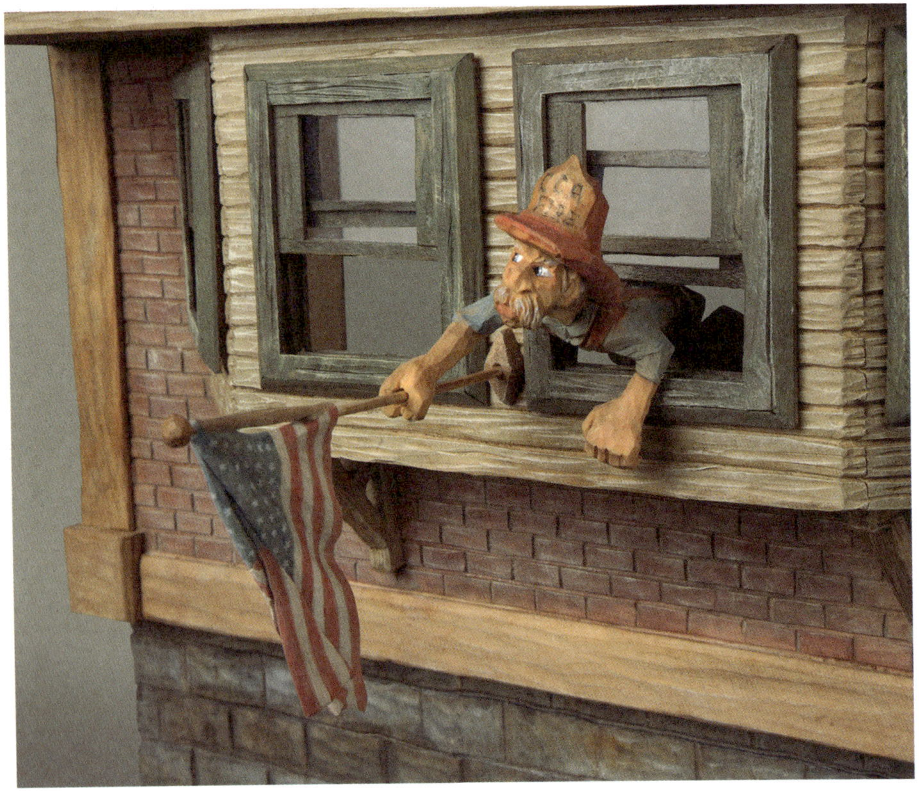

Fireman by PJ Driscoll, flag by Sandy Smith

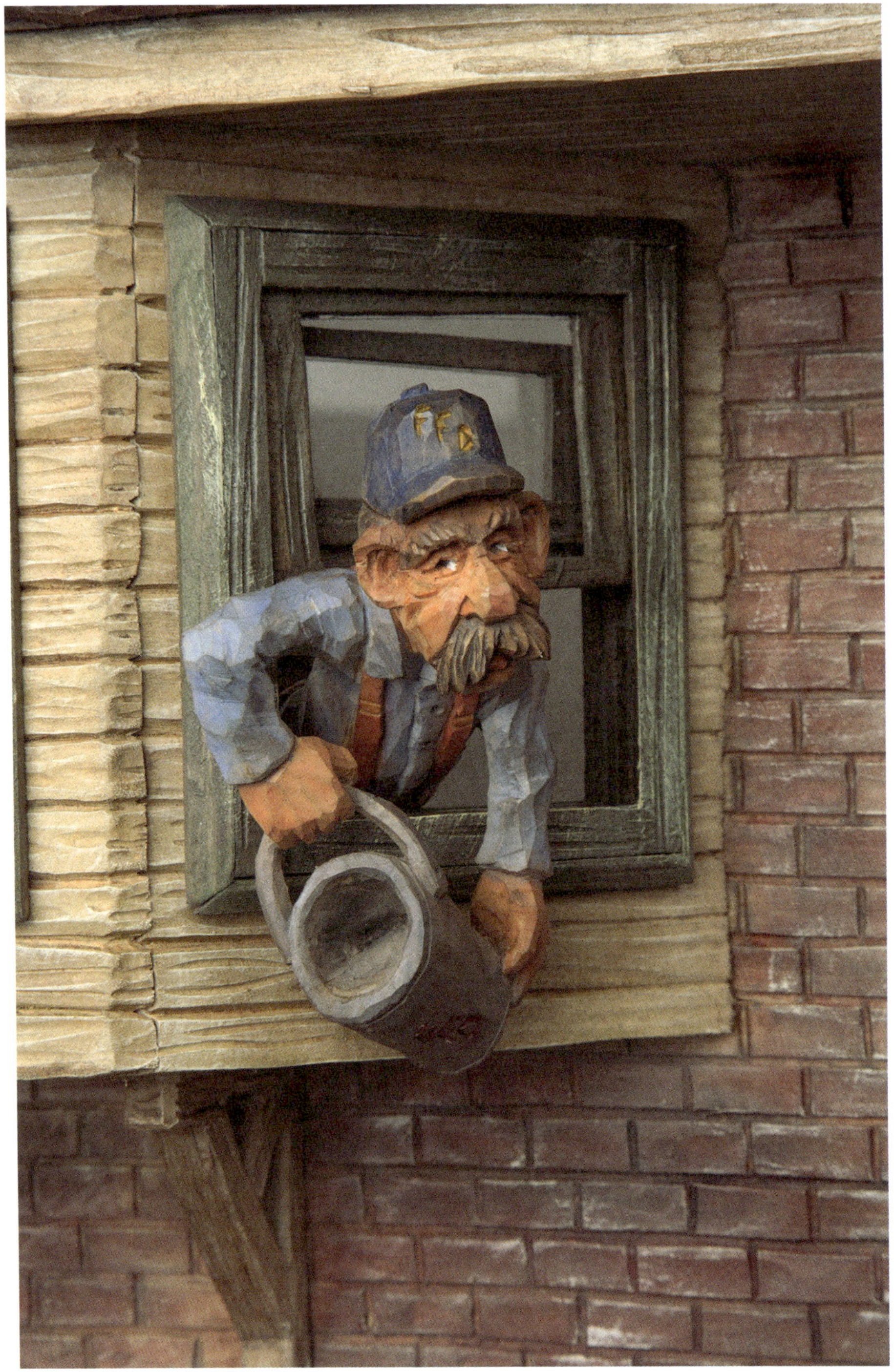

Fireman with bucket by Marv Kaisersatt

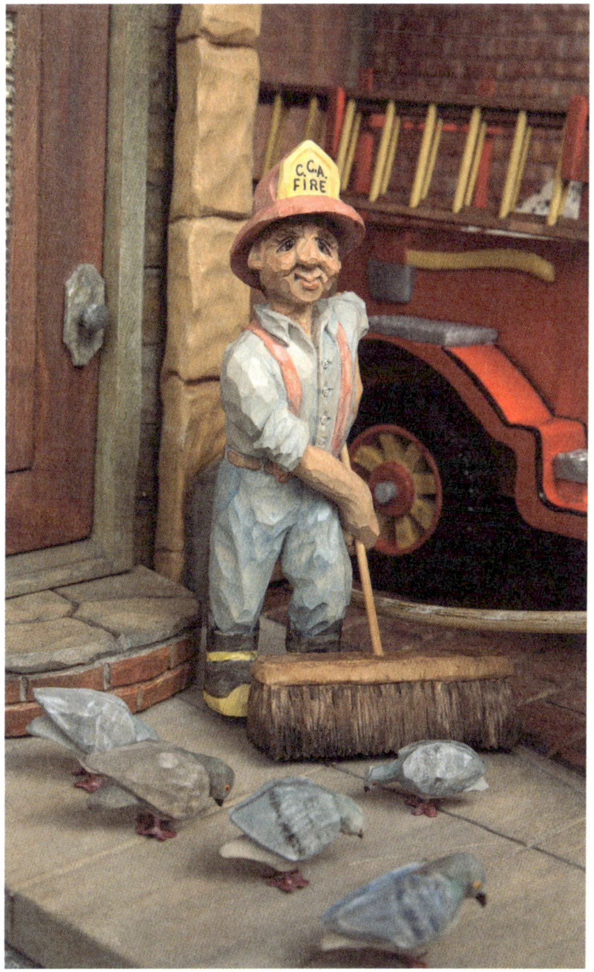

Fireman and pigeons by Sandy Smith

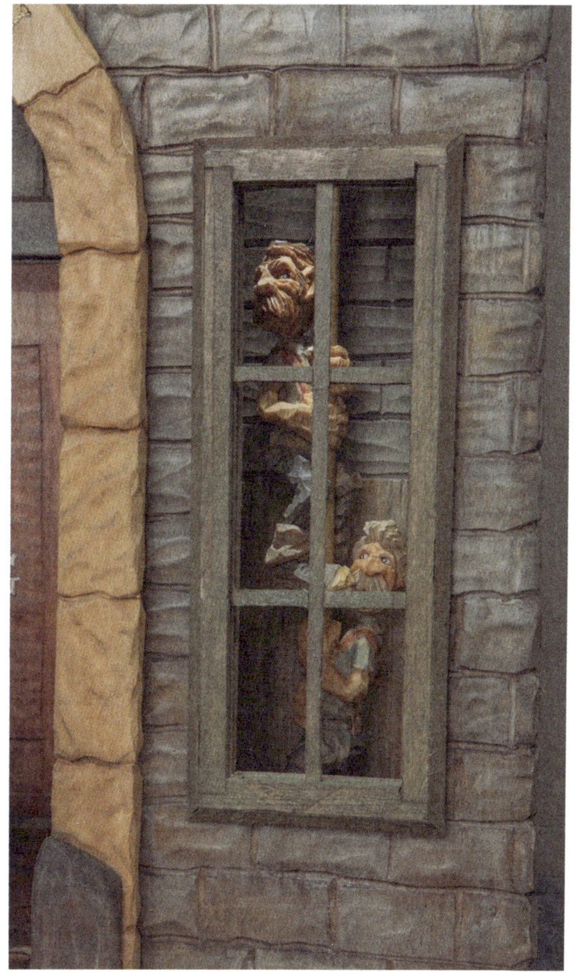

Firemen on pole by PJ Driscoll

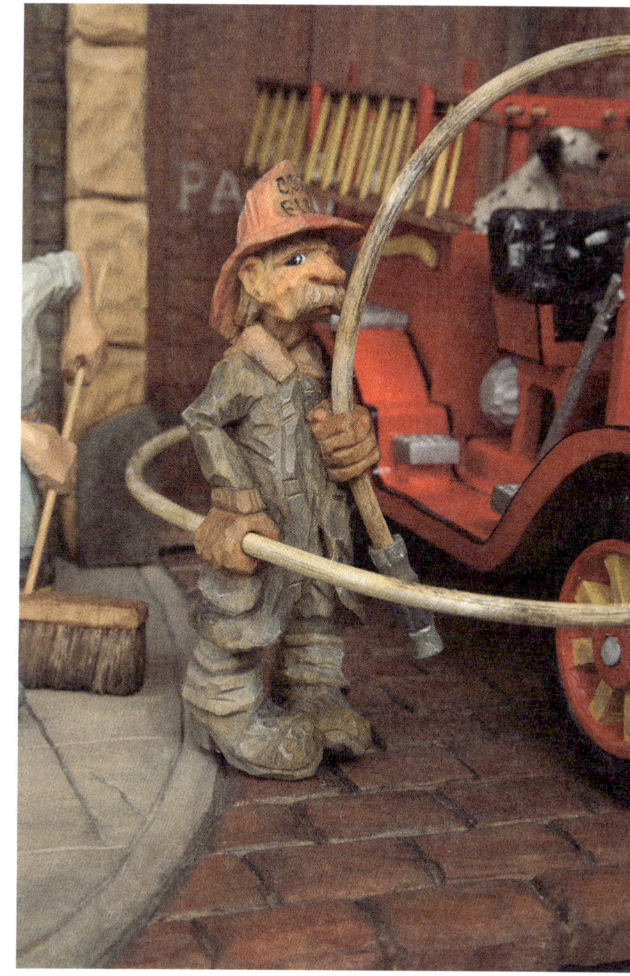

Fireman with hose by PJ Driscoll

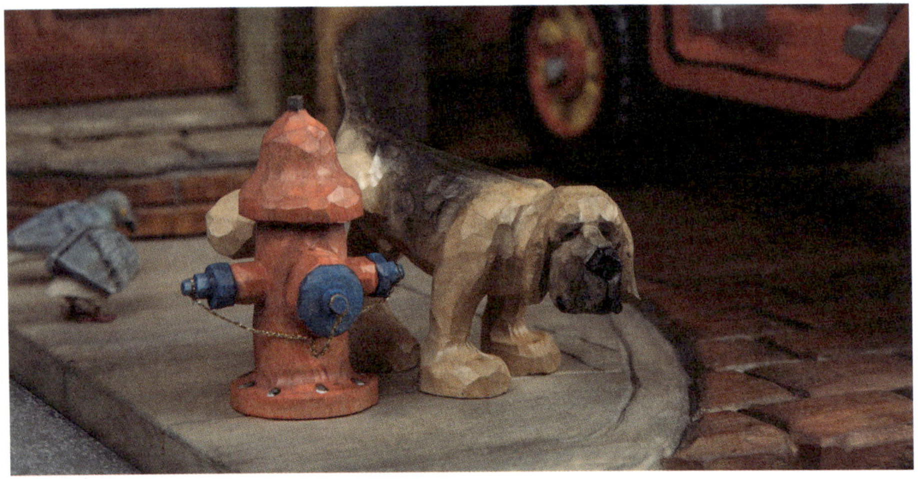

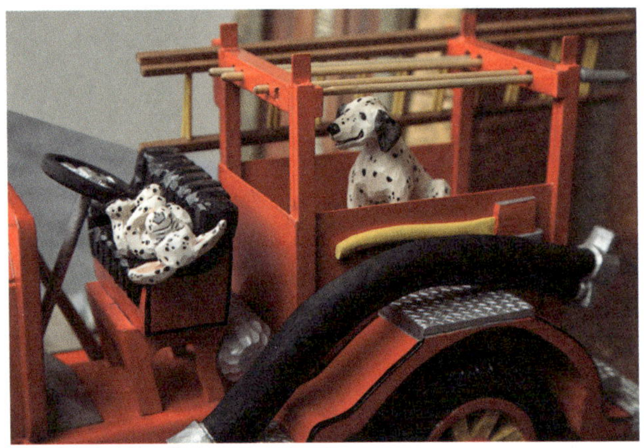

Hound, hydrant, and dalmations by Sandy Smith

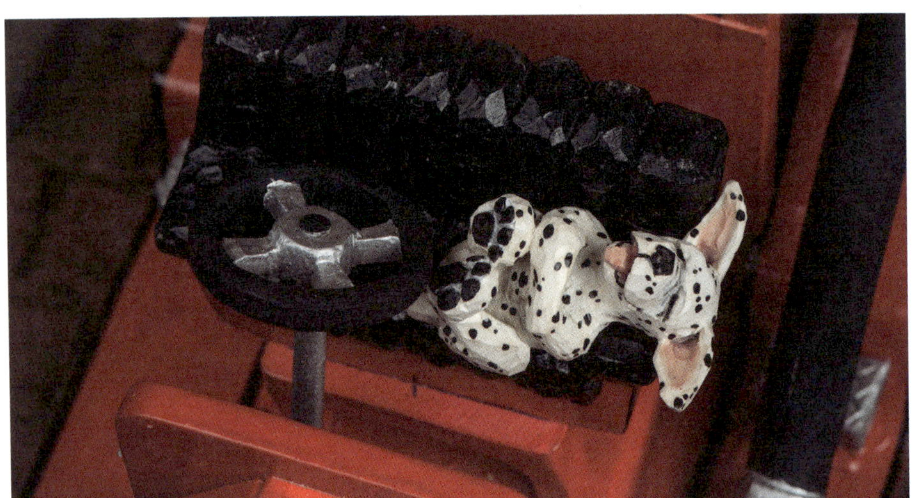

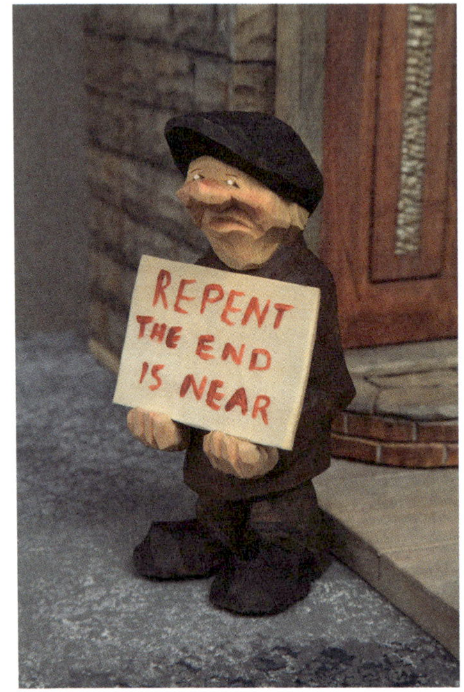

Repent by Harley Refsal

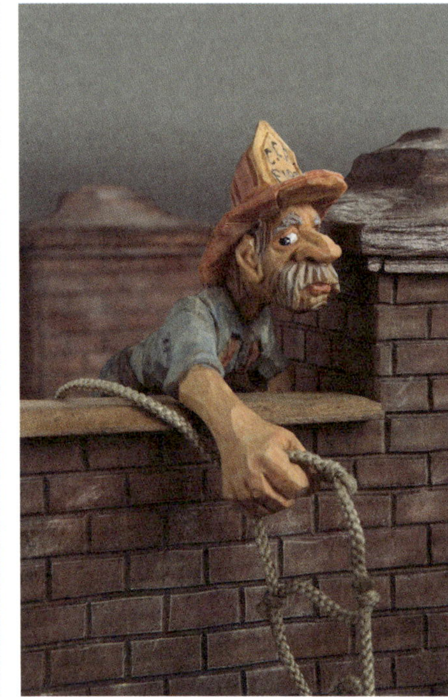

Fireman with rope ladder by PJ Driscoll

What? Do I want to be involved with the creation of a firehouse scene for the next CCA book, a 1930s city street? I didn't have to give it any thought at all. My answer to PJ Driscoll, another retired firefighter like me, was, "Yes, yes, yes." He also said that we would be teaming up with one of our newest members, Sandy Smith. What a great team it was. With PJ taking over as OIC (Officer In Charge), we collaborated on a very good design. I volunteered to build a period fire truck. Having some knowledge of what a 1930s fire truck looked like, all I needed were some measurements from the architects (PJ and Sandy) as to the size of the apparatus entrance doors. Using the scale of 1 inch to 1 foot, I began to design our truck. Older fire truck body styles were very boxy, compared to the sleek, smooth trucks of today. After drawing the pattern and cutting out the parts, it all came together very well, with a little nip and clip here and there. Once the fenders, lights, seat, and engine compartment were formed and shaped, they had to be painted before assembly.

—Peter Ortel

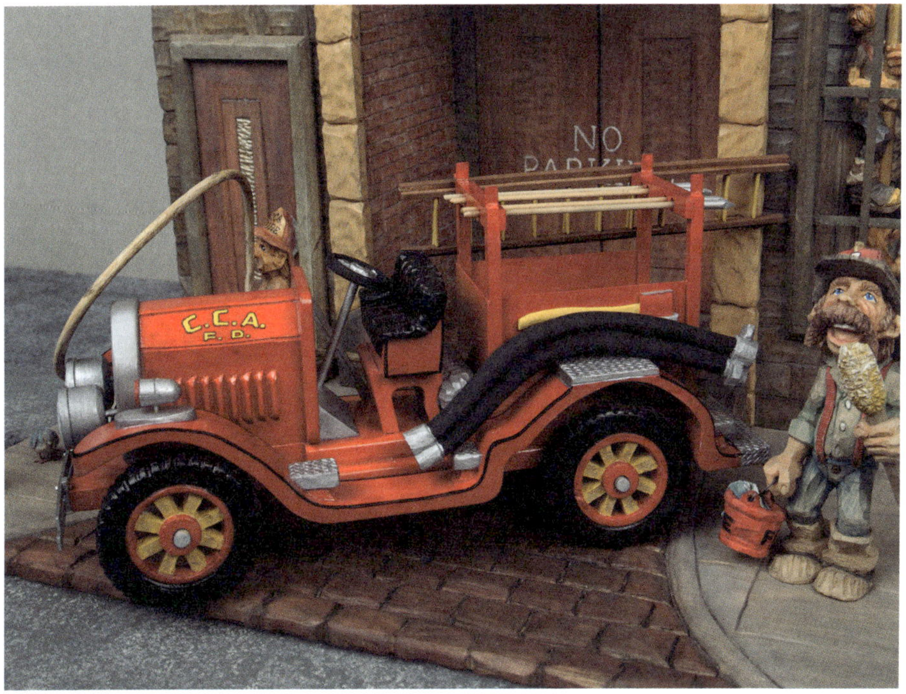

Creating the Fenders

One tip that I'd like to share is on forming the old style fenders. On old fire trucks, the fenders started at the front bumper, connected to the side running boards, and transitioned to the rear fenders at the back of the truck. This was my first fire truck to build (but it won't be my last), so my first thoughts were to shape all three pieces out of one thin strip of wood and use steam to soften and bend the wood.

I thought of my friend, Bob, who builds beautiful ship models that require some wood bending, and wondered if he had any suggestions. He suggested cutting the fenders and running boards from one block of wood. That makes the running boards and front and rear fenders, including "the back step," all one piece. No steaming necessary. "Back step" is a phrase used by firefighters to describe where they stood while they were responding to a fire call. A firefighter would hold on with one hand and continue to put on his coat and boots while the truck was rushing to the call for help, be it a fire or other emergency. Nowadays we're all much smarter and firefighters sit inside the truck and even use seat belts. Who'd a thought?

—Peter Ortel

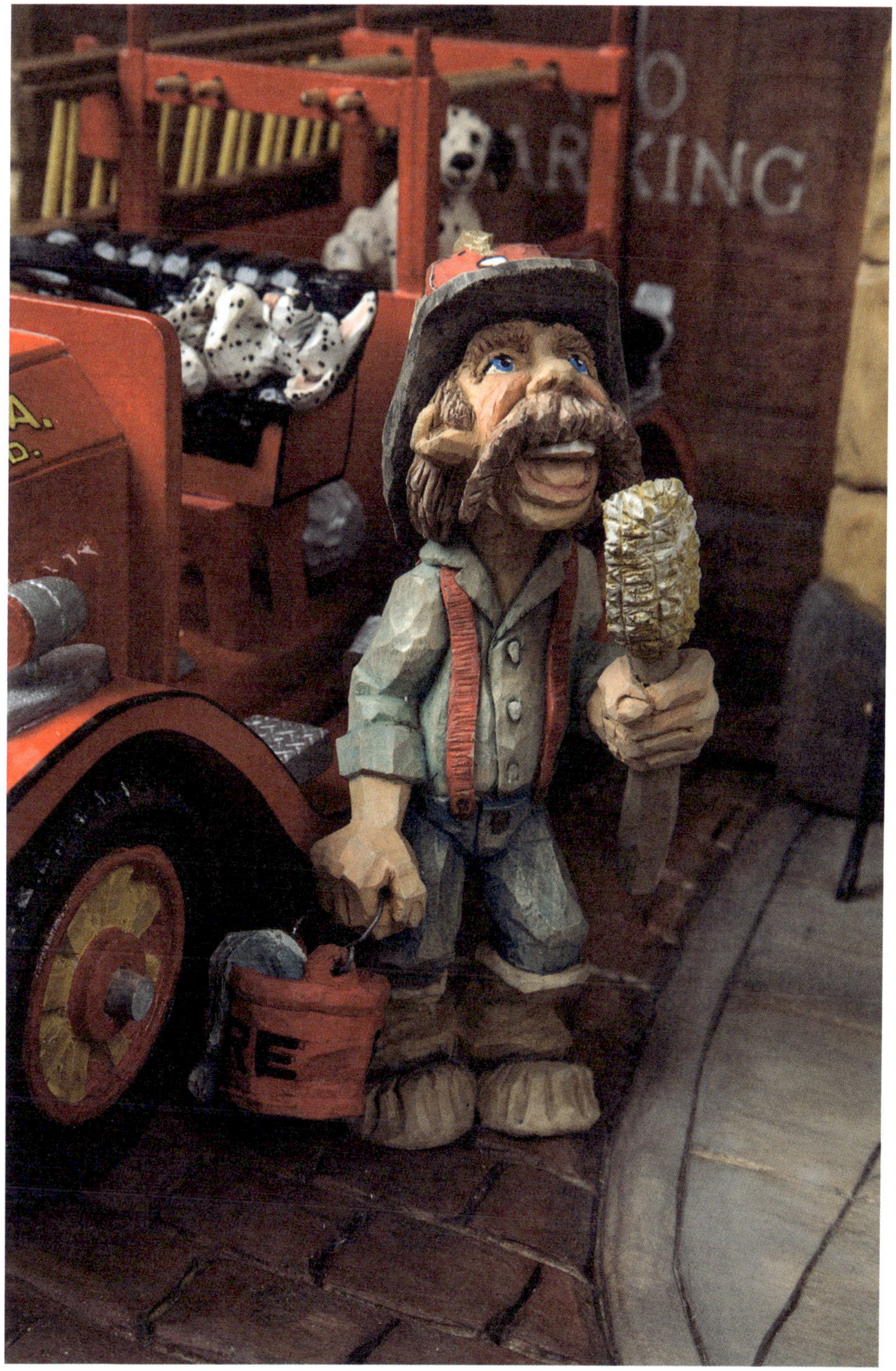

Fire truck and fireman with bucket and brush by Peter Ortel

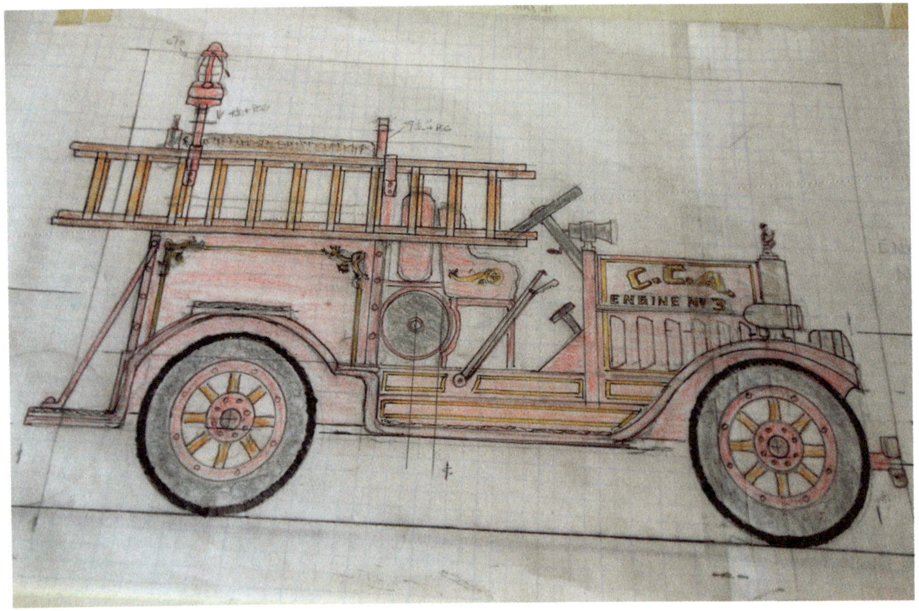

Plans, side view

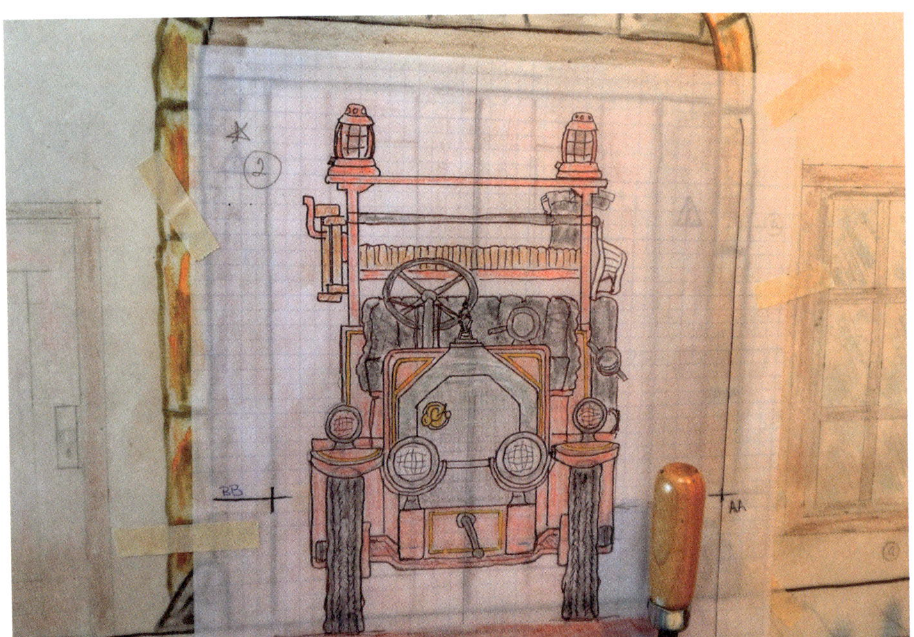

Plans, front view

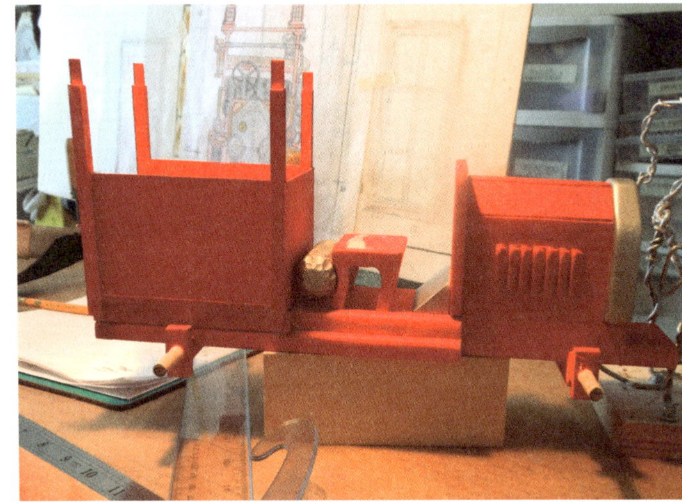

Body construction

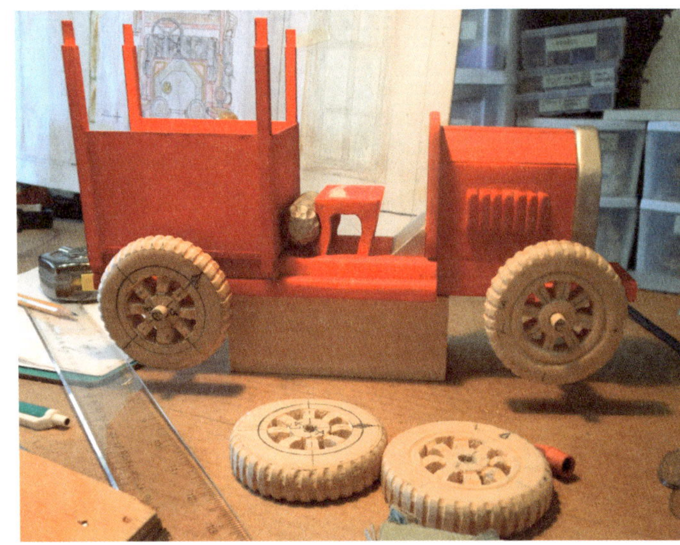

Wheels added

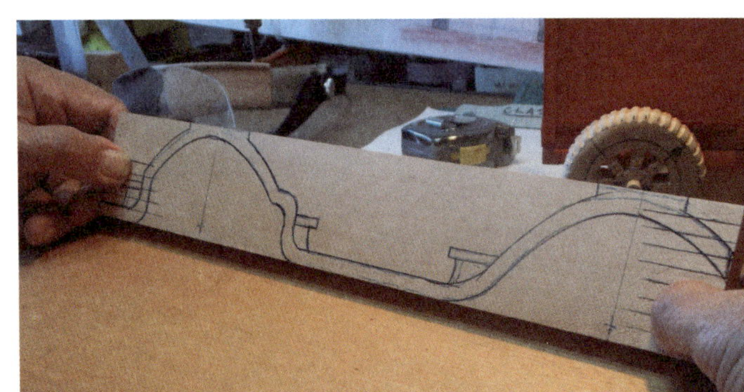

Fenders

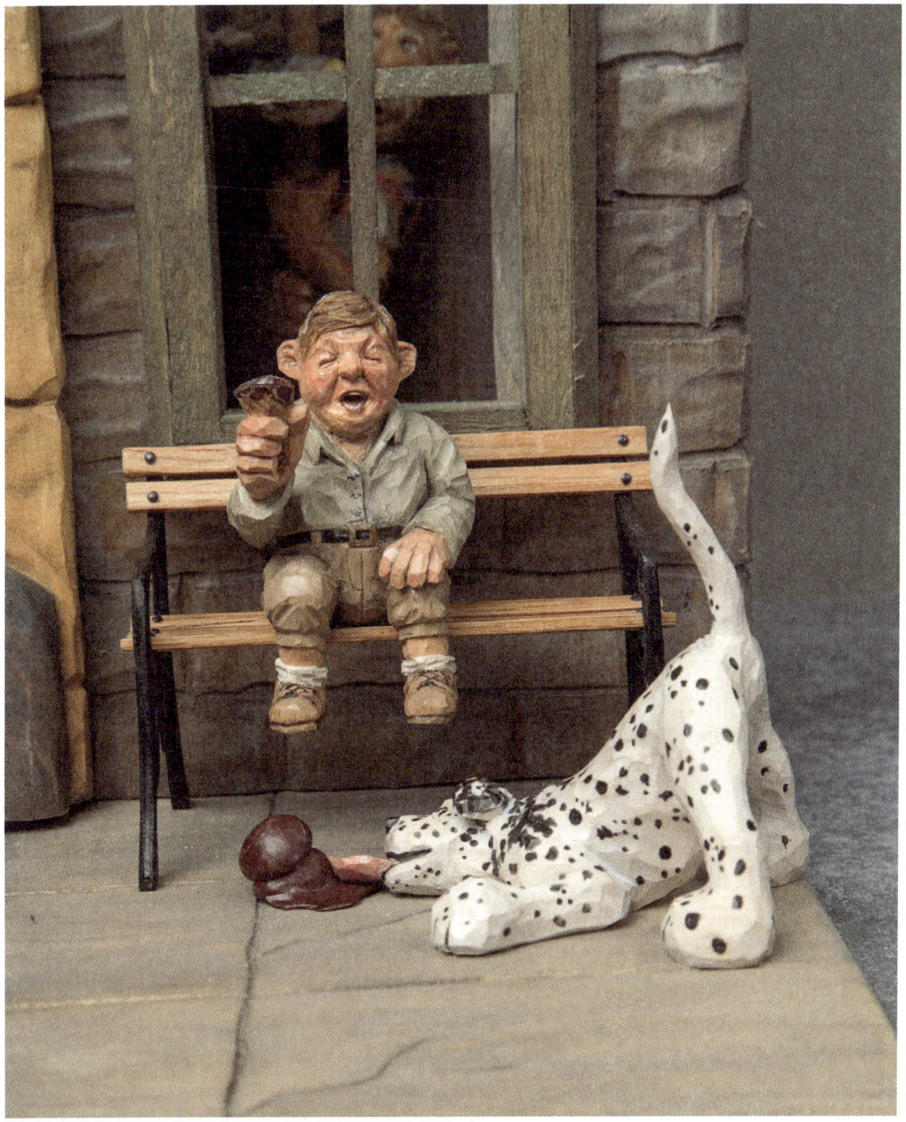

I told Sandy that the neighborhood children loved hanging around the fire station. That inspired her to carve the little boy with the ice cream cone and the dog licking up the spills.

—PJ Driscoll

Note: See Sandy's shopper in Bishop's General Store for a method of creating a pattern from the clay model.

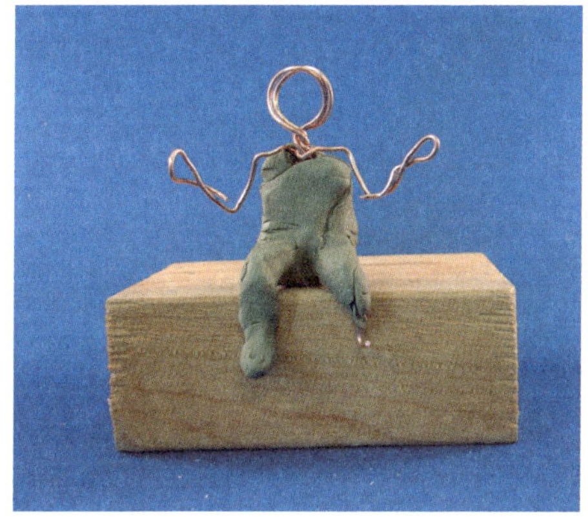

Clay on armature

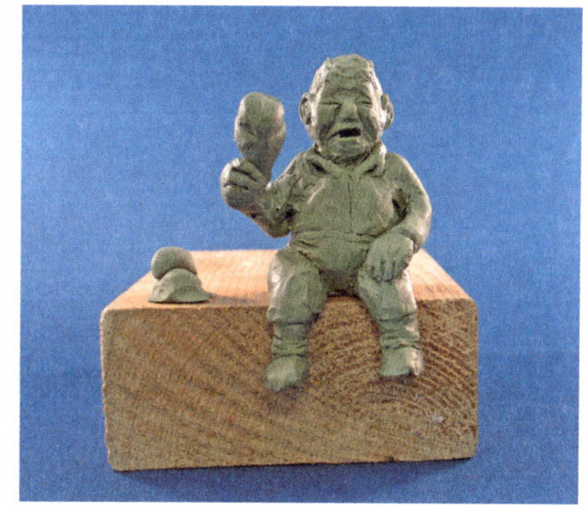

Crying boy, clay

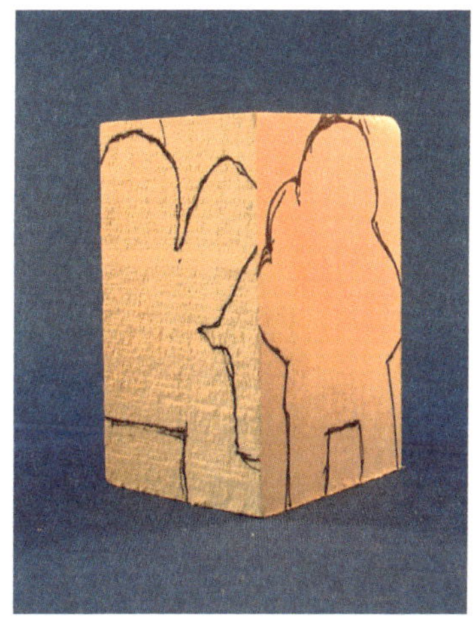

Pattern on wood

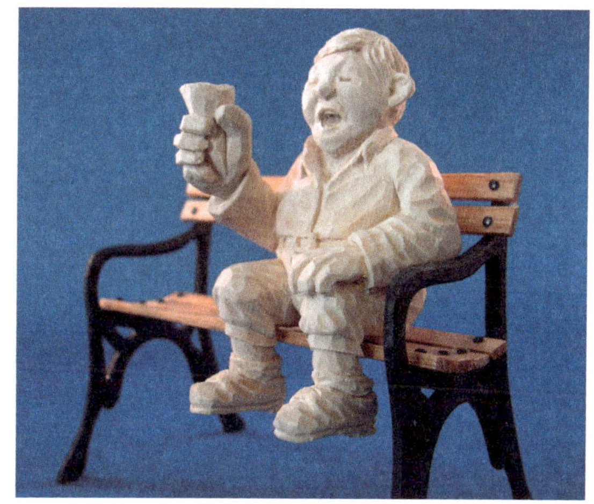

Ready to paint

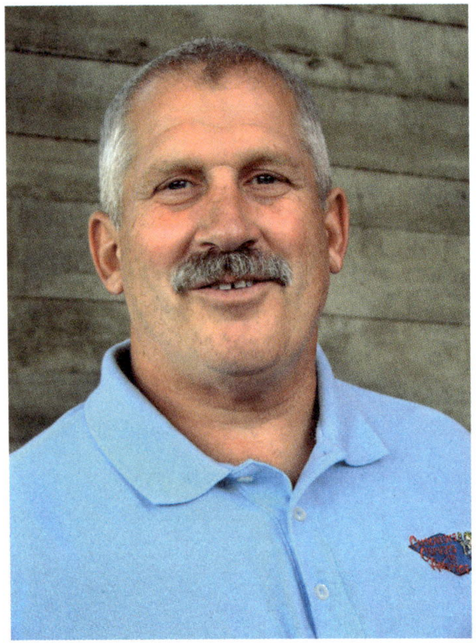

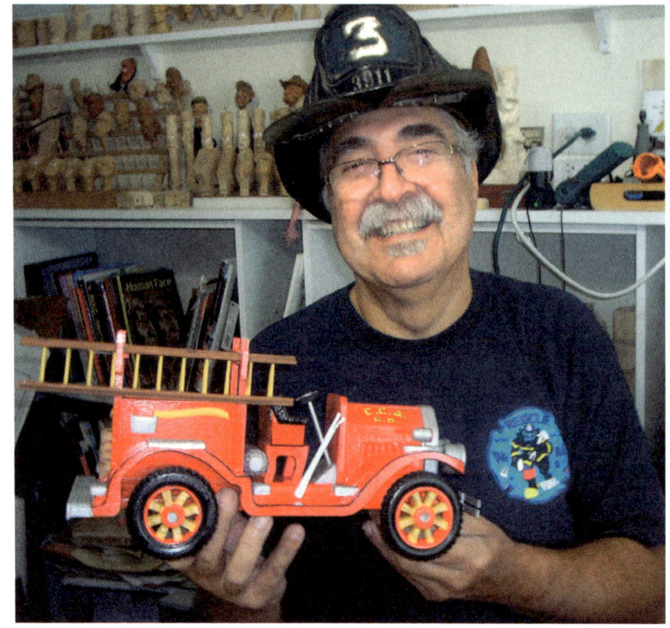

PJ Driscoll

PJ began woodcarving in 1992. Next to his family, he considers his induction into the CCA to be one of his greatest achievements. He is honored and very proud to be a member.

PJ has been a frequent blue ribbon winner at woodcarving shows. When not spending time with his family, PJ is busy teaching or taking woodcarving classes. He has made numerous friends and feels very lucky to have met so many great people through woodcarving.

PJ and Marge, his wife of 40 years, live in LaVista, Nebraska. He retired from the Omaha Fire Department at the rank of Captain after 24 years. They have one daughter and two sons, both firemen. Their greatest enjoyments are their children and grandchildren. They like traveling, spending time together and babysitting the grandkids.

Peter Ortel

Peter was born and raised in the Bronx, New York, where he met and married his wife, Madelyn. They moved to Monroe, New York, to raise their three sons, while he commuted to the city for twenty-one years, where he served as a firefighter on the New York City Fire Department.

After retiring, Peter used his artistic talent by decorating fire trucks in the "old style" with gold leaf scrolls and striping.

He began woodcarving in 1989, after taking his first woodcarving class and becoming completely hooked on this new found expression of art. His mentors were Claude Bolton, Harold Enlow, Marv Kaisersatt, and Dave Dunham. Peter was inducted into the Caricature Carvers of America in 1992. Peter's carvings have won many first place awards including the prestigious Best of Show and People's Choice awards at the International Woodcarvers Congress. Because the fire department is "in his blood," carvings of firemen are his area of expertise.

Peter and Madelyn now reside in the Myrtle Beach area of South Carolina, where he continues to teach woodcarving, carve for his own pleasure, and enjoy life.

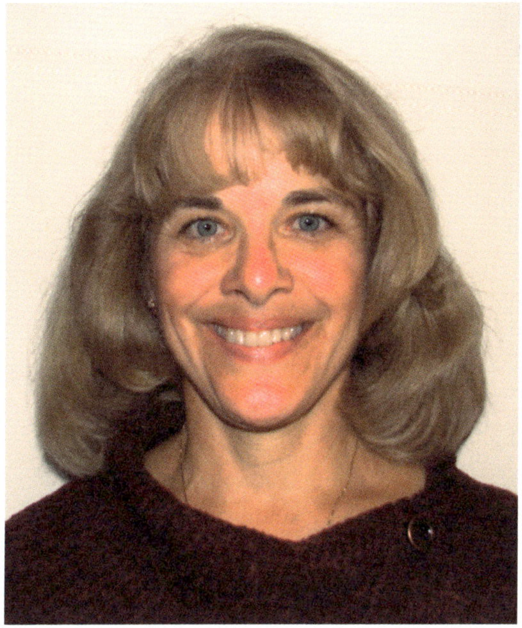

Sandy Smith

Retiring from a career in typesetting and graphic arts, Sandy and her husband, Gary, moved to the North Arkansas Ozarks in 1999. Following a brief endeavor with intarsia, Sandy was a "hooked" woodcarver after her first lesson in the spring of 2001, taught by Jack Ryan. Classes with Ron Wells and Harold Enlow strengthened her newfound "compulsion," and several months later she attended her first Woodcarving Rendezvous II in Branson which converted her compulsion into an obsession.

Sandy has been influenced by all of her carving instructors and her classmates, in learning and sharing carving and painting techniques. She's had several step-by-step projects published in *Woodcarving Illustrated*, and feels incredibly honored to have her carving of a Yorkshire terrier "Dusty" chosen as cover art for *Carving Magazine* and "Passing Preflight Inspection" on the cover of Fox Chapel Publishing's *"Handcarved Christmas"* book.

Her most revered woodcarving honor was to have been elected to the CCA in 2011.

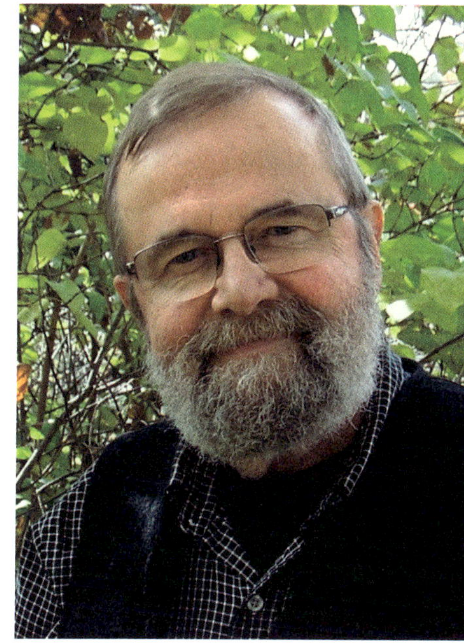

Harley Refsal

Born and raised on a farm near Hoffman, Minnesota, settled by his Norwegian-immigrant grandparents, Harley has been exposed to a fine handcraft of one kind or another his entire life.

Harley became smitten with Scandinavian style flat plane figure carving in the late 1960s. By the early 1980s, and many, many carved figures later, he began to receive invitations to teach courses in his favorite style of carving. Since then he has taught hundreds of courses throughout North America, as well as in Norway, Sweden, and Iceland. He has also conducted research and written several books and magazine articles on Scandinavian-style figure carving. In 1996 he was decorated by King Harald V of Norway, receiving the Saint Olav's Medal, for his contributions to Norwegian and Norwegian-American traditional culture and art, especially figure carving.

Harley has held a variety of positions at Luther College, Decorah, Iowa, since 1972, and now holds the title Professor Emeritus in Scandinavian Folk Art.

RIALTO THEATER

Doug Raine

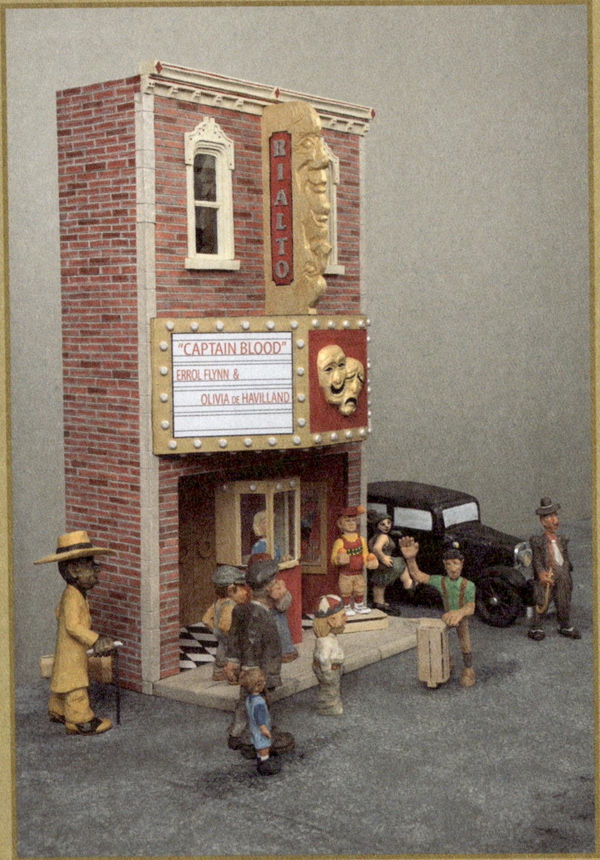

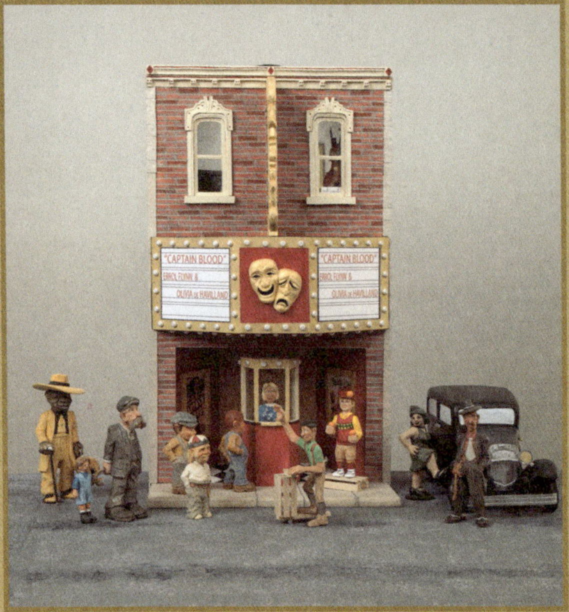

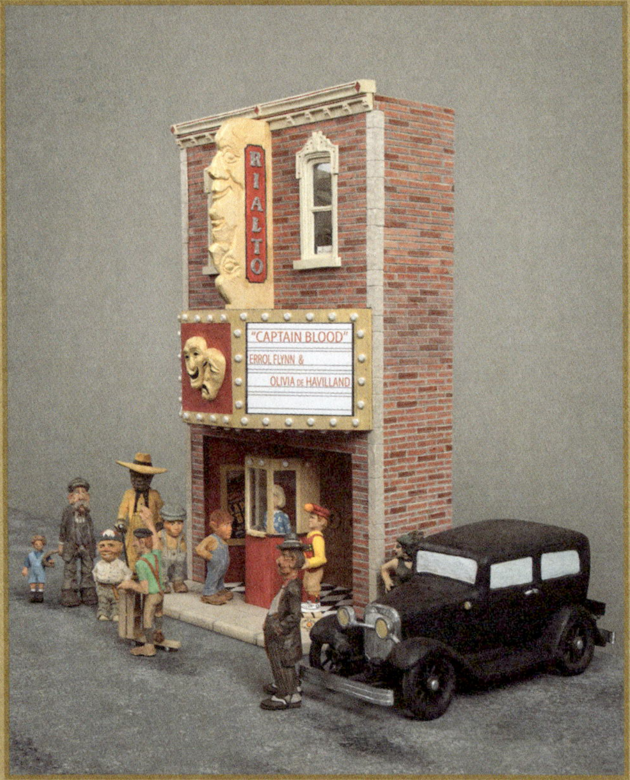

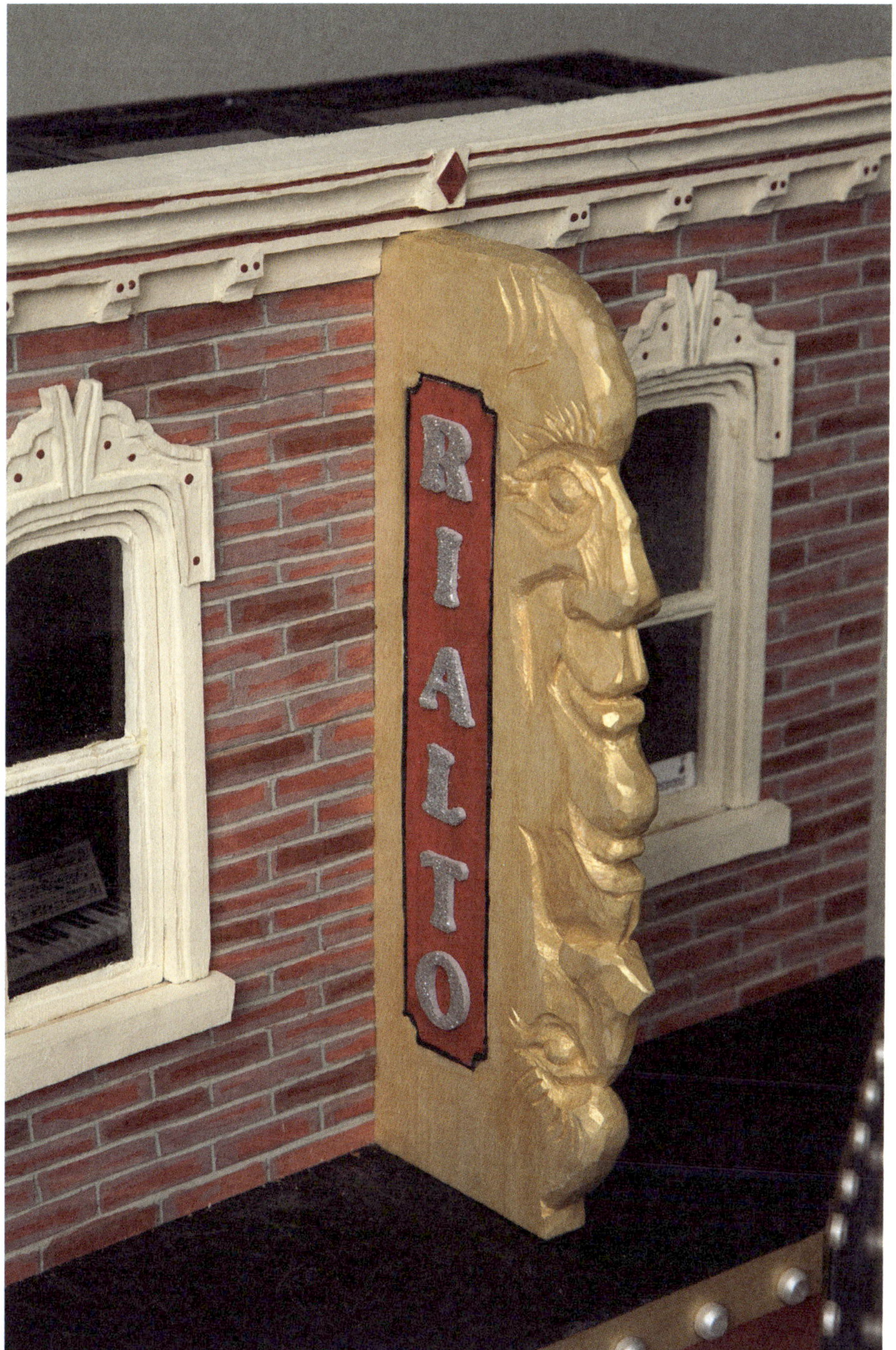

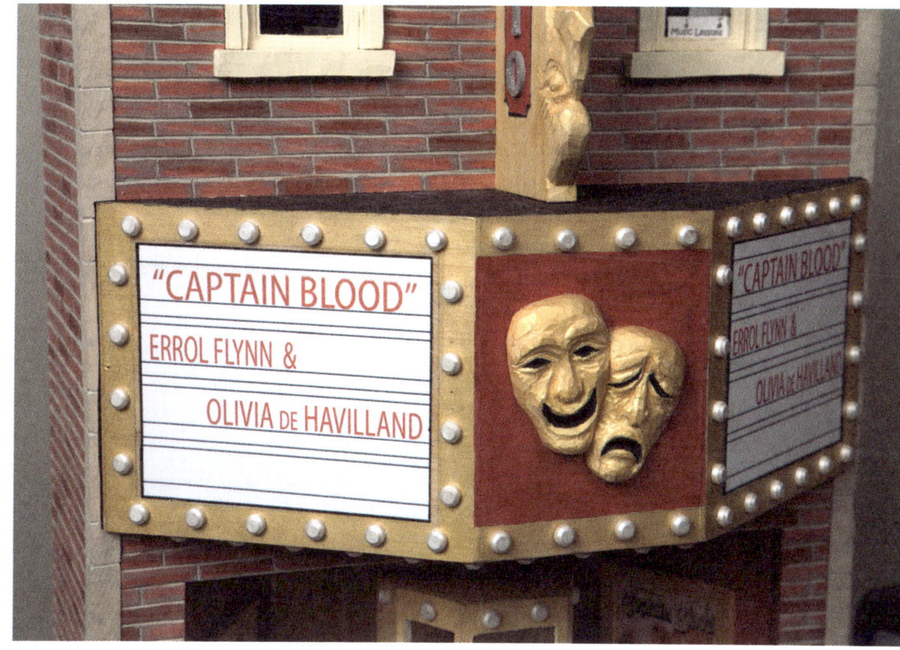

In 1922, Rafael Sabatini wrote a novel about an English doctor named Peter Blood. The story took place in the late 17th century. Dr. Blood attended to a patient wounded in a conflict with the king's men and was accused by the crown of treason. He was sent to a colonial island as a slave. In true swashbuckling fashion, he escaped his captors and became a Robin Hood-type pirate. It was a perfect story for Hollywood in the depression era. The movie premiered in December 1935. Recently, the Phoenix Museum of Art had a showing of old movie posters, and "Captain Blood" was one of them. This gave me the idea for the Rialto Theater in the 1930s street scene.

—Doug Raine

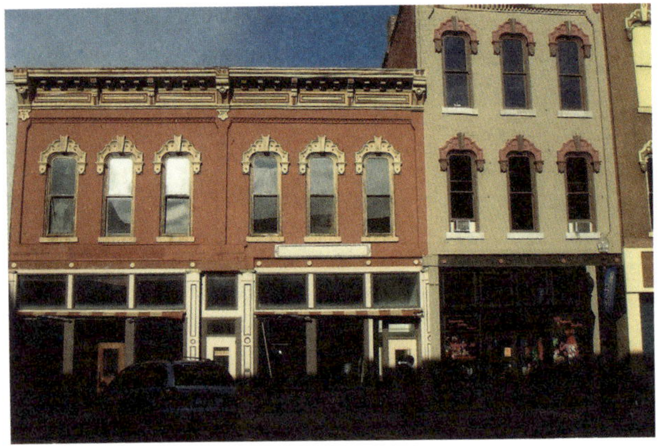

Main St., Faribault, MN

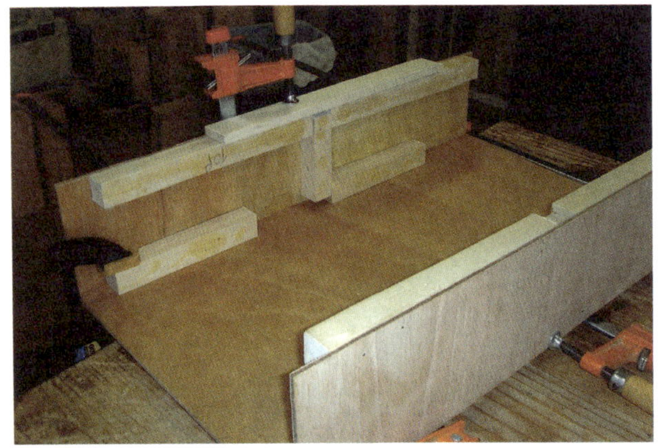

Beginning construction

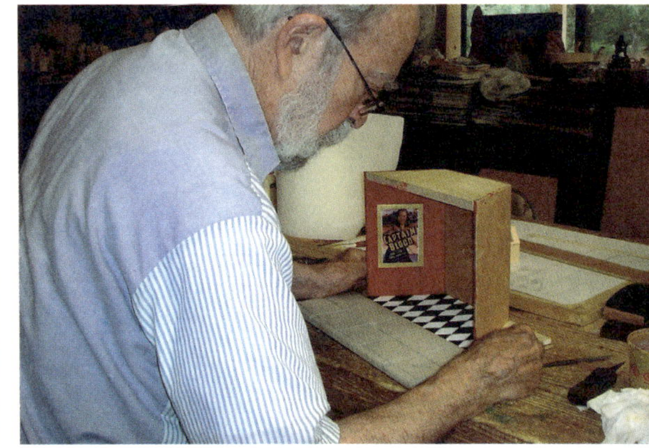

Theater entrance

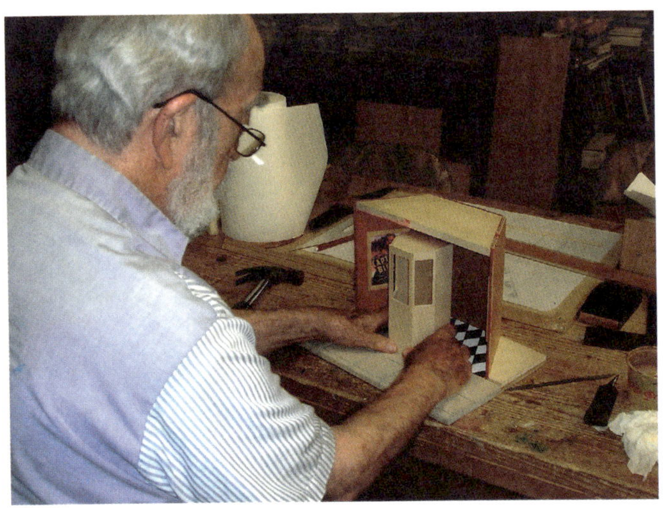

Ticket booth

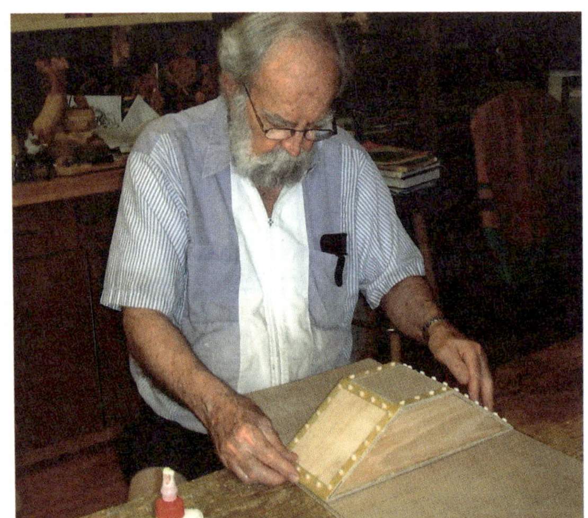

Theater top

The theater is constructed of quarter inch plywood, reinforced on the corners. The bricks were made with a number 11-1.5mm gouge on 1/16-inch basswood. The mortar and cement were painted grey, with some of the paint intentionally slopped on the bricks. I used a "brick" color for the individual bricks. I followed this by mixing a little burnt umber with the brick color and randomly painting a few bricks.

The window caps and the cornice at the top of the building were modeled after buildings I photographed in Faribault, Minnesota. To add some character to the building, the marquee features the mask of comedy and tragedy. The Rialto sign also has the caricature profile of an upside-down face.

—Doug Raine

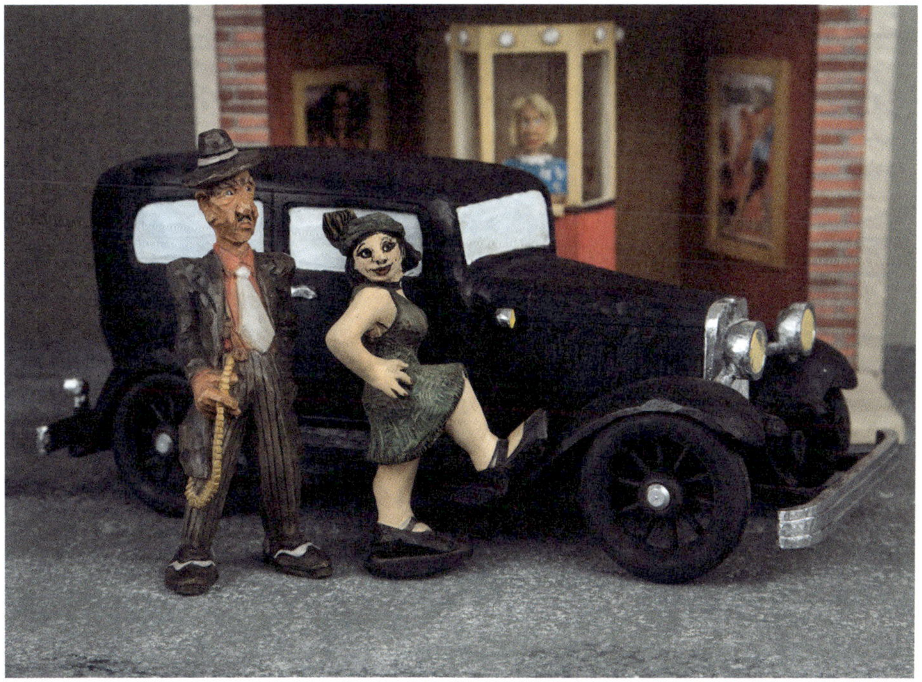

Car by Doug Raine, man by Marv Kaisersatt, and woman by Desiree Hajny

Tips from Desiree Hajny

• Don't be afraid to try new things and work in areas that are of interest to you. If I try to do something that isn't in my area of interest, I'm not happy with the end result and the piece is a struggle throughout.

• Take classes from instructors who are specialists in what you like to carve. I learn things along the way from carvers taking my seminars, and, hopefully, they pick up some things, not to mention the fun of sharing time with people that are interested in the medium.

I wanted a car in the scene, and the 1932 Ford is the result. Marv Kaisersatt carved the zoot suiter and Desiree Hajny carved the sassy gal.

—Doug Raine

I heard about this project from Doug Raine. He asked if I would carve a small piece to interact with his wooden car. I was honored and tickled. After measuring the height of the running board on the car, I sketched several flirting gals and chose this pose. She was a fun and simple balancing project.

—Desiree Hajny

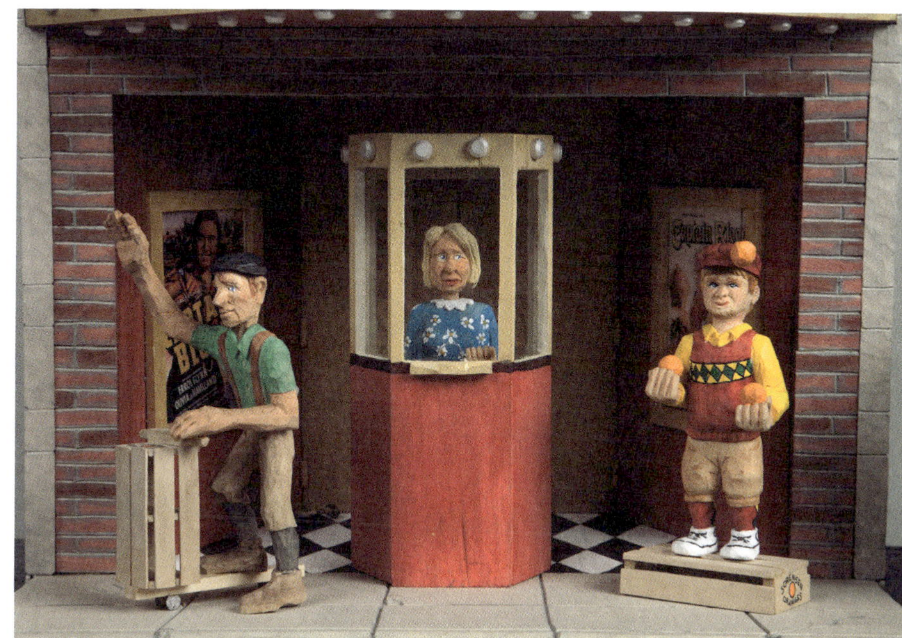

Carvings by Doug Raine

The boy juggling on the orange crate is a tribute to Bob Sorenson, a good friend and two-year survivor of a double lung transplant.

I also carved a boy with a 1930s version of a skateboard. The orange crate was nailed to a 2x4, and mounted on a pair of roller skate wheels (a box scooter). It was great fun. I hope you enjoy the scene.

—Doug Raine

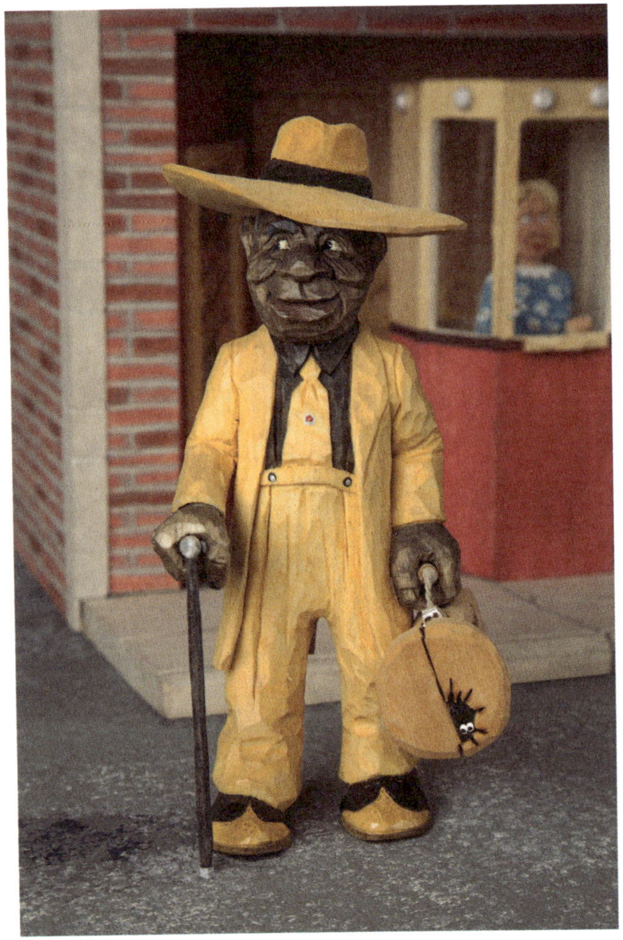

Always in style

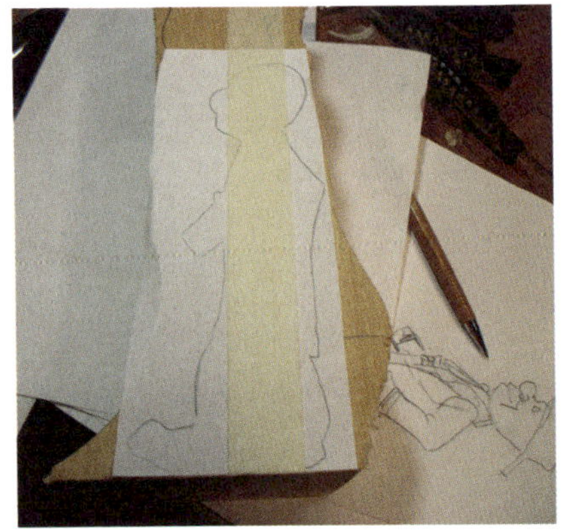

Pattern on wood

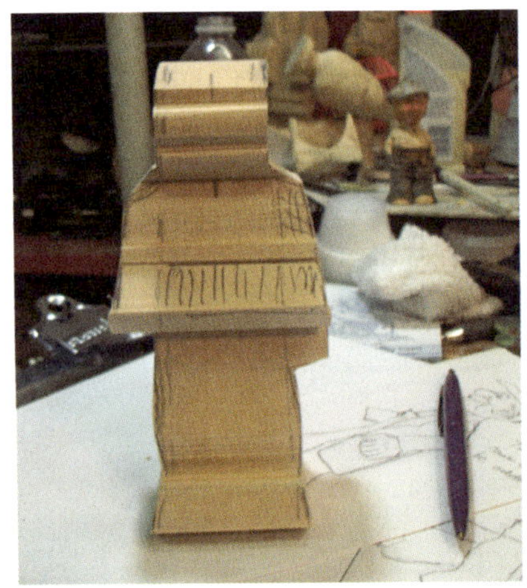

Cut out, front

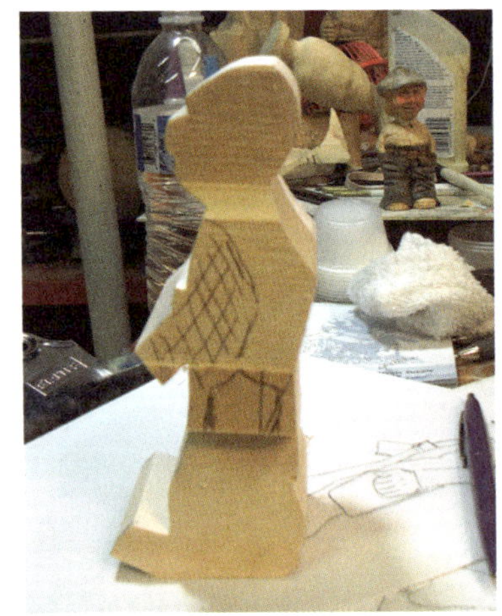

Cut out, left side

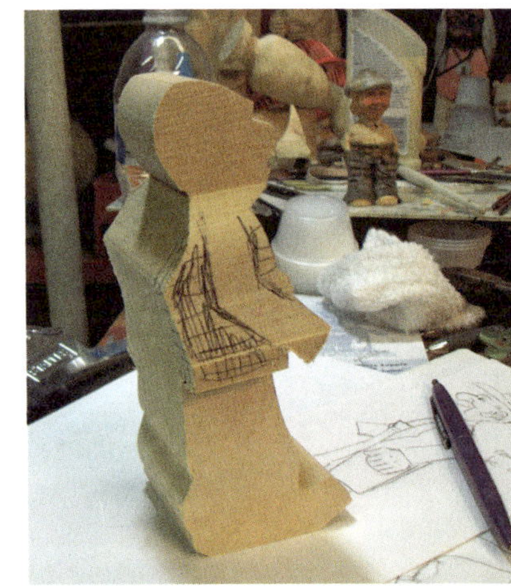

Cut out, right side

The idea for this carving came from a zoot-suited blues player. Although zoot suits didn't become fashionable until the 1940s, I thought he would look neat in the scene.

Beginning with a rough profile sketch, I trace the parts of the sketch I like, rework the sketch, and repeat this process until I am satisfied with the design. I learned this method many years ago from a "relatively" famous carver named Harold Enlow.

Cut the profile out on the band saw allowing extra wood for tweaking the carving. I use #9 and #2 gouges and knives to rough out the carving before carving the details.

—Gary Falin

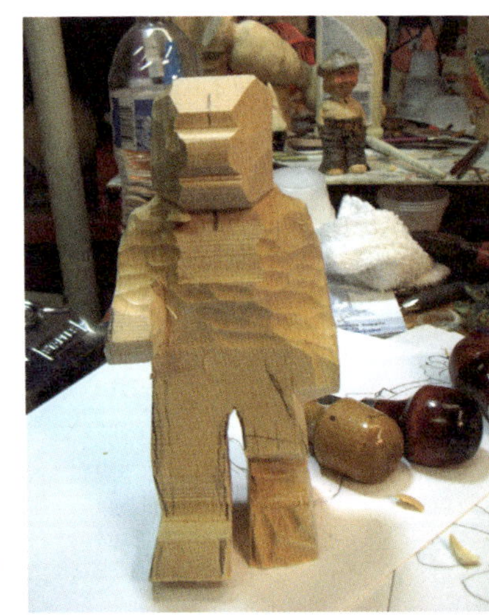

Roughing out

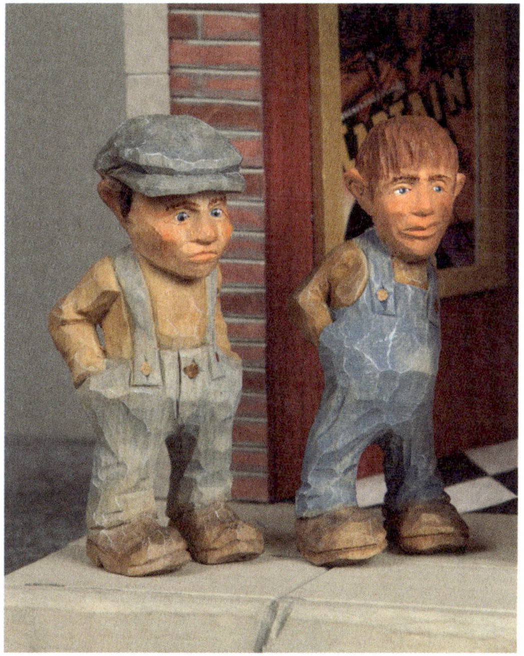

Two young boys by Gene Fuller

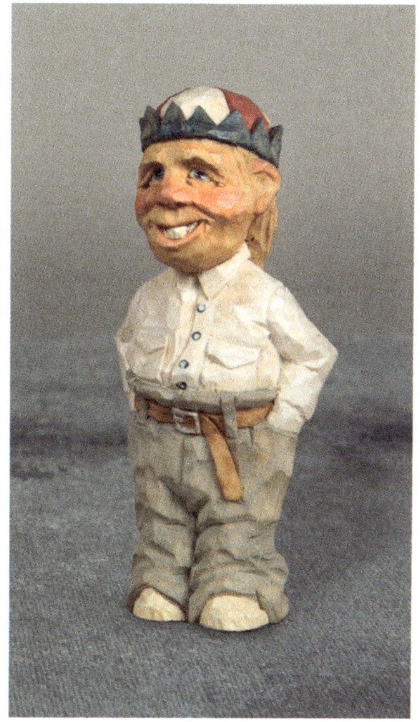

Young boy by Gary Falin

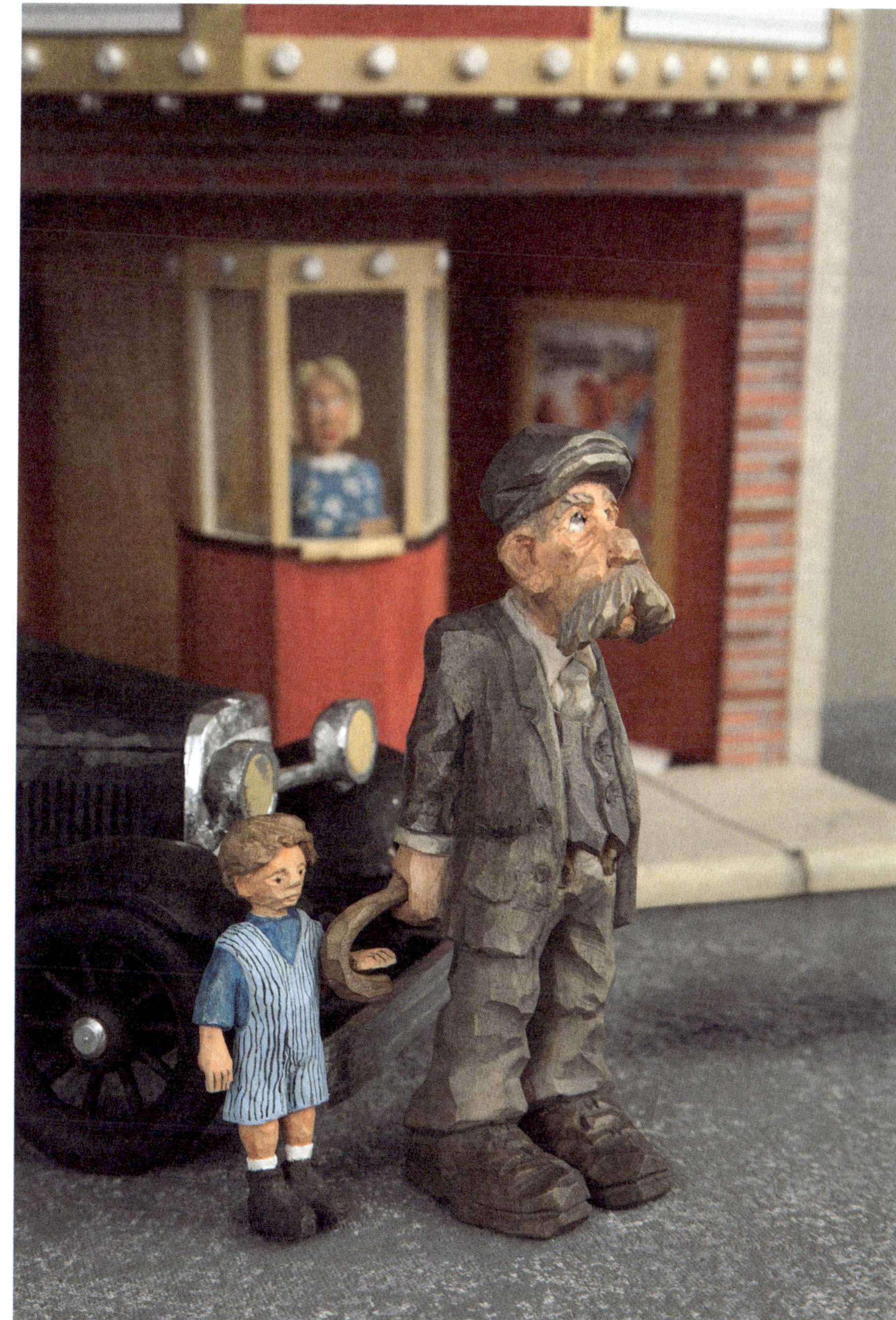

Man by Marv Kaisersatt, boy anticipating the movie by Doug Raine

Children of the 1930s were largely left to their imagination to create play situations. It was a special day when they could attend the local cinema and see their favorite cowboy in action against the desperados of the day. The good guy always won and was adept at shooting the gun out of the hand of the bad guy so no blood was spilled. As was often the case, clothing was ill-fitting, so youngsters were faced with dislodging the offending underwear or scratching an itch on their behind as inconspicuously as possible. The other youngster has both hands in his pockets so that he can clutch the eighteen pennies that his mother gave him for admission with his right hand. His head is down because he is shy, but eager to get inside for the movies and the candy bar he will buy with the nickel in his left pocket. You might try carving the boys with knickers and long socks or add a floppy hat. Have fun being creative.

—Gene Fuller

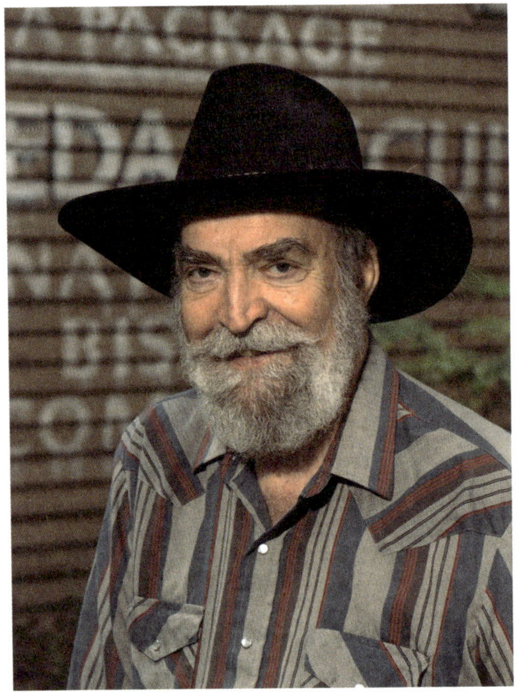

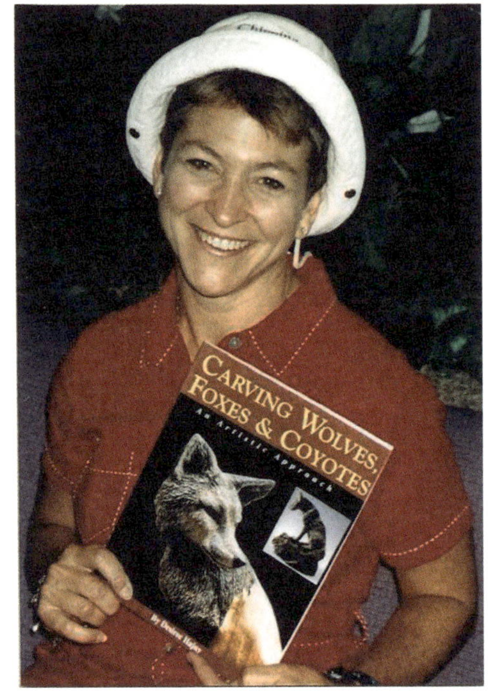

Doug Raine

Doug Raine has been carving since he was 10 years old. His first full figure was of Daniel Boone, carved out of a pine 2x4. The carving is still on display, although the rifle is long gone.

In 1997, with the help of good friends, he built his dream workshop. Doug has hosted seminars taught by many CCA members, and other nationally known carvers.

Every Wednesday, he hosts an open shop for as many as sixteen carvers. It used to be beans and cornbread every noon, but now it's coffee and cookies. Everyone enjoys carving, tall tales, and camaraderie.

If you are in Tucson, give him a call. If you like, you may bring your tools and join in on the carving, fellowship, and fun.

Desiree Hajny

Desiree Hajny has been involved in the arts her entire life and in carving since 1979. She has authored six books and contributed to eight others. She continues to teach seminars throughout North America and produce her wildlife sculptures for collectors and exhibitions. Her works can be viewed at hajny.fineartworld.com.

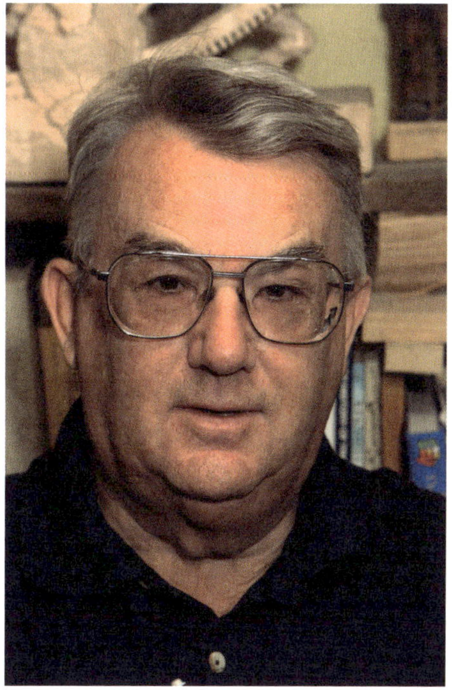

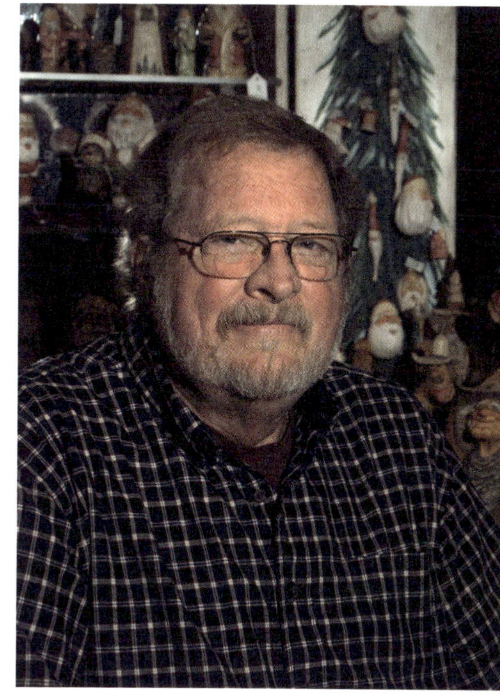

Marv Kaisersatt

After leaving the U.S. Army, Marv Kaisersatt taught junior high math in Faribault, Minnesota, until his retirement in 1995. With time on his hands, during a work stoppage in 1976, he turned to woodcarving.

Marv prefers the challenge of carving scenes from a single piece of basswood. This allows the carving to take on a sculptural quality through the interplay of mass and space.

He teaches classes at the Whillock Studio in Faribault. The emphasis is on designing in clay and carving the caricatures from band sawn blanks.

He has written a book, *"Creative Caricature Heads in Wood and on Paper."* It takes the carver through yet another approach for carving caricature heads, but more importantly, it lays out a detailed procedure for designing them.

Marv has amassed a variety of awards and honors at the International Woodcarvers Congress, considered by many as the premier general woodcarving competition.

Gary Falin

After 30 years teaching high school vocational classes, Gary retired to pursue the hobby he loves. He has been a carver for over 35 years and has taught for the last 21 years. He teaches regularly in the southeastern states. Gary teaches at the Midland, Michigan, Rendezvous and at the Renegade Roundup in Lebanon, Tennessee.

He has been a winner at the International Woodcarving Congress, Dayton Artistry in Wood Show, and Dollywood.

Gary is a very versatile carver. Not only has he won whittling competitions at Dollywood, he has demonstrated pumpkin carving at Dollywood's Harvest Festival for 5 years. He was a featured carver in the books *Carving Found Wood* and *Extreme Pumpkin Carving,* and has written two step-by-step articles for *Woodcarving Illustrated* magazine.

Gary and his wife, Marilyn, enjoy two grandchildren, Jole and Zach.

BUILDING UNDER CONSTRUCTION

Dave Stetson

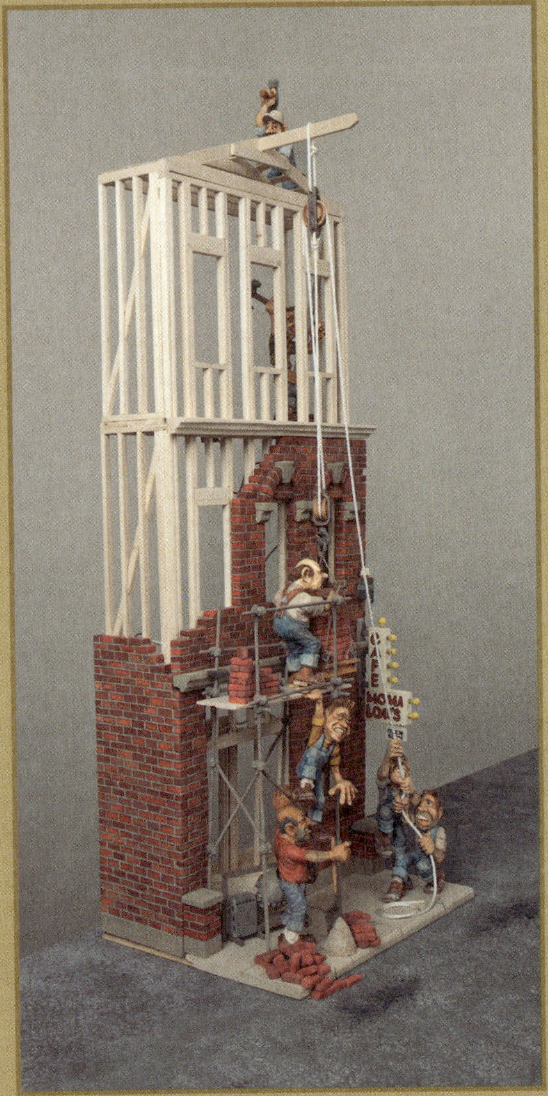

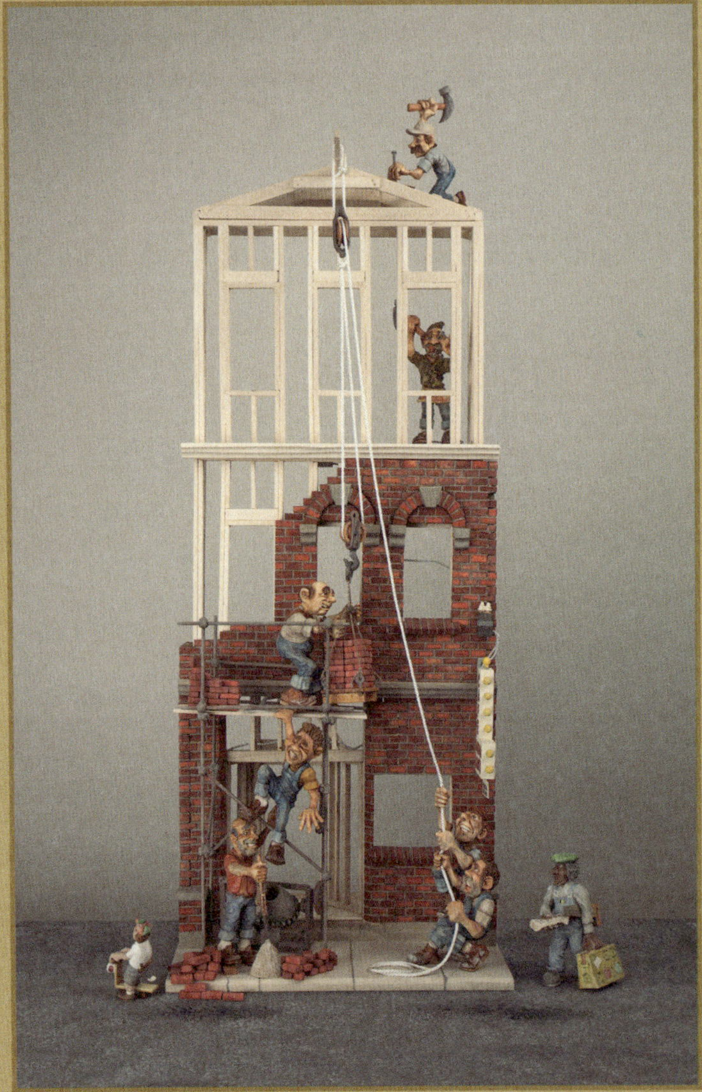

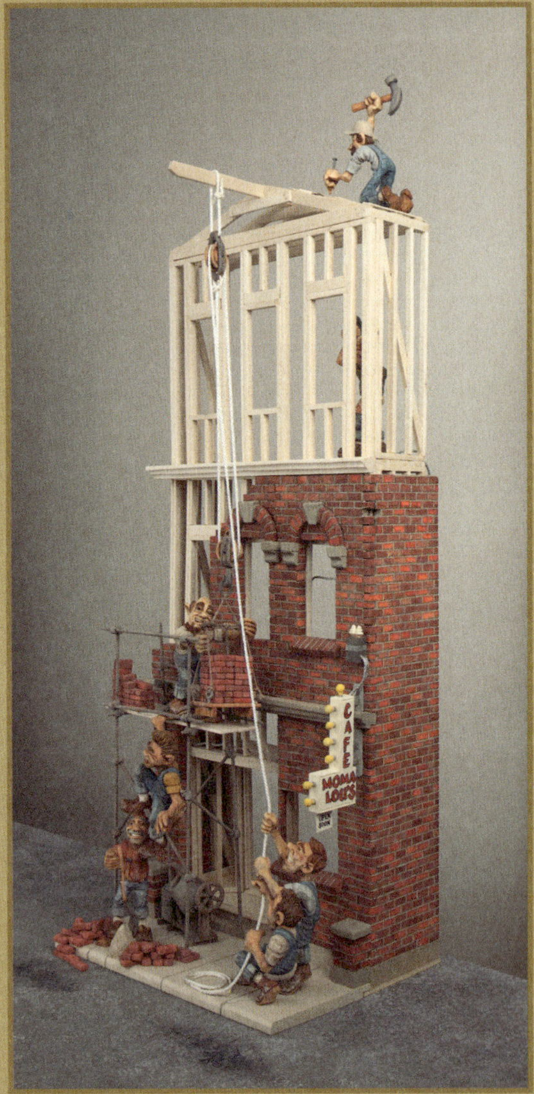

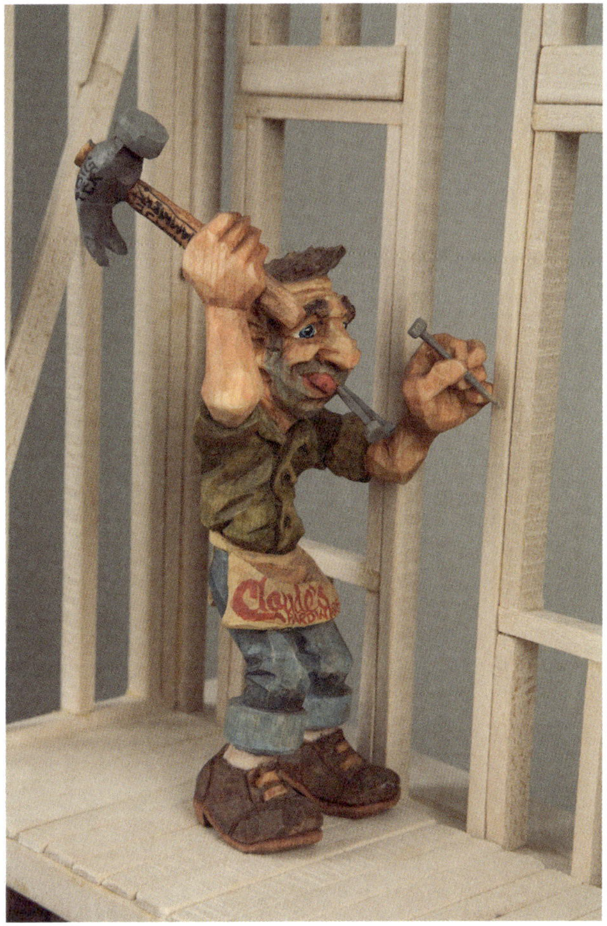

Framing in a window

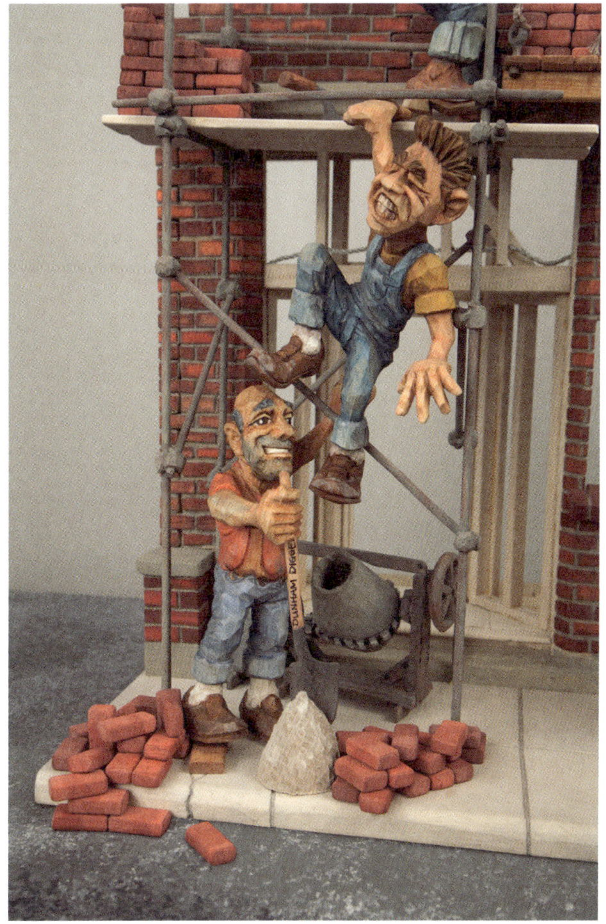

Hangin' in there

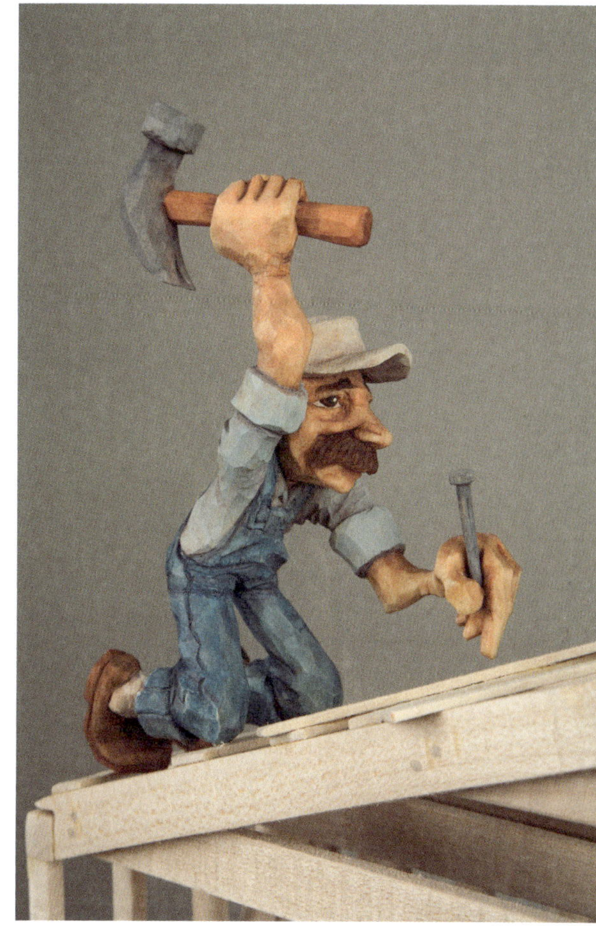

Framing in the roof

When the idea of creating a 1930s Street Scene was first presented to us, my original thought was to do something I'd tried in the past. I'd carve a few figures and let them construct the building. All went well at first, until construction seemed to slow down and eventually ground to a halt. When I confronted the figure in charge, he described the situation as a protest of sorts. They called it a strike; meaning they wouldn't work on the project until some sort of fair and equitable settlement could be reached between them and me…heck, I'm thinking that without me, they got nothing. I felt that the only thing to do was to carve a new crew to do the job left by the first bunch, only this time I'd carve them better so there wouldn't be any problems like the first figures created. Once the second group was carved and set to work, the first group decided to join in and go back to work (seems that one of the things they wanted was more help in the first place). Go figure. Woodenheaded workers are really hard to depend on. Hence, the building remains unfinished and I cleverly titled it a "Building Under Construction." Maybe someday they'll finish what they started, but I doubt it. It didn't seem to work out so well the last time I tried this idea, either.

—Dave Stetson

The construction crew at work

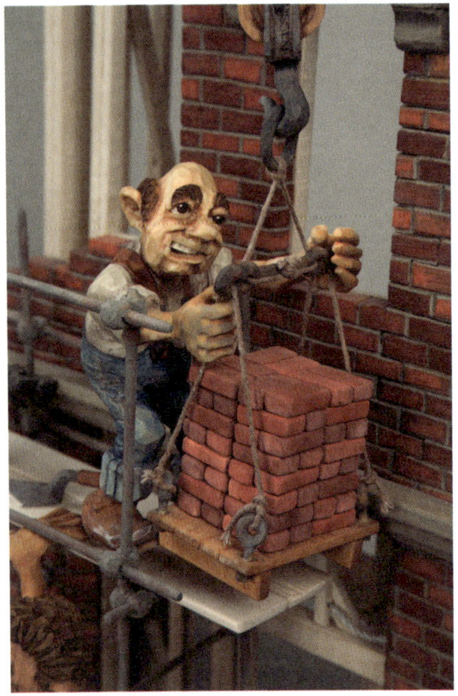

Another load of bricks

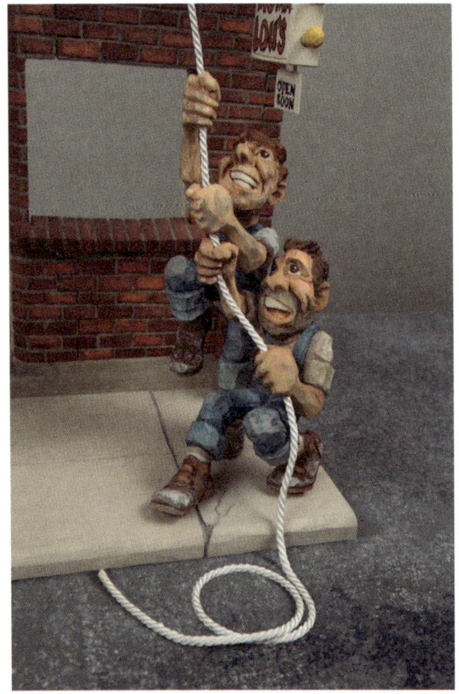

Those bricks are heavy

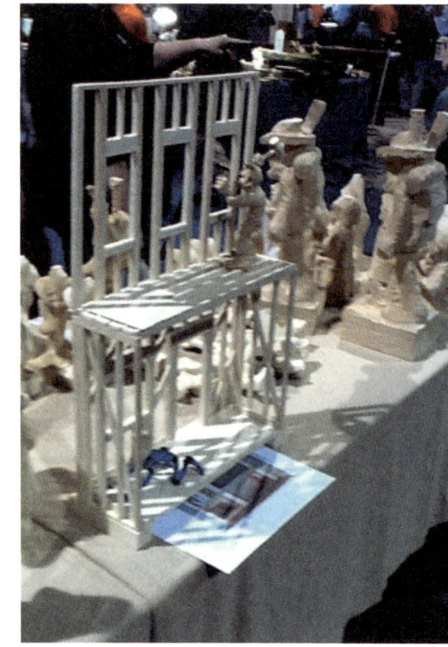

Construction under way

The sign at the corner of the building says "Moma Lou's Café." It represents the place where we had Sunday lunch during our organizational meeting in Ft. Worth, Texas. Dave Dunham and Claude Bolton thought it would be fun to dine in a soul food café. The food was great, but the Bail Bondsman advertisement on the wall is something I'll never forget.

The deceased members of our organization are remembered and represented in the building scene: Tex Haase by the Haase Hammer Company's "Big Tex" model hammers that the carpenters are using; Dave Dunham by the "Dunham Digger" shovel; Dave Rasmussen by Rasmussen Roofing Equipment; and Claude Bolton by Claude's Hardware on the carpenter's apron. Our dear friend Joe Wannamaker is remembered on the cement mixer. There is also a brick with each emeritus member's name. I don't ever want to forget the contributions that past members have made to our organization, and I attempted to honor them in the best way I know how...through the carvings.

—Dave Stetson

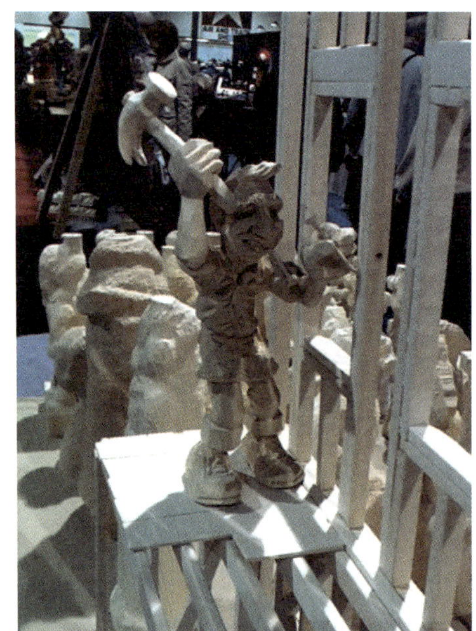

Work in progress

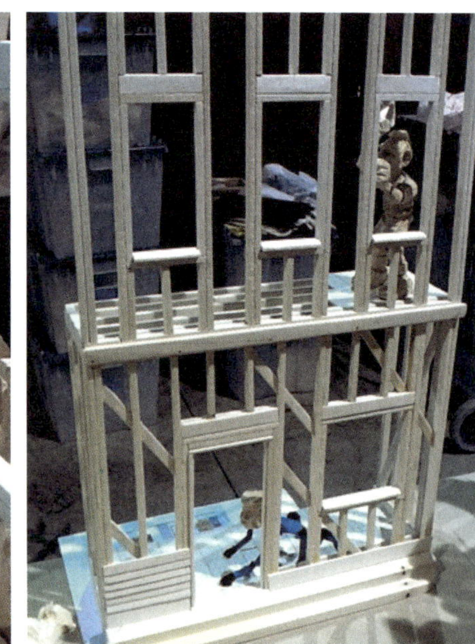

Still working

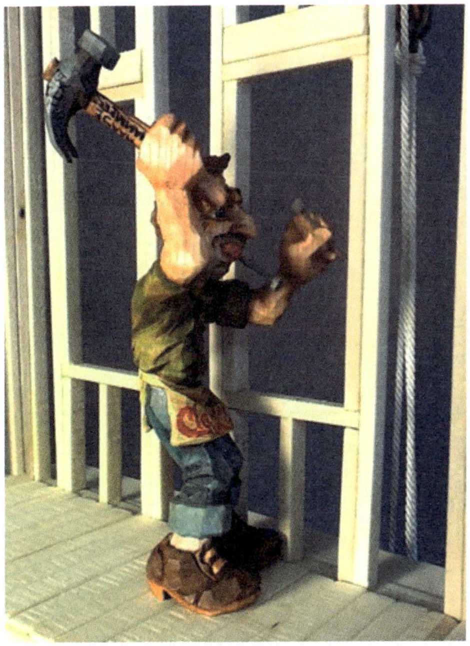

A big nail!

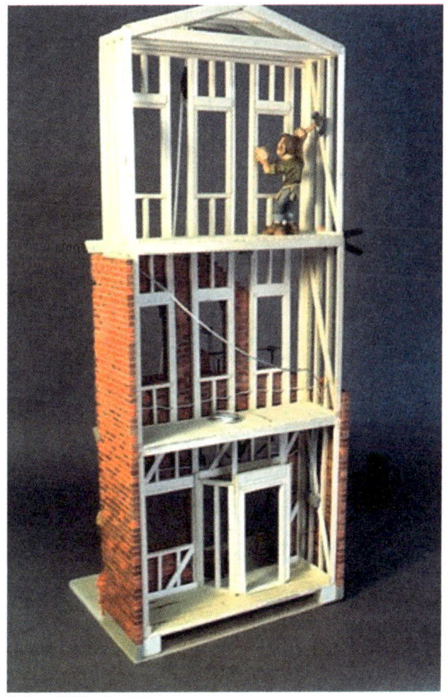

Brick layers at work

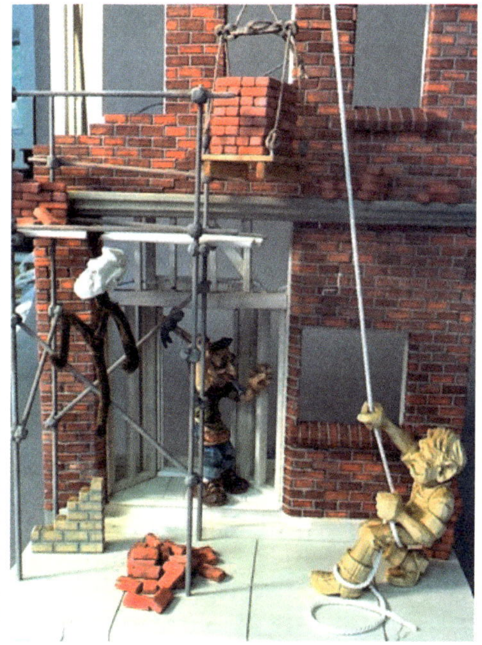

Bricks goin' up

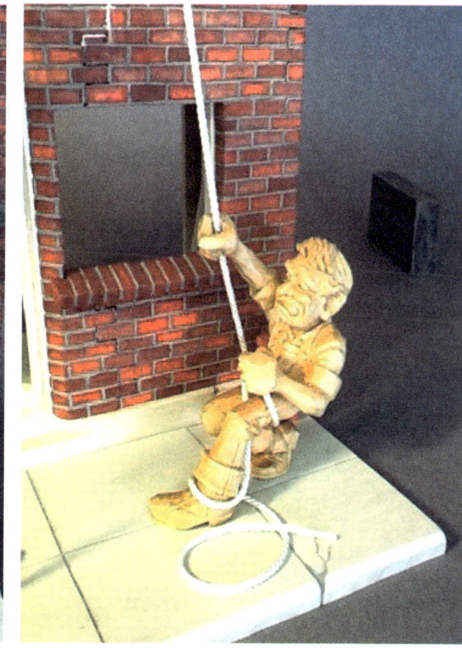

Bricks still goin' up

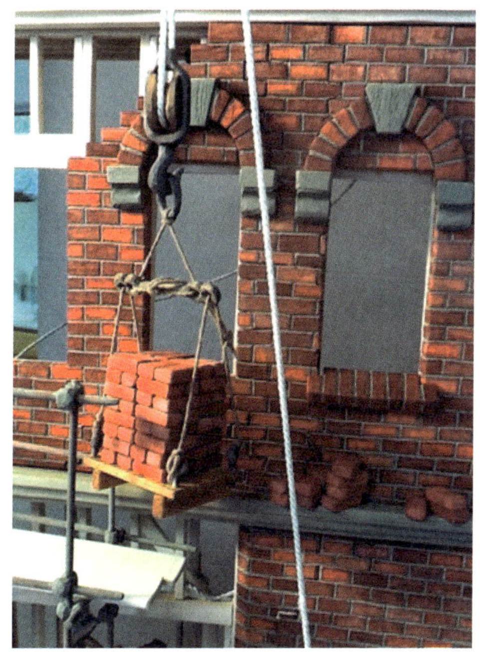

Those bricks are heavy

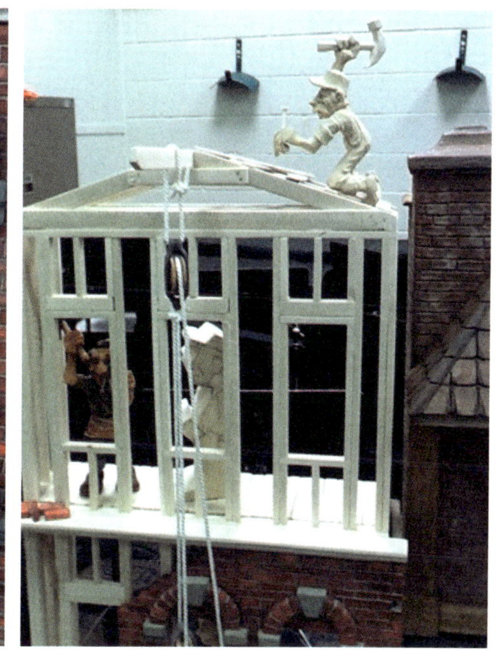

Roofer at work

The idea for the man looking for work came after a discussion with Dave Stetson about his "building under construction" concept. He said he was looking for a few workers to go with the project, so I thought a man looking for work would be a good fit.

The figure started as a rough sketch and then progressed to a refined drawing. I did not need a clay model because the figure is small and I had a clear vision for carving him. After a quick turn on the band saw, my blank was ready for carving. The final carving differs slightly from the original design, because that's where the wood and inspiration took me.

After the carving phase was completed I cleaned the carving using mild soap and water, which removes any dirt and oil left on the wood.

—Joe Schumacher

Pipe cleaner mannequin

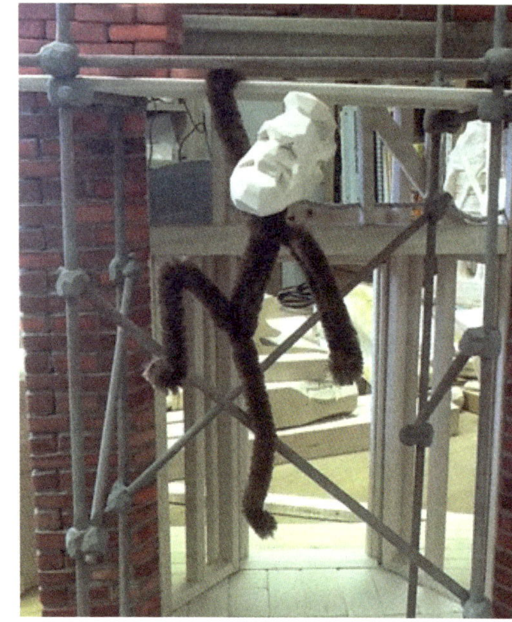

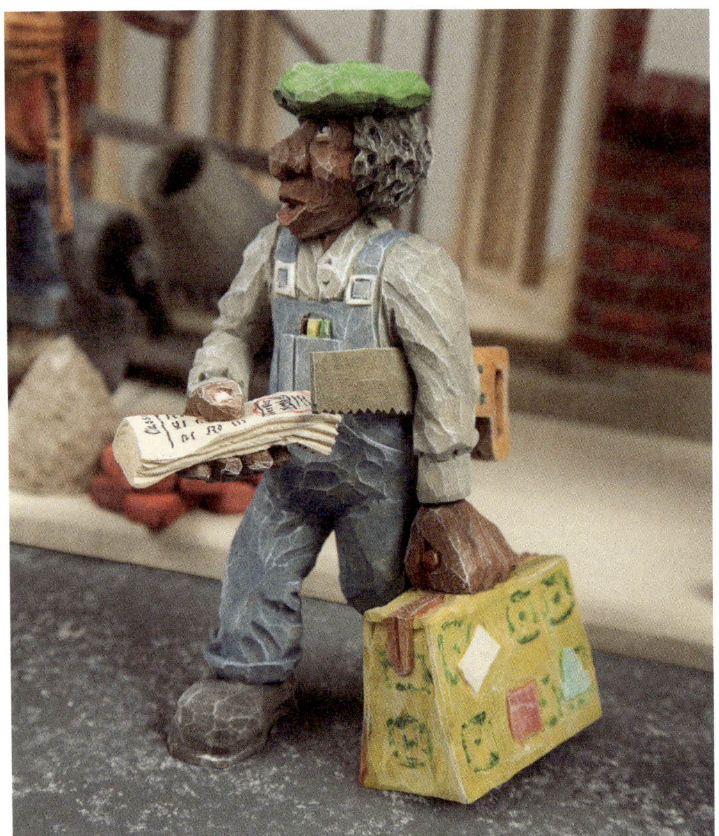

Man looking for work

I've found through many trials, that the most effective and easiest way to create a figure interacting with other figures is through the use of mannequins from pipe cleaners. Be sure to make the mannequins the same size as the final figures. Pipe cleaner mannequins are easily posed and traced for a cutout, as seen in the photos. They will give you the basic shape and size, and detail can easily be added once the basic figure is roughed out. Another method of design uses a clay figure modeled onto an armature. However, that's a lot of work for a small figure. I reserve clay models for larger figures. Either way, a model of the final carving will save on wasted wood and time. I can't begin to tell you how many times I thought I knew where I was going with a carving, only to throw it out halfway through the process, because I didn't allow enough wood or my proportions were off. That problem is easily remedied by making a model before starting. Planning ahead is even more critical when you add motion to your figure.

I used pipe cleaner mannequins for the figures in this project. Wrap the major torso and limb sections with blue painters' tape to keep the joints bending in the same place. I tried to work as much action and interaction as practical into the scene. Originally, I had only one figure pulling the rope to lift the pallet of bricks, but I thought that he probably needed some help or he might complain about working too hard. The first guy that caused trouble can be seen hanging from the scaffolding with his hand being stepped on...just a little reminder for any other crew members who may wish to stir up discontent.

—Dave Stetson

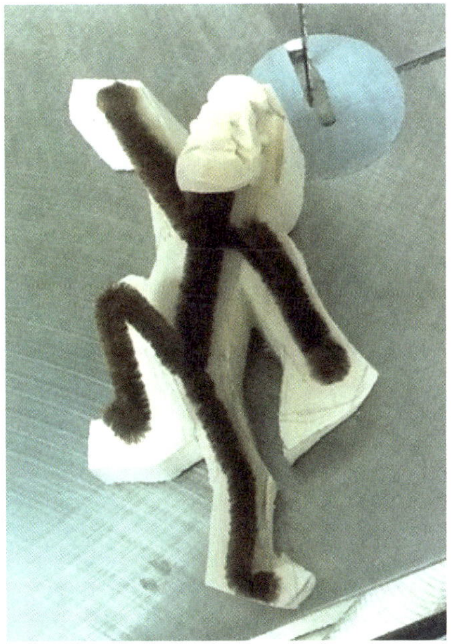

Mannequin pattern on wood

Tips from Bruce Henn

- Buff or strop your knife and gouges before carving final details.
- Take classes – Learn to sharpen your knives and tools.
- Research your subjects and have fun carving.

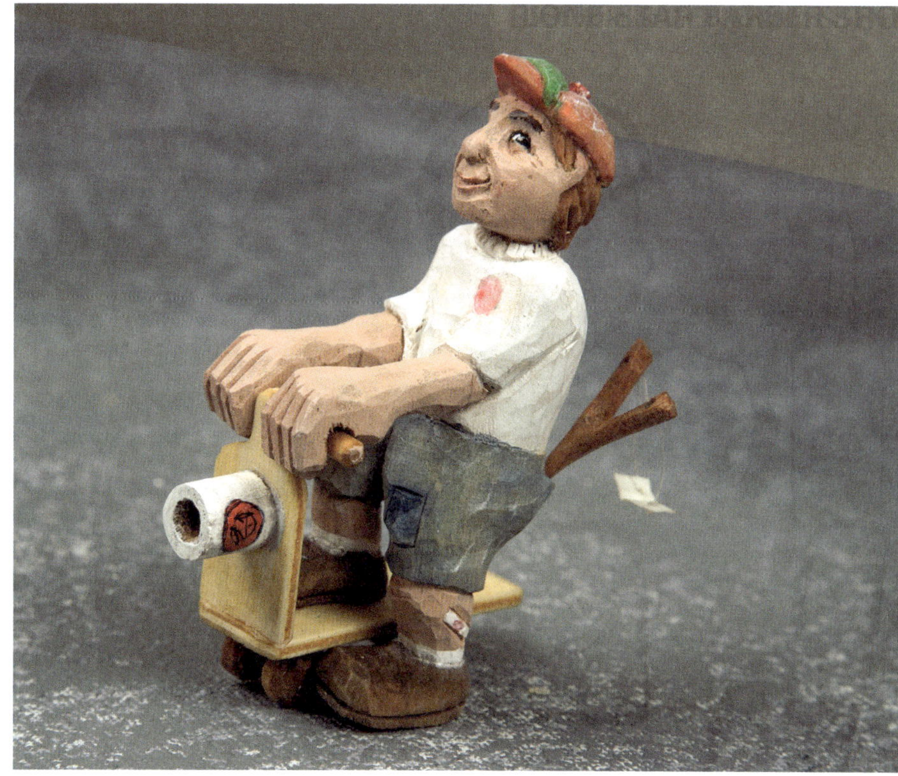

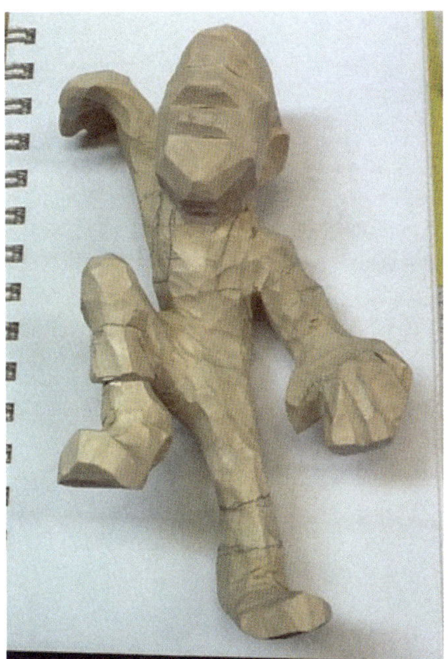

Partially carved

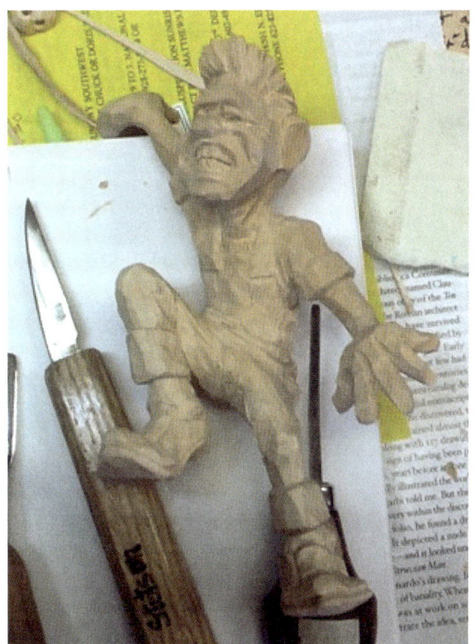

Ready to paint

Scooter Boy

I started with an idea of making a boy on an old-time scooter. I use a wooden mannequin to develop a pattern, or draw a stick figure and add detail for the final design. I transfer the pattern to the wood, normally only drawing the side view of a figure. Using wood approximately twice the width of the body, I band saw the side view which gives me the width of the shoulders on the front view. On this project, I removed wood on the shoulders to get the width for the head, leaving enough wood for the ears and the hat. I have the head tilted back like he's looking up inquisitively at the men working on the second floor of the building. I removed wood between his arms and legs, and carved his right leg in front of his left leg with his left toe touching the ground. I put a patch on his left trouser knee and a sling shot in his back pocket, because boys are always going to be boys. The scooter was made by the boy out of scrap wood and is a little wider than his foot. It has a tin can for a light and roller skate wheels.

—Bruce Henn

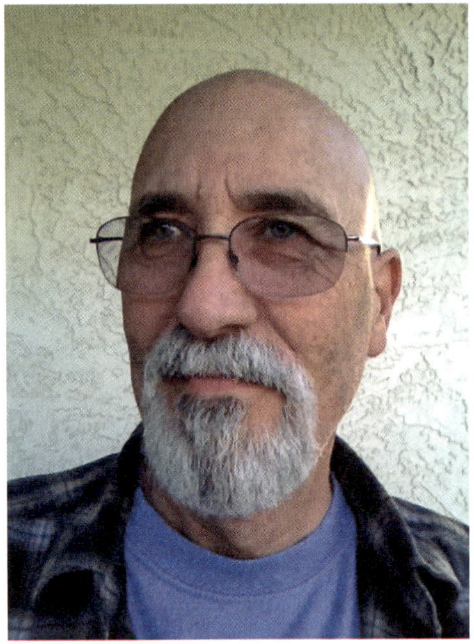

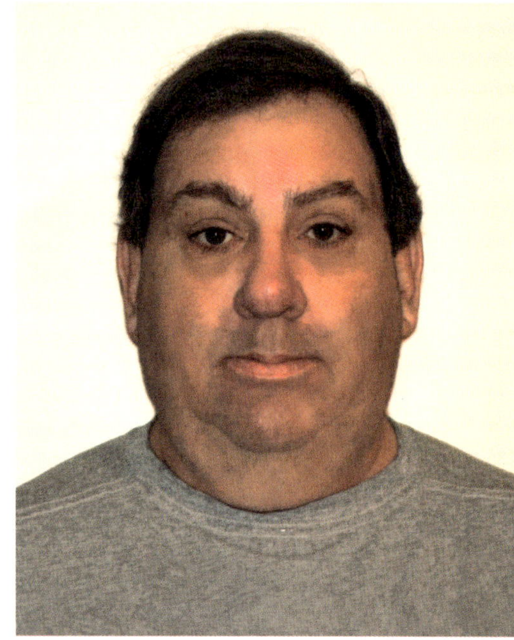

Dave Stetson

Once upon a time, a woodcarver born to a poor European family was stranded high up in the Peruvian Andes. It happened that there was an expedition of Spanish conquistadors searching for Inca treasures who stumbled upon the remains of what would become known as "the ark of Yesah" (mentioned in an old copy of *National Geographic*). In the excitement and confusion surrounding the archeological find, Stetson's ancestor became engrossed with one of his carvings and was separated from the troop of conquistadors. He managed to survive on the fringe of a forested area just above the tree line and spent his remaining days carving and tending to the local ladies. Many, many, many generations later, and a long journey north, David's mother gave birth to a son who, as it turns out, became a woodcarver in the tradition of his absent-minded ancestor. David often becomes so engrossed with carving that he seems to be lost in the Andes, and makes up stories to update his biography. After all, his bio is what it is, and history can only be changed through exaggeration and made up stories.

Joe Schumacher

Joe Schumacher began his carving career in 1990 at the age of 40. Since he began carving he has taken over one hundred seminars encompassing all types of carving. He has been involved with a variety of clubs and organizations. With his wife Fran, Joe enjoys traveling, teaching woodcarving, and judging carving competitions. He was inducted into the CCA in 2005.

PATTERNS

Many of the patterns created for this project are unique, in that, rather than a pattern for a caricature figure, they are plans for buildings. As with any pattern, there are a variety of styles and approaches to the development of the design. For the buildings, we used line drawings, mock ups, and the ever popular trial and error method. The same is true for the caricature patterns. They range from simple line drawings to detailed sketches. The design can be as uncomplicated as transferring the line drawing to the wood, and as complex as creating a complete design in clay and using it as a template. One of the more contemporary approaches is to use a child's action figure. Some of our members actually create miniatures in wood and then replicate them in larger versions for their final carvings. There is no definitive method. In the end, it's simply a matter of what works best for the carver and allows them to transfer an idea to the wood.

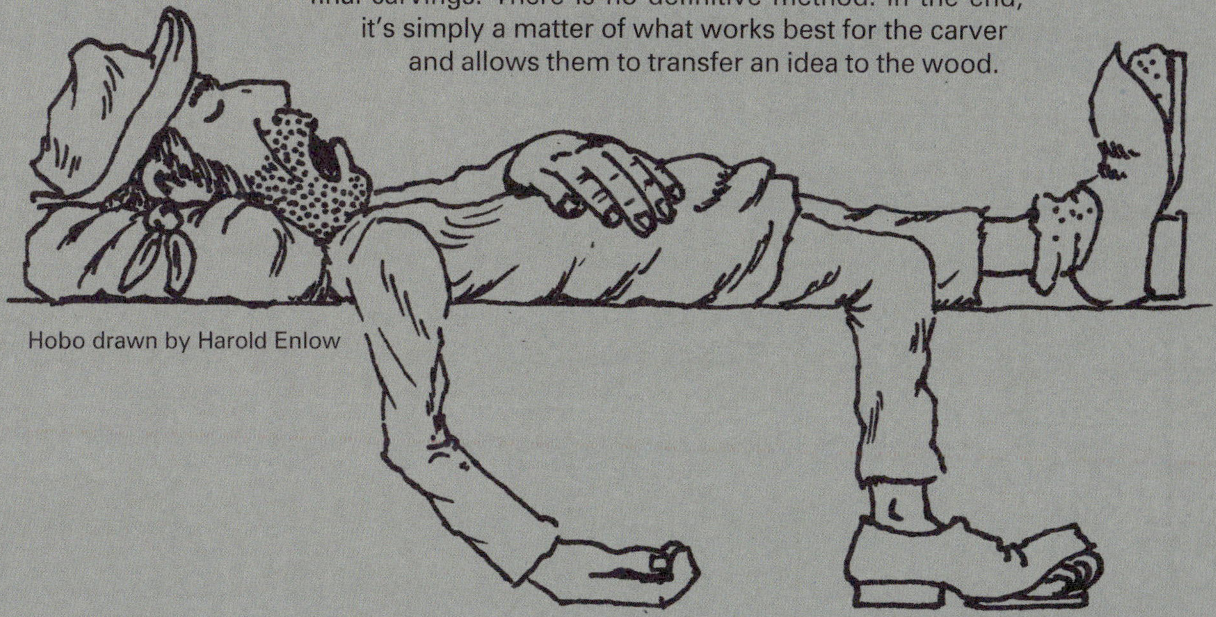

Hobo drawn by Harold Enlow

The Street Sweeper—
Don Mertz

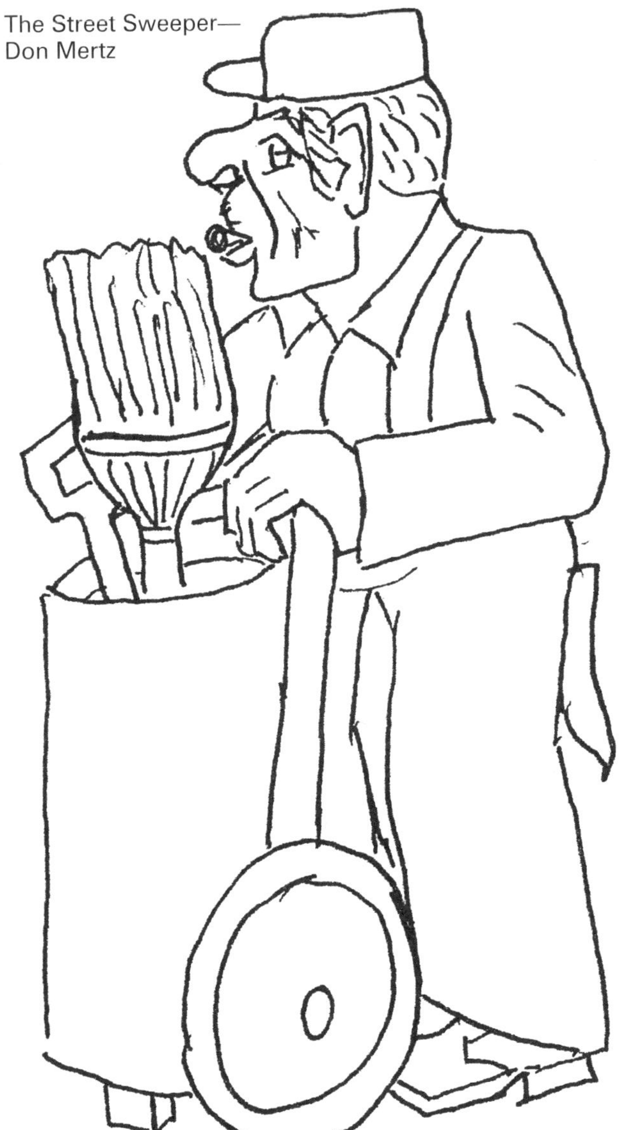

Mechanic and Boy—
David Boone

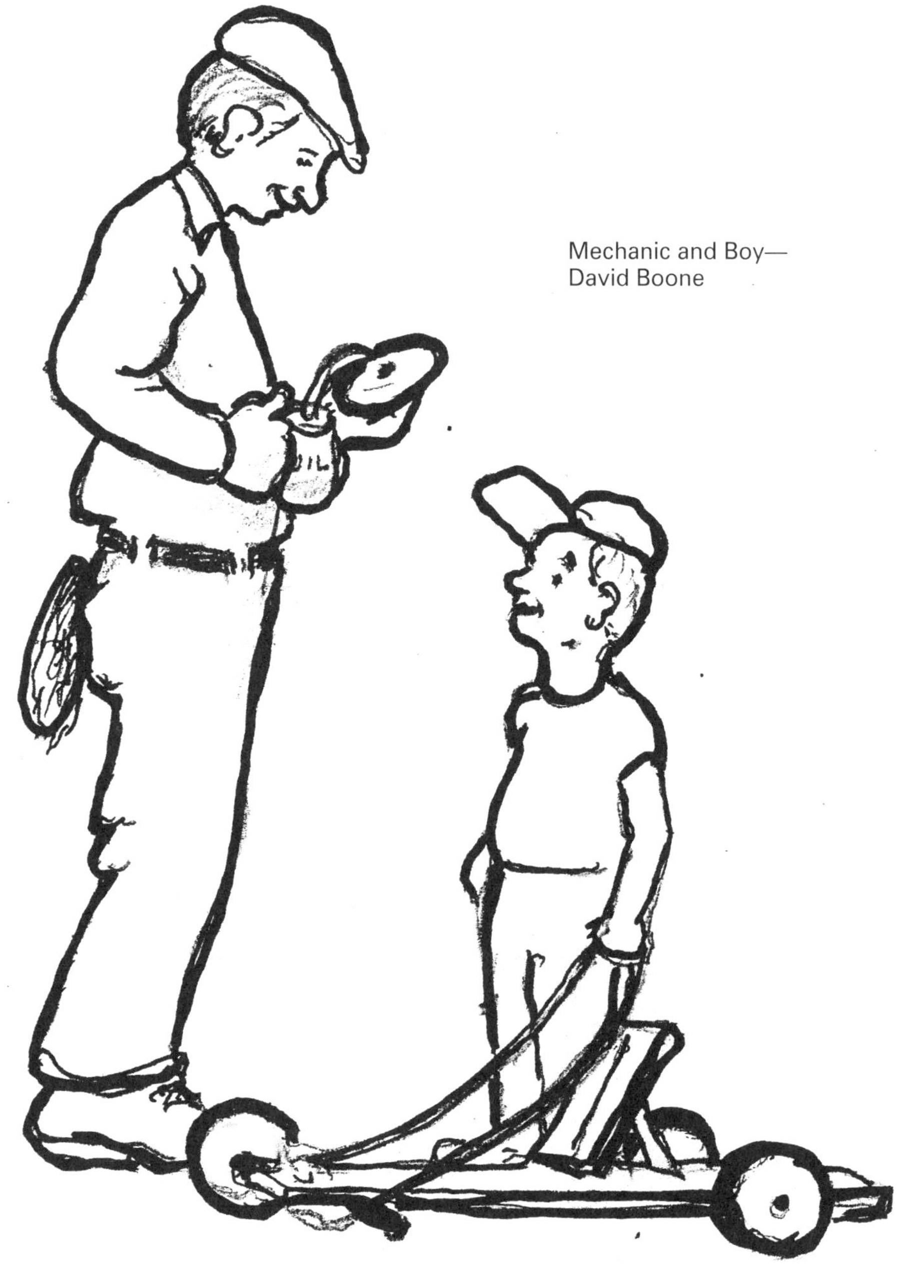

CLYDE'S AUTO REPAIR

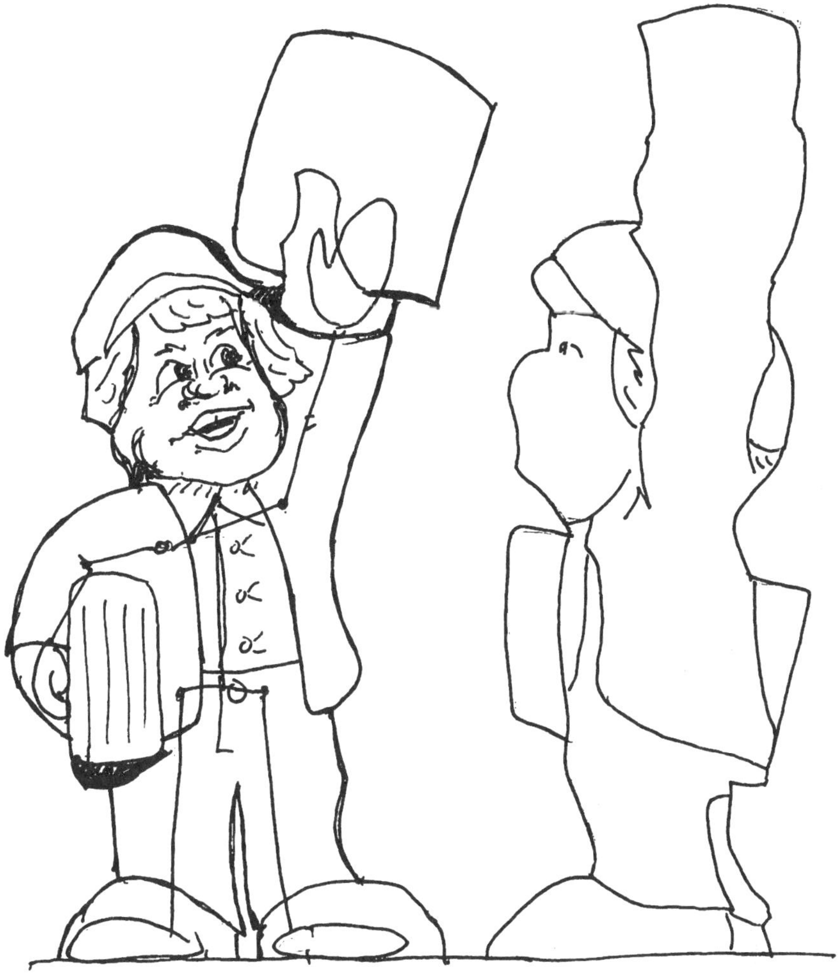

Newspaper Boy—
Mitch Cartledge

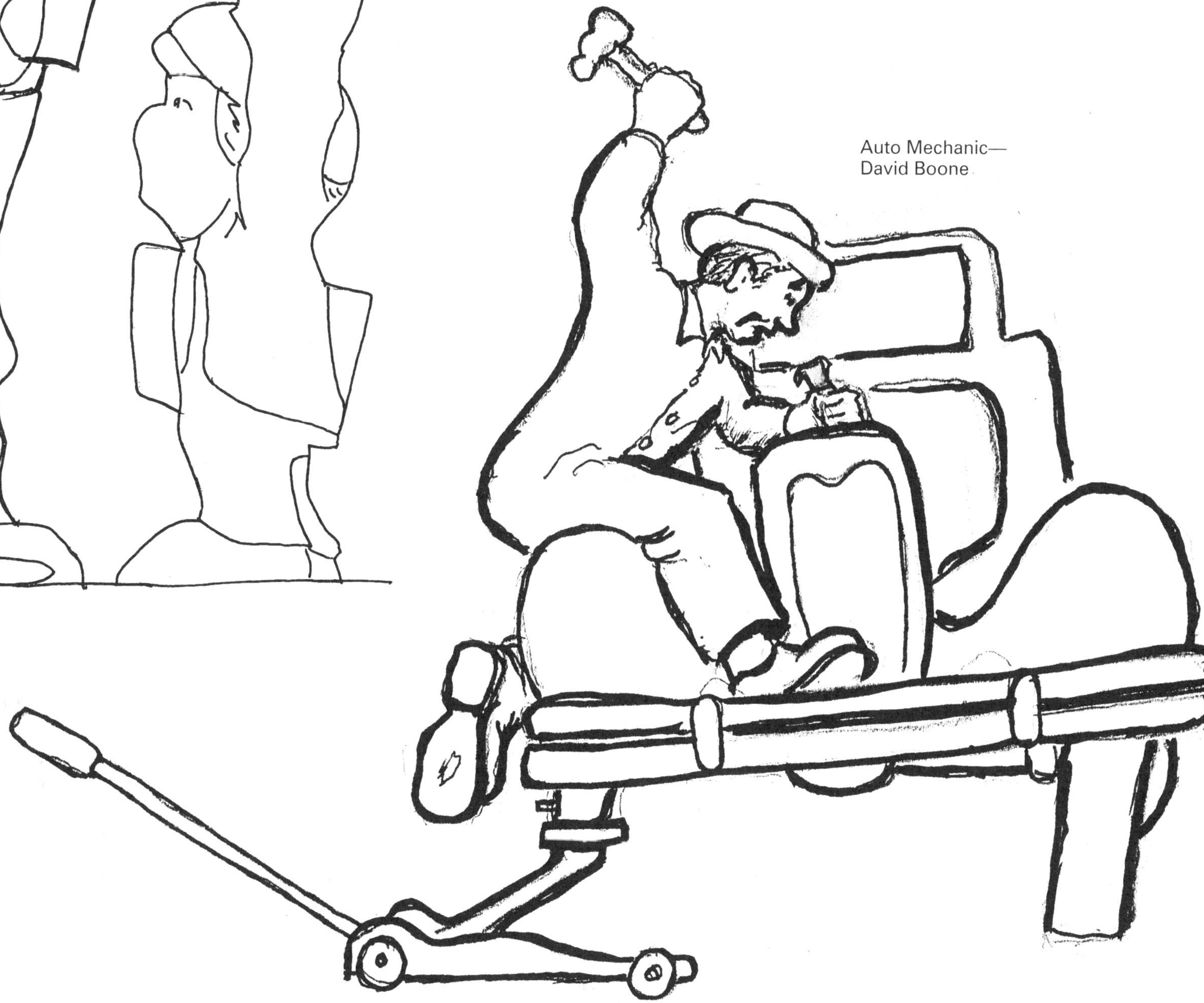

Auto Mechanic—
David Boone

A & K BOARDING HOUSE and GUISEPPE'S RESTAURANT

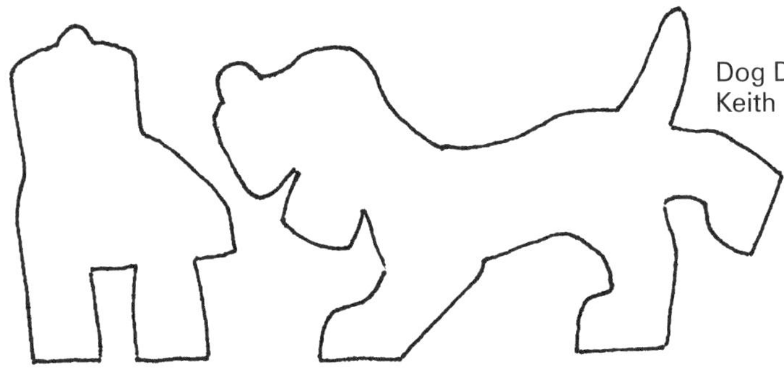

Dog Doing His Thing—
Keith Morrill

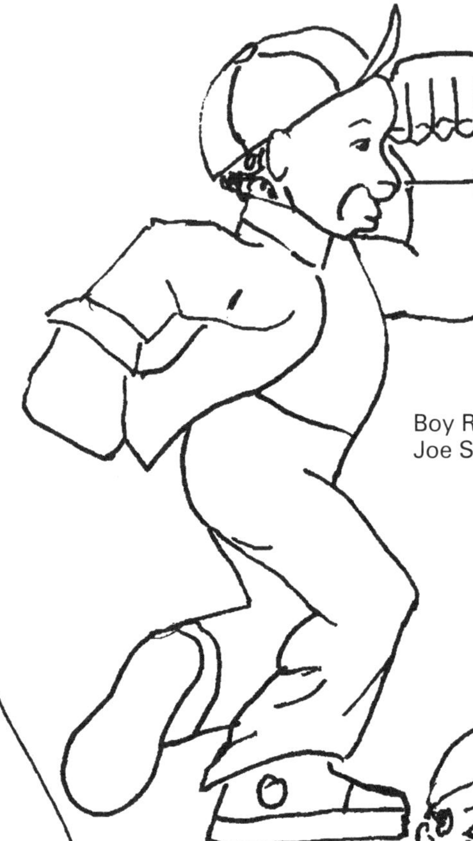

Boy Running—
Joe Schumacher

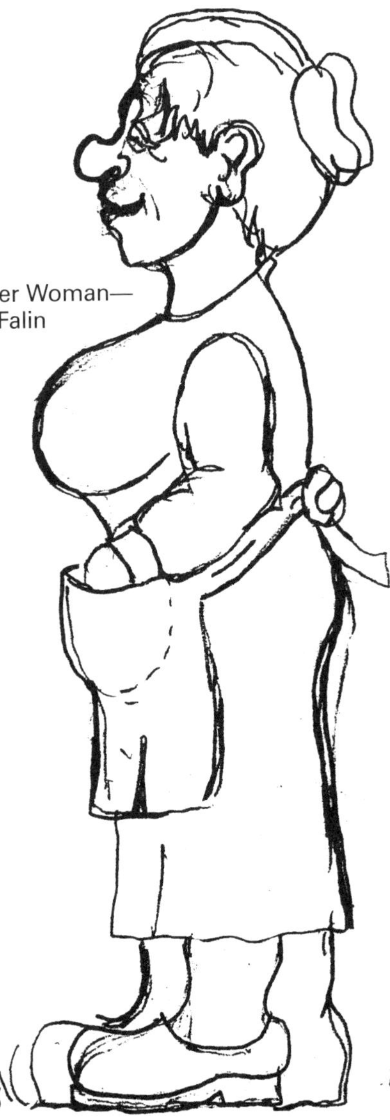

Washer Woman—
Gary Falin

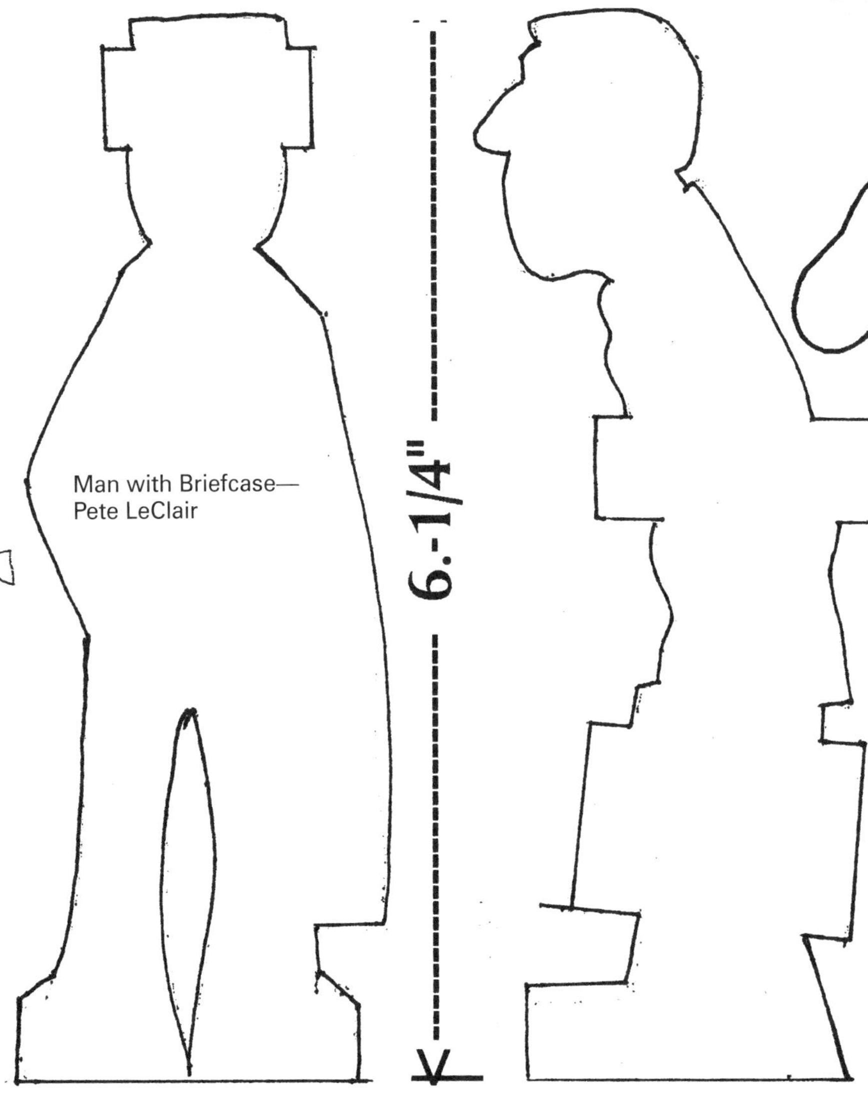

Man with Briefcase—
Pete LeClair

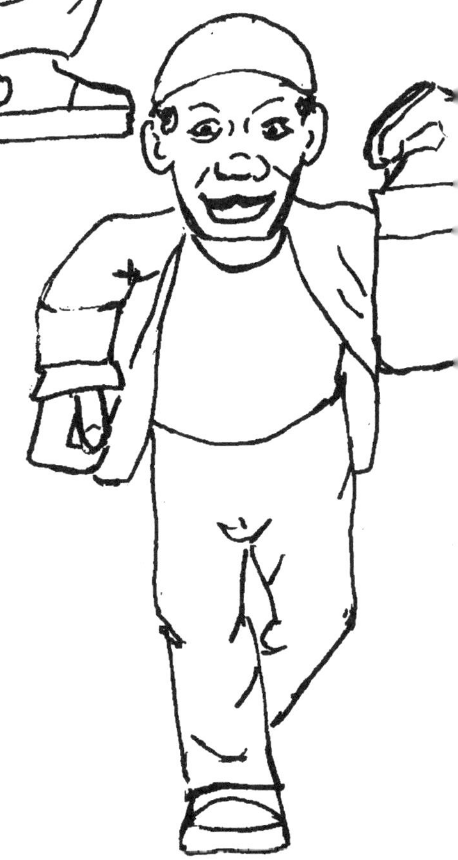

A & K BOARDING HOUSE and GUISEPPE'S RESTAURANT

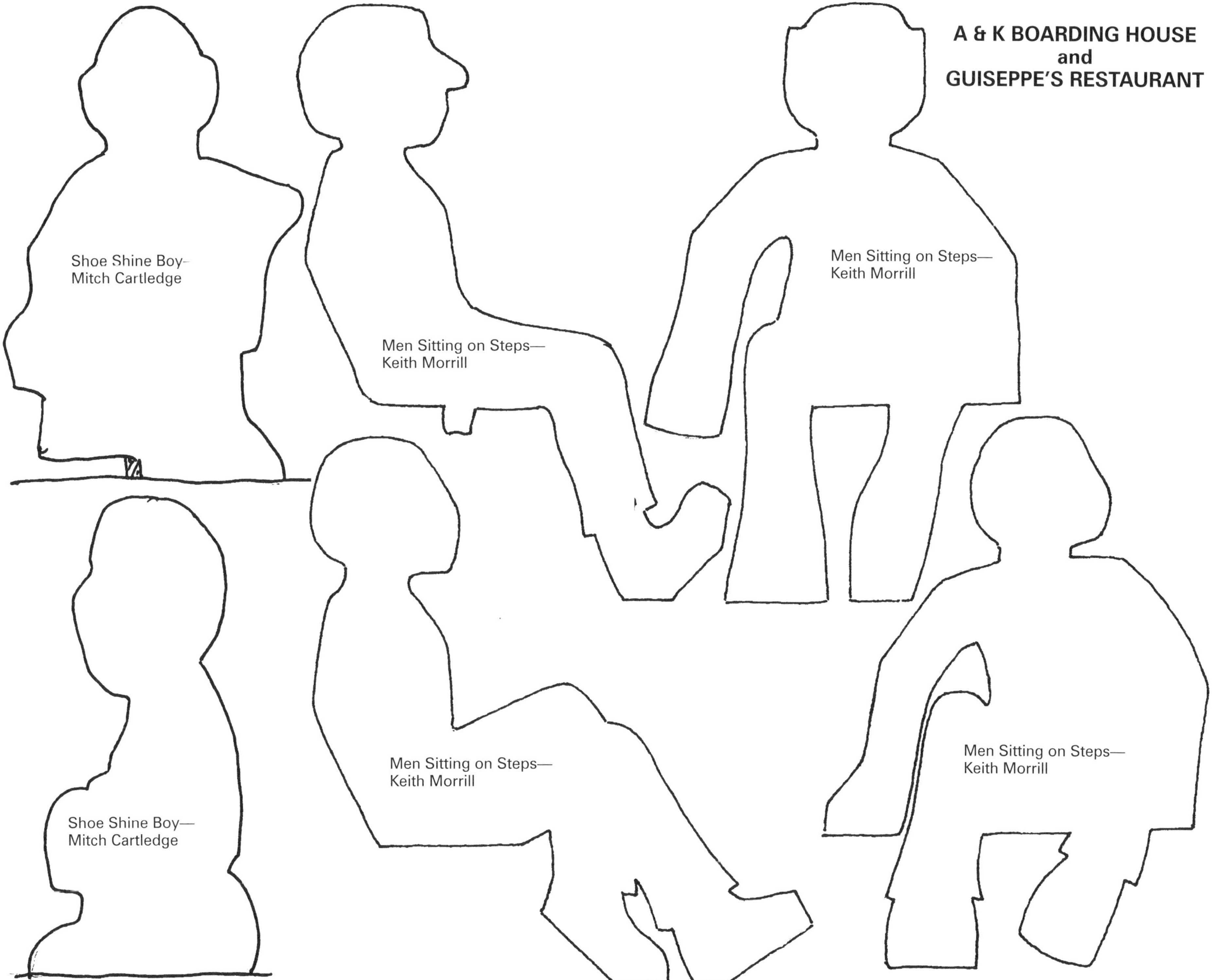

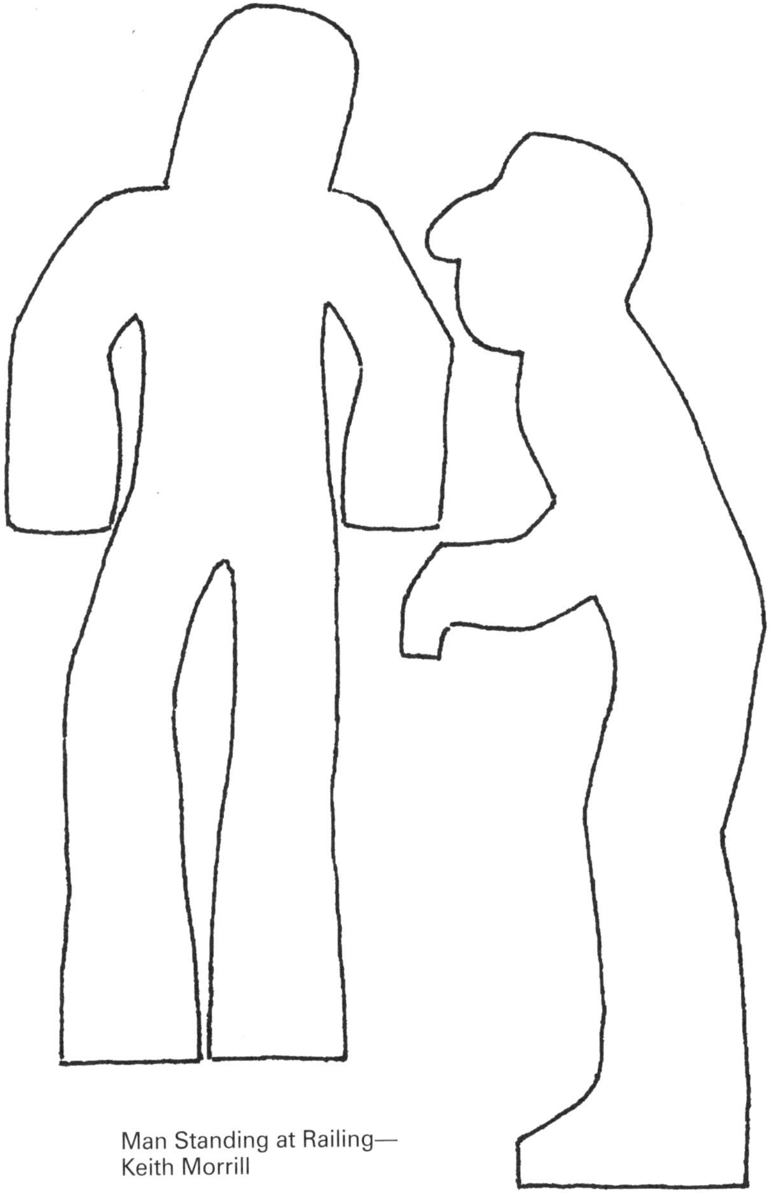

Man Standing at Railing—
Keith Morrill

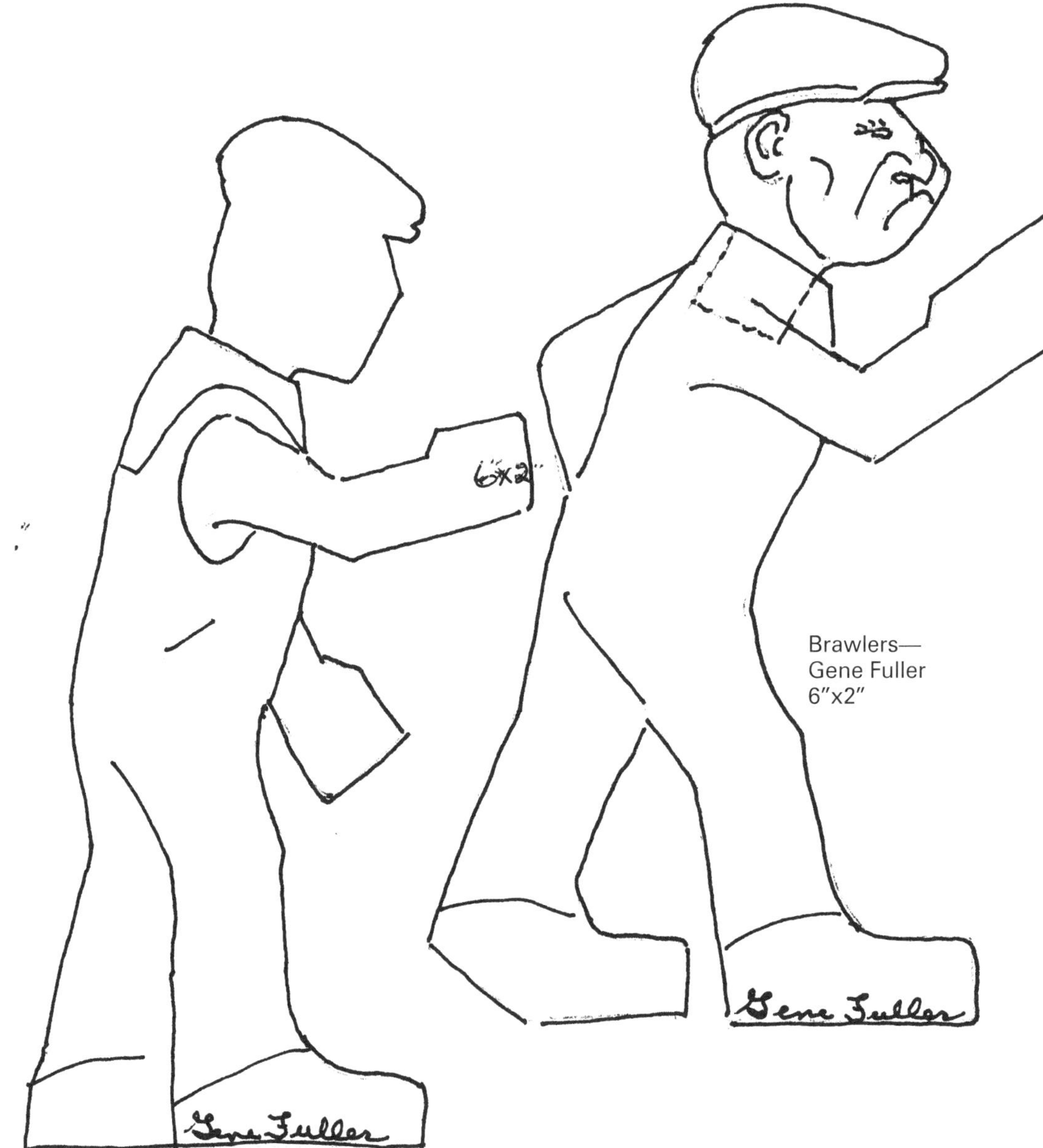

Brawlers—
Gene Fuller
6"x2"

A & K BOARDING HOUSE and GUISEPPE'S RESTAURANT

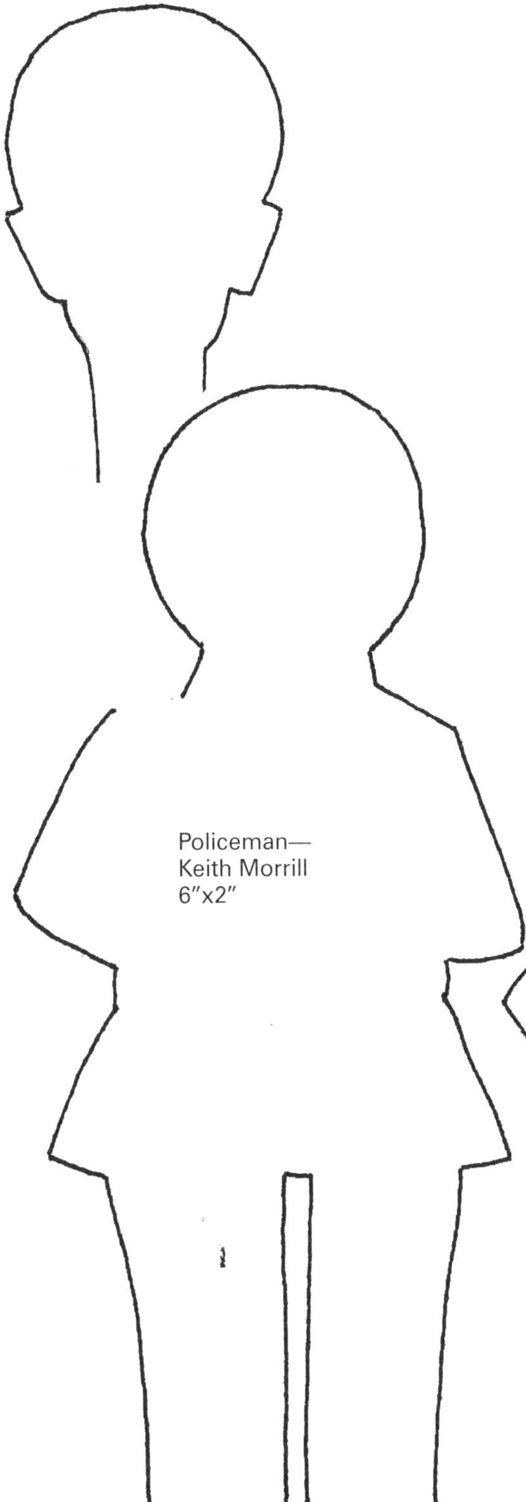

Policeman—
Keith Morrill
6″x2″

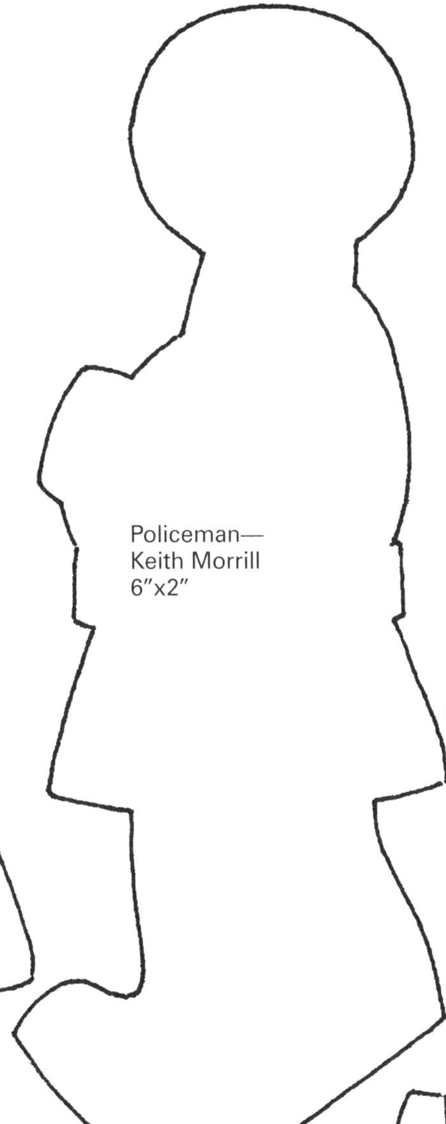

Policeman—
Keith Morrill
6″x2″

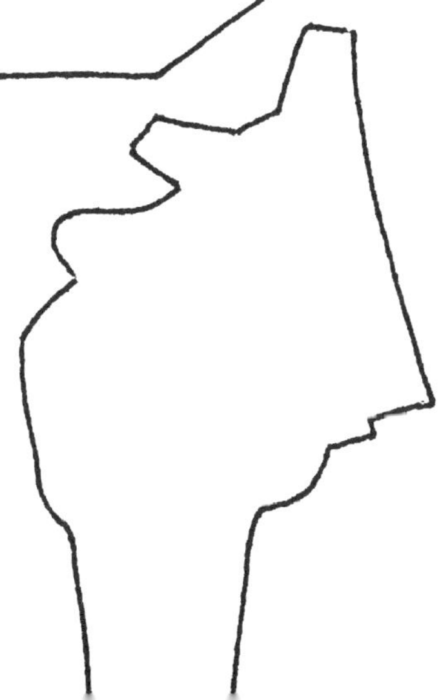

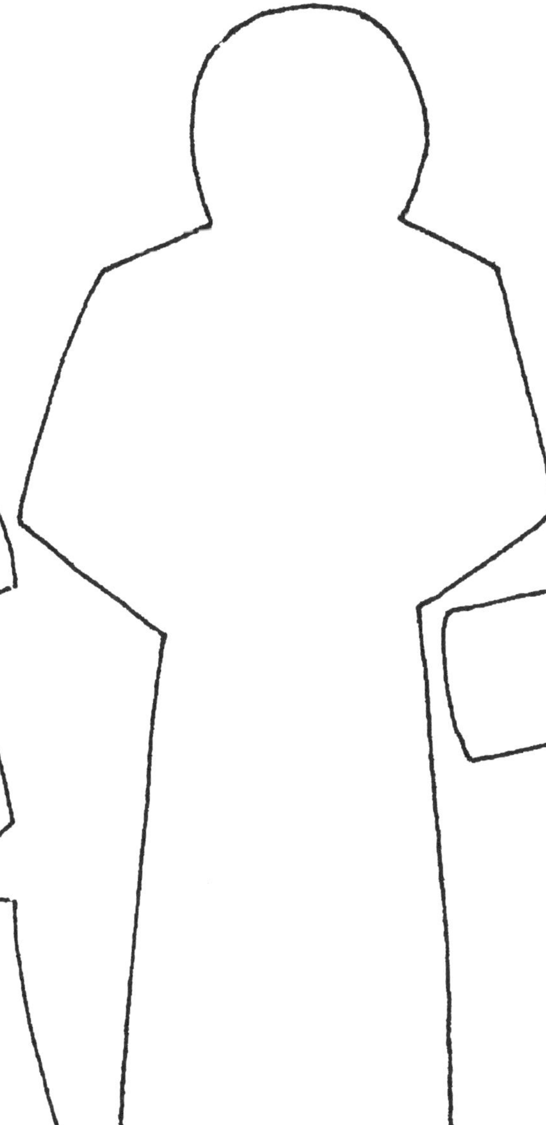

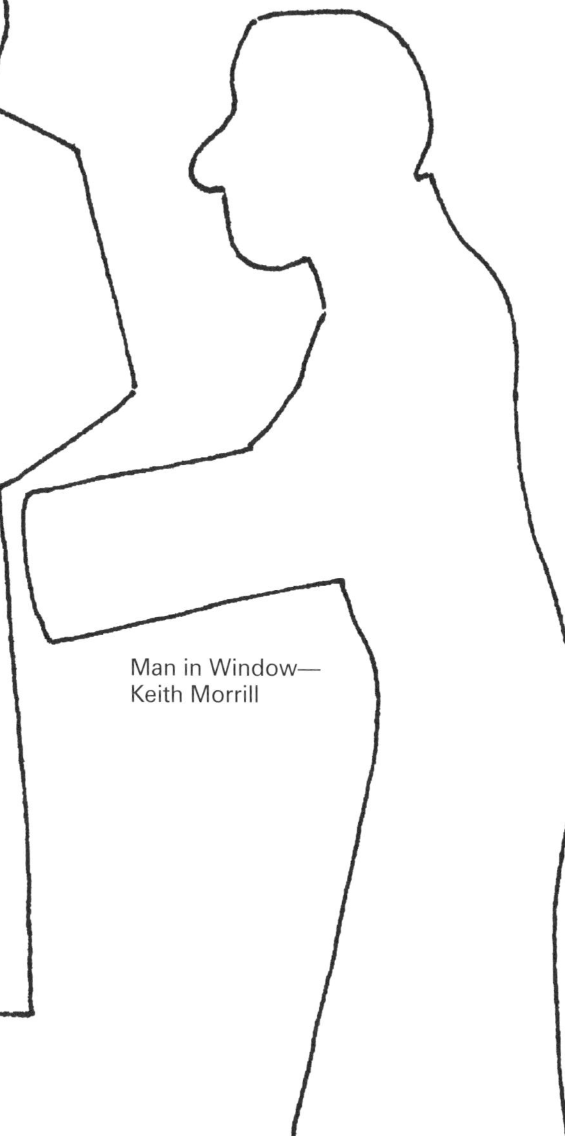

Man in Window—
Keith Morrill

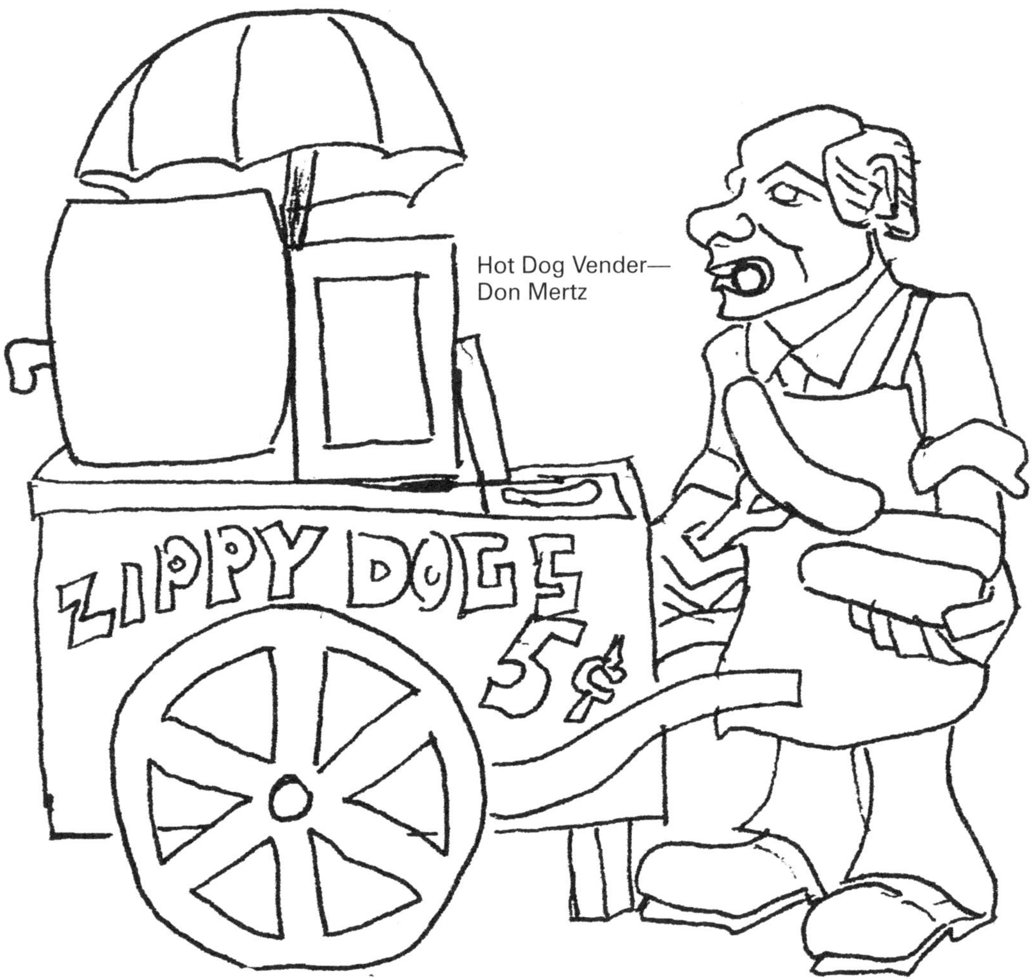

Hot Dog Vender—
Don Mertz

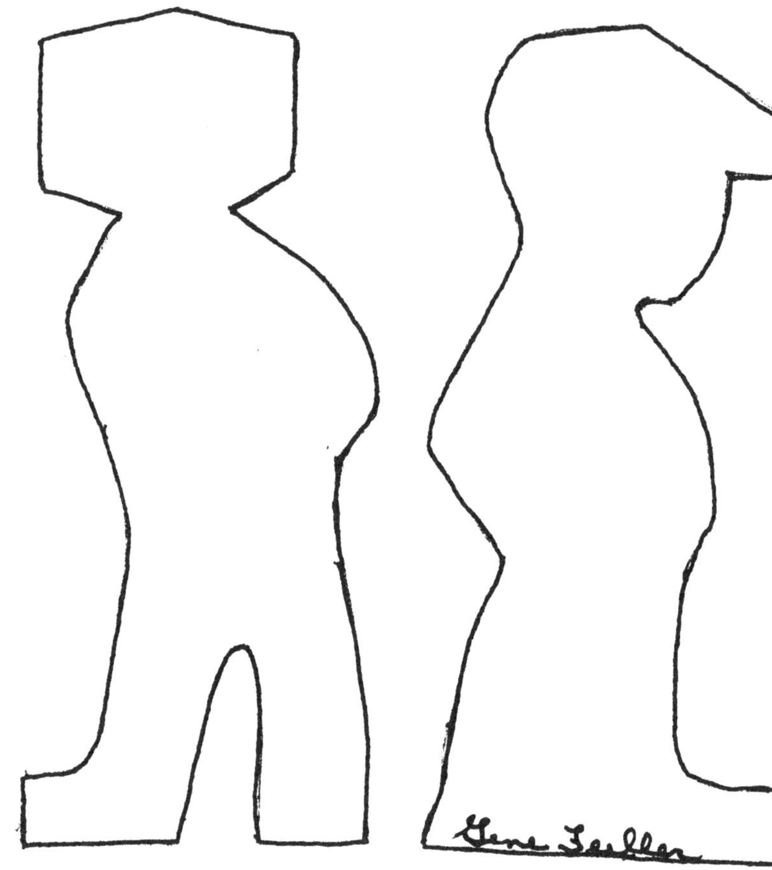

Boy Scratching his Butt—
Gene Fuller

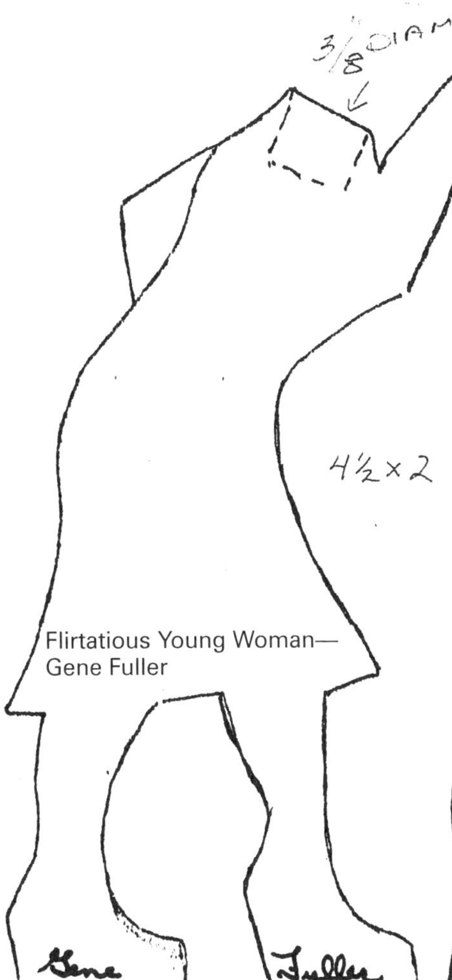

Flirtatious Young Woman—
Gene Fuller

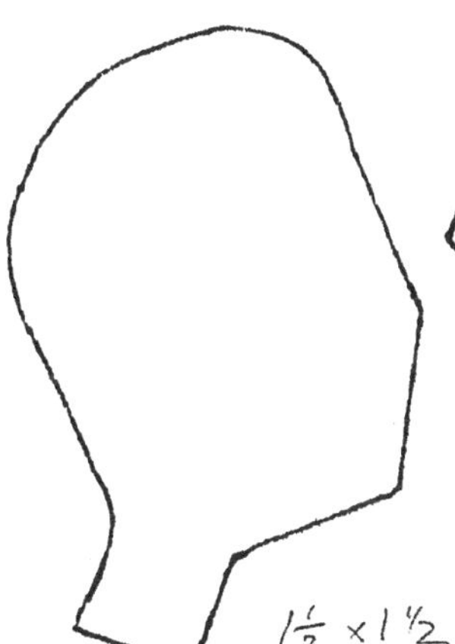

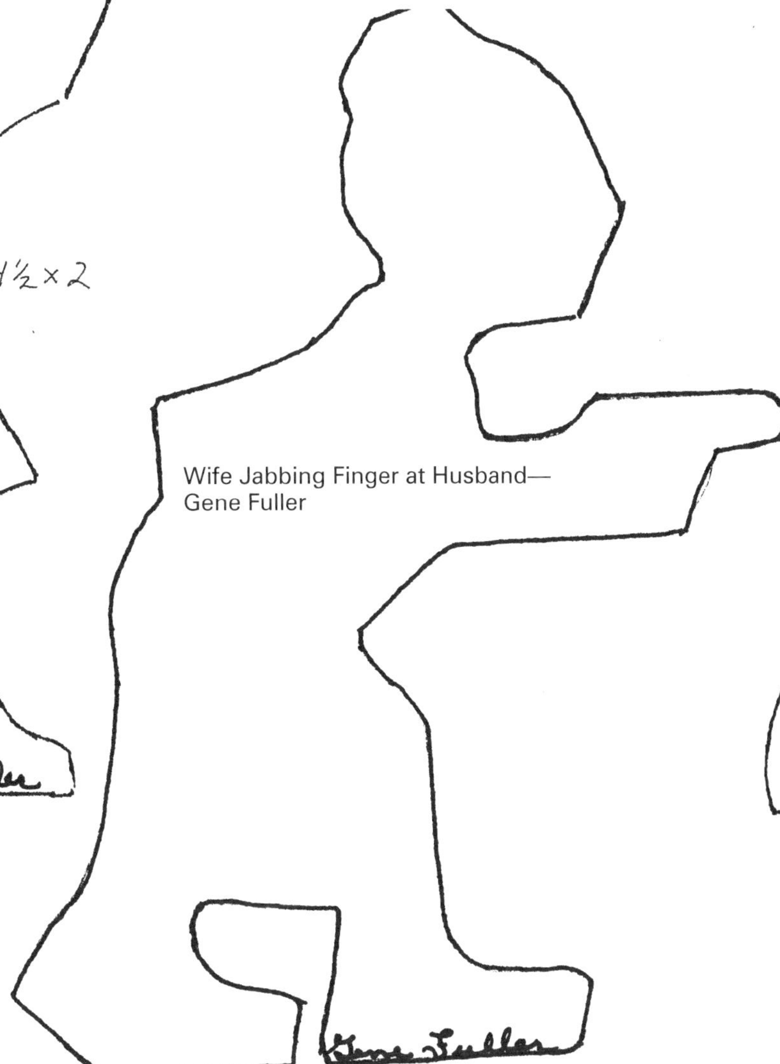

Wife Jabbing Finger at Husband—
Gene Fuller

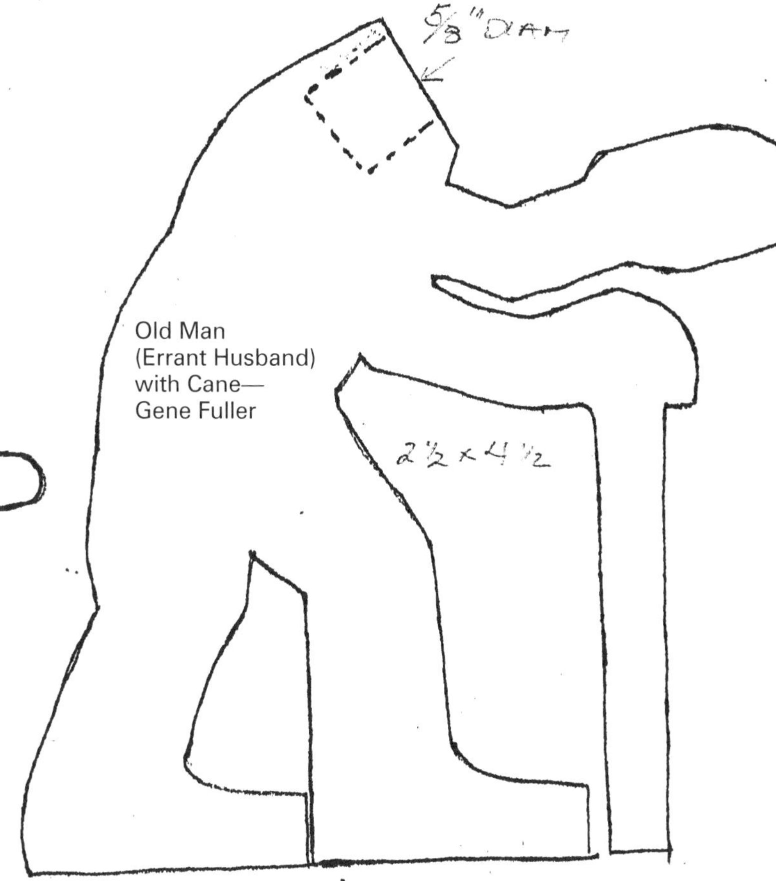

Old Man
(Errant Husband)
with Cane—
Gene Fuller

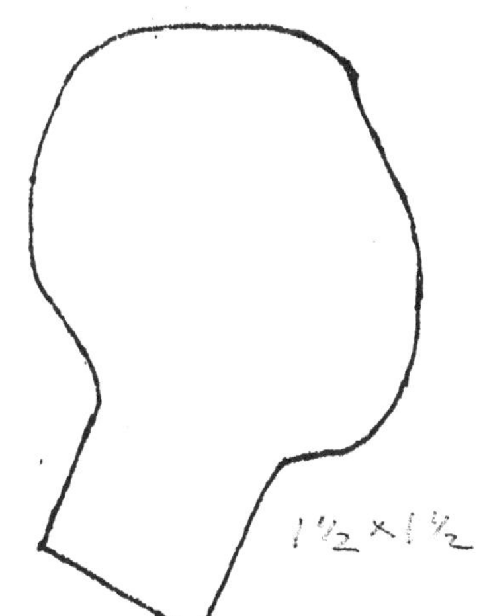

LONE STAR BARBER SHOP

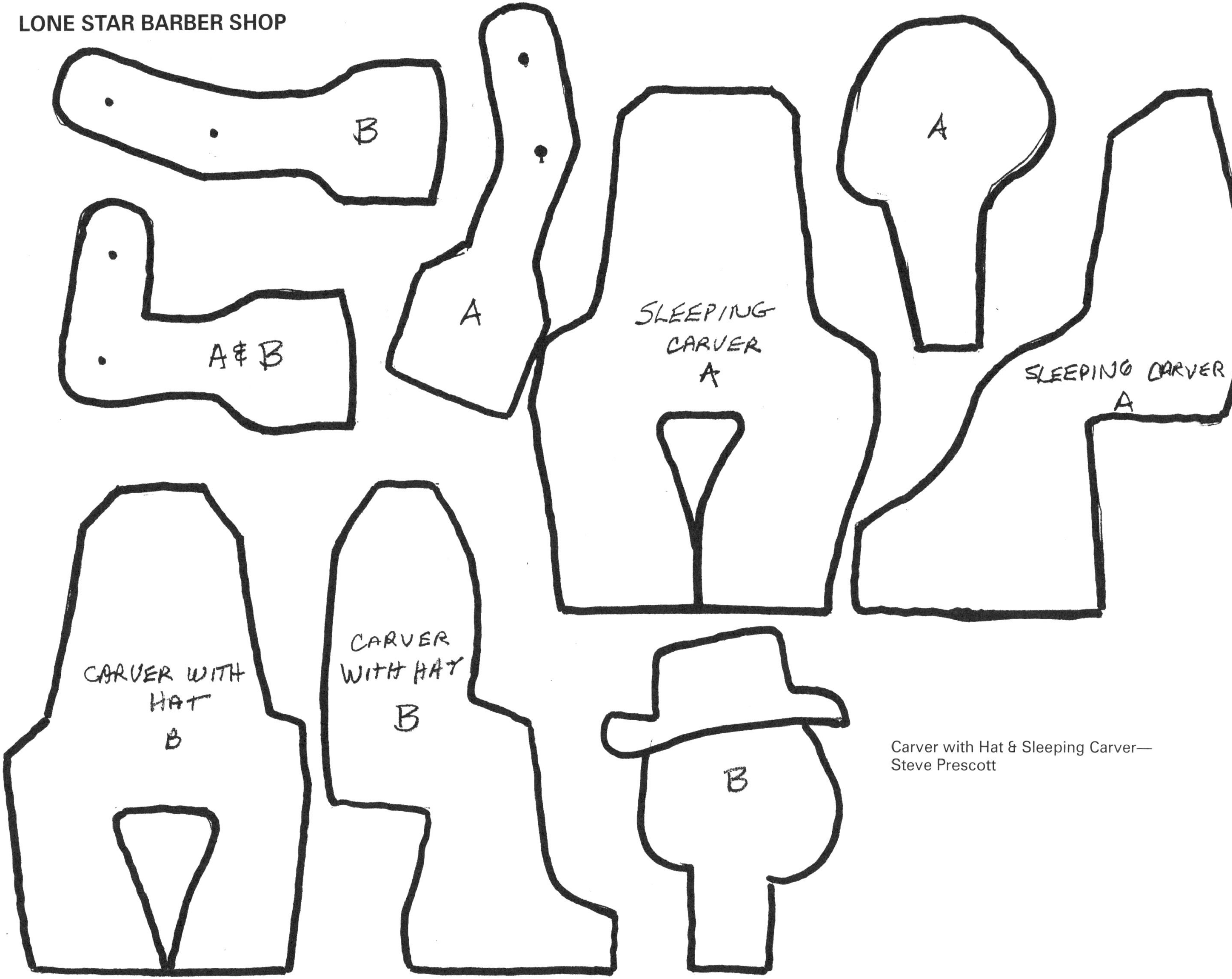

Carver with Hat & Sleeping Carver—
Steve Prescott

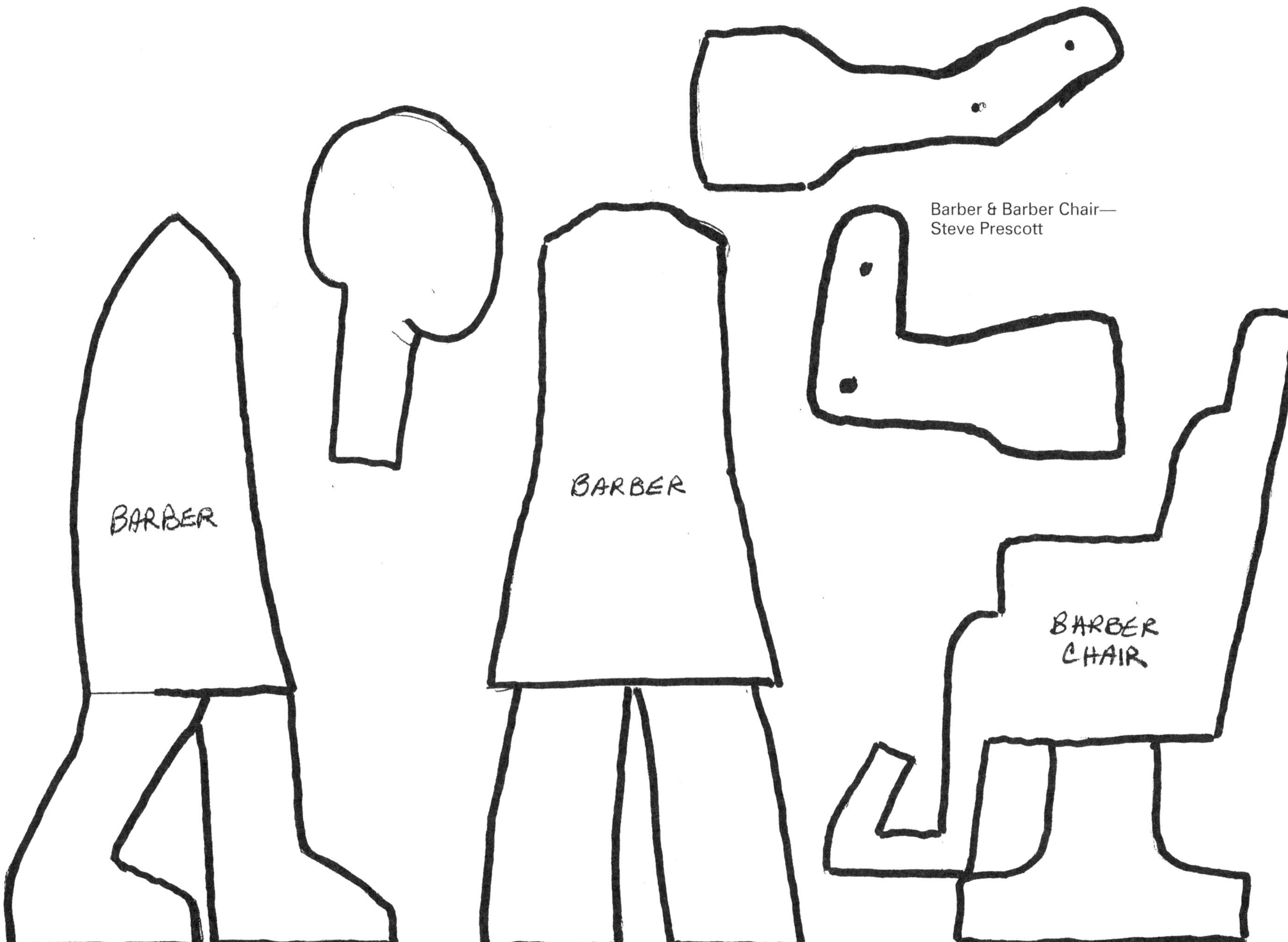

Barber & Barber Chair—
Steve Prescott

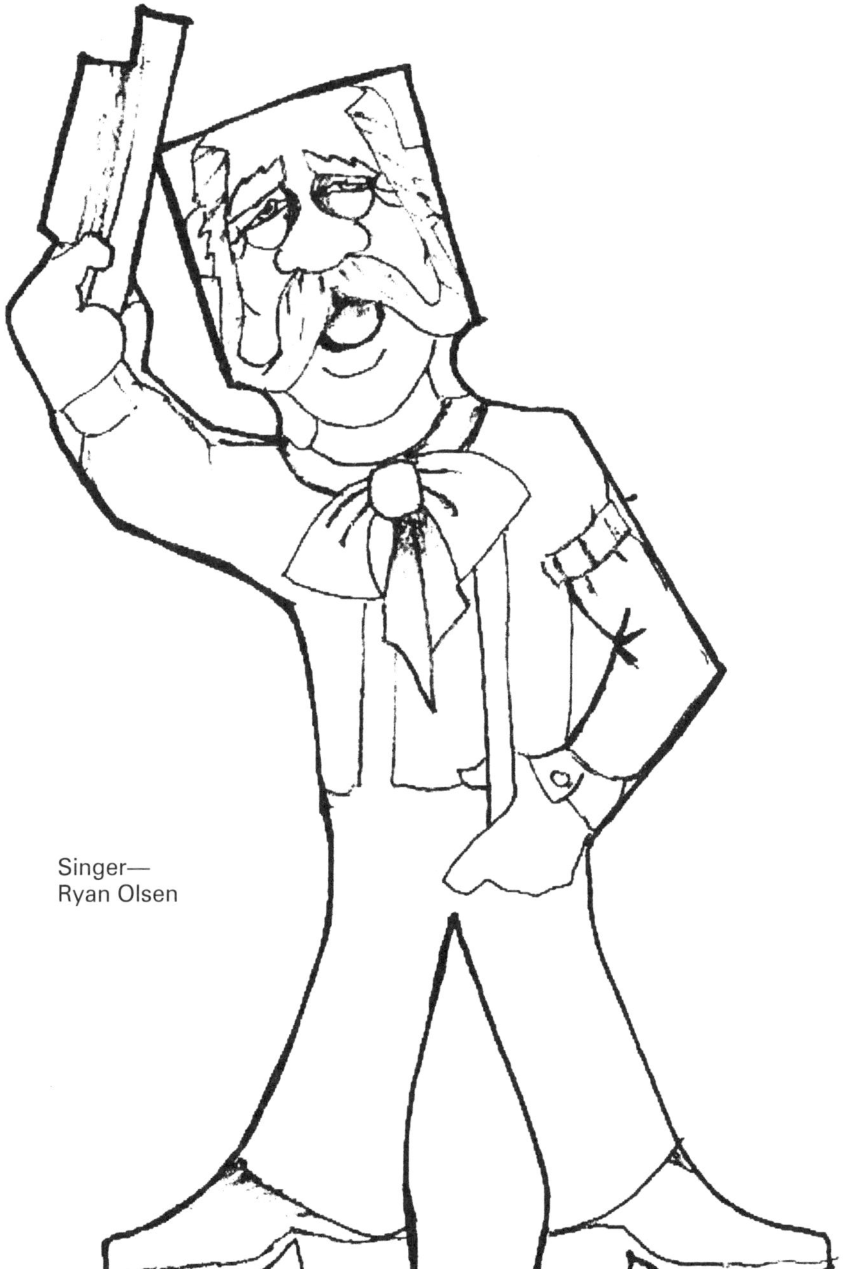

Singer—
Ryan Olsen

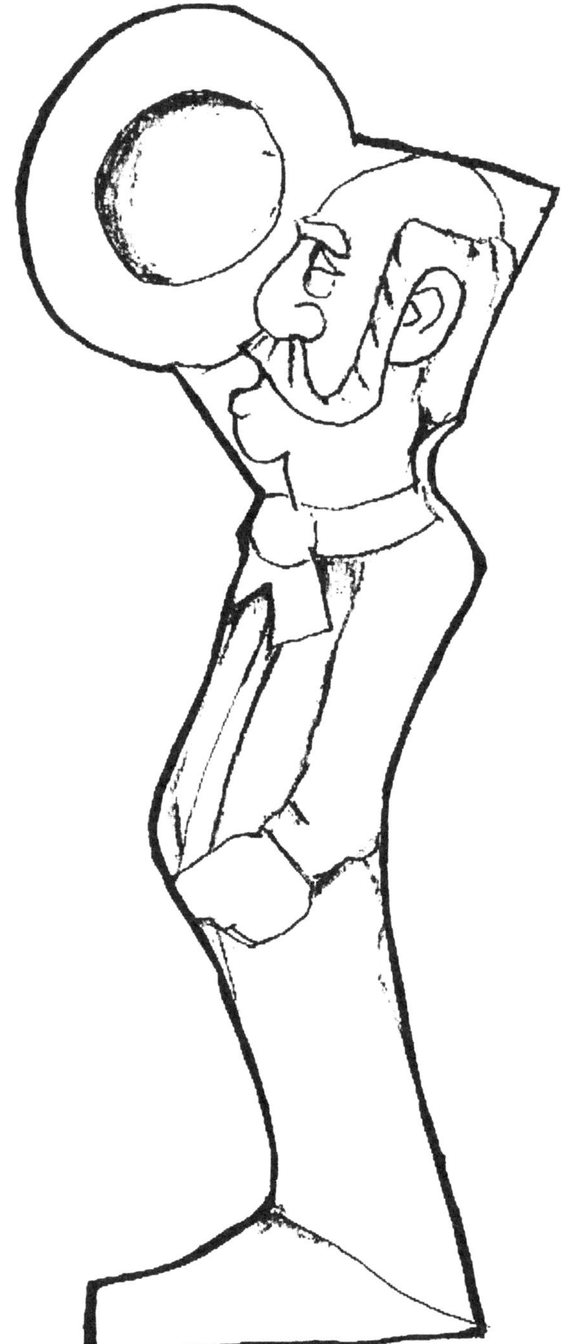

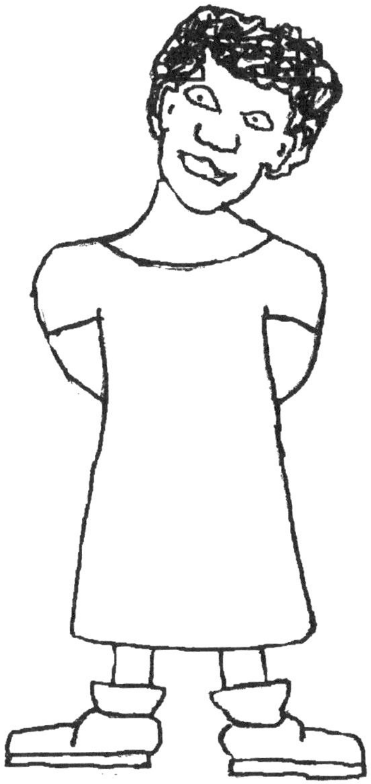

Girl with Doll—
Joe Schumacher

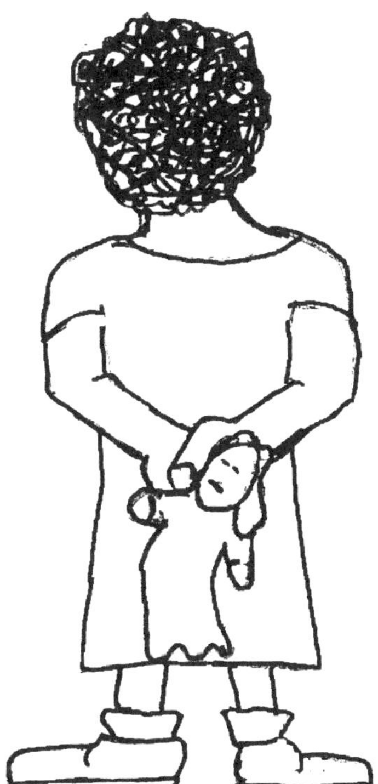

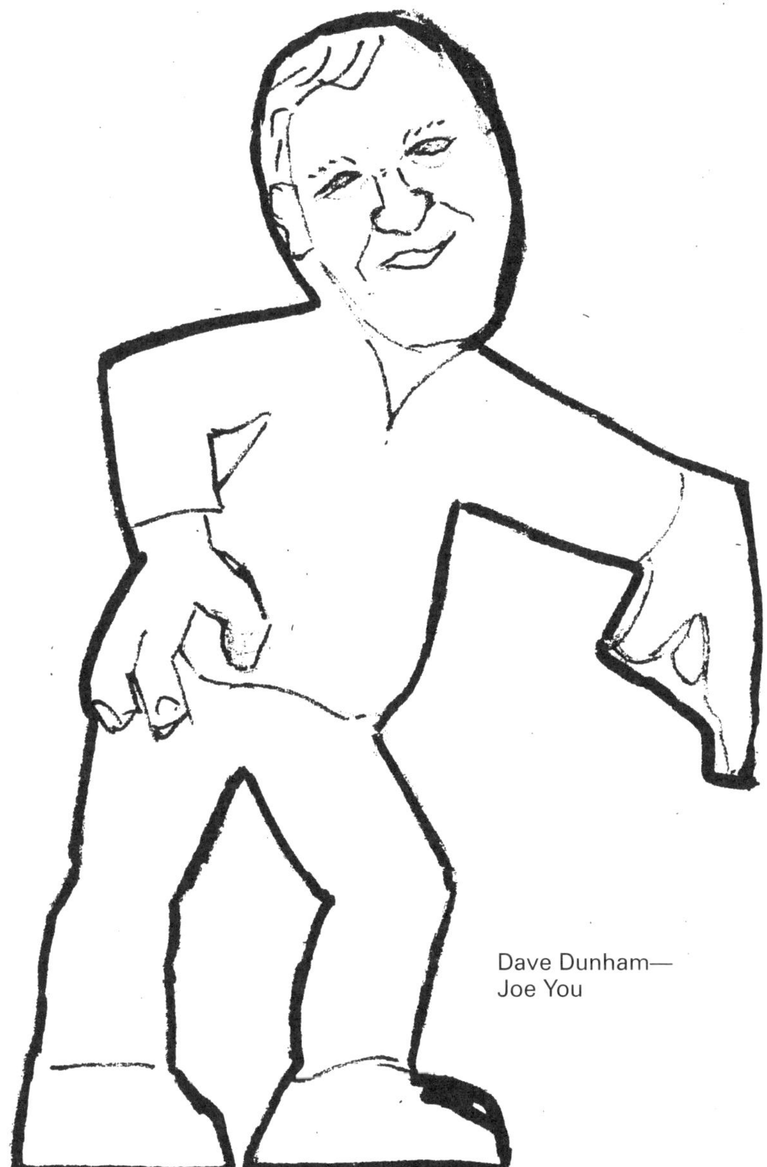

Dave Dunham—
Joe You

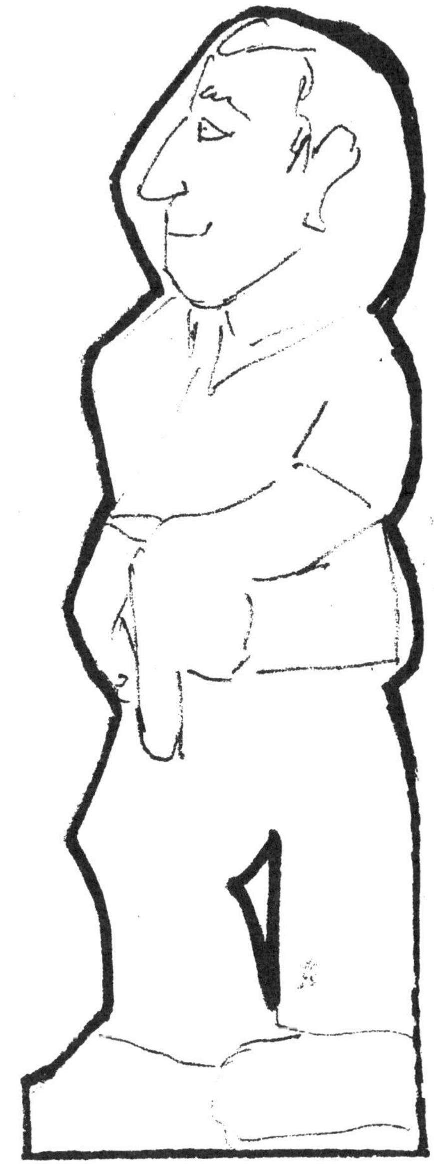

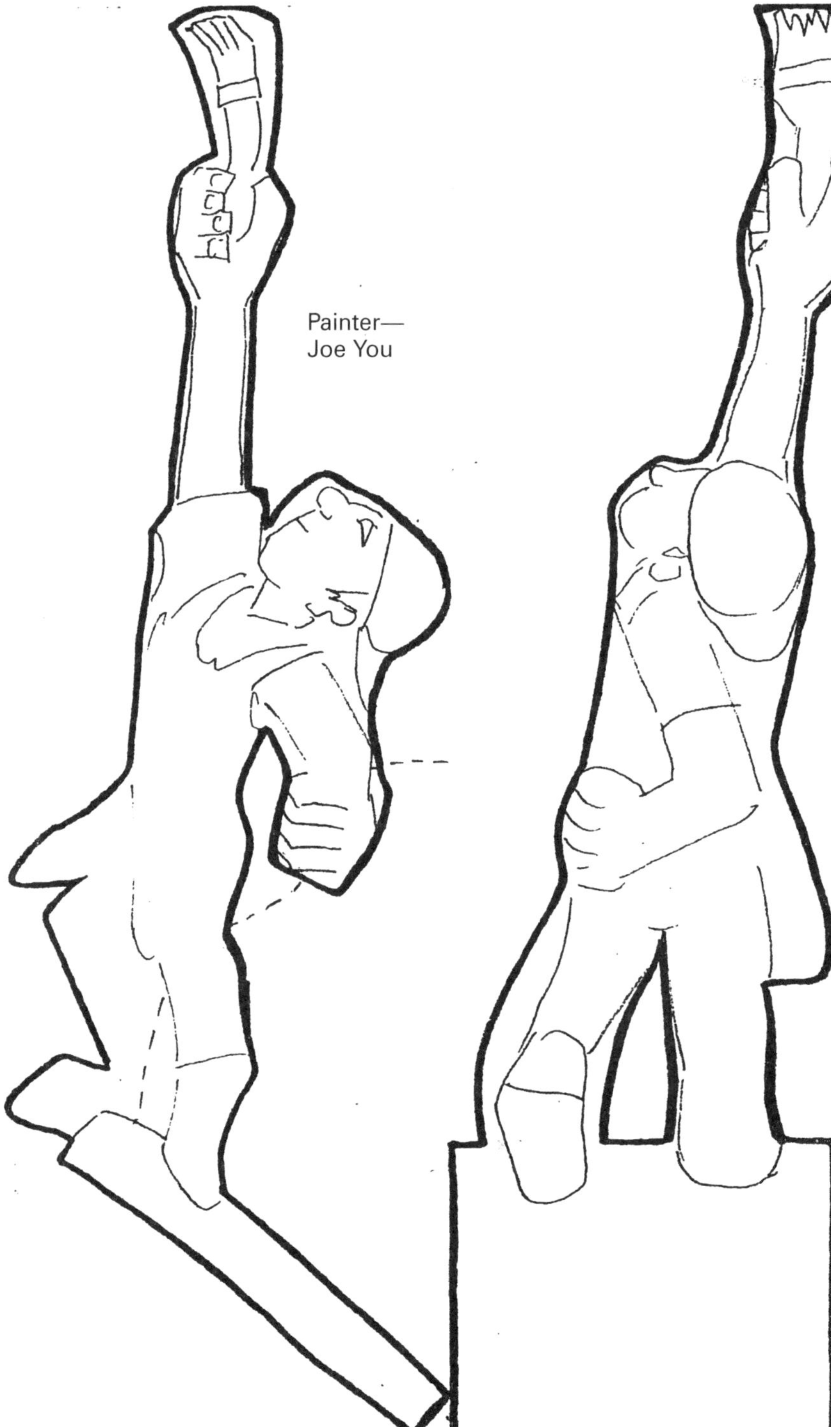

Painter—
Joe You

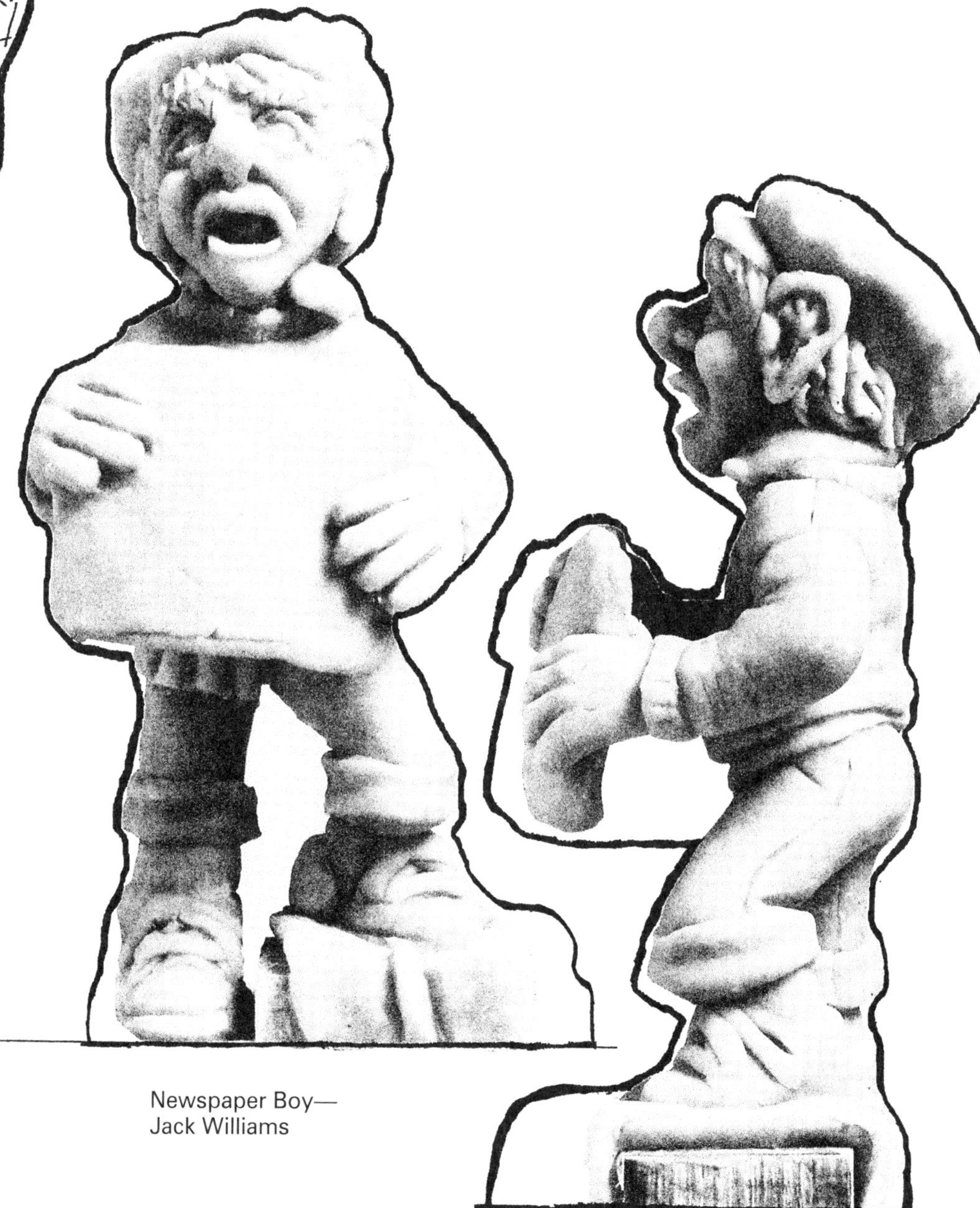

Newspaper Boy—
Jack Williams

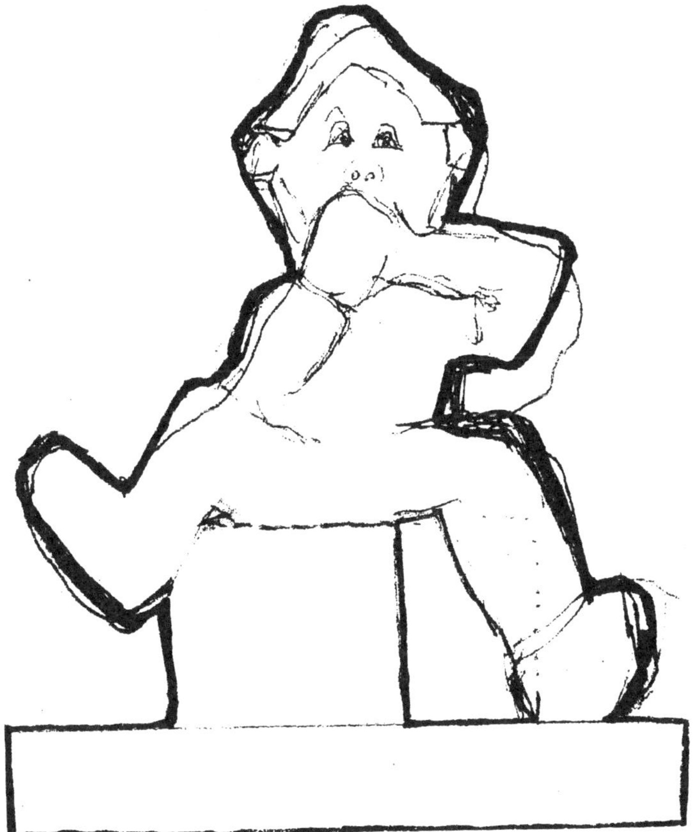

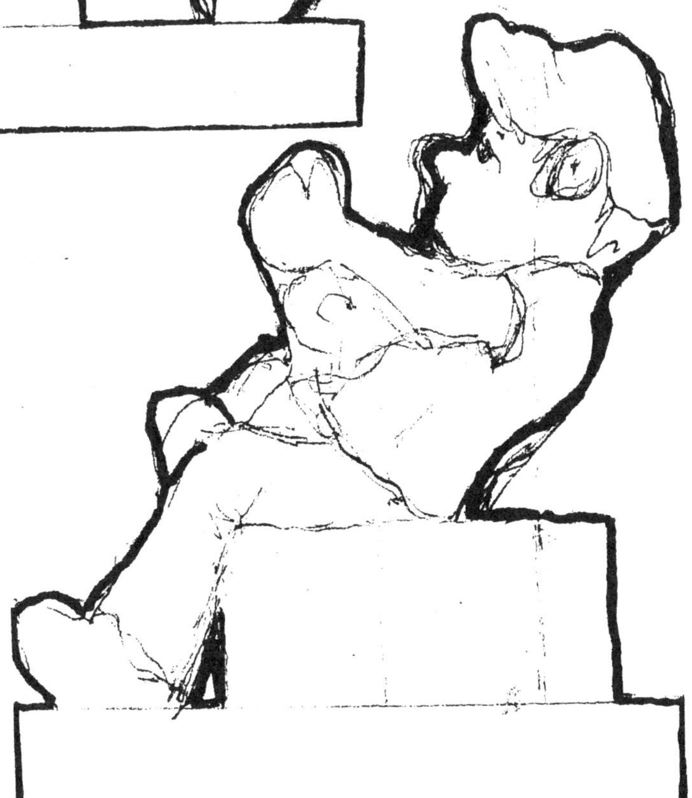

Boy Fishing—
Joe You

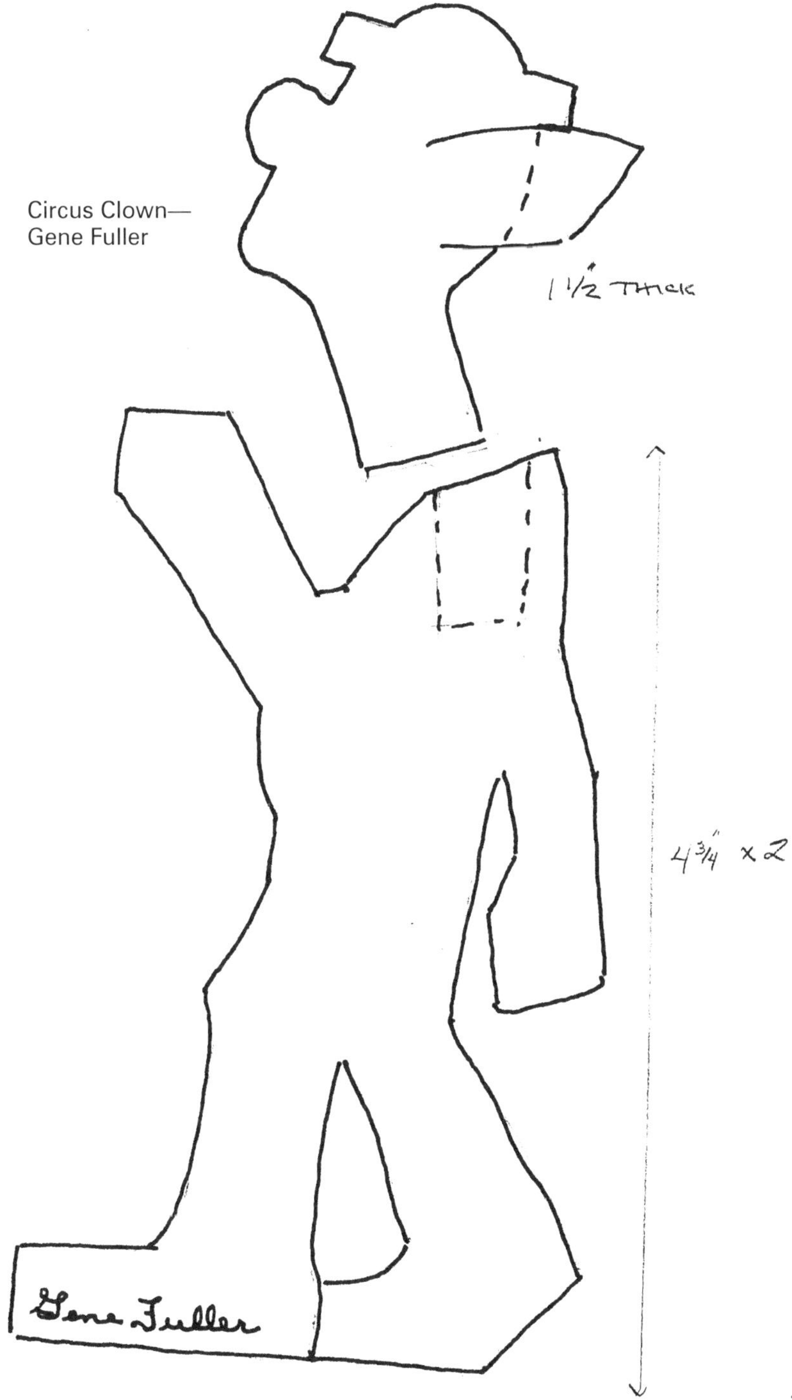

Circus Clown—
Gene Fuller

DUNHAM'S DENTISTRY & FRED'S MEAT MARKET

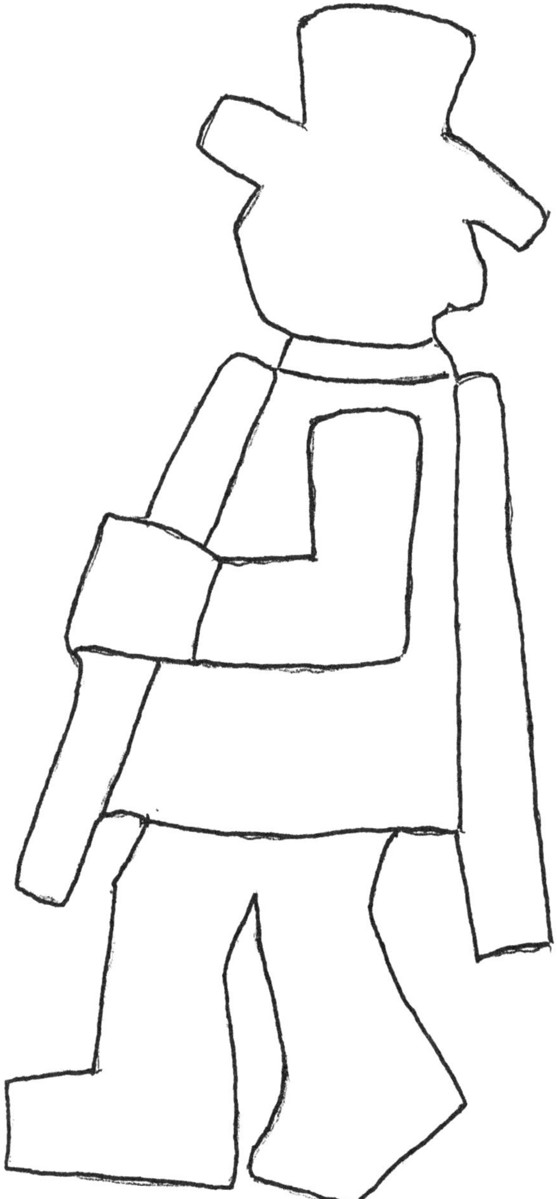

Sandwich Board Man—
Bob Travis

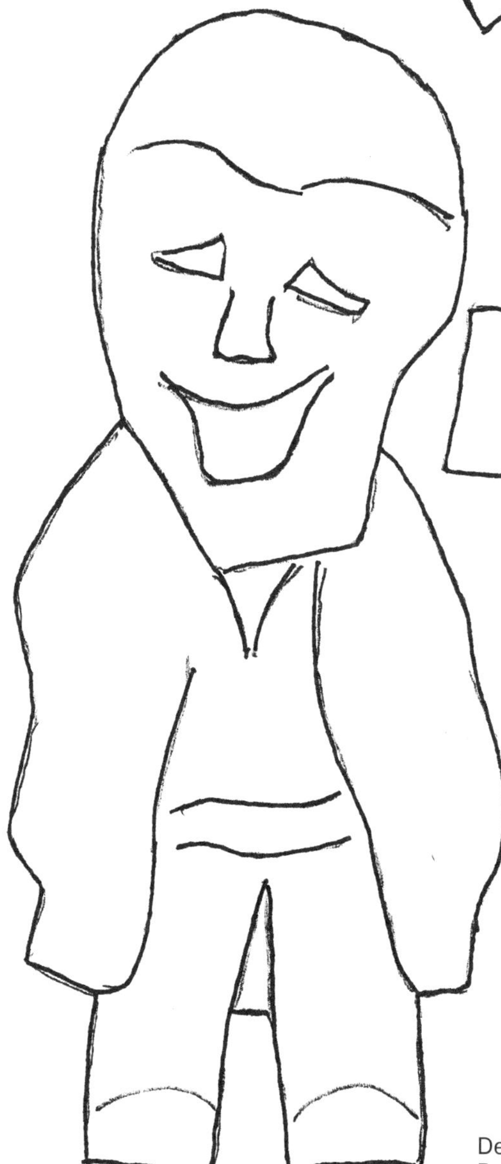

Dental Patient—
Bob Travis

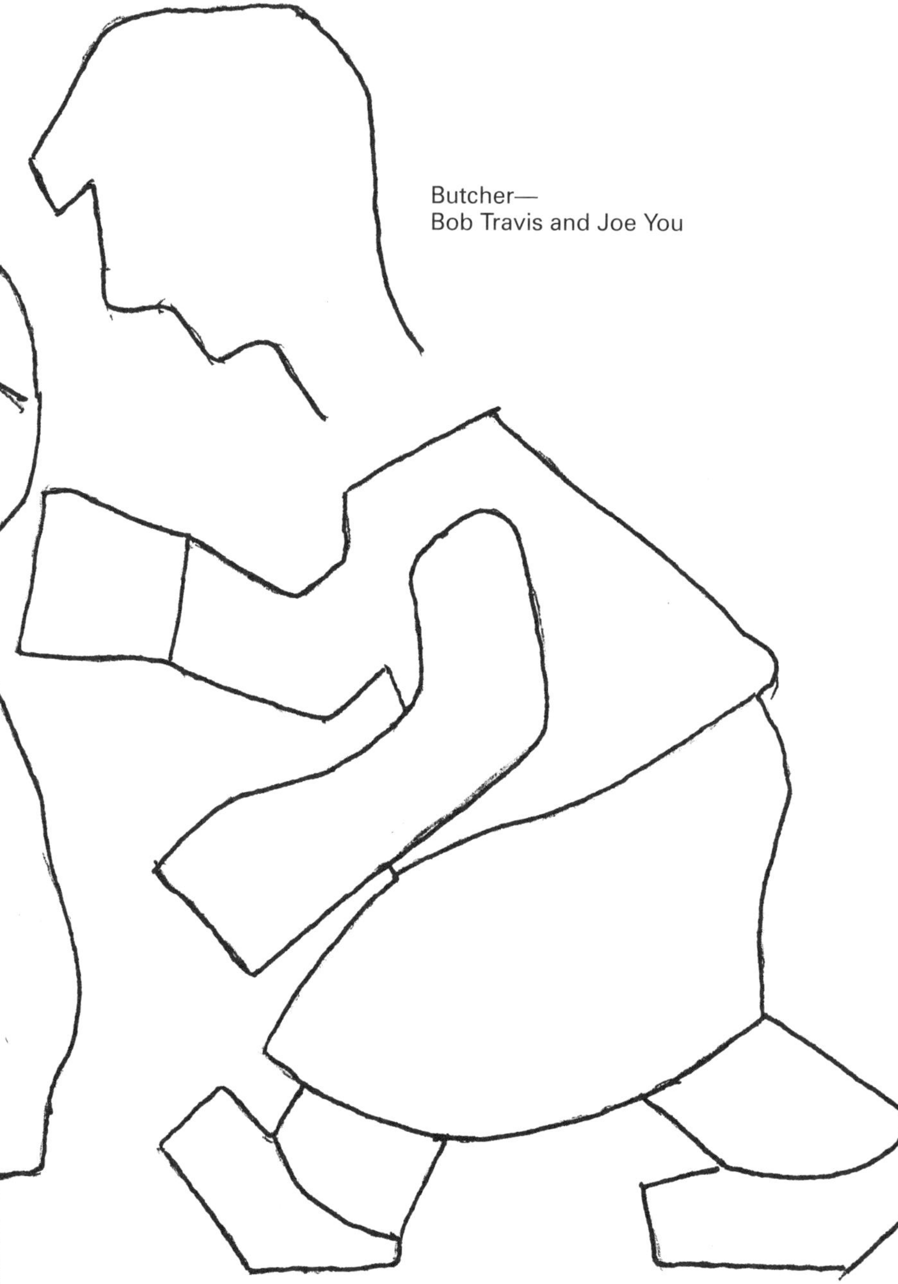

Butcher—
Bob Travis and Joe You

CCA BANK & TRUST

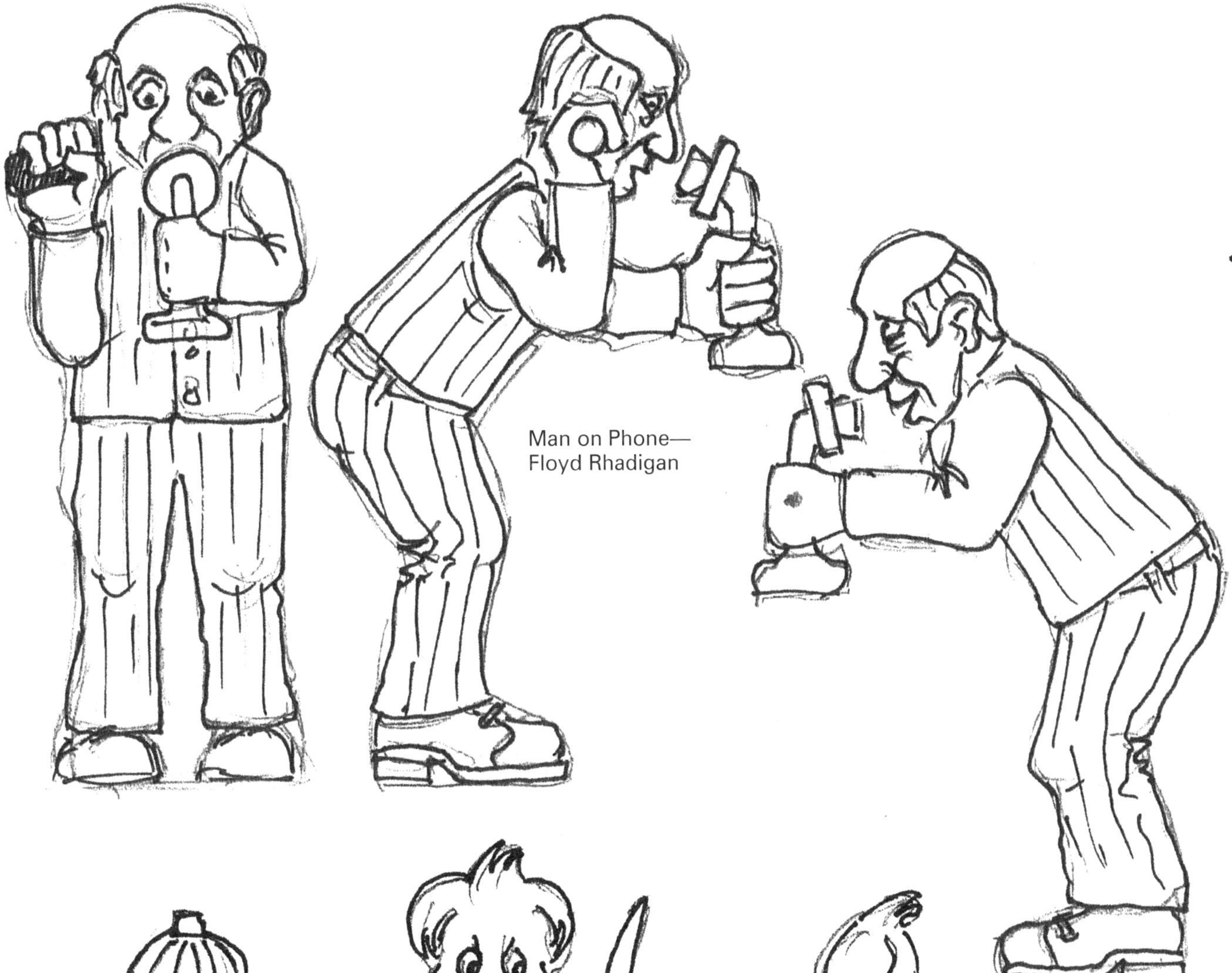

Man on Phone—
Floyd Rhadigan

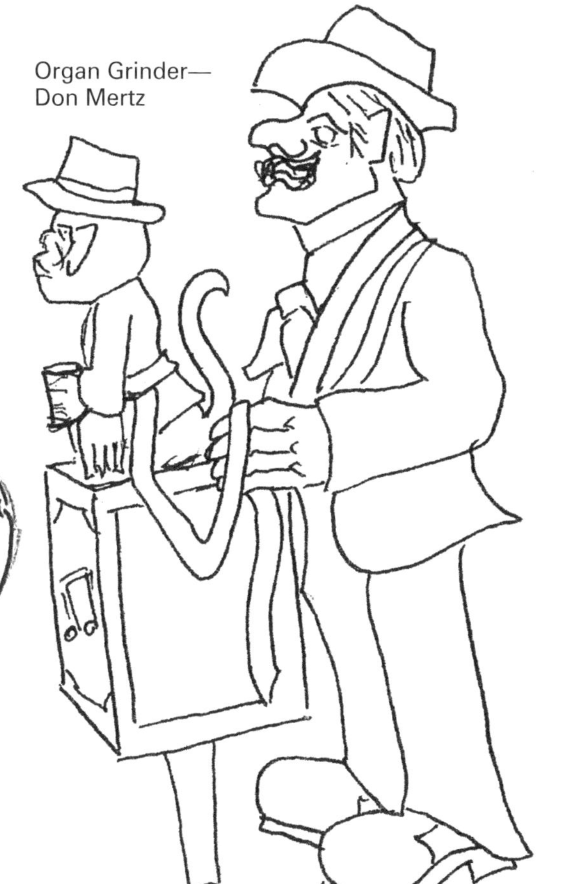

Organ Grinder—
Don Mertz

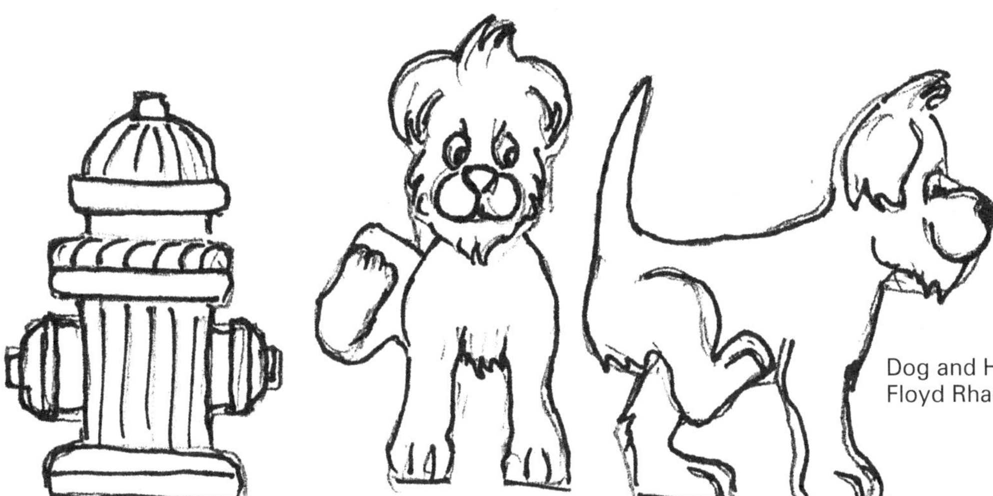

Dog and Hydrant—
Floyd Rhadigan

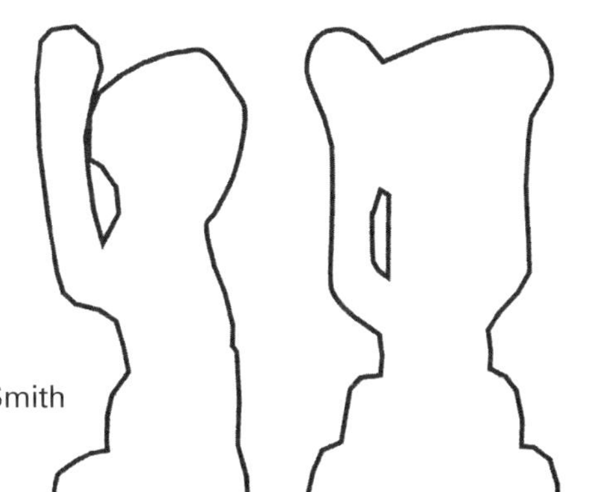

Dog—
Sandy Smith

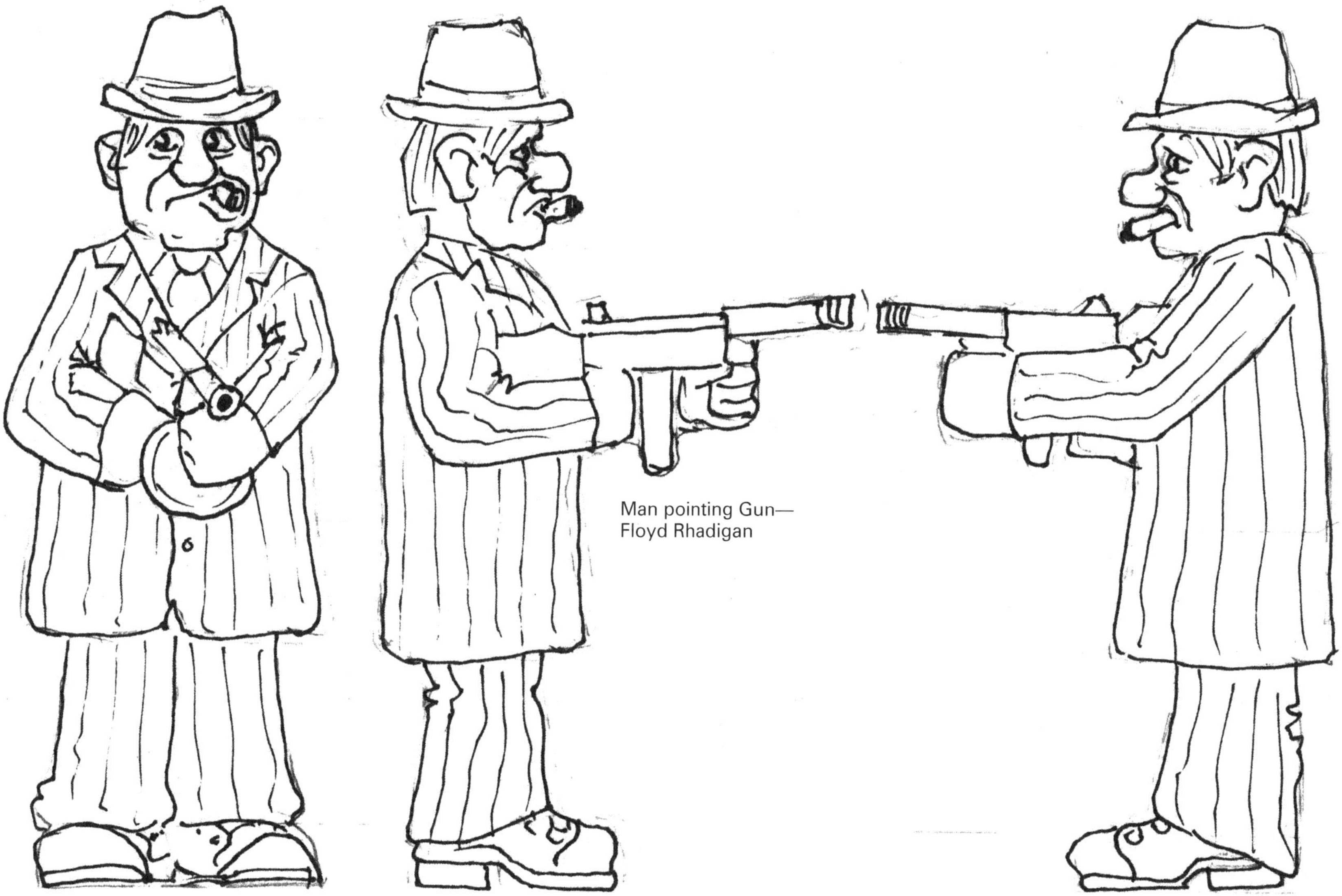

Man pointing Gun—
Floyd Rhadigan

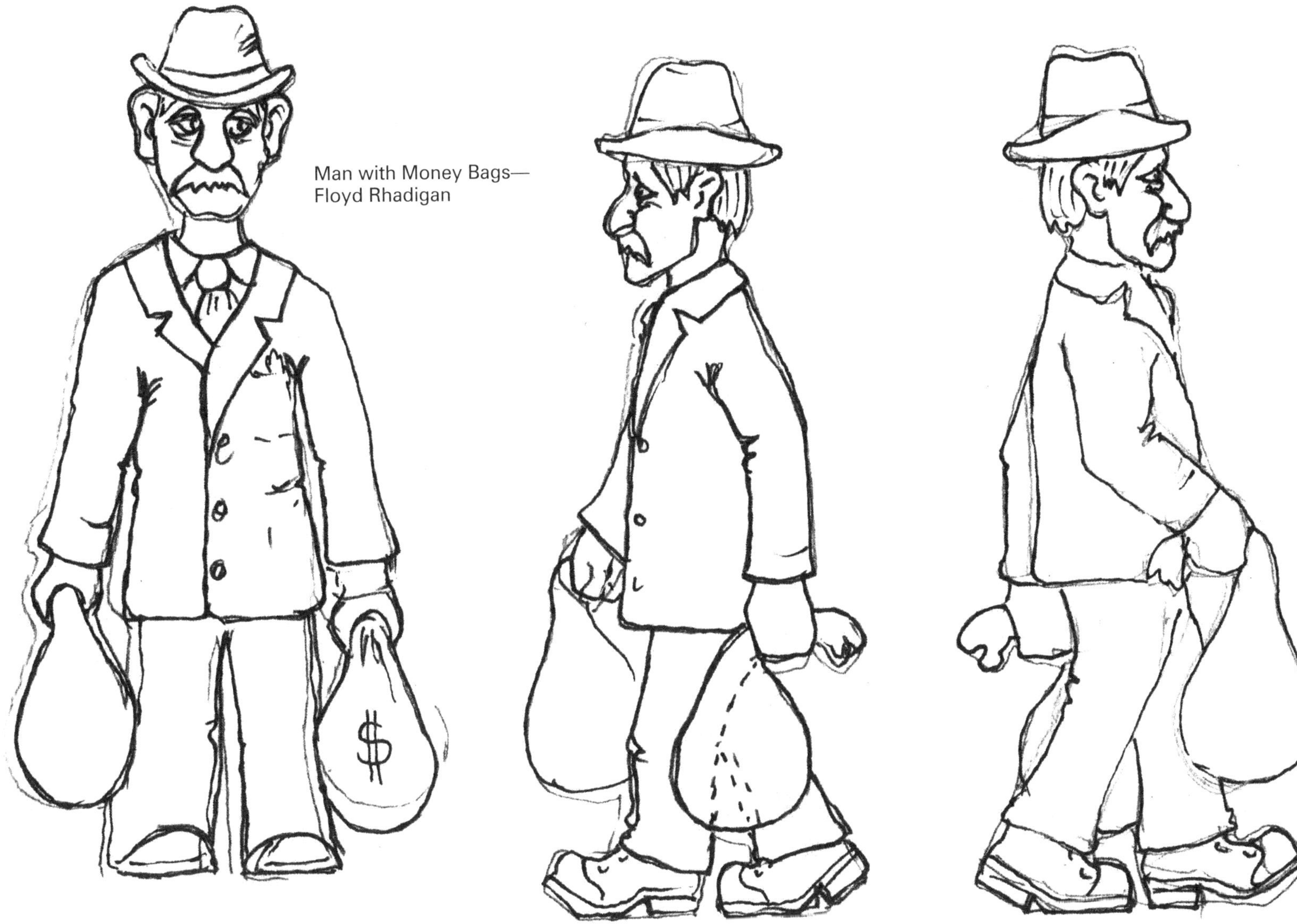

Man with Money Bags—
Floyd Rhadigan

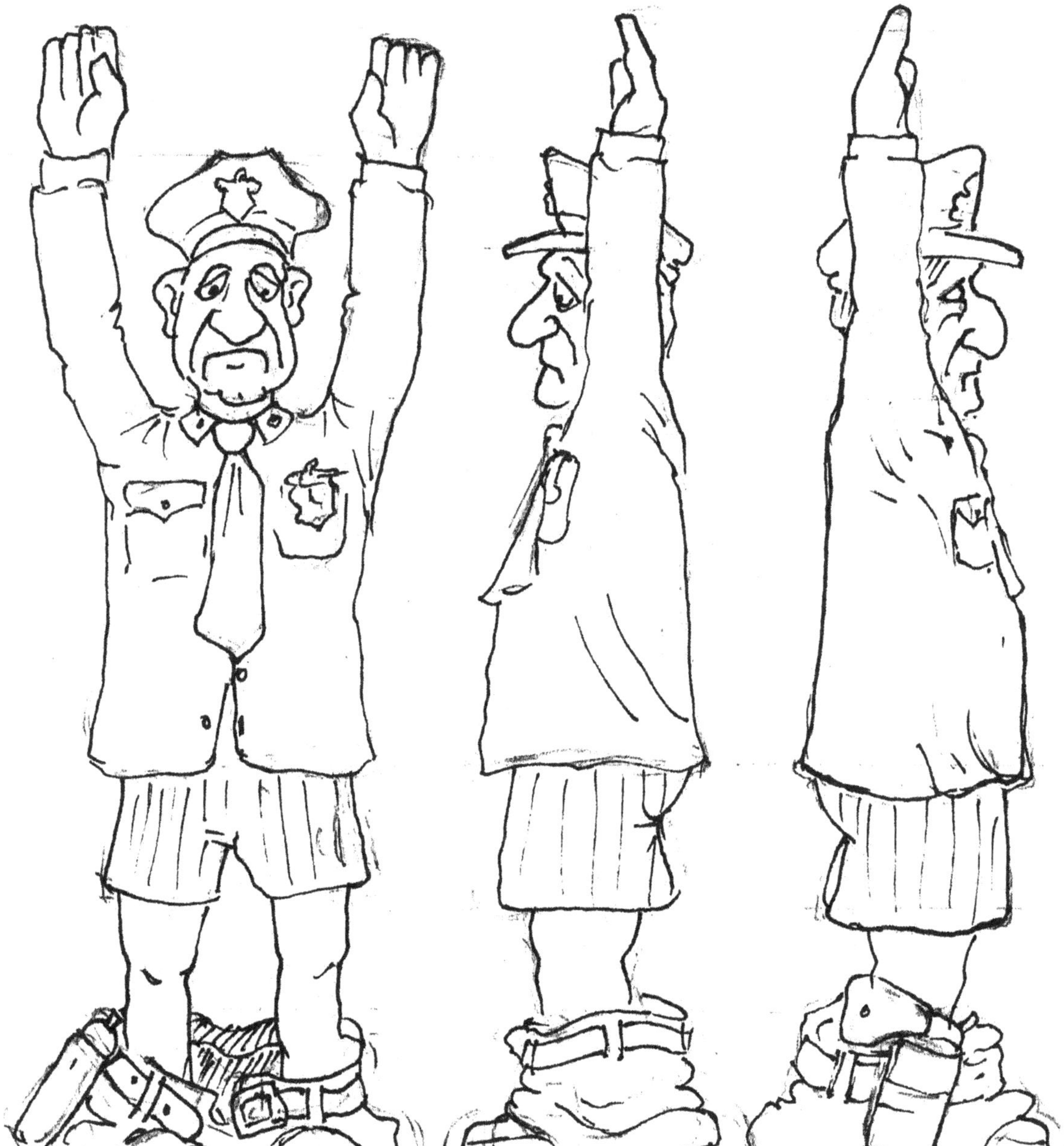

Policeman with Hands Up—
Floyd Rhadigan

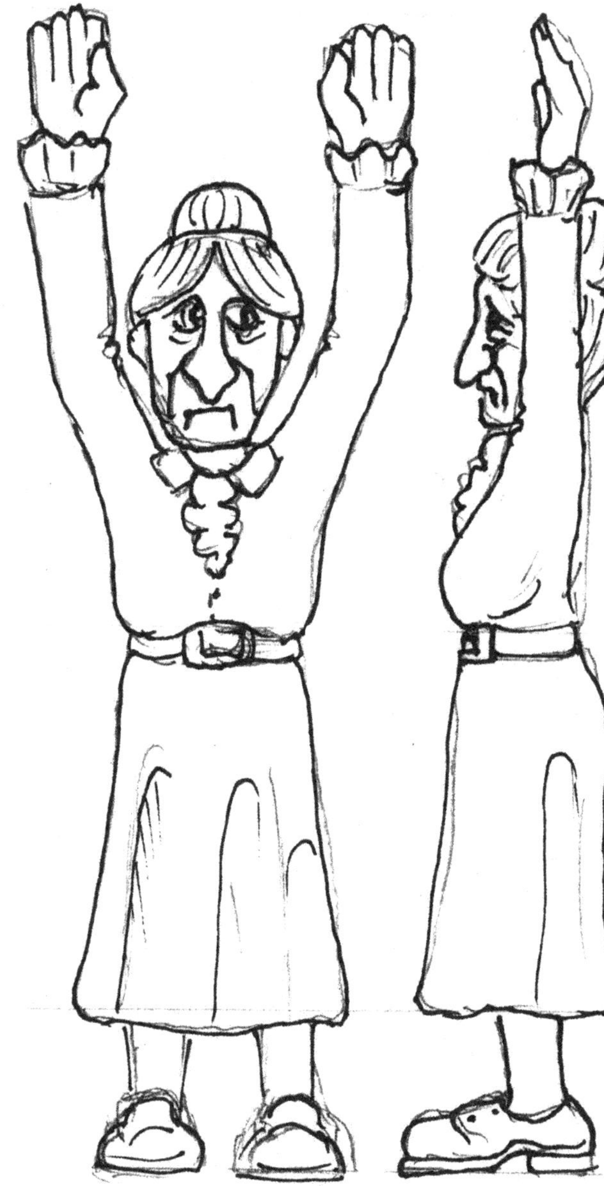

Woman with Hands Up—
Floyd Rhadigan

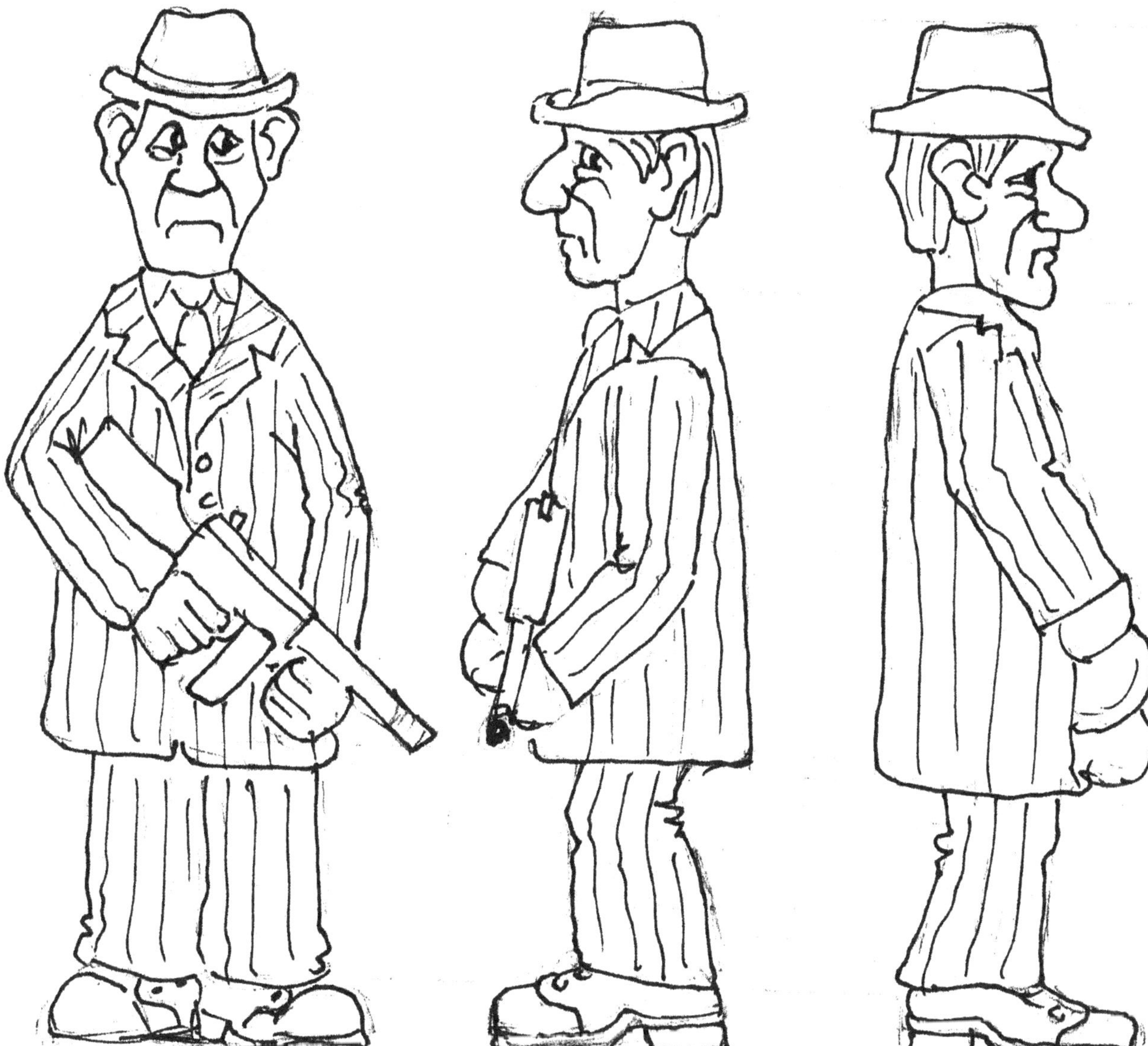

Man carrying Gun—
Floyd Rhadigan

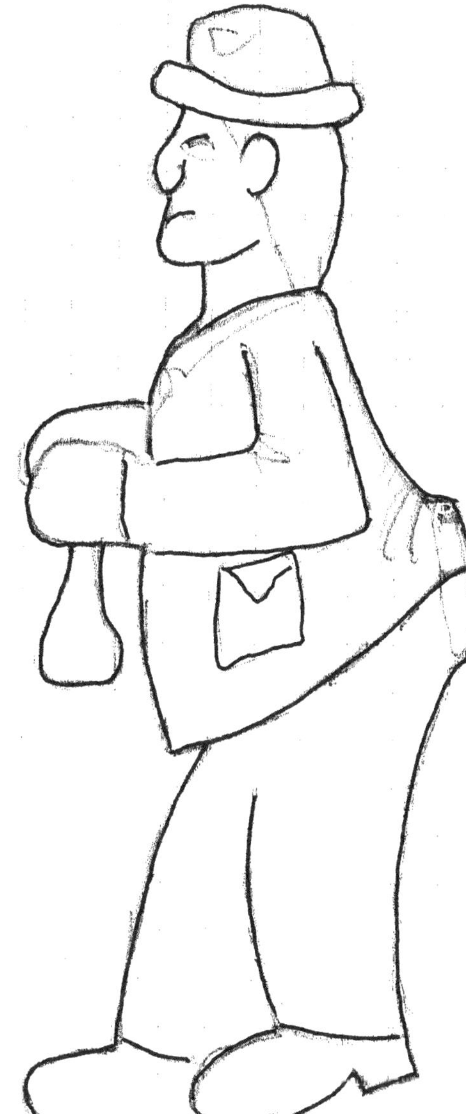

Man with Bag—
Bruce Henn

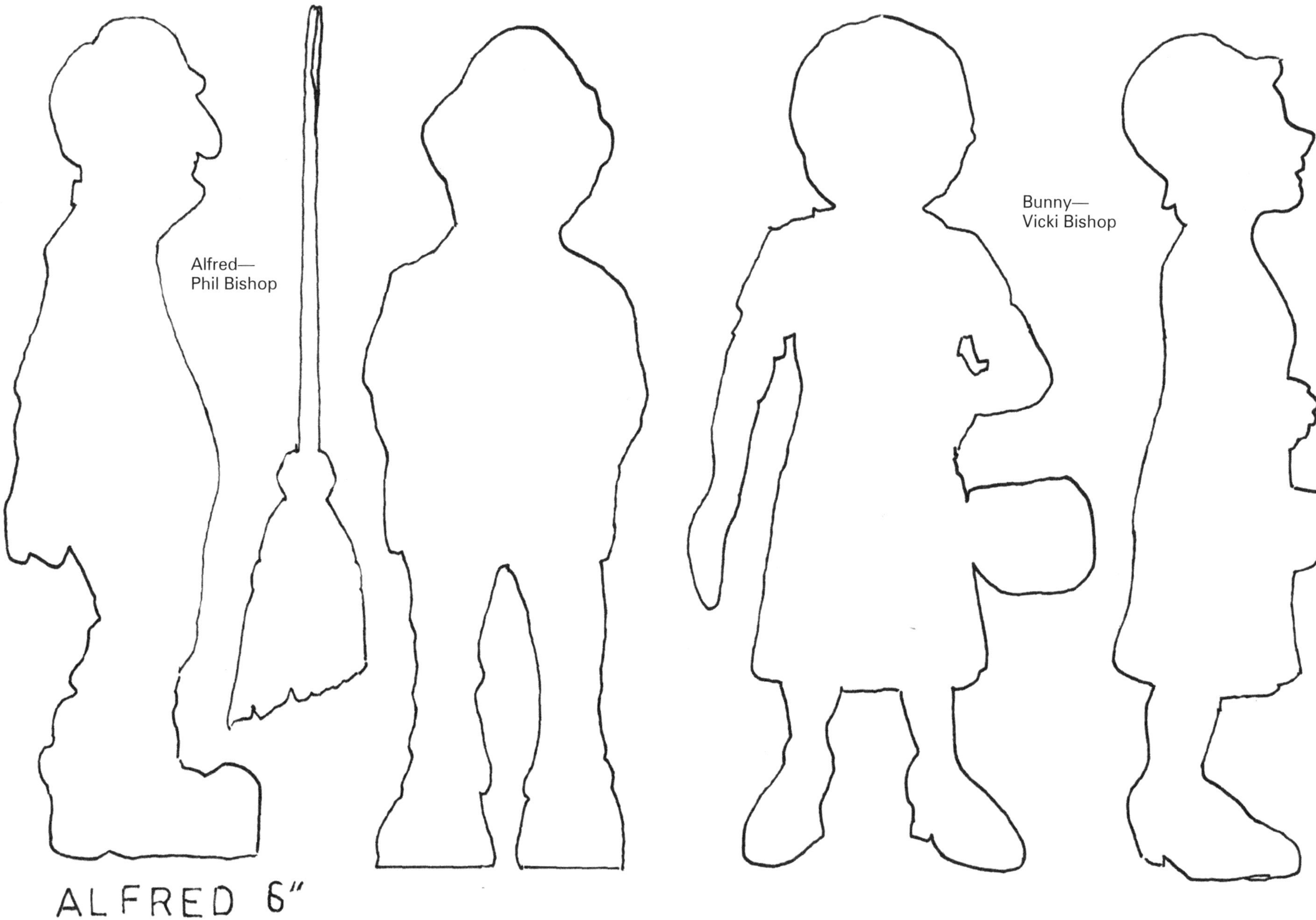

Alfred—
Phil Bishop

Bunny—
Vicki Bishop

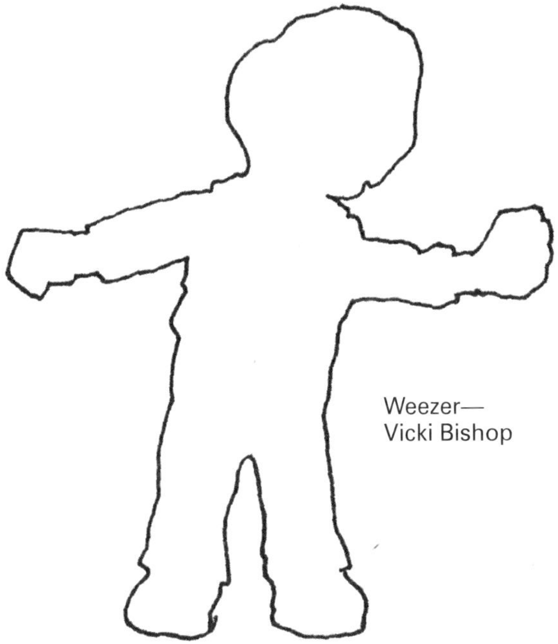

Weezer—
Vicki Bishop

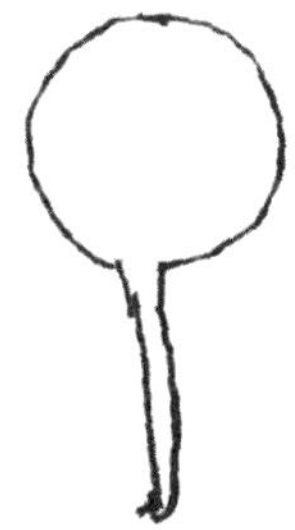

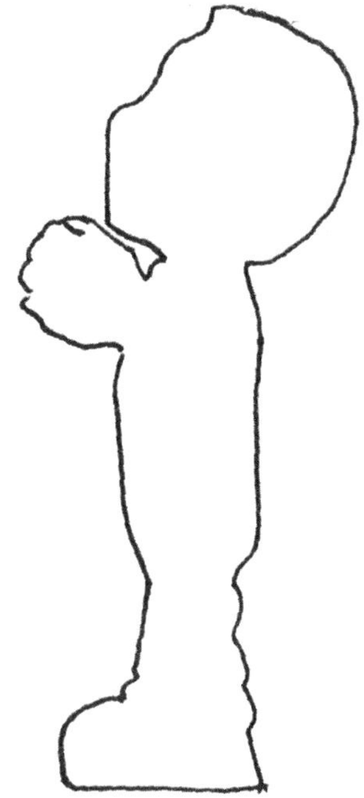

WEEZER 3 3/8"

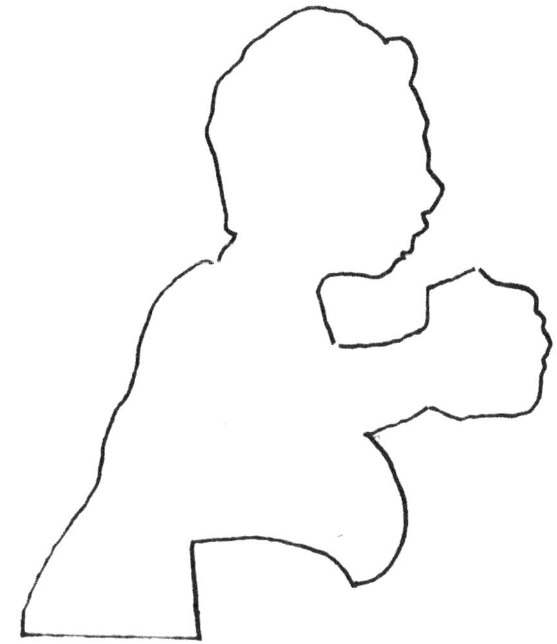

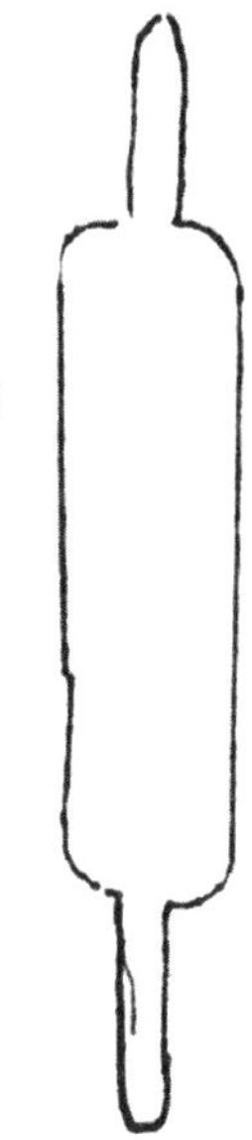

ELLA MAE 3 1/4"

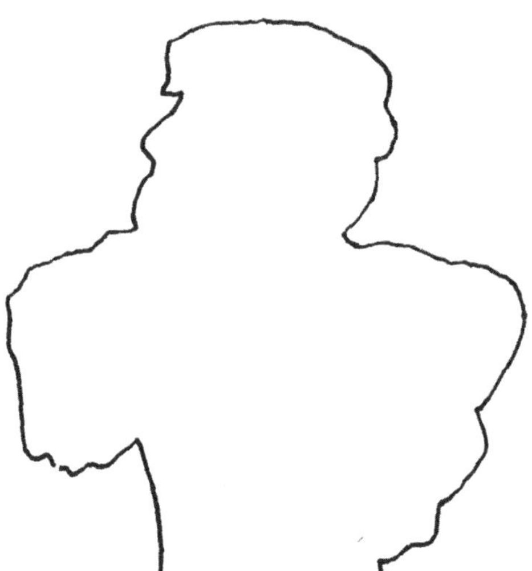

CLAUD 2 1/2"

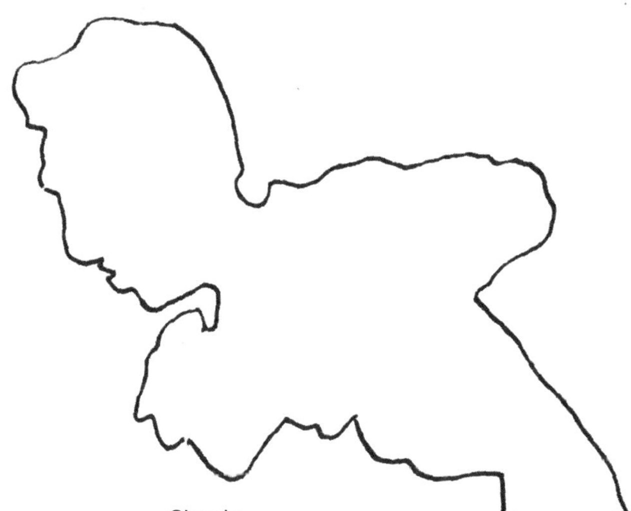

Claude—
Phil Bishop

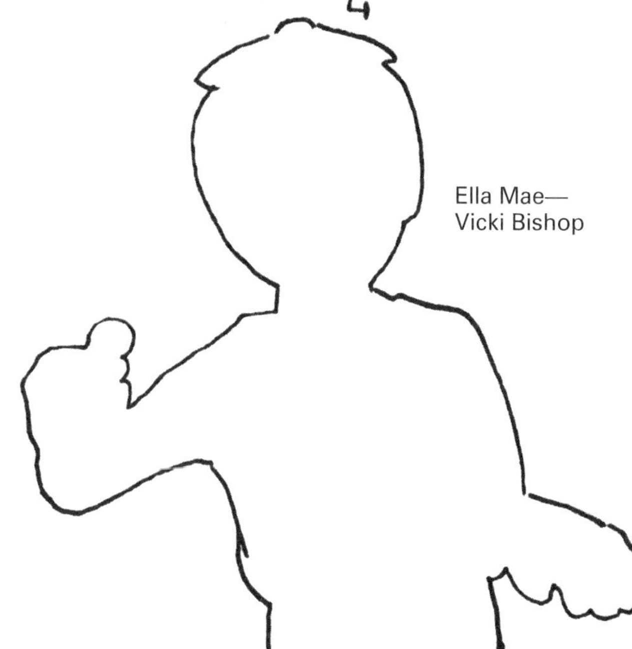

Ella Mae—
Vicki Bishop

BISHOP'S GENERAL STORE

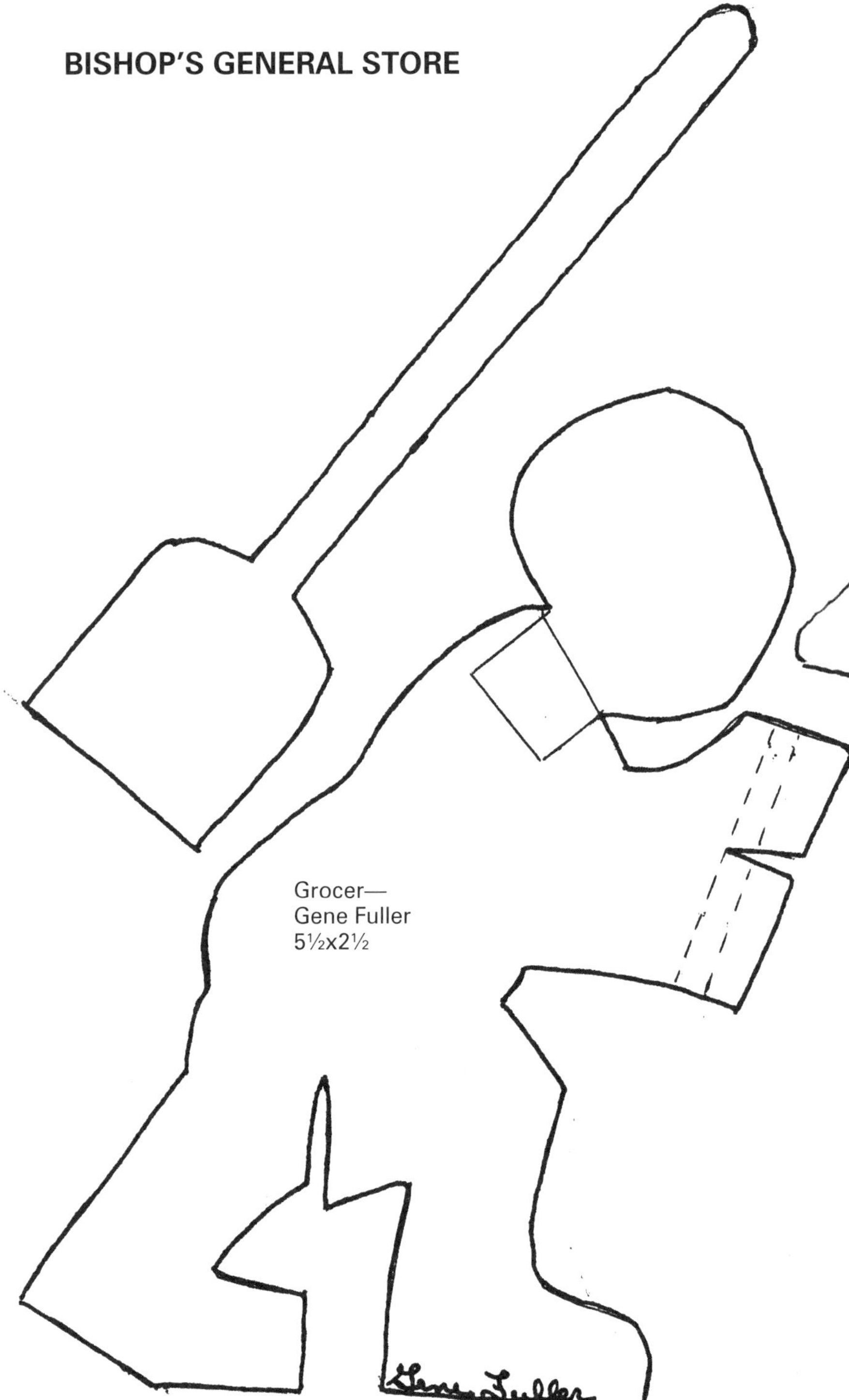

Grocer—
Gene Fuller
5½x2½

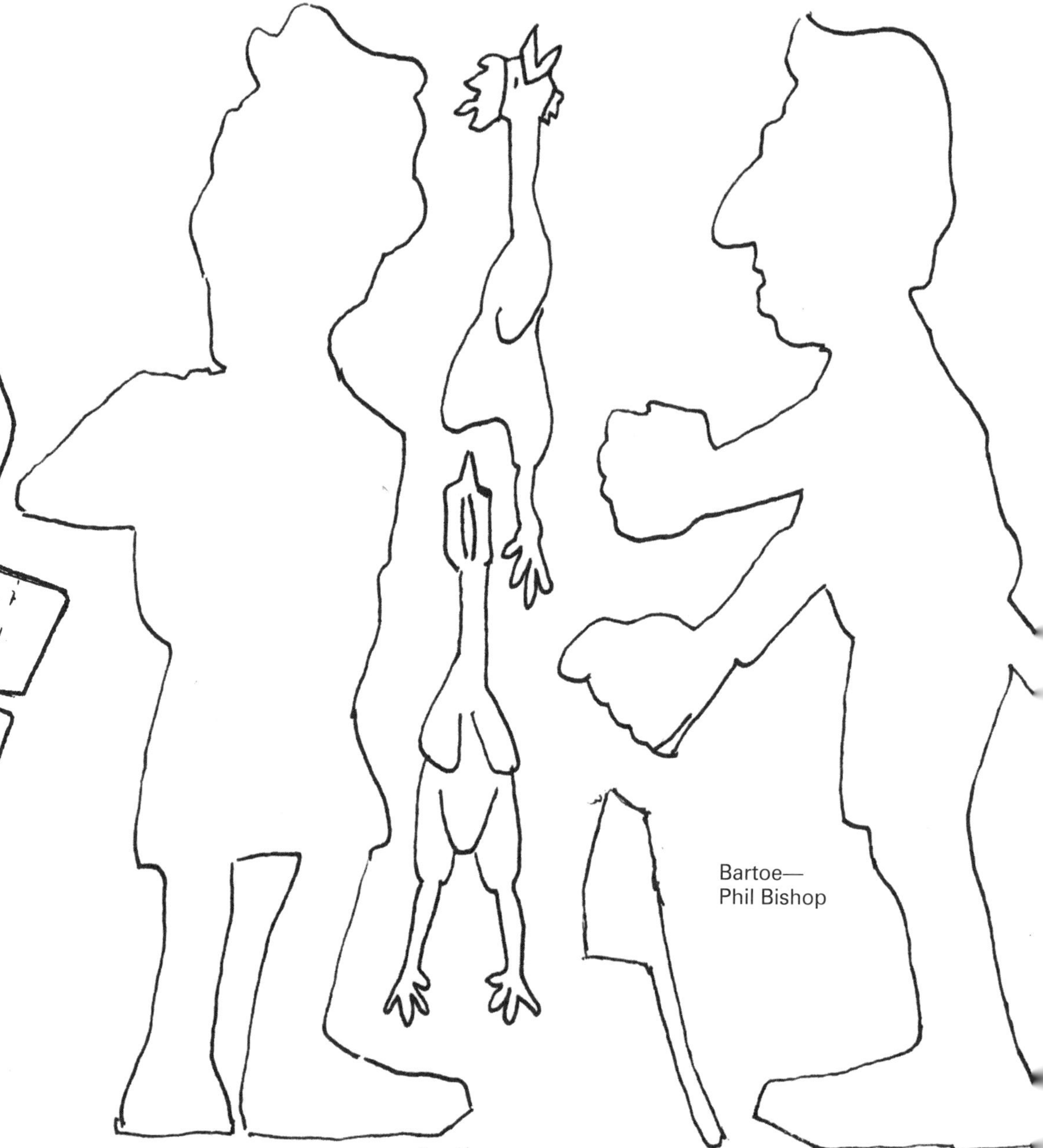

Bartoe—
Phil Bishop

BARTOE 6½"

BISHOP'S GENERAL STORE

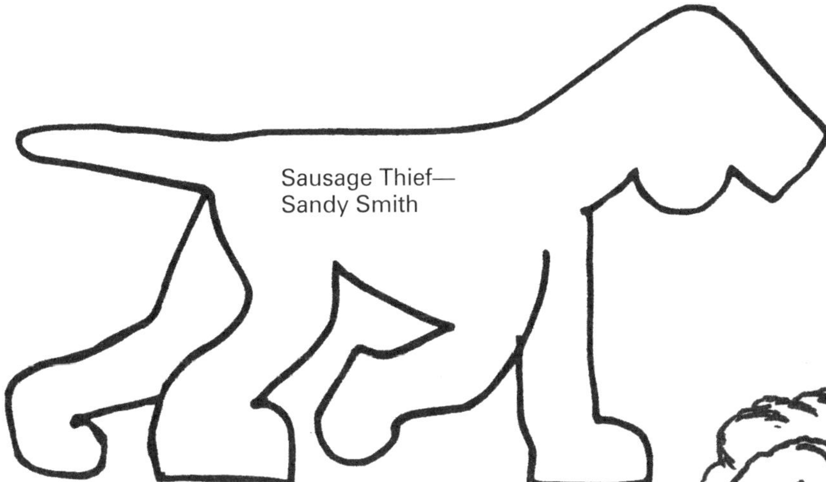

Sausage Thief—
Sandy Smith

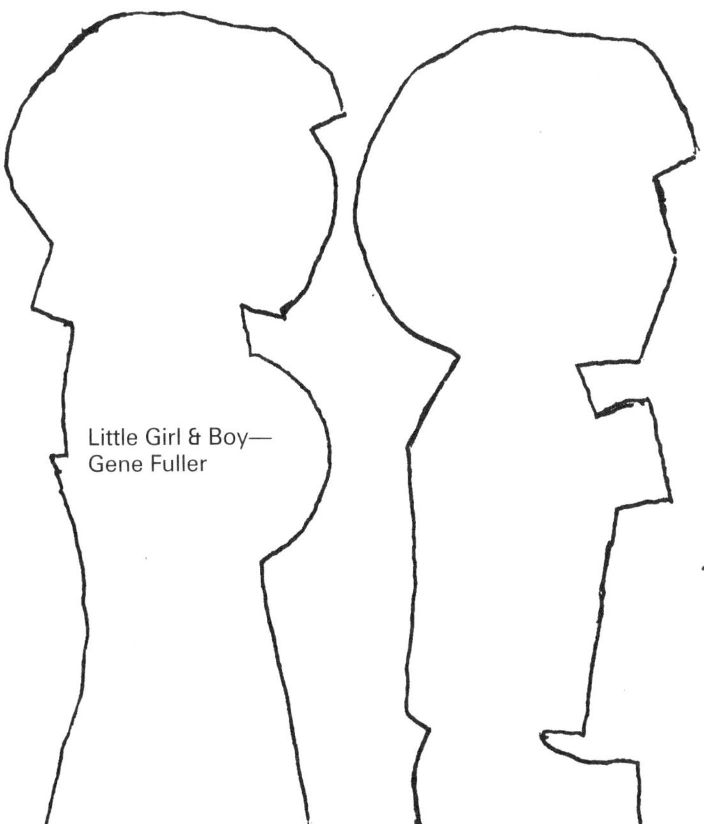

Little Girl & Boy—
Gene Fuller

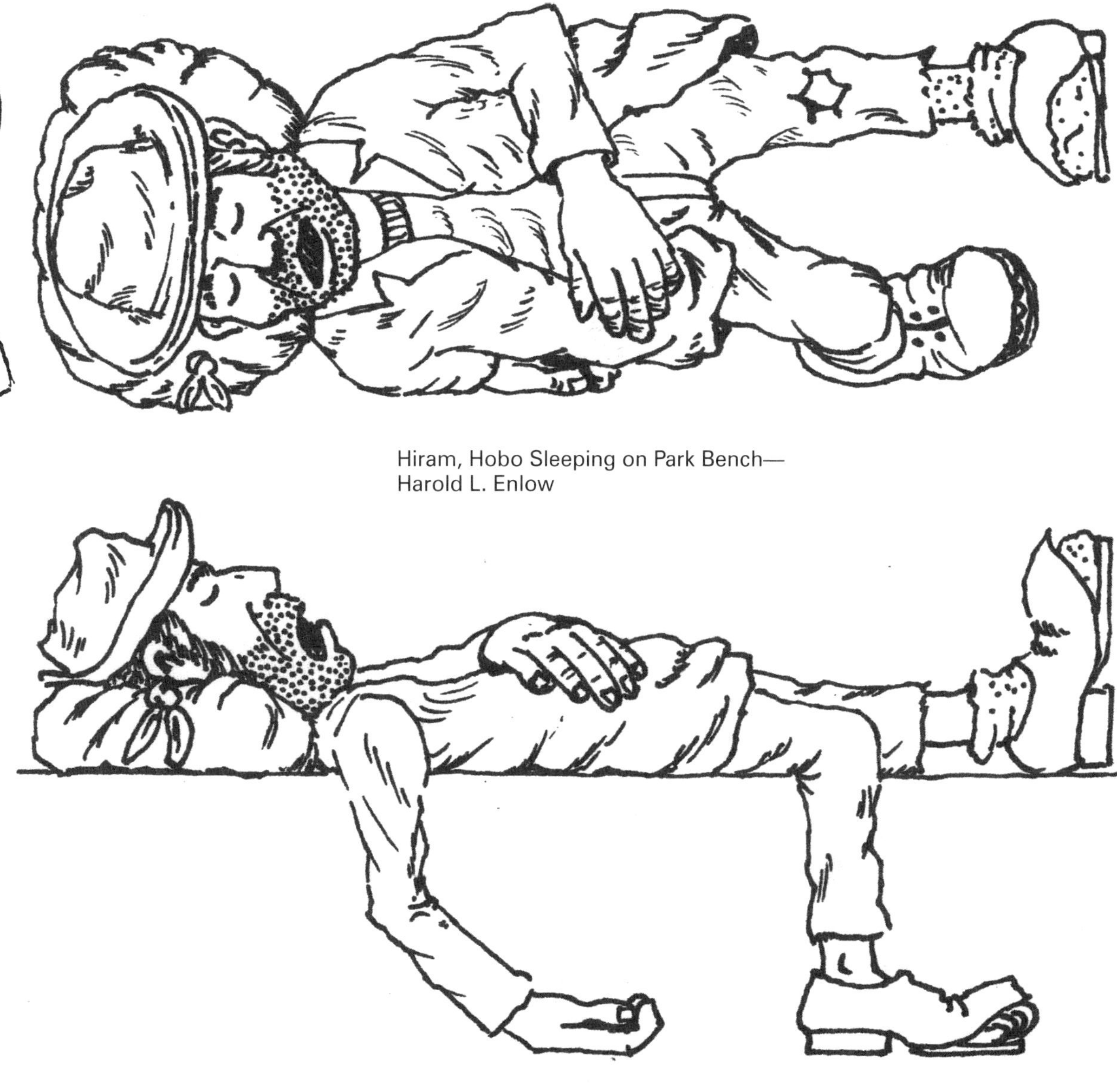

Hiram, Hobo Sleeping on Park Bench—
Harold L. Enlow

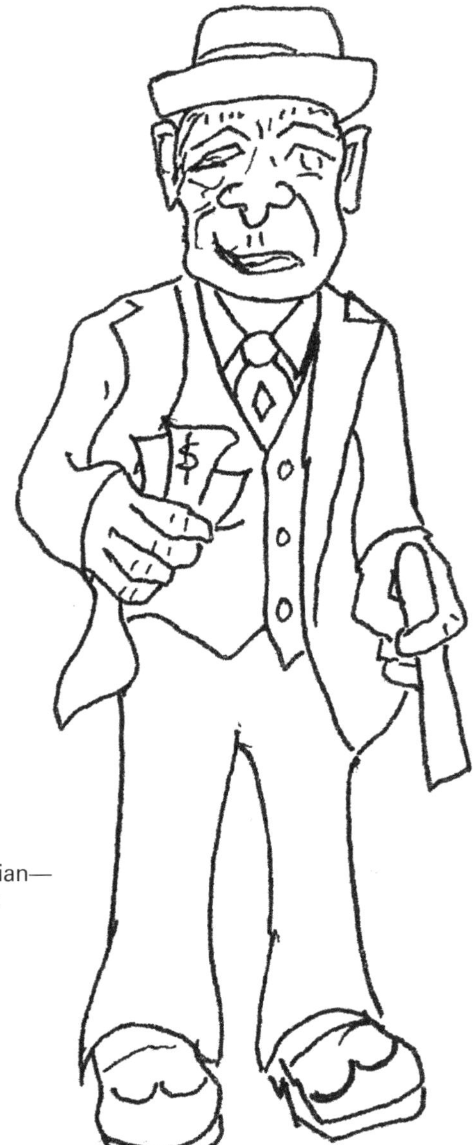

The Politician—
Don Mertz

Policeman—
Eldon Humphreys

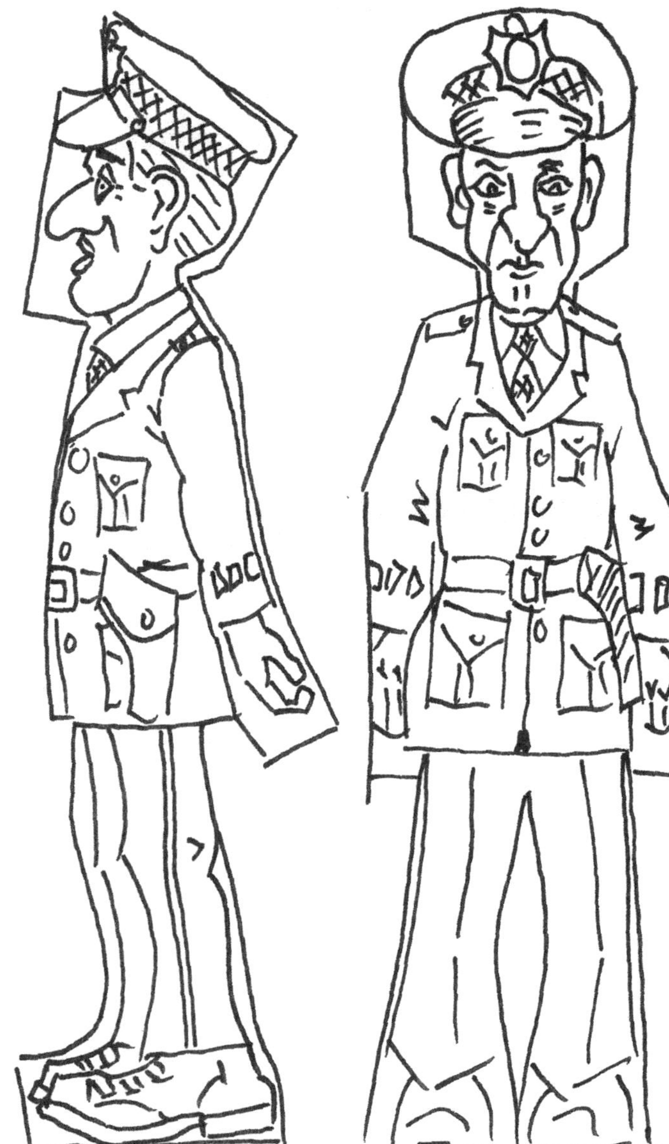

Trash Talk—
Dennis Thornton

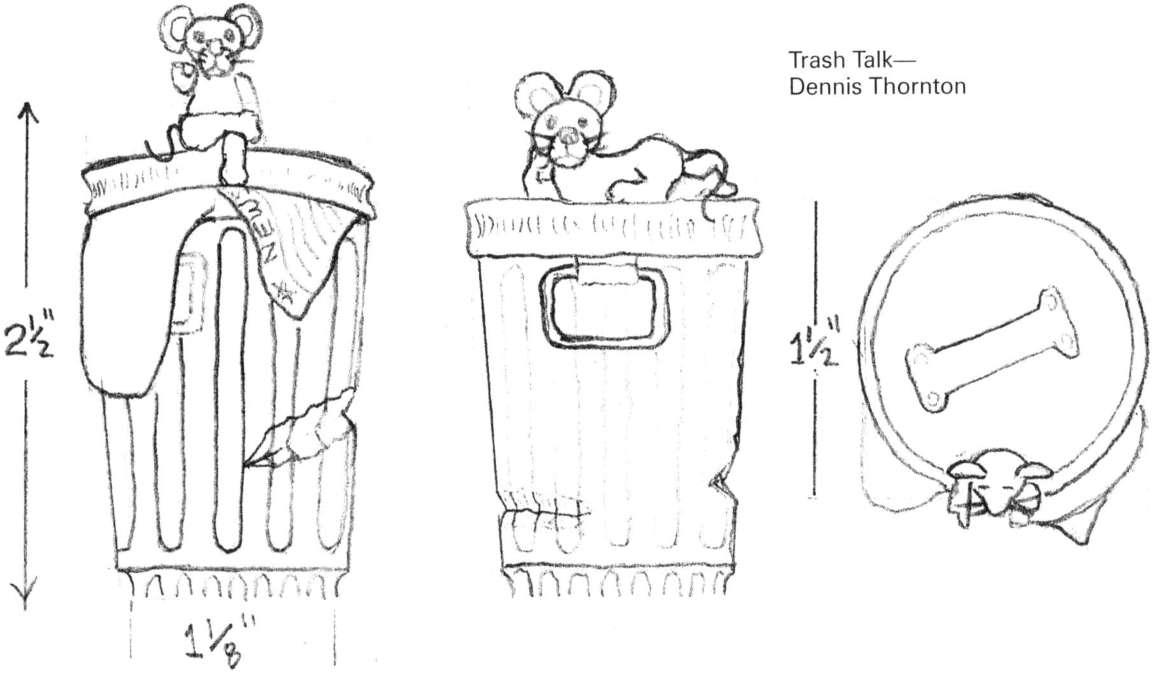

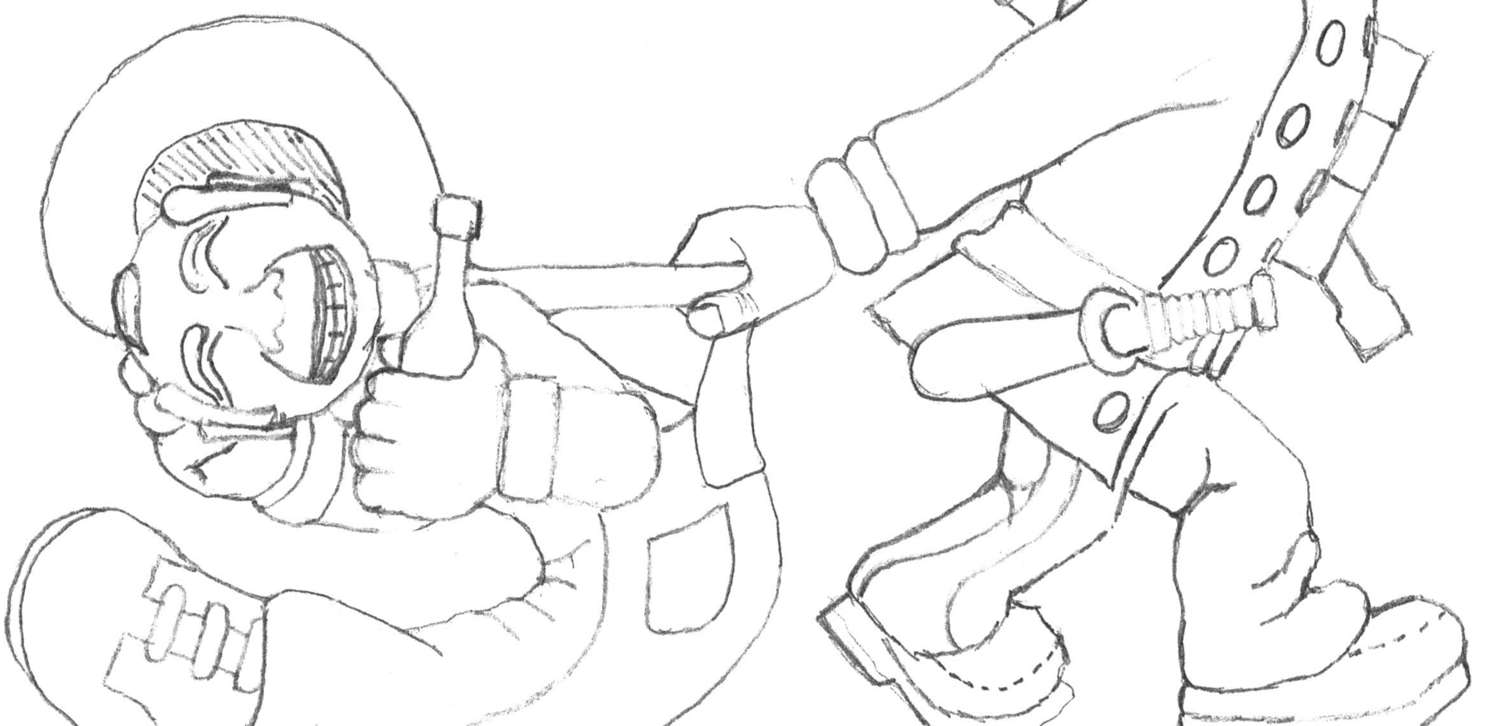

Home James—
Dennis Thornton

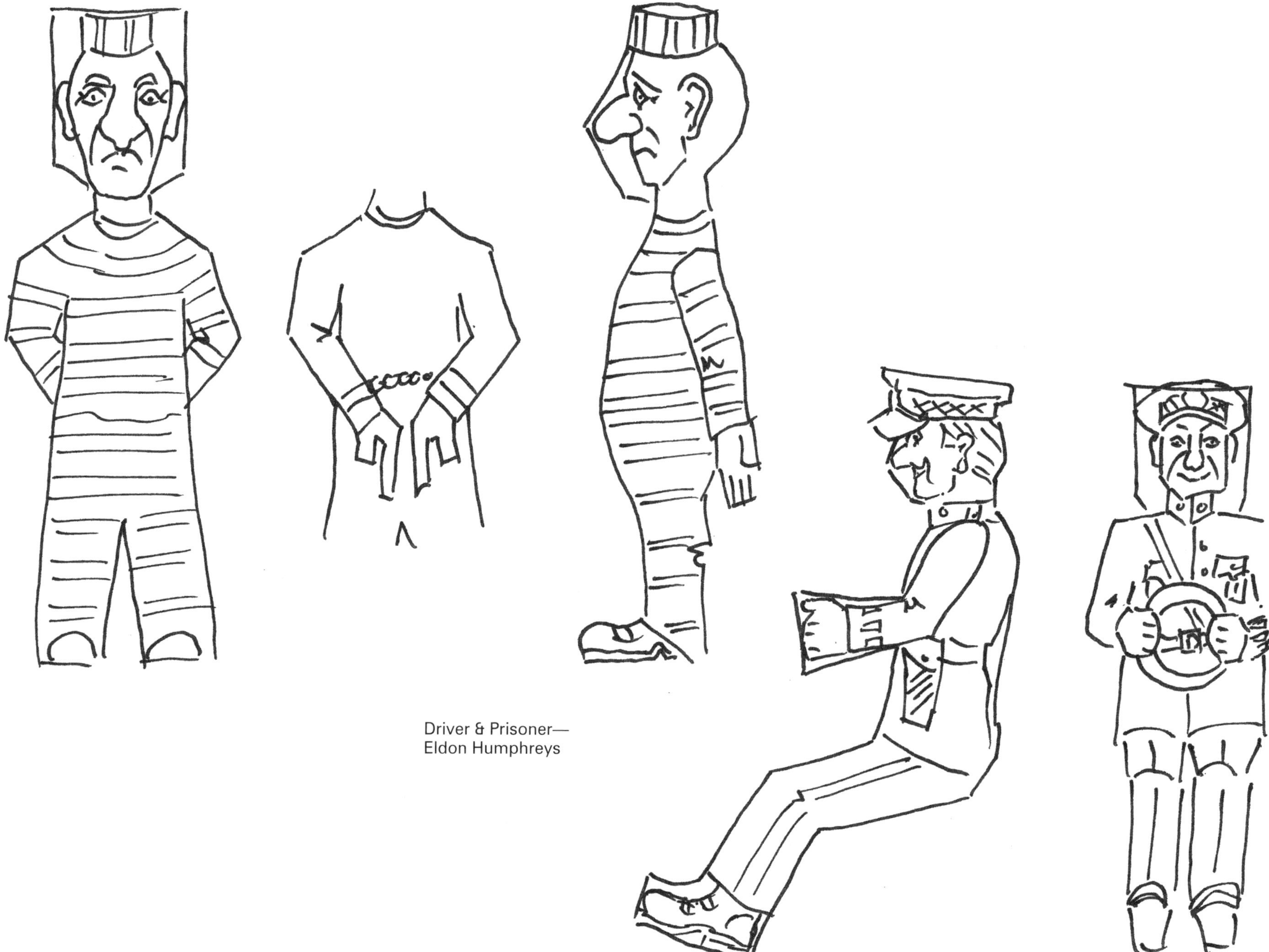

Driver & Prisoner—
Eldon Humphreys

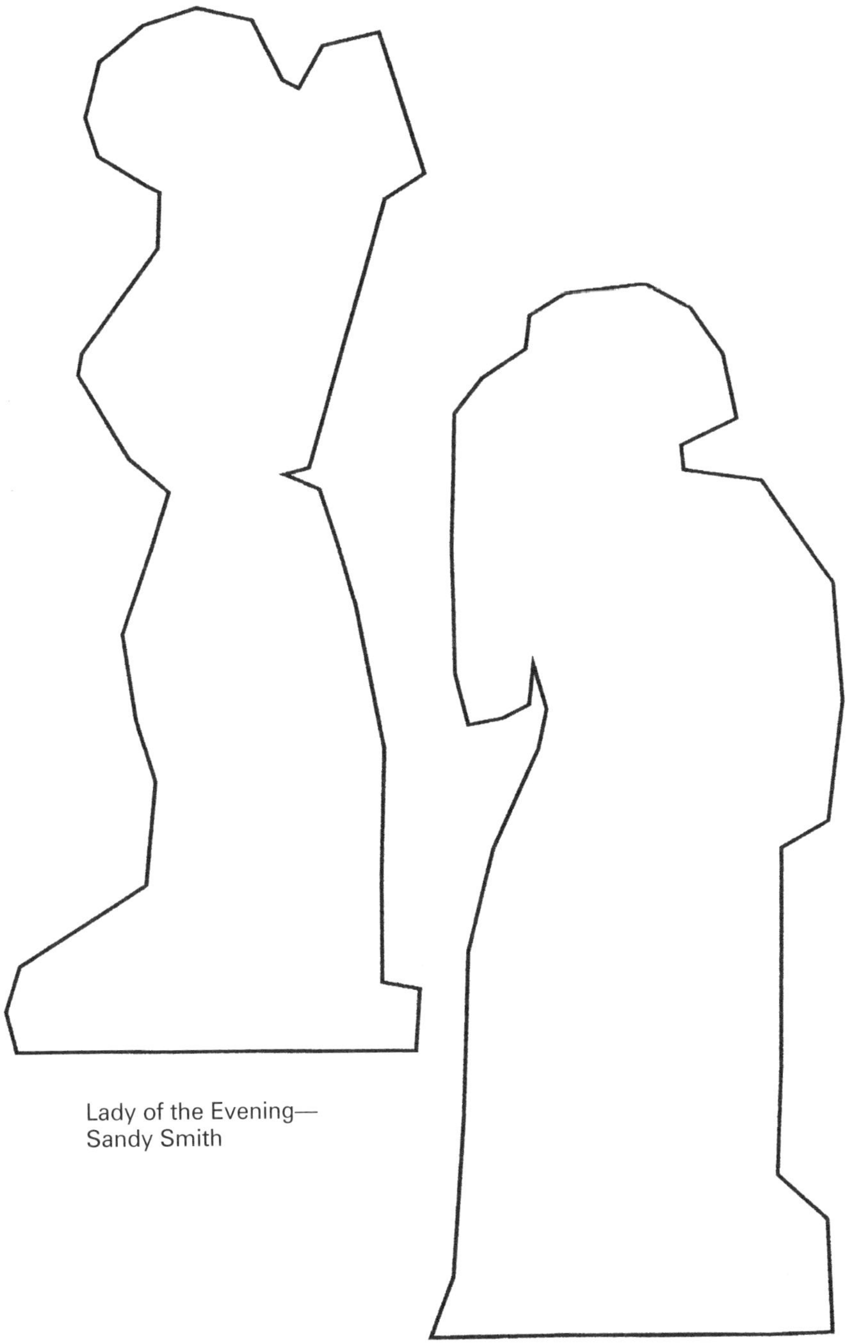

Lady of the Evening—
Sandy Smith

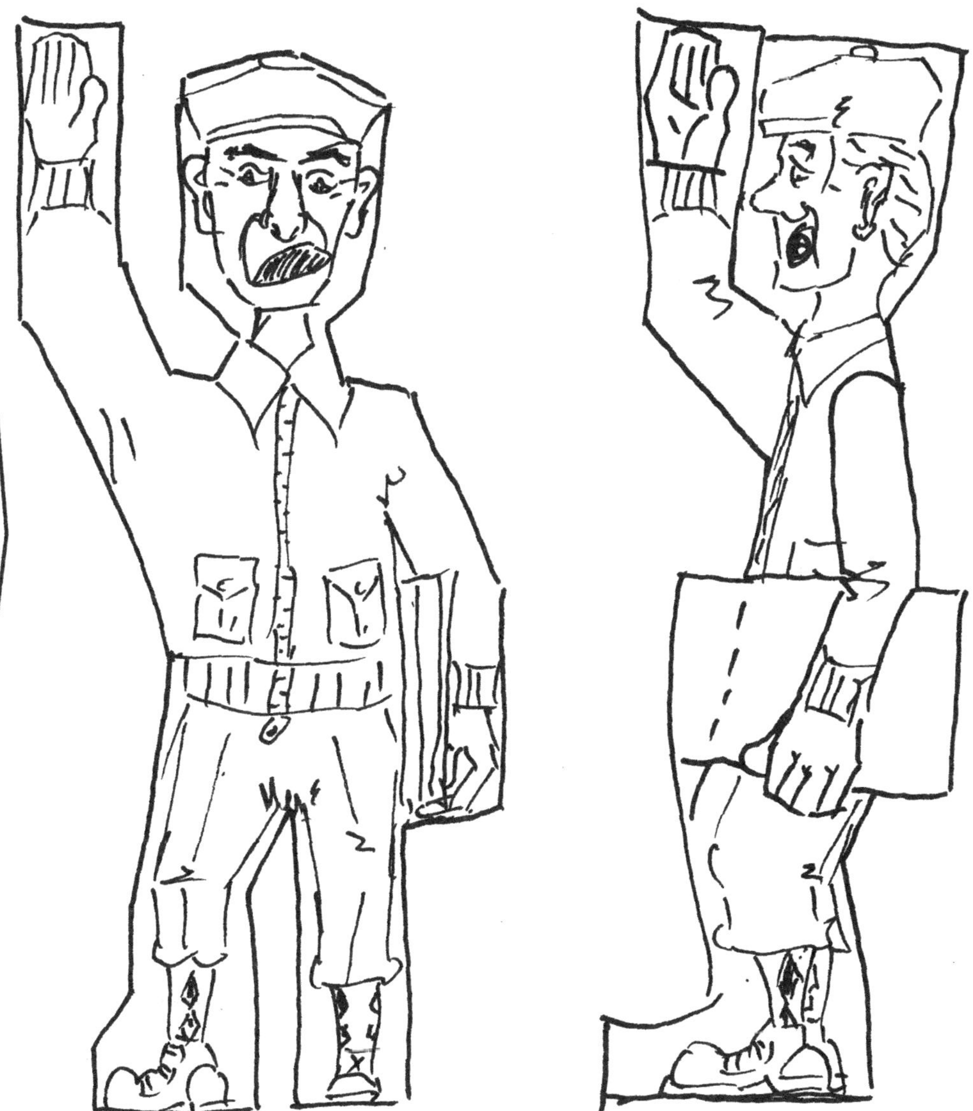

Paper Hawker—
Eldon Humphreys

POLICE STATION AND JAIL

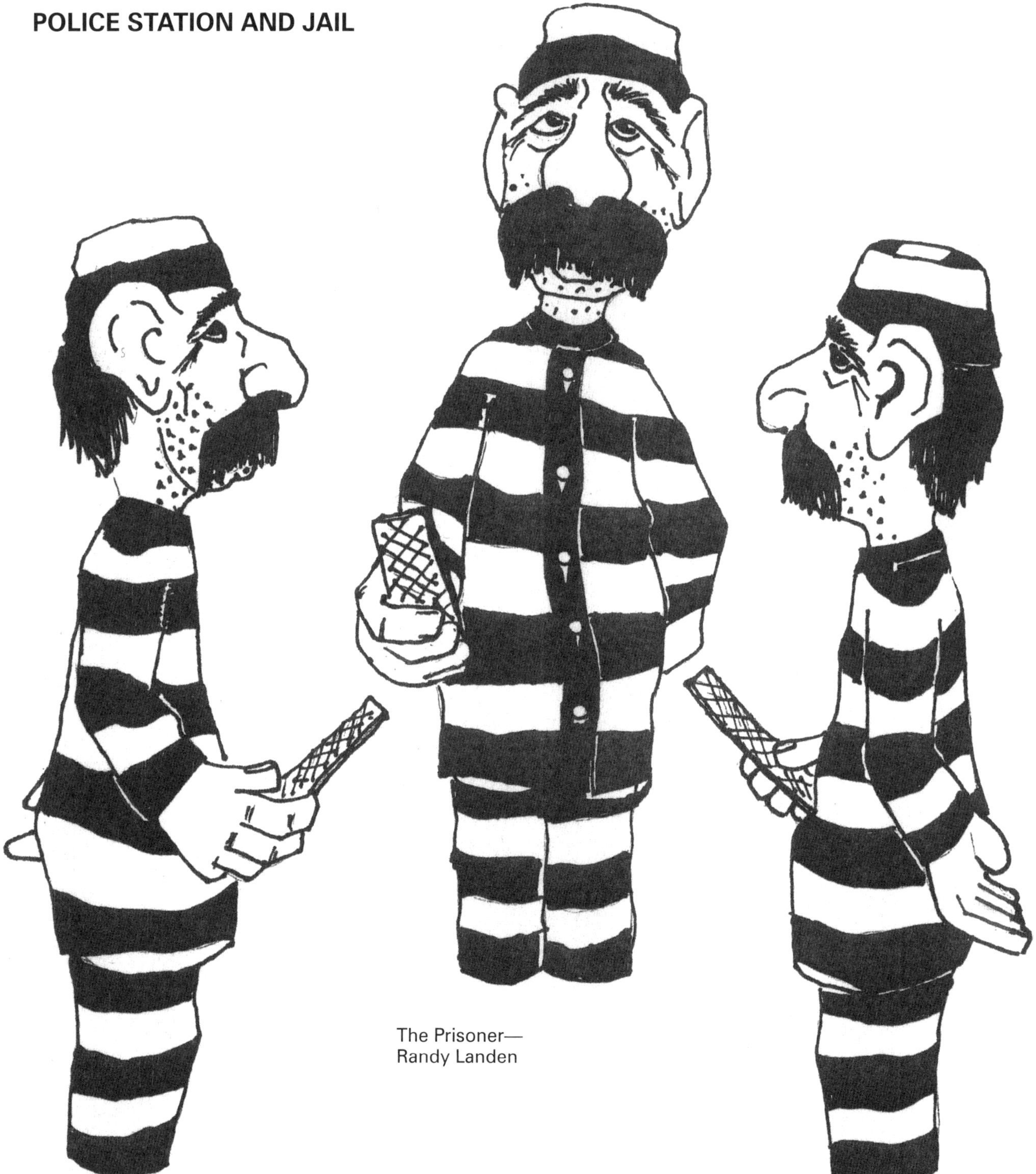

The Prisoner—
Randy Landen

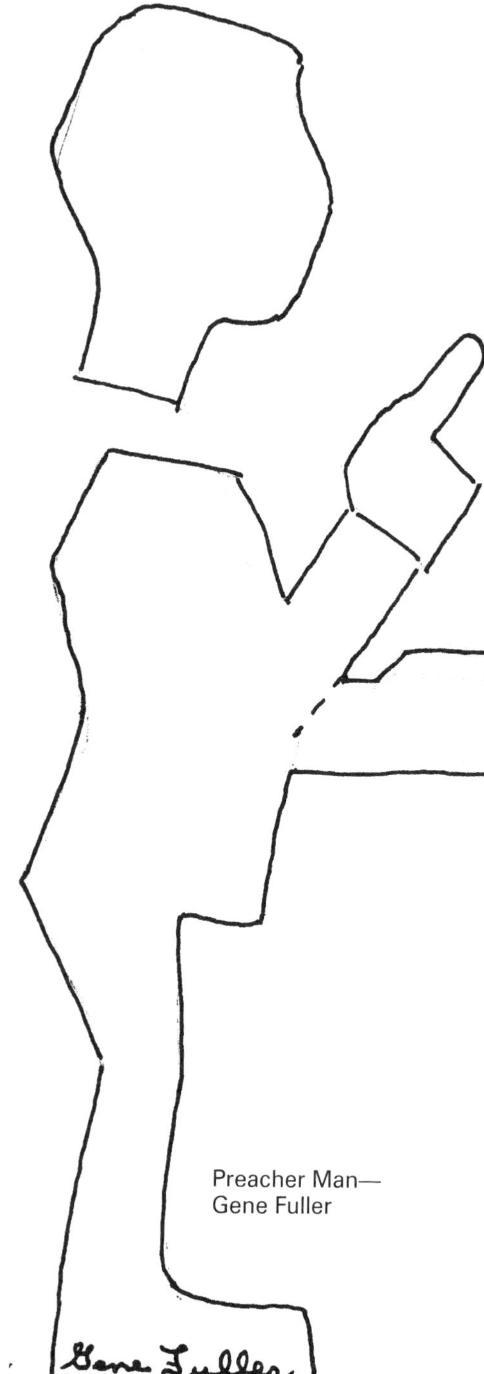

Preacher Man—
Gene Fuller

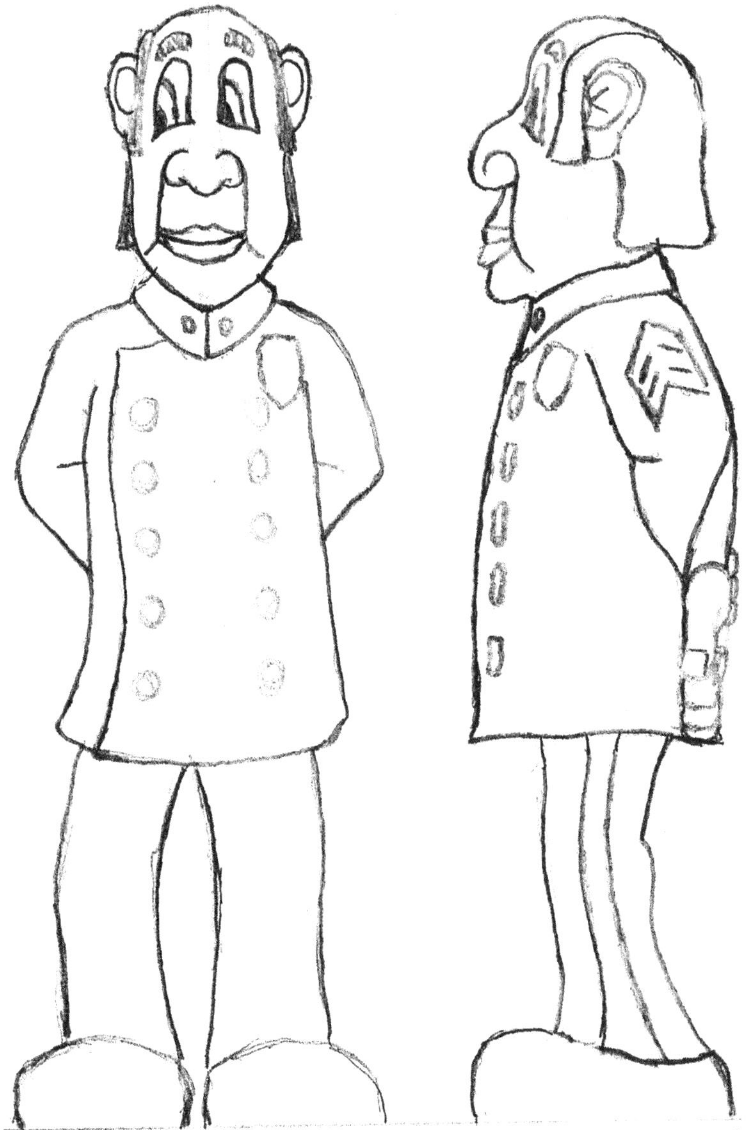

Sergeant Jimmie O'Dea—
Dennis Thornton

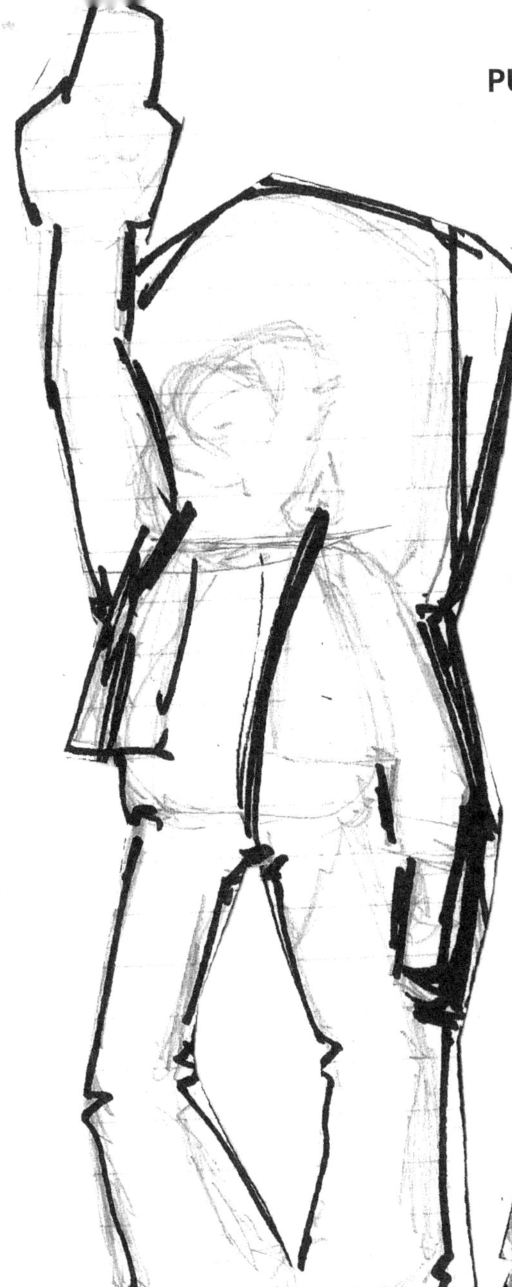

Negotiating Cowboy—
Chris Hammack

Masseuse—
Chris Hammack

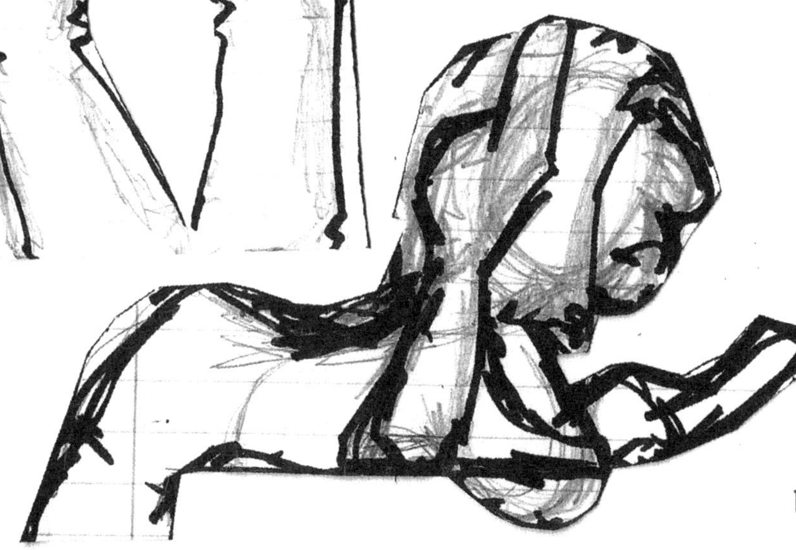

FIRE STATION

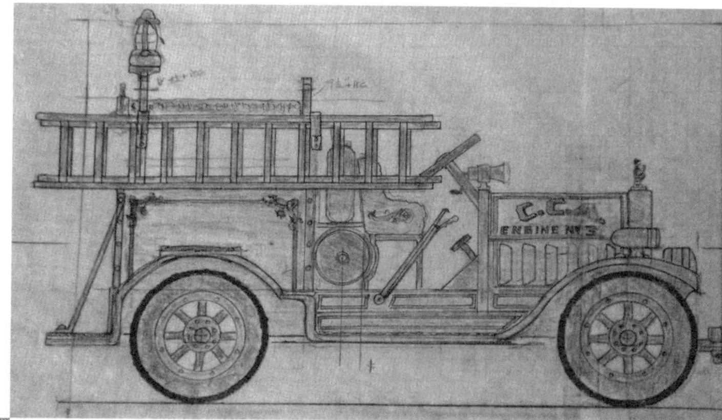

Fire Truck—
Peter Ortel

Man with Hose—
Peter Ortel

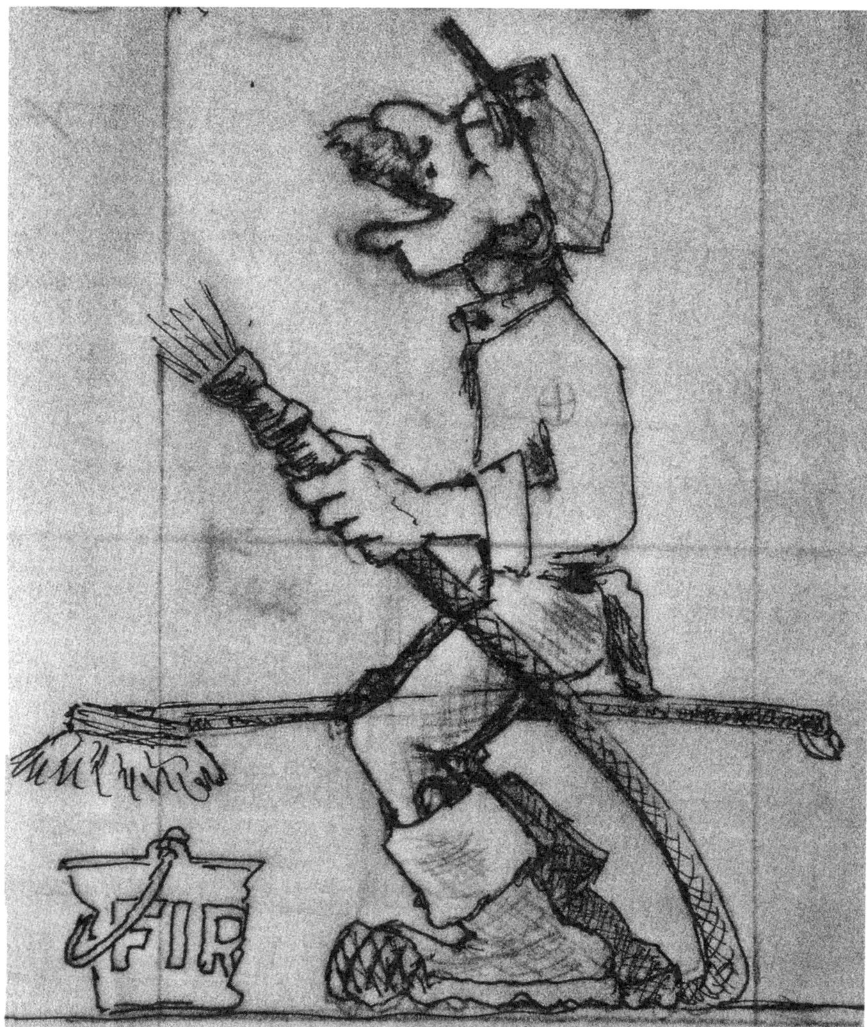

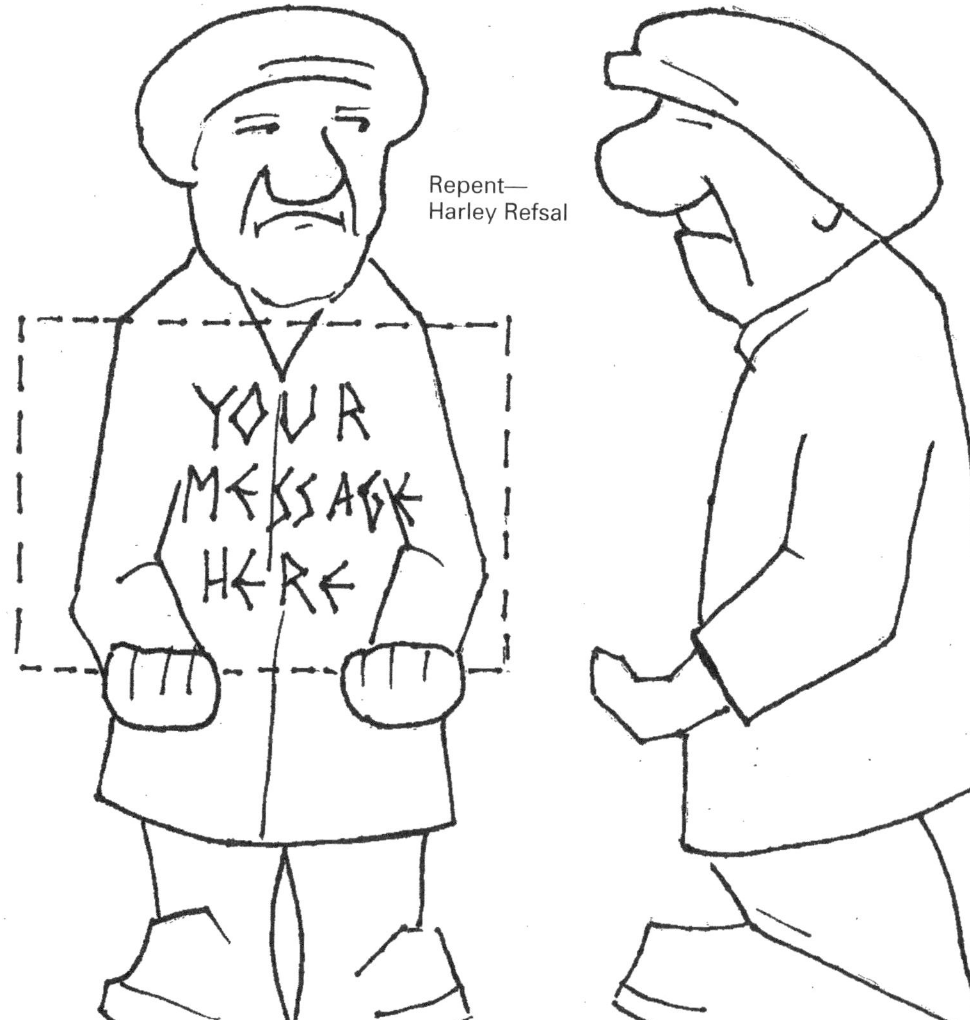

Repent—
Harley Refsal

Fireman with Hose—
PJ Driscoll

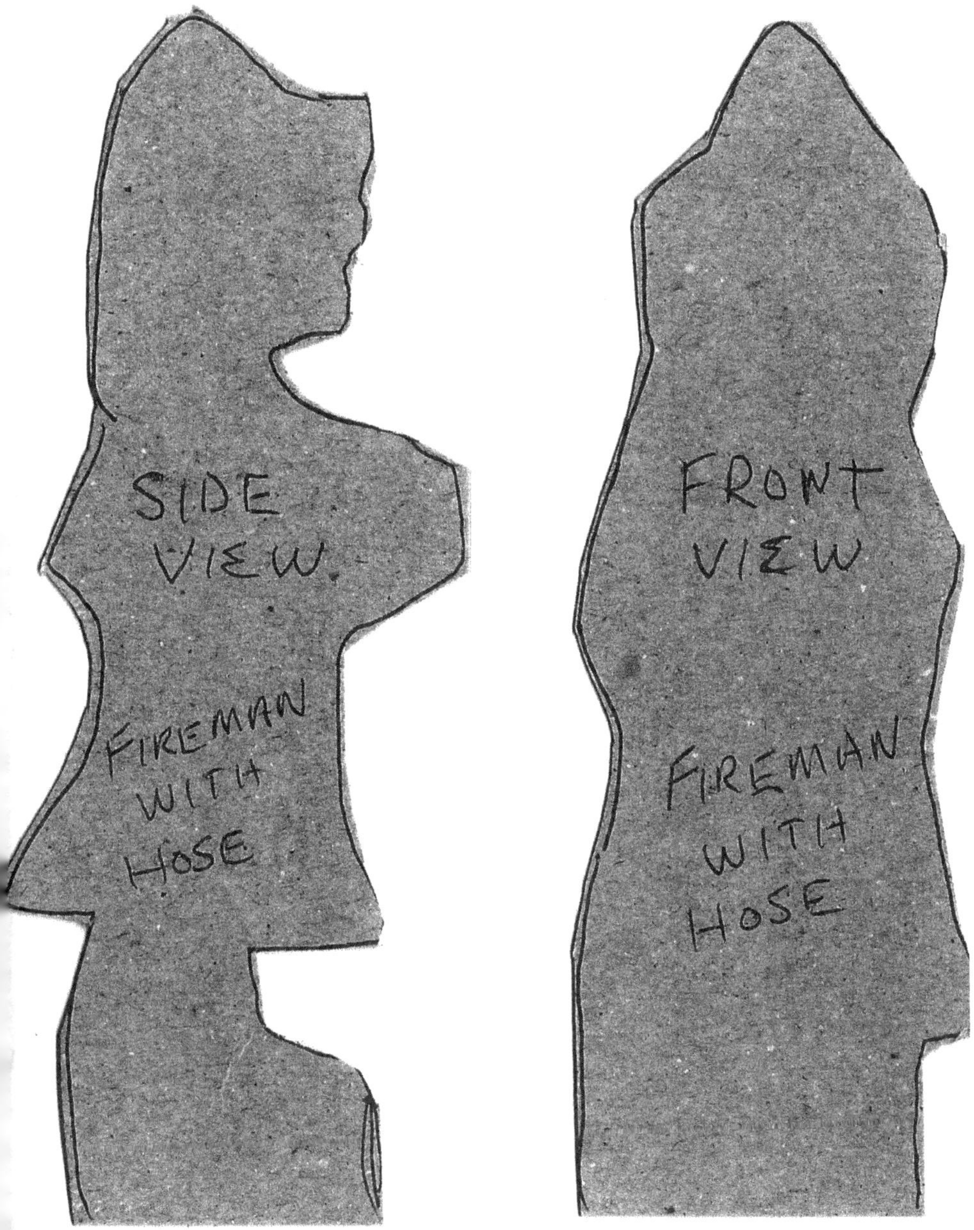

Fireman Sliding Pole—
PJ Driscoll

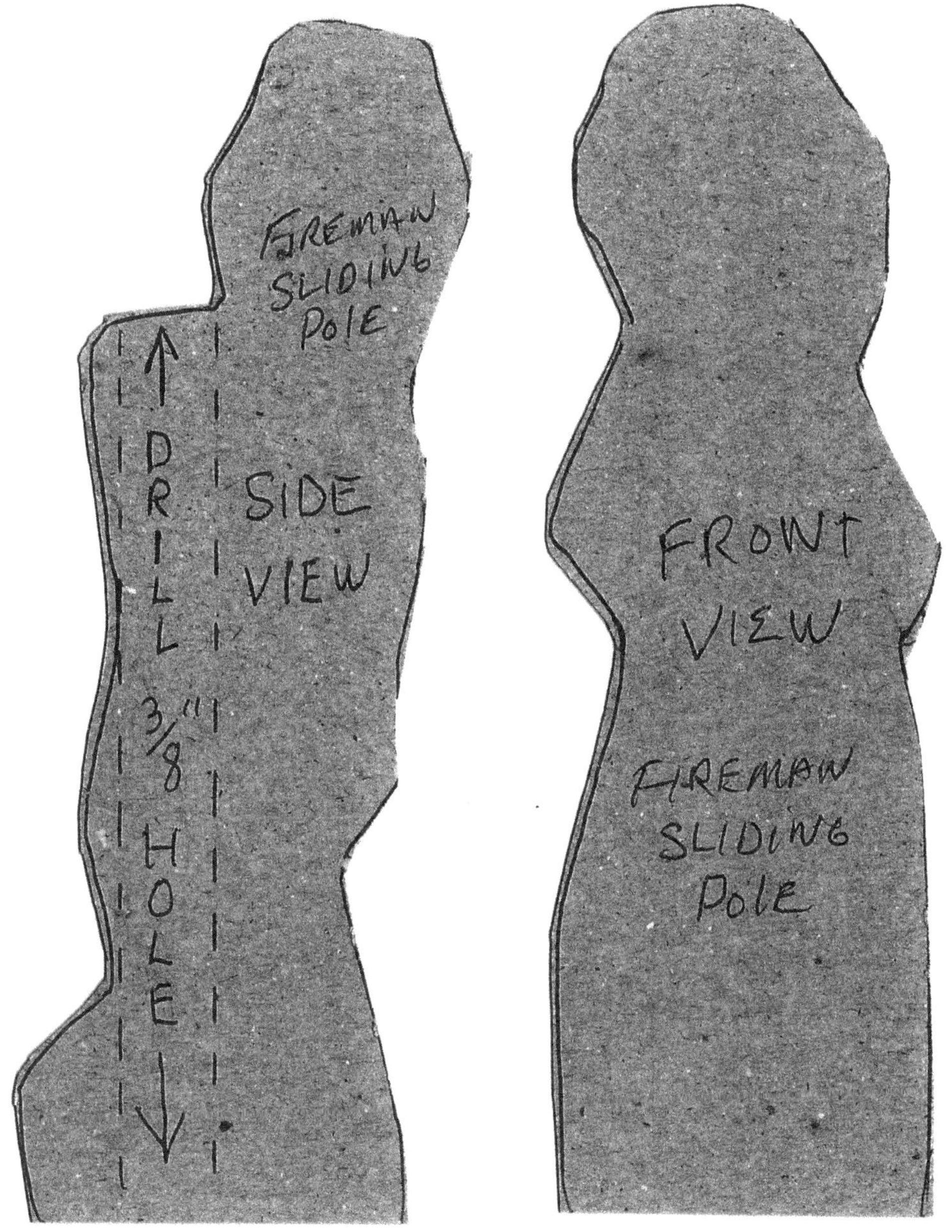

RIALTO THEATER

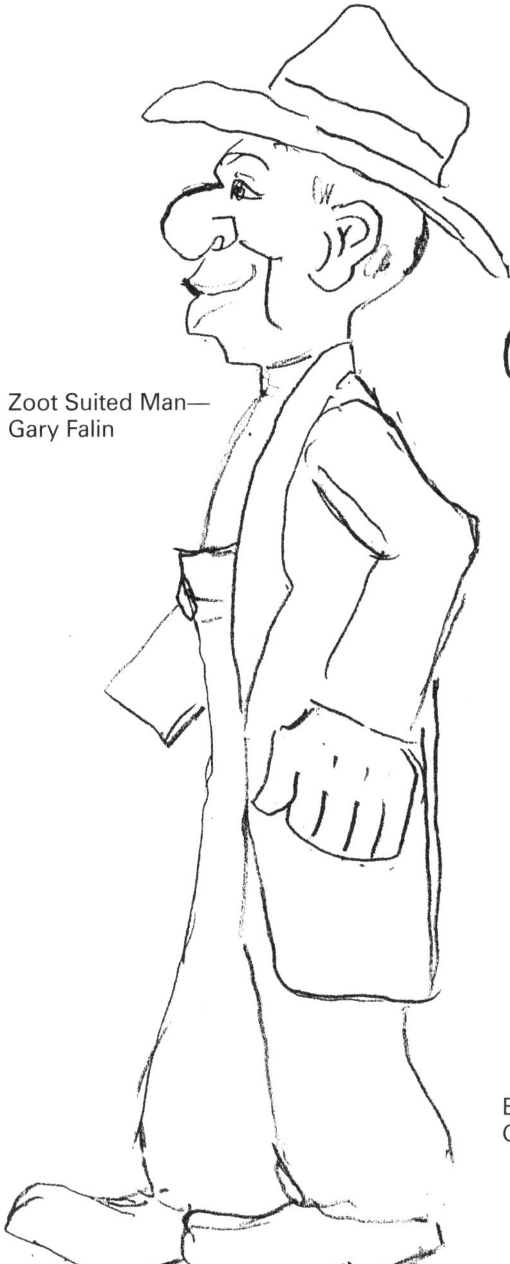

Zoot Suited Man—
Gary Falin

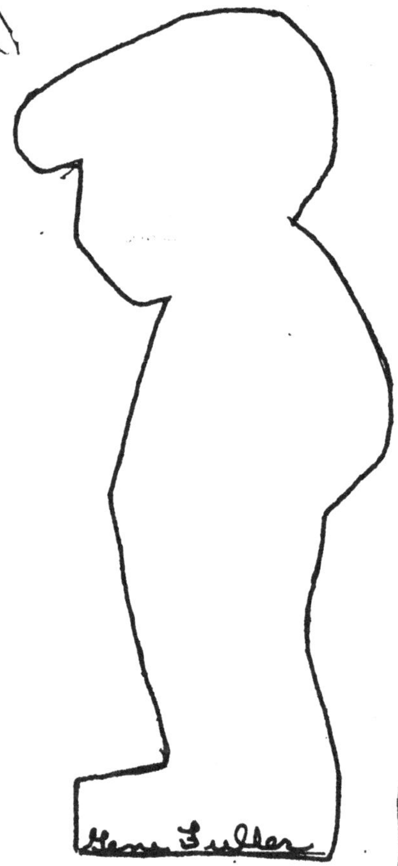

Boy with Hands in Pockets—
Gene Fuller

BUILDING UNDER CONSTRUCTION

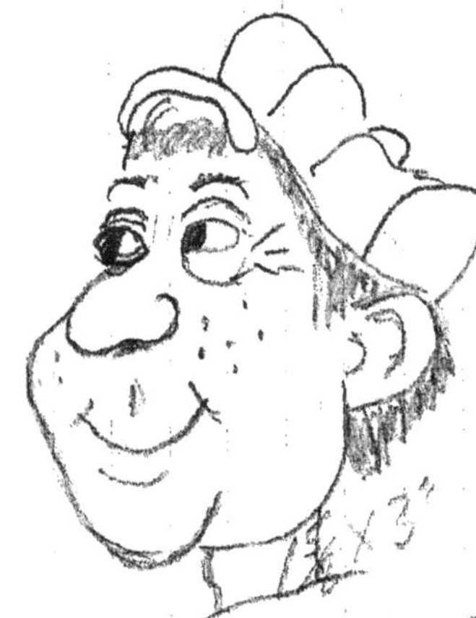

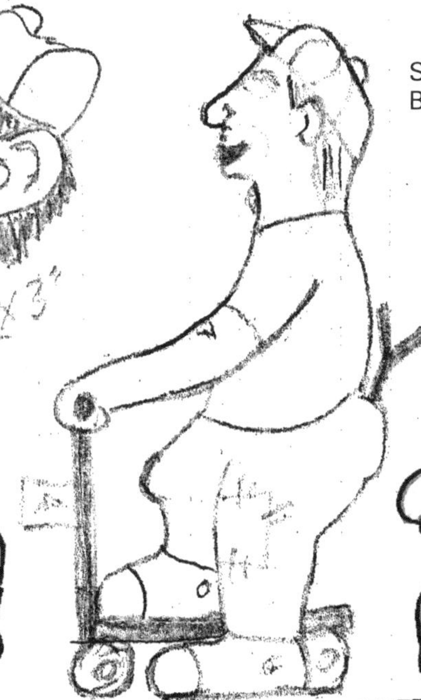

Scooter Boy—
Bruce Henn

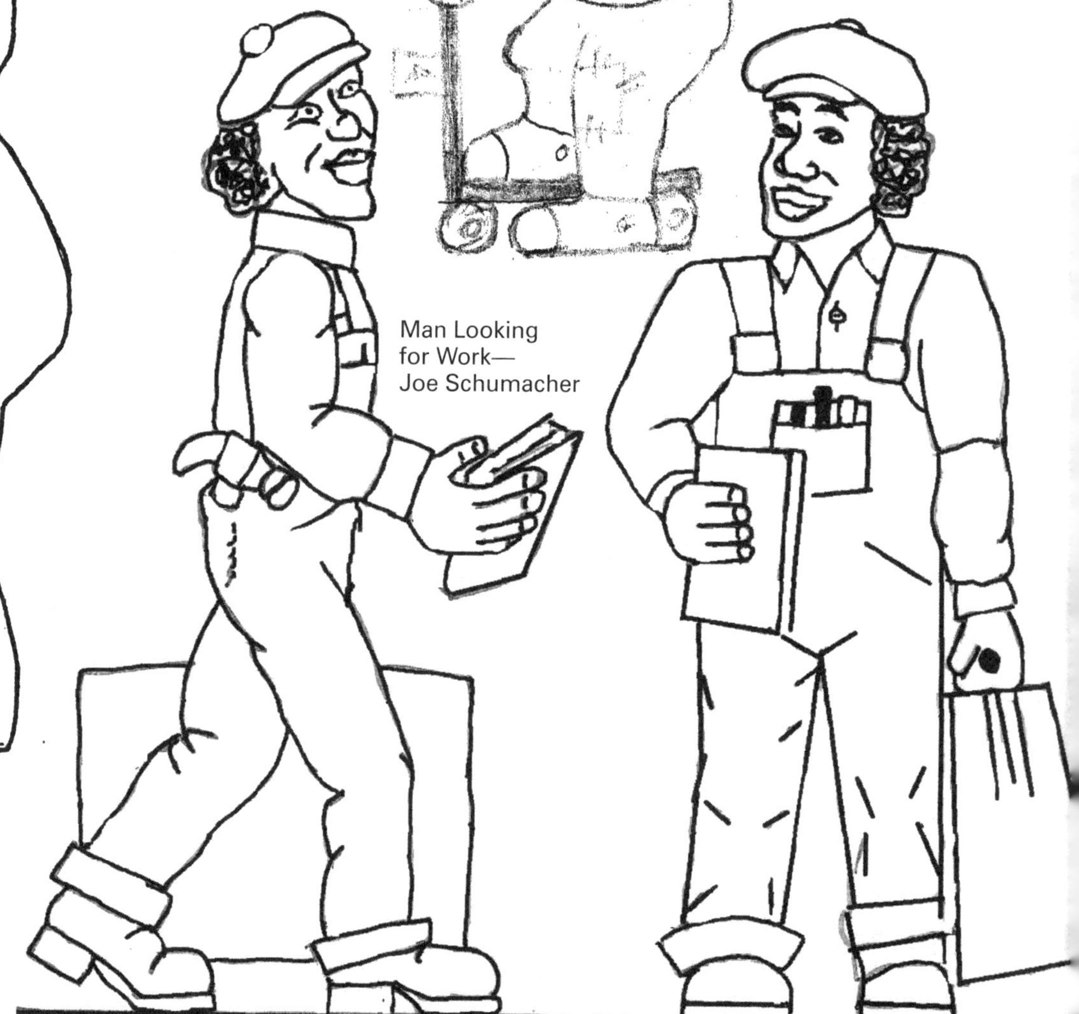

Man Looking
for Work—
Joe Schumacher